POLICY FORMULATION AND
ADMINISTRATION

Policy Formulation and Administration

A Casebook of
Top-Management Problems in Business

GEORGE ALBERT SMITH, JR., A.B., D.C.S.
Professor of Business Administration
(1905–1969)

C. ROLAND CHRISTENSEN, A.B., D.C.S.
George Fisher Baker, Jr., Professor of Business Administration

NORMAN A. BERG, S.B., D.B.A.
Professor of Business Administration

MALCOLM S. SALTER, A.B., D.B.A.
Associate Professor of Business Administration

All of the
Graduate School of Business Administration
Harvard University

SIXTH EDITION • 1972
RICHARD D. IRWIN, INC. *Homewood, Illinois 60430*
IRWIN-DORSEY INTERNATIONAL *London, England WC2H 9NJ*
IRWIN-DORSEY LIMITED *Georgetown, Ontario L7G 4B3*

SIXTH EDITION

First Printing, July 1972
Second Printing, May 1973

Case material of the Harvard Graduate School of Business Administration is made possible by the cooperation of business firms who may wish to remain anonymous by having names, quantities, and other identifying details disguised while basic relationships are maintained. Cases are prepared as the basis for class discussion rather than to illustrate either effective or ineffective handling of administrative situations.

ISBN 0–256–00482–X
Library of Congress Catalog Card No. 72–77062
Printed in the United States of America

To
GEORGE ALBERT SMITH, JR. (*1905–1969*)
Friend
Colleague
Teacher to all

Acknowledgments

IT IS NOT POSSIBLE for the authors of this book to acknowledge specifically and individually all of the people to whom we owe thanks for their help and encouragement in the development of this sixth edition of *Policy Formulation and Administration*. We are indebted to our colleagues here at the Harvard Business School and our colleagues in other schools of commerce and of business administration in this country and throughout the world. We are indebted to the business leaders and their associates who have contributed so generously of their time and experience to these case studies. They have shared their failures as well as their successes with all of us who learn and teach in the Policy Area.

Case research and writing is a demanding discipline—a blend of rigorous research method and artistry of presentation. We are especially indebted to the men and women who researched and developed these case studies. Some of these cases are the product of individual effort; others grew out of collective efforts. Some of them we have written or supervised ourselves. Others have been written by our colleagues. Without attempting to assign names to cases, we will simply list the authors. We congratulate them for their work well done, and we extend them our gratitude for their cooperation in making this book possible. In addition to specific cases, these colleagues have helped us in clarifying the basic concepts and objectives of our book. The contributors are: K. R. Andrews; J. F. Archer; N. H. Borden, Jr.; J. S. Garrison; T. Gearreald, Jr.; W. K. Harper; C. W. Hofer; C. A. Hogg; T. C. Kienzle; P. R. Lawrence; E. P. Learned; G. L. Marshall; R. A. Pitts; T. C. Raymond; D. C. D. Rogers; D. Schofield; B. R. Scott; Mrs. A. T. Sproat; H. H. Stevenson; and S. Tilles.

We are also grateful to the administrative officers of the Harvard Graduate School of Business for their encouragement of this effort. Dean Lawrence Fouraker, Dean George F. F. Lombard, Mr. A. R. Towl, and Professor Robert Merry have been most supportive. Miss Josepha Perry and Miss Juliet Muenchen have carried the main editorial burden of this book; we are in their debt.

The cases in this book are, with two exceptions, copyrighted by the

President and Fellows of Harvard College. Two of the cases are copyrighted by the Directors and Trustees of the Management Development Institute of Lausanne, Switzerland, and we thank the Directors and Trustees of that Institute for allowing us to include them here.

Finally and most importantly, we acknowledge our great debt to George Albert Smith, Jr., who passed away October 12, 1969. Professor Smith had been the senior author of this book during its first five editions. His ideas are still critical to the organization and content of this book. He personally influenced and taught each of the present authorship group. We hope to honor him by carrying this book forward.

In that continuing voyage, Professors Christensen and Berg are pleased to have the help of Professor Malcolm Salter, a colleague at Harvard. He brings to the authorship new insights and experiences which will be helpful to all.

June 1972   C. ROLAND CHRISTENSEN
NORMAN BERG
MALCOLM SALTER
(GEORGE ALBERT SMITH, JR. 1905–1969)

Contents

Section 4. Managing the Administrative Organization

Section 5. Follow-up and Reappraisal

PART III. Corporate Response to Social Change

Section 6. The Business Leader and Public Responsibility

Introduction

THE PURPOSES of this sixth edition of *Policy Formulation and Administration* are essentially the same as those of the previous editions. The book provides a selection of cases that can assist men and women preparing for a career in business administration to become acquainted with the opportunities and challenges confronting the top manager of a firm. The case material also provides ample opportunities for learning for middle managers and senior managers enrolled in university or corporate management development programs.

The educational objectives of this edition are the same as for earlier editions. Its orientation is managerial. It seeks to encourage the development of leadership skills. Men and women who can "take charge" of organizations are a scarce resource. The hope of the authors is that the study of these situations may encourage interest in general management skills and may provide an opportunity for academic practice of skills requisite to this organization position via discussion of selected case problems.

Specifically, the study and discussion of these cases offer opportunities:

1. To learn what the functions of top management are.
2. To develop skill in envisaging goals; to delineate the functions that must be performed to achieve the goals; and to determine what activities are needed in workable combination to carry out the functions necessary to goal achievement.
3. To become familiar with "risk" and its place in top-management thinking.
4. To learn to identify—and to attract to a business—personnel with the requisite technical and emotional abilities and to build them into a thinking, living, acting organization.
5. To develop the ability to divide the work of a firm into logical and understandable assignments, with limitations on authority and, at the same time, with provisions for individual decision-making powers and opportunities for cooperation.

6.   To learn to set standards for measuring performance.

7.   To understand how to provide motivation for the members of the management group so they will apply their skills (which the organization needs) and in doing so find nutriment for their own needs.

8.   To gain insight, self-confidence, imagination, and the ability to furnish leadership to the organization. Coupled with leadership is the willingness to take ultimate responsibility not only for the results of one's own decisions but also for the results of the decisions and actions of all to whom the leader has delegated authority.

9.   To anticipate and accept the responsibilities of the leader and those of the organization to the various sectors of society that are affected by the organization's actions: the investor, the worker, the supplier, the community, and the country. Our private enterprise system is on trial in 1972 probably more than ever before, and it is clear that the leader of the organization must play an instrumental role in shaping his own organization to meet these responsibilities.

The cases take their viewpoint primarily at the level of top management, including directors, where companywide objectives are set and departmental policies and activities are coordinated. This is the point of view of the Business Policy course at the Harvard Business School (the only required second-year course in the two-year program) and of the many similar courses (although the names may be different) at other universities, colleges, and business organizations here in the United States as well as throughout the world.

Each case in this book describes an actual situation as of the time the case was written. To preserve confidences, fictitious names have been used in some instances, and sometimes the geographical locations have been changed. Only on rare occasions has the industry been changed or the size of the company materially altered. Almost always the case contains information about the industry and its competitive conditions; some historical background about the company itself; financial and statistical data; information about products and production, and marketing methods and facilities; the organization plan; and executive personnel. These cases are the raw materials that permit simulation in the classroom of the actual discussions carried on informally among managers and in board and committee rooms.

In the tradition of earlier editions, this volume contains a selection of "seasoned" cases used in previous editions as well as a selection of new cases not heretofore published. In selecting these cases we have been dependent upon the advice and counsel of our colleagues working in the Policy area throughout the world. We appreciate their help. All of the cases have been used here at the Harvard Business School in our various Policy courses.

Again, as in earlier editions, we have selected cases from a wide variety of corporate organizations. Cases range in size from the small, new enterprise to the large and very complex conglomerate organization. In addition to cases covering problems of the overall enterprises, we have included, in this edition, some cases focusing on the problems of the individual manager as he attempts to survive and to influence his organization. We believe institutions and students will find this material to be highly challenging.

It should be emphasized that our cases are not intended to be "examples" of right and wrong, good and bad. In no instance was a particular company selected because we believe it to be the "best" or the "worst" in its industry, or because we thought it was "average" or "typical." Obviously, some of these firms had been well managed; others not so well. Some were in very good condition; others in critical condition. The important thing was that in the actual situations the persons responsible for the particular ventures were obligated to recognize and deal with the problems as they were. The problems might be desperate emergencies calling for drastic action. They might be basic policy decisions of long-range significance, even though not requiring emergency handling. Or they might be the somewhat less dramatic, but nonetheless important, problems of routine administration, keeping things going on an even keel from day to day.

It has been our experience and the experience of many other teachers that, by using cases such as these, a teacher and his students can together create "ways of thinking," "ways of feeling," and "ways of doing" that accelerate tremendously both intellectual growth and emotional development.

An important by-product of case study and discussion is the accumulation of much information about business affairs. The main, though more elusive, products, however, are: insight, intellectual power, judgment, imagination, practical common sense, leadership ability, responsibility, and self-confidence.

THE QUESTIONS OR PROBLEMS IN THE CASES AND THEIR SOLUTIONS

At the top level, an executive does not have any "all-wise" adviser to inform him what problem or problems he should be watching or working on at a particular time. That he must decide himself. And he has no reference book to look into, no infallible aid to give him *the* solution. He must, nevertheless, find *some* solution, some workable solution. This he does by the use of experience and the exercise of his judgment, usually after discussion and consultation with others. And neither before a decision is made, nor after, can he be absolutely sure what action is *right* or *best*.

The administrator must be willing and able to work in a climate of uncertainty, which is often uncomfortable. He must accept the responsibility for reaching decisions under time pressure, on the basis of limited facts, and in the face of many unknowns. He must work with people who, like himself, are imperfect. Almost always, some of his associates or other parties involved will disagree with him. He should take their disagreement and their views into account. His is the usually lonesome situation of the possessor of ultimate responsibility. He inevitably will make some mistakes. If he is experienced and mature, he will expect this and will allow for it. He will hope to reach wise decisions most of the time. If he does, he is a successful business leader.

This clearly suggests that the cases do not include any "official" or "demonstrably correct" answers. We do not have either "official" questions or "approved" solutions. It is part of the student's task, as it is part of an executive's task, to discover questions and to distinguish the important from the unimportant. In some instances, we do not agree among ourselves as to exactly what the most fundamental problems or opportunities are; and in still more instances we do not agree on the best possible course of action. If we did, we would question the reality of our cases and perhaps also the quality and integrity of our own views. Complicated business situations such as are presented here are episodes taken out of business life. Since we are all different people, with our own special backgrounds and experiences, we will attach to these problems at least somewhat differing interpretations and envision somewhat differing or substantially differing solutions or courses of action.

We do have our own ideas about each of the cases we are offering; so do our colleagues who use them. In some instances, we hold our views with strong conviction. In others, we are much less sure of what we think. And we change our views from time to time. So we certainly do not feel that we *know* what should be done in each of the situations presented. The value of the cases in the classroom lies in their discussion, not in the giving or finding of an "authoritative" answer.

ORGANIZATION OF THE BOOK

The edition contains the basic organizational features of its predecessor efforts with some modifications. We have divided the book into three major subsections: Part I, Policy Formulation; Part II, Administration; and Part III, Corporate Response to Social Change.

The introduction to each of these three sections provides instructor and student with a statement of educational objectives and a suggested format for the study of those cases. We believe these suggestions may be of value to all. But we would also say immediately that there are many other ways to "map" the general manager's terrain. And the student of the policy process, as with a general manager, will want to develop his own specific way of dealing with these kinds of problems. We urge experimentation.

This organizational plan with its selected distribution of cases can give you as students a sense of the atmosphere in which top-level executives work and can make real to you the individuals in top management, with their range of human frailties and strengths. It also will make clear to you that the manager must work through and depend on other people; that he must engage in much routine work; that virtually all he can be sure of is "change" and the "unexpected." You will learn also that policy formulation is not always a formal process; that there often is a discrepancy between "stated" policy and policy as "practiced"; that much policy making is done (and should be) at fairly low levels in organizations; and that effective authority or leadership is not conferred from above but is earned and awarded from below.

As you progress in your study of the cases, many other important things will become clear. For example, you will be disabused of any idea that the executive discovers and solves one problem at a time. On the contrary, he deals with many problems concurrently, each at a different stage of development. Furthermore, the route of travel from size-up, through planning, organizing, putting plans into action and control, to reappraisal is not a straight line. The route is much more like a circle. Even in dealing with one problem, the administrator goes around the circle many times. And, as we have said, he is busy with many circles. His job is never really finished.

PREPARING A CASE FOR CLASS

The question of how students should prepare a case for class has been put to us many times by our own students and also by people studying and teaching these cases elsewhere. Actually, the question is often phrased: "What is the *best* way to prepare a case?" That one we cannot answer, inasmuch as we do not think there is any *best* way. There are, no doubt, many good and useful ways. Each of us must develop the methods that serve him best. Moreover, we all must change our approach somewhat to deal with each new situation. And each case is a new situation. So there is no formula, no basic pattern, that we can pass on. We can, at most, make a few observations.

We recommend, with the qualifications just stated, the following to the student: We suggest you first read the case through to get a general impression of what it is about, how it seems to come out, and what kinds of information it contains. We think there is a real advantage in doing this first reading a day or two before the time when you must do your thorough and final preparation. There is value in having the general situation in mind in time to mull it over, both consciously and subconsciously, for a while. That is true of any important problem one has to deal with—in school, in business, anywhere.

For the second reading, we suggest you take the time to proceed slowly and carefully, studying the tables and exhibits and making notes as you go. Perhaps some headings will occur to you under which you want to summarize what you believe are especially pertinent factors. The headings, of course, will vary from case to case. Moreover, what at first looks like a basic fact or issue may come to seem less important than something else as you work longer.

When going through these two steps, it may be helpful to use the format of general questions detailed in the introductory material of each of this book's major subdivisions. The questions we have cited, we stress, are only suggestions. You will think of others, and the sequence in which you put them to yourself is up to you. Perhaps, however, when you feel you are about at the end of your preparation, it will be well to ask: "Have I worked this thing through to the point where, if I really had a chance to talk to the persons responsible for this company, I could (1) talk intelligently with them about their company and their job in managing it; (2) show them why the main issues I have distilled out as a result of my analysis are really of first importance; and (3) give them a coordinated program of action that would be practical and would have a reasonable chance to succeed?"

We urge students to discuss the cases with one another while preparing them. Managers in business discuss their problems with other key people. But be sure you do your own independent work and independent thinking. Do not be too stubborn to recognize a better idea than your own, but be sure you really understand and believe in it before you adopt it.

One more observation. Not infrequently, students express the wish for more information than is in a case; they feel they cannot make a decision without more facts. Do not hide behind that bogeyman. For one thing, business leaders never have all the facts they would like to have. And, as far as the cases are concerned, they all contain enough information to enable you to decide and recommend something sensible. Be sure you learn how to use, and do use, all the information you have.

OUTSIDE READING

While the cases in this book make up the subject matter of a complete course, an instructor may wish to assign outside readings which reinforce the concepts brought out in class discussion. Several works, in particular, are relevant to the cases presented in this book:

Andrews, Kenneth R. *The Concept of Corporate Strategy*. Homewood, Ill.: Dow Jones-Irwin, 1971.
Ansoff, H. Igor. *Corporate Strategy*. New York: McGraw-Hill Book Co., 1965.
Chandler, Alfred D. *Strategy and Structure*. Cambridge, Mass.: The M.I.T. Press, 1962.
Galbraith, John Kenneth. *The New Industrial State*. Boston: Houghton Mifflin Co., 1967.
Selekman, Benjamin. *Power and Morality in a Business Society*. New York: McGraw-Hill Book Co., 1956.
Selznick, Philip. *Leadership in Administration*. New York: Harper & Row, Publishers, 1957.
Sloan, Alfred P. *My Years at General Motors*. Garden City, N.Y.: Doubleday & Co., Inc., 1963.
Zaleznik, Abraham. *Human Dilemmas of Leadership*. New York: Harper & Row, Publishers, 1966.

The work by Andrews provides a good overview of the range of policy problems which will be addressed in this casebook. Zaleznik's book complements Andrews by shedding light on the human problems of top-level decision makers. The works of Ansoff, Selznick, and Sloan are particularly relevant to Part I of the book, while the Chandler study will provide an important perspective for looking at the cases presented in Part II. Finally, Galbraith and Selekman will provide the kind of viewpoints which can usefully be discussed in connection with the cases appearing in Part III.

Each instructor, of course, will be able to add to this list. In doing so, the relevant criteria for selection should be whether a given work sharpens the focus of policy problems or helps students of administration broaden their perspective in analyzing the cases presented for study.

Quite apart from "course specific" readings, there is a world of literature relevant to the study of policy formulation and administration. Biographies and autobiographies offer a rich account of policy formulation and decision making. Similarly, history and political science present innumerable opportunities to study the evolution of policy and organization. Accounts as diverse as those on the administrative organization set up in France by Napoleon in the 17th century, the development of the railroads in the 19th century, and the path of the social revolutions in the 20th century all offer clues about how organizational leaders manage their affairs.

No less important are current affairs, political as well as economic. In many ways the study of the Cuban missile crisis will reveal to the careful student insights as relevant to business policy and decision making as the study of the Penn Central crisis. When reading such news, try to look at events through the eyes of the persons who head the organizations in question, noting what kinds of decisions they make and what actions they have to take. In addition, you might also ask yourselves what you would do if you were in their positions.

Business leaders are more effective and more useful to society the better they understand human nature and the more fully they are acquainted with past and present movements in the arts, the sciences, and the humanities. Thus, while an active personal library transcends the purposes of this casebook, it unmistakably reinforces them.

PART I
Policy Formulation

THIS CASEBOOK invites you to enter into a process of policy formulation and administration. This process, as will become apparent from class discussion, depends upon a melding of intellectual and administrative skills. For example, identifying problems that affect the long-term position of the firm calls for the ability to select and relate disparate bits of information so that an inclusive statement of key problems can be made. Making such a statement requires, however, more than the intellectual skill of analyzing environmental trends and data on internal corporate operations. It also requires the ability to articulate problems in such a way that suggests actionable alternatives which can be submitted to careful evaluation. This ability reflects what we can call an administrative sense. Similarly, setting objectives and formulating a plan of action require both the sense of what is needed and what will work.

The cases presented in this book are not meant to stand alone. They are not research documents which describe important aspects of policy formulation and administration. Nor are they studies which suggest how policy should be formulated and administered by top corporate executives. Rather the following cases have been designed to provide the raw material for students to work out for themselves, under the guidance of a trained instructor, what business policies are appropriate for particular firms. It is intended that a course based upon these cases will help the student develop an analytical approach to broad business policy problems.

Part I of this book contains cases that require the student to define and assess corporatewide problems affecting a firm's long-run performance. The most important long-run problems are not necessarily obvious after a first reading of the case. Nor do the statements of managers quoted in the cases always reveal the scope of issues to be faced. Given this realistic setting, developing the ability to identify the critical or strategic problems facing a firm constitutes the primary objective of

Section 1. The cases are broad and require the student to "size up situations" from the top manager's perspective.

The "size-up," as we like to call it, starts with an identification of the nature of the company's business; its economic goals; its key operating policies; its organizational structure; its economic, social, and political environment; and the values and administrative procedures used by top management. This process of identification is a kind of intelligence operation which should lead to a general status report on the company in question. This process relies heavily upon the skills and knowledge developed in functional courses in finance, marketing, manufacturing policy, organizational behavior, and the like. The added challenge presented by the first cases of this book is the need to relate and to synthesize disparate bits of information in an overall assessment of a company's current position.

In preparing the cases in Section 1 for class discussion, each student should consider as a start the following kinds of questions: What kind of company is this? Is there an identifiable strategy? What are the environmental factors affecting the company today, and what can we foresee as potential changes in the company's environment? What are the company's greatest opportunities and risks? What are the company's strengths and weaknesses in light of the industry trends and apparent opportunities and risks? How are the values of management affecting the strategy and performance of the company? What, if any, social responsibilities should be recognized in evaluating the current position of the company?

A complete and well-thought-out status report on a company will inevitably suggest future alternatives or courses of action. While the first cases provide ample opportunity for the exploration of such alternatives, the cases presented in Section 2 are cast in such a light that particular attention must be paid to establishing objectives and formulating future plans of action. Moving to this aspect of corporate planning requires that the student develop criteria for establishing meaningful goals and evaluating alternative strategies. The development of such criteria is a major goal of Section 2.

Each class should aim at developing such criteria for itself. In addition, each class should be able to develop a feel for when specific criteria are most relevant. There is no checklist which can be usefully applied to every company situation. This feel can be developed through the process of informed discussion in the classroom. In preparing for this discussion, each student should start by doing the kind of overall corporate assessment suggested above for the cases in Section 1. On the basis of this broad-gauged assessment, major strategic alternatives should be identified. In addition, each student should come to class with a recommended course of action based on his analysis of the company's principal alternatives. The following questions may be a useful point of departure for individual preparation: What constitutes a reasonable set of goals for this company? Given these goals, what are the company's major alternatives? Which alternatives build on the company's existing strengths? Under which alternatives are profit opportunities best exploited and risks properly hedged? Which alternatives fit most closely with existing corporate values? If selected, what are the implications of each alternative for the company, and can the company accommodate these new demands?

The cases in Section 2 present situations where concrete recommendations are required. They are sequenced so that the problems and decisions become increasingly complicated. Pharmalab and Mathatronics focus on the straegic problems of two relatively small firms in highly fractionated industries. In contrast, the cases on the light aircraft industry deal with larger companies with broader product lines operating in a highly concentrated industry. Here the problems and dynamics of interfirm competition are accented. The case on Tensor Corporation complicates the process of recommending a set of objectives and a plan of action by providing substantial data on the personal values of the key managers of the company. Heublein focuses on the issue of strategic diversification, and CML Group concentrates on the strategic problems of a widely diversified firm.

In working through the cases in Part I of this book, the student should keep in mind the primary task of formulating and evaluating corporate purpose. He should remember that policy formulation requires the capacity to recognize and deal with numerous relations between the firm and its environment. He should recognize that the power to mold multiple, complex relations into an integrated plan must build upon specialist training but cannot be considered the result of that training. He should therefore see the classroom discussion of these cases as the vehicle for developing a generalist's point of view, one which can identify not only the complexity of strategic problems facing a firm but also realistic goals and feasible courses of action.

Section 1
The Top Management Perspective: Sizing up Situations

1. Merlin-Microwave, Inc.

IN FEBRUARY, 1970, Merlin-Microwave, Inc., of Bridgeport, Connecticut, reported that its first two years in business had ended with cumulative losses in excess of cumulative sales, which in 1969 had totaled just over $100,000. Nevertheless, management had been able to increase MM's initial capitalization (under $55,000 in cash, mostly from relatives and business associates) by a successful public offering. Early in 1969, 50,000 shares of common had been marketed at $6 per share, with proceeds to the company of $225,000. (See Exhibits 1 and 2 for financial statements.) Furthermore, MM's management believed that they had devised a strategy capable of making their company a viable competitor in the $161 million microwave tube market, which was seen as headed toward rapid expansion.

As an early major step toward its objective, management had decided to try to obtain a substantial military contract. The thinking on this matter was described as follows by Mr. Albert Olsen, marketing vice president and (along with Dr. Edwin Merlino, president, and Mr. Harold Rhodes, treasurer) one of the company's three co-founders:

We see many favorable things about the military market. The procurement rules are well established; on sales of replacement tubes, for example, the low bidder will win as long as he can demonstrate financial and technical capability. Various government circulars make it easy to find what bids are outstanding. Finally, the market is large and it is possible to strike at certain tubes where prices are high and there is a good chance of winning a contract.

In the long term, we see the primary benefit of the military market as a springboard. If we can win a large contract and deliver, we will prove that MM is a real company. We will develop a product history and a good name for commercial and government contracts. We will also very importantly be building up a technology base with government money. By producing tubes we will be gaining invaluable R&D experience and knowledge of tricky vacuum and brazing technologies. With this base we can move naturally into commercial areas with a minimum of investment on MM's part.

We feel that if we concentrate on the military replacement market we can win contracts and build a reputation. Then we can offer new services such as refurbishing other companies' tubes. By this process we can earn a profit in the short term and build expertise to make successful bids on other military and commercial contracts.

Exhibit 1

MERLIN-MICROWAVE, INC.

Balance Sheets as of January 31, 1969–70

	1969	1970
Current assets:		
Cash	$23,386	$ 18,571
Accounts receivable	504	33,488
Inventories	8,891	71,468
Other	2,879	1,541
Total	$35,660	$125,068
Fixed assets, net:		
Machinery and equipment	9,874	40,425
Other	1,639	3,990
Total	$11,513	$ 44,415
Capitalized research and development*		56,884
Other assets	250	450
Total assets	$47,423	$226,817
Current liabilities:		
Accounts payable, trade	$ 5,840	$ 44,071
Accrued payroll and expenses	1,066	7,520
Other	1,352	4,317
Total	$ 8,258	$ 55,908
4% Notes, convertible at $2 per share, due 1973	25,000	25,000
Capital:		
Common stock ($.01 par value)	981	1,481
Paid-in capital in excess of par†	76,413	375,913
Accumulated deficit	(63,229)	(231,485)
Total	$14,165	$145,909
Total liabilities and capital	$47,423	$226,817

* R&D costs incurred in 1970 were to be amortized over five years.
† Included $52,312 received from exchange of stock for cash and $24,101 received from exchange of stock for salary in 1969. The increase in the following year mainly represented proceeds from the public issue of 50,000 shares of common at $6 per share.
Source: Company records.

The Microwave Tube Industry

In their 1969 stock *Prospectus,* MM's management defined their company's business and industry as follows:

The Company's business is the design, development, manufacture, and sale of tubes for the generation and amplification of microwave power.

Microwaves are waves of electromagnetic energy. . . . They fall in the spectrum between the long waves used in radio communication and the very short waves of visible light. Although the term "microwave" [does not define] an exact frequency range, the frequencies most commonly associated with this term are between 1 billion and 100 billion cycles a second. Due to the unique properties of waves in this frequency range, they are useful for radar, communications, and, more recently, for rapid cooking and special industrial [heating] processes.

Exhibit 2

MERLIN-MICROWAVE, INC.

Operative Statements, 1969, 1970

	Eleven Months to January 31, 1969	Twelve Months to January 31, 1970
Gross sales		$ 98,980
Returns		474
Net sales	$ 3,591	$ 98,506
Cost of goods sold:		
Materials used	5,041	10,929
Direct labor	8,735	50,858
Factory overhead*	31,462	44,305
Total	$45,238	$106,092
Gross loss	$41,647	$ 7,586
Operating expenses:		
Selling		57,835
General and administrative		60,251
Total	21,542	$118,086
Loss from operations	$63,189	$125,672
Interest and other income	60	7,550
Total loss	$63,129	$118,122
Provision for state taxes	100	642
Net loss for period	$63,229	$118,764

* Included expensed research and development costs of an undisclosed amount for 1969 and of $1,966 for 1970.
Source: Company records.

PRODUCTS AND APPLICATIONS, R&D, PRODUCTION

Microwave tubes fell into three generic types: magnetrons, klystrons, and traveling wave tubes (TWTs). Although more than one of these types might be used in some applications, each type had certain properties which normally gave it an advantage for a particular purpose. Thus, the magnetron was characterized by high efficiency and low weight per unit of power output; these properties gave it an advantage in the application of airborne radar. The magnetron was also relatively low-cost, which gave it an advantage in heating. The klystron was characterized by extreme stability of operation; that is, it could receive a signal, amplify it, and send it without distortion. This property gave it an advantage in ground-based, high-power radar and in many types of communications. The TWT was characterized by its ability to carry signals over a broad band width; this property gave it an advantage in communication systems like cross-country telephone transmission, since thousands of conversations could be simultaneously sent through one tube.

By 1970 all three types of microwave tubes had been long established, though magnetrons had been the first to achieve importance. Invented in England in 1939 and further developed at MIT, they had performed an invaluable service in radar during World War II. Early in the war, Raytheon became the top producer, and in 1945 a Raytheon scientist was credited with discovering the cooking application of the magnetron. The klystron, like the magnetron, had first appeared in 1939; it was an invention of Dr. Russell H. Varian of Stanford. The market for this type of tube did not open up until after the war, however, when high-powered versions were developed. The TWT was a postwar creation of the Bell Laboratories; it had come into use by 1948.

Exhibit 3

MERLIN-MICROWAVE, INC.
Tube Price Data

Tube Type	Price Range	Average Price Range	Comments
Klystrons:			
Reflex..........$ 70–$500		$ 300–$400	Tubes in the $400–$500 price range were for specialized uses.
Power..........$500–$250,000		$1,000–$1,200	Tubes in the higher price ranges were for specialized uses and included high development costs.
Magnetrons........$100–$4,000		$ 600–$700	Tubes in the lower price range were for heating purposes. The majority of tubes were used in radar.
TWTs.............$700–$50,000		$1,500	Tubes in the higher price range included high development costs.

Source: MM management estimates.

In line with this long history, MM's management said that future advances in the state of the art for microwave tubes were not expected. Development rather than research would be required to create new tubes capable of meeting new specifications. Another change predicted was lower unit costs. Eventually, microwave tubes might be coupled with solid-state devices, but MM's management saw this change as occurring in the distant future and thus as posing no present competitive threat.

In terms of production, intraclass differences among tubes could be at least as significant as differences among different tube categories, since tubes within each major type might differ greatly in complexity and size. To some extent this variety was reflected in the wide range of prices at which tubes in each category were sold (Exhibit 3). The very high prices of some tubes, however, could only be interpreted as reflecting the inclusion of substantial development work.

According to MM's management, the production of microwave tubes, regardless of generic type, had been likened to "black magic." Many complicated technologies were necessary, and extremely close tolerances were required in most applications. Several types of exotic metals and brazing alloys were used, and many scientific disciplines were required. While the formulae involved in the creation of the desired power, frequency, etc., could be calculated at the drawing-board stage with considerable accuracy, the number of relevant variables was so great that finalization of the design could usually be accomplished only after varying degrees of "tinkering" or experimentation. Even if the design was right, management had further found that failure to perform as expected might be due to such production "bugs" as minute differences in cavity size or contamination by miniscule particles of cigarette ash or dust. In addition, tube assembly had a "learning curve" as technicians became more proficient in putting together intricate components. Therefore, the larger the quantity of a given tube produced, the faster and more efficient production became.

MARKETS AND COMPETITION

In 1970 the three main markets for microwave tubes continued to be radar, the original use; communications, to which the tubes had spread from radar; and heating, including cooking. Markets could be further subdivided into military and civilian, and the civilian heating market could be broken down into industrial, commercial, and home use.

In one market estimate for 1969, the total market size was put at $161 million, of which radar (using all three types of tubes) accounted for $88 million; communications (using klystrons and TWTs) accounted for $66 million; and heating (using lower-priced magnetrons almost exclusively) accounted for $7 million (Exhibit 4). Growth rates were available only for tube types rather than for markets (Exhibits 5 and 6), but these figures showed that volume as a whole had grown 9.5% in units and 2.9% in dollars from 1968 to 1969. Commenting on the 2.9% dollar growth, MM's management suggested that it reflected the general economic downturn. For future years they estimated that a realistic growth rate would be 7%.

MM's management further believed that the radar and communication markets were not only the oldest and largest, but the most mature in terms of potential expansion, new applications, established competi-

Exhibit 4

MERLIN-MICROWAVE, INC.
The Microwave Tube Market in 1969
(Dollars in Millions)

MARKET SEGMENT	ESTIMATED APPLICATION BREAKDOWN			REPORTED TOTAL*
	Klystrons	Magnetrons	TWTs	
Communications.........	$19	—	$47	$ 66
Radar.................	19	$36	33	88
Heating:				
Industrial............	1	1	—	2
Domestic............	—	3	—	3
Commercial..........	—	2	—	2
Total............	$39	$42	$80	$161

* Not projected to total industry figures. Represents factory sales data from reporting firms.
Source: Aggregate tube sales by class are Electronic Industries Association figures from *Electronic News*, May 6, 1970, p. 2. Sales breakdown by market segment based on management estimates.

tion, and market shares. On the other hand, management saw the heating market as very young, with a large growth potential and with competition not yet firmly established.

Overall, management believed that 90% of the tube market was shared among the three top suppliers: Varian Associates with 50%, Raytheon with 25%, and Litton Industries with 15%. Other suppliers included Hughes Aircraft, Sperry Rand, Amperex (of Holland), Microwave Associates, and Microwave Electronics Co. Most of these companies were very large (see Exhibit 7) and had been making tubes for up to 25 years.

Although the three major competitors were in all three generic tube

Exhibit 5

MERLIN-MICROWAVE, INC.
Factory Sales in Units and Dollars, 1968–69*
(Units and Dollars in Thousands)

Tube Type	1968 Units	1969 Units	Per Cent Change	1968 Dollars	1969 Dollars	Per Cent Change
Klystron...............	153.0	142.6	(6.8)	$ 41,413	$ 39,107	(5.6)
Magnetron............	94.3	135.4	43.6	38,440	42,004	9.3
TWT.................	49.6	47.0	(5.2)	76,512	79,758	4.2
Total...........	296.9	325.0	9.5	$156,364	$160,870	2.9

Note: Failure of figures to add is due to rounding.
* Not projected to total industry data. Represents data from reporting firms.
Source: Electronic Industries Association figures in *Electronic News*, May 6, 1970, p. 2.

Exhibit 6

MERLIN-MICROWAVE, INC.
Tube Shipments by Type, 1959–68
(Dollars in Millions)

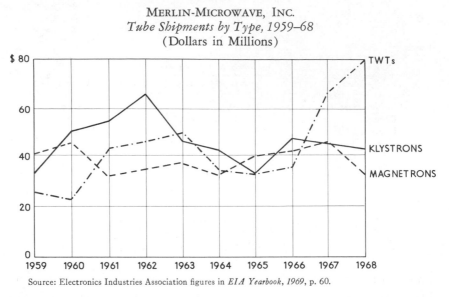

Source: Electronics Industries Association figures in *EIA Yearbook, 1969*, p. 60.

types and in all three basic markets, no company blanketed the market for all subtypes and applications. Most kinds of military tubes, for example, were manufactured by only one supplier. In the commercial area, tubes made by different manufacturers were not interchangeable within systems. Thus, once a buyer had designed his equipment around a particular supplier's tube, he could not easily switch his source, since he could not purchase an alternate tube off some other supplier's shelf. As a result, the market tended to be monopolistic and prices and profit margins were high. MM's management saw in this situation an opportunity for a small company to make a profit for itself by attacking the flanks of large companies with substitutable designs at lower prices. Alternatively, it might try to get its tubes selected for new or "second-generation" systems.

Management further believed that competition was restricted by the difficulty of changing from one tube field to another with very different requirements. For example, Hughes made sophisticated radar tubes where very close tolerances were required to meet power and frequency specifications. It would not have been easy to switch this production to the manufacture of heating magnetrons where tolerances and the pride of craftsmanship were not as critical. Therefore management believed that, although Litton, Raytheon, and Varian were large, they did

Exhibit 7

MERLIN-MICROWAVE, INC.

Size and Product Data for Companies Competing in the Microwave Tube Market, 1969

(Dollars in Thousands)

Company	Total Sales and Ending Date of Fiscal Year	Net Income	Microwave Sales/ Total Sales*	Major Product Lines
Amperex (Holland)............	—	—	—	—
Hughes Aircraft Co...........	—	—	—	Weapons systems, equipment and controls, missiles, space vehicles, communications and guidance systems, electronic components, etc.
Litton Industries, Inc........	$2,176,598 (7/31)	$82,258	1 + %	Computers and controls, automatic guidance systems, data processing, radar, communications, business machines, electronic and other components, shipbuilding including nuclear submarines, etc.
Microwave Associates, Inc....	27,756 (9/27)	839	—	Microwave energy components, semiconductors, solid state devices, transmission line devices, subassemblies, TV relay equipment, etc.
Microwave Electronics Co., Inc. Division of Teledyne, Inc...............	1,294,755 (10/31)	60,103	—	Electronic control systems and components, electrical products, services for the oil industry and oceanographic service, specialty metals, metal working machinery, etc.
Raytheon Co.................	1,285,134 (12/31)	35,232	3 + %	Electronic systems, subsystems, equipment, and components; heating, cooking, and cooling appliances, etc.
Sperry Rand Corp............	1,607,340 (3/31)	77,036	—	Information handling and retrieval systems; aerospace products; industrial, agricultural, construction, and materials-handling equipment, office machines, consumer and marine technology products, etc.
Varian Associates...........	186,172 (9/30)	7,004	43 + %	Microwave tubes and other electronic equipment and solid-state devices.
Miscellaneous "uni-tube" companies†....	—	—	—	—

* Based on management's assumption that Varian had 50% of the 1969 market, or $80.5 million; Raytheon had 25%, or $40.3 million; and Litton had 15%, or $24.2 million.

† Believed by MM management to be undercapitalized as well as narrowly based.

Source: Standard & Poor's *Corporation Records* and *Poor's Register of Corporations, Directors and Executives,* 1970.

not represent as formidable competition as appeared. Transfer of talents did occur, however, from military contracts to commercial activities within related tube classes.

MILITARY AND CIVILIAN MARKETS FOR RADAR AND COMMUNICATIONS

Looked at in another way, the market for microwave tubes could be divided into military and civilian segments. MM's management stated that the military was by far the largest buyer of all three types of tube, although its proportion was expected to decline, as is shown in Table 1.

TABLE 1

Tube Type	Volume 1969 (Millions)	Estimated Military Share		Estimated Commercial Share	
		1970	1973	1970	1973
Magnetron	$42	80%	50%	20%	50%
Klystron	39	90	90	10	10
TWT	80	70	50	30	50

Source: Exhibit 4 and MM management estimates.

Based on these estimates and a total dollar volume of $161 million in 1969, the military was spending $34 million for magnetrons, $35 million for klystrons, and $56 million for TWTs, for an overall total of $125 and an 80% combined market share.

Of the three applications for microwave tubes—radar, communications, and heating—the first two were predominantly military; only the third had no specific military importance.

So far as radar applications were concerned, the market was almost wholly military, since the major use for radar was in defense systems— in the air; on the ground, including landing fields; and on ships. Military demand for a particular type of tube was relatively easy to assess. Essentially, each defense system required a set number of tubes (for example, each B–52 airborne radar system used one particular coaxial magnetron), and the number of systems in use was fairly constant, as was the rate at which tubes were replaced. (For example, tubes for the B–52 radar system were replaced every four months, and 1,200 tubes were purchased each year.) How long military demand could continue to be confidently predicted was, however, doubtful, owing to changing defense needs and to budgetary constraints.

Nonmilitary uses of tubes for radar included weather reconnaisance, surveillance of commercial airports and air traffic control, airport landing systems, and navigation systems for ships and small boats. These commercial uses had come into being as military needs were satisfied and as engineers were freed to investigate nondefense applications. New segments were appearing and growth was accelerating, so demand was not easy to predict—except that the small boat market was expected to show the fastest gains. Overall, however, the radar market was expected to expand at a slow pace.

So far as communications applications for microwave tubes were concerned, the military market was believed to account for 65%–70% of sales. Here the major use was long-distance voice and ground-to-air communications.

The principal nonmilitary use of microwaves for communications was in telephone and television relay links. Microwaves performed 90% of all TV transmission and two-thirds of all long-distance communication, including telephone data transmission and facsimile. The principal purchasers were Bell Telephone, Western Union, Microwave Communications, Inc., and the UHF–TV stations. Annual sales ran approximately $20 million.

For military and nonmilitary uses combined, MM's management predicted that the communications market would be growing at 7%, the industry average. Over the long run, microwaves might encounter some competition from lasers, which had an even greater capability for carrying information. So far, however, technical difficulties with laser systems had prevented their extensive use. For the foreseeable future management believed it probable that the bulk of communication transmissions would continue to be carried out at microwave frequencies. Microwave systems were finding greatly expanded use in satellites for transcontinental communications.

SELLING THE MILITARY MARKET

Sales to the military might be direct—i.e., to military procurement offices, or indirect—i.e., to manufacturers who made defense systems incorporating tubes. Indirect sales, MM's management believed, were the more difficult type to make. Not only did some major systems manufacturers produce their own tubes (e.g., Raytheon, Hughes, Microwave Associates, and Sperry), but key sales factors in this area were longstanding intercompany relations, reputation, and past performance.

Direct military sales were made to user agencies which employed two methods of procurement: Invitations for Bids (IFBs), and Requests for Proposals (RFPs). At the government's option, a bidder might be required to have previously qualified his product as acceptable by meeting standards contained in a Qualified Product List (QPL) for the item. By qualifying a tube at a cost of approximately $30,000 for development and testing expenses, a company could always bid on the tube without having to meet test standards to insure that the tube was acceptable.

If an IFB was used, all terms of the contract were final as bid, and the low bidder won provided he passed certain tests as a "reliable" supplier. Under a RFP, terms and prices were negotiated both before and after the award, and the low bidder did not always win. If a QPL was stipulated, a non-QPL vendor could not bid. Contracts could be let with or without a QPL stipulation.

Direct military sales broke down into sales of tubes for new equipment, for replacement, or for R&D. Each of these segments varied in terms of procurement methods used, ease of entry, market effort required to win the business, and potential profit payoff. The least difficult segment to enter, MM's management believed, was the replacement segment. Here the purchaser stated the specifications, followed well-established procurement regulations, and purchased on the basis of price. In this segment, QPLs were often but not always used. Profits, however, were generally lowest. As one moved into military sales for original equipment and R&D, contracts became harder to obtain since factors such as new design and innovation were important. Profits increased, but so did costs and capital investment.

As previously noted, MM was interested in entering the military market, especially the replacment sector, not only as an end in itself, but also as a "springboard" to greater visibility for the company and to more business elsewhere.

Besides these advantages, company management also saw some problems in the military market. These were identified by Mr. Olsen as follows:

There are some drawbacks, too, in the military market. First, there is the cyclicality of defense spending. Second, there is the risk of choosing a line of tubes for qualification on QPLs and then not receiving a bid for the tubes. Third, the profits are generally not as high as in the commercial market. They are high in some areas now, but if we enter the market, we will be forced to underbid the competition to win.

THE HEATING MARKET

Unlike radar and communications, the $7 million heating market for microwave tubes was civilian. In this market purchasers used the product for heating nonmetallic materials, including food. The advantage in this technique arose from the ability of microwaves to dissipate energy uniformly throughout the mass of the substance being heated. In conventional heating, energy was applied only to the outside surface of the material and was carried to the inside by conduction. This process limited the amount of energy that could be applied without burning the outer surface of the material. The microwave tube, though, could supply energy at a sufficient rate to heat a nonmetallic substance without burning in a fraction of the time required by conventional methods.

The ability to heat rapidly was the principal promise of microwave heating. Mainly because of this feature, microwave heating had three basic applications: industrial, domestic, and commercial. Of these, both of the last two featured the heating or cooking of food. In this application, as in others, speed was a prime consideration: For example, a microwave oven could cook eight strips of bacon in three minutes or bake a cake in four minutes. In addition, a secondary value of the process was the ability to cook food in its own juices without drying it out. Lastly, since no conventional heat was used, grease would not burn onto the side of the oven and therefore could be wiped off easily with a sponge.

Industrial Heating Applications. The industrial segment of the heating market used microwave systems to produce rapid drying and curing of products. These applications were practically endless. Microwave heating had been used to dry paper, leather, baseball bats, tobacco, glue, and foundry sand cores. In the field of medicine it had been used for diathermy treatments where deep heat penetration was required. Experiments were being performed by several industries to determine the usefulness of microwave heating. For example, Kodak was attempting to dry film and PPG Industries was looking into microwave heat to dry fiberglass.

MM's management believed that no clear-cut competition had yet appeared in the industrial segment. Varian, as the largest tube producer with 1969 tube sales of approximately $80 million, appeared to be the most likely leader. Raytheon was known to have a small share of the market with one of its tubes (they had shipped a potato chip dryer to

Frito-Lay). Litton might be a source for some end-users, but MM's management believed that Litton's heating tubes were mostly geared to the commercial and domestic oven markets and that Litton probably had no extant working tubes that would be especially efficient if transferred to the industrial scene.

Summing up MM's assessment of the industrial heating market segment, President Merlino spoke as follows:

The primary advantage of microwave heating is its time saving. General Motors, for example, has found that foundry sand cores can be dried in five minutes with a microwave oven versus over an hour with a conventional oven. Additional benefits are a saving of floor space, greatly improved consistency since the cores dry at the same rate all the way through, and lower capital investment and operating expenses.

The industrial market has been an enigma for years. Since 1945 technicians and scientists have recognized the vast potential savings and have been attempting to adapt microwave power to industrial uses. Yet sales of tubes for these purposes increase only slightly each year. Everyone wants to know what the magic word is to open this potentially enormous market.

There are two keys to the market. First, tubes must cost less. One system being designed to dry a single type of fiber will use 150 tubes and require four replacements a year. The system will be used on 20 lines. Therefore, 12,000 tubes a year will be needed. A tube today costs approximately $300 in this quantity; the user, though, looks to a $100 tube, or savings of nearly $2.4 million.

Second, a systems approach must be taken in developing a heating process. The microwave engineer cannot design a system without a good knowledge of the nature of the product being heated. Each product has particular characteristics that alter cavity size, heating time, and the power frequency required. The heating system must also be capable of being incorporated without disruption into the overall production process. Therefore, the microwave specialist must work very closely with the product technicians and the mechanical engineers.

In spite of these problems, some facts are obvious about this market. Its potential is tremendous, if just *one* application for *one* company requires 12,000 tubes a year. Thus, a supplier must have a sufficient amount of automated equipment and capital to produce tubes in the quantity and at prices required by customers. Finally, a company like us with microwave expertise must find people to provide a "systems approach" to the market.

Domestic Oven Applications.   Of all the uses for microwave tubes, the domestic oven market appeared to have the greatest growth potential, since domestic ovens were used in the home for daily cooking. Table 2 shows the tremendous projected growth of this market.

For comparison, past growth in unit sales of some other appliances are reported in Table 3.

TABLE 2

Year	Units Sold (Thousands)	Estimated Oven Sales Price*	Estimated Total Sales (Thousands)
1966...................	2	$1,000	$ 2,000
1967..................	4–5	700	3,000
1968..................	15–20	500	8,000
1969..................	30	500	15,000
1970 est.†.............	80	475	38,000
1971 est................	200	375	75,000
1972 est................	375	300	112,500
1973 est................	600	275	165,000

* The tube was approximately 15% of the selling price in 1969.
† Raytheon and Litton both said they were building 50,000 ovens apiece for 1970.
Source: For units sold, *Appliance Magazine*, February, 1970, p. 62; for estimated prices, MM management.

Several tube manufacturers were already in the domestic oven market, and others were planning to enter. Some produced the total system (ovens plus tubes), though in different divisions or subsidiaries (e.g., Raytheon); others sold their tubes to independent oven manufacturers (e.g., Amperex), while others handled oven tubes both ways (e.g., Litton). Management's knowledge of competition is summarized in Table 4.

Any plans which other large appliance manufacturers might have for marketing a domestic oven were not known to MM's management team, nor were the plans of foreign manufacturers.

In at least one foreign country—Japan—microwave ovens had made

TABLE 3

	1960 (Thousands of units)	1969 (Thousands of units)	Per Cent Change 1968–69
Dishwashers........................	555	2,157	10%
Food waste disposers................	760	1,880	8
Electric ranges.....................	1,495	2,468	7
Gas ranges.........................	1,814	2,499	10
Electric refrigerators................	3,475	5,485	1
Washing machines...................	3,364	4,482	2
Dryers.............................	1,260	3,120	9
Electric irons......................	6,410	10,000	
Vacuum cleaners....................	3,313	7,144	10
Electric fans.......................	4,687	9,257	1
Freezers...........................	1,045	1,135	1
Wholesale price index (1957–59 = 100).................	97.0	94.1	2

Source: Bureau of the Census, Bureau of Labor Statistics, and *Merchandising Week*, in Business and Defense Services Administration, *U.S. Industrial Outlook*, 1970, p. 109.

TABLE 4

Oven Source	Tube Source	Date of Entry	Estimated Annual Sales
Tappan Co.*	—	1954	About 2,000 (until 1968)
Amana Division of Raytheon Co.	Raytheon	1967	2,000–3,000 in 1967; 15,000 in 1968. Objective of 50,000 in 1970.
Litton Industries, Inc.	Litton	Late 1969	Planned to sell through Montgomery Ward under the "Signature" label. Objective of 50,000 in 1970.
Norris Industries, Inc. "Thermador" ranges†	—	March 1970 (planned)	—
General Electric Co.	—	—	—
Roper Corp.	Litton	—	Five-year exclusive agreement to use Litton tubes in an oven to be sold through Sears Roebuck.
Husqvarna Corp.‡ (Sweden)	—	Planned to enter U.S. market after 1970	—

* Microwave and regular oven combination.
† Microwave in combination with an infrared unit to brown food, at a price of $680, or $1,200 with a self-cleaning feature.
‡ Round-shaped oven, which some industry observers believed would be particularly appealing to housewives.
Source: MM management.

much greater progress than in the United States. Unit sales were already 250,000 by 1969, with 500,000 to 750,000 predicted for 1970. Several Japanese suppliers were already established, the principal ones being Toshiba, Sharpe (Hayakawa), and Matsushita.

The rapid acceptance of microwave ovens in Japan was deemed due to some local market factors. Thus, Japanese food was readily adaptable to microwave cooking—vegetables, rice, and fish being more easily cooked than roasts. Japanese homes were traditionally small, so a microwave oven fitted better into the kitchen than a large stove with oven. Urban husbands and wives in Japan usually worked, so an oven became important as a time-saving device. By nature the Japanese also loved gadgets. Finally, very few of the older generation in Japan had possessed stoves. Therefore, in contrast to the United States, none of the younger Japanese had been taught by mother to cook on a conventional appliance, so they had no reluctance to cook with microwave.

Summing up MM's assessment of the U.S. domestic oven market, President Merlino spoke as follows:

First of all, the demand for microwave ovens is increasing rapidly as TV shows give them away as prizes and as full-page ads are run in large magazines like *Ladies' Home Journal* and *Life* [September 19, 1969, Amana oven]. This publicity, of course, works in our favor, since it develops a market for us to enter.

Second, the conventional appliance companies are very interested in the microwave oven market. There are a lot of these companies: Hotpoint, Whirlpool, Frigidaire, Corning Glass Works, Hamilton Beach, Hupp Corp., and others. They will not be satisfied to see their markets taken away by microwave ovens, nor will they be happy to see these oven manufacturers making a very healthy profit in areas where they consider they have expertise. Many are not sure exactly what product to sell: Should it be an oven, a sandwich grill, or a unique device for the kitchen? It is certain, though, that several of them will enter the market.

The major tube producer, though, may not as yet have appeared. Litton and Raytheon are working at capacity for their own needs, and the other tube companies either show little interest or have little expertise in this area. Therefore, a supplier must come forth to meet the demand.

On the negative side, four factors have restricted growth in this market. First, there is the tendency for all girls to prefer to cook the way their mothers did. We are dealing here with personal tastes, and some people are reluctant to eat food prepared by a fantastic machine that shoots electricity into food and cooks it in a few minutes.

There is also the basic problem of selling the oven, a radically new product, to the public. A particular problem here is the recent HEW allegation of radiation leakage from ovens. Its statement that radiation above certain levels can cause cataracts and chromosome damage and that oven leakage is not being properly controlled has significantly cut sales in the first few months of 1970. We feel that by the time we are in the market, firm regulations will be in effect and we will take them into account in our designs. [See the Appendix for a more complete discussion of this problem.]

Third, the microwave oven, by the nature of its heating process, does not brown food. A steak is cooked the same all the way through and does not have the conventional "charcoal-broiled" look. Finally, there is the problem of packaging food for use in the oven. Not all food can be cooked in the oven and each type and amount of food requires different cooking times. When you speak of baking a potato in four minutes, it is critical that food not be left in the oven too long. This problem is being solved with the planned introduction by frozen food companies [Stouffer] of food packaged for microwave ovens, with cooking times on the package.

MM feels that the combination of these factors leads to a basic conclusion: the domestic microwave heating market has come of age and is ready to explode. The lead time in developing, testing, and getting approval of an oven is about two years. Therefore, the time to act is today before another tube manufacturer appears and before the market matures around the existing oven manufacturers.

Commercial Oven Applications. The commercial market for microwave ovens was mainly composed of a restaurant segment, with some demand also from a fast growing automatic food-vendor segment.

Since the primary advantage continued to lie in the saving of time, restaurant users tended to be those that prided themselves on fast service. Such customers included some important franchise chains: e.g., Howard Johnson's Sizzlebord, and Pewter Pot. These used the ovens to reheat precooked foods.

Besides speed, a secondary advantage of microwave heating for commercial use lay in the fact that the ovens gave off no grease, thereby eliminating the need for exhaust hoods and easing sanitary problems with boards of health. Additionally, the consistent cooking time in an oven allowed for better planning, more extensive menus, and more consistent tasting food.

Litton was the principal producer of ovens for restaurants and cafeterias. It had been in this market since 1965, and, according to MM's management, Litton had been able to prove itself as a source of dependable, quality ovens. The original market entrant had been Raytheon, which had started this business in 1945. After putting millions into its "Radarange" venture, however, Raytheon dropped out in 1968. Increased competition from Litton plus a desire to concentrate on the domestic market potential of its own Amana oven were the factors that reportedly led to its decision. More recently, the restaurant market had been invaded by Magic Chef with an oven similar to Litton's and using Litton tubes. In addition, two small companies sold commercial restaurant ovens: Welbilt Corp. and Thermo Kinetics, Inc. Welbilt (Garland Oven) used an oven manufactured by Husqvarna (Sweden) and was believed to have a problem in obtaining replacement tubes. Therefore, it was selling the oven to restaurants only in the northeast United States and had not sold over 500. Thermo Kinetics sold a large oven that was used for bulk processing of food. They had sold only about 20 ovens, and MM's management believed that there was no real market for the product. It used an Amperex tube.

In the vending segment of the commercial market, the microwave oven was used to heat sandwiches and other foods. For example, an oven could cook a frozen hot dog or it could thaw (yet not heat up) a frozen milk shake. Since cooking was accomplished in a matter of seconds, machines could be used in many types of location: gasoline stations, airports, or even special microwave areas on a turnpike.

So far, microwave cooking for vending machines was accomplished by separate vending mechanisms and ovens rather than by an integrated system. Although the technology for the latter had been available for many years, no one had yet placed it on the market.

Each of the three principal competitiors in the food-vending business had made an exclusive agreement with a microwave oven supplier. Thus, Rowe International Co., the largest, had an exclusive agreement with Litton to place Litton's oven next to Rowe's vendor; Vendo, the second largest, had a similar agreement with International Crystal Manufacturing Co.; and National Vendors, the third largest, had a similar agreement with Sage Laboratories, Inc., of Natick, Massachusetts. Of these oven suppliers, Litton and Sage used the Litton tube, while Crystal used the Amperex from Holland.

Although Rowe, Vendo, and National were the only vending machine companies that had national coverage, many other smaller competitors (for example, the Cornelius Company) were anxious to enter the market with microwave equipment and were looking for a microwave oven supplier. In addition, Vendo was reportedly interested in an integrated vending-oven arrangement. Its present oven supplier, Crystal, was considered too small to develop such a product, and consequently Vendo was seeking another source to develop and produce this equipment.

Commenting on prospects in the commercial market, Mr. Rhodes, MM's treasurer, expressed himself as follows:

There is a great range of possible customers to consider in this area. We can sell our microwave expertise to vending machine companies, food-processing equipment manufacturers, food processors, or conventional appliance makers. Likewise, the variety of food that can be heated is enormous, and each type requires a different oven configuration.

We must be careful in this market, though, because some of these ideas for dispensing food are novel and require sizable capital to develop machinery and back-up systems. Also we cannot design an oven to heat, say, cheeseburgers without ensuring that the cheeseburger has a uniform size and consistency [fat and meat content]. Because of the nature of the heating process, the set machine time, and the automation of the machinery, cheeseburgers of differing sizes would have very uneven quality and would not sell. This "systems" aspect goes one step further in a situation like, say, McDonald's, which has uniform kitchens at each location. While a microwave oven might work well, installing an oven would necessitate a change in the rest of the kitchen and therefore would not be worth its savings.

The systems approach requires coordination with food suppliers, but this is not an insurmountable problem. Large and small frozen-food companies are producing food for microwave ovens. We feel that since the system is being attacked by others and the technology and desire are here, microwave heating in the commercial area has finally come of age. [See Exhibit 8 for data on the potential market for microwave cooking capability.]

Exhibit 8

MERLIN-MICROWAVE, INC.

Major Firms in the U.S. Market for Microwave Cooking Capability, 1969*
(Dollars in Thousands)

Company	Current Participation in the Microwave Oven Market	Total Sales and Ending Date of Fiscal Year	Net Income
Amana Division of Raytheon Co......	✓	$ 1,285,134 (12/31)	$ 35,232
Automatic Vendors of America, Inc....	✓	32,016 (9/30)	129
Cornelius Co........................	—	39,309 (12/31)	d(989)
Corning Glass Works...............	—	350,568 (12/28)	50,029
Crystal Mfg. Co....................	✓	—	—
Frigidaire Division of General Motors Corp...........................	—	24,295,141 (12/31)	1,710,695
Hamilton Beach Division of Scovill Mfg. Co.........................	—	444,490 (12/31)	15,616
Hotpoint Division of General Electric Co..............................	✓	8,447,967 (12/31)	278,015
Hobart Mfg. Co....................	—	201,016 (12/31)	13,102
Hupp Division of White Consolidated Industries, Inc....................	—	767,601 (12/31)	29,853
Litton Industries, Inc..............	✓	2,176,589 (7/31)	82,258
Magic Chef, Inc...................	—	90,067 (6/30)	3,018
National Vendors Division of UMC Industries, Inc...................	✓	136,469 (12/31)	7,284
Roper Corp.......................	✓	205,412,976	4,972,453
Rowe International, Inc., Division of Triangle Industries, Inc.........	✓	67,237 (12/31)	2,844
Seeburg Corp. of Delaware..........	—	—	—
Sage Laboratories, Inc..............	✓	3,763 (6/30)	200
Tappan Co........................	✓	133,877 (12/31)	3,441
Norris Industries, Inc................	(planned) (7/31)	281,800	14,400
Thermo-Kinetics, Inc................	✓	—	—
Vendo Co.........................	✓	99,326 (12/31)	2,408
Welbuilt Corp.....................	✓	56,842 (12/31)	882
Whirlpool Corp....................	—	1,153,530 (12/31)	45,943

* Excludes a Swedish firm with a microwave oven in the U.S. market (Husqvarna) and three Japanese suppliers (Sharpe-Hayakawa, Matsushita, and Toshiba).
Source: MM management and Standard & Poor's *Corporation Records*.

Merlin-Microwave in 1970

MANAGEMENT AND KEY PERSONNEL

In 1970 MM's management and key personnel included the company's three co-founders and three outside members of the board (see Exhibit 9 for details on their experience and education). Dr. Merlino, as president, was responsible for overall administration. In reality, he indicated, all decisions were made on a consensus basis by the three principals, with no individual attempting to sway the others to his own opinions. The group worked very closely as a team and rarely made a decision, other than one of a minor administrative nature, without agreement.

Like Dr. Merlino, Mr. Rhodes, the treasurer, and Mr. Olsen, the marketing vice president, both had engineering backgrounds. Dr. Merlino, who was a listed inventor on several patents in the field of high-power microwave tubes, was considered the company's expert in klystrons. Mr. Rhodes was considered its microwave heating specialist. Mr. Olsen was relied upon for his knowledge of machinery, material, mechanical engineering, and drafting. Ten patents in various fields had been granted to Mr. Olsen, and he had others pending.

Outside members of the board also had specialized expertise. Thus Professor ———, the head of the electrical engineering department in a local Ivy League university, acted as technical advisor; Mr. ———, the treasurer of a successful restaurant franchise chain, was the financial individual on the board; and Mr. ———, a recent graduate of the Harvard Law School, was an associate of MM's firm of legal advisors.

PRODUCTION AND SALES ORGANIZATION

After raising some $225,000 through its public issue, MM increased the number of people employed from 6 to 21. By early 1970 the production group included four experienced tube technicians, a test engineer with an Associate in Engineering degree, a factory superintendent, a senior engineer with a BS degree and 12 years of experience in microwave tube development, and a physicist with an SM degree from MIT and 12 years of experience in electrical and mechanical engineering and particle physics.

The selling group included a retired Army procurement colonel who consulted on government procurement, a Washington representative, and a national network of 18 sales offices (manufacturers' representatives).

Exhibit 9

MERLIN-MICROWAVE, INC.

Background Data on Founder-Managers and Key Board Members

Name	Office	Age	Holdings of MM Shares*	Education	Previous Positions
Dr. Edwin Merlino	President	36	25,000	BS (Engineering) Pennsylvania State MS (Electrical Engineering) Stanford PhD Northeastern	Microwave engineer, Varian Associates, 1957–61 Manager of Advanced Tube Development, Microwave Associates, 1961–67
Mr. Albert Olsen	Marketing Vice President	45	18,525		Chief Engineer, Joseph Pollak Corporation, † 1959–62 Manager of Engineering, Waters Manufacturing, † 1962–65 National Radio Co., 1965–67 Consultant 1967–68
Mr. Harold Rhodes	Treasurer	38	10,000	BS (Physics) Geneva College MS (Physics) MIT	Engineer, Raytheon Microwave Power Tube Division Engineer, Microwave Associates Director of R & D, Contek, Inc.,† 1963–68
Professor———	Head of the Department of Electrical Engineering, ———University since 1966	—	1,000		
Mr.———	Treasurer and Director, [snack chain] Management Corp.; Director, [pizza] Management Corp.	—	1,000		International Vice President, [Snack-bar chain]

Note: The only available information on Mr.—, the lawyer, is p. 25.
* Out of 148,129 common shares outstanding.
† Small companies in the Bridgeport area.
Source: Interviews with company management.

Although management noted that MM lacked sufficient assets to step into large-scale tube production, management believed that the company had established a nucleus of capable people and administrative and control systems.

PRODUCT LINE AND SALES TO DATE

At the time of MM's stock offering, the *Prospectus* told investors that management had had experience in the design, development, and production of all three generic types of mcirowave tubes and that the company intended to develop products in each of these fields. Products already developed included a line of heating magnetrons for home and restaurant ovens, plus other models having direct application in industrial processing. Of the proceeds to be raised by the public offering, about $50,000 was intended for "tooling and cost reduction engineering" relating to these heating tubes.

Besides its magnetrons, the company reported that it had also developed a klystron for use in the receiver portion of an airport radar system; this klystron was also believed to be potentially useful in transmitting and receiving communications.

By the end of its second year, MM had been involved in two major contracts, both of which had been successfully completed. One of these was with the Federal Aviation Authority (FAA) and involved a $65,000 order for 185 reflex klystrons of a type on which the company had had little previous experience. This contract had lasted 12 months, during the last of which the yield had been 85% of all tubes put into production, while shipments totaled 64 tubes. MM had had no rejects from the FAA.

The second major contract had been a $21,500 order from Westinghouse for two magnetrons. Also, under contract, the company had developed three industrial heating tubes for Bechtel Corporation, and it was working on an integrated hot dog oven-vendor for a major machinery manufacturer which was contemplating this product as a possible diversification.

As of February, 1970, MM had no contracts for commercial products, but it had spent approximately $45,000 on travel and communication in order to get in touch with potential microwave tube users, especially those interested in heating applications. To demonstrate the workability of its heating tubes, the company had put them into several Litton and Raytheon ovens. Management believed that the company had made many valuable contacts with potential customers.

THE DESC ORDER

Early in 1970 management indicated that the most significant event in MM's immediate future would be the outcome of a $222,500 military order from the Defense Electronics Supply Corps (DESC), obtained in October, 1969. This order involved 310 coaxial magnetrons to be used in an Air Force airborne radar system.

The decision to go after this contract stemmed directly from management's strategy of penetrating the military market as a way to get established in the tube industry. The contract thus successfully pursued had been one for a replacement tube, though not for a type of tube which MM had so far produced. The contract had involved an Invitation for Bid (IFB) rather than a Request for Proposal (RFP), so management was sure that the low bidder would be successful. Also, the contract had not stipulated that the tube must be purchased from the Qualified Product List (QPL), and thus a non-QPL vendor could bid. Instead, the contract terms had required a First-Article Test and a Systems-Compatibility Test.

At the time of bidding on this contract (August, 1969), management had known that both Raytheon and Varian would also bid. Moreover, both had previously won awards for this same tube, though Raytheon's version had not yet passed its First-Article Test. On these earlier occasions, Varian's price had been $1,200 a tube and Raytheon's $1,250 (the latter set on a negotiated basis).

To insure that MM would win, management bid a price of $750, or enough to cover estimated variable costs of $730 per tube and to make a minor contribution toward estimated allocated unit costs of $225 for selling and administration. Thus, MM's management decided to accept a $60,000 loss as a necessary "investment" to enter the military market. As it turned out, the company's bid was just a few dollars a tube below Raytheon's at the 310 volume level.

Before the final award, MM had to pass a pre-award survey to determine its productive, financial, and technical capability. By September all phases of the survey had been completed and a favorable report had been sent by the New York Region of the Defense Contract Administration Services (the contract administrator) to DESC, which had the final contract authority.

According to MM's management, DESC was very unhappy with the favorable report, since they wanted a known tube company as the supplier. They had never expected MM to win and were not anxious to nurse the company through financial and technical problems. Furthermore, the head of procurement at DESC was about to be promoted and he did not want MM to damage his chances. Nonetheless, MM could not be disqualified, and the award was made on October 31, 1969.

The contract had the following schedule:

Date	Event
April 9, 1970	Completion of First Article Test
April 30, 1970	Completion of Systems Compatibility Test
April 30, 1970	Shipment of 50 tubes
May 30, 1970	Shipment of 100 tubes
June 30, 1970	Shipment of 100 tubes
July 30, 1970	Shipment of 60 tubes

The contract also had a 50% "follow-on" option for another 155 tubes, exercisable by the supplier until April 15, 1970. Given the "learning curve" on tube production, management believed this would be very profitable.

FUTURE PLANS

Having implemented the first major step in its strategy by obtaining the DESC contract, MM's management had to turn its attention to planning its succeeding steps. By this time it had already been decided that the heating tube business would be the next area on which to concentrate, and MM had already got in touch with several possible clients in this field. Early in 1970, the company was engaged in active negotiations with one supplier of domestic ovens (Corning Glass Works) and with several sources in the commercial field (Vendo, Cornelius, Sage Laboratories, and Crystal Manufacturing Co.). (See Exhibit 8 above for data on the potential oven market.)

In addition, several tubes had been sold to a company (Bechtel Corporation) active in industrial heating tubes.

Management said that while "military sales were bringing in profits and a reputation," all segments of the heating market would be attacked by means of cooperative ventures with nationally known companies. All companies that might have an interest in microwave heating would be contacted, and MM would work with as many partners as it could to reach the home-oven and industrial heating markets. In the commercial market, in contrast, what seemed needed was a single partner who could provide a distribution system, marketing ability, and a willingness to invest. MM's executives indicated that their company, by itself, did not have the capital and expertise to compete with the extensive marketing organization of Litton, Raytheon, G.E., etc.

As for product and production plans, MM's market entry would occur in two phases. First, the company would continue to refine its current heating tube designs, and it would build prototypes. Also in this phase, designs of ovens, electronic packages, and heating systems would be accomplished. Whether the company would eventually move forward into actual production of such electronic packages and/or total systems remained an open point to be decided. In the second phase of its market entry, MM would create automated equipment capable of producing up to 100,000 tubes a year. The development of such equipment was seen as being within the "state of the art," although none had actually been constructed.

Besides working out their marketing and product approach to heating tubes, MM's management had some financial planning done for these and other longer-range objectives. To implement the company's goals, an estimated $2 million would be needed: $500,000 in 1970, $800,000 in 1971, and $700,000 in 1972. Applications would be as follows:

Domestic and Commercial Heating

$350,000	Tooling and product development
150,000	Automated production line
100,000	Marketing

Industrial Heating

$150,000	Product development
70,000	Control circuitry and power supply modules
85,000	Marketing

Military

$250,000	TWT development
150,000	Magnetron development
100,000	Marketing
250,000	Working capital

Special Products

$150,000	Solid state coupling of tube devices
250,000	Oven electronics, transformers

MANAGEMENT'S LONG-RANGE PERSONAL GOALS

Over the longer run, each of the three founder-managers had in mind a picture of what kind of company he wanted MM to become and what personal satisfactions he expected to derive from working for this kind of firm. Dr. Merlino, the president, expressed himself as follows:

I had three reasons for starting MM. First, I have a particular personality trait of being unable to work for someone else. I have always been in trouble with my bosses, and in fact that was the reason I parted from my previous employer, Microwave Associates. Second, my wife is a biology professor and has a good salary. Therefore, 30%–40% of any money I make goes to the government in taxes. In order to make my time worthwhile, I must have either a high salary to get sufficient take-home pay or a capital gains situation. MM offers the latter alternative. Third, I desire to be independently wealthy by 40, and I am 36 now.

Besides these personal goals, I have certain corporate objectives. First, MM must be a profit-making device. Second, I want to make a profit without exploiting employees. In fact, if there is anything unique about the company, I want it to be a feeling of responsibility toward the employees. Varian, for example, shows real respect for its employees and they in turn work hard for the company. Most of the employees have considerable longevity; they are rarely laid off because management anticipates the market and does not overhire so that it will not have to release people. I hope to do the same within the constraint of survival and profits. If MM has to, we'll reduce profits to keep employees.

I also want to apply my knowledge of microwave tubes and physics in a company. I feel that there is great potential in the microwave heating market and that we can make a contribution to it. MM should use this area as a springboard to make contributions elsewhere, probably in the technological areas, since our expertise lies there. Essentially, we hope to be a technical company that is trying to sell products in the commercial world.

I do not want MM to be a very small company. It is not difficult to be a $1,000,000 tube firm, and such a company could operate well until I retire. But this is not my goal. I want a large business that grows as fast as it can. One problem we might have is wanting to grow too fast, in the sense that we are not sufficiently aware of the outside world to realize that our goals are not realistic.

Mr. Rhodes, treasurer, described his desires for MM as follows:

As for my personal objectives, I want to build a successful small company out of nothing. A small company has great interest to me. First, there are very few experts in small companies because either these companies fail or get large. Second, I am interested in the total process of building and managing a company. If one can manage a small company well, there is satisfaction from having done a successful job. Third, I am looking forward to drawing together all aspects of business—finance, psychology, marketing—within a technical area and making a success. Expertise to me is not science or business but the ability to join the two together.

Mr. Olsen, marketing vice president, described as follows what he hoped to achieve through MM:

In relation to the company, I am interested in seeing it have a significant and profitable place in a market with a product that does something for people. I am not interested in the aerospace or military market. These areas do advance technology faster than would normally occur, but I am not sure whether all their product spin-offs are worth the expense. Some of the output, though, is very helpful in the commercial market, and we plan to take our share of these advances. I would like to take these advances and turn them into something that makes people's lives easier and more significant.

This country is in need of a new industrial revolution based on the last 20 years of technology. Scientists and engineers today are too interested in advancing the state of the art, and not in giving people products they want and need. In the microwave heating area we have seen an evolution in the last 25 years based on advances in material technology. I would like to see MM extend this evolution by producing better products for microwave heating.

Eventually we should expand into related areas, e.g., all aspects of microwave heating and producing better power supplies. But the microwave heating area is so large that MM could spend all its life in the field and not even make a big dent.

Personally, I enjoy making products better and/or cheaper by manufacturing or application engineering. I also enjoy finding new uses for products. I should like to be able to motivate people along these lines so that there would be a group of people to make better products and not just myself. We must, though, find people that are interested in this type of work.

There are many ways to approach making a better product: working on the product itself, using better tooling, or making more investment in tooling. We must be careful, though, to relate our manufacturing effort to marketing feedback and find out how good a product we can make based on what people want. Only after we know what to make can we finance it.

I expect to make a profit for myself and the company if we go about our product development correctly. Profit should be a natural evolution from this process. If we have good marketing and production, everything else will fall into place.

IMMEDIATE PROSPECTS AS ASSESSED BY MM's PRESIDENT

In looking to the near-term future, Dr. Merlino assessed MM's prospects as follows:

In spite of the size of Litton, Raytheon, Varian, and other tube companies, we feel that we have certain assets we can sell. Litton and Raytheon have Japanese subsidiaries they originally hoped would make tubes for the U.S. market. But with Japanese sales increasing dramatically, the subsidiaries cannot export tubes. They are working at capacity making tubes for their own use. On the other hand, MM has the necessary talent, capability, and desire to produce tubes for appliance and vending machine companies. We can move very quickly in contrast to the long time it takes a large company to act. We also can underprice the large companies in a market where price is important. Finally, our tubes have a ceramic seal rather than a conventional glass one and can therefore be baked at higher temperatures, which leads to a longer life and quicker, less costly production.

A final asset is the fact that there is a limited pool of talented microwave tube engineers. For many years this area has not been a glamour field like solid-state physics, and there have been few new engineers. Additionally, few people in the universities have been interested in microwave tubes. With normal attrition, then, the pool has shrunk, and nearly all qualified people are tied in with present companies. To enter the field from scratch would require hiring engineers away from other companies, which is difficult, since they are needed in their present jobs. The fact that we have three qualified microwave people and have no capacity constraints makes us an important entity.

We have been purposefully open-minded about our entry into the market. Our expertise is the design of tubes, but a microwave system requires, in addition, a power supply, transformer, miscellaneous electronic equipment, and the oven itself. Therefore, we are not limiting our entry to microwave tubes only.

When you look at the market [Exhibit 8], it is evident that a certain amount of stratification has occurred. Three vending machine companies are set with tube sources. Varian has stated that if they get any portion of the microwave heating market it will be the industrial segment; Raytheon is already entrenched in the domestic oven market; Litton has contracted with Montgomery Ward to sell domestic ovens and they also have a strong reputation in the commercial oven market. Therefore, time is a very precious commodity to us. If you look at the picture of a normal product life cycle [see graph below], we feel that we are not too far into it yet to be hurt. For example, on the ROI curve of the graph

NORMAL PRODUCT LIFE CYCLE

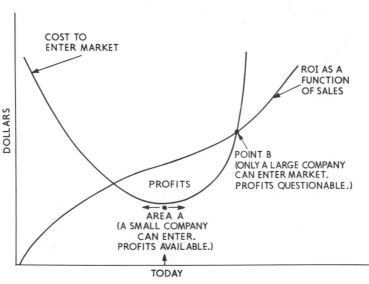

we are probably in Area A, where we can still invest a small amount and make good profits. But Point B, where the costs of entry will be very high and profits questionable, is only nine months to one year from now.

We are now faced with the question of whether it was wise to bid on a large contract with the prospect of a $60,000 investment. We have never made these tubes before. Going after the commercial market will take a lot of money, and we are not positive that we can raise capital. If we do not, it will be difficult to finance delivery of the government tubes. We also wonder whether we have guessed correctly that the microwave heating market is ready to take off. Does everyone else believe this, too, or are the well-heeled "partners" we are looking for still not ready to move ahead?

Appendix: Merlin-Microwave, Inc.

PROBLEMS OF RADIATION LEAKAGE IN DOMESTIC MICROWAVE OVEN*

One of the more serious problems facing microwave oven producers in early 1970, particularly producers of domestic ovens, was the recent allegation that microwave ovens were releasing harmful amounts of radiation.

The problem had two aspects: one political, the other biological. The political aspect centered around a disagreement in the Bureau of Radiological Health of HEW as to how strict rules for products under BRH's jurisdiction should be. With the appearance of Ralph Nader, who had effectively publicized the ineffectiveness of certain regulatory federal agencies, plus the revelation of some disturbing facts on certain ovens, the proponents of more stringent requirements found the perfect time to proselytize for their position. As a result, HEW tested some ovens in the field and found that in fact some of the ovens (one-third of 155 tested) had leakage of 10% to 20% above the commonly accepted 10 milliwatt-per-square-centimeter (MW/CM^2) level. (This standard had been set by the Department of Defense for radar, based on Atomic Energy Commission research.) HEW, however, admitted that these results did not reflect the nationwide picture because of sampling inaccuracies.

In essence, the industry (that is, the Association of Home Appliance Manufacturers) claimed that they had been monitoring all their ovens and that they were all within the accepted limits. Furthermore, the Association claimed in testimony in Washington on October 1, 1969, that these appliances were "not unreasonable hazards to health and safety."

---

*Sources: Edward Gross, "Microwaves and Health Effects," *The World*, February 18, 1970. (Reprinted from *Science News*); Association of Home Appliance Manufacturers, *Newsletter*, December, 1969; *The Wall Street Journal*, March 3, 1970; *Microwave News*, February, 1970, pp. 17–24.

The testimony continued, "However, if the Commission [National Commission on Product Safety] concludes some products are unreasonably hazardous, requiring mandatory safety standards, AHAM suggests the expertise in industry, and in nationally recognized standards-setting organizations, be used to initiate and develop them. . . ."

The biological side of the argument was not clear-cut. It had been known for a long time that microwaves in *sufficient* amounts and over a *long enough* period could cause harmful heating in human systems, particularly in eyes, testes, gall and urinary bladders, and in the digestive tract. But these harmful effects stemmed from large doses of microwaves, and scientists were uncertain about the effects—either short-term or cumulative—of low-level doses. Scientists were not even certain if all effects were thermal; Russian scientists claimed that microwaves caused changes in heart rhythm and neurological activity in the brain. Western scientists variously agreed and disagreed with the Russian theories. Apparently, the Russian experiments were conducted on a different basis from similar studies elsewhere. One problem with the studies underlying the HEW allegations was that scientists considered them "ancient," and therefore questionable—given today's more sophisticated testing procedures and consumer concerns.

Against this backdrop, discussion had shifted to what the maximum permissible level of microwave leakage should be. Early in 1970 HEW was expected to release a new standard under the authority of the Radiation Control for Health and Safety Act (1968). It was expected to say that not over one milliwatt per square centimeter of leakage could exist when the oven was shipped and that no oven could *ever* remain in service with over five. The manufacturers (AHAM) suggested on October 31, 1969, that a 10 MW/CM^2 level was "reasonable, conservative, and completely adequate to protect the public health and safety." The crux of the problem was seen as being that no manufacturer could guarantee a 5 MW/CM^2 level for life. For example, what happens if the oven is dropped by the owner?

The problem facing manufacturers at this point was more serious than simply meeting a government requirement. While manufacturers had 30 days to comment on the standard after it was published in the *Federal Register,* they would also have to test their ovens in the field and change their design specifications. Sales dropped off, and, as one industry expert stated, "Any publicity is bad publicity." Once a standard was agreed upon, there was still a question as to whether the product environment would have changed so as to make selling the ovens an unprofitable venture.

2. United Industries

UNITED INDUSTRIES was founded in 1945 by Mr. Peter Amato under the name of Middlesex Pattern Works. Mr. Amato, age 57, had been a craftsman in wood and metal for many years, having served a rigorous apprenticeship in his youth. For many years he had worked for General Electric at its Lynn, Massachusetts, plant.

From the date of its founding until 1956, the company's major product had been patterns. These were made primarily for the local foundry of General Electric but also for many of the other foundries in the Greater Boston area.

Patterns are solid pieces which are placed in a mold in order to impart the desired shape to a casting. A typical casting process would be to use a pattern to create, in sand, a depression of the size and shape of the desired casting. This is done by packing sand around the pattern. The pattern is then removed and the depression in the sand filled with molten metal.

United Industries made patterns of wood, metal, plastic, and clay. Since a single pattern can be used to produce many castings, patterns are often made in very small quantities; and an order for only one pattern of a particular kind is very common. Consequently pattern making is a highly skilled handcraft activity.

After 1956, the company's major product shifted from patterns to models and mockups. Net sales went from about $125,000 in 1957 to about $207,000 in 1961 (see Exhibit 1). Earned surplus went from $27,849 in 1957 to $81,191 in 1961 (see Exhibit 2). Financial ratios for this period are shown in Exhibit 3.

Models and mockups are three dimensional imitations of a device which differs from the real thing in several important ways. One important difference may be in actual size. A model may be either much smaller or much larger than the thing itself. Small-scale models are commonly used in architecture, factory layout, and chemical plant design. Large-scale models are used in product development.

A second important distinction between a model and the real thing may be in terms of the materials from which it is made. A full-scale model (often called a mockup) of wood or plastic may be desired as a

Exhibit 1

UNITED INDUSTRIES
Profit and Loss Statement
January 1 to December 31
(Thousands of Dollars)

	1957	1958	1959	1960	1961*
Gross sales	$127.1	$201.9	$257.2	$264.8	$211.4
Loss: Returns & allowances	1.2	1.1	6.8	4.1	4.0
Net sales	$125.9	$200.8	$250.3	$260.6	$207.4
Less: Labor	$ 58.2	$ 82.3	$107.3	$121.4	$102.7
Materials	19.5	32.4	40.9	40.6	23.9
Cost of goods sold	$ 77.7	$114.8	$148.2	$162.0	$126.6
Operating income	$ 48.1	$ 86.0	$102.1	$ 98.6	$ 80.7
Other income	1.8	..	..	5.5	5.4
Total income	$ 49.9	$ 86.0	$102.1	$104.1	$ 86.2

Operating expenses:

	1957	1958	1959	1960	1961*
Admin. salaries	$ 16.9	$ 20.0	$ 25.3	$ 20.5	$ 13.6
Office salaries	4.0	5.2	5.5	5.6	10.1
Rent	3.6	4.2	4.4	13.0	24.6
Repairs	2.0	2.8	2.3	4.4	10.1
Taxes	2.7	4.9	6.2	7.4	5.7
Contributions	..	0.2	0.3	0.2	..
Depreciation	2.9	4.6	6.0	5.5	4.3
Advertising	0.7	1.0	1.4	1.9	3.5
Travel expenses	1.3	1.6	1.7	1.5	0.4
Electricity, gas & fuel	1.7	1.9	2.2	3.2	3.7
Telephone	0.4	0.5	0.7	0.7	0.7
Office expenses	3.1	3.3	3.2	3.8	3.1
Freight	0.2	0.4	0.9	0.6	0.4
Insurance	1.0	1.3	1.6	2.6	2.0
Bad debts	..	..	0.4	..	..
Research & product development	..	..	4.1	..	..
Employee benefits:					
Insurance	0.6	0.9	1.6	3.2	2.3
Profit-sharing retirement plan	..	7.0	7.0	4.5	0.1
	$ 41.7	$ 60.6	$ 75.7	$ 78.5	$ 85.6
Profit before income tax	8.2	25.3	26.3	25.6	0.5
Federal income taxes	2.4	7.6	8.2	7.8	0.1
Net profit	$ 5.7	$ 17.6	$ 18.1	$ 17.7	$ 0.4

* Figures for 1961 reflect expenses incurred in the relocation of plant from 746 Broadway to 1901 Revere Beach Parkway.

less expensive way of reproducing a metal device for either display, instruction, or some other purpose where the durability of the actual material is not necessary. For example, United had made an aluminum and wood mockup of a jet engine for General Electric which was used to check the completed design, and subsequently for sales and exhibition purposes.

Exhibit 2

UNITED INDUSTRIES

Balance Sheet—December 31

(Thousands of Dollars)

Assets	1957	1958	1959	1960	1961*
Cash	$16.7	$27.1	$32.2	$ 47.4	$16.7
Receivables	9.8	21.3	27.7	30.1	28.1
Inventory	7.8	8.5	8.2	8.3	13.3
Total current assets	$34.3	$57.0	$68.1	$ 85.9	$58.1
Prepaid expenses	0.2	0.2	0.2	0.3	0.3
Deposits	0.6	0.6	0.6	0.6	0.1
Machinery & equipment	23.1	31.3	41.2	42.3	59.4
Less depreciation	13.6	18.3	19.5	25.1	26.0
Life insurance cash surrender value	1.0	1.8	2.5	3.4	4.3
Total assets	$45.8	$72.7	$93.2	$107.4	$96.2

Liabilities

	1957	1958	1959	1960	1961
Accounts payable	$ 0.6	$ 3.6	$ 3.3	$ 1.9	$ 5.1
Accrued payroll	7.8	2.4	3.1	0.9	0.6
Accrued taxes	1.9	2.5	3.3	6.2	3.7
Accrued profit-sharing contribution	..	6.0	7.0	4.5	0.1
Federal income taxes	2.4	7.6	8.2	7.8	0.1
Total current liabilities	$12.9	$22.3	$24.9	$ 21.4	$ 9.9
Capital stock	5.1	5.1	5.1	5.1	5.1
Surplus	27.8	45.2	63.2	80.9	81.2
Total liabilities	$45.8	$72.7	$93.2	$107.4	$96.2

Reconciliation of Surplus

	1957	1958	1959	1960	1961
Surplus at start	$22.5	$27.8	$45.2	$ 63.2	$80.9
Add: Tax income	8.2	25.3	26.3	25.6	0.6
Add: Increase in life insurance value	0.5	0.6	0.7	0.9	0.8
Total	$31.2	$53.8	$72.3	$ 89.7	$82.3
Less: Federal income tax	2.4	7.6	8.2	7.8	0.1
Less: Premium on life insurance	0.9	0.9	0.9	1.0	1.0
Total	$ 3.3	$ 8.6	$ 9.1	$ 8.8	$ 1.1
Surplus at end	$27.8	$45.2	$63.2	$ 80.9	$81.2

* Figures for 1961 reflect expenses incurred in the relocation of plant from 746 Broadway to 1901 Revere Beach Parkway.

Exhibit 3

UNITED INDUSTRIES

Selected Financial Ratios

Ratios	1957	1958	1959	1960	1961
Current assets/current liabilities	2.7	2.5	2.7	4.0	5.8
Operating income: % of net sales	38.0	43.0	41.0	38.0	39.0
Net profit after tax: % of net sales	4.5	8.8	7.3	6.8	0.2
Net profit after tax: % of net worth	17.3	35.1	26.6	20.8	0.4

The magnitude of the shift to models and mockups may be seen from the following table:

	Percentage of Total Sales
1956	15%
1957	30
1958–61	70

In explaining this shift in product mix, Mr. David E. Miller, marketing manager, said:

The shift wasn't planned—it just happened that way. Models and mockups have much higher margins than patterns, so we pushed in that direction when the opportunity arose.

The opportunity arose primarily because General Electric felt that Atkins & Merrill was high on price. Also, Atkins & Merrill was making models in fiberglass, and General Electric was interested in having them made of aluminum, which is much sturdier. We were in a position to do this because of our pattern-making experience and our casting facilities.

Our big problem was convincing GE that we could do the job. Atkins & Merrill had that big, fancy plant, and we were just a cellar operation at the time.

However, they were in the midst of developing the engine at the time, and they wanted quality models in a hurry. We were able to do the work. We were glad to have it because it came along just at the time when the pattern business was slack. It permitted us to keep the shop going.

In 1961, the name of the company was changed from Middlesex Pattern to United Industries. This took place at the same time that the company moved from the basement where it began operations to a two-story industrial building on Revere Parkway in Everett.

MANAGEMENT

The president, treasurer, and sole owner of United Industries was Mr. Amato. The other members of management in 1962 were Mr. R. H. Adams and Mr. David E. Miller. Mr. Adams, age 37, was production manager and had been with the company for over 15 years. Mr. Miller, age 26, was marketing manager. He had joined the company after having had previous marketing experience in other firms. Mr. Miller had an undergraduate training in engineering, and was a graduate of a leading eastern business school. He was also Mr. Amato's son-in-law.

MR. AMATO LOOKS AT HIS JOB

In an interview with the case writer, Mr. Amato made the following comment about his job:

I like this kind of work, and would do it even if I wasn't making any money. When you do something just for money, you don't always do the best job—you don't do it as well as something you do because you like it.

I couldn't stand a job where I did the same thing day after day. It's challenging to run this place, to solve the variety of problems we are faced with.

In fact, one reason I left the big company I used to work for as a pattern-maker was that I felt I couldn't grow any more. So I decided to leave.

If I had had more schooling, I might be working in a research group. I'd never get rich at it—but I'd be happy.

In the past, we have never refused a job because it was difficult—and we have never had a job that we couldn't do. I would say that the major strength of our organization is our ability to see the customer's problem and to have enough ingenuity to develop a solution for it.

I can see where, as a president, I have to project growth. After all, you either have to grow or fall by the wayside.

PERSONNEL

In 1962 United had 26 full-time employees. Twenty-one people worked on direct production activities, as follows:

Production Manager	1
Pattern Makers	7
Molder	1
Machinists	2
Apprentices	10
	21

In addition, there was one person assigned full time to maintenance. The remaining four employees were Mr. Amato, Mr. Miller, a clerk, and a typist.

Mr. Amato felt that one of his major problems was the lack of skilled craftsmen. Because most of the orders were either for a single item or a relatively small number of items, they had to be shaped and finished by relying almost entirely on simple tools and the worker's skill.

Craftsmen were very much in demand in the area and no pool of such men existed to meet the demand. On one occasion Mr. Amato inserted an ad for a patternmaker in a local newspaper. The only response was received from a 79-year-old man who was a retired patternmaker. One of the things that Mr. Amato was doing to remedy the situation was working with the vocational school in Everett in order to interest more young men in considering this kind of career. Mr. Amato was very much interested in training young men to be craftsmen. However, he had difficulty in doing this because of a shortage of qualified applicants.

The shortage of craftsmen was intensified by the unpredictability of orders being received. Also, there was a great deal of variation from month to month in the amount of work on hand (see Exhibit 4).

Employees were not unionized, but wage rates were approximately union scale for each craft. Time-and-one-half was paid after 40 hours, and double time for Sundays. The standard workweek was 48 hours, but because of the variations in orders received, it could be as low as 40 or as high as 60.

Exhibit 4

UNITED INDUSTRIES

Monthly Sales as a Percentage of Annual Sales, 1957–61

	1957	1958	1959	1960	1961
January	9.7	5.6	5.4	7.8	7.8
February	7.7	7.4	6.0	5.0	8.4
March	21.7	5.7	6.4	10.2	7.7
April	3.2	5.7	6.4	10.2	7.7
May	6.9	18.8	12.3	11.7	9.8
June	12.6	7.9	8.9	8.3	7.5
July	5.6	3.8	6.1	3.0	5.8
August	5.0	2.4	8.6	12.7	7.7
September	3.9	3.0	5.3	9.2	9.1
October	5.0	14.0	11.2	6.3	3.9
November	5.9	15.7	13.1	7.6	13.6
December	12.8	9.9	10.3	8.0	11.0
Total	100.0	100.0	100.0	100.0	100.0

All production employees participated in a profit-sharing fund into which 15% of profits before tax of each year were placed. Each employee's share was payable to him only upon termination of employment or retirement.

PRODUCTION

The building in which United was located was a two-story brick structure. There were 12,000 square feet on the first floor and 10,000 square feet on the second. The second floor was leased for a three-year period beginning in January, 1962, at an annual rental of $7,200. United occupied the entire first floor but currently used only 7,000 square feet of the total available space. The remainder was available to meet the needs of expansion. The building was owned by a trust set up by Mr. Amato; United paid an annual rental of $22,000 to the trust.

The work space was divided into four general areas: office, woodworking, metalworking, and foundry. Appropriate modern equipment was available in each of the areas.

The management felt that 1961 net sales of $207,000 could be doubled without requiring more than $15,000 in new equipment.

PRODUCT LINE

United had done work in a wide variety of fields and felt competent to provide a diversity of services, if orders could be obtained. Among the fields in which it had successfully provided service were developmental tooling, machine development, industrial design, and commercial exhibitions.

Developmental Tooling. Developmental tooling refers to tools made of materials that are less durable than those required for extensive production runs. They are less durable because they are made of materials which are easier to cut and form. This keeps the initial investment in tooling low until the final decisions concerning the production process are made. In addition, developmental tooling may be the only tools made for a job when the total expected production volume is low. Developmental tools are most commonly used in press operations, such as stamping and forming, since the cost of press dies is directly related to the durability of the die materials.

In explaining how the company got into developmental tooling, Mr. Miller said:

In 1960, we developed a way of making tools of kirksite, which is a good material for tooling on short-run jobs. We are the only ones in this area who do this kind of work. General Electric was especially interested in this service since they wanted to experiment with low-cost dies while they were getting their engines into production. However, now that GE is in full-scale quantity production, we have not only lost a lot of mockup business from them, we have also lost a lot of business for experimental tooling. In fact, we haven't had any mockups from them since April, 1961.

Prototypes. Prototypes are first-of-a-kind working models. They are, in a sense, the final phase of the design process—the tangible manifestation of the engineer's ideas. Many engineers felt, however, that a drawing of what they had in mind was as far as they had to go, and one of United's sales missions was to convince engineers of the desirability of a prototype model.

In its advertising, United presented the virtues of its prototype service as follows:

We at United feel that in creating prototypes—first-of-a-kind working models—we most fully demonstrate our unlimited imagination, flexibility, and skill. Many designers and engineers have come to realize that our ingenuity and experience can play an integral part in their planning of new or revised products, components, processes, and equipment. Our expertly modeled prototypes offer that vital opportunity to actually prove the feasibility of a two-dimensional plan or calculated theory before extensive commitments are made. Prototypes enable the designer and engineer to study the physical relationships of component parts, one to another, and their cumulative relationship to the envelope design. They offer the opportunity for revisions, for additions, for improvements—without prohibitive expense.

.   .   .   .

In addition to their technical applications, prototypes aid the market research team. Prospective customers can actually try the new product, evaluate its usefulness, indicate its design appeal, and offer suggestions which might broaden the range of the product's sales potential.

United Industries had actively promoted its service of building prototypes, especially to manufacturers and designers that did not have their own manufacturing facilities. One of the groups toward whom this service was directed was small electronics firms. However, this business did not prove to be as great or as profitable as United had anticipated. The chief difficulty, Mr. Miller said, was "it costs a lot to do, and you have to bid more than most shops are willing to pay."

Product Development and Industrial Design. United had an arrangement with an industrial designer whereby they would build either models or prototypes of designs that he developed and would charge him a fixed rate. In return, he would provide them with industrial design services at a fixed rate.

In promoting this service to prospective customers, United's brochure described this service as follows:

The United Industries product development team produces ideas far enough advanced to stimulate the consumer and close enough to his purchasing habits for him to feel confident in buying it. Industrial applications are approached from a less aesthetic, more functional point of view.

We would welcome an opportunity to meet with you to discuss objectives and establish a general approach to your particular product design or redesign problem. Our well-rounded specialists adopt a practical approach to design. By designing within the limitations of your shop, our designers and engineers enable your company to hold production costs within reasonable limits.

Exhibits and Training Aids. United had prepared a number of displays for companies interested in exhibiting at trade shows.

Engineering Consulting. Recently, Mr. Miller had also taken on a job as engineering consultant to a company which had a machine that was not working properly. There was no manufacturing required on the job, which required several days of Mr. Miller's time.

Small Lot Production.   United was also ready to supply plastic fabrications and castings in limited quantities.

MARKETING

Customers.   In the years 1958–61, General Electric had been by far the company's major customer, with 65% to 70% of total sales being made to this one company. In the preceding years, this percentage was much lower since United had then been predominantly a pattern shop.

In addition to GE, most of United's sales were to a small number of firms. Ninety-four per cent of sales were to 20 customers in 1959, and 96% of sales were to 25 customers in 1960. No data were available for later years, but United estimates that from mid-1960 to mid-1961 it had from 75 to 100 active accounts who regularly submitted repeat orders, and from mid-1961 to mid-1962 from 100 to 125 active accounts. United had been actively striving to increase the number of active accounts it served in order to get some stability of work. Since an individual company did not have a continuous need for this kind of service, it felt it needed a greater number of customers.

Plastic fabrications were made by United to special order. They were usually completely handcrafted since only one or two might be ordered at a time. An example of such a fabrication was the air inlet duct used in the static testing of jet engines.

One adverse effect of increasing the number of accounts was that sales costs rose appreciably, reducing the profit margins. Another problem introduced by having a larger number of accounts was that a bunching of orders could have serious repercussions. Either work would have to be subcontracted, which was generally unprofitable, or the shop would have to go on a "crash" basis—with subsequent loss of quality, or else the bid on the job would have to have either a long delivery date or high margin—both of which were detrimental to United's relationship with its customers and to its general reputation.

Advertising.   Early in 1962, 10,000 copies of a brochure describing United's products and facilities had been prepared at a cost of $5,000 for artwork and printing. United distributed these brochures in two ways: mailing and through McGraw-Hill's direct mail service. McGraw-Hill sent the brochures together with a covering letter to design engineers in Massachusetts. United's mailing was sent to firms all over New England selected from the *New England Directory of Manufacturers.* Speaking of this mailing in October, 1962, Mr. Miller said:

Unlike the covering letter on the McGraw-Hill mailing, the one we sent out was typed on an autotyper, with the man's name inserted and his product referred to specifically. We received ½% return in terms of inquiries on both mailings. Oddly enough, the personalization of the letters we sent did not seem to help.

We spent about $13,000 on the advertising, including my own time but not the overhead, and received about $11,000 in work.

In terms of actual business received, we got more out of McGraw-Hill's mailing than from our own. I think it's because we emphasized the engineering end more in that mailing.

Most of our quotes aren't coming from the advertising at all—they are coming from the yellow pages. We ask people how they happened to hear of us, and most of them say because of the yellow pages.

Exhibit 5 gives two examples of text from some of United Industries' recent advertising.

Manufacturers' Representatives. In the spring of 1962, five manufacturers' representatives were appointed: one for Washington, D.C., for federal government work; one for the state of Pennsylvania; one for the state of Maryland, and two for the states of New York and New Jersey with each covering a part of each state. These representatives would receive a commission of 10% of all sales originating in their

Exhibit 5

UNITED INDUSTRIES

Text from Recent Company Advertisements

Example 1

IMAGINATION

AND ABILITY TO FOLLOW THROUGH

United Industries enthusiastically looks for and accepts assignments which require exceptional ingenuity, inventiveness, resourcefulness and experience.

Since our beginning, nearly twenty years ago, it has been this imagination which has stimulated our growth. We at United are convinced that our greatest potential lies in our willingness and ability to exploit the knowledge and experience gained from past assignments. Such continual evaluation leads to new approaches, new materials and new methods with which to do those "impossible" jobs.

With several specialized departments working under one management, United offers a fully coordinated effort on all client problems. United's "first-of-a-kind" experience and service in the fields of product development, presentation and manufacture meet customer requirements for know-how, quality, delivery and cost.

Exhibit 5—Continued

Example 2

United's modern, well-equipped facilities plus the skills of our craftsmen enable us to assume complete responsibility for an entire project. For example: we can take an idea of any complexity, expressed in words or blueprints, and give it shape in the form of wood, metal, plastic or any other material. The coordinated efforts between our various shops cut costs, eliminate delivery delays and enable the customer to deal with a single responsible supplier.

In effect, we are saying that customer satisfaction is of primary importance at United Industries. We continually strive for this through the following four point program.

1. We believe "there is a better way to do it" . . . and we find it!
2. We deliver on time! Extra effort to meet customer expectations is assured.
3. We maintain a quality control system which insures customer acceptance.
4. Our quotations reflect our resourcefulness.

United's imagination—resourcefulness—skill can help your company improve its products and competitive position. We would welcome the opportunity to prove it!

CALL UNITED INDUSTRIES FOR ANY JOB WHICH REQUIRES AN UNUSUAL COMBINATION OF SKILLS, SUCH AS:

Engineering mockups · Prototypes · Scale models · Cutaways · Exhibits and displays—still and animated · Training devices · Low cost development tooling · Precision castings—aluminum and steel · Patterns · Reinforced plastic fabrications

---

territories whether or not they played any part in securing the sales. Their function was to seek out prospects and to make arrangements for United to submit bids on jobs. Job specifications would be sent to United and price proposals on all jobs would be made by United. Mr. Miller said of his representatives:

Most of our reps have not been productive. There is a lot of customer resistance to having this type of work done at plants located at some distance. The only rep to overcome this is the one working on the government account out of Washington, D.C. The government, being the government, will not generally use distance as a factor in disqualifying a vendor. As to the other reps, either our line is too broad or we haven't given them enough support.

Pricing. United Industries arrived at its proposed price for any job by estimating the number of hours of direct labor required, multiplying this number by $6.50, and adding to this figure the estimated cost of materials for the job. This formula was normally used, but $7 was substituted for $6.50 in proposing prices to customers who, it was believed, would accept the resultant higher price. The proposed price was also adjusted according to whether the plant was then working at or below capability with a 48-hour week. In the former case, a higher dollar rate would be used and in the latter a lower dollar rate. This adjustment was employed to a large degree as a means of regularizing production by discouraging new orders when at capacity and vice versa. Orders were not customarily turned down by admitting to the customer an inability to handle the job at the time but in effect by quoting a noncompetitive price to him. Due to the importance of General Electric as a customer, this policy was not followed on bids for this company; the price proposed on any job for this company was that secured by the formula with the $6.50 or lower rate inserted. The job, if awarded by General Electric to United, was, of course, accepted regardless of capacity considerations; if necessary, the plant was put onto a longer work-week or even onto a "crash" basis.

Due to the custom nature of the products, no two jobs were identical, and preparing price proposals involved considerable guesswork. Frequently a price proposal was made without benefit of exact specifications or detailed blueprints but instead on the basis of a sketch, a photograph, or a rough print. For each job undertaken, cost records were maintained to be compared upon completion of the job with the price agreed upon for the job.

Actual results on individual jobs varied from price equal to as much as twice the cost at one extreme to cost equal to twice the price at the other extreme. This wide range followed both from errors in estimating direct labor costs and from prices deliberately set either above or below the price indicated by the pricing formula (with the $6.50 per hour rate) as a means of either discouraging or encouraging the prospective customer to award the job to United. About one half of the jobs for which bids were submitted were awarded to United Industries.

Speaking of pricing in October, 1962, Mr. Miller said: "We've been running at breakeven, which is about $250,000 per year. Right now, we are quoting jobs to break even, without any profit in the estimates at all."

Competition. The firms listed in the yellow pages under "Model Makers" are shown in Exhibit 6.

Exhibit 6

UNITED INDUSTRIES

Firms Listed in Yellow Pages of Boston Phone Book
under Classification "Model Makers"

Firm	Employees	Location	Products and Services
Atkins & Merrill, Inc........	180	Sudbury	Industrial scale models (architectural, chemical, and engineering), product design, training and sales aids, mock-ups, prototypes, and production parts of reinforced fiberglass
Carlson Pattern Works.......	n.a.	Boston	Metal and wooden patterns
F. W. Dixon Co.............	25	Cambridge	Pattern and model shop
C. H. French Co.............	n.a.	Boston	Industrial models—aluminum molds for rubber and plastics
Harman F. Ward Associates..	n.a.	Halesite	Plant layout, architectural models, chemical components, product design
Morton Hollis Industrial De-signers, Inc..............	n.a.	Boston	Product design and model making
J. P. Hussar................	n.a.	Boston	n.a.
C. M. Jenkins Co............	n.a.	Boston	n.a.
Mendall Pattern Works......	n.a.	Boston	n.a.
Madewell Co., Inc...........	60	Boston	Exhibits, point of sale displays, scale models
Master Model Co...........	n.a.	Boston	n.a.
Micro-Mechanics Co........	n.a.	Wakefield	n.a.
Nelson Pattern Works.......	n.a.	Boston	n.a.
Norwood Pattern Works.....	n.a.	Norwood	n.a.
Pitman Studios.............	n.a.	Cambridge	n.a.
Scott Bros. Pattern Works....	n.a.	Somerville	n.a.
United Industries...........	26	Everett	(Large advertisement in center of page) mockups, prototypes, models, cutaways, training devices, development tooling, reinforced plastic products, aluminum precision products—Quality, satisfaction, prompt service
Van Buren, Inc.............	n.a.	Walpole	n.a.
Worcon Poli-Arts Co........	n.a.	Boston	Industrial and architectural scale models, product development, and model-making, prototypes, exhibit models, mockups

United considered its major competition to be Atkins & Merrill, Inc., the largest firm of this kind in the Greater Boston area.

Speaking of competitive conditions in October, 1962, Mr. David Miller said:

Since June we have had it very tough. The companies are all tightening up on costs. Things like exhibits are considered a luxury, and one of the first things to be chopped in a budget squeeze. Also, many engineers don't want to ask for a model, in order to keep their outside expenses down. The pinch is being felt by everyone. Even the little guy in the garage is cutting prices. And not only the little fellow—we recently lost a job to Atkins & Merrill—by 5%. They have traditionally been much higher than us on competitive bids because of their greater overhead. This means that they have been aroused and are really fighting for orders.

GOVERNMENT BIDS

One of the things that United was doing in October, 1962, in order to raise its volume was bidding on government jobs which required models or mockups. This work, however, was intensely competitive since firms from all over the United States submitted bids. One such job was an order for a number of full-scale mockups of space capsules to be made of fiberglass. Speaking of this job, Mr. Miller said:

> I went down to Washington to look at it, and there were 31 companies down there participating in the bid. One of these is Lockheed, which has a couple of plants idle on the West Coast.
>
> One of our problems now is how to bid on this job for NASA. If we get the job, we'll have to hire more people—and that's a problem. But we really need the work.

THE QUEST FOR A PROPRIETARY PRODUCT

In the summer of 1962, United had been apprehensive about its operating level, which was below its break-even point. In order to raise the operating level and in order to introduce a greater measure of stability into its operations, it began to think about having a product of its own.

At about this time, they sent out a mailing to architects who frequently use scale models. One architect gave the brochure to his son who is an agent for inventors. This man brought United a product, in prototype form, which appeared to have some commercial possibility.

Speaking of the product in October, 1962, Mr. Miller said:

> We hope to develop and manufacture it. We have redesigned the original prototype, and quoted on making 100 units. We think the total market could be as much as one million units over the next five years. While we are primarily interested in manufacturing it, we would also be willing to take on the marketing, if the backer wants us to. The backer is simply a source of capital. He has the money, and has teamed up with the original inventor.
>
> We have trimmed our estimate on this job as far as we could. We have cut the cost so much that it probably would not pay for them to try to go elsewhere to have it made. If we get the job, it will probably pay for all our overhead.

LOOKING AHEAD

Speaking of the company's future over the next few years, Mr. Miller said:

Three years from now, I see the model and mockup business as a small part of our annual volume—which by then should be about $2 million a year. Most of that will come from manufacturing small lots, although we have recently quoted on an order to produce 10,000 units of one small teaching machine.

If I take the most optimistic assumptions, next year's business might be as much as $1 million. But as it stands now, we don't have the equipment, or the people, or the money to do it. On the most pessimistic ones it could be as little as $300,000.

Mr. Amato saw the future of the company as follows:

Recent events indicate that our policy should be to encourage production business. If we could do that, we could increase our sales, and fill in the dips in our production volume. Also, the shortage of skilled personnel limits our expansion in our traditional product lines.

If we could get enough production business, there would be no limit to how large we could get. And we might even develop something of our own. We often spend a lot of time and effort on developing something far above what we get paid for, because we like to see it work. I see no reason why we couldn't do it for ourselves.

3. Hammond Tire & Rubber Company, Inc.

IN AN INTERVIEW with the case writer in mid-September, 1965, Mr. Henry Hammond, Jr., Chairman of the Board of the Hammond Tire & Rubber Company of Plainville, Ohio, remarked:

There were over 300 manufacturers of tires in the United States when my grandfather founded this company in 1915; today there are only 12, and some of these may not last much longer in this intensively competitive industry. We have succeeded, I believe, because we have not tried to be a little Goodyear. To try to do everything the big boys do but on a small scale is a sure way to go broke in the tire business.

During most of the last 50 years, the company was run by a two-headed management "organization" consisting of my father in charge of sales and my uncle in charge of production. To some extent, neither side knew what the other was doing. In addition, I would say that neither of them was to any great extent *personally involved* in the company as a growing business operation. They ran it pretty much as a hobby, and although it was pretty successful as a hobby, it didn't show much growth as a business. Decisions were made on the basis of how these decisions would affect the personnel involved, rather than on a purely businesslike basis. As a result, our only significant periods of growth took place during World War II and the Korean conflict. We actually faced bankruptcy in 1936 and were saved by a $50,000 loan from the old Reconstruction Finance Corporation. The whole atmosphere was one of a relaxed, "don't-rock-the-boat" type of approach to business problems. There was absolutely no sense of urgency. By 1950, we'd been in business for 35 years, and I'm sure that everyone felt we could survive—just as we were—for another 35 years.

I joined the company in 1950, and this attitude of utter complacency disturbed me greatly. I felt we were just drifting. I also felt that my father's and uncle's relaxed approach to business showed most plainly in the quality of the other management personnel. We were very weak, anywhere you looked. Our criteria for selecting management personnel were almost nonexistent. I set about changing that; and since 1953, we have been extremely selective in *all* our hiring—factory, clerical, and management. Our organization has been transformed from a two-headed monster into a smoothly running team. Our production facilities have been modernized, and our sales organization has been completely reorganized. We have developed a sound technical capability, which has led to completely revamped product lines.

51

But above all else, Hammond is strong today because of the people we have attracted. Of course, Goodyear probably has more geniuses working for it than we have total employees. But the point is that we have a much higher percentage of top-notch people. If we don't make a lot of progress in the future, it will probably be because we got lazy or self-satisfied; it won't be because we weren't smart enough.

Now, as we start our second 50 years of operation, I believe it is important that we review our past and present development and evaluate our strategy for the future. Such a review is needed because of several changes that have recently taken place or are imminent in both major areas of business—truck tires and passenger tires.

In recent years, there has been a marked trend toward increased concentration in the trucking industry. Large, well-organized, and highly sophisticated firms are rapidly replacing outfits largely run by ex-truck drivers who were lucky enough to save some money and buy a few rigs. These large firms want to buy directly from the tire manufacturer. Hammond, however, has traditionally sold through independent tire dealers. Thus, if we agree to sell directly, we run the risk of damaging our dealer relationships; if we don't, we may lose a lot of business.

We also face the possibility of a major technological change in the production of truck tires. I am referring to the introduction of radial truck tires, which some people in the industry expect to account ultimately for 80 per cent of all truck tires produced. To produce radial tires we must develop new production skills and techniques, as well as invest large sums in capital expenditures.

In the passenger tire business two closely related changes have recently occurred, and two more will eventually have a major impact on our industry. The first change took place in 1957, when department stores discovered that they could make money selling tires. Since that time, the mass merchandisers have really moved in, and there has been a relative decline in the importance of the independent dealers. Since we presently sell about 80 per cent of our passenger tires to the independents, this trend is of great importance to us. As the sale of tires on a volume basis developed, a second trend became clear—the advertising and sale of passenger tires on a price basis. This has led to the introduction of undersized, understrength, third-line and fourth-line tires selling for as little as $9.95. Hammond, on the other hand, has traditionally produced only first-line and premium quality tires.[1]

Very much related to the cutthroat price competition and the introduction of low quality tires is the impending regulation of tire standards by the federal government. I have enthusiastically supported the idea of legally enforced standards, not only because I believe the consumer has a right to know what he is buying, but also because I believe these standards will materially improve our competitive ability.

Lastly, there is a real possibility—indeed, a probability—that one of these days we'll see the introduction of a 100-thousand-mile tire as original equipment on all new cars. When this happens, you can imagine the impact it will have on

---

[1] Although no uniform grading standards exist, first-line tires are generally the equivalent of original equipment tires.

firms like ours which sell exclusively in the replacement market. When cars begin going to the junkyard with their original tires still in place, our passenger tire sales will disappear almost overnight, and we must be prepared to survive this development. This is the reason why I have turned over all operating responsibilities to our president, William Porter, while I devote all my time to a search for companies we can acquire as part of a major diversification effort.

In September, 1965, Hammond was one of the smallest of 12 tire producers in the United States. In 1964 the company earned $317,000 after taxes on a sales volume of $10.3 million. Balance sheets and income statements for the 1957–64 period are presented in Exhibits 1 and 2, and a financial comparison between Hammond and four other small tire producers during the 1955–64 period is presented in Exhibit 3. Financial data on the major tire producers are presented in Exhibit 4.

In 1965 the company's sales were divided among its major product lines as follows:[2]

	Sales (in thousands)	Percentage	Units
Passenger car tires	$ 2,778	27	199,856
Heavy truck tires	4,631	45	77,950
Light truck tires	617	6	25,235
Tread rubber	1,441	14	. . . . .
Tubes, tire repair materials, and nontire products	823	8	. . . . .
Total	$10,290	100	303,041

Unlike most firms in the industry, Hammond sold all its tires under its own brands. Information on the company's four lines of passenger car tires and seven lines of truck tires is presented in Exhibit 5.

The company's 32-man sales force sold to about 900 active accounts in 21 states—all, with the exception of a large dealer in St. Louis, east of the Mississippi. Of these, about 700 were independent tire dealers, and the remainder were trucking firms to whom the company sold direct. In addition, some sales were made to dealers in 15 states where business was not actively solicited, and about 3% of the company's tires were sold through an agent in the export market. Although some Hammond dealers sold gasoline and oil products as a sideline, in all cases their major volume was in tires. No sales were made directly to automotive supply chains or through other channels of distribution, although some Hammond dealers resold the company's tires to service stations.

---

[2] These proportions had remained relatively constant during the previous five years.

Exhibit 1

HAMMOND TIRE & RUBBER COMPANY, INC. Balance Sheets as of December 31, 1957–64 (Dollars in Thousands)

Assets	1957	1958	1959	1960	1961	1962	1963	1964
Cash (including U.S. treasury bills)	$ 382	$ 342	$ 263	$ 190	$ 92	$ 384	$ 327	$ 410
Accounts and acceptances receivable (net)	$1481	$1336	$1534	$1483	$1657	$1325	$2076	$1996
Inventory:								
Finished goods	$ 705	$ 752	$ 772	$1031	$ 800	$ 813	$ 805	$1050
Work in process	322	119	137	153	165	168	170	188
Raw materials	125	220	372	337	240	402	204	347
Total inventory	$1152	$1091	$1281	$1521	$1205	$1383	$1179	$1585
Prepaid expenses	$ 6	$ 13	$ 14	$ 14	$ 81	$ 16	$ 14	$ 18
Total current assets	$3021	$2782	$3092	$3208	$3035	$3108	$3596	$4009
Investments	$ ...	$ ...	$ ...	$ ...	$ 68	$ 134	$ 161	$ 53
Cash surrender value of life insurance	$ 42	$ 46	$ 52	$ 32	$ 53	$ 46	$ 54	$ 47
Property, plant & equipment:								
Land	$ 12	$ 12	$ 12	$ 12	$ 12	$ 12	$ 12	$ 12
Buildings	{1014	{1425	{1669	440	496	522	557	664
Machinery and equipment				1484	1354	1439	1673	2200
Molds and drums					408	435	473	547
Total (at cost)	$1026	$1437	$1681	$1936	$2270	$2408	$2715	$3423
Less depreciation	514	654	879	1016	1407	1610	1822	2046
Net fixed assets	$ 512	$ 783	$ 802	$ 920	$ 863	$ 798	$ 893	$1377
Total assets	$3575	$3611	$3946	$4160	$4019	$4086	$4704	$5486

Liabilities

Current liabilities:	1957	1958	1959	1960	1961	1962	1963	1964
Accounts payable	$ 451	$ 429	$ 514	$ 379	$ 409	$ 527	$ 304	$ 617
Accrued salaries, wages, commissions	...	...	...	...	107	102	160	153
Accrued taxes & other expenses	374	490	439	457	276	211	244	226
Federal & state income taxes	...	...	...	...	18	6	259	190
Current portion of long-term debt & notes payable	785	241	341	485	435	499	45	120
Total current liabilities	$1610	$1160	$1294	$1321	$1245	$1345	$1012	$1306
Long-term debt	346	571	483	396	310	225	925	1160
Net worth	1619	1880	2169	2443	2464	2516	2767	3020
Total liabilities	$3575	$3611	$3946	$4160	$4019	$4086	$4704	$5486

Source: Company records.

Exhibit 2

HAMMOND TIRE & RUBBER COMPANY, INC.

Income Statements Years Ending December 31, 1957–64

(Dollars in Thousands)

	1964	1963	1962	1961	1960	1959	1958	1957
Net sales	$10,290	$9,563	$9,078	$7,620	$9,573	$10,686	$9,075	$7,720
Cost of goods sold	7,459	7,103	7,212	6,012	7,085	8,232	7,045	6,190
Gross profit	$ 2,831	$2,460	$1,866	$1,608	$2,488	$ 2,454	$2,030	$1,530
Selling, shipping, administrative, and general expenses	2,179	1,897	1,772	1,533	1,878	1,646	1,369	1,206
	$ 652	$ 563	$ 94	$ 75	$ 610	$ 808	$ 661	$ 324
Other income (deductions)	(37)	(17)	(32)	(37)	157	(156)	(83)	21
Earnings before taxes	$ 615	$ 546	$ 62	$ 38	$ 453	$ 652	$ 578	$ 345
Provision for taxes	298	296	9	18	229	356	313	190
Net earnings	$ 317	$ 250	$ 53	$ 20	$ 224	$ 296	$ 265	$ 155

Source: Company records.

Exhibit 3

HAMMOND TIRE & RUBBER COMPANY, INC.

Financial Comparison—Hammond and Four Competitors, 1955–64

(Dollars in Thousands)

	Lee National Corporation	Mansfield Tire & Rubber Company	Mohawk Rubber Company	Seiberling Rubber Company	Hammond Tire & Rubber Company
NET SALES					
1955...............	$45,912	$74,556	$14,330	$45,987	$ 7,188
1956...............	46,582	61,558	15,127	46,634	7,238
1957...............	48,601	59,722	20,842	46,934	7,720
1958...............	46,559	63,634	25,513	48,134	9,075
1959...............	52,164	68,950	31,657	54,788	10,686
1960...............	44,299	61,958	32,326	48,026	9,573
1961...............	44,683	62,210	36,379	46,653	7,620
1962...............	45,592	70,335	37,575	45,232	9,078
1963...............	26,056	74,246	37,678	51,535	9,563
1964...............	n.a.	75,230	38,386	49,748	10,290
NET PROFIT					
1955...............	$ 1,750	$ 1,768	$ 321	$ 1,127	$ 220
1956...............	1,613	1,377	371	1,051	163
1957...............	1,763	1,523	563	943	155
1958...............	1,798	2,311	1,065	1,070	265
1959...............	1,522	2,282	1,219	1,191	296
1960...............	323	705	1,068	131	224
1961...............	212	870	1,751	(684)	20
1962...............	(840)	925	1,004	(826)	53
1963...............	(2,307)	972	1,281	102	250
1964...............	n.a.	532	1,304	(1,630)	317
CURRENT RATIO					
1955...............	4.26	2.07	2.89	2.48	1.94
1956...............	4.54	2.00	2.28	2.44	2.66
1957...............	6.18	2.09	1.83	2.27	2.34
1958...............	6.45	2.49	2.06	2.40	2.39
1959...............	5.83	2.74	1.99	3.53	2.37
1960...............	6.86	2.48	2.01	3.35	2.41
1961...............	6.07	2.41	2.14	3.19	2.37
1962...............	5.57	2.28	1.81	2.31	2.30
1963...............	9.85	2.30	3.49	1.86	3.55
1964...............	n.a.	3.66	3.35	1.45	3.07

Exhibit 3—Continued

	Lee National Corporation	Mansfield Tire & Rubber Company	Mohawk Rubber Company	Seiberling Rubber Company	Hammond Tire & Rubber Company
NET WORTH/TOTAL DEBT					
1955.	3.88	1.29	3.19	1.53	1.12
1956.	4.69	1.41	1.23	1.57	1.70
1957.	6.78	1.57	1.02	1.50	1.16
1958.	7.30	1.09	0.96	1.61	1.08
1959.	6.66	1.08	0.87	1.28	1.22
1960.	8.13	0.97	0.89	1.25	1.42
1961.	7.25	0.98	0.83	1.21	1.58
1962.	6.67	0.92	0.69	0.91	1.60
1963.	12.70	1.00	0.83	0.72	1.43
1964.	n.a.	0.95	0.80	0.53	1.23
INVENTORY TURNOVER*					
1955.	3.21	4.71	4.93	3.98	6.74
1956.	3.23	4.20	3.51	3.82	6.76
1957.	3.69	4.08	4.65	3.89	5.37
1958.	2.95	3.66	4.59	4.19	6.46
1959.	3.26	3.72	4.29	3.91	6.43
1960.	2.90	3.91	4.44	3.22	4.79
1961.	3.40	3.24	4.13	3.87	4.99
1962.	4.40	3.16	3.50	3.40	5.21
1963.	7.30	3.34	4.54	3.44	6.03
1964.	n.a.	2.85	4.90	3.40	4.70
SALES/WORKING CAPITAL					
1955.	2.55	6.09	4.54	4.44	7.72
1956.	2.48	5.57	4.16	4.43	6.29
1957.	2.59	5.25	5.75	4.47	5.50
1958.	2.39	4.16	4.65	4.31	5.61
1959.	2.69	3.89	4.78	3.12	5.93
1960.	2.37	3.88	4.58	2.98	5.08
1961.	2.51	3.62	3.93	3.11	4.46
1962.	2.73	3.82	4.10	2.68	5.20
1963.	1.68	4.22	2.71	3.93	4.86
1964.	n.a.	3.12	2.63	5.77	3.81
NET SALES/NEW PLANT					
1955.	6.46	12.56	7.06	7.38	14.98
1956.	6.75	8.53	4.46	7.38	16.83
1957.	6.94	8.78	5.71	7.28	15.05
1958.	6.05	7.52	6.80	7.79	11.52
1959.	6.07	5.89	5.37	8.98	13.14
1960.	5.15	4.05	4.89	6.86	10.44
1961.	5.14	4.35	5.78	6.40	8.44
1962.	5.07	5.29	4.88	5.79	11.38
1963.	3.08	5.76	5.13	6.42	10.71
1964.	n.a.	5.92	5.41	7.10	7.47

* Based on cost of goods sold.
Source: Company records.

Exhibit 4

HAMMOND TIRE & RUBBER COMPANY, INC.

Selected Financial Data of Major Tire Producers, 1955–64

	1964	1963	1962	1961	1960	1959	1958	1957	1956	1955
Net Sales (in millions of $)										
Goodyear	$2011	$1731	$1592	$1473	$1551	$1579	$1368	$1422	$1359	$1372
Firestone	1449	1382	1278	1183	1207	1188	1062	1159	1115	1115
U.S. Rubber	1087	980	1007	940	967	977	871	874	901	926
B. F. Goodrich	872	829	812	758	765	772	697	735	724	755
Net Income (in millions of $)										
Goodyear	$100.2	$81.2	$71.1	$76.2	$71.0	$76.0	$65.7	$64.8	$62.5	$59.7
Firestone	79.0	63.4	60.0	63.6	65.0	64.6	53.8	61.7	60.5	55.4
U.S. Rubber	30.1	22.1	25.7	27.1	30.7	35.6	22.7	29.7	31.9	33.6
B. F. Goodrich	34.0	27.1	26.3	31.0	30.0	37.6	35.5	39.4	43.8	46.7
Per Cent of Net Income to Net Sales										
Goodyear	5.0%	4.7%	4.5%	5.2%	4.6%	4.8%	4.8%	4.6%	4.6%	4.3%
Firestone	5.5	4.6	4.7	5.4	5.4	5.4	5.1	5.3	5.4	4.9
U.S. Rubber	2.8	2.3	2.6	2.9	3.2	3.6	2.6	3.4	3.5	3.6
B. F. Goodrich	3.9	3.3	3.2	4.1	3.9	4.9	5.1	5.4	6.0	6.2
Net Income per Share of Common Stock										
Goodyear	$ 2.81	$ 2.28	$ 2.00	$ 2.44	$ 1.99	$ 2.13	$ 1.85	$ 1.82	$ 1.75	$ 1.68
Firestone	2.75	2.21	2.09	2.22	2.27	2.26	1.89	2.18	2.17	1.99
U.S. Rubber	4.27	2.90	3.50	3.80	4.45	5.30	3.05	4.31	4.74	5.04
B. F. Goodrich	3.71	2.95	2.87	3.39	3.33	4.18	3.95	4.40	4.90	5.26

Source: Company annual reports.

In those states where sales were actively sought, the company's share of the passenger car replacement tire market ranged from .01% in Illinois and Rhode Island to 1.53% in Missouri, and in truck tires from .15% in Illinois to 4.39% in Ohio (see Exhibit 6).

Hammond Organization. Since March, 1963, when Henry Hammond, Sr., and his brother Paul Hammond retired as president and chairman, respectively, Henry Hammond, Jr., and William Porter had held the positions of chairman and president. Other members of the

Exhibit 5

HAMMOND TIRE & RUBBER COMPANY, INC.

Selected Data on Hammond Product Lines

Passenger Car Tires	Quality	Dealer Price*	"No Trade-in" Retail Price*
Eagle..................	Premium	$14.42	$38.60
Hawk..................	First-line	12.33	30.35
Falcon.................	Second-line	11.09	24.30
Winter Master..........	Premium	13.33	30.30

Truck Tires	Quality	Range of Sizes	Range of Retail Prices (Nylon)†
Super Highway..........	First-line	8.25–20—11.00–22	$ 95.30–$184.15
Super Distance..........	First-line	8.25–20—11.00–24	95.30– 191.25
Super Tread.............	Premium	8.25–20—10.00–22	100.50– 163.80
Duralug.................	Premium	7.00–15—12.00–24	41.15– 387.95
Roadmaster 100..........	Premium	6.70–15— 7.50–20	31.50– 75.45
Super Master...........	Premium	7.00–15— 9.00–20	46.55– 121.35
Super Winter Master......	Premium	6.70–15— 7.10–15	32.35– 35.80

* All prices shown are for 7.75–14 nylon cord, tubeless, blackwall tires, not including federal excise tax.
† Prices are for tube-type tires and do not include federal excise tax.
Source: Company records.

company's top management in 1965 were Philip Edwards, vice president of sales; Robert Gray, vice president of administration; George Roberts, vice president of manufacturing; and Peter Douglas, vice president of finance. All of these men had been hired since 1954 as part of an effort to strengthen the company's management. An organization chart is presented in Exhibit 7.

Company Ownership. Of the 60,000 shares of common stock outstanding, over 54,000 shares were owned by members of the Hammond family, with the remainder owned largely by (nonfamily) members of the management. No dividends had ever been paid on the common stock, and no future dividend payout was anticipated. The stock had

Exhibit 6

HAMMOND TIRE & RUBBER COMPANY, INC.

Market Penetration, in Percent—1964

	Passenger Tires and Inner Tubes	Truck and Bus Tires and Inner Tubes	Tread Rubber and Repair Material	Total Replacement Sales
Connecticut.................	0.33%	1.46%	1.23%	0.64%
Delaware....................	0.25	2.12	0.75	0.80
District of Columbia..........	0.22	0.06	1.68	0.26
Georgia.....................	0.27	0.77	0.03	0.38
Illinois.....................	0.01	0.15	0.17	0.06
Indiana.....................	0.36	2.19	1.42	1.00
Kentucky....................	0.19	1.08	2.09	0.64
Maryland....................	0.10	1.07	0.53	0.40
Massachusetts................	0.24	1.29	0.60	0.51
Michigan....................	0.06	0.68	1.28	0.30
Missouri....................	1.53	1.14	...	1.24
New Jersey..................	0.09	0.54	0.05	0.19
New York...................	0.19	1.24	2.04	0.55
North Carolina..............	1.11	3.58	2.09	2.01
Ohio.......................	1.47	4.39	5.72	2.69
Pennsylvania................	0.23	1.14	0.76	0.52
Rhode Island................	0.01	1.24	0.34	0.33
South Carolina..............	0.59	2.30	1.52	1.16
Tennessee...................	0.23	0.46	0.26	0.30
Virginia....................	0.62	2.24	2.93	1.34
West Virginia...............	0.60	0.45	2.67	0.85
Wisconsin...................	0.07	1.08	0.19	0.33

Source: Company records.

never been traded, and a public offering in the foreseeable future was not expected. Of the 16,200 outstanding shares of $100 noncumulative 4% preferred stock, 13,560 were held by Plainville College and the Hammond Foundation, with the remainder owned by members of the Hammond family.

THE FIRST TWO GENERATIONS OF HAMMOND MANAGEMENT

For the first 15 years of its experience, the Hammond Tire & Rubber Company was operated as a sole proprietorship by its founder, Henry Hammond. During this period his two sons, Henry and Paul, graduated from college and entered the business. When their father died in 1930, each son inherited a 50% share of the company. At that time, Henry Hammond, Sr., assumed the title of president and the responsibility for the sales activities of the company. Paul Hammond became executive vice president in charge of all production activities. In describing the

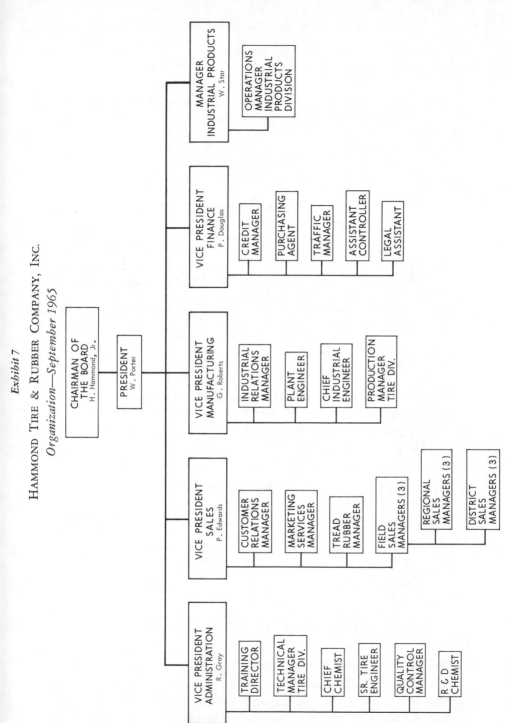

Exhibit 7

HAMMOND TIRE & RUBBER COMPANY, INC.

Organization—September 1965

CHAIRMAN OF THE BOARD
H. Hammond, Jr.

PRESIDENT
W. Porter

VICE PRESIDENT ADMINISTRATION
R. Gray

- TRAINING DIRECTOR
- TECHNICAL MANAGER TIRE DIV.
- CHIEF CHEMIST
- SR. TIRE ENGINEER
- QUALITY CONTROL MANAGER
- R & D CHEMIST

VICE PRESIDENT SALES
P. Edwards

- CUSTOMER RELATIONS MANAGER
- MARKETING SERVICES MANAGER
- TREAD RUBBER MANAGER
- FIELD SALES MANAGERS (3)
  - REGIONAL SALES MANAGERS (3)
  - DISTRICT SALES MANAGERS (3)

VICE PRESIDENT MANUFACTURING
G. Roberts

- INDUSTRIAL RELATIONS MANAGER
- PLANT ENGINEER
- CHIEF INDUSTRIAL ENGINEER
- PRODUCTION MANAGER TIRE DIV.

VICE PRESIDENT FINANCE
P. Douglas

- CREDIT MANAGER
- PURCHASING AGENT
- TRAFFIC MANAGER
- ASSISTANT CONTROLLER
- LEGAL ASSISTANT

MANAGER INDUSTRIAL PRODUCTS
W. Star

- OPERATIONS MANAGER INDUSTRIAL PRODUCTS DIVISION

Source: Company records.

operation of the company under the management of his father and uncle, Henry Hammond, Jr., remarked:

Evidently my grandfather never specified which son was to be the boss, with the result that our company grew up in the form of two totally separate organizations with no real coordination between them. The worst thing about working for such a company is that every now and then you're going to find yourself caught in the middle between the two bosses. After this has happened a few times, it will begin to dawn on you that you have three alternatives—quit, choose sides, or become a good tightrope walker. You can learn to stall on making a decision and can even train your bosses to make your decisions for you.

Now, do you see what kind of a management team you're liable to develop in a two-headed company? Do you think that really top-notch men will stay very long in a situation like that? Well, in our company's case, they didn't. In fact, it's amazing that good people were ever hired in the first place. It used to be a joke around town that the way to get hired by Hammond was "to be a good Lutheran boy and to have three or four relatives already working there." If you could pass these two criteria, you were in.

World War II Saves the Company.   Hammond was severely hurt by the intense price competition initiated by the major tire producers during the Depression as they fought bitterly for the remains of a replacement tire market which decreased from sales of 43.9 million units in 1929 to 27 million units in 1936. Company records for 1934 showed a loss of $9,000 on a sales volume of $217,000, and although sales had increased to over $760,000 by 1940, profits in that year were only $1,490. This situation was radically altered, however, by a large increase in sales during World War II, as shown by the data below:

Year	Sales	Profit
1941	$1,097,145	$29,806
1942	1,539,368	23,806
1943	2,483,310	13,252
1944	3,086,385	20,280
1945	4,291,032	51,713

The Postwar Period—Continued Prosperity and Sudden Crisis. After the end of the war, the large pent-up civilian demand for replacement tires created a seller's market, and the company was forced to ration its tires among its dealers. At the same time, a profitable export market developed as a result of the severe damage suffered by European tire manufacturers during the war. Hammond rapidly expanded its export business to the point where it accounted for over 30% of total sales in 1947. In 1948, however, the availability of Marshall Plan dollars was sharply curtailed, and the company experienced the sudden loss of almost its entire export volume. In 1948 Hammond lost $5,000 on sales of $3 million, and the loss increased to over $58,000 in 1949, when sales fell to $2.2 million. The situation was considered to be so bad that the owners of the company gave serious consideration to selling out to one of its larger competitors.

The Korean War. Before a final decision to liquidate the company was made, however, the Korean War broke out in 1950, and the company benefited from a situation similar to the one experienced 10 years earlier during World War II. Once again it became necessary for Hammond to ration tires among its dealers while at the same time being able to expand production. Sales and profits during this period were:

Year	Sales	Profit
1950	$4,208,461	$146,468
1951	6,446,171	114,860
1952	5,625,997	117,155

THE THIRD GENERATION OF HAMMOND MANAGEMENT

In the summer of 1950, just after the start of the Korean War, Henry Hammond, Jr., joined the company after receiving a degree in business administration from the University of Illinois. He entered the production side of the company, and it was expected that he would eventually replace his uncle when the latter retired. In the interview with the case writer, Mr. Hammond described his first reactions in the firm:

When I joined the company I was appalled at the low caliber of our management people. Today, 15 years later, I am more convinced than ever that my first impression was correct. If I live to be a hundred, I'll never forget a remark made by Uncle Paul during my first week at Hammond. We were looking for an assistant to our lab technician, and the question of the proper salary for the job arose. Uncle Paul told me that it was company policy to pay a man one half of what he was worth for the first few years to see if he really wanted to work for the company. On the other hand, once a person was hired, he was never fired. We were sometimes called the "west-end branch of the Salvation Army."

Furthermore, our hiring procedures were about as crude as you can imagine. To hire people for work in the plant, for example, the production manager kept a large stack of completed applications on one corner of his desk. As new applications came in, his secretary added them to the top of the pile, and when the pile became too high, she would throw away the bottom three or four inches. Then, when a foreman announced that he needed one or two men to start work in his department "tomorrow," the production manager would start at the top of the pile and work his way down until he had found one or two men who could, literally, start the next day. Thus, we were hiring from a population of men who were currently unemployed or didn't have the courtesy to give their present employers any notice.

The situation hadn't hurt us too badly, however, since we did little hiring between World War II and 1950. And from the middle of 1950 until the end of 1952 we were completely occupied just trying to fill all the orders that were rolling in. Then the war boom started to collapse, and we found ourselves back in a competitive civilian economy. I realized then that major changes would have to be made in our operations if we were to escape another postwar crisis.

New Hiring Procedures. In 1953 Mr. Hammond convinced his father and uncle that the firm's method of hiring personnel, both plant and management, needed to be completely overhauled. To do this, the services of the Psychological Service of Cleveland (PSC) were engaged. PSC was a nonprofit organization specializing in the use of psychological tests for personnel selection. Starting in 1953, each potential employee of Hammond was required to take a battery of tests, and potential management personnel were intensively interviewed by a PSC psychologist, in addition to interviews by company executives. The first member of management hired using the new procedures was William Porter, Hammond's president in 1965. He entered the company as an industrial engineer, with the task of bringing the company's wage incentive system up to date.

PRODUCT DEVELOPMENT

Prior to 1958, Hammond relied almost exclusively on its major suppliers for the technical assistance needed for product development. A particularly close working relationship had been established with E. I. du Pont de Nemours & Company, suppliers of rayon and nylon tire cord, Neoprene synthetic rubber, and several rubber chemicals used in tire compounds. In exchange for Du Pont's technical assistance, Du Pont engineers used Hammond's production facilities and tires to test new Du Pont products. As a result of this outside help, Hammond's previous management had not felt it necessary to develop the company's own technical organization.

To strengthen the technical organization, Mr. Hammond hired Mr.

Robert Gray in November, 1958, to serve as chief chemist, and it was expected that Mr. Gray would eventually assume the position of technical director. Prior to joining Hammond, Mr. Gray had served for 8 years with the Seiberling Rubber Company as a rubber compounder, determining the proper mix of rubber, carbon black, and chemicals to be used in particular tires. When he talked with the case writer, Mr. Gray was 39 years old and held the position of vice president of administration. In this capacity he had formal responsibility for the company's product development, quality control, and training activities.

When I joined the company in 1958, I was amazed by the weakness of its technical organization. We were dependent upon our suppliers for technical advice; quality control activities were concerned almost exclusively with finished product inspection; no records were kept on product performance; and no knowledge existed about the actual applications in which our most important product, truck tires, were being used.

At that time, the company had a complacent attitude towards its products. People seemed to assume that Hammond tires were of the highest quality, and even though this assumption was false in several ways, the absence of knowledge about product performance made it difficult to challenge their position. Even our supposedly appealing advertising slogan, "Quality Since 1915," got us into trouble because it was interpreted by our employees as expressing a policy of producing the best tires possible, without any relationship to economic factors.

I believe the company was really trying to follow two conflicting product policies at the same time. On the one hand, we were trying to produce a quality product, able to compete with the best products of Goodyear and Firestone, while on the other hand we were trying to produce a tire which could be sold at a price 10% below the prices of competing lines. Furthermore, we assumed that because the name Hammond was not well-known, and because we did not have a sophisticated sales force, we had to make our tires larger and heavier in order to sell them.

It was my contention that a small company like Hammond could do something unique and get away with it. For instance, I suggested that we design a special tire to be sold as original equipment on a car such as the Chevy Corvette or the Ford Thunderbird. Bill Porter supported this idea for a while, but Henry Hammond, Sr., was violently opposed to it, and when a lot of internal friction developed, the idea was dropped.

The TX–35 Experience. In early 1960 the major tire producers initiated a 20% across-the-board decrease in the wholesale and retail prices of their tires. When Hammond's management determined that the company's premium tire, the Super Ride, could not be sold profitably at the new price levels, they ordered the development of a new premium product, the TX–35. This tire was both lighter and smaller than previous Hammond tires and thus represented a significant departure from the company's traditional products. In addition, it had a radically different tread design, with only three tread ribs, compared with the conventional five to seven rib construction. Unfortunately, the reduced number of ribs produced a high-pitched squeal during turns. The company's management believed that the competitive disadvantage which resulted from the tire's higher noise level was increased by the fact that the TX–35 was introduced at about the same time the major producers introduced their "Bucron" tires and promoted them largely on the basis of the quiet ride they delivered.

Hammond's dealers were extremely unhappy with the TX–35, and their failure to push the tire was believed to be a major factor behind a decrease in total sales from the 1959 high of $10.7 million to only $7.6 million in 1961.

When the full impact of the TX–35 failure became known, the company reintroduced the Super Ride tire, after making some modifications to lower its manufacturing cost. In addition, a new first-line tire, the Hammond Hawk, was added to the company's product lines. In order to introduce the Hawk as quickly as possible, it was originally manufactured using secondhand molds purchased from another tire company. Although the Hawk was considered to be old-fashioned in appearance, it was large and heavy, and dealers seemed to be pleased with it.

Recognizing that the steps described above were insufficient to place the company's passenger tires on a sound long-run competitive basis, Hammond started to develop a completely new Hawk tire, along with a new premium tire called the Eagle. These new lines were introduced in the spring of 1965 in conjunction with the company's 50th anniversary promotion.

Mr. Gray believed that the most important result of the company's product development program had been the parallel development of a sound technical capability. In September, 1965, Hammond employed six university-trained technical specialists and anticipated hiring more each year.

Product Development—Truck Tires. Mr. Gray also described problems of product development in the company's truck tire lines:

In 1958, Hammond was the only company in the industry still using Du Pont's Neoprene rubber in its truck tires—the result of the close relationship between the two companies. Although Neoprene originally had the advantage of good resistance to "channel cracking,"[3] by 1958 it was priced considerably higher than other synthetic rubbers on the market, in spite of the fact that it performed less satisfactorily at high operating temperatures. This latter characteristic was particularly important, because over the years there has been a steady increase in the length of truck trailers and, thus, in their weight. Their greater weight along with higher operating speeds has led to higher operating temperatures. As a result, the continued use of Neoprene rubber had a harmful effect on our ability to compete in the truck tire market. Unfortunately, however, our lack of knowledge of the field performance of our products prevented us from recognizing this problem as early as we should have. It was only when we began to lose a lot of truck tire business in 1960 that we stopped buying Neoprene and got off the Du Pont hook.

Additional difficulties have resulted from our failure to define the correct application or end-use of our truck tires and to insist that they be sold by our dealers only for this proper application. Last year, for instance, we had a problem with our "Duralug" tire—a tire with heavy "lugs" or cross ribs running perpendicular to the tread. We assumed that these tires were being used almost entirely in "on-the-road," or highway, applications, and we made several product changes to improve their high-speed performance. The result was a lighter tire that did not experience as much heat buildup in the tread. As soon as we started to distribute these modified tires, however, we began to receive many complaints of stone penetration—a type of damage that could only take place in "off-the-road" applications. We have therefore had to change our assumption, and we now believe that up to half of our Duralug tires are being operated off the road. Mistakes like this will be repeated unless we can develop a system which will give us much better feedback from the field.

PLANT MODERNIZATION PROGRAM

The only significant change which has taken place in the method of manufacturing tires during the last 10 years has been the introduction of the "Bag-O-Matic" curing press in 1952. Before this development, an airbag had to be manually inserted into each "green," or uncured, tire before the tire was placed in the curing press. The airbag, when inflated, served to hold the tire in the proper shape during the curing process. With Bag-O-Matic presses the uncured tires were placed in position without airbags, and the press, with its own airbag which automatically shaped the tire, was closed to complete the cure. As a result of eliminating the manual insertion of the airbag, the productivity of the curing department could be significantly increased.

Up until 1964, however, Hammond's management had not under-

---

[3] Channel cracks were splits that developed inside the grooves of a tire's tread. Combined with sufficient wear these cracks could lead to tire failure.

taken to modernize its production facilities, believing that machines did not have to be replaced as long as they were operating satisfactorily. During the late 1950's and early 1960's, therefore, Bag-O-Matic presses had been installed only at a rate of one press every two or three years, as the older presses wore out. By 1963, however, Hammond's management had become convinced that a major plant modernization program was necessary to lower production costs, and during 1964 ten Bag-O-Matic presses were installed at a cost of $50,000 per press.

At the end of 1965, there were 17 Bag-O-Matic presses in operation, and all but three of these incorporated equipment for the automatic loading and unloading of green and cured tires. The resulting increase in curing efficiency is shown by the fact that in 1964 only nine workers were required to cure 1,400 tires per day, while in 1954 there were 27 workers in the Curing Department when output was only 550 tires per day.

THE FINANCIAL CRISIS OF 1960

In 1959 the company's sales of tread rubber to tire recappers had grown to about 20% of total sales, and the machine which processed the tread-rubber compounds were being operated close to their capacity. Rather than expanding capacity at the Plainville plant, it was decided to build a tread-rubber plant in the southeastern U.S. Hammond's management believed that such a plant would enable the company to expand its tread-rubber sales in the Southeast by putting the company in a position to offer quicker delivery times to recappers in that area. In late 1959 a site in Palmerville, Georgia, was selected, and preliminary design work for the new plant was started in January, 1960. All plans for a new plant had to be abruptly terminated, however, as a result of a financial crisis which soon developed. Mr. Hammond described the crisis to the case writer:

We didn't realize it at the time, but we were at that moment skating on thin financial ice. As a result of a failure to develop adequate financial controls, we had granted extended payment terms to too many dealers for too many dollars' worth of business in our "spring dating" program. Under this program, tires needed to build up dealer inventories for the spring selling season were sold and shipped during the first few months of the year although dealers were not billed for these tires until the late spring.

By April of 1960, our cash position had deteriorated to the point where we simply could not pay all our bills. When we realized the seriousness of our situation, we immediately quit granting extended terms to dealers, much to the dismay of our salesmen. They were competing with companies only too happy to sell tires and not get paid for them for 90 days. Unfortunately, we had exactly no alternatives, and our spring dating program disappeared overnight.

We managed to squeak through April, and in May the incoming cash flow was sufficient to enable us to pay all creditors. Obviously, any company which can't even pay its bills is not in shape to be starting a branch plant, and our Georgia adventure was indefinitely postponed. The experience showed us just how little we really knew about our financial situation and how poorly organized we were in our Financial Department. Actually, I'm being generous when I refer to a department because we really didn't have one then. Fortunately, we do now.

THE DEVELOPMENT OF A MARKETING ORGANIZATION

In September, 1965, Mr. Hammond believed that the major tasks in the development of a sound marketing organization had been accomplished. The last step in this process had been the appointment a month earlier of a field sales manager reporting to the vice president of sales, Mr. Edwards. It was hoped that without the responsibility to supervise the company's three regional sales managers, Mr. Edwards would have sufficient time for sales planning and the development of marketing policies.

Marketing Background. From 1930 until his retirement in March, 1963, Henry Hammond, Sr., was formally the director of the company's sales effort. Prior to World War II, however, he spent most of his time in the field as one of the company's two salesmen, and many important marketing decisions were made by Mr. M. P. (Flip) Jones, Hammond's sales office manager, when he talked with customers on the telephone.

In 1940 Mr. Hammond, Sr., hired three salesmen and returned to the home office. During the war and the immediate postwar period, sales problems were minimal, the result, first, of production for the armed forces and, later, for the tire-short domestic and overseas markets. Although the size of the sales force grew as additional salesmen were hired, the company continued to rely on a system of paying salesmen on a straight commission basis to provide an incentive for the sales effort, and no steps were taken to strengthen the sales organization in the home office.

In 1951 Henry Hammond, Sr., suffered a near-fatal heart attack. Realizing that a qualified replacement for his brother was necessary, and convinced that Mr. Jones was not the man for the job, Paul Hammond hired Mr. Frank Fairly as vice president of sales. Mr. Fairly made no significant changes in the marketing area, however, devoting almost his full attention to the company's advertising program.

In 1956 Henry Hammond, Jr., became alarmed about the situation. He described his feeling to the case writer:

Although I had no intention of getting into sales when I joined the company, the thought suddenly struck me in mid-1956 that I didn't know anything about sales at a time when we were exceedingly vulnerable in our Sales Department. No sales management people had been hired since Mr. Fairly became vice president of sales, and there were no qualified management candidates among our salesmen.

Therefore, with Bill Porter coming along well in production, I decided that if I were ever going to learn anything about sales, it had to be then. Acting on the theory that the best way to learn about sales is to get out and sell, I left Plainville, and for the next three years I worked as a salesman for the company in the field. By mid-1959 I thought I was ready to return to Plainville and take over our sales organization.

Upon my return I assumed the title of vice president of sales and started to run the sales end of the company. Fairly had already retired and Flip Jones resigned soon after I returned, so I immediately started to look for someone to work as my assistant and eventually become our sales manager. In the spring of 1960, I hired Philip Edwards for this job. At that time he was part owner and manager of the Pittsburgh branch of a retreading-equipment manufacturer, after previously starting his career in tire sales with the U. S. Rubber Company.

Our personnel problems in the marketing area were certainly not solved, however, when we hired Philip. By 1961 I realized that in addition to having a sales manager to supervise our field sales organization we needed a manager of marketing services, responsible for such things as advertising and promotion, sales planning, sales forecasting. Thus, in the fall of 1961, I hired Frank Williams for this position. Mr. Williams turned out to be neurotic and oversensitive, and he was simply unable to establish good working relationships within the company. Shortly after Bill Porter assumed total operating responsibility in the company, it was necessary to let Mr. Williams go, and he left in the fall of 1963. Bill can pick up the story from this point, and I suggest you talk to him.

Interview with William Porter. Following Mr. Hammond's suggestion, the case writer talked to Hammond's president, William Porter, about the recent development of the company's marketing organization:

My first attempt to replace Mr. Williams as director of marketing services failed. The man I hired in the fall of 1963, Mr. Peters, turned out to have a big "I" complex. Not content to run his own show, he attempted to exercise direct authority over our salesmen who reported to Philip Edwards. We could not tolerate this, so he left after just one year in the job.

Since we had failed twice to place someone in our marketing organization on a par with Philip Edwards, I decided that what we needed was a director of marketing in charge of all marketing activities with Philip reporting to him. For this job, I hired Paul Henderson in the fall of 1964. At first glance, Paul seemed to be a real world beater. He had been outstandingly successful as an account executive in our advertising agency and had made several brilliant presentations to us. Even though he had had no experience in the tire industry, I thought that his great sophistication in marketing was what we needed.

I was totally wrong. Soon after he joined the company, he started playing the "I've got a secret" game and refused to keep me informed about what he was doing. For example, one of the people in our Industrial Products Division convinced Paul that we needed to have an ultrasonic testing machine. I told him that we could not afford to purchase this expensive piece of equipment. Shortly thereafter, however, I began to hear people talking about ultrasonic experiments and was shocked to learn that, contrary to my orders, Paul had purchased the machine and had had it secretly installed in a garage he had rented downtown.

Paul also behaved in ways which I considered to be unethical—particularly when it came to recruiting people. For instance, one of his favorite tricks was to call the company of a man he wanted to hire and, pretending to be the representative of a credit agency, he would discover the man's address and telephone number. Then he would contact the man and try to get him to leave his present position.

This kind of behavior gradually began to undermine our entire organization. During the last few months before he left, I noticed that our weekly management meetings had deteriorated to the point where people were unwilling to discuss any of their problems with their associates. I wasn't aware of the reasons behind this, however, until I asked Paul to leave two months ago. As soon as he left everyone started to talk freely again. You can hardly imagine how this company bubbled over with joy when his dismissal was announced.

In describing my analysis of this development, I like to use the analogy of the behavior of airplane passengers when they pass through a severe thunderstorm. While the storm is around them, an almost complete silence descends upon the plane, but as soon as the storm is behind them and the plane emerges into blue skies, you can hear a great sigh of relief and everyone begins to speak.

Part of the difficulty we have had in getting a satisfactory marketing team probably stems from a failure to define the job to be done. In thinking about the case of Henderson, you must also remember that for several years Philip Edwards, Robert Gray, and I have formed a kind of inner group in our company. Therefore, to try to bring someone into a small organization and interject him between two members of such a group puts this person in a difficult position. I know that Paul thought that there was too much communication directly between Philip and me, and to some extent his criticism was probably valid.

Since Philip has only been in the sales vice president's position for a month, it is still too early to judge his effectiveness. He is probably the best tire salesman in the industry, but he has yet to prove himself as a manager.

Interview with Philip Edwards. To learn of the specific changes that had been made in Hammond's marketing operations, the case writer interviewed Mr. Edwards:

When I joined the company in May, 1960, I entered the most screwed-up sales organization I had ever seen. There were no quotas, no sales forecasts, no sales goals, no sales reports. No one in the home office even knew where the salesmen were. With no control over our sales activities, our salesmen were the real customers of the company, not the dealers who sold our tires. Obviously, it was impossible to plan with such a system.

Mr. Edward's first action was to require the salesmen to fill out route sheets and submit a weekly call report. Even these minor controls were resisted, however, and one salesman quit rather than "stand all that dirty paperwork." He then created the positions of three regional sales managers, each with a maximum of 12 salesmen under his supervision. And finally, Mr. Edwards instituted a salary-plus-commission compensation system to replace the straight commission system previously in force. Under the new system, which had been completely installed by January, 1963, each salesman was assigned a quota for his territory. When a salesman reached 90% of his quota, he began to earn a bonus of 1% of his salary for each percentage point increase in his sales, up to his assigned quota. Beyond this point, a salesman received a bonus of 2% of his salary for each percentage point gain in sales. Mr. Edwards said that he usually increased quotas 10% each year in those territories which were fully developed. In newly established territories, he said the annual quota increases were much larger, sometimes amounting to as much as 40%.

In late 1964, Mr. Edwards introduced a further modification in the company's sales compensation system whereby a salesman's bonus was raised or lowered on the basis of how the average gross margin of his sales compared with the average gross margin achieved by all salesmen. For each percentage point that a salesman's gross margin was higher than the company average, his bonus was increased by 10%; and for each decrease of 1% below the average gross margin, his bonus was decreased by 5%. This last change was designed to encourage the salesmen to push Hammond's high-margin products. For example, although the average gross margin on sales was 37.3% in 1965, tread-rubber sales to tire recappers, which represented 14% of total sales, earned a gross margin of only 22.7%. "Thus," Mr. Edwards remarked, "a salesman who sells a larger than average percentage of tread rubber will get clubbed when his bonus is computed."

Mr. Edwards had also devised a salary-plus-bonus compensation system for the three regional sales managers. When sales in a region reached 90% of quota, the regional managers received a bonus equal to

5% of their salary, and their salaries were increased an additional 2.5% for each 2% increase in the sales of their region. Eventually, Mr. Edwards planned on paying the regional managers a bonus based on the profits earned in their regions rather than on total regional sales. He believed, however, that it would be January of 1967 before this profit-center plan could be implemented.

With the appointment of a field sales manager to supervise the three regional sales managers, Mr. Edwards anticipated spending considerable time during 1966 on what he considered to be the two most important problem areas remaining in the company's marketing program—sales training and market research. The position of company training director had recently been created and a man hired to fill it. The new training director, reporting to Mr. Gray, was to be responsible for all training activities at Hammond. Mr. Edwards did not expect him to take a direct part in training salesmen, however, since he had had no previous experience in the tire industry. Mr. Edwards believed that such training should continue to be a responsibility of the regional sales managers.

In 1965 the company performed no market research on a continuing basis. Although Mr. Edwards believed that a market research program was needed, he was not yet sure how this function should be fitted into his sales organization.

PRODUCTION OPERATIONS, 1964–65

Mr. George Roberts, Hammond's vice president of manufacturing, discussed recent developments in the company's production operations. Before joining Hammond in May, 1964, Mr. Roberts had been vice president of operations of a large, plastic toy company for two years, after working 12 years as production manager and industrial relations manager at the Toledo, Ohio, plant of the Rockwell Manufacturing Company. While working for Rockwell, Mr. Roberts attended night school, receiving a bachelor's degree in industrial engineering from the University of Toledo in 1959.

During his first four months with Hammond, Mr. Roberts served as assistant to the president. In August, 1964, he was named production manager, and in the spring of 1965 he was promoted to the newly formed position of vice president of manufacturing. At the time of the interview, Mr. Roberts was 33 years old.

As vice president of manufacturing, I am responsible for coordinating the activities of our managers of production, industrial engineering, and industrial relations. Previously, these three men, plus our plant engineer, reported directly to the president, and my position was established to take this load off his shoulders.

When I became production manager, the most critical area needing improvement was labor relations. A few years previously, we had overhauled our incentive system and had eliminated many loose standards. But I think the pendulum had swung too far in the other direction. For example, in July, 1964, our curing room workers were being paid their hourly base pay of $2.11, even though under the previous incentive system these men had earned $3 per hour. Through an investment of $340,000 we had built a new curing room, and a dozen people had been taken off their jobs and assigned to other production operations. The result was a marked increase in efficiency accompanied by a lowering of morale.

To improve our labor relations, I adopted the use of union-management meetings, where I sit down with the executive board of the union four times a year to go over their problems and complaints. I think that their attitude has improved considerably in the past year because we now work together on common problems.

Our average incentive wages are now $2.50 per hour and some go as high as $3.55 per hour. I think, however, that we have lower labor costs than the major producers. We are the only company in the industry that does not negotiate with the Rubber Workers Union; we deal instead with the United Mine Workers Union. Although I don't have any specific data, I think that our lower wages are offset by our higher raw material and shipping costs. Normal raw material prices are f.o.b. Akron, and we have to pay the added costs of having our materials shipped to us here in Plainville.

The second most critical problem I faced when I took over this job was the need for better analyses of manufacturing requirements. In the past, the company had taken the attitude that they would follow the other fellow in the industry, doing what others did whether or not it was appropriate for Hammond. In addition, the production manager had taken upon himself the task of performing all economic analyses, making all decisions about plant layout, and handling the problems of industrial engineering. At present, however, the Industrial Engineering Department carefully analyzes the costs of any proposed changes in our production operations, and the plant engineer is responsible for making a careful economic evaluation of any new equipment purchases.

I believe that the major problems I encountered have now been eliminated, and we are making smaller refinements in our operations. My major goal is to develop a high-quality attitude among the workers. By making it right the first time we can reduce our scrap and rework costs. I recently hired a top-flight engineer to work on ways to reduce scrap costs, and I expect that this step will pay off very quickly. We also have a plant engineer second to none in the country.

One of my major concerns now is the need to increase our capacity. We are working three shifts a day, producing twice the output for which the plant was designed. We have real plant layout and material handling problems. For example, raw materials now enter the plant in six different places.

In the past three years we have made capital expenditures of over $1.8 million, but this is only the beginning. During the next five years we expect to spend $4 million on additional plant and equipment which will double our capacity. At the end of this program we shall have a much more rational flow of production.

We are presently experimenting with the development of a radial tire. If we introduce radials, it will require a complete change in worker training because of the precision required in radial construction. In some places where we now produce to tolerances of $\frac{1}{8}$ of an inch, radial production requires tolerances of $\frac{1}{100}$ of an inch.

I believe that a 100-thousand-mile tire will come along eventually, and that it will probably be made out of a plastic replacement for rubber. For instance, urethane tires were produced by the Germans in World War II, and many small industrial truck tires are now made from urethane. Because of urethane's high abrasion resistance, these tires last three to four times longer than conventional tires. There have also been some promising developments in the use of a mixture of rubber and styrene plastic.

RECENT FINANCIAL DEVELOPMENTS

In 1961 Mr. Peter Douglas joined Hammond as vice president of finance. Prior to that time, following a career as a CPA with a national accounting firm, Mr. Douglas had been the president of several smaller companies, each of which he had developed into profitable operations before selling to larger companies. At 57, Mr. Douglas was the oldest member of Hammond's management. Mr. Douglas described the financial development of Hammond:

When I joined the company, we had a controller but no financial man. We had a pretty good cost accounting system but very poor financial controls. Furthermore, the loans we had at that time were secured by warehouse receipts, a very expensive form of financing.

In 1962 we started a major plant modernization program, financed by a revolving loan from local banks. In 1964, however, we refinanced with loans of $600,000 from the Pittsburgh National Bank and $1.2 million from the Metropolitan Life Insurance Company.

I believe that anything that is sound can be financed and that one of the most important reasons why we have been able to secure adequate financing is the high caliber of the management group. With the exception of myself, this is a very young, dynamic organization. I've never been with a company that has the vim and vigor of Hammond, a company continually pushing ahead but, at the same time, keeping its feet on the ground.

The last three years have been spent in trying to educate our managers to use the accounting data we now give them. We make sales forecasts for each type of tire in our line, and these are translated into a manufacturing budget. Budget variances are analyzed monthly and the budget is revised every three months if necessary. I believe we have as many sales statistics as any of the larger companies in our industry, and we are very proud of what we are doing. Our main task now is to get more timely information to our management people.

Our earnings in the last few years have been somewhat understated because we have been taking as much depreciation as possible. Our plan now is to go for profits, and we are aiming at profits of $800,000 in 1966. You will also notice that we are highly leveraged, and I don't think you'll find another company of our size which has borrowed so much in relation to its net equity.

Credit Policies. Hammond was the only company in the industry using trade acceptances in its sales to dealers, and at the end of 1965 over $1 million in acceptances had been drawn on the banks of the dealers. Mr. Douglas credited this form of financing sales with holding down the company's bad debt losses to a level of about $35,000 per year. "Our credit policy is one of aggressive collections," he said, "but with a selling orientation. I believe our collection manager knows our customers better than our salesmen, and there is close coordination between our sales and credit departments."

THE OUTLOOK FOR THE FUTURE

In the spring of 1965, in an effort to stimulate his associates to think about the long-term future of the company, Mr. Hammond asked each of them to complete a "secret ballot" listing how he believed the sales of the company would be divided among its major product classifications in 1980. The estimates of the Hammond management in millions of dollars were as follows:

	1980 Sales	Passenger Tire	Truck Tire	Industrial Products
H. Hammond	200	1	39	160
W. Porter	400	150	50	200
P. Edwards	640	160	160	320
R. Gray	575	130	145	300
G. Roberts	680	204	136	340
P. Douglas	200	15	35	150

The 100-Thousand-Mile Passenger Tire. There was no doubt in Mr. Hammond's mind that a 100-thousand-mile passenger car tire would be introduced as original equipment on all automobiles at some time in the 1965–80 period. As a result, he anticipated the virtual elimination of the company's passenger car tire business and had decided to devote his energies to a major diversification program. Mr. Porter agreed with Mr. Hammond that a 100-thousand-mile tire would eventually be developed, but he did not believe this would take place during the next 15 years. He told the case writer: "Because I see this event taking place further in the future, I do not see the urgency of our phasing out of the passenger tire business as fast as Henry does, and unlike Henry, I am quite willing to spend money in the tire business as long as we can have our investments pay back within the next five years." Mr. Edwards, on the other hand, believed there were several reasons why a 100-thousand-mile tire would not be introduced. He explained his position as follows:

Henry has tried to impress everyone in the company with the fact that products come and go in business. He talks about the 100-thousand-mile tire and even a form of hover craft which will not use tires at all. However, I believe we are fairly safe with our present products through 1980.

Although the 100-thousand-mile tire has already been researched, the cost of producing it now is so high that people would not be willing to pay for it. After all, most new car buyers intend to drive their cars for only about 25,000 miles before trading them in.

Another reason why the 100-thousand-mile tire will not come along in the foreseeable future is the fact that the automobile manufacturers don't want it; they like to have things begin to go wrong with their cars at about 25,000 miles. The first three things that start to go wrong are usually the tires, the battery, and the muffler, in that order. As soon as most car owners have to start putting money into their cars, they begin to think of trading them in on a new model. Automobile manufacturers are quite happy to have tires be the first things to go because they are able to disassociate themselves from the performance of a product made by other companies.

Changes in Channels of Distribution and Pricing Policy. In his opening remarks to the case writer, Mr. Hammond had mentioned the relative decline of the independent dealer as a distributor of tires and the growth of the mass merchandisers. He amplified his remarks as follows:

In spite of this relative decline, most industry experts see a continued growth in the tire sales of the independents on an absolute basis, and I believe we should continue to sell mainly in this market. The mass merchandisers in the big cities sell almost exclusively on a price basis and do not depend upon satisfied customers for repeat business. They also rely on the highly promoted reputation of the major producers. Because we are so small, however, we cannot engage in extensive consumer advertising, and we must rely on the personal relationship between the dealer and his customers to sell our tires. For this reason, our best market is and will continue to be in small-sized or medium-sized towns, where dealers know their customers personally. This also explains why we put almost all our advertising dollars in trade magazines aimed at the dealers and in cooperative newspaper advertising undertaken by our dealers.

I believe we should continue to give our dealers a tire which they can sell at a price a little below the price of the major brands but with a higher margin for themselves. We should make no pretense of being a full-line producer, but should take advantage of our small size by pointing out to our dealers that this permits us to produce a high-quality product at a lower cost. We should tell them, for instance, that we do not have multiple layers of branch management, have no expensive offices to maintain on the West Coast, do no expensive television advertising, and refuse to spend money flying blimps. Above all, we should continue to develop our ability to give our dealers fast action on their requests and quick answers to their questions, even though these answers may have to be "no." Right now, for example, we are setting up to handle all adjustment claims from our dealers in a maximum of 48 hours, compared with our old system which sometimes took as long as four to six weeks to process a claim.

Nor do I believe we should attempt to increase our geographical distribution west of the Mississippi. Even $20 million in sales is nothing in this industry, and it is much more efficient for us to try to increase our share of the market in our present area than to spread ourselves thin all over the country. Another reason for not expanding our area is that we can now dispose of our excess production at low prices outside our area if we get into a difficult situation without running into conflicts with our existing dealers.

Mr. Porter agreed with Mr. Hammond that the company should continue to attempt to expand its distribution through independent dealers in small towns and to limit its activities to its present geographic area. Mr. Edwards, however, was less sure about the wisest course of action for the company:

I am convinced that we cannot continue to do just more of what we have been doing. In the large cities it has become almost impossible to find an independent dealer for our products. Therefore, I have been investigating the possibility of selling to department stores or going into the private brand business. Many of the mass merchandisers have learned that it doesn't pay to sell inferior quality tires, and they may be ready to change to the higher quality levels we produce.

I am also concerned about our ability to continue to sell our truck tires through independent dealers. It is possible to divide truckers into two groups—those who operate about 20 rigs and those who operate more. The smaller outfits will continue to utilize outside services and will probably need to go through middlemen in buying their tires. Truckers operating more than 20 rigs, however, usually service their own equipment and want to purchase tires directly from the manufacturers. For the small trucker, the tire dealer or our own salesman can actually go around checking on such things as proper inflation, wheel alignment, and whether the tires are being removed at the right time for retreading. That is, they can act as maintenance departments for the truckers.

The large truckers, on the other hand, purchase tires mainly on a cost-per-mile basis, and they are particularly interested in the number of retreads they can get on a carcass. Selling on a cost-per-mile basis requires skilled salesmen who can analyze operating costs. I have thus told my salesmen to speak frankly with our dealers, telling them that if they cannot make the sales to the large trucking companies, we want to go in directly. Direct sales already make up 20% of our truck tire business, and the percentage is going up every year. I have already started to hire truck tire specialists for each region. These men will be responsible for all truck tire sales in their region, and in addition to working with the regular salesmen, I expect they will eventually spend a lot of time in direct selling.

One problem we face in truck tire sales is that of reciprocity. That is, the large truckers buy tires from those producers who use their trucks to transport their own materials. This practice has just about kept us out of the market composed of the ICC licensed operators.

While I agree that it would be unwise for us to attempt nationwide distribution all of a sudden, I believe some expansion is necessary. I thus plan on setting up sales territories in the states immediately west of the Mississippi in the coming year.

I believe we have some cost advantages over the major producers because of our lower wage rates and lower distribution costs. We don't have an expensive branch office type of operation. On the other hand, I have had to increase our distribution costs in the last year by establishing three branch warehouses. This step was necessary to give quicker delivery to our dealers.

We have traditionally followed a policy of pricing our tires at a level about 10% lower than the prices of the major producers. I believe that most of this saving has been passed along to the tire purchaser, even though we have no control over the final retail price. In recent months, however, price competition has grown so intense that we have had to abandon this policy, and I do not see us returning to it in the near future.

On the other hand, I do not intend to change our policy of not publishing a "Hammond price," or suggested retail price as most producers do. Last year one of the major producers was offering a suggested retail price only 14% higher than the dealer price. I don't see how their dealers could possibly operate profitably under those conditions. We just publish a "no trade-in price" and allow our dealers to mark our tires up to what the traffic will bear.

Introduction of a Second-Line Tire. At the end of 1965, plans were well under way to introduce a second-line tire for the first time in the company's history in the spring of 1966.[4] In commenting on this action, Mr. Porter said:

We claim that we have never made a second-line tire, but I'm not sure if we really believe this. For instance, the first Hawk tire was sold to our dealers for the same price they paid for the second-line tires of the major producers, and even though it was promoted as a 100-level tire, I'm sure many dealers sold it at a normal second-line price. In fact, the normal competitive situation in this industry is for the smaller producers to sell their tires at a price one level below

---

[4] Shortly after the preparation of this case, the company's second-line "Falcon" tire was introduced. The Falcon was sold at a dealer price of $11.09 and a "no trade-in" retail price of $24.30 (for the 7.75–14, nylon cord, tubeless, blackwall).

those of the major brands. Thus, the level of a tire is mainly one of price; as a measure of quality it is a relatively meaningless term. If our second-line tire turns out to be what I think it will, it will be a safe tire that represents a good customer value, and as far as I'm concerned, that's exactly our traditional product policy.

Mr. Gray was even less concerned about this proposed departure from tradition:

I believe our product policy can be expressed as producing tire products with a quality equal to or better than the average products of the major producers in the same price levels and for the same applications. Thus, as far as I'm concerned, we could go so far as to produce fifth-line tires and still be consistent with our policy.

Government Regulation of Tire Standards. By the fall of 1965, many industry observers expected that a federal law would be passed in 1966 establishing minimum standards of tire safety and perhaps including a uniform system of grade labeling. For several years, Mr. Hammond had been a leading spokesman among those pressing for such standards. In a statement submitted to the Federal Trade Commission in January, 1965, he said:

The average new car buyer can probably be pardoned for assuming that he can fill up his vehicle with people and baggage and then drive off—safely. If he had just bought a six-passenger wagon, he might be very surprised to learn that if he put six 170-pound men in it, each of whom had placed his 30-pound suitcase in the back of the vehicle, the tires might be overloaded by as much as 20%. If any one tire on this vehicle was underinflated by as little as four pounds, a three-hour turnpike trip at 65 m.p.h. would be a rather dangerous one.

At present, the average car driver is completely uninformed with regard to (1) the maximum rated load for his particular tire size, and (2) the empty weight of his car. These two rather important figures are not furnished to him by the vehicle manufacturers.

Our company feels that every new car should have in it a placard, easily visible from the driver's seat, showing the net number of pounds or people and/or baggage that can be put into the vehicle before the tires become loaded to the maximum allowed. Drivers would at least know then when they were skirting the danger area. As things stand now, the average driver simply doesn't give any thought to the matter—because no one has ever told him that he was placing himself, his passengers, and every oncoming driver in a potentially dangerous situation.

We think it's time somebody gave him some facts.

In his discussion with the case writer, Mr. Hammond explained the reasons behind his support of tire safety legislation:

When the third- and fourth-line tires were first introduced a few years ago, we were shocked that any reputable tire manufacturer would turn out such a product and allow it to fall into the hands of the poor unsuspecting consumer. For a while, we thought that this situation was a fad which would soon pass. Unfortunately, we were incorrect in that assumption.

Since our company only manufactures tires in the higher priced end of the spectrum, we quickly discovered that it was very difficult for us—being unknown to the consumer—to compete with the very low-priced tires. Our company policy on product quality would not allow us to "join them"—so we decided to beat them. Our approach was to start beating the drum for some kind of minimum tire quality standards. The industry bigwigs kept saying that it couldn't be done, but we had some very logical reasons as to why it could be done, and I am happy to say that our position will prevail. Our position has been that when the average American driver suddenly gets the idea that he needs some kind of protection when he goes to buy a tire, said American driver is going to get his legislators to pass some kind of a law which will provide the desired protection. There are only 12 tire producers, but there are millions of voter–drivers. Thus, it doesn't make any difference what the major rubber companies think.

The main social responsibility issue here is the need to protect the consumer from himself. In this industry, under present laws, a manufacturer can make tires out of chewing gum and old ties, and there is no way he can be prosecuted. It so happens that in this case a real need on the part of the public coincides with the competitive ax we have to grind in Hammond. Once the unsafe "cheapie" tires are off the market, we can breathe more freely here in Plainville.

Mr. Porter agreed that legally enforced tire standards would be established, but he was less sure about their impact on the company:

I am not sure that it is practicable to develop meaningful safety standards for tires, but since we are going to have these standards anyway, I believe we should take part in their formulation. In resisting tire standards against what appears to be an overwhelming public demand for them, I believe the industry has made a great mistake. All the industry has succeeded in accomplishing is a great deal of ill will.

I am afraid that the minimum standards will be set at a quality level somewhere around the present third-line tire. If so, there is a danger that the tire buyer will say, "If these tires are OK with the government, they are OK with me." This kind of reaction might well result in the reduction in sales of premium tires. The average car owner doesn't intend to keep his car until the second set of tires wears. Therefore, if he can be assured of the safety of his replacement tires, he may purchase the cheapest "approved" tires he can find.

Messrs. Gray and Edwards were also concerned about the effect of the concern for tire safety on their company. Mr. Gray believed that the government standards would be set at a quality level between that of present second- and third-line tires, and that as these tires gained public acceptance, manufacturers such as Hammond would have less to sell. That is, the company could no longer promote its products on the basis of their greater safety. Mr. Edwards believed that people who were worried about tire safety were more likely to purchase a tire made by a major producer than to take a chance with the product of a company with a less well-known name and reputation.

Diversification. Each member of Hammond's top management team believed that the company should make a major effort to diversify its activities. Mr. Hammond believed that the company's future development would take place in the field of industrial rubber products, and during the past year he had investigated over 40 companies which appeared to be potential acquisitions. He had reached his present position after analyzing the company's first attempt at diversification, which had been made in 1962 when it purchased the Willow Corporation, a manufacturer of fiberglass boats. He described this unsuccessful venture to the case writer:

Somewhere in about my second or third week with the company, the subject of diversification came up. We had just come through a bad year in 1949, and the subject of this particular meeting was the desirability of getting into other fields which would presumably remain profitable during the periodic slumps in the tire business. The meeting broke up on a theme of "everybody keep his eyes open for something new that we could get into, and when you see something interesting, bring it in and we'll look at it. If it looks good, we'll give it a try." Thus, getting us into new fields was everybody's business, and since everybody's business is nobody's business, it's no wonder that it took us 12 years before we made the first step.

In 1962 a consultant we were using mentioned a friend of his who was making fiberglass boats in his garage. This friend suggested that we get into the fiberglass boat business with himself as manager. We might actually have gotten started this way, if a representative of an investment banking firm hadn't casually mentioned that he knew of a fiberglass boat plant in Des Moines, Iowa, that was about to go broke. He was right, but we were hot for some kind of diversification, and the glamor of the boat business temporarily got the better of our business judgment. We bought the Willow Corporation for 15 cents on the dollar, and in looking back I can say that that was considerably more than it was worth.

Three years later, we came to the reluctant conclusion that we had gotten into the wrong business in the wrong place at exactly the wrong time. We were selling a big-ticket luxury item which had an extremely seasonal sales pattern, and we couldn't learn enough about selling boats fast enough to pull Willow out of the red. We finally sold off all the parts except the industrial fiberglass end of it and gave up the effort.

What did we learn from this experience? One thing was simply that if you are considering going into a field that requires a completely different marketing approach than you're used to, it might be a good idea to go out and call on some dealers who are presently in this particular business. You might learn pretty quickly just what some of the selling problems actually are. We also learned that if there isn't any fit between your present sales organization and the new field, you might ask yourself if you can afford to build up a completely new sales organization. A final lesson we learned was that taking a business which is losing money and then making it profitable is a skill that very few companies have. We may eventually develop such skills, but we don't have them yet.

By September, 1965, Mr. Hammond had developed a list of 13 criteria for the evaluation of potential acquisitions. These criteria were:

1. *Size of Company Being Acquired.* Prospects should have net sales between $500 thousand and $5 million.
2. *Management of Company Being Acquired.* The management must have similar basic philosophies to our own regarding product quality, desire for future growth, and honest dealing. Psychological Service of Cleveland evaluation of key management people must be satisfactory. Service companies (as opposed to product companies) should generally have a stronger management team. In general, one-man company situations should be avoided.
3. *Prospect's Field of Operations.* One-product companies should be avoided, unless the management team has enough demonstrated depth to come up with new (replacement) products as present product becomes obsolete. Prospect should offer either economies of manufacturing or economies of marketing when combined with our company. A qualified person in our own management must have some personal knowledge of and interest in the prospect's field—either through previous work experience or through some personal (hobby) interest in same. (This depends to some extent on the size and competence of the management team being acquired. The bigger and better, the less need for our "personal" involvement.)
4. *Prospect's Geographic Location.* Prospect should be in eastern half of U.S. and should be readily accessible, meaning that total air-ground travel time should not exceed three hours.
5. *Prospect's Financial Condition.* Prospect must be a profitable operation with at least a five-year history of same. Avoid businesses less than five years old.
6. *Prospect's Physical Facility.* Physical facility must present an appearance which indicates some effort being made toward keeping things shipshape. Sloppy housekeeping indicates sloppy management.
7. *Prospect's Reasons for Selling.* These must sound reasonable to us and must be subjected to as close a scrutiny as circumstances will allow. Those of our management who make this investigation must write, and circulate to our Board, a formal opinion as to the reasons why the prospect wishes to sell out. (Depends on the apparent "bargain" being offered.)
8. *Financial Feasibility of the Acquisition.* All deals are to be for cash only. We do not presently contemplate exchanging stock.
9. *Prospect's Union Relations.* These must be at least average or better. We are not interested in situations with a history of poor union relations.

Restrictive contracts which encroach on management prerogatives are grounds for our rejecting the deal.

10. *Moving Prospect's Physical Facilities.* We do not contemplate buying a company and then moving it to another location, except in very unusual circumstances. Too many valuable personnel are lost in the process. If we acquire a company for its marketing organization (field), we could consider moving the company without risking loss of field personnel.

11. *Long-Term Commitments.* Investigation of the prospect's long-term obligations must be made. Onerous leases, pension, retirement, profit sharing, or union contract items must be carefully evaluated in terms of our willingness to live with same.

12. *Complete Control.* We are probably not interested in anything less than 80% control of any prospective acquisition.

13. *Our Management Representatives.* No acquisition should be undertaken unless we have a qualified member of our management who can be assigned to the operation on a full-time basis for at least one year.

Using these criteria, Mr. Hammond had narrowed his list of potential acquisitions in the industrial rubber field from 40 down to four, and in early 1965 negotiations had been initiated with two of these companies. By the end of 1965, however, both negotiations had been terminated for various reasons, and no specific diversification steps were under way. The loan agreement with the Metropolitan Insurance Company provided that all acquisitions had to be approved by Metropolitan.

Mr. Porter also discussed the company's need to diversify:

Ever since 1956 I have felt very strongly about the need for our company to diversify, for it is basically unsound for a business to be so dependent upon one product—particularly a replacement product. I think it is still an open question, however, as to whether our diversification will be only in industrial rubber products. I hope it will not, for I do not see this kind of business as having as large a profit potential as some other things we could do.

For instance, I believe there are real opportunities for making money in the areas of education, recreation, and services. These are relatively undeveloped areas where someone can start something new. Growing in industrial rubber products, on the other hand, means taking business away from firms already well established. A steel mill, for example, which spends a few hundred dollars on rubber roller coverings will be very reluctant to change to an unknown supplier and take a chance on a shutdown that could cost thousands.

Recently I have been fooling around semiseriously with the idea of starting some kind of industrial education program. We had some experience in this kind of work when we conducted a training program here for Du Pont salesmen who were going to be selling to the rubber industry. Similar programs might be successful because with the exception of some work at one university there is no place where a man can learn about the rubber industry even though there is a great scarcity of such people as tire designers and tire developers.

In general, I believe our diversification should aim towards supplying a service rather than a product. For example, we might get into the management of a private hunting preserve, fishing preserve, or skiing area. In my opinion, skiing areas today are designed exclusively for the very good and very wealthy skier, and they are too fancy for the vast majority of people. If we could develop an area with gentle slopes which would appeal to a mass market and provide our service at a reasonable price, we might be able to do very well. I must admit, of course, that my interest in such activities is directly related to the fact that I am an outdoorsman. I can't think of any time when I would not prefer to be outdoors than indoors.

In addition to increasing sales of nontire products through acquisitions, Hammond was expanding its own production of nontire products, and an Industrial Products Division had been established in 1964.

At the end of 1965, this division was organized as a separate company, the Hammond Industrial Products Corporation. It was housed in a separate plant, financed by a $400,000 guaranteed mortgage from the Ohio Industrial Development Organization.

The Hammond Industrial Products Corporation produced rubber covered rolls, used primarily in the steel, paper, and glass industries. It also produced rubber and fiberglass linings for tanks and molded urethane products. Because of urethane's high abrasion resistance, it was finding increased applications in products ranging from protective shields for crane hooks to bearing seals.

Hammond's industrial product sales had amounted to about $100,000 in 1964, and they were expected to increase to about $200,000 in 1965. Although the company had not earned a profit on its nontire business, it was expected that profits would be generated in 1966.

MR. PORTER'S DILEMMA

Mr. Porter described what he considered to be a strategic dilemma facing his company:

I mentioned earlier that as a result of the coming government standards, I believe there may be a rush to the production of tires coming closer to the minimum standards. Thus, we may see a fading out of our Eagle and even our Hawk lines. After all, these tires have no really distinctive characteristics with which we can compete in the higher priced market. Thus, there is a real possibility that our second-line Falcon tire will become our major volume producer.

In the face of a diminishing market for our higher priced lines, we are caught on the horns of a dilemma. On the one hand, we could concentrate on the truck tire market, using a rifle versus a shotgun approach to sell people who recognize the cost-per-mile factors. We realize, however, that there is little possibility for significant growth in truck tire business, and thus, we would be pursuing a stagnant market.

On the other hand, we do not have consumer acceptance in the passenger tire market, and we would have to make a major investment to gain it. Our main hope here is the independent tire dealer. At present these dealers do not have the proper merchandising skills, and they are not being helped by the major producers. Perhaps we could put together some kind of package which would enable them to compete.

Section 2
Establishing Objectives
and Formulating
Plans of Action

1. Pharmalab, Inc.

In January, 1969, Dr. Robert Carlo (age 36) was facing some critical decisions about the future of Pharmalab, Inc., of which he was majority owner, president, and treasurer. From a three-year loss position, this small manufacturer-packer of pharmaceuticals and chemicals had recently turned the corner to substantial sales gains and profits (see Exhibit 1). As a result, the company had been offered a $150,000 line of credit by one of Boston's largest banks. At the same time, Dr. Carlo had received an acquisition offer from a profitable and aggressive small conglomerate, Nomad Engineering, Inc., which was Pharmalab's third largest customer (25% of sales in 1968). As another possibility, operations might be expanded by using funds generated from profits.

Dr. Carlo believed that a choice among these routes for expansion should be made fairly quickly. He realized, too, that not only the pace of growth but also its direction would differ, depending on the avenue chosen.

EARLY HISTORY IN DENTAL PHARMACEUTICALS

After four years as an assistant professor of Pharmaceutical Technology in one of Boston's professional pharmacy schools, Dr. Carlo quit teaching to start a one-man pharmaceutical manufacturing concern in the basement of a drugstore which he and his brother had recently bought. His objective at this time was to try out some of his own innovative ideas about pharmaceutical product form, dosage form, packaging, and manufacturing methods.

During the first three years of the young firm's operations (1960–63), sales were confined to Greater Boston and eastern Massachusetts. Moreover, only three products were produced: sodium fluoride tablets, sodium fluoride drops for the prevention of tooth decay, and toothache drops.

Besides producing this line himself, Dr. Carlo did his own "detailing." That is, he called on dentists to acquaint them with the merits of his products and to urge them to recommend these items to their patients. In addition, Dr. Carlo acted as his own sales force, covering

Exhibit 1

PHARMALAB, INC.

Statement of Income and Retained Earnings, Fiscal Years Ending June 30, 1963–69

	Last 3 Months 1963	1964	1965	1966	1967	1968	First 6 Months 1969
Net sales*	$ 3,188	$ 18,629	$ 76,301	$118,062	$130,899	$164,617	$111,106
Beginning inventory	0	2,170	8,554	13,492	16,787	19,282	27,909
Purchases	2,472	17,527	39,008	61,372	66,552	75,749	33,928
Goods available for sale	$ 2,472	$ 19,703	$ 47,562	$ 74,865	$ 83,339	$ 95,031	$ 61,837
Ending inventory	2,176	8,554	13,492	16,787	19,282	27,909	25,851
Cost of goods sold	$ 296	$ 11,149	$ 34,070	$ 58,078	$ 64,057	$ 67,122	$ 35,986
Gross profit	$(4)	$ 7,480	$ 42,231	$ 59,984	$ 66,842	$ 97,495	$ 75,120
Operating expenses	1,868	30,318	42,713	51,490	53,698	69,175	40,910
Net operating income	$(1,872)	$(22,838)	$(482)	$(8,494)	$ 13,144	$ 28,320	$ 34,210
Selling and administrative expenses	1,111	2,938	6,199	8,947	6,353	9,833	8,614
	$(2,983)	$(25,776)	$(6,681)	$(453)	$ 6,791	$ 18,487	$ 25,596
Other income (expenses)	1	27	322	89	(1,073)	(1,820)	(547)
Net income	$(2,982)	$(25,749)	$(6,359)	$(364)	$ 5,718	$ 16,667	$ 25,049
Retained earnings:							
Beginning	$ 0	$(2,982)	$(29,319)	$(36,943)	$(38,628)	$(34,230)	$(18,928)
Preferred dividend	—	588	1,265	1,321	1,320	1,365	704
Profit (Loss)	(2,982)	(25,749)	(6,359)	(364)	5,718	16,667	25,049
Ending	$(2,982)	$(29,319)	$(36,943)	$(38,628)	$(34,230)	$(18,928)	$ 5,417

* In fiscal 1968, sales were divided among customers approximately as follows:
Giles Brothers $53,000 (32%) Nomad $42,000 (25%) Other $18,000 (11%)
Cary $45,000 (27%) Weber First Aid $7,000 (4%)

Source: Company records.

drugstores in those localities where dentists were favorably impressed with his products and making arrangements with drug wholesalers.

After about eight months of detailing, the three dental-care products were moving well. And, after initial contacts with wholesalers, reorders automatically took care of that portion of the distribution.

With only three products to consider, Dr. Carlo had time to spend on his interest in developing attractive and innovative packaging and on acquiring an education in the mechanics of detailing. In addition, he was able to study pharmaceutical wholesale and retail distribution patterns. During these early years his main aim was to learn about the drug manufacturing business and thus to develop ideas for setting up a larger manufacturing laboratory.

To enhance his learning, he engaged in consulting work during 1962. For example, he was asked by a drug wholesaler, Giles Brothers, to study an unprofitable in-house manufacturing operation that produced the Giles line of private-brand pharmaceuticals. Here Dr. Carlo discovered that, in spite of a low sales volume ($140,000 in 1962) and a number of unprofitable items, the laboratory was able to operate at an overall loss of only 5% to 8% a year, and the relatively large parent company was willing to sustain this loss because the possession of a lab enabled it to perform extra services for its customers. From this consulting job, Dr. Carlo was able, as he put it, "to learn a good deal the way a lab should *not* be operated." He also gained additional knowledge of large-scale pharmaceutical production, raw materials sources and handling, and markets. As a result he was able to develop further his own ideas on how a pharmaceutical lab should be run.

Looking back in 1969 on his early dental lines, Dr. Carlo said he believed that he had found a niche in which to start his pharmaceutical business against minimal competition. For one thing, contacts would be limited to dentists, since the products were purely dental items. In contrast, the large pharmaceutical manufacturers tended to focus their detailing efforts on physicians, since these provided the major market for prescription drugs. Moreover, although several large pharmaceutical houses were producing fluorides with vitamins added, dentists did not consider themselves qualified to prescribe the combined products. The American Dental Association (ADA) did not believe physicians should prescribe the combined products either, since adminstration of vitamins with fluoride might give a child in one area a proper dosage of fluoride and a child in another area a harmful overdose when combined with natural or artificial fluorides occurring in some water supplies. The ADA made the following comment on the combined products:

> On the basis of effects observed with fluoride in water supplies, tablet preparations containing calcium fluoride or bone meal, often with one or more vitamins such as C and D, have been advocated for dental caries therapy. Convincing clinical evidence of the value of fluoride in such forms is lacking.[1]

INCORPORATION, AND EXPANSION INTO CONTRACT MANUFACTURING

Early in 1963, Dr. Carlo was approached by Mr. Frank Pandol, also a retail pharmacy operator, with an offer to help expand Pharmalab. Pandol had a friend, Mr. Harry Gerard, with a new building, and another friend, Mr. Frank Ventres, a CPA, who was willing to perform accounting functions and to provide financial know-how. Gerard offered not only to make the necessary leasehold improvements but also to provide the first six months rent-free. Six persons—Ventres, Gerard and his brother, Pandol, and Dr. Carlo and his brother, John—each invested $3,000 to provide Pharmalab's initial capitalization. Incorporation was completed in April, 1963, with the six investors serving as the board.

With this backing, Dr. Carlo planned a large-scale approach to manufacturing and selling pharmaceuticals. When asked about his aims and expectations at that time, he replied as follows:

> Looking back to 1963, when I was formulating the structure of Pharmalab's future, I felt that my first objective was to build up a record of credibility. A good track record and sales of $1,000,000 would be my goal of achievement. At this point, if necessary, I would offer my company to the public for the purpose of raising the necessary capital for a much faster rate of growth and profits.
>
> My plan called for three successive areas of growth: (1) finance, (2) marketing, and (3) research.
>
> The first task, on which the others would depend, was to create a financial base and to obtain a rapid cash flow, once our business operations commenced. The financial plan would be built around the sale of 1,000 shares of preferred stock, representing 10% of the stock outstanding. Successful sale of all the shares would yield a total of $100,000. With these funds, plus a satisfactory cash flow, I felt that the other two areas of growth, namely, marketing and research, would be established within a two-year period.
>
> Raising funds through a preferred stock offering was very important to me. I sincerely felt that I would gain a sense of moral support from those purchasing

---

[1] *Accepted Dental Remedies 1961* (Chicago: American Dental Association, 1961), p. 136.

the stock. When a person finds himself alone in all decision making, he looks for a type of moral support from friends. The faith people will place in a person's capabilities can usually be measured by their willingness or desire to buy into the company.

Based on his interest in packaging innovation and his previous experience and learning, Dr. Carlo felt that the best approach to sales expansion would be through contract manufacturing for outside companies. What he had in mind was a relatively unsophisticated line of nonprescription pharmaceuticals based on common drugs as listed in the *U.S. Pharmacopoeia* (USP) or the *National Formulary* (NF). Either the products themselves or the necessary fine chemicals could be bought in bulk from a variety of suppliers, and no initial R&D would be needed. Once processed into dosage forms, the products would pass to drug wholesalers for resale under their own private brands.[2]

Putting this idea into effect proved easy, once news of the service to be offered got about. Dr. Carlo recalled his first contact with a private-brand customer as follows:

Soon after we had organized our small company, we found potential customers seeking our services. By word of mouth, within the relatively local pharmaceutical community, people were being informed that a pharmaceutical laboratory had been established in the area. A most important call came from a large drug distributor within weeks after opening our doors. Cary, Inc., of Lynn, Massachusetts, wanted us to manufacture a private line of pharmaceuticals. This inquiry materialized into our first piece of contract work on a private basis.

As a means of explaining to Cary, Inc., just what benefits Pharmalab could offer as its new source of supply, Dr. Carlo followed up his exploratory talks with a written proposal which read in part as follows:

This report uses the phrase "a manufactured drug line" throughout. This phrase should be interpreted as meaning a line of drug preparations that are manufactured for your own private-brand distribution. The line will not include any drug products that are not directly related to your present products and markets. But all your products, now so different in appearance, will be given a "family" resemblance by means of more uniform and attractive container shapes, container materials, and distinctive labels.

In addition, if you adopt the "manufactured drug line," we will put our laboratories at your disposal. We are in a position to develop and manufacture special hospital formulations as well as to supply standard hospital formulations in bulk. Not only will you be offering hospitals an unusual service, but- you will also be increasing your hospital sales volume, which is an important part of the overall drug wholesale business.

---

[2] For trends in pharmaceutical sales and distribution, see the Appendix.

There is a definite need for a "manufactured drug line" by large wholesale drug houses. This need has become more predominant during recent times. Obviously, large drug manufacturers are in a position to dictate distribution policies of their own product line. Several drug manufacturers have within the last year or two restricted the distribution structure of the drug wholesaler by reformulation of their own selling policies to the retailers.[3] Such action has put the squeeze on all wholesalers.

It is our opinion that the drug wholesaler must combat this squeeze by seeking new activities that are guaranteed, that is, guaranteed in the sense that they cannot be taken away by someone else. A "manufactured drug line" offers you this guarantee because it belongs to you alone.

The future could hold an unlimited business opportunity for your company. If you were to have your own "manufactured drug line," you could easily expand your dollar volume with retail accounts, and certainly you would be in an excellent position to recruit new business from the many hospitals that you serve. At present, no drug wholesaler in this geographical area is offering a development and formulation program to hospitals. Hospitals would welcome such a program, especially the smaller hospitals that lack manufacturing facilities. Such a program could be tailored to the needs of any hospital.

Once Cary, Inc., had accepted his proposal, Dr. Carlo proceeded to acquire the necessary raw materials, containers, and labels. He also developed an inventory control system for the Cary line of 50 items. This activity took about four months. A full-time employee was hired in September, and Pharmalab began producing the Cary line in October, 1963. By the end of fiscal 1964, nine months later, sales of $18,000 had been achieved, of which $16,000 was from Cary.

Early in fiscal 1965, Dr. Carlo was approached by the same Giles Brothers for which he had previously worked as a consultant. Giles Brothers had become aware of the work that Pharmalab was doing for Cary, and, having become dissatisfied with their own manufacturing, they asked Dr. Carlo to help phase out their operation and to start producing their private brands for them.

For Dr. Carlo, this request posed major questions: Should he become more heavily dependent on private labeling at the expense of committing some resources to a more independent approach? And if he did decide to commit himself entirely or almost entirely to private-label contract manufacture, what kinds of business ought he to accept? Looking back as of 1969, Dr. Carlo described the alternatives that confronted him, and his reasoning, as follows:

---

[3] Besides continuing to increase the percentage of direct sales to retailers, major pharmaceutical manufacturers had recently started to give retailers a larger discount from quoted prices than wholesalers could give.

After we had established the Cary line of pharmaceuticals, we began to receive new inquiries from other people and firms, and these inquiries became more frequent as the Cary line began to find its way into more and more drugstores and hospitals. It appeared that our products as well as our customers were becoming a sort of referral system over which we had no control—this despite the fact that our products never had our name on the label, since our work was private contract packaging.

Since we had not yet created any type of sales department, it was a pleasant feeling to have people looking for us at this stage of the game. Because potential customers had been seeking us instead of our seeking the customers, we were becoming more confident of our abilities, and we felt that we could grow on the basis of our past performances.

After the first year's operation, one fact became obvious. Although we did not have a single salesman and did not advertise our company in any way, we continued to receive inquiries from potential customers. Two logical assumptions were made at this point. First, we realized that the type of manufacturing we were involved in was not readily available, and, second, we realized we were capable of producing quality products for our customers. Had this not been so, we certainly would have had to sell our company's services more aggressively, by means of the normal selling tools such as salesmen, advertising, etc.

Confidence that we could put quality products in the hands of our customers was felt immediately. Without exception, customers would return to us with complete assurance and, in most instances, with praise for our services and output. This feeling of being needed as well as wanted had a rather strange effect on our business. I had originally planned to organize a sales department in the latter part of our first year. But I changed my mind about this positive approach to selling and adopted what could be considered a rather precarious philosophy towards sales growth. This philosophy proved to be both challenging and self-rewarding for me.

I took the risk that if the company could continue to offer good service and good quality, in all probability a referral system created by both customers and products could serve to increase sales without increasing selling expense. Eventually we could build to a profit-generating business. I realized that dollar volume would not grow nearly as rapidly as could be expected with a positive sales program. Nevertheless, I felt that new accounts could be personally selected using a rigid set of criteria for acceptance.

Resigned to the concept of gradual but steady growth using a negative sales approach, I was determined to analyze each potential customer in order to establish good and, by all means, lasting accounts. I formulated a set of criteria which, if closely adhered to, would guarantee steady growth as well as profitability:

1. We would extend our services to people, institutions, and companies only after their background was investigated and was proved to be ethical.
    This is of most importance in the pharmaceutical field because of narcotics, stimulants, and barbiturates.
2. The product or product line we were to manufacture must be suitable to inhouse production and quality control procedures.

In this way we could assure deliveries and control product quality. Subcontracting could have improved our growth; however, the uncertainties and lack of control could be troublesome.

3. We would not manufacture products unless we had control of the ultimate packaging.

We refused to manufacture any products that would leave our plant in a poorly designed package. Our products were *our salespeople* and we knew that a silent selling job of a well-packaged product was priceless. If a poorly packaged product was brought to us, we would redesign the package until we had satisfied our customer, but, of more importance, we had to satisfy ourselves. If the potential customer had a poorly packaged product that was successful in the market and he would not allow us to redesign the package, we would without exception refuse to take on his work. In all instances we worked within the budgets of our customers; however, it was an absolute must that the final package meet with our approval.

4. The companies we selected as accounts should have good growth patterns and should also have good promotional efforts behind the products we were producing for them.

This was extremely important because we felt the growth rate of Pharmalab depended greatly on how well the products we produced were promoted. If a potential customer lacked the vehicle for good product promotion, he was of no value to us.

5. The profit, in every instance, should be of proper structure.

Work would never be accepted at no profit or at an unacceptable profit. Regardless of the circumstances, we had to generate satisfactory profit from every item manufactured. If this could not be achieved because of competition, we would refuse to produce the product(s). We knew what our expenses were, and it was mandatory that these be covered by accurate costing and pricing procedures.

6. The accounts selected should be prompt in paying their bills.

Excellent payment records have allowed Pharmalab to operate on an extremely efficient cash-flow structure. Pharmalab has discounted 85% of all payables for the past three years.

"It may be definitely stated that, unless each of the above criteria was satisfied, Pharmalab would not accept the account," added Dr. Carlo. "As a direct result of this procedure, today we manufacture for prestige accounts, and our so-called 'referral system' for new business continues to gain impetus. Today our 'referral system' is based on excellence in *service, quality,* and *customer relations.*"

Dr. Carlo found that Giles Brothers met the tests which he felt were important for a private-label customer. They agreed to let him pare the line to the items he considered important for a private-label customer as well as profitable (about two-thirds of the former dollar volume). They also agreed to his procedures and encouraged him to redesign and repackage their line, just as he had done for Cary. In addition to giving their private-brand business to Pharmalab, Giles Brothers agreed to sell Pharmalab some of their equipment at very favorable prices and payment terms.

In order to protect the Cary business, Dr. Carlo informed Cary that Pharmalab was about to start private branding for Giles. The two lines would contain many duplicate items. Since these would require the same formulation regardless of the company for which they were prepared, the acquisition of an additional private-brand customer increased the volume of Pharmalab's sales significantly without correspondingly increasing the complexity of its operations. Fiscal 1965 drew to a close with sales almost four times those of the previous year and losses only about one-fourth as high.

In fiscal 1966, Pharmalab added another drug wholesaler and a safety equipment manufacturer as major customers. The latter had sought out Pharmalab as a supplier of first-aid medications after becoming aware of Pharmalab's excellent packaging capabilities.

As Pharmalab continued to expand, Dr. Carlo said that he was able to follow his philosophy of being selective in choosing customers and to concentrate on adequate margins and good quality control and packaging. New business was added at a regulated rate, and quality was never sacrificed for volume. At the end of fiscal 1966, sales were up almost 60% and losses for the year were not more than nominal.

CHEMICAL FILLING

In January 1967, Pharmalab was approached by the Nomad Engineering Company about undertaking a new type of contract-filling business. This would involve packing chemicals in scholastic chemistry kits sold by Nomad's Educational Division. Nomad had learned of Pharmalab's capability for attractive packaging through a bottle-cap supplier who called at both companies. After visiting Pharmalab, Nomad Educational's general manager asked Dr. Carlo if he would be interested in this business. At first Dr. Carlo's reply was negative for a variety of reasons: he was in pharmaceutical manufacturing, not chemical filling; price competition in the chemical filling business would not allow for his usual margins; he was accustomed to the stricter quality control required for pharmaceuticals; and he did not like Nomad's present packaging, which would have to be improved to reflect Pharmalab's standards. He agreed, however, to submit quotations on six items, informing Nomad that the quotations would reflect his relatively high margins and additional costs for improved packaging.

Nomad management believed that most of Pharmalab's quotations were comparatively high, but livable, especially since their present suppliers were located outside the New England area. Although some of Pharmalab's prices were definitely too high and out of competitive range, management was very much impressed by the plastic bottles and the new label designs which Pharmalab submitted. As a result, it was agreed to let Pharmalab redesign the entire line and to give Pharmalab 50% (or $30,000) of Nomad's filling business for the year.

In the autumn of 1967, Pharmalab was approached by the educational division of one of Nomad's major competitors to perform the same type of redesigning and filling that had been done for Nomad. Since Dr. Carlo was interested in obtaining all of Nomad's filling business for 1968 and also in maintaining an excellent relationship with Nomad's management, he turned down this new offer. In the event, Pharmalab received only $42,000 of Nomad's $60,000 filling business for 1968, but this accounted for 25% of Pharmalab's 1968 sales.

In addition to the Nomad contract, Pharmalab's other business continued to expand rapidly through fiscal 1968 and the first half of fiscal 1969. Following its first profitable year in 1967, the company increased profits to $17,000 (10% of sales) in 1968, and to a healthy $25,000 (22% of sales) for the first half of fiscal 1969.

FINANCE

While obtaining materials and setting up for his first private-label contract for Cary, Dr. Carlo began to realize that Pharmalab's initial capitalization ($18,000 in 1963) was much lower than his early $100,000 target and that it was inadequate to support the transition to the new line of business. Success with the Cary line, however, convinced the original investors that an additional commitment should be made. During fiscal 1964 an extra $32,500 was raised, $20,500 of it in preferred stock (see Exhibit 2). With this infusion of capital and another $7,500 the following year, net stockholders' equity was maintained at a positive figure in spite of interrupted production and start-up costs in fiscal 1963–64, plus operating losses in each of the next two fiscal years.

Once the company turned the corner during fiscal 1967, profits were protected from income taxes, at least temporarily, by the previous period

Exhibit 2

PHARMALAB, INC.
Balance Sheets as of June 30, 1963–68 and January 1, 1969

	1963	1964	1965	1966	1967	1968	January 1, 1969
Assets							
Cash	$ 3,188	$(1,415)	$ 3,153	$ 736	$ 716	$ 372	$ 4,790
Receivables (trade)	72	3,028	10,077	11,314	16,320	17,890	17,793
Notes receivable	—	1,000				—	
Inventories	2,175	8,554	13,492	16,787	18,283	27,909	25,851
Prepaid expenses, deposits	642	2,459	2,385	2,319	2,594	3,272	1,846
Total current assets	$ 6,077	$ 13,626	$ 29,107	$ 31,156	$ 38,913	$ 49,443	$50,280
Net fixed assets*	33,235	39,594	43,601	39,666	33,833	35,181	46,275
Other assets	1,775	2,127	741	500	500	500	500
Total assets	$41,087	$ 55,347	$ 73,449	$ 71,322	$ 73,246	$ 85,124	$97,055
Liabilities							
Note payable (bank)	$ —	$ 5,000	$ 15,000	$ 13,500	$ 11,000	$ 7,000	$ 5,000
Accounts payable	1,596	3,549	10,277	9,521	10,317	9,476	5,955
Accrued expenses	509	1,652	2,663	2,426	3,195	2,784	3,763
Accrued interest†	—	—	488	1,038	3,274	3,602	3,930
Total current liabilities	$ 2,105	$ 10,201	$ 28,428	$ 26,485	$ 27,786	$ 22,862	$18,648
Notes payable (stockholders)	23,965	23,965	23,965	25,465	21,690	21,690	13,490
Stockholders' equity:							
Preferred‡	—	20,500	22,000	22,000	22,000	23,500	23,500
Common§	9,000	9,000	9,000	9,000	9,000	9,000	9,000
Capital and paid-in surplus	9,000	21,000	27,000	27,000	27,000	27,000	27,000
Retained earnings (deficit)	(2,983)	(29,319)	(36,944)	(38,644)	(34,230)	(18,928)	5,417
Net equity	$15,017	$ 21,181	$ 21,056	$ 19,372	$ 23,770	$ 40,572	$64,917
Total liabilities	$41,087	$ 55,347	$ 73,499	$ 71,322	$ 73,246	$ 85,124	$97,055

* Machinery and equipment, leasehold improvements, motor vehicles, furniture, and fixtures.
† On stockholder note.
‡ Par value, $100. Number of authorized shares, 1,000.
§ Par value, $1.00. Number of authorized shares, 10,000.
Source: Company records.

of losses. Partly as a result, Dr. Carlo felt that he could afford to buy out three of the original investors who were dissatisfied with the rate at which their money was growing. Thus he emerged as the owner of 75% of Pharmalab's common in the first half of fiscal 1969—or some six months ahead of Nomad's first acquisition offer.

PRODUCTION AND PRODUCTS

A one-man operation until incorporated in 1963, Pharmalab had hired its first full-time employee just before starting production for Cary. With occasional part-time help from the other co-investors, Dr. Carlo was able to operate on this basis until fiscal 1966. Then increased volume, a wider range of products, and a growing number of customers necessitated hiring two more full-time workers and two part-time high school students. During fiscal 1967 and 1968, Pharmalab further enlarged its work force by hiring a packaging supervisor plus a manufacturing supervisor to take charge of formulating, mixing, and preparing all products. Both men reported directly to Dr. Carlo.

By mid-fiscal 1969, the work force had expanded to 10 full-timers, including Dr. Carlo and his bookkeeper-secretary, plus six part-timers, all of whom were high school students. Manufacturing and packaging occupied most of the plant personnel, with machine maintenance and cleaning being the only other operations.

As for plant, in 1965 Pharmalab outgrew its 1963 accommodations (3,000 square feet at $3,000 a year). It then expanded in the same three-story building to 5,500 square feet at a $4,800 rental. By June of 1968, the company was ready for still another move—this time to a modernized building where Pharmalab took over 10,000 square feet, all on one floor, with an option to lease another 13,000 on the floor above by 1970. This new building offered substantially improved conditions. Besides office space, there were separate rooms for packaging, warehousing, and manufacture, with sections in the latter for preparing liquids, powders, tablets, and ointments. Acquisition of some manufacturing equipment and good maintenance of older equipment actually gave the manufacturing area more machines than could be kept operating continually by the supervisor and his part-time help. Such excess capacity added flexibility for producing a variety of products with rapid customer service.

Capabilities included the manufacture of liquid preparations in quantities from one gallon to 950 gallons in a single batch. The separate powder-filling and tableting areas met stringent requirements concerning cleanliness and ventilation. In the packaging room Pharmalab employees used semiautomatic machinery to fill, cap, and label the many sizes and shapes of bottles, jars, and tubes. As in the manufacturing room, the variety of machines required for the many types of containers could not all be utilized continually.

In 1968 Pharmalab manufactured and packaged 257 pharmaceutical products, including USP and NF formulations, plus formulas developed by Pharmalab for its customers. Of these products, some 40% were merely repackaged from bulk with no formulation involved. Of the 257 products, about 30% were produced in scheduled production, while the others were manufactured and/or packaged upon customer demand.

MARKETING AND DISTRIBUTION

By manufacturing mainly private brands for distributors who routinely picked up their orders from Pharmalab, the company had greatly simplified marketing and distribution. In addition to the complete pharmaceutical line for Cary, Inc., and Giles Brothers, Pharmalab produced private-brand items for three distributors of veterinary products, produced a line of first-aid products for two distributors of unit first-aid kits, and filled educational chemicals for Nomad. (A sales breakdown for 1968 is shown in a note to Exhibit 1 above.)

RESEARCH AND DEVELOPMENT

Besides his interest in developing attractive and related "families" of bottles and labels to distinguish a customer's line, Dr. Carlo was also interested in developing a "pack" of individual liquid doses for hospital use. Dr. Carlo believed such dosage forms were not commonly available and yet might offer significant assistance in the prevention of maladministration by harried hospital personnel.

In the area of drug research, Dr. Carlo was one of perhaps only two U.S. manufacturers who had applied to the Food and Drug Administration for permission to investigate the therapeutic effects of a mental drug used for some years in Australia and Europe, where it was said to be achieving remarkable results. This drug, lithium carbonate, had been hailed by the U.S. Surgeon General, who said it "appears to be the best specific agent yet found for the treatment of any mental disease." Research on it had been supported by grants from the National Institute of Mental Health, and hopes had been expressed that uses might include not just the treatment of manic states (the original indication) but also the control of depression and other emotional disorders tending to occur in periodic cycles.

In spite of its high medical potential, lithium carbonate had found its U.S. market to date as an industrial chemical compound; so far, it had not been of interest to the large U.S. prescription-drug houses. Reasons for the latters' lack of interest have been summarized as follows:

> For the psychiatrist, lithium's easy and inexpensive availability in nature poses somewhat of a paradoxical problem of supply; no company has wanted to market it. There is nothing to synthesize and nothing to process; the pharmacist—or his after-school assistant—simply puts the material into capsule form. Most important of all, there is nothing about lithium in any of its present forms that can be patented; consequently, no one can make any money marketing it. In the absence of patent protection, a company could not charge more than a few cents a tablet—about the cost of aspirin.[4]

THE NOMAD ACQUISITION OFFER

Late in calendar 1968, Nomad Engineering, for whose Educational Division Pharmalab had packaged chemicals for the past two years, informed Dr. Carlo of its desire to acquire his company in return for stock. Although Nomad asked Dr. Carlo what price he would ask for Pharmalab, he would not quote a figure. Instead, he suggested that Nomad make an offer based on Pharmalab's growing profitability and the value of Dr. Carlo and his personnel to Nomad. As a result, initial discussions concerned topics other than the amount of the acquisition offer.

One of the topics discussed was Pharmalab's role in Nomad's total operation. Besides being in the educational field and making control devices for machines, Nomad had recently acquired a number of laboratory facilities for running diagnostic medical tests, and Pharmalab could produce some of the reagents required in this business. From Nomad's point of view, there would be a product cost advantage in owning its own source of supply, plus a transport cost and delivery time advantage in having that source located near the heart of its regional market, or at any rate closer to several of its labs than alternative sources.

Besides supplying chemicals to Nomad's testing laboratories, Pharmalab would continue to fill and package chemicals for Nomad's Ed-

---

[4] *New York Times Magazine*, January 13, 1969.

ucational Division, and would, Dr. Carlo believed, get 100% of this business. About 100 chemicals were involved, and Pharmalab would be entrusted not only with furnishing the supply but also with in-house development and troubleshooting. This activity would, Nomad said, give Nomad Educational an advantage over its competition, who had their chemical kits filled by outside contractors.

Another Pharmalab responsibility would be product development in the pharmaceutical field. For example, unit dosage work for hospital items, which Dr. Carlo had already developed to a great extent could proceed toward market introduction at a much faster pace when the resources of Nomad were added to Dr. Carlo's talent.

As for Pharmalab's plant and employees, Nomad offered to take over the 10-year lease and to keep Pharmalab in its present location. All employees would receive at least as much pay as at present, plus the added fringe benefits offered by the larger company. After his initial conversations with Nomad, Dr. Carlo informed all the Pharmalab employees that acquisition was a possibility, but that their jobs and pay were secure.

In further negotiations with Nomad, Dr. Carlo insisted that, if acquisition were accepted, his contract should limit his work to the Boston area, since he had just built a large new home in a Boston suburb and he and his family wished to stay there. Nomad agreed to this, and in turn required Dr. Carlo to sign a three-year contract and to bind himself not to compete with Nomad in any way for two additional years. Nomad further stated that Dr. Carlo would not be limited to Pharmalab work. He could be assigned to other projects to make full use of his talents.

Negotiations about acquisition price resulted in the following offer: Nomad would deliver 4,000 shares of its common stock at the time of closing the acquisition, plus an additional 2,000 shares on July 31, 1969, provided that Pharmalab sales exceeded $180,000 during the fiscal year ending June 30, 1969. Nomad stock had been fairly steady around $50 per share, even though this meant an exceptionally high EPS (80 times earnings in January, 1969), reflecting the company's rapid past growth and its current plans for continued expansion (see Exhibit 3). As part of the offer, Dr. Carlo would receive both a com-petitive salary (considerably higher than his previous drawing of $10,000) and an attractive qualified stock option plan. Pharmalab had reported sales of $111,000 and profit of $25,000 for the first half of fiscal 1969.

Exhibit 3

PHARMALAB, INC.
Data on Nomad Engineering Company

History. Founded in 1961, Nomad increased its sales fivefold from fiscal 1963 through fiscal 1967, while net went from a negative figure to almost 10% of gross. Early in the following fiscal year, the stock was split 10 for 3, and a public offer followed of 125,480 shares at $15. Four months later, Nomad acquired a medical instrument company (CED) on a pooling-of-interest basis, and this move was a major factor in raising sales from the $3 million to the $16 million level during fiscal 1968.

Early fiscal 1969 was in some respects a repetition of the previous year. The number of authorized common shares was increased from 1.5 million to 10 million; the stock was split again 3 for 2, and another public offering was effected: 141,335 shares at $50. Shortly thereafter (March, 1969), the company announced that it had agreed in principle to purchase two medical laboratory companies in Philadelphia; one in New York; another with facilities in Washington, Maryland, and Virginia; and one in Latin America on a half-interest basis. All these acquisitions would be for shares, and they would give Nomad biomedical facilities.

Business. The company's business was carried on by four divisions, with sales broken down as follows for fiscal years ending August 31:

Division	1967	1968
Electronics	17%	24%
Educational	7	16
Medical⎫ Plastics⎭	76	60

In December, 1968, the company incorporated a subsidiary to engage as its Biomedical Sciences Division in the business of providing medical diagnostic testing services and analytical chemical analyses for industry.

Finances. Some highlights of Nomad's finances were as follows:

Selected Operating Data for Fiscal Years
Ending August 31
(Dollars in Thousands)

	Sales	Net Profit (Loss)
1963	$ 599.7	$ (37.2)
1964	852.9	90.5
1965	1,239.5	141.5
1966	1,542.5	127.1
1967	3,137.0	297.2
1968	5,708.7	1,045.5

Exhibit 3—Continued

Selected Balance Sheet Data for Fiscal Years Ending August 31
(Dollars in Thousands except EPS)

	1967	1968
Total assets............................	$2,316.7	$9,248.3
Current assets........................	1,583.8	6,954.3
Current liabilities....................	800.6	2,365.9
Long-term debt.......................	388.4	1,239.5
Owners' equity:		
Common (par $0.25)................	192.3	477.3
Paid-in surplus.....................	456.6	1,887.7
Earned surplus.....................	442.8	3,277.9
Total........................	$1,091.7	$5,642.9

Note: Figures are for company only through 1967; consolidated in 1968. After including CED (acquired April, 1968), consolidated sales for 1967 would have been $13.1 million; net $0.6 million.

Per Share Earnings and Dividends for Fiscal Years Ending August 31

	Adjusted Earnings* (Loss) per Share	Dividends
1963....................	$(0.03)	nil
1964....................	0.90	nil
1965....................	0.14	nil
1966....................	0.11	nil
1967....................	0.26	nil
1968....................	0.57[†]	nil

  * After adjustment for 3 for 2 stock split of December 12, 1968, as well as 10 for 3 split in 1967 and issuance of shares for minority interest.
  † As reported. Assuming exercise of all stock options as originally granted in 1961, EPS for 1968 would have been $0.55.

Stock Prices

	Bid	Asked
1967*........................	24⅜–20½	24⅝–20⅝
1968		
First quarter...............	29⅛–20⅜	29⅜–21⅛
Second quarter..............	47⅜–25⅝	48⅛–26
Third quarter...............	50⅝–37⅜	52⅝–38⅝
Fourth quarter†	54⅝–45⅜	56⅝–47⅜

  * From December 19, when shares were first publicly traded.
  † Through December 17
Source: *Moody's Industrial Manual.*

CHOOSING AMONG ALTERNATIVES FOR GROWTH

Early in 1969 the case writer asked Dr. Carlo how he envisioned Pharmalab's future operations, assuming acceptance of the line of credit or of the acquisition offer, and what advantages and disadvantages he foresaw from each alternative. Dr. Carlo replied as follows:

At this point it must be stated that I am enthusiastic over the fact that we have been offered the line of credit. This is certainly an indication that we have created a good track record. The credit would allow me to continue my growth trend. It would also allow me to build management stability through "people expansion." Were I to accept the line of credit, I could look forward to adding more wholesaler customers such as those I already have, and perhaps to adding some chain-type retail customers as well. If so, of course, I would have to build something in the way of a marketing organization. An additional possibility would be geographic expansion—that is, getting in touch with customers serving more of the regional market than I already indirectly sell.

But my situation is unusual. Two alternatives are open that would be very influential on our future. Do I take advantage of the bank's offer, or do I allow my company to be acquired? I have done some thinking about the circumstances under which I might sell out and about the kind of company I might sell to. Sellers all too often do not think this problem through. The aggressiveness is all on the part of the buyer—the buyers are the swingers because they seem to hold the royal straight flush. The buyer has usually had an opportunity to search out and investigate the seller's company very carefully. They usually calculate their timing perfectly; they time for primary choice and favorable financial arrangements.

In our own case, though, timing is definitely in our favor. We have better earnings, more assets, fewer liabilities, a good lease with leasehold improvements, a good cash flow, controlled expenses, that $100,000 dollar offer from the bank. . . and all our accounts have good growth rates. Pharmalab can, therefore, sell from strength. You may be sure this will be pointed out in any discussions or negotiations.

And we will point up the trends. The seller frequently sells in the wrong way for the wrong reasons. The greatest error on the part of any seller is to sell at today's value and to completely ignore the future. Should we sell out, we will not ignore our own future or that of Nomad either.

The essential thing in selling is to sell constructively and to the proper party. This means that the value of the owner's equity must grow faster in the future if he sells than it could possibly have done if no sale took place.

Another important thing is a match between the buyer's and the seller's objectives. If only one party can be helped, then there is a mismatch. The buyer must be interested in the seller's objectives as well as his own. The buyer must be made aware of the seller's objectives, so that he will not fail to fulfill them.

Another thing to remember is that selling out is really an investment decision, for if a company is sold for stock the decision is identical to purchasing the stock for the same amount in dollars.

The potential acquiring company in my case is what I would consider as being a well-balanced, dynamic concern. The financial community has much praise for Nomad Engineering, and the investment community reveals a great deal of faith in the company, as evidenced by the increase in the price of their stock over a one-year period.

Fortunately, I have been close to this company, since they have been a substantial account of Pharmalab. I know the type of people in management and have a very good feeling about their capabilities. In addition, it was revealed in the negotiations that Pharmalab would have business autonomy if it were acquired.

If I decide to go the bank route, I recognize my biggest difficulty is building a good management team. Where would I find the right people for the key positions on the team? Would I be able to afford a management team immediately? Do I possess the background that would be necessary to direct a management team efficiently? The more I study the bank route, the more complexities I discover.

The final conclusion would, of course, rest on a measure of advancement. Once I determine which method would allow my personal holdings as well as my company to grow at the most rapid rate, I would be in a position to decide without doubt.

Appendix: Pharmalab, Inc.

INDUSTRY TRENDS

In Pharmalab's industry environment, a number of external trends appeared relevant to prospects for the company's future. These included the continued survival of about 1,000 pharmaceutical firms even though the top 50 did about 90% of the business; the relatively rapid sales and profit growth of the pharmaceutical industry, particularly of its major firms; the tendency among the latter to by-pass wholesaler channels in the distribution of at least their "ethical" drugs; the increasing importance of drugs and other health aids to the retail drugstores through which these products were still mainly sold in spite of increasing competition from other types of retail outlets; the trend toward increased market dominance by chain drugstores versus independents; and the relatively strong position of large wholesale drug houses compared with the small ones.

These trends are illustrated by figures in the following tables:

A. *Concentration in Pharmaceuticals*
(Ethical and Proprietary)

Year	Number of Companies	Value of Company Shipments* (Millions)	Percent of Shipments Accounted for by:			
			4 Largest Companies†	8 Largest Companies	20 Largest Companies	50 Largest Companies
1954............	1,128	$1,643.1	25%	44%	68%	N.A.
1958............	1,064	2,533.4	27	45	73	87%
1963...........	944	3,314.3	22	38	72	89
1966...........	N.A.	4,432.0	24	41	N.A.	N.A.

* Shipments include nonpharmaceutical products.
† Largest companies are determined by each company's value of shipments in the industry specified.
Source: U S Bureau of the Census, *1963 Census of Manufactures*, Vol. I, pp. 11–41; *Statistical Abstract of the United States, 1970*, p. 708.

B. *Relative Growth in Shipments of Pharmaceutical Establishments*
(Dollars in Billions)

Year	All Manufacturing Establishments	Establishments in Chemicals and Allied Products	Establishments in Drugs	Pharmaceutical Establishments*
1958................	$326.7	$21.0	$3.0	$2.6
1963................	420.5	31.8	3.7	3.3
1967................	555.9	42.2	5.3	4.7
Per cent change, 1958–67............	+73.6	+100.9	+76.7	+80.8
Average annual growth............	5.1	6.5	5.3	5.5

* These shipments include some nonpharmaceutical products. In 1967, all-industry shipments of pharmaceuticals were $4.1 billion, of which about 70% were "ethical" drugs (promoted only to the medical profession), while the rest were mainly proprietaries (drugs promoted to the general public).
Source: U.S. Bureau of the Census, *1963 Census of Manufactures; 1967 Census of Manufactures, Industry Series 1, Preliminary Reports;* and *Statistical Abstract of the United States, 1969*.

C. Sales and Financial Trends for Leading Pharmaceutical Companies
(Dollars in Millions except for Price)

The companies used for this series of composite data are: Abbott Laboratories; American Home Products; Bristol-Myers; Merck; Parke, Davis; Chas. Pfizer; Richardson-Merrell; Schering; Searle (S.D.); Squibb Beech-Nut; Sterling Drug; and Warner-Lambert.

	1958*	1963	1967*
Sales..................................	$26.12	$34.87	$ 44.27
Operating income......................	4.65	6.29	9.44
Profit margins %.....................	17.80%	18.04%	20.65%
Depreciation..........................	$ 0.39	$ 0.66	$ 0.98
Taxes................................	2.18	2.80	3.80
Earnings.............................	2.29	2.96	4.39
Dividends............................	1.24	1.68	2.49
Earnings as a % of sales.................	8.77%	8.49%	9.92%
Dividends as a % of earnings............	54.15	56.76	56.76
Price (1941–43 = 10)—High.............	$51.75	$75.16	$136.87
—Low..............	27.79	61.71	102.71
Price/earnings ratios—High.............	22.60%	25.39%	31.18%
—Low..............	12.14	20.85	22.40
Dividend yield % —High.............	4.46	2.72	2.42
—Low..............	2.40	2.24	1.82
Book value...........................	$11.05	$15.84	$ 18.55
Return on book value...................	20.72	18.69	23.67
Working capital†......................	7.29	9.55	14.73
Capital expenditure....................	1.24	1.06	2.67

Note: Per share data are expressed in terms of the S & P Stock Price Index, i.e. stock prices, 1941–43 = 100. Each of the items shown is first computed on a true per share basis for each company. Totals for each company are then reconstructed using the same number of shares outstanding as was used to compute our stock price index as of December 31st. This is done because the shares used on December 31st, although the latest known at the time, may differ from those reported to the annual reports which are not available for six or eight weeks after the end of the year. The sum of these reconstructed totals is then related to the base period value used to compute the stock price index As a double check, we relate the various items to the dividends, as these are the most stable series. So, for example, if total sales amount to 15 times the total dividend payments, then, with per share dividends at 3.50 the indicated per share sales will be (15 × 3.50) $52.50 in terms of the S & P Stock Price Index. For comparability between the various groups, all data are on a calendar year basis, corporate data being posted in the year in which most months fall. Fiscal years ending June 30 are posted in the calendar year in which the fiscal year ends.

* McKesson & Robbins was added to the group in 1958 and dropped in 1967.
† Current assets less current liabilities, without allowance for long-term debt.
Source: Standard & Poor's *Industry Surveys*, "Drugs, Medical Care, and Cosmetics, Basic Analysis," May 8, 1969, p. D 25.

D. Use of Wholesaler Channels by Ethical Pharmaceutical Manufacturers in Different Size Classes, 1967

PHARMACEUTICAL MANUFACTURERS BY SALES SIZE CLASS	SALES AS A PERCENTAGE OF CATEGORY TOTAL			
	To Wholesaler	To Retailer	To Other*	Total†
Over $100 million......	39.2%	37.3%	23.5%	100%
$30 to $100 million.....	61.1	13.7	25.2	100
$5 to $30 million.......	70.4	13.5	26.1	100
Under $5 million.......	49.8	24.6	25.6	100
Average, all firms.......	47.8	29.3	22.9	100
Volume (in millions)...	$1,540.7	$944.4	$840.4	$3,225.5

* Hospitals, government, doctors, other manufacturers, and repackers.
† Dosage form ethical drugs for human use only.
Source: Pharmaceutical Manufacturers Association, *Yearbook, 1968*, p. 106.

E. *Relative Importance of Drugs and Other Health Aids**
to Drugstore Sales Volume
(Dollars in Billions)

Year	Total Sales in All Retail Outlets†	Drugstore Share of Total Retail Sales		Product Category as a Per Cent of Total Drugstore Sales
		Dollars	Per Cent	
Prescriptions				
1958............	$1.86	$1.82	98%	27.22%
1963............	2.62	2.54	97	28.90
1966............	3.57	3.35	94	31.80
1967............	3.93	3.63	93	32.78
Packaged Medications				
1958............	$1.55	$1.05	68%	15.64%
1963............	1.90	1.23	65	13.96
1966............	2.17	1.41	65	13.36
1967............	2.27	1.47	65	13.28
Other Health Aids				
1958............	$1.42	$1.55	—	8.26
1963............	1.74	1.69	—	7.14
1966............	1.58	0.69	—	6.59
1967............	1.24	0.72	—	6.49
Total‡				
1958............	$4.43	$3.03	68%	45.18%
1963............	6.09	4.25	70	48.37
1966............	7.32	5.45	74	49.63
1967............	7.48	5.51	74	49.61

* Other categories of drugstore products include toiletries, tobacco, confectionery, ice cream, and miscellaneous.
† Excludes purchases in noncivilian outlets.
‡ Owing to duplication of 2%–6%, subtotals do not add to totals.
Source: *Drug Trade News*, July 17, 1961, August 1, 1966, and August 12, 1968.

F. *Growing Importance of Large Chain-Store Operations
in the Retail Drug Trade*

	1958	1963	1967
Sales ($ billions)			
Chain drugstore.............	$2.56	$3.59	$ 5.35*
Nonchain...................	3.75	4.16	5.09
Total.....................	$6.31	$7.75	$10.44
Chain store per cent...........	40.6%	46.3%	51.3%
Number of chain stores........	8,925	12,047	14,159
Average chain-store sales........	$286,683	$298,000	$377,498

* Classified by size of chain, total sales broken down as follows in 1967:

Size of Drug Chain in Units	Sales Volume	Per Cent of Drugstore Total	Per Cent of Chain-store Total
11 or more..........	$3.47	33.3%	64.9%
4–10...............	.94	8.9	17.5
2–3................	.94	9.0	17.6
Total........	$5.35	51.3%	100.0%

Source: Chainstore Age, Drug Editions, *1968 Annual
Report of the Chain Drug Industry*, pp. 4, 5.

G. *Relative Importance of High-Volume Merchant Wholesalers in Drugs,*
Drug Proprietaries, and Druggists' Sundries, 1963
(Dollars in Millions)

MERCHANT WHOLESALERS by SALES SIZE CLASS	ESTABLISHMENTS 1963		ESTABLISHMENTS 1967		SALES 1963		SALES 1967	
	Number	Per Cent	Number	Per Cent	Volume	Per Cent	Volume	Per Cent
$2 million and up...........	520	15.5%	623*	20.4%	$2,552	70.5%	$3,729	78.7%
Under $2 million...........	2,715	81.9	2,360	77.4	1,010	28.0	941	19.9
Operating less than a full year........	86	2.6	70	2.2	58	1.5	78	1.4
Total................	$3,321	100.0%	$3,053	100.0%	$3,620	100.0%	$4,748	100.0%

* Includes 272 establishments in the $5 million and up size class, with combined volume of $2,562 million.
Source: U.S. Bureau of the Census, *Census of Business, Wholesale Trade, 1963, 1967.*

2. Mathatronics, Inc.

"Like a Good 5¢ Cigar"

MATHATRONICS, INC., a small electronics firm located in Waltham, Massachusetts, manufactured and distributed a low-cost, electronic, desk-top, digital computer called the Mathatron. Sales brochures described this machine as providing "the benefits and convenience of automatic digital computation without the high cost." The machine could be used both for fully automatic computation or could be operated like a desk calculator using ordinary mathematical notations.

Mathatronics, Inc., had been organized by Mr. Roy Reach, Mr. Dave Shapiro, and Mr. William Kahn, the designers of the Mathatron, in February of 1962 for the purpose of developing, manufacturing, and distributing the machine. They believed the machine would fill what they saw as a "gigantic void" in the data-processing market between the $1,500 rotary calculator and the $20,000 full-size computer. According to Mr. Reach, president and treasurer, the needs of this void "were too complex for calculators but were not such as to require a $20,000 computer. For a long time there has been a saying in the electronics world that what the country needed most was a 5¢ cigar and a $5,000 computer. We believe we have the computer."

By December, 1962, the first prototype had been built. Within one year orders had been received for 40 Mathatrons.

Both Mr. Kahn and Mr. Reach as well as Mr. Shapiro had had extensive technical training and experience in the computer industry prior to their formation of Mathatronics, Inc. Mr. Reach had been associate director of research and systems for Minneapolis-Honeywell's computer division, having specialized in the development and design of electronic computers throughout his career. Mr. Kahn had been a senior engineering analyst at Raytheon, specializing in electronic systems analysis before organizing Mathatronics. His cohorts described him as a "genius at program and system design." Mr. Shapiro had been a project director in charge of production planning and design for RCA's data-processing group. At one time all three men had worked at

Honeywell. It was during this period that the idea of entering business together had first arisen.

THE MATHATRON

The Mathatron had been designed for use in scientific and engineering calculations, accounting procedures, and specialized business problems where speed, accuracy, low cost, and simplicity of operation were important. The recognition of the lack of machinery available to fill these needs had been an outgrowth of "many informal after-hour bull sessions" between the three men. The product itself had resulted from what Mr. Reach described as a "concentrated, nine-month design effort to try and fill these needs."

The Initial Concept. Mr. Reach described the group's initial thinking as follows:

We realized our primary skills were computer related. Consequently we concluded very early in our discussions that anything we did had to be connected with the data-processing industry. We also were certain that the financial requirements of pursuing the large data-processing market would leave us with little ownership or control. Working with computers, we knew that no one was exploiting the possibility of economy via reduced speed, i.e., everyone was building devices with greater capacity and speed. Therefore we decided to determine what data-processing needs we could satisfy, exploiting the cost advantages of lower speed systems, which were not being satisfied by available high-speed systems.

The conclusions of the three men were incorporated into presentations made to potential investors. Direct excerpts of these presentations follow:

The Need:. . . . . .Low investment.

The Problem:. . . . . .Present-day systems are economical only in large-scale, high-speed applications.

The Solution:. . . . . .Produce low-cost data-processing equipment by taking advantage of the low-speed requirements of the small user.

Proposal:. . . . . .Design and produce low-cost desk-top electronic computer and design expanded line.
Sell to scientific market—expand into business market.
Expand to full data systems by producing an expanded product line and selling to a captive market (captive in the sense of the machine's unique capabilities)—capture the massive, untapped, small business data system market.

The Market:.........Potential billion dollar—ultimate market—
measured in total number of small busi-
nesses.
Trends:..............Growing office machine market.

	Average cost per machine
1947	$288
1954	614
1959	833

Tendency toward quality.
Expected share of calculator market: 13,000 over 10-year cycle.

ESTIMATE OF SALES BREAKDOWN

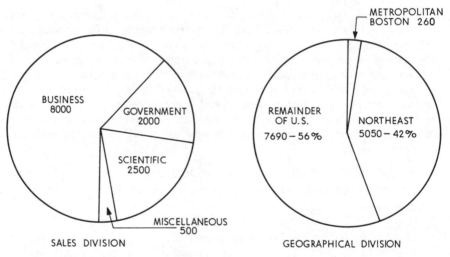

SALES DIVISION   GEOGRAPHICAL DIVISION

In 1959, 112,000 motorized calculators were sold. Mathatron sales of 100/month is 1.1% of 1959 sales.

According to Mr. Shapiro, the group concluded that to reach the
customer whose data-processing needs were beyond the capacities of a
calculator, yet were not large enough to efficiently utilize the
$20,000–$40,000 small computer, they had to design a machine
which:

1) Didn't require a large investment in programmers ("training
   people to fit the machine").
2) Would be "unfrightening" in appearance.

3) Could be mass-produced—one design covering the majority of applications.

4) Would require a modest investment, allowing even one individual to finance it easily.

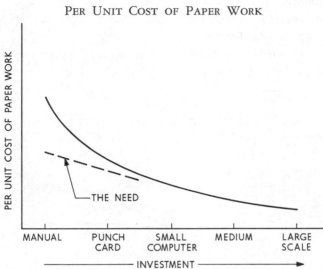

Figure 1

PER UNIT COST OF PAPER WORK

Mr. Kahn said that the Mathatron had been conceived of as essentially an extension of the electronic calculator. The basic advantage of the electronic calculator was its ability to perform all the functions of its mechanical counterpart faster and more quietly. The cost of the basic machine, however, was considerably higher than the standard rotary calculator, although the cost of expanding the electronic unit's capacity was relatively low (see Figure 2). Accordingly, the group's idea was to build an electronic calculator as cheaply as possible and then add to its features which would raise the machine's capability per cost ratio well above that of a mechanical calculator (point A).

Mr. Kahn explained:

Just the additional speed and quietness of an electronic calculator didn't seem enough to justify the higher cost of the basic machine. Consequently we added a program memory, automatic decimal point placement, and other operating efficiencies to our specifications. Now if the rotary calculator manufacturers were going to compete with us, it would have to be on an electronic basis.

By December of 1961, the three men had settled on what were to be the distinctive features of the proposed machine. These features were:

1) A very low price: $2,000–$2,700.
2) The high speed, quietness, and reliability of electronic components.
3) A printed record of all input and output data.
4) An ability to learn sequence of operations—to select a prewired sequence.
5) The ease of direct entry via "parenthication"—repeat data registers—push-button access.
6) The automatic placement of the decimal point and exponent.
7) An ability to be expanded to a full data system.

Figure 2

CAPABILITY PER INVESTMENT

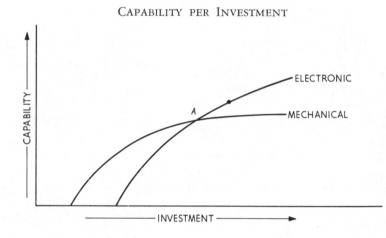

On the basis of this concept, Mathatronics was able to raise $250,000 during January of 1962. At that time no prototype or model had been built. As Mr. Kahn put it, "We were confident we could build it. Our uncertainty was how much would it cost to mass-produce it."

The Finished Machine.[1] The first prototype was completed in December, 1962. Except for changing the numbering and arrangement envisioned for the keyboard, the prototype did not vary significantly from the original technical conception. An underestimation of component costs, however, did result in an increase in price from $2,700 to $3,500.

Mr. Shapiro felt the maintenance of a disciplined design had been the

---

[1] See Exhibits 1 and 2.

Exhibit 1
MATHATRONICS, INC.

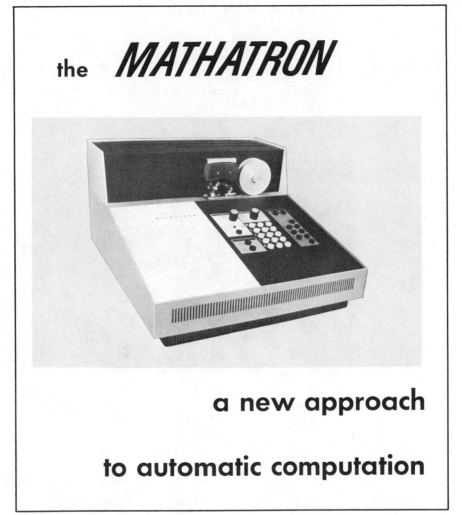

the ***MATHATRON***

a new approach

to automatic computation

major reason behind their ability to successfully implement the idea, and he said:

The usual thing for a large corporation is to add a little something here and another transistor there until you reach the point where it is a monstrous thing. This is a characteristic of the large corporation—an inability to stick to an original, careful specification.

Exhibit 2
MATHATRONICS, INC.
KEYBOARD LAYOUT

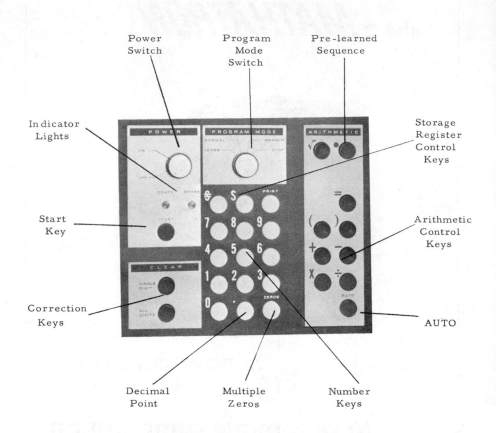

The Mathatron incorporated many of the computation abilities of large computers by adding to its desk calculating functions, storage registers, and magnetic memory units which allowed fully automative computation. The machine would accept direct entry of data using ordinary mathematical, algebraic notations (no preliminary programming was needed). Because of this feature, the three men had discovered that most individuals with a rudimentary understanding of algebra could learn to operate the Mathatron effectively within 30 to 45 minutes.

The Mathatron required no special wiring to operate. Its size (21 inches wide, 25 inches deep, 13 inches high) and weight (75–90 pounds, depending on peripheral equipment), in addition to the lack of special wiring required, made the machine relatively portable.

As each key was depressed, the corresponding number or symbol was printed out on a paper tape. Since the tape provided a continuous record of all data entered, written in conventional mathematical form, it was possible to intervene at any time during computation to display, modify, or correct formulas and numbers. The printer operated at 20 characters per second. In contrast, printer speeds in a large computer system ranged from 100 to 2,000 characters per second.

The printer had been developed along with the basic machine itself. The three men had planned to use a printer similar to those utilized by most adding machines, but due to an inability to find a printer which would meet required performance and cost specifications, they had designed their own. "This was our major technical change. It delayed us about three weeks."

Recently, the company had completed arrangements to sell 1,000 of these printers to a manufacturer planning to incorporate it into a special-purpose billing machine. Mr. Reach expected the independent sale of the printer to have a minor but a stabilizing influence on the company's growth. He stated:

Our major growth will come from the Mathatron, as the printer market requires extensive engineering coordination with the customer's design personnel—a service we are just not able to provide at the present time. In contrast, the Mathatron is ordered as an end-use item, thereby reducing to a minimum technical interface problems with the customer.

The Mathatron's unique ability was its capacity to solve the wide variety of problems that could not be worked on a mechanical calculator without the repeated reentry of intermediate steps, yet did not require the sophistication or capacity of the large computer. Some examples of these problems were:

> Calculation of mortgage payment tables
> Determination of bond prices
> Tax calculations
> Great circle calculations
> Surveying calculations
> Generation of random numbers
> Solution of cubic, quadratic, and fifth degree equations

Simultaneous equations (up to 3)
Correlations and distribution
Radic conversions

Exhibit 3 contains examples of applications.

Exhibit 3

MATHATRONICS, INC.

Representative Applications of the Mathatron

June, 1964

The MITRE Corp., Bedford, Mass., a technical consultant for the U.S. Air Force Electronic Systems Command at Hanscom Field, has two Mathatrons. One is being used for general research and development calculations. The other system is being operated by temporary office help from "Aid Employment" on a special project. (AID is a firm which specializes in providing temporary secretarial help to all types of organizations.) The engineer enters the formula with its several variables and then the AID girls spend the day working the formula by simply touching the AUTO key and entering the variable data.

Woods Hole Oceanographic Institution, Woods Hole, Mass., has been using two Mathatrons for the past eight months on the world-circling research vessel *Atlantis II.* These two Mathatrons have been operating satisfactorily under extremely difficult environmental conditions.

The MIT Instrumentation Laboratory, Cambridge, Mass., is using two Mathatrons for general engineering and design calculations. The Mathatrons, which are located in the same building as the Honeywell 1800 large-scale electronic data-processing system, are currently saving MIT time and money by providing a convenient, easy method for their engineers to do their own computations without waiting for data to be keypunched and scheduled on the large system.

Arthur D. Little, Inc., Cambridge, Mass., an industrial consulting firm, has been using the Mathatron as part of a service bureau to its outside consultants. Statistical clerks are doing the routine calculations which the consultants use for client reports. With desk calculators, a Mathatron, and an IBM computer at their disposal, these girls can now select the right machine for the size of job to be performed.

The Bell Telephone Co. of Canada, Montreal, Canada, has a Mathatron in its staff engineering headquarters. They have reported that a $3\frac{1}{2}$-day series of "great circle" type computations was completed in a single afternoon.

Boston University School of Medicine, Boston, Mass., has just established a medical statistical laboratory. Two Mathatrons equipped with nine prewired sequences were installed in this laboratory. With this prelearned sequence package, the researcher no longer has to be a machine operator to work his problems.

The MIT Lincoln Laboratory, Lexington, Mass., is doing contract research work for the government. Two Mathatrons have just been installed. One is being used by a group of R&D engineers and the other by a group of mathematicians.

Scientific Engineering, Waltham, Mass., a nonprofit research organization, is using the Mathatron to generate test data necessary to check out programs for its large computer in addition to performing their scientific computations.

United States Army Corps of Engineers, New England Division, Waltham, Mass., is using a Mathatron for civil engineering and river control calculations.

The Foxboro Co., Foxboro, Mass., a large manufacturer of industrial processing controls, is using a Mathatron in its circuit analysis group.

Polytechnic Institute of Brooklyn, Brooklyn, N.Y., is planning to use their Mathatron as a teaching tool to instruct engineering students in how to use a computer. Brooklyn Polytechnic has also completed installation of a large IBM computer which will be used for research; however, the IBM computer is much too large, sophisticated, and expensive to be used by the average engineering student. The Mathatron, on the other hand, can be used to teach the student the basic concepts of the computer, and just as important, the Mathatron can be used as an educational tool in teaching computer concepts from high school to Ph.D. level. (We have been in touch with the Department of Health, Education, and Welfare in Washington, D.C., and the Department of Education in Massachusetts. We find that 50% of the price of any educational tool will be paid for by the federal government, if it is to be used in secondary education. In many states the term secondary education extends through the sophomore year of college.)

Polaroid Corp., Cambridge, Mass., is using Mathatron to perform complex financial and production projections. Their Mathatron, which is located in the controller's department, is proving that the Mathatron can be used for business as well as a statistical and scientific application.

Emmons and Flemming, a small civil engineering organization located in Billerica, Mass., is using a Mathatron equipped with a special set of civil engineering prelearned sequences to compute automatically their closure, inverse, traverse, and all the other computations associated with surveying without the use of tables. This organization of approximately 10 employees expects the Mathatron to pay for itself, through timesaving alone, in less than two years.

Source: Company sales literature.

MARKETING

In March of 1963, a marketing manager was hired. According to Mr. Reach, the primary motivation in hiring such an individual was that "none of us knew anything about selling computers." The new manager, Mr. Charles French, was a graduate of the Harvard Business School. Mr. French had sold office machines for several years and before coming to Mathatronics had been the assistant manager of sales administration of Minneapolis-Honeywell's computer division. Mr. French was not a major stockholder, as were the three officers of the company.

In June of 1964, Mr. French described the Mathatron's markets as follows:

We have felt that the machine's greatest potential would be in the general business market, particularly over the long run, and that scientific and research applications would be significant only early in the game. But the response of the scientific market has proven to be much larger than we anticipated and to date we have concentrated on satisfying this demand. We still believe, however, that the small business, which can never afford the standard computer, is our largest potential market. But right now, the Mathatron does not do enough more, relative to the mechanical calculator, to justify its price to the small businessman. At the present time, it is primarily a scientific-engineering machine with only limited use in the business field. When we add the page printer and punched paper tape this fall, we will begin to get into more business applications.

Mr. Reach said that due to the uniqueness of the Mathatron, the potential business customer was usually unaware such a machine existed, and was therefore skeptical of its technical ability or its usefulness to him. In addition, he pointed out that the vast majority of small businessmen did not have any programming ability. As he stated it:

Selling to the engineer and the scientist greatly reduces these problems. Typically they are familiar with data-processing concepts and machinery, and they quickly recognize the innovation the machine represents. Also, because they are trained in mathematics they have no difficulty in operating the Mathatron. Consequently, the technically trained customer can make up his own mind as to how he will use the machine, greatly reducing our selling job. Such is not the case with the small businessman. It is difficult to get over to him why it is a better device than the calculator.

In response to a request by the case writer to characterize the Mathatron's distinctive abilities in layman's terms, Mr. Reach commented as follows:

The Mathatron is essentially a device which numerically evaluates mathematical functions automatically. You don't have to set the problem up for the machine, you just type in as you would write it down on a piece of paper. From this it gets answers easily and automatically, making the Mathatron different from the calculator. Certainly calculators get answers too, but not without a lot of intermediate help and mental figuring.

Mr. French explained that to overcome the difficulties in selling to the small businessman, "you have to show him the machine and how he can solve his own particular problems on it. You can't explain it to him in terms of generalized problems as you can with the engineer or scientist. The usual businessman's response to our sales literature is very small. In contrast, we have typically received from scientific-engineering firms a great deal of interest solely on the basis of promotional material."

Exhibit 4 illustrates the change in the company's market conception from 1962 to 1964.

Exhibit 4

MATHATRONICS, INC.

Predicted Composition of Sales 1962, 1964

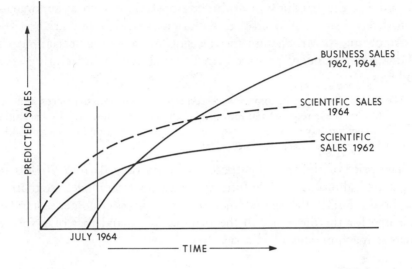

Shortly after Mathatronics incorporated in February, 1962, Mr. Reach had obtained a booth for the Northeast Electronics Research and Engineering Meeting (NEREM), held annually in Boston in November. The NEREM show was to be the company's first major promotional effort. In October of 1963, Mr. French obtained the services of a friend, for years a specialist in electronics publicity and advertising, to help prepare for the show. Company officers described the response to the Mathatron at the show as very enthusiastic. Reflecting the success of the show, front-page articles appeared in *Electronic News, Purchasing News,* and the *Electronic Design* magazines, describing the Mathatron's development and technical capabilities.

To capitalize on the interest of scientific and research firms three special-purpose models of the Mathatron were added to the product line: one for mathematical, one for statistical, and one for civil engineering computations. In essence, each model was the basic machine to which an expanded memory unit, containing several special-purpose prewired programs, had been added. Any of these internally stored programs could be used by simply dialing a program switch. The programs were selected on the basis of computations frequently utilized in each area. For example, the mathematical Mathatron contained prewired programs facilitating the automatic calculation of trigonometric ratios, the solution of simultaneous equations, the calculation of logs and antilogs, and so forth. The statistical model incorporated programs simplifying the handling of arithmetic operations such as summarization, determination of inverses, distributions, correlations, variances, etc.

According to Mr. Shapiro the decision to make the special-purpose Mathatron a standard product item had reduced manufacturing costs, and he said:

> We found that most customers were requesting prewired sequences and that 80%–90% of these requests fell into one of three categories. . . . By packaging it in this way we have also cut our spare parts problems in addition to making the marketing of the machine easier.

The price of the special-purpose machines ranged from $6,000 for the statistical model to $7,500 for the mathematical model. Mathatronics would install the special memory unit in a customer's standard machine for the difference in the original price and that of a special-purpose machine plus a $75 service fee.

DISTRIBUTION

During the spring and summer of 1963, electronics distributors who were interested in obtaining territorial franchises were told the company had not yet decided on how best to distribute the machine. However, just prior to the NEREM show, the company decided to use independent agents to sell and distribute the machine. Up to this time the principal sales effort had been confined to the direct contacts of Mr. French. The decision to use independent agencies was a result of a conclusion pushed by Mr. French that the size of the investment both in time and money which was needed to develop an effective sales and service force was too large. Described as not an insignificant factor was the immediate market created by requiring agents to purchase at least one demonstrator, if not two—depending on the type of contract agreed on.

The company offered two basic contracts. One, a distributor contract, required that the agent do the billing, assuming the credit risk. The distributor was required to buy two Mathatrons immediately. A discount was provided to him on all machines and parts. Another, a representative contract, provided a fixed commission and required the purchase of only one machine. The representative performed no billing or clerical functions. The distributor was required to carry a minimum stock of spare parts, the amount being determined by the number of machines operating within his assigned region. The representative was supplied spare parts by Mathatronics. Both contracts required the maintenance of service facilities and personnel. The initial agreements, for six months, were renewable on a year-to-year basis if all parties were satisfied. Initially agents had complained that the discount given on equipment was "tight." However, Mr. French said the company's participation in the NEREM show and a large electronics show held in New York in March of 1964 had generated a "tremendous enthusiasm" among the office equipment and machine distributors and scientific instrument dealers. His statement was:

We now realize that the demonstrator discount rates were tight for the distributor and the commission representative. However, the product was selling fast enough to provide us with a strong bargaining position. In addition, when an agent invests $5,000 to $10,000 in machinery, not counting the one-week service training we require of his personnel, he is likely to move quite quickly to recover his money. We are now planning to adjust our discount policy so it will conform more closely with standard practice.[2]

Mr. French sought agents who had the capacity to serve large regional areas as he planned to cover the United States with 10 to 11 large dealer organizations.[3] With a minor exception every agent was familiar with the scientific market. Often they were already calling on potential scientific and research oriented organizations with other lines. He added:

In each region we have tried to select the top distributors on the basis of sales volume, reputation, and service capacity. In some areas, notably New York and Washington, D.C., we have gone with new groups who will be concentrating exclusively on our products. Of course, we are limited in our search by lack of time, as we want to get the country as quickly covered as possible, as much of our early growth will come in this manner. Coverage is also important to our becoming solidly established before competition appears, for in the computer business the man with an advantage is the one who is there first. For the customer there is no economic justification for going to another computer system if he can expand his existing line.

COMPETITION

In discussing competition, Mr. French admitted that while the company had gone into "a complete vacuum" between the nonprinting $1,500 rotary calculator and the $20,000 computer, competitors were

---

[2] Standard practice in the industry was to provide discounts at 30% to distributors and representatives.

[3] See Exhibit 5 for a description of the sales agents as of July, 1964.

Exhibit 5

MATHATRONICS, INC.

List of Distributors

July, 1964

(Listed Chronologically since September, 1963)

Distributor	Office Location(s)	Territory	Number of Sales (Service) Personnel	Other Types of Products Sold	Number of Mathatronics Sold
Company	Waltham, Mass.	Eastern Mass.	....	Office equipment	28 (2)
A*	Framingham, Mass.	Eastern Mass.	3	Rents student dormitories	3 (1)
B*	Boston, Mass.		2		1 (3)
C†	New Jersey, East New York, Pennsylvania	New Jersey, East New York and Pennsylvania	3 (½)	None	6 (3)
D†	Washington, D.C.	Maryland, Delaware and Washington, D.C.	2 (2)	None	6 (2)
E	Orlando, Fla., Huntsville, Ala., Greensboro, N.C.	Florida, Georgia, Alabama, Kentucky, Tennessee, Virginia, North and South Carolina	7 (2)	Electronic components and measuring devices	4 (3)
F	Dallas, Texas	Texas, Arkansas, Oklahoma, Louisiana	6 (2)	Computer service bureau	1 (3)
G	Toronto, Ont., Vancouver, B.C., Ottawa, Ont., Montreal, Que.	Canada	7 (2)	Electronic components and measuring devices	1 (2)
H	Albuquerque, N.M.	Rocky Mt. states	3 (1)	Electronic components	(1)
I†	San Francisco, Calif.	California	2 (1)	None	(1)

* Discontinued.
† Indicates distributors.
Source: Company records.

Exhibit 6

MATHATRONICS, INC.

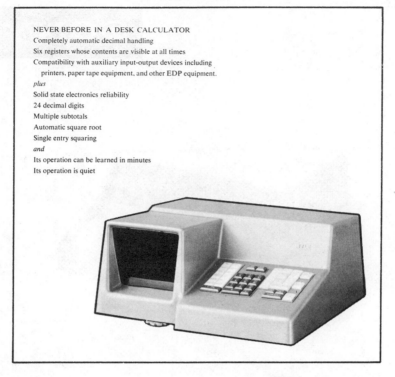

NEVER BEFORE IN A DESK CALCULATOR
Completely automatic decimal handling
Six registers whose contents are visible at all times
Compatibility with auxiliary input-output devices including
   printers, paper tape equipment, and other EDP equipment.
plus
Solid state electronics reliability
24 decimal digits
Multiple subtotals
Automatic square root
Single entry squaring
and
Its operation can be learned in minutes
Its operation is quiet

beginning "to adopt our concept of what a machine should be," and he pointed out:

Wyle Laboratories, for example, has just introduced a $4,000 electronic calculator which does have three storage registers (see Exhibit 6). However, it has no printer. Instead it utilizes a cathode ray tube display (like a TV tube) which doesn't allow you to maintain a record. But its biggest drawback, as far as we are concerned, is its lack of a program memory unit.

Mr. French expected the Wyle unit to have a program memory within 12 months, and a printer within 6.

Mr. French and Mr. Reach believed their closest competitors were companies making electronic calculators. Since mid-1962 several office and billing machine manufacturers, e.g., Sony, Friden, and Monroe, had introduced or announced development of electronic calculators (see Exhibits 7 and 8). Some of these machines featured automatic calculation of square root and decimal point placement. These machines ranged in price from $1,500–$2,500.

Exhibit 7

MATHATRONICS, INC.

SONY ALL-SOLID-STATE FULLY AUTOMATIC
ELECTRONIC CALCULATOR MODEL MD-V

SONY Electronic Calculator Model MD-V is a compact, handy, and light weight portable machine for general calculating purposes.

The MD-V can perform addition, subtraction, multiplication and division, and their serial calculation simply, instantaneously and silently.

The digits and directives for the calculation may be put into the calculator by pushing the keys according to the sequence of the mathematical expression to be calculated.

For example, to perform the following calculation:

$$[(123 \times 456) + 789 - 123] \div 456 = \quad ?$$

Simply push the keys in the following sequence:

$$1, 2, 3, \times, 4, 5, 6, +, 7, 8, 9, -, 1, 2, 3, \div, 4, 5, 6, =.$$

The answer is clearly visualized on the digital display tubes in a moment. ■ Calculation speed is almost instantaneous—within 0.5 sec. for every calculation. ■ Complete silence of operation is one of the most desirable features. ■ All solid state module construction provides compactness, light weight, reliability and long service life.

In March of 1964, Pacific Data Systems, Inc., announced a new computer priced at $21,500, designed for engineering computations (see Exhibit 9). In addition to its greater capacity, the machine provided (1) a typewriter printer, (2) a punch tape record of any pro-

Exhibit 8

MATHATRONICS, INC.

The new Friden 6010 is a low-cost electronic computer designed especially for business applications which require high-speed computation as well as descriptive alphabetic information. ■ In spite of its low cost, the Friden 6010 Electronic Computer has many characteristics of more expensive computer systems: it is fully transistorized; it has random access core storage; it performs logical functions; and it is capable of unattended operation. ■ The electronic processor of the Friden 6010 operates faster than many larger computers. For example, *in one second it can make over 750 additions—over 45,000 in one minute.* Yet, the machine takes up no more floor space than a secretary's desk and can be operated or monitored by any reasonably alert typist after a short period of instruction. ■ You can plug the Friden 6010 Electronic Computer into any standard wall outlet. Air conditioning is not necessary. ■ Friden computer specialists have devised a simple linear programming method which requires only sequential wiring on a removable program panel. You may have a separate program panel for each application, or you may wire a single panel for several applications, depending on the complexity of the programs involved. ■ The Friden 6010 Electronic Computer is versatile. It accepts input from punched tape, edge-punched cards, tabulating cards, auxiliary input units, or the familiar electric typewriter keyboard of the Friden Flexowriter* (the basic input-output unit). It produces output in the form of a printed document and punched paper tape or edge-punched cards. When required, it also controls auxiliary output units, such as tape- or card-punch machines. ■ Here is true automation, available now, at a practical cost within the range of even small companies. Let your local Friden Systems man show you how the Friden 6010 Electronic Computer can bring the benefits of automation to your company. Call him soon.

solid-state computer for business applications

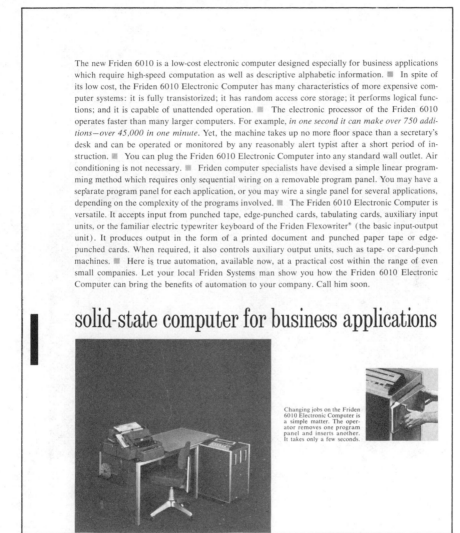

Changing jobs on the Friden 6010 Electronic Computer is a simple matter. The operator removes one program panel and inserts another. It takes only a few seconds.

gram entered, (3) typewriter or punched tape input, (4) interface connections allowing expansion and/or incorporation into larger systems, and (5) ease of programming due to the use of common arithmetic language. Mr. French expected this machine, as well as similar ones being developed by Monroe, Olivetti, and Friden, to become a

Exhibit 9

MATHATRONICS, INC.

- *Low cost, versatile computer designed to be used directly by engineers*
- *Keyboard operation for rapid problem solving*
- *Internal program storage for solving more complex problems*

more significant competitive factor as the basic Mathatron system was expanded. He said:

Within six months we will have, in addition to a typewriter printer and an expanded memory to be added this fall (1964), compatible interface connections and punched taped input and output. This will raise the upper end of our price range to $11,000.

In regard to the large computer manufacturers, Mr. French believed that the team concept of selling utilized by the large computer companies would delay their entry into the market. He explained as follows:

> I think that if a large computer company tried to develop a similar machine, it would become apparent that they would have no market force available to sell it. The machine is too sophisticated for their typewriter salesmen and too inexpensive to support the team-selling approach used with their computer products. The large computer salesman is a coordinator. He makes the contacts, defines the potential application areas, and then brings in his branch specialists. Since $10,000 won't support group selling, you need one salesman who combines the technical, programming, and application skills you find in the branch. The typical typewriter or calculator salesman does not have these skills.

To the best of the company's knowledge, none of the large data system companies were within three years of introducing a competitive machine. It was the conclusion of all four men, however, that the company would face direct competition within 18 months from Wyle Laboratories and Friden.[4]

PRODUCTION

The first Mathatrons had sold for $3,500. However, because buyers continually requested an expanded number of storage registers, an eight-register machine at a price of $4,990 had become the basic unit. The ability to produce and sell the machine at that price was a function, according to Mr. Shapiro, of an "integrated design," and he added:

> Rather than wait for basic design to be solidified before worrying about production and packaging problems (the usual thing), we designed lower production costs into the system. For instance, the Mathatron has several hundred logic circuits, each one of which has been designed to use the same kind of transistor; that way we can safely order them in batches of 100,000. It is difficult to integrate design functions in a big company as by its very nature you have to break up and separate various design functions, and efforts at reintegrating these activities never seem to overcome the difficulties.

Mr. Shapiro also pointed out that a preconception as to how the machine would be serviced had also influenced the basic design from the beginning. As he stated:

> We want the maximum amount of maintenance to be performed in the field by relatively low-skilled personnel. Therefore, we made malfunctioning compo-

---

[4] See Exhibit 10 for a comparison of the Mathatron with the Friden, Sony, and Wyle machines.

nents easy to isolate and replace by the use of five large, interchangeable, plug-in subassemblies. Thus, the maintenance man need diagnose only one out of five malfunctioning subunits rather than one out of 100 or 1,000 subunits.

Because several production techniques were unique to the industry, Mr. Reach believed there was as much innovation in the packaging and production of the machine as there was in its concept of application. He noted:

Low cost has not typically been a consideration in this industry. As a result, production costs have skyrocketed due to (1) the necessity of integrating on the production line the "pet" design concepts of several small research groups, and (2) the production engineer's ability to get involved in the overall design until it is already solidified.

Because of specialized design and production procedures, the cost of the Mathatron was substantially lower than it would have been using

Exhibit 10

MATHATRONICS, INC.

Comparative Summary

	Mathatron	Friden 130	Sony	Wyle Scientific
Selling price..............	$3,490	$1,900	Approx. $1,000	$3,950
Keyboard type.............	10 key	10 key	10 key	10 key
Number of digits of entry (listing columns)	9 plus exponent	13	10	24
Number of digits of total (totaling column)	9 plus exponent	13	. . .	24
Output..................	Printer (serial)	Cathode ray tube	Neon character tube—1 tube per digit	Cathode ray tube (like TV tube)
Individual subtotals and grand totals..........	Yes	Yes	Yes	Yes
Multiplication............	Automatic	Automatic	Automatic	Automatic
Division.................	Automatic	Automatic	Automatic	Automatic
Cumulative multiply.......	Yes.	Yes	Yes	Yes
Square root..............	Yes	No	No	Yes
Storage registers..........	4	1 plus 2 ltd. access	1	3
Program memory..........	24–48 steps	None	None	None
Electronic interface........	Yes	No data	No data	Yes
Transfer between registers...	Complete	Limited	Limited	Complete
Delivery.................	Immediate	Limited distribution	No data	July, 1964
Decimal point.............	Automatic/floating point	Adjustable fixed point	No data	Adjustable
Size (inches)..............	25 × 21½ × 13	c.20 × 22 × 9	20 × 20 × 8	20 × 22 × 1
Weight (pounds)..........	75	40	No data	50

Source: Mathatronics, Inc.

conventional design and procedures. Mr. Shapiro estimated that the machine would cost two to three times more if it had been designed and produced by conventional methods.

Mathatronics was located in a portion of the old Waltham Watch plant. The production area covered about 4,000 square feet, a large portion of which was used for inventory and test facilities. Except for the foreman and one mechanic, all production personnel were women. Conventional production procedure was for the computer to be wired almost entirely by hand. However, the Mathatron was wired almost entirely by semiautomatic methods which Mr. Shapiro felt to be several times more efficient than the best hand methods. Although a computer could be wired completely by machine, such wiring required several structural changes to be made in its physical design. A wiring machine cost approximately $45,000 and was considered to be about three times faster than the best hand methods, and better than the methods presently being used by Mathatronics. Mr. Shapiro estimated that the use of machine wiring would not be feasible for Mathatronics until their volume approached 200 machines per month. "Then it would be sensible to invest, say, $90,000 in machine wiring."

Partly in an effort to keep overhead as low as possible, but primarily as a result of "novel" production procedures, less than $5,000 had been invested in production tooling by July of 1964. At that time one girl required six working days to wire a machine. Mr. Shapiro indicated he would be able to reduce this to three to four working days by the use of better layout and fixtures, work flow procedures, etc. He said:

> At first I didn't have the time to take advantage of these efficiencies, as our priority was just to get the machines out the door. Now we are concentrating on steadying our production by building up our inventory of subassemblies, presently the cheapest way to level our production rate. As we have steadied our work flow and gotten the paper work squared away, I have begun to tighten up our methods and procedures. But, of course, you are always faced with the difficult question of "How do you do this without increasing overhead?"

In July of 1964, the production backlog stood at 90 days. The current rate of output was 20 machines per month. By September the production was expected to reach 40 machines per month and by the middle of 1965, 80 to 100 machines per month. To speed this buildup, Mr. Shapiro thought he might subcontract certain subassemblies. "However, I anticipate that by September our efficiency will be such that the cost of farming out our work will become unattractive to me. But I plan to do some of this in order to find a capable contractor who can help us in case of sudden peaks in our growth."

In June of 1964, Mathatronics exercised an option to lease a second-floor section of the building directly above their present facilities. The added space, 10,000 square feet, it was believed, would facilitate methods improvement which would eventually double efficiency, raising the existing production capacity to 140 machines per month. The new floor area was to be in use by September, but Mr. Shapiro didn't expect actual capacity to approach 140 machines per month until February, 1966.

PRODUCT DEVELOPMENT

Mr. Kahn, whose primary responsibility was system and application development, described the company's product development efforts as follows:

> So far our development effort has been to design attachments, special pre-wired sequences, etc., thereby increasing our capacity and moving toward the provision of a total data-processing system.
>
> Beyond the development of attachments, we have done some general thinking about what a new model of the Mathatron might look like. Our approach again has been to start from scratch and ask: "What would be the best and most needed machine we could build?" We still come up with something which is essentially a superimposure on the Mathatron. It would follow the same concept of ultimate simplicity by expanding on the language breakthrough of the Mathatron I.

Because the most serious competition was believed to be coming in from the "low end, not from the top," of the low-capacity data-processing market, Mathatronics planned to add as accessory units, a page printer, punch tape input-output, and expanded memory unit to its product line by January of 1965. The increased memory capacity would significantly extend the processing power of the Mathatron by allowing it to store longer problems and a large volume of data. This new capacity was expected to cut deeply into the abilities of the $20,000 computer. Mr. Kahn pointed out:

> With these attachments the Mathatron will still not do everything the $20,000 machine will, but it will perform the less complicated things more easily, e.g., surveying calculations. The expanded system will again allow us to pursue another vacant segment of the computer market—that of the $5,000 to $10,000 range which in turn will reduce the impact of the increasing competition at the lower end of the market.

As for the development of new applications, the company had begun to rely increasingly on the distributors for this service, and he added:

There is a bit of limit on what you want to work out here at the factory. However, we do provide a basic backup to the distributor, but we encourage him to define the needs. For example, we just finished a complete statistical program which one of them asked for. We have also made it available to all our distributors.

FINANCE

By midsummer 1964, the sales of Mathatronics were running at an annual rate of 240 machines per year. While financial figures were not available publicly, the company had been profitable since the last quarter of 1963 and the company was experiencing a substantial inflow of cash from its operations as of July, 1964 (see Exhibits 11 and 12).

The three founders held an estimated 60% of the common stock.

Exhibit 11

MATHATRONICS, INC.

Sales—Expense Statement

(Total Sales = 100%)

	Jan. 31, 1963	Jan. 31, 1964	April 30, 1964	June 30, 1964
Income:				
Sales	35.40%	97.35%	94.87%	95.94%
Rental	64.60	2.65	5.13	4.06
Total	100.00%	100.00%	100.00%	100.00%
Cost of sales	...	83.85	51.23	56.48
Gross profit	...	16.15%	48.77%	43.52%
Selling expense	305.88*	26.60	15.16	16.27
General and administration	...	48.40	13.85	14.78
Operating profit or (loss)	...	(58.85)%	19.76%	12.47%
Interest income	...	1.44	0.02	0.68
Net profit or (loss)	(205.88)%†	(57.41)%	19.78%	13.15%

* Total expenses since incorporation.
† Capitalized as net development cost to be written off over five years on the basis of electronic computers sold.

Exhibit 12

MATHATRONICS, INC.

Index of Total Sales & Total Assets

(January 31, 1963 = 100)

	Jan. 31, 1963	Jan. 31, 1964	April 30, 1964*	Aug. 31, 1964
Total sales	100.0	493.83	453.00	1293.57
Total assets	100.0	241.14	258.49	432.17

* 1964 fiscal year started on January 1.

The initial stock offering of $250,000 had been supported by a small group of private investors who, for each share of $100 preferred stock purchased, could purchase an additional 20 shares of common at $1. The 2% preferred stock, nonvoting and noncumulative, was callable at any time at its par value. Mr. Reach explained that the use of preferred stock had grown, to a large extent, out of "our [the founders] concern for maintaining control." In June an additional $150,000 had been raised when the original investors exercised options they held on 6,000 shares of common stock at a price of $25 a share. The majority of these proceeds were to be used to finance the expansion of production facilities.

JULY, 1964

By midsummer 1964, Mathatronics employed 60 people. In June an assistant sales manager had been hired to allow Mr. French to concentrate on the development and strengthening of the distributor organization. Also the services of the public relations consultant had been retained on a nearly full-time basis. In addition to these two gentlemen, two engineers were employed to write new program applications. However, the major growth in employment had come from the addition of testers and production personnel.

During July, a California distributorship was established and the company did not renew its contract with its first distributor. Assigned the New England territory, the distributor, an office equipment representative, had sold only three machines in a year's time. As Mr. French put it:

He was reluctant to call on the scientific-engineering types because of his nontechnical background. His difficulty in selling business firms reaffirms my belief that the primary market for the basic model of the Mathatron is the scientific-engineering firm. Fortunately, this weakness has shown up in our own backyard, where we are best equipped to handle it.

THE FUTURE

As to the future, Mr. French commented as follows:

I don't see any broad, integrated, general business applications where the Mathatron system takes care of the firm's entire data-processing needs.

We will, however, grow into segmented, specialist applications, such as estimating, bond calculations, certain billing work, etc. This will be in the foreseeable future as we add the full page printer and punch tape input. Because payroll and inventory control requires large storage capacity and the ability to sort and update data, these applications are a little further off. In the meantime we have found a potential market in process controls. The machine capabilities are as unique in this area as they were in the calculating market.

A real problem, I anticipate, is to expand at a rate which will allow our distributors to grow in their capacities as our product line grows. The complexion of our distributors will be increasingly system oriented. . . . Of course, my biggest worry is an automobile accident involving Roy, Bill, or Dave.

Discussing the future, Mr. Reach said:

Our biggest problem to date has been a matter of customer education and a difficulty in getting on people's budgets. Far too many people think a $5,000 computer just can't exist. In this respect competition will be an assistance as it will help to develop the market.

Our strength has been that we are thoroughly experienced in the digital field and we have the imagination to develop practical innovations and market them. Our ability to combine these skills with no interdepartmental squabbling is a big advantage. In this regard we try to hire bright people who are relatively inexperienced, not having been conditioned to the tight departmental boundaries found in larger organizations. . . .

As to our long-range growth we plan to get into other sorts of computers. We will try to keep ahead of the state-of-the-art, be the innovators—at least at the smaller, low-cost system level.

APPENDIX: GLOSSARY OF TERMS

Automatic Decimal Point Placement—Indicates the machine's capacity to carry the decimal point throughout its calculations, placing it correctly in the printed solution. In contrast, the standard rotary calculator prints only the digital composition of the solution, the operator being required to determine manually the proper placement of the decimal point.

Interface Connection—An outlet built into the machine which allows a "plug-in" connection with another electronic system, e.g., an electronic measuring device or a large computer system, etc.

Learning Ability—The ability to store a formula or sequence of mathematical operation in the machine's memory unit so that the operator is not required to re-enter the formula each time he wants to use it.

Memory Capacity—A general term used to describe the ability to retain either formulas or numerical data.

Program—A term used to describe the sequence of machine operations required to solve a problem.

Prewired Program—Indicates a program wired permanently into the machine's memory unit so that a specific formula and group of constants can be brought into use by the operator simply turning a switch. An example of a commonly used prewired program would be a program for the calculation of square roots.

Storage Registers—The ability to store a group of digits, each register storing only one digit at a time. A constant in an equation would be stored in such a register to be used as needed.

Typewriter or Punched Tape Input—Automatic methods of entering programs or numbers into a computer. Typewriter or punched tape input performs the same function as punched cards. Because the operator is not required to enter data manually via the machine's keyboard, the speed with which programs and numerical data can be entered into the computer is greatly increased.

3. Note on the Light Aircraft Industry

INDUSTRY DEFINITION AND STRUCTURE

ACCORDING TO the definition of the Aerospace Industries Association, the light aircraft industry in 1967 was composed of 15 firms that manufactured planes weighing less than 12,500 pounds.

The weight restriction in the industry definition reflected a standard set by the Federal Aviation Agency. Aircraft weighing over 12,500 pounds were required by the FAA to undergo much more comprehensive design certification, quality control, and product testing. As a result, no light aircraft manufacturer produced any models above the FAA limit.

Total light aircraft sales were $431 million in 1967. Approximately 80% of these sales were piston and turboprop aircraft, with the remaining 20% being jet aircraft. Three companies dominated the nonjet portion of the market: Cessna Aircraft, Piper Aircraft, and Beech Aircraft. These three companies, often referred to as the "Big Three," accounted for 85% of nonjet sales. The top five companies, which included Aero Commander and Mooney Aircraft, accounted for about 93% of nonjet sales.

Nine domestic and foreign manufacturers were actively competing in the jet portion of the market. Most were said to be experiencing unprofitable operations. The major reason for the unprofitability of jets was the small market (140 domestic and foreign jets sold in 1967), which prevented manufacturers from achieving basic economies of scale.

A breakdown of sales for 1967 is presented in Table 1 on page 143. Data for the 10 years from 1958 to 1967 are presented in Exhibits 1 and 2.

MAJOR COMPETITORS

The major companies producing light aircraft differed from each other not only in terms of size and market share, but also in terms of product line, size of dealership system, and degree of vertical integra-

Exhibit 1

NOTE ON THE LIGHT AIRCRAFT INDUSTRY

Unit Shipments and Percentage Share of Market of Light Aircraft by Selected Manufacturers, 1958–67*

	1958	1959	1960	1961	1962	1963	1964	1965	1966	1967
Cessna	2,926	3,588	3,720	2,746	3,124	3,456	4,188	5,629	7,909	6,232
	(46.0)	(46.6)	(49.0)	(40.5)	(46.5)	(45.5)	(45.0)	(47.5)	(50.0)	(46.0)
Piper	2,162	2,530	2,313	2,646	2,139	2,321	3,196	3,776	4,437	4,490
	(32.8)	(33.0)	(30.2)	(39.0)	(32.0)	(30.8)	(34.3)	(32.0)	(28.0)	(33.0)
Beech	694	893	962	810	840	1,061	1,103	1,192	1,535	1,260
	(10.9)	(11.6)	(12.6)	(12.0)	(12.5)	(14.0)	(11.7)	(10.0)	(9.8)	(9.2)
Aero Commander	97	148	155	139	121	114	109	110	229	362
	(1.6)	(1.9)	(2.4)	(2.1)	(1.8)	(1.5)	(1.2)	(0.9)	(1.4)	(2.6)
Mooney	160	182	172	286	387	502	650	775	779	642
	(2.6)	(2.4)	(2.3)	(4.2)	(5.9)	(6.7)	(7.0)	(6.5)	(5.0)	(4.7)
Other	377	348	266	151	86	115	70	370	889	614
	(6.1)	(4.5)	(3.5)	(2.2)	(1.3)	(1.5)	(0.8)	(3.1)	(5.8)	(4.5)
Total	6,416	7,689	7,588	6,778	6,697	7,569	9,336	11,852	15,768	13,600
	(100.0)	(100.0)	(100.0)	(100.0)	(100.0)	(100.0)	(100.0)	(100.0)	(100.0)	(100.0)

* Percentage share of market shown in parentheses.
Source: Prepared by case writer from issues of *Aviation Week and Space Technology*, 1959–69.

Exhibit 2

NOTE ON THE LIGHT AIRCRAFT INDUSTRY

Dollar Shipments and Percentage Share of Market* of Light Aircraft by Selected Manufacturers, 1958–67
(Dollars in Thousands)

	1958	1959	1960	1961	1962	1963	1964	1965	1966	1967
Cessna	$ 36,897	$ 45,703	$ 56,664	$ 42,266	$ 50,181	$ 55,662	$ 66,818	$ 97,238	$128,841	$116,558
	(35.8)	(35.2)	(37.5)	(34.0)	(36.6)	(36.4)	(33.6)	(30.5)	(26.2)	(27.0)
Piper	26,548	33,134	35,102	28,889	32,142	38,540	54,479	61,664	80,100	79,430
	(25.7)	(25.4)	(23.2)	(23.2)	(23.5)	(25.0)	(27.2)	(19.4)	(16.4)	(18.4)
Beech	26,660	35,701	43,061	37,072	37,359	38,594	54,923	72,211	97,284	91,961
	(25.8)	(27.5)	(28.5)	(29.8)	(27.4)	(25.2)	(27.8)	(22.6)	(20.0)	(21.4)
Aero Commander	6,902	10,626	N.A.	11,047	10,840	11,840	11,973	27,727	51,537	31,760
	(6.8)	(8.1)		(8.8)	(7.9)	(7.7)	(6.0)	(8.8)	(10.6)	(7.2)
Mooney	1,868	2,091	2,781	3,987	5,525	7,235	9,569	12,173	15,406	14,571
	(1.9)	(1.6)	(1.8)	(3.3)	(4.1)	(4.7)	(4.8)	(3.8)	(3.2)	(3.4)
Other	4,152	2,621	13,612†	1,062	784	1,544	1,114	47,253	115,242	97,636
	(4.0)	(2.2)	(9.0)	(0.9)	(0.5)	(1.0)	(0.6)	(14.9)	(23.6)	(22.6)
Total	103,027	129,876	151,220	124,323	136,837	153,415	198,876	318,266	488,410	431,916
	(100.0)	(100.0)	(100.0)	(100.0)	(100.0)	(100.0)	(100.0)	(100.0)	(100.0)	(100.0)

* Percentage share of market shown in parentheses.
† Includes Aero Commander.
Source: Prepared by case writer from issues of *Aviation Week and Space Technology*, 1959–68.

Exhibit 3

NOTE ON THE LIGHT AIRCRAFT INDUSTRY

Movements of Stock Prices and Price-Earnings Ratios, 1958–67

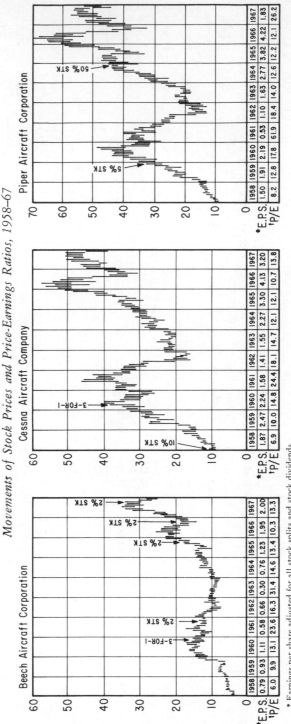

Beech Aircraft Corporation

	1958	1959	1960	1961	1962	1963	1964	1965	1966	1967
*E.P.S.	0.79	0.93	1.11	0.58	0.66	0.30	0.76	1.23	1.95	2.00
†P/E	6.0	9.9	13.1	23.6	16.3	31.4	14.6	13.4	10.3	13.3

Cessna Aircraft Company

	1958	1959	1960	1961	1962	1963	1964	1965	1966	1967
*E.P.S.	1.87	2.47	2.24	1.58	1.41	1.55	2.27	3.30	4.13	3.20
†P/E	6.9	10.0	14.8	24.4	18.1	14.7	12.1	12.1	10.7	13.8

Piper Aircraft Corporation

	1958	1959	1960	1961	1962	1963	1964	1965	1966	1967
*E.P.S.	1.50	1.91	2.19	0.53	1.10	1.63	2.77	3.82	4.22	1.83
†P/E	8.2	12.8	17.8	61.9	18.4	14.0	12.6	12.2	12.1	26.2

* Earnings per share adjusted for all stock splits and stock dividends.
† Price-earnings ratio computed on the mean of the high and low stock price for the year.
Source: *Moody's Handbook of Common Stocks,* fourth quarterly 1968 edition.

TABLE 1

BREAKDOWN OF 1967 LIGHT AIRCRAFT SHIPMENTS

	UNIT SHIPMENTS		DOLLAR SHIPMENTS	
	Number	Per Cent	$(000)	Per Cent
Cessna	6,232	46.0	$116,558	27.0
Piper	4,490	33.0	79,430	18.4
Beech	1,260	9.2	91,961	21.4
Aero Commander	362	2.6	31,760	7.2
Mooney	642	4.7	14,571	3.4
Other	614	4.5	97,636	22.6
Total	13,600	100.0	$431,916	100.0

Source: *Aviation Week and Space Technology*, March 18, 1968.

tion. A brief description of the industry's three major competitors follows below. Exhibit 3 gives data on earnings per share and stock prices.

Cessna Aircraft Corporation. With the most extensive product line in the industry, Cessna had accounted for between 40% and 50% of the industry's unit production ever since the early 1950's. Total Cessna sales were $213 million in 1967, of which $160 million were in light aircraft and related instrument sales and $53 million in military sales. $31 million of the light aircraft sales were export sales.

The dominant producer of single-engine aircraft since 1956, Cessna during the middle 1960's had made heavy investments in the twin-engine field. Thus, by 1967 Cessna's product line ranged from the $7,200 trainer to the $160,000 executive twin. The Cessna product line also included a STOL aircraft, and a business jet was scheduled for introduction by 1971. Cessna was the only one of the Big Three which followed a policy of annual model changes.

In addition to having the largest number of models, Cessna had the most extensive dealership system and was the only one of the Big Three to manufacture abroad. Versions of the Cessna 150 and 172 were manufactured in Rheims, France, and a plant in Argentina assembled parts shipped from the United States.

Cessna was more vertically integrated than its competitors in that the company manufactured many parts, components, and pieces of equipment such as propellers, propeller deicers and avionics. The company also manufactured a leading line of hydraulic pumps, actuators, and hydrostatic transmissions for the materials handling industry.

Finally, Cessna sold more light aircraft to the military than the other major manufacturers. Besides military versions of its civilian aircraft,

Cessna manufactured a jet trainer and jet combat attacker. No other light aircraft manufacturer produced military jets.

Piper Aircraft Corporation. Piper was the least diversified of the Big Three and ranked second in terms of unit volume. Piper's 1967 sales were $80 million, coming almost exclusively from light aircraft. Export sales accounted for $23 million.

The Piper product line was traditionally strongest in the lowest-priced segments of the market. However, Piper had recently designed a $100,000 executive twin and was planning to introduce a $200,000+ commuter airliner in 1970.

Beech Aircraft Corporation. Beech ranked third in the industry in terms of unit sales and was considered the "Cadillac" of the light aircraft industry. With sales of $174 million in 1967, Beech was also heavily involved in nonaircraft aerospace work. The Beech Aerospace Division accounted for over 40% of total company sales in 1967.

Beech was traditionally strongest in the middle and upper ranges of the aircraft market. The company was not considered to be as strong as either Cessna or Piper in the low-priced field. However, in 1962 Beech entered the low-priced market with the Musketeer, which was planned to sell for under $10,000. Beech did not offer an executive jet, nor did the company rely heavily on military sales.

INTERFIRM COMPETITION

A major area of competition among the Big Three was the fight for market share. One aspect of this competition concerned the development of distribution outlets. The number of large aircraft dealers in prime sales areas was limited by the ability of the airports in the area to supply revenue necessary to support large dealers. Also, with the recent growth in sales volume in the industry, finding a qualified dealer with the necessary capital had become a significant problem. As a general guideline, Piper Aircraft, which sold the least expensive product line, suggested a $100,000 investment for a single-engine dealership, $300,000 for a dealership franchise that included twins, and $500,000 to $1 million for a distributorship.

As of 1967 Cessna had 725 dealers in the United States and 175 abroad. In contrast, Piper had 412 domestic dealers and 176 abroad, while Beech had 140 and 77, respectively.

Normally, distributors of light aircraft received discounts of 25% off list price and sold to dealers at 20% off list. Industry sources indicated, however, that Piper offered a high rate of discount—and thereby a large "spread"—to its distributors. Piper was thought to have broken away from the industry pattern in an attempt to compensate its distributors for their special efforts to help dealers develop their markets and sell more planes.

Another aspect of the competition for market share was product

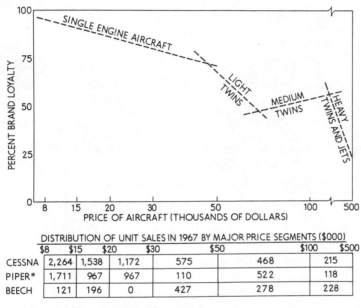

Figure 1

BRAND LOYALTY FOR LIGHT AIRCRAFT BY
MAJOR PRICE SEGMENT

DISTRIBUTION OF UNIT SALES IN 1967 BY MAJOR PRICE SEGMENTS ($000)

	$8	$15	$20	$30	$50	$100	$500
CESSNA	2,264	1,538	1,172	575	468	215	
PIPER*	1,711	967	967	110	522	118	
BEECH	121	196	0	427	278	228	

* Agricultural Aircraft not included.
Source: Data on brand loyalty summarized from company data and interviews with industry executives. Unit sales per price class estimated by case writer from statistics presented in *Aviation Week and Space Technology*, March 18, 1968.

positioning. Industry executives pointed out that product positioning was strongly influenced by the pattern of brand loyalty that characterized the industry.

Figure 1 summarizes company data and the opinions of various industry executives on the level of brand loyalty in the principal price segments. While the figure does not have statistical validity, it nevertheless represents an informed estimate of the degree of brand loyalty in the following types of purchases: first purchases by individuals having just learned to fly in a trainer, replacement purchases by both individuals and corporations, and additions to existing fleets. In this sense, it is a crude indicator of the percentage of purchasers who do not switch brands when moving from trainer to first-purchase aircraft and when trading up to more expensive aircraft.

Figure 1 also includes a distribution of major manufacturers' sales by price categories. These data include all types of first purchases—corporate as well as personal—along with replacement purchases and additions to existing fleets. In examining this distribution of sales in relation to brand loyalty for various price segments, it should be noted that the industry as a whole in 1967 offered fewer models above the $100,000 level than below.

TYPES OF LIGHT AIRCRAFT

Light aircraft was considered to be a highly differentiated product by both designer and pilot alike. In 1968 over 100 different models were

Exhibit 4

NOTE ON THE LIGHT AIRCRAFT INDUSTRY
Number of Light Aircraft in Use by Type

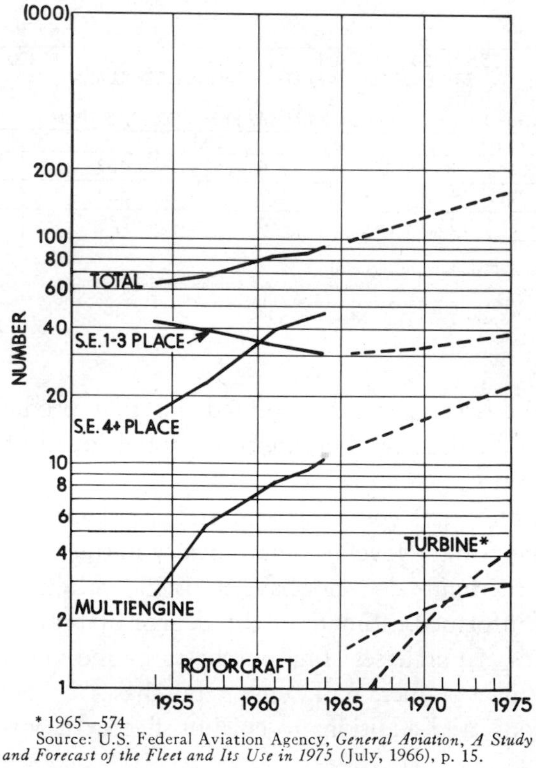

* 1965—574
Source: U.S. Federal Aviation Agency, *General Aviation, A Study and Forecast of the Fleet and Its Use in 1975* (July, 1966), p. 15.

Exhibit 5

NOTE ON THE LIGHT AIRCRAFT INDUSTRY
Principal Business Jets

Manufacturer and Model	Configuration	Basic Price
Dassault/Pan Am		
Fan Jet Falcon	10-pl, low-wing aft-mount turbofans	On request
Grumman Aircraft		
Gulfstream II	19-pl, low-wing aft-mount turbofans	$2,525,000
Hamburger Flugzeugbau		
HFB 320 Hansa	7–11 pl, forward swept, mid-wing aft-mount turbojets	700,000
Hawker Siddeley		
DH 125	6–10 pl, low-wing aft-mount turbojets	722,400
Israel Aircraft Industries		
Jet Commander	4–7 pl, mid-wing aft-mount turbojets	595,000
Lear Jet Industries		
Model 24	8-pl, low-wing aft-mount turbojets	649,000
Model 25	10-pl, low-wing aft-mount turbojets	795,000
Lockheed-Georgia		
JetStar	12-pl, low-wing aft-mount turbojets	1,650,000
North American Rockwell		
Sabreliner	10-pl, low-wing aft-mount turbojets	On request
Series 60	12-pl, low-wing twin jets	On request
Piaggio, S.P.A.		
PD–808	7–10 pl, low-wing aft-mount turbojets	760,000

Source: *Aviation Week and Space Technology*, March 18, 1968.

sold, and every major manufacturer had new models on the drawing boards.

Overall model design typically reflected both aesthetic and functional considerations. The functional considerations included size, speed, range, comfort, flexibility of use, and economy. Thus, wide ranges of alternatives existed for the designer in the combination of passenger space, aircraft weight, horsepower, and cabin design and convertibility. Aesthetics, while tied closely to functional requirements, also provided design options such as the low or the high wing.

Evidence that many of these options were influencing product policy can be seen in the rash of model proliferation undertaken by all major manufacturers during the 1960's. For example, from 1964 to 1968 Beech Aircraft's line grew from 11 to19 models while Cessna's jumped from 12 to 27 models.

For the purpose of statistical analysis, the principal industry association classified the various models of light aircraft according to five basic types: single-engine, one- to three-place; single-engine, four plus-place; multiengine; turbine; and rotorcraft. Exhibit 4 shows the number of aircraft in use by type from 1955 to 1964, along with a forecast through 1975.

Different types of aircraft were generally thought to have different rates of profitability for the manufacturer. Most members of the in-

TABLE 2

Average Annual Costs per Flight Hour

Type of Plane	Total Costs*	Direct Flying Costs†
Sabreliner (jet)........................	$668	$181
Gulfstream I (turboprop)...............	534	145
Beech 18 Series (large twin)............	159	47
Cessna 310 (small twin)...............	95	21

    * Total costs include all expenditures incurred in support of aircraft operation such as: fuel and oil, maintenance, landing fees, salaries, airport installations, depreciation, and spare engines, if any.
    † Direct flying costs include fuel and oil and all maintenance costs.
    Source: Edward P. Harkins, "Business Aviation in 1969," *The Conference Board Record*, December, 1969.

dustry were operating close to the break-even point in the manufacture and sale of the smaller single-engine aircraft, whereas as much as 25% of the factory selling price was profit in the case of the heavier twins. This profit differential reflected a declining price elasticity of demand for the larger and more powerful models.

Business jets[1] were the newest class of aircraft to appear on the market. As can be seen from Exhibit 5, business jets ranged from 4- to 7-place models selling at a little over a half a million dollars to 19-place models priced at $2.5 million. A comparison of average annual costs per flight hour for selected business aircraft appears in Table 2.

THE MARKET FOR LIGHT AIRCRAFT

Most light aircraft sales were made to the so-called general aviation market. General aviation is a term used to describe all aircraft not belonging to the military or to a commercial airline.

---

[1] Business jets, in a technical sense, were not light aircraft, since most models weighed over 12,500 pounds.

Exhibit 6

NOTE ON THE LIGHT AIRCRAFT INDUSTRY
Geographic Distribution of Light Aircraft Sales in the U.S., December 31, 1967

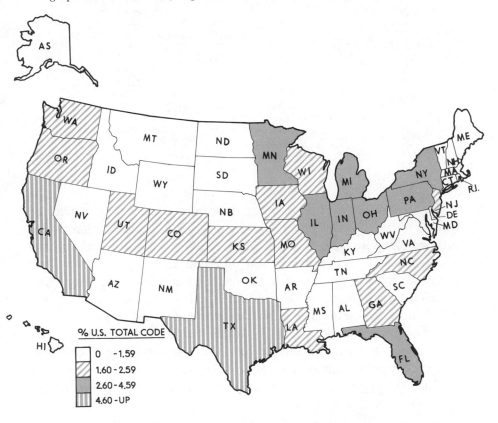

As of 1967 there were over 100,000 general aviation aircraft in the United States, compared with 66,000 in 1957 and 35,000 in 1946. By the mid-1960's these airplanes were logging four times as many hours as did the nation's airlines. In 1965 they carried over 39 million people, while U.S. commercial airlines carried about double that amount. Exhibit 6 gives the geographic distribution of general aviation aircraft sales in the United States as of 1967.

The general aviation market can be broken down into four segments by end use: business, commercial (which includes air taxi or third-level airlines), student instruction, and personal. Table 3 shows both the number of light aircraft by end use for selected years and an FAA forecast for 1975.

TABLE 3

NUMBER OF LIGHT AIRCRAFT BY END USE

Year	Business	Commercial*	Instruction	Personal	Other	Total
1953........	18,220	7,090	5,440	29,260	1,030	61,040
1954........	18,570	7,850	4,720	29,350	690	61,180
1957........	21,520	8,800	5,680	29,850	670	66,520
1961........	20,728	10,999	6,095	41,706	1,104	80,632
1963........	20,793	11,548	6,121	44,860	1,766	85,088
1964........	21,127	11,979	6,855	46,721	2,060	88,742
1965........	21,650	11,355	8,024	51,093	3,310	95,442
1975†.......	32,150	21,850	14,550	88,450	3,000	160,000

* Includes air taxis, crop dusters, and special applications, such as pipeline patrolling, aerial surveying, firefighting, and emergency rescue operations.
† 1965 FAA forecast. Previous FAA forecasts have often been conservative.
Source: U.S. Federal Aviation Agency, *General Aviation: A Study and Forecast of the Fleet and Its Use in 1975* (July 1966).

Business Use. While business firms purchased a wide variety of piston, turboprop and jet aircraft, they typically acquired aircraft for economic reasons. For example, most corporations owning their own planes found it less expensive and time consuming to transport their top executives in private aircraft. One reason for this was the geographic decentralization of many corporations' plants and divisions in areas where air service was either infrequent or nonexistent.[2] Another reason was the development of widely separated markets for individual firms. Thus, with an increasing number of local airports being constructed, more and more businesses felt compelled to purchase their own aircraft for the transport of management personnel between decentralized operations and widely dispersed markets.

Despite such economic usefulness, a survey indicated that the potential market for business aircraft remained virtually untapped. The survey pointed out that only 12% of the country's 3,000 largest companies owned their own aircraft. The survey also suggested that a total of 390,000 companies have both the need and the ability to buy planes, but only 8% actually maintained a company plane.

While corporate jets received great publicity in the late 1960's, the business market for smaller and lighter planes was still expected to expand rapidly. This was due to the fact that 77% of all business trips were 500 miles or less and therefore too short for jets to operate efficiently except on high-density runs.

---

[2] Since the end of World War II 9 out of 10 new plants have been constructed in cities of less than 50,000 persons.

Jet sales, however, were growing slowly and were expected by the Lycoming Division (aircraft engines) of AVCO to reach a total of 270 units per year by 1972 and a total of 550 units per year by 1980. While jets were initially a more expensive aircraft, maintenance and operating costs were lower for jets than for professionally piloted turbo-props of comparable capacity.

Commercial Use. The so-called commercial segment of the market included several types of noncorporate operators. The most rapidly growing type of operator was the third-level airline. Also known as air taxis, this segment of the light aircraft market was thought by industry experts to have exciting prospects, especially for those manufacturers offering a 15–17-passenger twin. From 1963 to 1967 the number of third-level and air taxi operators grew from 12 to 165. The number of aircraft of all types utilized by these scheduled operators grew from 72 to 685 during the same period. A wide variety of large single-engine and multiengine aircraft were used by commercial operators.

Third-level airlines were filling the gap created by the continuing abandonment of routes by regional airlines which did not generate sufficient passenger volume to fill large piston transports. In this way many scheduled operators were serving as extensions and link feeders to the trunk and local service airlines.

Most scheduled operators were located around air traffic hubs and serviced communities up to several hundred miles distance. Not only did these operators fill an important transportation need for moving people beyond normal air carrier terminals, but they were also used to transport air freight, mail, and commuters. Mail carrying was rapidly becoming a high-volume business. In 1966 the Post Office paid $180,-000 to these carriers for transporting mail. By 1968 annual dollar volume was estimated to be as much as $8 million.

Another important component of the commercial segment of general aviation was aerial application aircraft. Operators of these aircraft were typically involved in crop dusting, aerial spraying, seeding, and the like. Aircraft used for these purposes were specially designed. With the increasing industrialization of agriculture, the demand for special aerial-application aircraft was expected to grow.

Instructional Use. Following World War II instructional flying was stimulated by the interest in airplanes generated during the war and also by the liberal training provisions of the G.I. Bill. By 1947 flight training hours were up to 10.4 million from a prewar level of 1.5 million. However, a downward trend in hours of flight training set in as the Veterans Administration restricted the eligibility provisions for government-financed instruction. Aided by a renewed interest beginning in 1954, flight instruction settled to a two- to three-million-hour level by the late 1960's.

From 1954 to 1964 the number of aircraft used for instructional purposes increased by 45%, to 6,855 planes. While most aircraft used for instruction were specially designed single-engine trainers, almost all the increase in instructional aircraft was accounted for by the four-place and over models. The use of larger single-engine aircraft made it possible for flight schools to provide other services, such as air taxi, which increased both plane utilization and overall profits.

In 1967 FAA predicted an increase in demand for instructional aircraft of all types as older trainers continued to be replaced with newer ones and as training programs in high schools and colleges continued to expand.

Personal Use. The growth of the personal-use segment of the market was directly related to the number of students taking instruction at flight schools. While the number of individuals in flight training increased with the introduction of "Learn to Fly" programs by Cessna and Piper in the late 1950's, many analysts believed this market to be far from saturated. A recent study by a major aircraft manufacturer estimated that there were 10–15 million people in this country who could afford to fly but did not for one reason or another.

The inability of aircraft manufacturers to exploit this segment of the population was explained by three factors: lack of knowledge, cost, and time. In some respects it was felt the glamour of flying had tended to work against a radical upsurge in flight instruction. There is so little known about flying and so much adverse and uninformed publicity that the average person has come to believe there is a great deal of danger involved.

In addition, the beginner must spend between $600 and $1,000 to obtain a private license, which takes, on the average, anywhere from six months to a year. This must be accomplished before he can exhibit his new skills to his family or friends. This is a very significant expenditure in money and time compared to other potential outlets for his leisure time.

While the profile of a typical aircraft owner tended to vary with the price of his aircraft, a recent survey of individuals owning low-priced, single-engine models showed that approximately 80% were over 34 years old. With respect to family income, almost 70% of all owners had over $15,000. Occupations tended to be widely dispersed, with the majority being in management or one of the professions. Sixty-three per cent of the owners had flown less than 500 hours, and 42% had been flying for less than three years.

Every major class of aircraft was represented in the personal aviation fleet; however, in 1967 approximately 96% of the aircraft were single-engine models. Of these about 45% were one- to three-person models, while 55% could accommodate four or more persons. Thereafter, there was a shift to larger, faster, and more versatile aircraft. This trend was accompanied by an increasing tendency to install modern electronic navigation and communication equipment in aircraft for operation under IFR (Instrument Flight Rules) conditions.[3]

International Market.   Apart from the four segments of the market that can be differentiated according to end use, the geographic differentiation between the domestic and overseas markets was an important one for aircraft manufacturers. U.S. light aircraft manufacturers were estimated to account for about 90% of light aircraft sales outside of North America. Many export markets were expanding rapidly because of the lack of ground transportation systems, especially in the less-developed countries. As of 1967 the export market was about $100 million annually. The export market was expected to grow at least as fast as the domestic market.

One serious problem facing export expansion was an adequate distribution system. Qualified aircraft dealers were extremely scarce outside of the United States, and no light aircraft manufacturer could afford the capital outlays necessary for an adequate worldwide, company-owned distribution system.

Another problem posed by international expansion was that of tariffs. In many nations, light aircraft were considered to be luxury items and therefore were taxed at exceedingly high rates in order to discourage the use of foreign exchange for nonessential goods. Local manufacture was the principal means of developing substantial aircraft sales behind tariff barriers. No U.S. light aircraft manufacturer except Cessna had manufacturing facilities abroad.

Overseas sales also created problems with respect to special modifications required on standard aircraft. While foreign exchange in the less-developed countries was often made available for the purchase of light aircraft, expensive custom modifications often had to be made to equip planes for patrolling, surveying, ambulance work, and the like.

---

[3] Instrument Flight Rules can be contrasted with Visual Flight Rules, under which aircraft in fair weather can navigate and approach landings without use of instruments.

AIRCRAFT TECHNOLOGY

The rate of technological change in both product design and manufacturing process was restricted by the necessity for a safe product. Any aircraft manufacturer who acquired a reputation for an unsafe product was in serious difficulty. Therefore, technological change in the industry was almost always evolutionary rather than revolutionary.

Aside from the development of sophisticated avionics, the 1960's saw the development of three new approaches to flight which by the end of the decade had made only a slight impact upon the general aviation market: small jets and short take-off and landing (STOL) and vertical take-off and landing (VTOL) aircraft. STOL and VTOL aircraft did not need either long approach paths or extended landing strips, and were, therefore, seen as one solution to the serious congestion problem in large metropolitan areas. The possibility of landing areas much closer to the central city was considered another advantage.

However, aircraft manufacturers were not able to find an engine-airframe combination which would make either helicopters or STOL aircraft economical. In addition, the light aircraft industry did not feel the effects of the congestion so severely as the airlines. Light aircraft (even turboprops), because of their lower weight, could land at airports with shorter runways. For this reason, a large demand for the less economical STOL and VTOL did not develop in the light aircraft industry. Other reasons often cited as inhibiting the growth of the STOL and VTOL markets were lack of appropriate guidance systems and probable public reaction against a high noise level in the immediate vicinity of homes and business if airports were built near the central city.

From the point of view of the design of traditional aircraft, all planes were constructed mainly of aluminum by the 1960's. During the 1940's large numbers of planes were still being constructed out of wooden frames and canvas skins. This change had occurred because of the increasing importance of low weight and high strength as planes were redesigned for higher performance. To obtain even less weight, magnesium came into use on some parts of more expensive aircraft. In addition, fiberglass was often used for parts, such as the nose cone, which did not require great structural strength.

By the mid-1960's the light aircraft manufacturing and assembling process was showing signs of a shifting emphasis away from custom job shop toward mass production, which was thought to be economical with the increased unit sales volume. Cessna, the largest producer in dollar sales and in unit volume, led the way in the change to more mass production. A production-oriented product design, special-purpose machinery, and several production runs of a few weeks each to make a year's supply were the salient characteristics of this process change.

There were industry experts, however, who seriously doubted the potential of mass production techniques for the light aircraft industry. Limiting factors were claimed to be: (1) the quality characteristics of the finished product, (2) space and manpower requirements, (3) difficulties in scheduling incoming parts and components from outside vendors, and (4) an already low direct labor content (20% of total aircraft costs) that did not leave much room for increased labor economies.

In a forecast of developments by 1975 the FAA pointed out two constraints on technological innovation: economic feasibility and the capability of the average general aviation pilot. The FAA claimed that many sophisticated systems were available which could change the character of flying, but which also proved not feasible because of cost and/or pilot skill.

Barring a radical change in aircraft technology, the FAA forecast nevertheless included the following prognostications:

1. The aluminum stressed skin construction will continue to be the principal airframe structure.
2. Cabin pressurization, now found in some of the most expensive twin-engine piston and turbine-powered aircraft, may be anticipated in the more expensive single-engine aircraft.
3. Aerodynamic improvements can be anticipated, with resultant increases in speed and problems associated with low-speed flight. Systems designed to counter low-speed flight problems will add to the cost and complexity of aircraft.
4. The 1975 general aviation fleet will still be essentially a single-engine fleet.
5. Continued development of solid-state electronic gear, leading to reduced cost, weight, and power requirements and increased reliability, will stimulate wider use of avionics and more frequent flights under IFR conditions.
6. Use of certain V/STOL aircraft, mainly rotorcraft, will be continued for highly specialized purposes. For the purposes of general aviation flying, the capabilities of this type of aircraft will continue to be neither required nor particularly useful. Cost will also hinder widespread use of V/STOL aircraft through 1975.

THE AIRPORT CONGESTION PROBLEM

Congestion at large metropolitan airports, both on the ground and in the approach and takeoff patterns, was a problem of considerable interest to the manufacturers of light aircraft for the general aviation market. To the extent that anticongestion proposals affected the convenience, operating costs, and safety of general aviation operators, the potential sales of light aircraft were at stake.

While the FAA made several proposals in 1968 and 1969 to counter the dangerous congestion problem and develop an expanded system of airways and airports, general aviation was usually at odds with these plans. For example, the FAA's proposed limits on operations at five of the nation's busiest airports drew a storm of protest at a public hearing in September, 1968. The essence of the proposal was to limit severely the landings of scheduled air taxis and private aircraft at Kennedy, LaGuardia, Newark, Washington National, and Chicago-O'Hare airports to about 16% of total hourly landings (8% for air taxis, 8% for private aircraft). In addition, advance departure and arrival reservations would be required for all flights at these airports. Only if airlines did not use their full hourly allocations could additional slots be offered, first to scheduled air taxis and second to private aircraft.

The National Business Aircraft Association reacted by saying:

We cannot tolerate exclusion at specific hours at . . . Kennedy or any other airport. We believe it is fundamentally wrong to give exclusive use of public facilities to a handful of profit-making airlines at the expense of a part of the public which helps pay for those airports.[4]

The Aircraft Owners and Pilots Association promised to "forcefully oppose . . . with every means at our command" the "attempt to deliver the public airports of this nation to the airline corporations."[5]

Countering this reaction and addressing the larger question of developing America's airways, an Assistant Secretary of Transportation accused general aviation of "not now paying its way for the airways." In his indictment, M. Cecil Mackey made the following comments:

The Administration's airways proposal would have provided a $176,000,000 increase for the airways this fiscal year to finance badly needed facilities, equipment, and personnel. The revenues were to come from a higher airline passenger tax and an increase in the fuel tax on general aviation—seven cents a gallon

---

[4] *American Aviation,* September 16, 1968.
[5] *Ibid.*

(up from the present four cents), rising a penny a year to 10 cents. The reactions from general aviation were quick, almost unanimous, and in some cases almost irrational in opposition to the program and the user charges.

They seemed to ignore completely the fact that even a 10-cent-per-gallon fuel tax would increase the operating costs of a typical undepreciated single-engine aircraft by less than a penny a mile and add less than four percent to total expenses. For a two-engine aircraft, it would be less than two cents per mile and less than three percent added to total expenses. Considering the average prices of general aviation aircraft, their annual operating costs and the high percentage of general aviation flying that is tax deductible, the proposed charges hardly seem unreasonable or likely to have an adverse effect on general aviation growth.[6]

This kind of opposition and recrimination made it extremely difficult to develop the kind of consensus necessary to move ahead with a long-range program for airways and airports.

FUTURE PROSPECTS

Industry analysts generally agreed that the future prospects for light aircraft manufacturers were difficult to forecast with precision. The single-engine market depended in large part upon the number of student starts and levels of personal income. In addition, sales of multiengine and commuter aircraft were affected by a wide range of general business conditions, including industrial expansion, inflation, liquidity, and the level of interest rates.

The uncertainties created by these economic factors were reinforced by the possibility of future airport and airspace restrictions. At least one authority, writing in *Aviation Week and Space Technology,*[7] claimed that airport problems had already had an impact upon aircraft sales and that top managers intended to become more personally involved and to spend more to ensure that expanding aviation had the facilities for continued growth.

Appendix: Note on the Light Aircraft Industry

AIRPLANE SAFETY

In January, 1970, Ralph Nader released a 98-page report prepared by two Princeton University engineering students which claimed that small plane manufacturers are turning out "the most lethal of the major forms of transportation in the U.S." The report said that the

---

[6] *Flying,* January, 1969.

[7] March 9, 1970, p. 193.

nation's fleet of private planes (primarily single-engine aircraft) lacked many of the crash-survival features of automobiles, such as shoulder harnesses, padded instrument panels, or limited rearward movement of the control wheel, adding that "for years the Federal Aviation Administration has coddled the general aviation industry, providing the companies with comfortable minimum safety standards which they could parade to the public as a defense against criticism."

As reported in *The Wall Street Journal*,[1] the two students contended that light aircraft manufacturers could design and equip their small planes to ensure crash survival. The authors of the report claimed that this was possible, as shown by the safety-oriented design and low fatality record of crop-spraying planes like those made by Cessna and Piper and the "excellent crashworthiness" of Beech's relatively expensive Bonanza. In addition, the report claimed that in the early 1950's Beech moved to equip planes with shoulder harnesses and otherwise to push safety, but the attempt foundered on lack of market acceptance, and Beech gave up the idea.

The report quoted accident statistics indicating that at least 70% of the small aircraft in production would eventually have an accident. The report also quoted Dr. John J. Swearingen, chief of the FAA's protection and survival branch, as saying in an April, 1969, letter to Mr. Nader, "At the present time, anything more than a rough landing, and the occupants of a light aircraft have had it."

Most fatalities in small aircraft accidents result from the plane's structure collapsing or the occupants being thrown into protruding points in the cabin. Designing a plane to resist structural collapse in the event of a crash was considered by aircraft manufacturers to be technically feasible only up to a point. While models could be designed with more structural supports, the additional weight would, in some cases, require the development of new engines and reduce the performance characteristics of the aircraft. In addition, the price of small aircraft would increase significantly.

It was generally thought by people in the industry that the key to aircraft safety was reducing pilot error (which accounted for 90% of all aircraft accidents) rather than redesigning their aircraft.

---

[1] January 22, 1970.

4. Piper Aircraft Corporation

PIPER AIRCRAFT was the oldest of the Big Three light aircraft manufacturers. Founded in 1930, the company's first aircraft was the now legendary Cub. This aircraft was designed with canvas-covered wooden-frame fuselage, a "high" wing placed on top of the fuselage, and a landing gear consisting of two front wheels and a tail skid. In the decades following the company's founding, the Piper Cub and its successors were so popular that they became synonymous with small aircraft in the minds of many Americans. Yet despite this steadily increasing popularity, Piper's sales and earnings showed considerable fluctuation through the years. Exhibit 1 summarizes Piper's financial

Exhibit 1

PIPER AIRCRAFT CORPORATION

Financial History, 1938–57, Years ending September 30

(Dollars in Thousands)

Year	Sales	Net Income (Loss)	Total Equity	Percentage Return (Deficit) on Equity	Total Assets	Common Dividends
1938....	$ 768	$ 14	$ 248	5.6%	$ 438	$ —
1939....	1,769	94	365	25.8	672	—
1940....	3,230	206	749	27.5	693	—
1941....	4,680	211	945	22.3	722	—
1942....	5,308	301	1,057	28.5	3,280	—
1943....	11,479	315	1,361	23.1	3,203	—
1944....	10,646	260	1,529	17.1	4,359	80
1945....	7,701	86	1,684	5.1	3,871	—
1946....	11,197	(26)	3,131	(.8)	5,615	—
1947....	12,620	(223)	2,840	(7.9)	4,620	—
1948....	3,687	(543)	2,297	(23.6)	2,756	—
1949....	4,006	(75)	2,447	(3.1)	2,853	—
1950....	3,912	(178)	2,000	(8.9)	2,494	—
1951....	5,835	536	2,587	20.7	3,681	—
1952....	9,908	395	2,782	14.2	4,688	—
1953....	12,481	396	3,119	12.7	5,339	—
1954....	11,424	434	3,466	12.5	5,230	42
1955....	16,813	1,401	3,919	35.8	7,632	337
1956....	25,084	2,554	5,747	44.4	10,764	694
1957....	26,616	2,722	7,585	36.0	11,937	833

Source: Annual reports 1938–57.

history from 1938 to 1957, and Exhibits 2 and 3 give detailed financial statements for the years from 1958 to 1967.

Piper Aircraft's history had produced two attitudes which were still evident in the company in 1967. The first was a preoccupation with private and commercial aircraft sales as opposed to military aircraft sales. Piper was willing to sell standard aircraft to the military but preferred not to perform design modifications to encourage military sales. As a result, sales of aircraft to the military during World War II and the Korean War were limited, and wartime production did not bring Piper the 100-fold sales expansion experienced by Beech and Cessna. In addition, Piper's emphasis on civilian rather than military sales tended to restrain its development of highly sophisticated aerospace products for military and space programs.

The second attitude which had permeated the Piper organization was a strong commitment to selling small aircraft in large volumes at low prices. In order to sell these small airplanes, Piper had concentrated heavily on teaching people to fly and on promoting the construction of airport facilities. Another aspect of Piper's approach to selling small airplanes was to offer the best design and performance characteristics compatible with keeping a low price to the consumer. Consequently, Piper had traditionally concentrated on designing and producing the lowest priced model of any major manufacturer in each segment of the market that it entered.

It was in the context of this company background that W. T. Piper, Jr., took over from his father the presidency of the corporation in 1967. W. T. Piper, the 87-year-old founder of the company, retained the position of chairman of the board. Howard Piper, a brother of the newly appointed president, was executive vice president, and Thomas Piper, a third brother, was vice president.

With about 30% stock ownership in Piper Aircraft, the Piper family retained complete operating control even though it lacked the 51% ownership necessary for formal control. This combination of family ownership and management gave the Piper family the opportunity to set an informal work atmosphere and to determine corporate policy.

A great deal of family pride existed in having managed a pioneering light aircraft company to a sales level of nearly $100 million by the end of 1968. However, an extended period of future growth, more rapid than could be financed by retained earnings, was a serious threat to Piper family control. The recent expansion of the product line combined with a recent decline in profit margins was beginning to put a

Exhibit 2

PIPER AIRCRAFT CORPORATION

Income Statements, 1958–67, Years ending September 30

(000 Omitted, except for Dividends and Earnings per Share)

	1958	1959	1960	1961	1962	1963	1964	1965	1966	1967
Sales										
Light aircraft and related parts	$26,567	$33,777	$39,283	$30,744	$33,315	$38,033	$54,339	$69,048	$81,242	$80,421
Military	542	486	929	666	25	57	39	38	71	18
Total sales	$27,109	$34,263	$40,212	$31,410	$33,340	$38,090	$54,378	$69,086	$81,313	$80,439
Cost of sales	20,224	25,533	29,551	26,477	25,704	28,493	40,076	50,765	60,332	64,797
Depreciation	326	417	502	642	911	772	777	804	935	1,562
Gross Profit	$ 6,559	$ 8,313	$10,159	$ 4,291	$ 6,725	$ 8,825	$13,525	$17,518	$20,046	$14,080
Selling and shipping	1,134	1,471	1,798	1,980	1,995	2,337	3,004	3,648	4,628	5,566
Administrative and general	617	743	1,041	1,035	956	1,003	1,440	1,757	2,167	2,428
Interest and other income (net)	(30)	(58)	(278)	(394)	(145)	(168)	(290)	(275)	(343)	265
Profit before taxes	$ 4,838	$ 6,157	$ 7,598	$ 1,670	$ 3,920	$ 5,653	$ 9,371	$12,388	$13,594	$ 5,821
Taxes—Federal and State income	2,650	3,375	4,075	815	2,150	3,035	4,890	6,190	6,723	2,830
Net income	$ 2,188	$ 2,782	$ 3,523	$ 855	$ 1,770	$ 2,618	$ 4,481	$ 6,198	$ 6,871	$ 2,991
Common shares outstanding at end of year	927	927	1,072	1,072	1,072	1,073	1,080	1,623	1,628	1,638
Dividends	$ 927	$ 927	$ 1,040	$ 1,180	$ 1,072	$ 1,072	$ 1,614	$ 2,189	$ 2,439	$ 2,287
Dividends per share*	.63	.63	.70	.73	.67	.67	1.00	1.35	1.50	1.40
Earnings per share*	1.50	1.91	2.33	.53	1.10	1.63	2.77	3.82	4.23	1.83

* Based on common shares outstanding during each year adjusted retroactively for a 5% common stock dividend in 1960 and a three-for-two stock split in 1965.
Source: Annual reports, 1958–67.

Exhibit 3

PIPER AIRCRAFT CORPORATION

Balance Sheets, 1958–67, Years ending September 30

(Thousands of Dollars)

	1958	1959	1960	1961	1962	1963	1964	1965	1966	1967
Assets										
Current Assets										
Cash	$ 2,057	$ 1,006	$ 2,948	$ 2,603	$ 2,803	$ 3,640	$ 3,045	$ 2,996	$ 3,381	$ 3,715
Short term securities at cost		1,192	3,000		1,693	2,672	4,019	4,614		
Notes and accounts receivable	1,209	1,839	3,579	2,533	2,419	2,775	4,015	4,710	6,973	4,444
Inventories										
Finished airplanes	1,265	1,112	2,330	2,176	2,038	2,153	2,902	2,746	4,976	4,572
Service parts	517	638	778	708	872	1,014	1,326	1,504	2,128	2,759
Work in process	3,209	4,078	4,560	4,911	5,960	6,743	8,664	8,989	13,010	17,525
Raw materials, supplies and purchased parts	2,261	3,218	2,904	3,028	3,022	2,720	3,776	4,477	8,757	7,193
Less: Allowance for possible losses	(258)	(284)								
Total inventories	$ 6,994	$ 8,762	$10,592	$10,823	$11,892	$12,630	$16,668	$17,716	$28,871	$32,049
Prepaid expenses	105	96	101	258	113	123	227	266	264	159
Total current assets	$10,365	$12,895	$20,200	$16,217	$18,920	$21,840	$27,974	$30,302	$39,489	$40,367
Deferred charges and other assets	19	19	18	15	16	17	27	28	27	142
Fixed assets										
Land	30	41	41	43	44	92	287	340	451	522
Buildings	2,304	2,775	3,607	4,749	4,801	4,836	5,509	6,755	9,374	11,397
Machinery and equipment	1,750	2,182	2,670	3,204	3,250	3,320	3,266	3,834	5,230	6,649
Less: Accumulated depreciation	1,612	1,991	2,377	2,832	3,537	4,109	4,450	4,920	5,689	7,055
Total fixed assets	$ 2,472	$ 3,007	$ 3,941	$ 5,164	$ 4,558	$ 4,139	$ 4,622	$ 6,009	$ 9,366	$11,513
Total Assets	$12,856	$15,921	$24,159	$21,396	$23,494	$25,996	$32,623	$36,339	$48,882	$52,022
Liabilities										
Current Liabilities										
Notes payable									$ 5,000	$ 5,206
Accounts payable	$ 950	$ 1,568	$ 1,242	$ 1,052	$ 979	$ 1,342	$ 1,965	$ 1,871	4,847	1,128
Salaries, wages, etc.	748	797	920	749	729	993	1,715	1,639	1,906	785
Federal income taxes	1,791	2,147	2,222	410	1,664	1,782	3,196	3,559	3,289	250
Other taxes	203	309	349	109	197	315	481	424	440	
Customers' deposits and advance payments	318	399	333	307	459	545	1,215	747	792	1,178
Total current liabilities	$ 4,010	$ 5,220	$ 5,066	$ 2,627	$ 4,028	$ 4,977	$ 8,572	$ 8,240	$16,274	$ 8,547
5⅝% Notes due 1975–84										$10,000
Stockholders' Equity										
Common stock, par value $1.00 a share	$ 927	927	1,072	1,072	1,072	1,073	1,080	1,623	1,628	1,638
Capital surplus	1,347	1,347	9,058	9,058	9,058	9,064	9,223	8,719	8,791	8,944
Earned surplus	6,572	8,427	8,963	8,639	9,336	10,882	13,748	17,757	22,189	22,893
Total stockholders' equity	$ 8,846	$10,701	$19,093	$18,769	$19,466	$21,019	$24,051	$28,099	$32,608	$33,475
Total Liabilities	$12,856	$15,921	$24,159	$21,396	$23,494	$25,996	$32,623	$36,339	$48,882	$52,022

strain on the financial resources of the company, and in 1967 Piper sold $10 million in long-term debt. This represented the first long-term debt since 1945.

The possible need for additional capital to finance a further expansion led Piper's top management in 1968 to a reevaluation of the company's position in the industry. In reviewing past successes, the new president cited three contributing factors: (1) cost-conscious engineering and design, (2) concentration in market segments under $100,000, and (3) a lean management structure which had kept overhead expenses to a minimum. In discussing the future, however, Mr. Piper felt that it would be difficult to build upon these factors because of the rapidly changing nature of the light aircraft market.

A recent decline in earnings raised another important aspect of the company's current position for top management to consider: namely, the company's vulnerability to cyclical swings in industry sales. As noted by *Forbes,*

> Piper's vulnerability was painfully evident in 1967 when the whole industry suffered from a slowdown of corporate and personal orders. Piper sales declined only 1.1% to $80.4 million, but earnings dropped 57% to $3 million, largely because of writedowns on excess inventory. In contrast, Beech, because of its diversification, was able to increase sales and earnings. . . .[1]

The same article in *Forbes* also specified Piper's vulnerability in terms of new product introduction: "And because of the size of his industry and his company he [W. T. Piper, Jr.] doesn't have very much room for error. The marketplace can't absorb an unnecessary model or even a little overproduction, and the company can't absorb the loss of writing off a big mistake."

THE PIPER PRODUCT LINE

The main appeal of the Piper product line had traditionally been for sport, recreation, personal, and general utility purposes. Table 1 lists the 1968 Piper product line. Exhibit 4 details the product classification scheme used by Piper, and Exhibit 5 shows the market share in units held by Piper products in each segment from 1961 to 1968.

The Super Cub and the Pawnee were both special-purpose aircraft unrelated in concept to the modern low-wing aluminum aircraft which made up the rest of the product line. The Super Cub, a descendant of the original Cub, still retained a canvas skin and a high-wing design,

---

[1] *Forbes,* November 1, 1968, p. 46.

Exhibit 4

PIPER AIRCRAFT CORPORATION
Piper Light Aircraft Class Structure

CLASS 1: FLIGHT TRAINERS
  CHEROKEE 140
  Cessna 150
  Champion
  Alon
  Aero Commander 100

CLASS 2: SINGLE ENGINE, $12–$15,000
  CHEROKEE 150/160/180
  Cessna 172
  Cessna 175
  Cessna 177
  Beech Musketeer 19/23

CLASS 3: SINGLE ENGINE, $16–$22,000
  CHEROKEE 235
  ARROW 180/200
  Cessna 182
  Cessna 180
  Beech Musketeer 24
  Mooney 20–21 Series

CLASS 4: SINGLE ENGINE, $23–$30,000
  SIX 260
  SIX 300
  Cessna 185
  Cessna 205
  Cessna 206P/206U
  Cessna 207

CLASS 5: SINGLE ENGINE, $30–$40,000
  COMANCHE
  Beech E-33/E-33A/C Bonanza
  Beech 35/35TC Bonanza
  Beech 36 Bonanza
  Cessna 210/T210
  Bellanca
  Aero Commander 200

CLASS 6: TWIN ENGINE, $35–$45,000
  TWIN COMANCHE
  Cessna 336
  Cessna 337/T337
  Beech Travel-Air

CLASS 7: TWIN ENGINE, $45–$95,000
  AZTEC
  Cessna 310
  Cessna 320/T310
  Beech B55/C55/D55 Baron
  Beech 56 Baron

CLASS 8: TWIN ENGINE, $95–$200,000
  NAVAJO
  Cessna 401/402
  Cessna 411
  Beech Queen Air 65/70
  Aero Commander 500

CLASS 9: TWIN ENGINE TURBOPROP AND JET,
    $200,000–$1.2MM
  Beech King Air 90/100
  Beech Queen Air 60/80/88
  Beech 99 Airliner
  Beech Super H-18
  Cessna 421
  Aero Commander 680/680T/680 FLP
  Aero Commander 720
  Aero Commander 1121
  Mitsubishi MU-2
  Lear 24/25

CLASS 10: SINGLE ENGINE, AGRICULTURAL
  PAWNEE
  Cessna Agwagon
  Aero Commander Ag Cat
  Aero Commander Sparrow/Quail/Snipe/
    Thrush

CLASS 11: SINGLE-ENGINE, UTILITY
  SUPER CUB

Source: Prepared by case writer from company records.

but the frame had changed from wood to aluminum. The Super Cub was used for purposes such as pipeline patrolling, ranch work, and aerial surveying. It was particularly adapted for jobs requiring ground visibility and short takeoffs from and landings on unprepared strips.

The Pawnee was related to the Super Cub in that it was also constructed of canvas stretched over an aluminum frame, but unlike the

Exhibit 5

PIPER AIRCRAFT CORPORATION
Piper Market Share in Units, 1961–68

	CLASS 1		CLASS 2		CLASS 3		CLASS 4		CLASS 5	
	Units	%	Units	%	Units	%	Units	%	Units	%
1961	1035	69	136	10	...	...	...	...	558	43
1962	415	49	696	42	...	...	...	...	441	40
1963	264	35	653	29	47	4	...	...	307	40
1964	504	41	440	25	414	22	...	...	243	24
1965	753	29	898	34	225	12	97	16	367	34
1966	1055	23	897	29	48	2	660	55	266	23
1967	1572	37	638	28	308	15	513	50	134	15
1968	1167	30	797	25	1008	40	269	35	92	10

CLASS 6		CLASS 7		CLASS 8		CLASS 9		CLASS 10		CLASS 11	
Units	%	Units	%	Units	%	Units*	%*	Units	%	Units	%†
...	...	266	41	...	...			241	91	231	
...	...	268	39	...	...			275	100	138	
107	52	284	46	...	...			359	100	171	
466	75	250	32	...	...			472	100	143	
312	53	406	46	...	...			641	100	139	
380	56	419	38	...	...			453	61	141	
304	55	275	34	70	24			328	51	136	
161	42	276	32	209	44			358	53	139	

* No entry.
† No specific competition.
Source: Prepared by case writer from company data.

Super Cub, the Pawnee was designed specifically for agricultural use. It carried only the pilot and could be equipped with a sprayer or duster for chemical fertilizers and insecticides.

The Cherokee was introduced in 1961 as a four-passenger single-

TABLE 1

PIPER AIRCRAFT CORPORATION 1968 MODELS

Model	Suggested Base List Price
Super Cub	$ 9,925
Pawnee—235,260	16,490–16,990
Cherokee—140B, 180D, Arrow, 235B, Six 260, Six 300	8,990–22,900
Comanche B	24,990
Twin Comanche B, turbo-charged* Twin Comanche B	37,250–48,620
Aztec D, turbo-charged* Aztec D	57,990–72,400
Navajo 300, turbo-charged* Navajo	89,500–97,340

* Turbo-charged refers to a conventional piston engine that has been equipped with a super-charger to compress the air-fuel mixture in order to maintain performance in the thin air of higher altitudes. The supercharger is powered by an exhaust-driven turbine, hence the term "turbo." This engine is not a turboprop or jet engine.
Source: Company records.

engine airplane. By 1968 the Cherokee line had proliferated to include a two- to four-passenger trainer, three four-passenger models, and two six-passenger models. The trainer was purchased almost exclusively by aircraft dealers and flight schools for flight instruction; the three four-passenger models were purchased mainly by private individuals—about 50% as a first-purchase aircraft; the Cherokee Sixes were roomier, carried more useful load, and were often purchased by private individuals for business as well as pleasure use.

The Comanche was introduced in 1957 as a single-engine four-passenger aircraft. The Twin Comanche followed in 1963. In recent years the Comanche line had not been extended, and its usefulness in the Piper line was gradually being eroded by the proliferation of the more recently designed Cherokees.

The Aztec was the principal Piper twin-engine aircraft. It was used both by small and medium-sized businesses and by professional men for business and pleasure purposes. Very few Aztec owners bought this model as a first-purchase airplane, and over 75% had previously owned a Piper.

The Navajo was the most recent addition to the Piper product line. Like the Aztec line, the Navajo line was twin engine and contained two models, one with a standard engine and one with a turbo-charged engine. The Navajo had a range of about 1,500 miles with speeds up to 240 miles per hour. Because it had so recently been introduced, no data had yet been collected to determine exactly what type of corporation was buying the Navajo or for what purpose it was being used. Four Navajos had been bought by West Coast Airlines for use as commuter airliners.

In planning for the next five years, Piper proposed to enter one other new market—the commuter airliner market. The Piper entry to this market, the $200,000–$250,000 Pocono, would be available in 1970—two years after the introduction of the first domestically manufactured commuter airliner, the $375,000 Beech Model 99. Piper's airliner would be slower, would carry one more passenger, and, unlike the Beech 99, would not be a turboprop. Because the Navajo and the Pocono were both still nonpressurized piston-powered aircraft, an opportunity existed to extend the Piper product line upward into more expensive pressurized and turboprop models. Pressurization of an existing model line was estimated to require an investment of about $7 million, while converting the power plant to turboprop was expected to require approximately $4 million.

Table 2 gives the distribution of aircraft sales by major product categories for 1967 and the 1973 sales estimate made by marketing research.

Besides new aircraft sales, Piper had one other source of revenue—spare parts for the more than 30,000 Piper airplanes which were currently in use. Sales of spare parts amounted to about $6 million in 1967.

TABLE 2

PERCENTAGE DISTRIBUTION OF ACTUAL AND FORECASTED DOLLAR SALES
BY MAJOR PRODUCT CATEGORIES, 1967 AND 1973

	1967 (Actual)	1973 (Forecasted)
Cherokee..........................	47.4	40.4
Other single engine................	10.8	2.1
Navajo...........................	9.4	24.5
Pocono...........................	0	13.0
Other twins......................	32.4	20.0

Source: Prepared by the case writer from company records.

AIRCRAFT MARKETING

The basic tenet of Piper marketing was that flight instruction formed the basis for market growth. Piper believed that new pilots meant new sales in the pleasure, sport, and recreation markets and that corporate pilots or corporate executives who learned to fly in Piper planes were likely to recommend the purchase of an Aztec or a Navajo for business flying. Piper's research report on the flight instruction market stated it this way:

It is a documented fact that people have a strong tendency to continue flying in the type of airplane in which they learn to fly, and in addition loyalty is in evidence both to the fixed base operator where they learn to fly and also to the manufacturer.

It, therefore, is very important to us as a manufacturer to set as a goal the training of more pilots in Piper equipment than in that of any other manufacturer.

Because of this belief, Piper initiated the industry's first Learn-to-Fly program in 1961. For $5 and a coupon available in flying magazines and local newspapers, anyone could go to a Piper dealer and take his first flying lesson. Cessna had copied the Piper program, and Table 3 shows the growth of student starts, trainer sales, and first-purchase aircraft sales from 1961 to 1967 for the industry as a whole. Student starts were believed to have a direct effect on trainer sales, but, more importantly, were believed to be the main source of sales for the more profitable first-purchase class of aircraft.

In a continuing effort to raise the number of student starts, Piper in 1963 initiated the "Piper Airpark Plan." The major thrust of this plan was the distribution of both promotional and background material which discussed the economic costs and benefits of building a small airstrip. The plan was designed to encourage every community to have a general aviation airstrip. The Piper Airpark Plan succeeded in establishing some new facilities, but by 1968 Piper was concentrating prin-

TABLE 3

Student Starts, Trainer Sales, and First-Purchase Aircraft Sales
1961–1967

Year	Student Starts	Trainer Sales	First-Purchase Aircraft Sales*
1961	57,230	1651	2742
1962	60,627	751	3394
1963	69,130	830	3737
1964	84,629	1485	4007
1965	94,635	2670	4764
1966	128,000	4942	5244
1967	160,000	4124	4629

* Four- to six-passenger aircraft under $20,000.
Source: Piper Aircraft Corporation, company records; *Aviation Week and Space Technology, Annual Airpower Review*, 1961–67.

cipally on generating interest in and support for government-sponsored airport programs in metropolitan areas.

Another step which Piper had taken recently in order to increase the accessibility of its Learn-to-Fly program was to begin establishing Flite Centers. Each Piper dealer who had previously conducted student flight instruction as an ancillary dealer service was being encouraged by Piper to place flight instruction under the Flite Center program in order to give the Learn-to-Fly program more emphasis. A Flite Center consisted of a separate fixed base and new trainer aircraft bought by the dealer, plus instructional material and cooperative advertising supplied by Piper. Flite Centers could also be set up in areas in which Piper had not previously been represented. A Flite Center required only about $27,000 in original investment if the owner used a house trailer as an airport base. Piper was hopeful that these new outlets would expand the market for Piper trainers and that the more successful Flite Centers would eventually become dealers. The five-year Piper goal was to have 600 dealer-operated Flite Centers and 300 additional Flite Centers.

In 1968 Piper already had the second largest distributor-dealer organization in the industry. This distribution network consisted domestically of 412 dealers and 37 distributors. Piper believed very strongly that extensive distribution was an important asset and a major determinant of success in the industry. In order to make this asset more effective, Piper had continually concentrated on strengthening its distribution system. Some major policies in this regard included a requirement that distributors and dealers be separately managed to avoid a conflict of interest in the distributor's support of competing dealers in his territory and a requirement of quarterly financial statements from all Piper outlets. Unlike Beech and Cessna, who had recently experimented with distributor ownership or direct sales to dealers, Piper remained committed to a two-stage distribution system run by independent businessmen.

The function of Piper's distributors was to push the so-called Quality Dealers Program, which involved helping the dealer learn how to sell light aircraft, convincing the dealers to use and participate in Piper's promotional activities, and assuring that the dealers carried the appropriate line of demonstration models. In essence, Piper's distributors served a function analogous to that of a district sales manager.

When Piper introduced the Navajo in 1967, distribution was through the regular network. The previous contacts of these Piper distributors and dealers had been mainly with private flyers and "one plane" corporations. The result, as expected, was that most Navajo sales were made to corporations already owning an Aztec or to corporations whose chief executives flew privately in small Pipers. For the Pocono, however, Piper planned a separate distribution policy. The Pocono would be sold by corporate sales teams who would contact the commuter airlines directly. Distributors or dealers could also sell the Pocono, but the commission would take the form of a fee which varied according to the amount of work done by the distributor in securing the sale. Piper anticipated that most Pocono "sales" by distributors and dealers would involve only the payment of a finder's fee for designating an interested prospect to the corporate sales team.

Exhibit 6 is a study of the factors which Piper executives believed were important in selling the various portions of the Piper line.

Exhibit 6

PIPER AIRCRAFT CORPORATION

*Factors Considered Most Important In Selling Piper Products
as Ranked by Company Executives*

	AGRICULTURAL (PAWNEE)					FLIGHT INSTRUCTION (CHEROKEE 140)					SINGLE ENGINE 4-PLACE (CHEROKEE 180, 235)				
	P	VP–E	D–CP	D–M	D–DS	P	VP–E	D–CP	D–M	D–DS	P	VP–E	D–CP	D–M	D–DS
Advertising	3	6	6	4	7	4	6	2	3	3	5	6	6	4	4
Distribution network	5	3	2	2	1	1	3	1	2	1	1	1	2	3	1
Financing	4	5	3	3	4	2	5	3	5	5	7	5	5	5	6
Options	6	4	5	6	5	6	7	7	7	7	6	7	7	7	7
Price	2	2	4	5	3	3	1	4	6	2	2	4	4	6	3
Product styling	7	7	7	7	6	5	4	6	4	4	4	3	3	1	2
Product performance	1	1	1	1	2	7	2	5	1	6	3	2	1	2	5

SINGLE ENGINE 6-PLACE (CHEROKEE 260, COMANCHE)					LIGHT TWINS (TWIN COMANCHE, AZTEC)					CORPORATE TWINS (NAVAJO)					COMMUTER AIRLINER (POCONO)				
P	VP–E	D–CP	D–M	D–DS	P	VP–E	D–CP	D–M	D–DS	P	VP–E	D–CP	D–M	D–DS	P	VP–E	D–CP	D–M	D–DS
5	6	6	4	3	6	5	5	4	4	6	5	5	4	4	7	4	7	4	6
4	1	2	3	1	1	4	2	3	1	3	4	2	3	1	4	6	2	5	7
7	5	5	5	7	7	6	7	5	6	7	6	7	5	6	5	5	6	2	5
6	7	7	7	5	5	7	6	6	7	4	7	6	6	7	3	7	4	7	3
3	4	4	6	6	2	3	4	7	3	5	3	4	7	5	6	2	3	6	4
2	3	3	1	2	4	2	3	2	2	1	2	3	2	2	2	3	5	3	2
1	2	1	2	4	3	1	1	1	5	2	1	1	1	3	1	1	1	1	1

Key: P   = President
     VP–E = Executive Vice President
     D–CP = Director—Corporate Planning
     D–M = Director—Marketing
     D–DS = Director—Domestic Sales
Source: Survey by case writer.

One marketing approach which Piper's director of domestic sales, Wallis Smith, felt that the company could explore more fully was the annual model change. Mr. Smith argued that once consumers had learned to fly and had bought a Piper product, some impetus was necessary in order to encourage a trade-in for the newest model, or a trade-up to a more expensive model. The annual model change was currently being used by Cessna for precisely this purpose. In addition, Mr. Smith argued that the owners of light aircraft were usually more wealthy than the general population and often quite status conscious. Thus, an annual model change could be a constant reminder that an owner's present model no longer included the latest developments. Without a systematic annual model change, Mr. Smith argued that used Piper aircraft were the main deterrent to sales of new Piper aircraft. Mr. Smith consequently favored a program modeled after the automobile industry which called for minor changes every year and major changes every two years. This proposed program would mean a greatly increased amount of engineering time over that currently being spent on aircraft styling and modernization. While model changes were being made on some product lines, the annual cost of a systematic annual model change program was estimated to be between $500,000 and $1 million.

According to the director of export sales, another opportunity for developing the marketing organization was in the export distribution network. Although exports had increased substantially since 1963, as shown in Table 4, only 50% of the present 32 foreign distributors and

TABLE 4

PIPER AIRCRAFT CORPORATION EXPORT SALES, 1963–67

Year	Units	Dollars (Millions)
1963	547	$ 9.2
1964	669	13.1
1965	889	16.6
1966	935	17.6
1967	1135	20.3

Source: Piper Aircraft Corporation, annual reports.

10% of the present 114 foreign dealers were considered comparable to Piper outlets in the United States.

Some thought was therefore being given to Piper-owned foreign distribution as a means of merchandising more effectively abroad. One argument against corporate distribution was that production, and not sales, would be the future export bottleneck. For any particular model, the Export Sales Department contended that production was allocated between export and domestic sales on the basis of the proportion of sales of that model which each department had historically experienced. As a result, if the export sales of a model grew faster than domestic sales, and if that model was in short supply, export sales would encounter a more severe shortage than domestic sales. Because of this rationing process, export sales as a per cent of total sales changed very slowly.

As of 1967, Piper had established an international sales office in Geneva, Switzerland. The company did not dismiss the future possibility that partial or total assembly abroad would become a prerequisite for continued export expansion.

PRODUCTION

Piper's 1960 annual report summarized the production problems faced by light aircraft manufacturers.

Piper is faced with the same problem that confronts all aircraft manufacturers of private and business planes. The small total unit output and variety of models preclude the use of mass production methods. There is too much hand labor and the airplanes can almost be considered custom built. Modifications to the aircraft are numerous and closely supervised by the Federal government, in most instances require new tools, and add greatly to the cost of manufacture. The company is currently experimenting with a plastic bonded fiberglas model which, if successful, may solve many production problems, principally the multiple handling of aluminum in heat treating, forming, age hardening, drilling, and riveting.

In 1968 Piper was still investigating the possibilities of a plastic airplane, but was not expecting rapid results. Plastics under stress did not have as long a life span as aluminum, and the thermal shock of sizable temperature changes induced brittleness and cracking.

In terms of equipment, the manager of manufacturing for Lock Haven stated that Piper had "done more with less equipment" than any other manufacturer. However, the manufacturing tolerances, particularly for the larger airplanes, were tightening; and new machinery and special-purpose machinery were also becoming mandatory to effect the cost savings enjoyed by other manufacturers with more modern equipment. Without taking into account possible expansion, the company expected to have to spend $2.5 to $3 million in Lock Haven to update fully its present manufacturing equipment.

Piper's 1968 plant capacity was divided among four different sites. Almost 50% of Piper's productive capacity was located at the main plant and corporate headquarters in Lock Haven, Pennsylvania. A recent labor shortage coupled with Piper's own sales expansion had forced Piper to purchase two satellite plants, one 25 miles north at Renovo, and one 60 miles west at Quehanna. These two plants accounted for another 20% of capacity. The remaining 30% was an outgrowth of a research and development facility established at Vero Beach, Florida, in 1957 when the difficulty in attracting engineering talent to Lock Haven became critical. Vero Beach became a major production facility in 1961 with the introduction of its first new model, the Cherokee. In 1968 all Cherokee production took place in Vero Beach, and a second Florida plant was planned to house the assembly for the Pocono.

Because purchased parts amounted to 45% of 1967 sales, one possibility for Piper was a greater degree of vertical integration. The majority of purchased parts were engines and avionics equipment. Piper had made one attempt to purchase and operate an instrument manufacturing company, but other light aircraft companies had refused to continue to buy from a Piper subsidiary. In the purchase of engines, Piper products used engines made only by Lycoming, since the top management believed that a continuing relationship with one engine manufacturer was the best method of assuring the proper amount of attention to appropriate engine development. Thus, the general attitude of Piper management toward vertical integration through acquisition was that it was either impractical or too much of a burden. In addition, expanding aircraft sales appeared to occupy fully the available management effort.

As of 1967 Piper's manufacturing operations were characterized by job shop production. Walter Jamouneau, the chief engineer, did not believe that aircraft as currently designed could be produced by mass production techniques similar to the automobile industry. "The airplane is an excessively lightweight product, and even without this characteristic, mass production would need a much higher unit volume to be economical."

DESIGN, RESEARCH, AND DEVELOPMENT

Design and development engineering responsibilities in 1967 were split about evenly between Lock Haven and Vero Beach. Lock Haven did engineering work on the Comanche, Twin Comanche, Aztec, and Navajo lines, and Vero Beach was responsible for the Cherokees and for the development of the Pocono. The total engineering budget at Piper was $4 million in 1967, of which 40% went to the development of existing product lines and 60% to new product development. By comparison, the 1968 Beech engineering budget was estimated at about $9 million.

The principal focus of the Piper engineering effort had historically been to simplify product design and to reduce production costs. Bill Piper, Jr., the president, gave the following three examples of Piper's success in cost-conscious engineering:

It is interesting to note that the Cherokee 140, with the same Lycoming 150-hp engine as in the Tri-Pacer in 1958, was selling in 1968 for $8,990, just $100 more than the Tri-Pacer 10 years earlier. The Arrow, with a fuel injected 180-hp engine, sold for $16,900, compared to the carbureted 180-hp

Comanche at $15,000 in 1958; and the Twin Comanche, over 20 mph faster than the Apache, was priced at $37,250, compared to $36,900 for the Apache 10 years ago. So, we have made considerable progress in holding prices down in spite of constantly rising labor and material costs.

However, the new Navajo and the proposed Pocono required a different type of engineering expertise. Corporate purchasers tended to place more emphasis upon passenger comfort and product performance characteristics such as speed, range, product reliability, and availability of service than upon cost. Commuter airlines were also expected to be less interested strictly in the purchase price and more interested in the operating cost per mile. In addition, since Piper had no experience with either pressurization or turbine engines, any expansion of the Navajo or Pocono in these areas would require the acquisition of even more engineering skills.

In trying to develop the present engineering department to meet the new design requirements, two characteristics of Piper's engineering operation had to be taken into consideration. The first was the geographic split in R&D which had developed with the establishment of the Vero Beach facility. The 1,000-mile separation between Vero Beach and Lock Haven increased the probability that some duplication of effort might arise because of lack of coordination. For example, it was pointed out that such a possibility existed in extending pressurization to both the Navajo and the Pocono lines, since the development work on these two product lines was done separately—the Navajo in Lock Haven and the Pocono in Vero Beach.

A second characteristic of the engineering department was the lack of an aerospace division, with the attendant opportunities for beneficial technological and educational spillover. Processes such as honeycomb bonding were first used by Beech in aerospace products for the military and were later integrated successfully into light aircraft design. Cessna was using the knowledge gained in building a military jet to become the first of the Big Three light aircraft manufacturers to design a business jet. Both Beech and Cessna used their aerospace divisions to provide stable employment for their engineers. Whenever light aircraft sales fell off, more government contracts could be taken on until sales revived.

During the 1960's, Piper raised the percentage of sales spent on engineering from 3% to 5%. However, some executives believed that the allocation of these increased development funds was less than optimal and that too many design and development resources were being spent on the new corporate and commuter lines to the detriment of the development of private and pleasure model lines. One example given by the director of domestic sales was the development of a twin-engine Cherokee which Vero Beach had postponed in order to put more effort into the development of the Pocono.

Table 5 shows the percentage of engineering planned for each of the principal segments of the Piper product line for the next two years.

TABLE 5

PLANNED ALLOCATION OF ENGINEERING EFFORT
FOR 1969 AND 1970

Product	Percent of Engineering Effort
Cherokee	25
Other single engine	10
Navajo	30
Pocono	25
Other twins	10

Source: Company records.

Considering the engineering strain which the Navajo and the Pocono placed on Piper, the development of a corporate jet was ruled out by Piper management for the foreseeable future.

PERSONNEL

In 1939, 75% of Piper employees had voted to join the International Association of Machinists. Piper had subsequently given the IAM a union shop at Lock Haven in 1948, and as a result the 2,000 Lock Haven employees were all union members. Since 1948, Piper and the IAM had not agreed very often. Although Piper had experienced only two strikes, the union and management were constant adversaries. For instance, when Piper fell behind scheduled production of the Aztec in 1968, the union voted to refuse to work overtime. This 1968 production bottleneck was estimated to have cost at least $5 million in sales.

Another major personnel problem for Piper was the difficulty in shifting employees at the Lock Haven plant. As an example, when the production rate on any Lock Haven product line was lowered, an employee could not be shifted directly to fill another needed position. Rather he had the choice of any job held by a less senior employee, who in turn could pick any job held by an employee less senior than he. Lock Haven's manager of manufacturing stated that a change in manufacturing rate for any product required moving an average of six men for every one man whose job was changed. He believed that Piper suffered a disadvantage relative to its competitors by having a very militant union in a very strong labor state.

Just under 50% of the Piper work force was located in Lock Haven. The remaining 51%, located at Vero Beach, Renovo, and Quehanna, were not unionized and were considered by management to be substantially less obdurate than the Lock Haven employees. All of the planned output expansion would come from these other plants and from the new Pocono plant being built in Florida.

The wage scale paid by Piper was comparable to that paid for other similarly skilled jobs available in central Pennsylvania. (Piper's non-union employees were given the same wages and benefits as the Lock Haven employees.) However, this wage scale was not as high as the wages paid by other light aircraft manufacturers. From 1963 to 1967, the average Piper wage bill was only slightly above $5,500 per employee. This was about $500 per employee less than the average wage paid by Beech during the same period.

In 1967, Piper did not have any production incentive available to manufacturing employees. The company had used a piece rate during World War II, but this had been abandoned shortly after the end of the war.

MANAGEMENT ORGANIZATION AND CONTROL

Exhibit 7 is a 1968 partial organization chart of the Piper management structure. In general Piper had chosen an organization which stressed functional specialties and was organized along geographic lines. Coordination of the Florida and Pennsylvania facilities was achieved by virtue of Howard Piper's position as general manager of Vero Beach and Bill Piper's position as general manager of Lock Haven. Bill and Howard Piper had adjoining offices in the newly completed corporate headquarters and sales building in Lock Haven.

The new building was constructed just off the Piper landing field, with large bay windows overlooking the runway. Clearly visible take-offs and landings often occurred at the rate of more than 20 per hour. The four offices facing the runway on the top floor belonged to W. T. Piper, Bill Piper, Jr., Howard Piper, and Thomas Piper.

Bill Piper, Jr., and Howard Piper together occupied the five top

Exhibit 7

PIPER AIRCRAFT CORPORATION
Partial Organization Chart

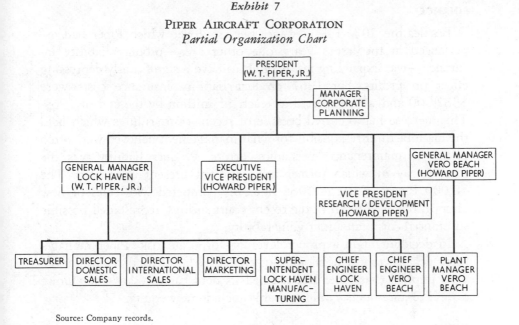

Source: Company records.

positions in the company. This situation was the result of the traditional Piper concentration on keeping down administration costs and the rapid expansion Piper had undergone in the previous five years. Recently the company had begun to enlarge and strengthen its middle management, but top management remained extremely thin.

Another unusual aspect of the Piper organization was the three-way division of marketing responsibility among the positions of director of marketing, director of domestic sales, and director of export sales. The present director of marketing had formerly been in charge of all aspects of marketing and sales, but ill health had forced him to relinquish direct sales accountability while retaining responsibility for market research, sales forecasting, and the overall direction of Piper's marketing approach. In the present organization all three area directors reported directly to the president.

In 1968 Piper did not have any formal system of rewards which varied directly with an individual manager's performance. Piper did, however, offer a bonus to all salaried employees; this bonus was computed from total corporate return on sales above a base level and was paid out to employees as a percentage of salary. No bonus was paid in either 1967 or 1968.

FINANCE

Besides the 20% rise in wages per employee which Piper had experienced in the last 5 years, one other area—product liability insurance—was expanding fast enough to have a significantly depressing effect on profits. For 1967 product liability insurance costs were $382,000 and were expected to reach $1 million by the end of 1969. This increase had occurred because of recent court rulings which held the manufacturer responsible for what management believed were often pilots' or maintenance mechanics' errors. Product liability was the second way in which former sales affected present operations. The 30,000 Pipers in use in 1968 not only competed with sales of new aircraft, but, as a result of the recent court rulings, represented possible substantial corporate profit vulnerability.

In deciding upon a proper level of corporate risk, Piper management decided that debt should not exceed 25% of total capitalization. This implied that Piper had reached its debt capacity and that future capital requirements would probably include new equity.

FUTURE

The most important problem facing Bill Piper, Jr., in 1968 was establishing objectives to guide the future of Piper Aircraft. A major issue in establishing these objectives was the question of family control. It was clear to the Piper family that if the growth of Piper Aircraft required new equity financing, it would become more difficult to maintain family control. In essence, the greater the growth objective, the less chance for the Piper family to retain operating control.

While family control was an important issue, Piper's president noted that his major concern was that the company might not be able to grow fast enough to keep up with the competition. Mr. Piper said in a *Forbes* interview: "I don't know if the aircraft industry has reached a point where merely being bigger makes one company better than another. But in the long run, I suppose, the bigger a company gets, the stronger a competitor it is."[2] In defining a sales level necessary for Piper to remain competitive, Mr. Piper estimated that at least 30% of industry unit sales and 20% of industry dollar sales were required for effective competition.

In order to get an idea of Piper's growth potential, a survey was conducted asking each member of top management to give his own esti-

---

[2] *Forbes,* November 1, 1968.

mate of Piper sales by principal market segment in 1973. Table 6 shows the results of that survey.

As indicated in Table 6, differences existed in management's thinking about the potential and probable mix of future growth. To some extent these differences reflected alternative concepts of how best to maintain an effective posture in the light aircraft industry.

TABLE 6

PREDICTIONS OF 1973 SALES BY PIPER MANAGEMENT
(Millions of Dollars)

	President	Director—Corporate Planning	Director—Marketing	Director—Domestic Sales	Manager—Market Research	Chief Engineer
Agricultural	$ 10	$ 10	$ 9	$ 10	$ 10	$ 10
Other single engine	68	100	70	50	55	85
Light twins	30	70	52	36	44	45
Navajo (all versions)	60	50	40	38	40	90
Commuter airlines	20	50	20	20	23	80
	188	280	191	154	172	310

Source: Survey by case writer.

From the point of view of one senior executive, the dilemma of how best to compete was expressed as follows:

Profits in the future will be in the more expensive aircraft. I have been hearing for 30 years that this industry is on the verge of blackening the sky with small aircraft. But it just isn't so, and it never will be. Small airplanes do not fit into the American way of life in the same manner as the telephone and the automobile do. You can't park an airplane in your garage, your wife can't fly it to the supermarket to shop, and an airplane is quite expensive and fragile.

Despite this, Piper has grown and outsurvived many of its former competitors. Yet, at present there is not a large market left to penetrate in segments where Piper has traditionally been strong.

It would therefore be a luxury for Piper to concentrate on selling low-priced planes, except for the market which builds for future sales of larger aircraft. Unfortunately, in order to take advantage of product loyalty in the small aircraft market, price is the big sales factor. But if a company gets a reputation for a low-priced product, the problem reverses itself in the large airplane market where price can be seen as a yardstick of quality.

Another high-level executive, however, saw the issue somewhat differently:

The potential of flight training is not adequately discerned by market research. The number of student starts would be almost unlimited if flight training opportunities were well publicized and made readily available. In addition, the growth of a company depends more on developing its own markets than on stealing customers from other manufacturers.

Therefore, if a concentration on flight training provides a practically unlimited number of new pilots, and if these pilots continue to prefer the brand they were trained in for 80% of their first purchases, then our small airplane markets have almost unlimited potential.

Company policy in 1968 reflected aspects of both points of view. The introduction of the Navajo, a six- to eight-passenger executive twin, represented the first time Piper had designed an aircraft solely for the corporate market. In addition, Piper planned to continue this upward broadening of the product line in 1970 with the Pocono—an 18-passenger third-level commuter airliner which was predicted to cost between $200,000 and $250,000.

As the same time it was clear that Piper had not decided to forsake its traditional areas of strength—the single-engine and lower-priced twin-engine market. Some Piper executives firmly believed that ultimately the success of the company depended upon training people to fly and then selling them Piper products to fly in. As one Lock Haven manufacturing executive put it: "Every one should have an airplane, and every airplane should have the Piper name on it. Everything else is wasting time."

In deciding what mix of policies was going to assure Piper of a profitable position in the light aircraft industry, Piper's management was fully aware of both the company's recent vulnerability to industry downswings and the substantial pressure for growth in sales and earnings. On January 24, 1969, Chris-Craft Industries, Inc., announced that it was making a tender offer to purchase up to 300,000 shares, or 18.3% of Piper's common stock at $65 a share.[3] While it appeared in February that the take-over bid would fail, Chris-Craft's move highlighted the critical importance of current as well as long-term performance for Piper Aircraft. Independent survival or merger on favorable terms in the future alike required sustained growth and increased profits.

---

[3] Piper Aircraft common stock traded as high as $72.25 in 1968.

5. Beech Aircraft Corporation

BEECH AIRCRAFT CORPORATION of Wichita, Kansas, was formed by Mr. Walter Beech in April, 1932, for the purpose of designing and building the first four-place, enclosed-cabin biplane. This first Beechcraft model, called the Staggerwing, set performance and dependability standards for the industry. Over 780 Staggerwings were built before production ended in 1948. Today it is regarded as a collector's item.

In the decades following the Staggerwing's first 200-mph flight over the Kansas plains, Beech Aircraft became the primary producer of twin-engine planes specifically directed toward the business, air-taxi, and newly developing airline markets. Throughout its development, Beech Aircraft had maintained the high quality standards initiated with the Staggerwing, and by 1968 Beech boasted one of the light aircraft industry's finest records. From 1963 through 1967 Beech Aircraft, under Chairman Olive A. Beech (co-founder with her late husband), 64, and President Frank E. Hedrick, 57, managed to triple its earnings per share on a 157% increase in sales. With $174 million in sales Beech was second only to Cessna ($213 million) in the light aircraft industry. Exhibit 1 summarizes Beech's financial history from 1937 through 1957, and Exhibits 2 and 3 give detailed financial statements for 1958 through 1967.

Based upon Walter Beech's commitment to innovative design and quality aircraft, the Beech company became through the years solidly established in the middle and upper ranges of the aircraft market. However, in 1968 Beech was not considered by industry analysts to be as strong as either Cessna or Piper in the low-priced field, and Beech had never sold a jet. Thus, with goals of at least doubling the company's sales and earnings during the next five years, Mr. Hedrick had to determine whether or not to modify Beech's old strategy of focusing its energies on aerospace operations (40% of sales) and the manufacture of medium- to high-priced ($50,000–$400,000) airplanes.

THE BEECH PRODUCT LINE

Traditionally, the Beech appeal had been directed toward taking advantage of the use of the flexibility of light aircraft for economic

181

Exhibit 1

BEECH AIRCRAFT CORPORATION
Financial History, 1937–57
(Dollars in Thousands)

Year	Sales	Net Income (Loss)	Total Equity	Percentage Return (Deficit) on Equity	Total Assets	Dividends
1937.....$	788	$ 14	$ 516	2.7%	$ 831	—
1938.....	1,141	(2)	614	(.3)	767	—
1939.....	1,328	(91)	735	(12.4)	1,277	—
1940.....	2,345	68	1,036	6.6	2,169	—
1941.....	8,062	472	1,539	30.6	13,760	—
1942.....	59,593	2,418	4,002	60.4	44,010	—
1943.....	126,578	4,036	7,021	57.4	58,782	$400
1944.....	90,469	2,705	7,569	35.8	52,688	400
1945.....	123,752	3,722	11,105	33.5	35,229	400
1946.....	24,396	(229)	8,517	(2.7)	19,281	400
1947.....	26,211	(1,816)	6,592	(27.6)	14,950	—
1948.....	24,141	2,214	8,366	26.4	14,228	400
1949.....	20,582	922	8,579	10.7	10,867	600
1950.....	16,454	589	8,662	6.8	12,238	480
1951.....	32,798	735	8,919	8.2	30,356	480
1952.....	90,912	1,693	10,252	16.5	40,040	360
1953.....	140,458	(2,321)	7,211	(32.2)	34,256	720
1954.....	78,033	3,386	9,997	33.9	29,778	600
1955.....	76,966	3,587	12,835	27.9	25,669	735
1956.....	74,539	3,331	15,267	21.8	32,533	900
1957.....	103,905	3,369	17,649	19.1	42,966	966

Source: Annual reports, 1937–57.

purposes. Consequently private businesses accounted for 95% of Beech's light aircraft sales. Table 1 lists the 1968 Beech product line.

The Beech single-engine model lines began with the two-passenger Musketeer Sport III, a trainer and first-purchase private aircraft, and

TABLE 1

BEECH AIRCRAFT CORPORATION 1968 MODELS

Model	Suggested List Price*
Musketeer—Sport III, Custom III, Super III	$ 13,750–17,950
Bonanza—E33, E33A, V35A, V35A–TC, 36	30,750–40,950
Travel Air—E95	53,500
Baron—B55, D55, 56TC	59,950–95,950
Duke—60	171,000
Queen Air—A65, B80, 88	144,500–259,500
Super H18	179,500
King Air B90	442,000
Beechcraft 99	415,000

* Includes standard avionics package.

Exhibit 2

BEECH AIRCRAFT CORPORATION

Income Statements, 1958–67, Years ending September 30

(000 Omitted except for Dividends and Earnings per Share)

	1958	1959	1960	1961	1962	1963	1964	1965	1966	1967
Sales										
Commercial*	$32,104	$37,915	$46,570	$43,110	$40,333	$45,303	$54,270	$74,329	$100,731	$103,919
Military	63,786	51,622	52,304	28,910	27,329	28,561	52,929	48,154	63,899	70,187
Total sales	$95,890	$89,537	$98,874	$72,020	$67,662	$73,864	$107,199	$122,483	$164,630	$174,106
Cost and expenses										
Wages, materials and other costs	81,138	73,049	79,246	58,314	53,035	60,790	89,994	100,897	133,070	140,123
Selling, general, and administrative	5,916	6,078	7,700	7,207	6,892	7,795	7,683	8,585	11,428	12,584
Interest	475	204	368	494	406	616	573	569	863	1,359
Depreciation and amortization	715	566	733	780	767	926	869	1,040	1,159	1,352
Taxes—Other than income	1,092	1,168	1,509	1,157	1,351	1,953	2,343	2,140	3,158	3,701
Total costs and expenses	$89,336	$81,065	$89,556	$67,952	$62,451	$72,080	$101,462	$113,231	$149,678	$159,119
Operating Income	6,554	8,472	9,318	4,068	5,211	1,784	5,737	9,252	14,952	14,987
Other income	741	846	981	1,269	1,192	1,725	1,000	1,382	1,593	1,939
Income before taxes	7,295	9,318	10,299	5,337	6,403	3,509	6,737	10,634	16,545	16,926
Taxes—Federal and State income	3,970	5,350	5,445	2,775	3,450	1,515	3,320	5,128	7,775	7,890
Net income	$ 3,325	$ 3,968	$ 4,854	$ 2,562	$ 2,953	$ 1,994	$ 3,417	$ 5,506	$ 8,770	$ 9,036
Shares outstanding at year end	824	838	897	2,720	2,803	2,807	2,816	2,818	2,882	2,953
Dividends	$ 1,235	$ 1,330	$ 1,403	$ 1,578	$ 1,677	$ 1,683	$ 1,686	$ 1,760	$ 2,078	$ 2,491
Dividends per share†	.50	.53	.53	.58	.60	.60	.60	.625	.725	.85
Earnings per share†	1.18	1.40	1.70	.89	1.01	.68	1.17	1.88	2.99	3.06

* Includes both aircraft and parts.
† Dividend rate per share is based on shares then outstanding, adjusted for a 3 for 1 stock split in 1960; dividends per share not adjusted for stock dividends. Earnings per share adjusted to reflect stock dividends of 5% in 1959, 2% in 1961, 2% in 1965, 2% in 1966, and the 3 for 1 stock split in 1960.
Source: Annual reports, 1958–67.

Exhibit 3

BEECH AIRCRAFT CORPORATION

Consolidated Balance Sheets, 1958–67, Years ending September 30

(Thousands of Dollars)

	1958	1959	1960	1961	1962	1963	1964	1965	1966	1967
Assets										
Current Assets										
Cash	$ 4,333	$ 4,250	$ 2,979	$ 3,185	$ 2,226	$ 2,013	$ 3,011	$ 2,864	$ 3,193	$ 4,086
Marketable securities at cost	4,007	4,612	6,794	7,950	4,926	1,704	1,813	4,400	2,341	2,312
Installment receivables	6,127	5,833	10,201	11,863	10,858	11,737	12,956	16,693	22,143	20,929
Accounts receivable—U.S. Government & prime contractors	5,468	6,468	5,773	5,640	6,108	7,861	4,291	6,812	9,608	8,190
Other accounts receivable— less reserve for losses	1,021	1,955	2,245	1,809	2,340	2,851	1,939	2,686	4,836	2,698
Inventories	17,245	19,338	21,412	18,304	24,526	26,639	32,896	29,901	40,362	46,633
Prepaid expenses	170	280	224	383	273	342	227	166	365	352
Total current assets	$38,371	$42,736	$49,628	$49,134	$51,257	$53,147	$57,133	$63,522	$82,848	$85,200
Other assets					380	380	380	530	510	435
Fixed assets										
Land	$ 363	$ 405	$ 424	$ 424	$ 525	$ 532	$ 534	$ 843	$ 843	$ 866
Buildings and equipment	12,428	12,997	13,780	14,312	15,119	16,047	17,155	18,191	20,235	21,892
Less: Allowances for depreciation	9,358	9,822	10,287	10,962	11,467	12,311	13,062	13,816	14,792	15,992
Total fixed assets	$ 3,433	$ 3,580	$ 3,917	$ 3,774	$ 4,177	$ 4,268	$ 4,627	$ 5,218	$ 6,286	$ 6,766
Total Assets	$41,804	$46,316	$53,545	$52,908	$55,814	$57,795	$62,140	$69,270	$89,644	$92,401
Liabilities										
Current Liabilities										
Notes payable to banks	$ 5,000	$ 4,600	$ 9,000	$10,000	$ 4,500	$ 5,825	$ 5,725	$ 8,475	$14,750	$11,000
Notes payable to others					4,500	7,500	5,350	4,185	6,500	11,500
Trade and other accounts payable	2,645	4,337	4,434	3,239	4,842	4,426	5,719	5,999	8,713	8,018
Payroll and payroll deductions	2,798	2,989	2,758	2,478	2,600	2,315	2,624	3,322	3,751	3,509
Accrued local taxes and expenses	550	550	891	801	821	920	1,420	1,234	1,479	1,073
Customer deposits	1,457	1,735	1,272	1,853	1,890	1,870	2,380	2,587	2,774	1,873
Provision for contract settlements*	1,758	1,093	925	681	722	19				
Income taxes estimated	4,115	4,621	4,506	2,906	3,534	2,167	4,320	5,092	6,501	3,481
Total current liabilities	$18,323	$19,925	$23,786	$21,959	$23,409	$25,042	$27,547	$30,894	$44,467	$40,454
Unearned Finance Charges†	412	394								
Stockholders' Equity										
Common stock, par value $1 a share	824	838	897	2,720	2,803	2,806	2,816	2,818	2,882	2,953
Capital surplus	9,252	9,528	11,328	9,711	10,812	10,846	10,945	10,980	12,491	14,068
Earned surplus	12,993	15,631	17,534	18,518	18,790	19,101	20,832	24,578	29,803	34,926
Total stockholders' equity	$23,069	$25,997	$29,759	$30,949	$32,405	$32,753	$34,593	$38,376	$45,176	$51,947
Total Liabilities	$41,804	$46,316	$53,545	$52,908	$55,814	$57,795	$62,140	$69,270	$89,644	$92,401

* Added to accrued expenses, 1964–67.
† Subtracted from installment receivables, 1960–67.
Source: Annual reports, 1958–67.

went up to the four- to six-passenger Bonanza V35A–TC, a turbo-charged aircraft which cruised at 230 mph. The Bonanza line was purchased mainly by businesses and by doctors, lawyers, and other professional men who used aircraft for business purposes.

The Travel Air was the lowest priced twin-engine Beechcraft, but in 1968 this model appeared to be going out of production. This was attributed to the gradual obsolescence of the 1957 design and to the 1961 development of the faster and more attractive Baron line. The Travel Air and the Baron were considered as the next logical "step up" from the Bonanza but were also first-purchase aircraft for many medium-size corporations. The Duke was introduced in 1968 to fill the gap between the smaller twins and the larger corporate line represented by the King and Queen Airs.

Beech had designed the original Model 18 in the late 1930's, and the present successor, the 7–11-passenger Super H18 was providing no appreciable sales volume. However, the 6–9-place piston-powered Queen Airs and the 6–10-place King Air had adequately taken the place of the Model 18 as large corporate aircraft. The King Air and its airliner counterpart, the Model 99, were turboprops which had cruise speeds of just over 250 mph.

Exhibit 4 shows the position of the Beech product line in the total industry market classification developed by Beech. Exhibits 5 and 6 detail sales by market segment from 1958 to 1967 for both the industry and Beech.

Besides having the greatest strength in the upper segments of the market, Beech also occupied the upper portion in both price and quality of each individual segment in which it participated. This was a result of the product upgrading which was the continual preoccupation of the engineering department. Prices were raised to cover the costs of these improvements, and accordingly major model lines had to be totally redesigned intermittently in order to keep from being priced completely out of the market.

The core of the Beech product line was the King Air. In 1967, the commercial and military versions of this single model line accounted for 33.5% of Beech's total sales. Beech had received a $35 million government contract for 129 units of the military (unpressurized) version of the King Air. By the end of calendar 1968, Beech expected to have completed delivery of all 129 units.

Beech had been quite successful at employing its skills in selling and servicing the King Air, and in the corporate market in general.

Exhibit 4

BEECH AIRCRAFT CORPORATION

Beech General Aviation Aircraft Class Structure, January, 1968

CLASS 1: SINGLE ENGINE, 2 PLACE, $8–$14,000
BEECHCRAFT MUSKETEER SPORT
Cessna 150
Champion
Mooney A–2 Aircoupe
Piper Super Cub 150
Piper Cherokee 140

CLASS 2: SINGLE ENGINE, 4 PLACE, $14–$17,000
Aero Commander 100
BEECHCRAFT MUSKETEER CUSTOM
BEECHCRAFT MUSKETEER SUPER
Cessna 172 Series
Cessna 177 Series
Piper Cherokee 150/160/180

CLASS 3: SINGLE ENGINE, 4–6 PLACE, $19–$25,000
Cessna 180
Cessna 182 Series
Cessna 185
Mooney Ranger Statesman, Executive
Piper Arrow 180R
Piper Cherokee 235
Piper Cherokee 6

CLASS 4: SINGLE ENGINE, 4–6 PLACE, $30–$40,000
Aero Commander 200
BEECHCRAFT BONANZA 33 & 33A SERIES
BEECHCRAFT BONANZA 35 SERIES
Bellanca Viking Series
Cessna 206 Super Skywagon & Super
  Skylane
Cessna 210 Centurion Series
Mooney Mustang 22
Piper Comanche 260

CLASS 5: LIGHT TWIN, 4–6 PLACE, $50–$100,000
BEECHCRAFT BARON 55 SERIES
BEECHCRAFT BARON 56 TC
BEECHCRAFT TRAVEL AIR
Cessna 310
Cessna 320 Skynight
Cessna 337 Skymaster
Piper Aztec 250
Piper Twin Comanche 160

CLASS 6: PROFESSIONALLY FLOWN MEDIUM TWIN*
Aero Commander 500
Aero Commander 560F
BEECHCRAFT DUKE 60
BEECHCRAFT QUEEN AIR 65
Cessna 401, 402, 411
Cessna 421
Piper Navajo

CLASS 7: PROFESSIONALLY FLOWN HEAVY TWIN*
Aero Commander 680F & 680FP
Aero Grand Commander 680FL
BEECHCRAFT QUEEN AIR 80
BEECHCRAFT SUPER 18

CLASS 8: PROFESSIONALLY FLOWN TURBOPROP*
Aero 680 FLP
Aero Turbo Commander
BEECHCRAFT QUEEN AIR 88
BEECHCRAFT KING AIR
Mooney MU–2 Series
Swearingen Merlin II

CLASS 9: LIGHT JET
Aero Commander 1121 Jet
Hawker Siddeley DH–125
Lear 23, 24, & 25

CLASS 10: HEAVY JET
Fairchild F-27
Falcon
Grumman Gulf Stream II
Hansa 320
Lockheed Jetstar
North American Sabreliner

* Aircraft in Classes 6–8 range in price from $100,000 to $480,000.
Source: Beech Aircraft Corporation market research, January, 1968.

Exhibit 5

Beech Aircraft Corporation
Industry Market Segmentation at Retail Value*
(Millions of Dollars)

	1958	1959	1960	1961	1962	1963	1964	1965	1966	1967
Owner-flown										
Single engine										
2 place, $ 8–14,000 (Class 1)............	$ 7.6	$ 11.8	$ 8.2	$ 13.0	$ 7.1	$ 9.3	$ 15.8	$ 25.8	$ 48.5	$ 43.5
4 place, $14–17,000 (Class 2)............	23.7	24.5	21.7	14.6	22.0	29.9	29.9	40.7	39.6	39.0
4–6 place, $19–25,000 (Class 3).........	28.4	27.4	25.8	24.7	30.6	29.2	40.4	47.8	61.7	59.5
4–6 place, $30–40,000 (Class 4).........	17.3	29.7	40.8	30.8	29.9	30.7	43.2	42.6	51.1	39.8
Light twin engine										
4–6 place, $50–100,000 (Class 5)......	36.2	38.8	48.8	41.5	49.2	62.1	80.4	88.8	116.0	85.3
Professionally flown										
6–11 place, $100–480,000 (Classes 6, 7, & 8).........	26.8	37.3	49.6	34.0	36.4	36.1	34.6	95.3	122.5	151.5
Total†................	$140.0	$169.5	$194.9	$158.6	$175.2	$197.3	$244.3	$341.0	$439.4	$418.6

* Typically equipped with avionics.
† Excludes jet aircraft.
Source: Beech Aircraft Corporation statistics (compiled from Aerospace Industries Association data).

Exhibit 6

BEECH AIRCRAFT CORPORATION

Beech Aircraft Segmentation at Retail Value*

(Millions of Dollars)

	1958	1959	1960	1961	1962	1963	1964	1965	1966	1967
Owner-flown										
Single engine										
2 place, $ 8–14,000 (Class 1)........	—	—	—	—	—	—	—	—	$ 2.2	$ 1.6
4 place, $14–17,000 (Class 2)........	—	—	—	—	$ 1.9	$ 5.4	$ 1.5	$ 4.3	4.2	5.5
4–6 place, $19–25,000 (Class 3)........	—	—	—	—	—	—	—	—	—	—
4–6 place, $30–40,000 (Class 4)........	$10.5	$15.0	$16.2	$13.0	10.9	10.5	18.4	15.7	19.9	16.3
Light Twin engine										
4–6 place, $50–100,000 (Class 5)........	9.7	8.0	8.5	15.6	13.0	15.2	21.8	16.2	25.0	24.2
Professionally flown										
6–11 place, $100–480,000 (Classes 6, 7, & 8)........	12.8	19.2	30.4	20.1	24.1	20.3	29.8	58.7	73.2	73.0
TOTAL†	$33.0	$42.2	$55.1	$48.7	$49.9	$51.4	$71.5	$94.9	$124.5	$118.6

* Typically equipped with avionics.
† Excludes jet aircraft.
Source: Beech Aircraft Corporation statistics (compiled from Aerospace Industries Association data).

However, in 1962 Beech had entered one completely new market—the flight training and personal pleasure flying market—with the introduction of the Musketeer.

Some Beech executives thought that Beech had entered the low-priced field without the necessary extensive distribution system. Dealers and distributors who were accustomed to selling very expensive and glamorous models were reluctant to put much effort into selling the Musketeer line. Also, previous dealer contacts had not been with the type of customers who would buy a Musketeer, and so Musketeer sales often involved a more than proportional effort to establish a new class of customers. Through 1968 the Musketeer had not developed the demand Beech had hoped for, and although there were three Musketeer models, 1967 Musketeer sales were below the 1963 level.

In 1968 Beech entered another expanding market—the commuter airliner market. Before 1968 Beech had sold Super 18's and Queen Airs as airliners, but with the development of the 17-passenger Model 99, Beech began to concentrate seriously on commuter airliner sales. The initial response to the Model 99 was encouraging. Beech had firm orders for almost 100 aircraft before the first Model 99 was delivered. Beech felt that the production rate which best balanced the risks of overexpanded production with the economies of mass assembly was about nine planes per month. Changing the assembly rate on any of its larger models was a major task for Beech, but the Model 99 product manager believed that the nine-per-month rate could be maintained indefinitely.

Mr. Hedrick's approach to product planning was founded upon two basic considerations, consumer loyalty and industry expansion. Concerning consumer loyalty, Beech research had shown a high probability that a customer would, as his needs evolved, "trade up" from a lower- to a higher-priced model produced by the same manufacturer. This implied that the manufacturer who first sold a customer a light aircraft was likely to benefit also from the future sales which that customer would generate over time. Table 2 details this brand loyalty in the light aircraft industry as it affected Beech model lines.

Beech had derived one other figure from its market research which demonstrated the shift of aircraft buyers from smaller to larger models. This figure was the per cent of owners of a given model line who were trading up from the product category immediately below, i.e., heavy single engine from light single engine, light twin engine from heavy single engine, etc. Beech research showed this figure was 25% for the

Bonanza, 40% for the Baron, 65% for the Duke/Queen Air, and 81% for the King Air.

Industry expansion affected product planning in two ways. First, the 15% annual growth in dollars which the industry was expected to experience would mean that the total industry would be growing stronger economically. Mr. Hedrick did not feel that Beech could expect to remain strong relative to the competition if Beech sales stagnated. Second, not expanding in the present meant fewer sales in the future, since the customers lost to the competition would tend to remain loyal throughout their subsequent aircraft purchases. Beech studies showed that only 10% to 15% of the corporations capable of economically employing a private aircraft currently owned one. This low saturation

TABLE 2

BEECH AIRCRAFT CORPORATION STATISTICS ON BRAND LOYALTY

MODEL	PERCENTAGE OF PURCHASERS		
	First time airplane owners	Previous Beech owners	Previous owners of other companies' products
Musketeer	65%	5%	30%
Bonanza	30	46	24
Baron	15	65	20
Duke/Queen Air	10	70	20
King Air	8	75	17

level was believed to offer almost unlimited expansion possibilities for the foreseeable future.

The combination of brand loyalty and industry expansion caused Mr. Hedrick to conclude: "We just can't afford not to be in every part of the market."

Light aircraft sales provided 59.7% of Beech's 1967 total sales; the remaining 40.3% were supplied by the Beech aerospace division. A major facility for this division was in Boulder, Colorado, and its external sales were contracted for by the U.S. government and a select group of prime companies. Major aerospace competences had been demonstrated in the mixing and testing of liquid gas fuels of very low temperatures for the Gemini and Apollo, and in the field of subsonic and supersonic missile targets with the latest contract for the development of the Sandpiper for the Air Force. The Sandpiper would fly at four times the speed of sound at an altitude of 90,000 feet and would feature new hybrid engines utilizing both liquid and solid propellants. Beech also did some subcontracting for the Lockheed C-141, the McDonnell F-101, and the Convair F-106. In 1968 Beech did not produce any light aircraft model lines solely for government use, although some Beech commercial planes were modified for use as military trainers. Table 3 gives the dollar value of new aerospace contracts received by Beech from 1961 to 1967.

TABLE 3

AEROSPACE CONTRACTS RECEIVED BY BEECH AIRCRAFT
(Millions of Dollars)

Year	Amount of Contracts
1961	$11
1962	29
1963	36
1964	54
1965	37
1966	40
1967	60

AIRCRAFT MARKETING

In 1968 the Beech domestic marketing organization was composed of 140 dealerships[1] and 24 distributorships. Four of the distributorships (each of which also operated a retail dealership) were company owned. The rest were owned independently. The function of the distributor was to arrange consumer financing and to stock display aircraft and spare parts. The dealerships were responsible for aircraft sales, maintenance, and repair. Beechcraft dealers were franchised for various models depending on their market potential, location, and financial strength.

Beech had often stated its support of a strong dealership system. A 1960 Beech study delimited 126 economic areas which could support one or more Beech dealerships. This study was the basis of the Beech distribution system. Beech dealerships received revenue from a number of sources, including new and used aircraft sales, instructional flying schools, charter flying, maintenance service and parts sales, and line sales of gasoline and related items. About 65% of the sales and 70% of the gross profits of a typical Beech dealership came from new aircraft

---

[1] Of the 140 Beech dealerships, approximately 50 sold single-engine aircraft only, 60 sold both single-engine and light-twin aircraft, and 30 sold the full product line.

sales. Typically, Beech sold to its distributors at 25% off list; distributors sold to dealers at 20% off list.

The strength of the Beech domestic dealership organization is shown by 1967 new aircraft sales per dealer of about $550,000. This compared with $175,000 per dealer for Cessna and Piper. On a unit basis, Beech dealers sold an average of 10 units—about the same number as Piper and two more than Cessna dealers. In order to assure that the dealer network remained strong, Beech received monthly financial statements from its dealers.

A Beech marketing executive stated that the justification for a distribution system composed of a relatively small number of large dealerships was that a large sales volume was needed to support the repair and maintenance that a customer corporation owning an expensive twin demanded. However, this type of distribution system also presented Beech with risks, in that a poorly managed dealership in a large metropolitan area could have a significant adverse effect on total Beech sales. Piper and Cessna, with 400 and 900 dealerships, respectively, were much less affected by the strength or weakness of any particular dealership.

The risk of a rapid ownership turnover and therefore less continuity of service in dealerships and distributorships had become more acute in recent years as Beech commercial sales had expanded. Owners who had had sufficient skill, and capital to run a $1 million distributorship-dealership in the early 1950's might not have the ability or the capital to run a $5 million operation in the late 1960's. Between 1960 and 1967, four of the Beech distributor-dealer franchises whose owners were retiring or wished to invest funds in other ventures, could not find a buyer with the capital and experience a Beech outlet demanded. These outlets in Los Angeles, Wichita, Houston, and Denver were acquired by Beech in order to protect their market share and to gain some experience in dealer and distributor problems.

Beech, Piper, and Cessna all used partial franchises which allowed an owner with limited capital or experience to handle only the single-engine portion of the product line. The strong single-engine dealerships often evolved into twin-engine dealers, but twin-engine dealers for the industry as a whole represented only about 10% of total dealers. Since many members of the Beech distribution system were permitted to sell twin-engine aircraft, Beech probably had a stronger network for selling twins. However, Beech had fewer dealers who concentrated on selling

Musketeers. This was one reason given for the relatively low market penetration of this model line.

Another possible reason for Beech strength in the higher-priced models was the extensive amount of factory support for the bigger aircraft. For instance, to sell the King Air, Beech had invested a substantial amount of resources in order to identify those firms that would find King Air ownership economically practical and financially feasible. The names of these firms were distributed to Beech dealers for contacting. Dealer aid in sophisticated selling techniques was available from corporate headquarters. When a firm finally bought a King Air, it also received free training for pilots and mechanics in order to assure proper aircraft care and handling. Furthermore, the puchaser became a member of the Beech King Air Club—a club whose members enjoyed the right to tour Beech production facilities, to visit corporate headquarters, and to obtain the personal attention of the chairman of the board or the president if any complaint arose. Exhibit 7 ranks the factors which Beech executives felt were most important in selling King Airs and similar models, as well as other portions of their commercial product line.

By comparison, the factory support given the Musketeer line was not great. The advertising budgets of the Big Three were all in the area of $2 million annually. However, Beech spent less than 10% of the 1968 advertising budget on advertising specifically aimed at the flight training and pleasure flying markets. In contrast, Piper and Cessna spent the majority of their advertising budgets on appeals to this private/pleasure market.

Furthermore, unlike Piper and Cessna, Beech did not have a national "learn-to-fly" program with which to interest prospective customers. Piper and Cessna each tried to bring new customers into the market by offering the first flying lesson for $5 plus a coupon available in almost any flying magazine. This offer was redeemable at any of their company dealers. In the fall of 1968, both Piper and Cessna began television commercials to promote further the learn-to-fly program. Once a customer had learned to fly, he was a prime candidate to buy a lower-priced single-engine airplane.

It was estimated that a competitive learn-to-fly program would cost Beech as much as $1 million to initiate and $500,000 annually in subsequent years. Beech believed that a learn-to-fly program at that time would be ineffective because its dealerships were not widely spread. It

Exhibit 7

BEECH AIRCRAFT CORPORATION

Factors Considered Most Important in Selling Beech Products
as Ranked by Company Executives

	Light Single Engine (Musketeer)				Heavy Single Engine (Bonanza)				Light Twin Engine (Baron, Travel Air)				Corporate Twin Engine (Duke, Queen Air, King Air)				Commuter Airliner (Model 99)			
	P	VP-M	VP-CP	VP-E	P	VP-M	VP-CP	VP-E	P	VP-M	VP-CP	VP-E	P	VP-M	VP-CP	VP-E	P	VP-M	VP-CP	VP-E
Advertising	5	5	5	6	5	6	5	6	5	6	5	5	6	7	6	7	7	6	6	7
Dealer network	2	4	1	4	2	2	1	4	2	2	1	4	3	2	1	5	6	7	7	6
Financing	3	2	4	3	3	4	4	3	3	5	4	3	5	6	3	3	3	3	3	2
Options available	6	6	6	5	6	5	6	5	6	4	7	6	7	4	7	4	5	5	5	4
Price	4	1	3	1	4	3	3	2	4	3	3	2	4	5	5	2	4	4	4	3
Product characteristics	1	3	2	2	1	1	2	1	1	1	2	1	1	1	2	1	1	1	1	1
Transportation consulting	7	7	7	7	7	7	7	7	7	7	6	7	2	3	4	6	2	2	2	5

Key: P = President
VP-M = Vice President—Marketing
VP-CP = Vice President—Corporate Planning
VP-E = Vice President—Export Sales: This ranking pertains to selling Beech products abroad.
Source: Survey by case writer.

was thought that private flyers would learn to fly only at locations convenient to them.

Supplementing the Beech domestic distribution network were a National Accounts Department and an in-house Beechcraft 99 Airliner sales force. The National Accounts Department had been necessitated by the purchase of aircraft "fleets" by large multiplant and often multinational firms. Few dealers had the skills necessary to analyze a firm's total transportation needs and recommend the product combinations which could satisfy those needs. The request for the transportation consulting done by National Accounts was usually initiated by the dealer with whom the firm had originally made contact. Using canceled airline tickets and expense reports, National Accounts first determined the departure and destination points of company executives. The substitution of light aircraft flying times for airline flying times or driving times would usually show a substantial savings in man-hours—often enough to justify purchase of a light aircraft even before benefits such as added flexibility and increased communications were considered. Any sales which developed as a result of the National Accounts Department were channeled through distributors and dealers to the franchise which would service the aircraft after the sale.

The 17-place Commuter Beechcraft 99 Airliner was sold directly to airlines by Beech. This generally required even more sophisticated techniques than National Accounts employed. Beech demonstrated the economics of the 99 Airliner by obtaining from a prospective buyer the end points, altitudes, load factors, and passenger revenue per mile of proposed routes. Beech combined these inputs with a computer program which would print out the annual income statement resulting if the Beechcraft 99 were used on the run. The Beech reputation for accurate reporting of product characteristics made this selling method effective. The 99 Airliner had a low break-even load factor of only three passengers at 12 cents per passenger mile; it was therefore generally suitable for almost all typical commuter airline runs. The separate selling force permitted Beech to sell the Beechcraft 99 Airliner at a lower price (and thereby to meet competition) because of the small number of identifiable prospects and the absence of used airplane trade-ins.

Exports accounted for approximately 25% of Beech light aircraft sales, one-half of which came from Europe. In many of the developing countries, light aircraft found a market because of the lack of a sufficient surface transportation network. Major markets of this type included Brazil, Australia, Japan, and the Philippines. Table 4 details the growth of export sales from 1963 to 1967.

The Beech international distribution network was composed of 41 distributors and 36 other dealers. Only about 10 of the total 77 dealers were comparable in size or in quality to Beech's domestic dealers.

The vice president of export sales felt that in general economic and political stability were more important determinants of export sales than the dealer network. Beech tried to insulate its export sales from overly violent fluctuations by selling and financing only in U.S. dollars and by retaining all manufacturing facilities in the United States. These stringent export sales policies meant that purchasing power abroad relative to the United States was a variable of major importance. Sales could be affected adversely by depression or devaluation abroad, or by price inflation domestically.

TABLE 4

BEECH AIRCRAFT CORPORATION EXPORT SALES
(Millions of Dollars)

Fiscal Year	Exports
1963	$10.8
1964	15.5
1965	17.7
1966	24.5
1967	24.5

The breakdown of export sales in 1967 was roughly 50% business and private sales and 50% public sector sales. The public sector included the military, government agencies, government corporations, and air taxi operators. Major future growth in Beech export sales was expected to come from the public sector. This sector was more able to obtain scarce foreign exchange, and Beech was more able than some other manufacturers to make the special modifications for hospital aircraft, photographic survey aircraft, or other specialized aircraft often required. The eventual export sales breakdown was projected at 30% business and private sales and 70% public sector sales.

AIRCRAFT PRODUCTION

Purchases from outside suppliers amounted to 45% of the dollar value of total Beech sales in 1967. Beech did not produce either engines or instrumentation, a policy which allowed the company to choose the highest quality product from a number of possible sources, rather than being locked into using one internal source. Beech bought engines from Lycoming, Continental, and Pratt & Whitney. Instrumentation could come from any approved source specified by the customer.

The basic materials used by Beech in aircraft production were aluminum, magnesium, fiberglass, and plexiglass. Although the highest military tolerances were not required in much of the fabrication, extensive quality control was maintained at many stages in production in order to assure that the tolerances that were necessary were being met. Beech quality control had an excellent reputation for minimizing defects.

The three Beech commercial production facilities in Wichita, Salina, and Liberal, Kansas, employed 10,350 of the 11,000 Beech employees.[2] Wichita, the main plant, had 9,000 employees and included fabrication for all product lines and final assembly for every product line except the Musketeer and Duke. Salina employed 1,000 persons, who worked mainly on the Duke and subassembly operations such as Bonanza and light twin-engine wing assembly. Liberal, with 350 employees, was the final assembly point for the Musketeer line.

The Wichita facilities consisted of the Beech executive offices, a private landing strip for Beech use, and three manufacturing plants. Fabrication of parts for all models and assembly of the King Air and Beechcraft 99 were located in Plant 1; Bonanza and light twin-engine assembly took place in Plant 2; aerospace subcontract work was done in Plant 3.

The light aircraft production process used in Wichita could be characterized as a custom job shop. Parts were purchased and fabricated in lot sizes which on the average would yield a one-month supply of parts in inventory. About 20% of the parts fabricated were common to more than one model line of aircraft. These parts could be produced in larger and more economical lot sizes than the parts which were unique to one model line. One Beech executive believed that other manufacturers had put more effort into obtaining a greater degree of parts commonality, whereas Beech engineers had concentrated more on design innovation and product performance. As a result, Beech designs were less standardized and, therefore, Beech was less able to take advantage of possible production economies.

Although parts fabrication was done in batches, each part was destined for a specific aircraft scheduled to begin assembly in the next month. A small tag designating the model line and production number

---

[2] Salina and Liberal were respectively 90 and 45 miles distant from Wichita.

was attached to each part as it moved from fabrication to the various subassemblies which were built up in preparation for final assembly. On its larger planes Beech allowed a wide variety of optional equipment, and by the time the components for a particular plane were beginning to reach the more complex subassemblies, the dealer order specifying the optional equipment desired on that aircraft had been received. Therefore, the necessary modifications could be made at the subassembly level, preventing reworking at the time of final assembly. This ability to produce individually customized aircraft on the same production line was not typical of the other light aircraft manufacturers. A more common practice was to produce only standardized planes. If the customer desired extensive options, the finished product was sent to a special modification shop for reworking.

Because of the emphasis on custom production, Beech did not produce a large number of aircraft for inventory. Dealers would order a relatively standard plane in anticipation of a future sale. This meant that the inventory risk for assembled aircraft was carried mostly by distributors and dealers. The Beech factory anticipated demand by scheduling long lead-time items such as engines and other components.

One reason that dealers ordered light aircraft for inventory was the long time lag between the order date and the factory shipment date. This time lag resulted from a Beech commitment to a policy of a level assembly rate. Because the demand for its product was seasonal and it did not carry a large inventory of assembled aircraft, Beech smoothed its production by variations in the time lag between order and delivery date. During the winter the waiting time was often less than a month, but during the spring and summer, the lag could extend to as much as four months. The Beech manufacturing executives believed that the customer would be more willing to accept the extra time between order and delivery than the extra cost a changing assembly rate caused. Beech would gradually change the monthly assembly rate if the order backlog rose or fell unreasonably.

In summary, the vice president of operations thought that the primary requirements for successful operation of the Wichita production process were: (1) sophisticated scheduling to plan and coordinate the more than one million manufacturing operations occurring per day, (2) general-purpose fabrication equipment to produce many types of low-volume parts for many models, and (3) a stable production rate to avoid the major inefficiencies which a change in the production rate caused. Beech met these three requirements by using a computer scheduling system, numerically controlled fabrication equipment, and an extensive system of demand forecasting.

The Musketeer final assembly at Liberal, Kansas, had moved away from the Beech concept of custom production and toward an assembly-line production process more similar to the automobile industry. This more standardized production was almost a requisite in order to keep costs low enough to compete in the small single-engine market. The emphasis on low-cost, high-volume production at the Liberal plant had changed the production requirements for success. Musketeer production was characterized by on-line subassembly, less flexible production equipment, and design changes made to obtain production ease and speed.

However, like Wichita, the Liberal facility tried to keep a level production rate (seven planes per week in 1968) and a minimum of assembled aircraft. This combination of policies did not allow nearly the economies of production available to Cessna, which produced the total year's output in a much shorter period of time and shipped the assembled planes to its dealers. Beech executives were skeptical of obtaining economies in this fashion, because Beech was reluctant to assume the inventory risk or to force its dealers to assume the additional inventory risk necessary to support extensive mass-production economies. Furthermore, producing the Musketeer over a short period of time would mean large fluctuations in employment in the Liberal plant. Cessna was able to avoid employment fluctuation because it produced a large number of high-volume, low-priced models. This allowed sequential production scheduling; one model line might be produced in January and February, another in March, and so on.

Concerning future production capacity and facilities distribution, the vice president of operations felt that the optimal plant size for fabrication was 5,000–6,000 employees. Optimal plant size for assembly operations was estimated at about 1,000 employees. One possible plan for future plant location was a "hub and spoke" arrangement. Wichita would serve as a fabrication center, with assembly operations occurring at separate but nearby facilities, such as Liberal, Salina, and possibly others. This type of arrangement would retain the mass-production economies available in fabrication, but would allow the Beech expansion to draw on labor forces outside the already strained Wichita area.

DESIGN AND RESEARCH AND DEVELOPMENT

Design and research and development were considered by Beech management to be key assets. Consistent high-quality production had given Beech a product reputation which Beech executives believed was a significant advantage. Mr. Hedrick believed: "The reputation for quality and service is the one asset which the competition tries to copy and cannot. Beechcraft on an aircraft is like sterling on silver." R&D made a continual effort to preserve this reputation through a close and constant monitoring of competitive products and through a perpetual upgrading of all products to the highest quality available in its particular market segment. Beech employed approximately 800 engineers. In order to retain the maximum amount of flexibility among development programs in light aircraft and aerospace, all of the Beech engineers were competent in the area of light aircraft design and development. The vice president of engineering stated that he was in the process of hiring an additional 200 engineers as fast as qualified personnel could be obtained.

The total 1968 engineering expense was $9 million, of which approximately $1.25 million was the allocation for upgrading the 1967 light aircraft product line. The importance given to high quality throughout the organization was so great that some executives doubted whether Beech could successfully design a low-price, lesser-quality aircraft for high-volume markets. One marketing executive believed that low Musketeer sales were partially attributable to an overemphasis on quality rather than on price.

Concerning new product development, the basic Beech philosophy was to search out an unsatisfied portion of the market and design an aircraft to fill that demand. The King Air and the Beechcraft 99 were recent examples of aircraft which had opened up new segments of the aircraft market. Marketing was therefore frequently the initiator of new product ideas. Lead times from conception to delivery were about 1½ to 2 years for a completely new model line, and from 6 months to 1 year for a major modification of an old model line. The vice president for R&D estimated that the total investment required before the first plane could be sold was as much as $20–$30 million for a heavy twin and $2–$5 million for the smaller single-engine planes.

AEROSPACE

Aerospace sales were composed of nonaircraft government contracts, modified light aircraft sold to the military, and subcontracting work done on military planes. Expansion of the Beech Aerospace Division had not been considered a prime goal since the contract cancellation which had occurred on June 10, 1953. After Beech had hired personnel and produced the prototypes of a T-36 trainer on a $300 million per year contract, the Air Force canceled the order. This marked a major turning point in the outlook of Beech Aircraft by causing a desire for less military dependence and a stronger commercial base. Fortunately, commercial production had been continued during the Korean War, and as a result Beech sales fell only to a $75–$80 million plateau level. However, even after receiving cancellation penalty payments from the government, Beech lost over $2.3 million in 1953. This loss was almost one-third of 1953 stockholders' equity.

For fiscal 1968, aerospace sales were down to 30.7% of total Beech sales, from 40.2% in fiscal 1967. Although the aerospace division was considered a desirable financial diversification, Beech believed very strongly that the main contribution of the aerospace division was not sales volume, but rather talent, ideas, and new processes available for use in commercial production. With this conception in mind, Beech demanded five tests which a contract must meet to be acceptable:

1. That the contract be relatively long term, preferably five years or more, so that Beech would not have the typical aerospace problem of boom or bust.
2. That the contract require an intermediate level of technology so that Beech could continue to have the transference of engineering and technical skills between aerospace and commercial production.
3. That the contract area be specialized enough so that Beech could compete on an equal basis with larger competitors for future contracts in this area.
4. That the contract have a possible overlap in either technology or product with commercial sales.
5. That the contract be profitable in and of itself.

These five conditions had been very successful in the past in giving Beech the quality and quantity of aerospace contracts desired. New processes for commercial production such as chemical milling, honeycomb bonding, and electron-beam welding had grown out of past aerospace contracts. Some specific competences such as the cryogenics work being done with liquid hydrogen had not yet yielded any direct commercial benefits but were a continuing source of profitable contracts until a commercial application for liquid-gas fuels could be developed.

Mr. Roy McGregor, vice president of aerospace marketing and contracts, emphasized that the skills necessary to operate the aerospace division were different from the skills necessary to compete successfully in light aircraft. Successful bidding on aerospace contracts required very close communication between marketing and engineering. Marketing must know the product thoroughly from an engineering point of view. Even then, "You have to get 5,000 signatures from people spread all over the world; 4,980 have the power to say no, but no power to say yes." For larger, more comprehensive contracts, teaming arrangements were used. A typical team might include Westinghouse, Raytheon, Boeing, and Beech. Each would be responsible for designing the proposal for a specific aspect of the total contract. In these instances, poor team communication or one weak link in the team might cause unsuccessful contract competition, even though an individual member on the losing team was better qualified than his counterpart on the winning team. Another problem with teaming arrangements was that aggregate differences between competing teams were usually extremely small, and the final choice was therefore often based on considerations other than maximum economic efficiency.

The production and engineering skills necessary for a successful aerospace division were also different from those necessary from light aircraft success. Closer tolerances, tighter scheduling, less emphasis on styling, and higher engineering content per sales dollar were four of the specific differences. A more general difference was the ability to manage production discontinuities and diverse production processes. Depending on the contract, output could be required at the rate of one unit every five years, or 13,000 units every month.

A final important difference was that the government was seen as an idea market. A superior idea could provide the basis for a contract even when the government had not previously planned to spend resources in that area. Therefore, the aerospace division had the additional ability to create new demand as well as to satisfy existing demand.

FINANCE

Two conservative policies characterized the Beech financial stance. One was the practice of writing off all development expenses as they were incurred, and the other was the reluctance to use long-term debt.

Beech had been a leader in its financing operations, which were conducted through its financial subsidiary, Beech Acceptance Corporation,

Inc. Beech Acceptance had begun dealer financing in 1956 and customer financing in 1958. At that time most commercial banks were unwilling to accept an aircraft as collateral for a bank loan, but in the years since the founding of Beech Acceptance, banks had changed their attitude toward the acceptability of aircraft as collateral and had become Beech Acceptance's chief competition. In fact, in 1968, banks were generally more liberal than Beech Acceptance. Examples of Beech Acceptance conservatism were a turndown rate of one in four corporate loans and one in three individual loans. In the summer of 1968, Beech Acceptance interest rate charges to distributors were about 8% and to individuals about 11%. In addition, a net worth of five to six times the amount being borrowed was required. The combination of these policies had caused a recent decline in domestic financing volume, but a new area was opening up in export financing. The future role of Beech Acceptance was seen as mainly a financer of export distributors, while it continued to finance a few special domestic sales not accepted for financing by local banks.

One recent development in the Beech financial area was the August, 1968, offering of $30 million of subordinated convertible debentures. Part of these funds was used to replace the $18 million in short-term debt owed by Beech Acceptance, and part was allocated for facilities expansion. It was anticipated that Beech would need substantially more long-term financing to meet its five-year growth goals.

PERSONNEL

Beech employees had been represented by the International Association of Machinists since the 1930's. During that time Beech employees had received continual wage and benefit increases, and Beech in turn had never experienced a work stoppage.

In 1968 the only incentive available to production workers was a suggestion system which generally yielded $5 or $10. Beech had previously introduced a major wage incentive in December, 1941, called the Beech Efficiency Incentive Plan. This plan was based on pounds of airplane production per hour and had served as a model for incentive production plans in other companies. By 1967 continual wage increases had converted these variable wage costs into standard and universally received benefits.

Beech had always been proud of the loyalty and long service of its employees. However, rapid expansion in recent years had caused a generation gap to develop. The most senior 3,000–3,500 of Beech production employees, the main reservoir of Beech's production skill, had an average age of 55, whereas the average age of the remaining 7,000 less-skilled employees was only 27. Beech was trying to remedy this situation through the use of an extensive manpower development and training program whose average cost in 1968 was $24 per employee. Beech would need many more skilled employees in the future to meet its expansion goals.

The Beech management organization would also have to be expanded to manage effectively the planned level of future sales. For the 54 Beech executives in 1967 the average term of employment with the company was 22 years. Many of these executives had been with Beech since World War II and would retire in the next five years. It was doubtful that the traditional Beech practice of promotion from within would be able to fill all the positions which would become vacant. As a result, Mr. Hedrick listed this problem of executive scarcity as the biggest obstacle toward the continuance of a rapid growth rate.

ORGANIZATION

Beech had been organized around functional expertise until 1968. However, in response to the need for a focus of attention on each part of the increasingly complex product line, in January, 1968, Beech created the position of program manager, with multifunctional responsibilities. The program manager, together with a product sales manager who was responsible for marketing that segment of the product line, was responsible for all phases of design, scheduling, production, and marketing. The five program managers appointed in 1968 were for the Musketeer, Bonanza, Light Twins, Corporate Twins, and Beechcraft 99.

Exhibit 8 attempts to show how the product responsibility was shifted downward in the Beech organization between 1967 and 1968. Program managers were constantly working to coordinate engineering, manufacturing and product reliability in order to hold down costs, to meet production schedules, and to retain product styling and engineering desirability. The product sales managers, in turn, tried to coordinate advertising, export sales, domestic sales, and financing in order to achieve the maximum sales volume. The initial indications were that this system had produced improved results in reducing production lead times and in selling more aircraft. Another new element in the Beech organization was the autonomy given the Musketeer program manager by moving his production to the Liberal plant. The vice president of operations speculated that if this initial experiment proved successful,

Exhibit 8

BEECH AIRCRAFT CORPORATION
Organization Schematics, 1967 and 1968

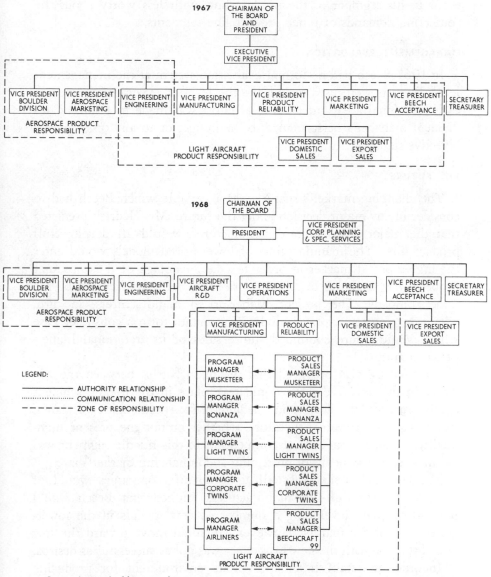

Source: As perceived by case writer.

other divisions might be organized with the program manager as the division head. Possible geographic decentralization would then allow a division manager to develop and marshal expertise particularly relevant to his segment of the product line, with less worry about the conflicting demands of other product line segments.

MANAGEMENT EVALUATION

In 1967 Beech had no formal evaluation system at the management level. Budgets were used to indicate the level of expenses expected in each functional area, but no formal effort was made to relate an individual manager's performance to the budget or to any other purely objective standard.

THE FUTURE

The changing market structure was a variable which Beech had to consider in any major decision about the future. Mr. Hedrick predicted that the major light aircraft manufacturers would all develop full product lines. The manufacturers of lower-priced models would enter the higher-priced market in order to take advantage of the consumer propensity to trade up to a higher-priced model manufactured by the same company. The present higher-priced manufacturers, in turn, would develop lower-priced models in order to form a consumer base which would insure continued future sales of its traditional higher-priced aircraft.

Mr. Hedrick also predicted that the main battles between the Big Three in the next five years would take place in the middle segment of the market, the low- and medium-priced twin-engine airplanes. Beech had to determine, therefore, whether or not the present high-quality, high-price method of competition in this middle segment was the most effective means of protecting and enhancing market share.

Mr. Hedrick's belief that all light aircraft companies would of necessity become full-line manufacturers implied that Beech would have to consider developing a number of new models in the lower-priced part of the market. However, an initial move toward the low end of the line with the new Musketeer was not as successful as desired.

In order to establish an appropriate environment for producing lower-priced models, Beech was in the process of expanding the number of Beechcraft single-engine dealers and also the number of light twin-engine outlets. The domestic sales manager thought that through this program Beech would get better exposure and coverage in its retail sales, and also that financially and managerially overextended franchises could be supplemented by new franchises in the same geographic area, with responsibility for different parts of the product line being split among them. In addition, many areas which could not justify a full-line Beech dealer could justify a small single-engine dealer with less extensive supporting service responsibilities. There was also a general feeling among Beech executives that selling single-engine aircraft to owners required different advertising and selling techniques than selling twin-engine aircraft to corporations. Expanding the Beech franchise organization would allow a particular dealer to concentrate more effectively on the skills necessary to sell to his particular segment.

The jet market was a second area for product expansion. It was estimated that a $25 million investment was required to develop a business jet. In September, 1968, Cessna became the first of the light aircraft manufacturers to announce a planned entry into the business jet market. Cessna predicted sales of 1,000 Cessna jets from 1970 to 1980 at a price of $590,000. Beech had been studying the business jet market for some time, but was apprehensive because, to its knowledge, none of the domestic business jet manufacturers showed a profit in 1968. Further, no available jet engines gave the combination of comfort, speed, range, payload, and price which Beech felt their customers wanted. Beech realized that entry into the jet market was an eventual necessity but felt that the timing was a crucial issue.

A third possible area for product expansion was a medium-size commuter airliner which would fill the gap between present 100-passenger jets and the 17-passenger Beechcraft 99 turboprop. Presumably Beech could use the marketing contacts and experience gained in selling the 99 Airliner to sell a much larger aircraft (probably jet to take advantage of lower operating costs) in three to five years. The same basic airlines would form the market for both planes.

While this potential opportunity to sell about 100 units per year of a 20–30-passenger jet commuter plane for about $1–$1.5 million per unit was very attractive in terms of sales volume, it presented three serious risks:

1. Required investment in airframe development, plant and inventory would probably be $25–$50 million, requiring a major portion of available resources—financial and engineering. The attention given to this product might cause other product areas to suffer.

2. If annual sales of $100–$150 million in this product did ma-

terialize, the structure of the company might have to change in order to accommodate the needs of such a large new product area.

3. Beech would have unmistakably entered an area previously dominated but since vacated by Douglas, Lockheed, and Boeing, all of whom are many times the size of Beech.

Short takeoff and landing aircraft (STOL) were becoming increasingly talked about as a way to solve airport and airspace congestion. This type of diversification presented another alternative for Beech sales expansion. Indeed, Beech was monitoring STOL developments and constantly reassessing the advisability of entering this market. One possible drawback was the special-purpose nature of a STOL which caused a higher operating cost per mile and was only potentially advantageous for very short runways or for very crowded airports. Beech did not believe that the aircraft usage of most businesses was presently of a nature which would justify the extra cost. Beech also believed that the design and production skills and the technological capability necessary to produce a STOL were presently available in the Beech organization. This capability could be tapped if the environment changed to one of substantial demand for this type of aircraft in place of the present Beech product line.

Vertical takeoff and landing (VTOL) technology presented more of a problem for Beech. It was thought that corporations might find the added flexibility of this type of aircraft advantageous. To prepare for this eventuality, Beech was performing development and substantial production work for a major helicopter manufacturer. In return for Beech developmental costs, the helicopter manufacturer committed to Beech the right to production of future sales of this model. This arrangement enabled Beech to master VTOL technology on a profit-producing basis.

Major growth in the export market was another expansion possibility. Unfortunately, Mr. Neuburger, vice president of export sales, felt that growth much more rapid than the present 15% compound rate would require a much better foreign distribution network, and possible foreign manufacture. Acquiring a strong foreign distribution system was definitely not a short-term proposition, as Mr. Neuburger thought that 70% of the foreign market was being unsatisfactorily serviced in 1968. Concerning foreign manufacturing, Beech was wary of establishing a facility in any country, since no one foreign country alone had the sales volume to support efficient production. It was assumed that intercountry rivalry would then demand manufacturing in more and more countries, resulting in many small inefficient production operations. Another concern raised by foreign manufacturing was the problem of repatriation of profits. Mr. Neuburger commented on this point, "An Indian manufacturing facility might corner the Indian market, but what are we going to do with all those rupees?"

A final possibility for extensive growth was in government contracts. Beech Aerospace had a good cost and delivery record as a government contractor, and this reputation would undoubtedly succeed in securing a greatly expanded aerospace volume if Beech relaxed its stringent contract requirements. However, the type of contract that could give Beech rapid extensive volume increases was almost certain to have a lower margin, or lower technology, or shorter duration, or be less likely to produce beneficial side effects on Beech commercial technology.

A variable which might seriously affect Beech in the future was the problem of airport and airspace congestion. This problem would become particularly acute if Beech decided to produce a business jet, which presumably would be used mainly for long trips to major airports. To date, the air congestion problem had not affected the Beech outlook in any major way. Beech felt that the travel restrictions being contemplated would principally affect the smaller aircraft segment, where Beech had very few sales. Beech contended that its larger aircraft were generally used at less crowded "closer in" airports such as Meigs Field in Chicago or Lakefront Airport in Cleveland.

Another relatively recent addition to the light-aircraft manufacturing environment was foreign competition. For instance, the Beechcraft 99 had no competition from domestic manufacturers but did lose some sales to the De Havilland Twin Otter. Foreign competition, it was believed, would take place primarily in the upper end of the market. It was much easier for a foreign manufacturer to sell a small number of larger planes than a large number of smaller planes. Furthermore, the labor content was higher for larger planes, allowing foreign manufacturers with low wage rates an extra advantage in the higher-priced segments. Beech expected increasing foreign competition in the future.

In October of 1968, Beech announced for the fiscal year ending September 30, sales of $176 million, including $54 million in aerospace sales and about $30 million in export sales. Mr. Hedrick had also received projections for annual sales which were expected to be achieved by the present product line through 1973. These sales fell substantially short of the 1973 goal of over $350 million, and Mrs.

Beech, Mr. Hedrick and the other top Beech executives were debating what combination of product commitments and major operating policies was best able to meet the goals which had been established for the next five years. Top management was aware that any decision affecting the future strategy of Beech Aircraft would have important implications for the allocation and management of the firm's resources.

6. Tensor Corporation

Tensor History to 1969

MR. JAY MONROE, PRESIDENT, summed up the early history of Tensor Corporation as follows:

I had a considerable amount of mechanical aptitude as a kid and always wanted to be an engineer. But in the 1930's engineering was still a closed field to Jews. Jewish kids just did not grow up to be engineers. Sperry Gyroscope was the largest hirer of engineers in New York City, and they did not hire Jews.

Consequently I decided to be an inventor so that I could be an engineer. I attended Cornell and majored in electrical engineering. At the end of my senior year in 1945 I went to Western Electric to apply for a job. Even though I got a perfect score on the engineering employment qualification test, Western Electric could not figure out what to do with me.

This inability to find a meaningful job at many of the large companies is one of the reasons for the existence of the large number of small companies in the New York City area. Of the 10 members of my Cornell Jewish fraternity in my graduating class, all are now presidents of small companies.

Shortly after I got out of school, there was a marked change of attitude in the country in general, and anti-Semitism was no longer condoned or tolerated by most Americans. I took a variety of jobs for short periods to gain experience and in 1949 was a partner with Gerald Starr in the formation of Tensor Electric Development Company.

Tensor Electric Development was solely a government contractor for the first 10 years of the company's history. A number of consumer products were tried during that period, but none was successful enough to justify continued production. The idea remained, however, that the only way to be free to guide your own destiny was through developing and marketing a consumer product. It took 10 years to invent that product, but finally in 1959, we thought we had developed the basis for a profitable company from a consumer product: the Tensor lamp.

THE TENSOR LAMP

High intensity lamps consisted basically of a step-down transformer built into the base of the lamp, an automobile headlight bulb, and a reflecting cone. Mr. Jay Monroe had designed the small transformer in order to power a lamp whose light would be bright enough to compensate for his poor vision and focused enough to keep from

Figure 1
TENSOR CORPORATION
Officers—1970

JAY MONROE
President
b. 1927. Graduated from Cornell in 1945. Majored in Electrical Engineering. Founded Tensor Electric Company in 1949.

GEORGE SAVITSKY
Vice President—Sales and Marketing
b. 1938. Graduated from Pace College in 1960. Worked as an accountant with a N.Y.C. accounting firm before joining Tensor in 1964.

STANLEY JARET
Treasurer
b. 1930. Graduated from City College of New York in 1953. Worked in public accounting with a N.Y.C. accounting firm until joining Tensor in 1964.

WALTER GLOUMAKOFF
Director of Manufacturing
b. 1934. Attended Rutgers University. Concentrated on engineering courses. Worked for Rotobroil. Joined Tensor in 1964.

EDMUND SOVATSKY
Vice President—Engineering
b. 1934. Attended Brooklyn Vocational High School. Joined Tensor in 1950.

disturbing his wife's sleep while he read in bed. The first lamp, which used a tin measuring cup for a reflecting cone, was designed by Mr. Monroe in 1959. The *Lamp Journal* for August, 1964, reviewed the physical characteristics of the high intensity lamp:

Its chief advantages are: white light, high intensity, and size, perhaps in that order. Each of these three features was available before the advent of high intensity lamps, although not all at the same time from the same lamp.

The advantages of white light, high intensity, and [small] size in the high intensity lamps are achieved at the sacrifice of bulb life. The shortest bulb life of a 75-watt bulb in common use is 55 hours. At 25¢ retail per bulb this amounts to ½¢ per hour bulb cost; power cost is ¼¢ per hour. The equivalent conventional lamp, using a 200-watt bulb, would cost approximately ¹⁄₃₀¢ per hour for the bulb and 1¢ per hour for power. In general, short bulb lives notwithstanding, the miniatures are cheaper to operate than equivalent incandescents, but considerably more expensive than equivalent fluorescents.

TABLE 1

Tensor Lamp Sales, 1960–65

Year	Sales
1960	$ 1,000
1961	50,000
1962	285,000
1963	850,000
1964	3,893,000
1965	6,863,000

When his friends began to ask him to make lamps for them also, Mr. Monroe decided that the new lamp had commercial possibilities. He set up a production line inside the Tensor factory to begin small-scale manufacture. The Tensor lamp encountered rapid success from the start of its commercial introduction in 1960. Table 1 gives sales of Tensor lamps from 1960 through 1965.

During this period of expansion, Tensor was constantly pressed by the necessity for more management personnel and larger facilities. In 1964, Tensor sold off the government contract division to Mr. Gerald Starr and concentrated completely on the Tensor lamp. A December, 1964, article in *Business Week*[1] detailed some of the changes which had taken place at Tensor since the introduction of the high intensity lamp:

[1] "The Little Lamp that Grew Up," *Business Week*, December 19, 1964, pp. 64–65.

Tensor is showing a growth pattern typical of rapidly growing small companies. Early in their growth they usually rely heavily on outsiders to beef up a slim executive staff. As they grow, they soon find they can afford larger administrative overhead to handle much of the farmed-out work.

Just six months ago Monroe ran Tensor with only four other executives— an executive vice president, two marketing executives, and a treasurer. Ten outsiders helped run the company. Two full-time consultants reshaped production lines to fit Tensor's hodge-podge plant that rambles through eight floors of three adjoining buildings in Brooklyn. Legal counsel handled most business dickering, such as adding new plant space, as well as legal problems. Two advertising agents handled last year's $300,000 advertising campaign and also acted as material purchasing agents. New equipment and design changes were recommended by other consultants.

While most of the outsiders still work with Tensor, many of their extra duties have been turned over to a beefed-up home office executive team. Tensor has recently added a comptroller, a production director, and a troubleshooting presidential assistant.

Still Tensor's shape, like its lamps, is something less than classic, but it seems to be paying off. A consultant-tailored incentive labor plan cut pre-lamp costs in half; bookkeeping and inventory controls are working smoothly; plant security is being tightened—losses so far have been cut in half; and this year Tensor lamps are expected to show a healthy profit.

As sales of Tensor lamps continued to expand in 1965 and 1966, Tensor added to corporate overhead by (1) leasing new executive offices in Great Neck, Long Island, (2) leasing a new one-story manufacturing plant in Brooklyn, which replaced the old manufacturing facility, and (3) investing in new mass-production machinery which for some operations could handle 10 times the company's 1965 lamp volume. The new Great Neck office included a much expanded laboratory for Mr. Monroe, who believed he could turn his attention away from administration and back to inventing.

During the 1965–66 period the company was receiving letters from many of its customers praising the high intensity lamp for its ability to give sufficient light to allow older persons and persons with poor vision to read and carry on other visually detailed operations.

The success of the Tensor lamp did not go unnoticed by other lighting manufacturers. A mid-1965 investment report by du Pasquier & Co., Inc., summarized the competition as follows:

There are now at least 15 manufacturers of high intensity lamps and this number is expected to increase. Tensor estimates that it had some 50% of the market for high intensity lamps in 1964 and that this percentage is currently being maintained (total industry sales of high intensity lamps in 1964 are estimated to have been $8.0 million).

Tensor feels it is now over the critical period where a competitor could come out with a single design that would capture the bulk of the market. There is considerable speculation of the effect a large manufacturer such as Westinghouse or G.E. would have entering the market with a major advertising campaign. It is doubtful, however, that a major company will enter the arena until the total market is larger and in the meanwhile Tensor is continuing to achieve broader distribution and the name to provide effective competition. Of incalculable value is the fact that all high intensity lamps are increasingly becoming known as Tensor lamps regardless of their manufacturer.

Tensor's major competitor is the Lampette, which is manufactured in Japan and Germany for Soss Manufacturing. Some $2.5 million worth of Lampettes were sold in 1964. Lightolier, a leading manufacturer of lighting fixtures, and Rotobroil are shortly expected to introduce high intensity lamps.

As Tensor faced the future of the high intensity lamp market at the end of 1965, many uncertainties remained about the eventual size of the industry and Tensor's role in it. The Tensor lamp was the only high intensity lamp manufactured in the United States. This gave competitors who used foreign suppliers a cost advantage which was reflected by being able to offer a lower price to the consumer or higher margins to the sales and distribution network.

Furthermore, although Tensor had advertised heavily and established a brand name with the consumer, that brand name had been built on the basis of product utility. Recent competition, however, seemed to emphasize styling. Mr. Monroe disdained this attempt to turn the high intensity lamp into a "fad" item. He believed that the market would respond best to an appeal to utility rather than style. Mr. Monroe therefore continued to emphasize utility, and Tensor was the last major marketer of high intensity lamps to introduce a telescoping lamp neck into their product line.

Tensor's goal in the high intensity lamp market was to maintain the 50% share of market the company held in 1965. In order to assure the financial ability to support a higher forecasted sales level, Tensor sold 100,000 shares of stock at 11⅛ per share net to the company. This new stock, issued in the summer of 1966, gave Tensor a wide ownership and a listing on the American Stock Exchange. It also gave the company the necessary cash to finance the advertising budget ($100,000 in 1963, $300,000 in 1964, $1,000,000 in 1965 and 1966) and the new building and equipment expenditures.

But 1966 and 1967 did not produce the high level of sales the company had been forecasting. Sales increased slightly in 1966 to $7.4 million, but fell more than 30% in 1967. Net income plummeted from earnings of over $0.5 million in 1965 to a deficit of $0.5 million in 1966 and a similar loss in 1967.

Looking back on those two years, Mr. Monroe commented that the stupidest thing he had done was to "lose contact with the plant" and to allow overexpansion:

It was extremely painful to me and to the company and its employees to undergo the major contractions of late 1966 to early 1967. We closed down the Great Neck offices and moved back to the plant in Brooklyn. Both salaried and hourly employees were cut back drastically in order to allow the company to survive.

The major cause of our misjudging the market size was the erroneous belief that the high intensity lamp was an all-purpose lamp which would replace many other forms of lighting. We interpreted the letters we were receiving as a sample of the reaction of the general public. Actually the bright light of the high intensity lamp was not needed by younger people with good eyesight. It was no more useful to them than a good incandescent lamp, and it made their eyes tire more rapidly. One rumor which was current in 1966 and 1967 was that the more rapid tiring of the eyes caused by high intensity lamps resulted in permanent eye damage. This rumor was subsequently proved to be completely false, but it did nothing to improve our declining sales.

Another problem we had with our demand forecasts is a common problem with any new product area: the boundaries of our forecasts were so wide that the forecasts themselves became almost useless as a planning tool.

Two demand factors contributed significantly to our inability to assess accurately future high intensity lamp sales. The first factor was our lack of ability to predict sales to the consumer as opposed to factory sales to wholesale and retail outlets. In mid-1966 we ran a trade promotion. Shortly thereafter we received a significant number of reorders, and we concluded that consumer demand was remaining strong. The large number of retail and wholesale outlets that began to carry Tensor in 1964 and 1965 were all well stocked for the mid-1966 demand level. But in late 1966 consumer sales fell off sharply, and our distribution channels were stuck with an inventory appropriate for a much higher demand level. Consequently, factory orders did not recover for some time.

The second factor which affected our forecasts was the extra consumer demand generated by the large amount of advertising and promotion. We "over-advertised" to try to build up our name while the market was still immature, and this contributed to a larger final demand than would have been experienced in a time of less aggressive promotion. In addition, a number of new competitors entered the market in 1964–65. Each new entrant needed a large promotional campaign in order to carve out an initial market share; promotional campaigns often increased the total market rather than resulting in "conquest" sales from other manufacturers. These campaigns stimulated some demand which was not sustainable when the promotion level became more normal.

Figure 2 shows schematically the unsustainable demand on which Tensor based its 1966 and 1967 sales forecasts. Mr. Monroe estimated that the dotted line represented the sustainable demand for high in-

Figure 2

TENSOR CORPORATION

A Comparison of Theoretical Tensor Lamp Sales under Normal Conditions versus Actual Experienced Demand, 1960–68

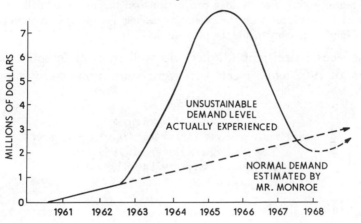

tensity lamps which Tensor would have experienced without unusual pipeline and promotional sales.

THE TENSOR TENNIS RACKET AND DISPOSABLE FLASHLIGHT

Mr. Monroe commented on Tensor's expansion into a new product line:

In late 1967 it was clear to me that the drop in high intensity lamp sales was not just a temporary phenomenon. Tensor lamps, because of our strong brand name, retained a 50% market share. However, total high intensity lamp sales were contracting to meet a stable level of demand which represented the share of market for high intensity lamps in the total lamp market. From that point, I expected that high intensity lamp sales would only increase as fast as population growth.

I did not want to take the risk that stabilized Tensor lamp sales would not be sufficient to support the company's organization. I was also displeased that sales in the high intensity lamp market were becoming more dependent on product styling than on product utility. This trend emphasized fad rather than lighting improvement. Consequently, I began to look around for other new product possibilities. The Tensor lamp had helped the company to build a valuable national name, and I believed that our reputation would be a big help in any new area we entered.

My major source of recreation is playing tennis, and early in 1968 I noticed that the waiting list for metal rackets at pro shops was growing longer and longer. This was an indication to me that metal racket production capacity for the major producers of tennis rackets was lagging behind demand. Metal tennis rackets did not seem to represent any major manufacturing innovation, and by early 1968 the contraction in lamp sales had left us with plenty of spare production capacity.

In February we made the decision to go ahead with the design work on a metal tennis racket, and by May production had begun on a small-scale basis. We priced our racket with the premium models put out by the competition, and evidently our name made the price stick.

The Tensor steel tennis racket sold well from its inception, and by the end of 1968 tennis racket sales were contributing a substantial part

Exhibit 1

TENSOR CORPORATION

Tensor Corporation and Subsidiaries: Income Statements,
Year Ending December 31, 1962–69

(000 Omitted except for Last Three Items)

	1962	1963	1964	1965	1966	1967	1968	1969
Net sales	$ 757	$1,415	$4,263	$6,863	$7,445	$5,135	$3,262	$3,825
Cost of goods sold	518	765	2,454	4,137	5,649	4,040	2,259	2,393
Gross profit	$ 239	$ 650	$1,809	$2,726	$1,796	$1,095	$1,003	$1,432
Selling, general and administrative expense	321	495	1,238	1,711	2,669	1,513	914	1,206
Operating profit (loss)	$ (82)	$ 155	$ 571	$1,015	$ (873)	$ (418)	$ 89	$ 226
Interest expense	—	—	6	41	80	42	29	27
Other income (expense)	(31)	5	3	13	(8)	13	43	42
Income before taxes	$(113)	$ 160	$ 568	$ 987	$ (961)	$ (447)	$ 103	$ 241
Taxes (refund)	(24)	74	270	450	(465)	(200)	45	125
Profit (loss) before extraordinary items	$ (89)	$ 86	$ 298	$ 537	$ (496)	$ (247)	$ 58	$ 116
Extraordinary income (loss)	—	—	—	—	—	(195)	45	60
Net income	$ (89)	$ 86	$ 298	$ 537	$ (496)	$ (442)	$ 103	176
Shares outstanding	300,000	300,000	313,535	325,200	425,200	425,200	430,200	434,700
Earnings (deficit) per share*	$(.30)	$ .29	$ .95	$ 1.65	$(1.17)	$ (.58)	$ .14	$ .27
Return on stockholders' equity*	(28.1)	21.3	40.2	40.8	(25.7)	(16.7)	3.6	6.4

* All returns based on profit (loss) before extraordinary items.
Source: Annual reports.

Exhibit 2

TENSOR CORPORATION

Tensor Corporation and Subsidiaries: Balance Sheets,
Year Ending December 31, 1962–69
(000 Omitted except for Book Value and Price)

	1962	1963	1964	1965	1966	1967	1968	1969
Assets								
Cash	$ 29	$108	$ 336	$ 79	$ 104	$ 124	$ 329	$ 90
U.S. government securities	—	25	—	—	—	344	325	350
Accounts receivable	127	302	777	1,382	1,177	501	700	743
Inventories	137	159	677	1,383	1,643	649	563	889
Claims for refund of income taxes	35	—	—	—	531	227	21	
Prepaid expenses	2	13	110	19	30	18	43	40
Total current assets	$330	$607	$1,900	$2,863	$3,485	$1,863	$1,981	$2,112
Machinery and other equipment	78	74	123	419	669	630	529	489
Leasehold improvements	5	10	45	128	177	111	112	112
Accumulated depreciation	26	29	59	133	234	281	275	288
Total fixed assets	$ 57	$ 55	$ 109	$ 414	$ 612	$ 460	$ 366	$ 313
Other miscellaneous assets and deposits	4	3	64	205	163	118	104	159
Total assets	$391	$665	$2,073	$3,482	$4,260	$2,441	$2,451	$2,584
Liabilities and Stockholders' Equity								
Accounts payable	$ 38	$102	$ 751	$ 614	$ 668	$ 385	$ 320	$ 226
Notes payable	—	—	—	550	1,000	—	—	—
Current portion of noncurrent liabilities	—	—	15	4	47	43	43	43
Accrued liabilities	21	72	151	146	138	126	124	127
Federal income taxes payable	15	88	280	350	—	—	—	65
Total current liabilities	$ 74	$262	$1,197	$1,664	$1,853	$ 554	$ 487	$ 461
6½% promissory note payable	—	—	135	450	412	375	338	300
Due under contract for purchase of leasehold	—	—	—	33	28	23	17	12
Deferred federal income taxes	—	—	—	20	35	—	—	—
Total noncurrent liabilities	$—	$—	$ 135	$ 503	$ 475	$ 398	$ 355	$ 312
Common stock: Par value 10¢ per share	30	30	31	33	42	42	43	43
Additional paid-in capital	253	253	292	327	1,431	1,431	1,447	1,473
Retained earnings	34	120	418	955	459	16	119	295
Total stockholders' equity	$317	$403	$ 741	$1,315	$1,932	$1,489	$1,609	$1,811
Total liabilities and stockholders' equity	$391	$665	$2,073	$3,482	$4,260	$2,441	$2,451	$2,584
Book value per share	$1.06	$1.34	$2.36	$4.04	$4.54	$3.50	$3.74	$4.17
Stock Price Range*								
High	Not	Not	14	18.375	15.75	9.625	10.25	11.25
Low	traded	traded	3.375	10.5	3.75	4.25	4.125	6.0

* Price on March 2, 1970 = $6.875.
Source: Annual reports.

of Tensor's sales. The only miscalculation apparent in the introduction of the Tensor tennis racket was the use of a soft gauge of steel in the very early rackets. This caused a large number of customer returns of rackets with snapped handles. Tensor quickly changed to a harder gauge of steel and customer returns subsequently declined to less than 2%.

Largely because of the tennis racket, Tensor became profitable in 1968 and 1969—even though 1969 sales remained substantially below the 1964 level. Exhibits 1 and 2 detail Tensor's financial statements from 1962 to 1969.

Tensor had introduced one other new product in 1968—a disposable flashlight retailing for $1.98 and guaranteed to last for at least one year. Mr. Monroe had first seen the product as a French import, but when the French company would not issue Tensor a license to sell the flashlight under the Tensor name, he designed his own version.

Mr. Monroe had not been enthusiastic about the disposable flashlight, but at the time of its introduction in mid-1968, it had helped to fill some of Tensor's excess production capacity. Most of the disposable flashlight sales were "premium sales." Under this arrangement Tensor printed another company's name as well as its own on the product. The other company could then use large quantities of the product in consumer or trade promotions and as prizes in sales contests. Although Tensor continued to make minor design and packaging improvements in disposable flashlights, the specialty nature of the premium market made a stable sales level above $1 million annually extremely unlikely.

Tensor in 1969–70

COMPETITION

By 1969 Tensor's competition in the high intensity lamp market had dwindled to only two other firms with national distribution and a number of smaller firms with regional distribution. The two nationwide competitors were Lightolier—a company with $40 million in annual lamp sales, of which 5%–8% were high intensity—and Universal. Universal, a high intensity lamp company with headquarters in Chicago, had an annual sales of $1 million. George Savitsky, Tensor's vice president of sales and marketing, estimated the high intensity lamp market, including the regional firms, at about $7 million. Tensor's line of high intensity lamps sold at retail for prices ranging from $8.95 to

$50.00. A major portion of the volume was concentrated at two points in this range—$12.95 and $19.95. By comparison, some of the private-label brands imported from Japan sold for as little as $3.99. The Lightolier price range was $12.95 to $25.00.

The metal tennis racket market was much more difficult to estimate. All manufacturers wished to withhold from competitors possibly helpful information on the size of the market and the unit volume that each manufacturer was selling.

The three brand names in the market were Wilson, Spalding, and Tensor. In 1969 Tensor had introduced a lower-cost model of its metal racket under the brand name of Melbourne. This was an effort to broaden the appeal to new market segments without diluting the Tensor brand name. Tennis rackets which carried the Tensor brand name ranged in price from $34 to $60 at retail. The aluminum racket was the least expensive at $34; the steel racket sold for about $40; a new 24K gold-plated line sold for $50; and the new top-of-the-line stainless steel racket was priced at $60. Tensor's Melbourne brand was produced in both aluminum and steel with selling prices from $19.95 to $29.95. Although the Tensor steel racket at $40 was competitive with Wilson and Spalding, private-label rackets sold as low as $12. A 40%–50% retail markup on factory price was considered normal in sporting goods distribution.

Although estimates were only approximate, Mr. Savitsky believed that Tensor in mid-1969 was selling 10%–20% of the market in comparison to 45%–70% for Wilson, 10%–15% for Spalding, and 10%–20% for the combined small private-label manufacturers. He also estimated that Wilson had 60% of the wooden racket market, while Spalding had 30%, and all others accounted for the remaining 10%.

Mr. Monroe had a different estimate for market share based on the metal rackets he observed at country clubs and on some information he had heard about the total market size. Mr. Monroe believed that four million tennis rackets were sold annually and that recently 35% of tennis racket sales were metal rackets. Combining these figures with his own observations, Mr. Monroe reasoned that Wilson metal rackets were outselling Tensor 10 to 1. Wilson Sporting Goods, Inc., was a $100 million subsidiary of a $3.5 billion conglomerate. Spalding had annual sales of $65 million and had recently been acquired by a $220 million conglomerate.

MARKETING

Mr. Monroe saw marketing as the key area in Tensor's recent recovery. He believed that Tensor's quality image had allowed the company to market successfully a second and third consumer product. Exhibits 3 and 4 give sample advertising and pictures of lamps and flashlights; Exhibits 5 and 6 do the same for tennis rackets. George Savitsky commented on Tensor's image:

> We established our image with the customer by advertising and with the dealer by not allowing price cutting. Our advertising was quite heavy as a per cent of sales, but it helped us maintain our market share in periods of expansion and later contraction. Perhaps we even "overadvertised" on Tensor lamps, but the name we developed gave us an image which we could trade on to our advantage in 1969.
>
> As far as our channels of distribution were concerned, we initially avoided discount stores as much as possible. We didn't want to do business in areas of severe price cutting. Whenever that happens we'll leave the business to others. I believe Tensor was 98% effective in stopping price cutting on Tensor lamps. We brought suit under fair-trade laws, cut off distributors who were cutting their prices, coded our lamps so we could determine which distributors were selling to the retail price cutters, and even bought up some of the discounters' lamps to dry up their supply.
>
> We feel we are continuing to enhance our image with tennis rackets. Recently we refused a large order from a major retailer because they wanted us to put our name on the tag and cut the price. This willingness to turn away business that is not on our terms is what establishes a reputation. Perhaps we will soften our stance in tennis rackets after this reputation is firmly established.

Tensor's allocation of margin to the various aspects of its distribution network depended on the product involved. In the lamp business, where Tensor had a narrow margin, most of this margin was allocated to the channel of distribution. The manufacturers' representatives received only a 5% commission.

For tennis rackets, on the other hand, Tensor was able to allow more margin to the sales force. At present the tennis rackets were being sold on a 10% commission basis.

Tensor's two sales forces consisted solely of manufacturers' representatives. The first group, numbering about 25, sold high intensity lamps to 30 department stores and chains and to 300–400 wholesalers. Retail outlets serviced by these wholesalers probably averaged 100 per wholesaler. The second sales force, also numbering about 25, sold tennis rackets to sporting goods stores, specialty stores, and pro shops. This sales force serviced about 2,000 accounts.

In addition, Tensor was in the process of developing a 25-man "premium" sales force to sell the disposable flashlight and other Tensor products to companies for use in sales contests and promotional campaigns.

As manufacturers' representatives, Tensor's salesmen served the same distribution outlets with non-Tensor products. Mr. Savitsky was uncertain of the extent of the increase in volume on present product

Exhibit 4

TENSOR CORPORATION

Lamp and Flashlight Sample Pictures

| Tensor Model 6500 | Tensor Model 7200 | Tensor Model 100 Disposable Flashlight |

lines that Tensor could obtain by raising sales commissions or by developing additional Tensor product lines appropriate for sale by the present sales force.

FINANCE

Stanley Jaret, the treasurer, outlined the company's 1969 financial position as follows:

Now that we are back in the black again, our problem is not cash. We had almost $450,000 in cash and marketable securities at the end of 1969. Most of this cash resulted from our failure to expand sales—and therefore inventories and receivables—as fast as we had anticipated when we acquired new equity in the summer of 1966.

Our real problem is to assure that we retain control of the company. Jay owns 26% of the stock, but none of the rest of the management owns more than a nominal amount of Tensor's equity. As far as we are able to determine now, the stock is widely distributed with no other party owning any significant per cent. We could use our cash to repurchase some of the stock on the open market and virtually assure control, but our stock price doubled with our return to profitable operations, and any significant volume of buying seems to boost the price sharply.

We have made some structural changes to keep Tensor from being taken over. For instance, at our next stockholder meeting we will propose cumulative voting for positions on our expanded nine-man board of directors. Directors will have staggered three-year terms, allowing management to retain control for two years even in the eventuality of a raid. With our large cash position and our deficits for 1966 and 1967, a raid was a distinct possibility. Also, we

Exhibit 6
TENSOR CORPORATION
Sample Metal Tennis Racket Pictures

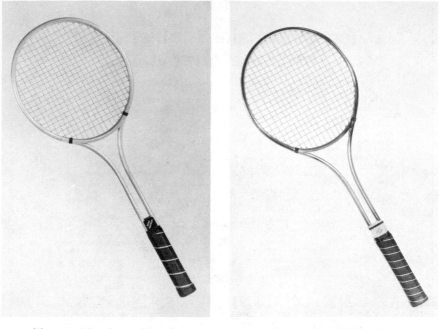

Tensor Aluminum Tennis
Racket

Tensor Steel Tennis
Racket

recently voted an employee stock plan. The employee stock fund buys shares on the open market. This should put more shares in friendly hands. Finally, a management stock bonus plan has been started. The four officers of the company received 5,000 shares of stock (restricted for 10 years as to sale) in 1968. Forty-five hundred additional restricted shares were given to management in 1969.

I would say our biggest area for present improvement of financial management is internal control. We should be able to avoid the capital expenditure errors we made in the past, and also to remain more current in our sales projections.

PRODUCTION

In 1969 Tensor employed approximately 200 persons in its Brooklyn headquarters and plant facility. Most of the production jobs required only short training periods, and manual dexterity was the major requirement for many of them.

The lamp section of the plant consisted of a couple of subassembly lines, a small amount of in-process inventory to smooth the work flow, and finished inventory at the shipping end of the plant.

Tennis racket production started with precut metal rods. These rods were bent, drilled, and finished. A handle and grip then were added at the end, and the racket was strung and stored on a long rack by size and type. As orders were received, they were filled by picking the rackets off the easily accessible storage rack and sending them to shipping.

Walter Gloumakoff, the plant manager, summarized the Tensor production operation as simple and flexible:

> Our strength is in keeping operating costs low and in not sinking resources into production tooling. We have quite experienced toolmakers who save us time by cooperating in the product design stage. As a product is being designed, they simultaneously create the tools to produce it. That way we don't create any new products we can't produce. Our toolmakers also save us money by designing more economical limited purpose tools instead of general purpose tools which do more than is required. A good example is the $2,000 drill rig made up to drill the string holes for our rackets. A general purpose tool to perform the same task might have cost as much as $10,000.
>
> We are essentially a design and assembly business with low fabrication content. We did bring some of the lamp fabrication in-house when sales dropped off, but that was mainly to fill idle production capacity.

One production decision which was a continuing possibility was the transference of some manufacturing to Japan. This was an alternative available not only for lamp production, but also for any other electromechanical devices which Tensor developed in the future. Because of the original uncertain nature of the lamp market and the need to make design improvements, Mr. Monroe had considered it unwise to make the large fixed-volume and design commitment necessary to secure Japanese production at a low cost. Recently, however, design maturation and cost competition had forced a reconsideration of the desirability of lamp importing.

In the area of new products, Mr. Monroe continued to believe that the best course to follow was to retain start-up and initial production in the Brooklyn plant until the design could be stabilized and some estimate of the demand was possible. Using this production strategy, original Tensor selling price would be based on eventual Japanese production costs rather than actual Brooklyn production costs. Tensor would make little or no profit on any new electromechanical product until production could be transferred to Japan.

RESEARCH AND DEVELOPMENT

Tensor's research and development was concentrated entirely in the hands of Jay Monroe. He had 10 other people working for him on development projects. Every couple of months Monroe made out a list of ideas that were of current interest to him. Then he and the development staff worked on that list until each item was either finished or discarded. The February, 1969 list, shown in Table 2, consisted solely of innovations concerned with tennis.

Mr. Monroe believed that Tensor's product development was less fruitful than would be possible if he could find a larger congenial staff

TABLE 2

FEBRUARY, 1969, R&D LIST

1. Improved tennis ball
2. Nylon tennis string
3. Deep groove in hardened frame
4. Flanged eyelets
5. Fiberglass racket
6. Stainless steel racket
7. "U" channel for aluminum racket
8. Lithographed nameplate
9. Box to hold string

Source: Company document.

to do development work. The general problem was that sophisticated research and development personnel often required the freedom to conceive and independently execute their own ideas rather than execute engineering details under someone else's direction. Mr. Monroe had found only one tool and model maker (known throughout the company as "Mac") who was a major help to him in his development work. Mr. Monroe stated the personality problem this way:

I know I don't have the easiest personality to work with, and many qualified applicants will not like development work at Tensor because of the way I run it. I do feel, however, that my talent is being underutilized, and that I could direct much more extensive development work.

By June of 1969 Tensor had completed all the projects on the February list except the "U" channel, which had been dropped, the fiberglass racket which was waiting for completion of final testing, and the improved tennis ball, which was still pending. The delay on the tennis ball was attributed to the inability to find a molding method which did not require a capital investment of $1 million or more. However, in

April of 1970, Tensor finally finished the design of a hairless rubber ball which had the characteristics on a cement or composition court that a regular tennis ball had on a clay court. Mr. Monroe had designed this ball in the belief that tennis had become too fast a game on nonclay courts and that his ball would allow a normal clay court speed on a non-clay court. The new ball could be mass-produced with less than $100,000 in equipment investment.

Tensor was uncertain about the company's ability to market tennis balls with such radical characteristics. Consequently, Tensor planned first to gain experience by introducing under the Tensor name a conventional tennis ball manufactured in Ireland.

Telephone Message Recorder. During early 1970 Tensor was also planning to announce the introduction of a $200–$250 (a firm price had not yet been decided) telephone message recorder. Jay Monroe had invented the recorder so that he would not have to take messages personally for his children when they were not at home. With his message recorder all he would have to do was turn on the recorder; it was designed so that it could be attached to his children's telephone, which had its own separate number.

The telephone message recorder consisted of a cassette recorder, a tape to give messages to the caller, a tape on which the caller can leave messages, and an automatic on/off mechanism. The breakthrough in the Tensor product was a low price achieved through simple design and the use of recent advances in the size and capability of cassette recorders. Tensor also planned to market a lower-priced model which would not include its own cassette recorder. Any tape recorder could be attached to this model.

The present message recorder market had four brand entrants. Three of those four were priced far above the Tensor level, and the fourth was a very recent entry priced at $150–$200.[2] Mr. Monroe was hoping that his latest product would have wide acceptance by individual consumers. Previous message recorders were used mainly by businesses. Exhibit 7 shows a photograph of a Tensor message recorder unit.

Mr. Monroe estimated the present message recorder market at $10 to $15 million annually and growing extremely rapidly. One question being debated by Tensor management in late 1969 was how to finance the introduction of the message recorder. Management estimated the

---

[2] This recent entry was imported from Japan and was roughly competitive with Tensor in its product characteristics.

Exhibit 7

TENSOR CORPORATION
Photograph of Tensor Telephone Message Recorder Unit

capital required at $1 million and was not anxious to jeopardize the existence of the company by risking internal operating capital. One possible solution was to form a majority-owned subsidiary and issue stock to the public. The subsidiary could then develop separate management and production facilities.

This strategy of public capitalization of the message recorder did not seem to Mr. Monroe likely to succeed, however, because of the lackluster state of the U.S. economy and the low level of the stock market in early 1970. An alternative to public capitalization was for Tensor to introduce the recorder over a period of time which would cause less financial risk. A slow product introduction would have less market impact but would allow Tensor to cut its losses earlier if the product was not accepted by the consumer. Under this alternative Tensor planned to manufacture the first recorders at the plant in Brooklyn. If the product were successful, mass production could be shifted to Japan to keep costs down.

Paddle Tennis Racket. In late 1969, Tensor began production on a paddle tennis racket. Tensor management predicted that this market, although only $50,000–$100,000 annually, would be highly profitable. Exhibit 8 is a photograph of the Tensor paddle tennis racket.

Exhibit 8

TENSOR CORPORATION

Photograph of the Tensor Paddle Tennis Racket

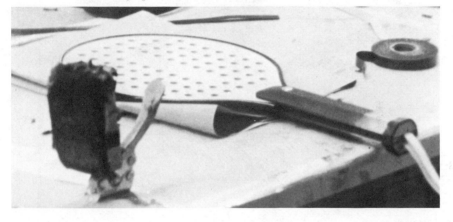

Sportsmen Inc. In order to expand into additional sporting goods areas, in February, 1970, Tensor acquired Sportsmen Inc., a small Long Island manufacturer of fiberglass billiard cues, archery sets, and fishing equipment. The Tensor 1969 *Annual Report* stated that Tensor planned "to utilize the sporting goods distribution channels we have established to increase the sales of Sportsmen's existing products while developing new products combining Tensor's technology and Sportsmen's manufacturing facilities." In particular Tensor hoped to employ the fiberglass manufacturing techniques which the president of Sportsmen had developed. Mr. Monroe believed that fiberglass usage in consumer products was expanding and that these techniques might be useful in any number of future Tensor products.

Sportsmen Inc. sales had previously been as high as $1 million, but lack of marketing expertise had resulted in a 90% sales decline and in unprofitable operation. Tensor purchased Sportsmen for approximately

Exhibit 9

TENSOR CORPORATION

Photograph of the Sportsmen Inc. Product Line

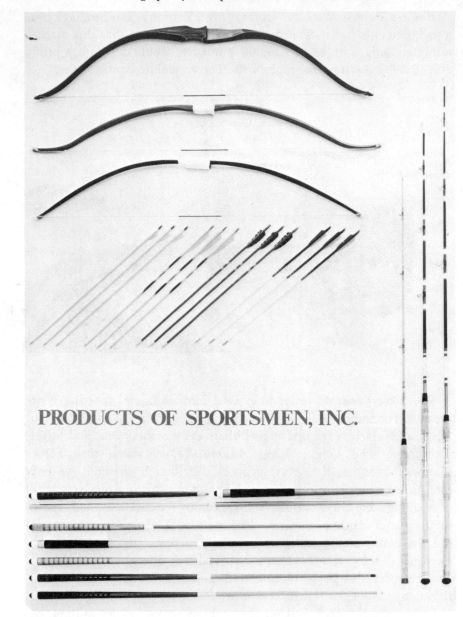

PRODUCTS OF SPORTSMEN, INC.

$15,000 cash and 5,500 shares of stock. Valuing Tensor shares at the closing price of $6.75 recorded on the purchase date, Tensor paid about $30,000 below book value. Exhibit 9 shows the Sportsmen product line.

As opposed to the 1960–67 period, when Tensor seemed content to confine new products to new lamp models, the 1969 approach was spread out in a number of diverse product areas.

ORGANIZATION

Tensor's organization at the end of 1969 was similar to its pre-expansion organization in 1964. It consisted of Mr. Monroe and one

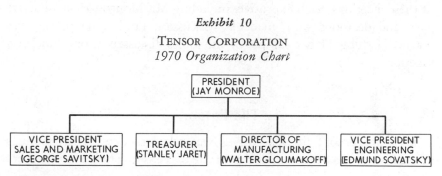

Exhibit 10

TENSOR CORPORATION
1970 Organization Chart

Note: All five executives served as Tensor directors.

executive each in marketing, finance, manufacturing and development engineering. Exhibit 10 gives the 1970 Tensor organization chart. These five executives had a five-year contract for compensation totaling $147,000 annually.

The interrelations among the five executives were frequent and informal. The financial job consisted of a preliminary financial profit forecast for the company derived from marketing and production estimates and a monitoring of operations to assure that the company was not below forecast.

Production scheduling was a combined effort of marketing and production. Marketing supplied forecasts and production scheduled on that basis. Marketing forecasts were continually revised on the basis of orders being received. Production, which was not set up to derive economies from long runs, was able to adjust rapidly to changes in demand.

The central coordinating device in the Tensor organization was the daily lunch meeting of the five top executives, which took place in the

Exhibit 11

TENSOR CORPORATION

Topics of Discussion at One Lunch Meeting in February, 1970

A recent speech by economist Pierre Rinfret
Tennis racket returns
Logo and printing on Tensor-marketed tennis balls
Sportsmen acquisition
Financing the message recorder introduction
Deciding where to invest development time
Trading-off risk and gain in development decisions
What the executives want to sell regardless of the return

company conference room. Almost all corporate decisions were made at these meetings. Each executive, including Mr. Monroe, took an active part, and decisions were made by discussion until a consensus was reached. Exhibit 11 is a sample of the topics discussed at one luncheon meeting.

The Future

Each of Tensor's five executives was asked to express his feelings about his job and his goals for the future of Tensor. Their answers were as follows:

JAY MONROE, PRESIDENT

I think of the whole company as a toy. My motive for establishing and operating Tensor is for the sheer fun of running it. I have no official duties of any kind and feel that management on a day-to-day basis is boring and not worth the time it takes.

I feel it is a tragedy that the present economic system has made my motivations unacceptable. Product decisions in the United States are being made more and more on the basis of return on investment. This means that industrial art and creative technical development suffer. The state of product development of consumer products would be higher if business were willing to make decisions on aesthetic rather than return on investment criteria. The creative guy wants to gamble, but the professional manager stifles him.

From my own point of view, I want to be able to produce a product I like even if it did not show any chance of an acceptable level of return. Above all, I don't want to have to take my ideas to a professional manager and have to convince him economically of the idea's worth. This may not be in the short-term best interest of the other stockholders, but I believe that the company will contribute better and more interesting products.

My goal for new products is to market only "classy" products which contribute to the image of the company. For instance, we could probably profitably expand into tennis clothes, but I am determined to avoid the bad image of the garment industry.

One element of management I don't like is the constant degradation of ethics necessary to restrain a competitive operation. It seems that no matter how low you sink, someone is always more unethical. This cycle is repulsive. For instance, kickbacks to marketing channels and questionable advertising claims may become increasingly necessary to continue to compete. I believe this practical necessity is unethical and very objectionable.

In terms of size, I am happy to have Tensor remain at its present volume. We have four other executives, all roughly the same age, who are content to spend their lives with this company. Perhaps we should grow enough to keep up with expanding wages and overhead, but I've experienced rapid expansion once, and I don't want to go through that again. In addition, any major expansion that required new equity would seriously endanger management control of Tensor's ownership.

STANLEY JARET, TREASURER

My goals from the company are a responsible position, a good living, security, and a job I can enjoy. I would like to see Tensor stabilize at around $6–$7 million sales. Any further increase would probably necessitate a major organizational change. I am content with the present arrangement and do not feel that the company needs to try to cope with an expansion larger than $3–$4 million.

One of my personal goals for the company is to assure that Tensor remains above break-even. If we can stay profitable, we substantially reduce the threat of takeover or insolvency.

GEORGE SAVITSKY, VICE PRESIDENT—SALES AND MARKETING

My job is to tear apart everything Jay wants to do and figure out what parts we can do and what parts we can't. The general pattern is his ideas and my exploitation.

As far as new products, I'd like to see more products which fit into our present channels of distribution. We have a fairly meager volume per store, and I would like to increase our worth to our distribution channels.

I would like to see steady growth for Tensor through product diversification. I don't believe I would enjoy the impersonality of a $50 million business, but I would like the excitement of a $20–$30 million company.

EDMUND SAVITSKY, VICE PRESIDENT—ENGINEERING

My greatest pleasure is to finally put a product into production after fooling with the design for a few months. I like sporting goods as a product area because the time from idea to market is exceptionally short.

My sales goal for the company is $10 million per year or a little over. I dislike emergencies and feel that a company that size is still small enough to be controlled. Also, I like the freedom I have to make decisions, and I believe that freedom would be impaired if the company grew too large.

WALTER GLOUMAKOFF, DIRECTOR OF MANUFACTURING

My objective for Tensor is profitability with a reasonable growth curve which would include diversification in products and in manufacturing assets. I am particularly fond of electromechanical consumer products. They represent more of a challenge than strictly mechanical products.

I would like to see Tensor achieve a sales level of $30–$50 million. At that volume production would be a lot more complicated. Production is always a rat race, but I love it.

Supplement: Tensor Corporation

The following article appeared in the January 8, 1970, issue of the evening edition of the *Boston Globe.* Additional information relating to the controversy described is included in Exhibits 1–3.

TENSORS'S FRIEND AT CHASE TOO FRIENDLY WITH ARABS[1]

NEW YORK—An advertisement bearing the headline "Tensor Corporation no longer 'has a friend at Chase Manhattan' " appears in today's edition of *The New York Times.*

Tensor's president, Jay Monroe, said in the quarter-page ad that the company would close out its account at the New York City bank whose slogan is, "You have a friend at Chase Manhattan."

Monroe, president of the company which manufactures high-intensity lamps and tennis rackets, said in the ad the action was being taken as a protest to reported efforts of Chase Manhattan's chairman of the board, David Rockefeller, and a former chairman, John J. McCloy, to induce President Nixon to reshape Middle East policies to mollify the Arab states because of what Monroe said was the bank's "considerable economic interests in the oil-rich region."

When informed of the ad's contents, Rockefeller issued a statement in which he said, "I believe, as I always have, that the United States must do everything it can to safeguard the security and sovereign existence of Israel.

"My sole interest," he added, "is in seeing that hostilities are ended and peace is achieved, a peace taking fully into account the legitimate aspirations of the parties involved."

Monroe, who is of Jewish origin, said in the advertisement: "Now Mr. Rockefeller has apparently decided it is best to put his mouth where his money is. I feel that turnabout is fair play. Accordingly, Tensor's account is being withdrawn from the Chase."

A source close to Tensor said the company maintained an account with the bank that was "in excess of $50,000." He said the cost of the ad was about $2,200.

Monroe said he based his statement about the Rockefeller's advocacy of a

---

[1] The *Boston Globe,* evening edition, January 8, 1970. Reproduced with permission.

new Middle East policy on a story in the Dec. 22 issue of *The New York Times*.

The *Times* article had reported that a group including Rockefeller and McCloy had discussed the Middle East political situation at an unpublicized meeting with President Nixon at the White House Dec. 9.

The article said: "According to officials familiar with the discussion, the consensus in the group was that the United States must act immediately to improve its relations with oil-producing and other Arab states. The group was said to feel this was necessary to deflect what the group feared to be an imminent loss of United States standing in the Middle East that might be reflected politically as well as in terms of American petroleum interests in the area."

Exhibit 1

TENSOR CORPORATION SUPPLEMENT
Article from The New York Times, *December 22, 1969*

U.S. POLICIES IN MIDEAST ARE UNDER FIRE
Industrialists Reported to Warn Nixon on Loss of Influence with Arabs
TAD SZULC

Special to The New York Times

WASHINGTON, Dec. 21—President Nixon is reported to have received warnings from a group of top American industry leaders with oil and other interests in the Middle East that the United States is rapidly losing political and economic influence in the Arab states because of its present policies.

The industrialists' concern over the deterioration of the United States position in the Middle East and over the proportional growth of the Soviet importance there—attributed by them in part to Washington's past support for Israel—was expressed at an unpublicized meeting at the White House on Dec. 9.

Bankers Attended

A White House spokesman has confirmed that Mr. Nixon had asked the group to discuss with him the "political situation in the Middle East." The members included David Rockefeller, president of the Chase Manhattan Bank; John J. McCloy, former president of Chase Manhattan, and Robert B. Anderson, former Secretary of the Treasury and a director of Dresser Industries Company, which has oil interests in Kuwait and Libya.

Administration officials said that the President had invited them to hear their views on the eve of the Dec. 10 session of the National Security Council, which was dedicated to a review of the United States policy in the Middle East.

Attending the industrialists' meeting with Mr. Nixon was Henry A. Kissinger, the President's special assistant for national security affairs. White House officials emphasized that those conferring with the President were "people with a political knowledge of the Middle East situation and the oil situation in the Middle East."

Exhibit 1—Continued

Action Was Urged

Administration officials declined, however, to disclose what specific advice the industrialists had offered Mr. Nixon and none of the participants were available today for comment.

According to officials familiar with the discussion, the consensus in the group was that the United States must act immediately to improve its relations with oil-producing and other Arab states. The group was said to feel this was necessary to deflect what the group feared to be an imminent loss of United States standing in the Middle East that might be reflected politically as well as in terms of American petroleum interests in the area.

The group was said to feel that United States weapons deliveries to Israel, including the recent shipment of supersonic Phantom jets, and Washington's alleged support of Israeli policies in the Middle East conflict were turning moderate and conservative Arab leaders as well as radical Arabs against the United States.

That basic evaluation was presented to Mr. Nixon early this year by William W. Scranton, former Governor of Pennsylvania, who toured the Middle East on a presidential mission.

But the increase in Middle East hostilities in the intervening period and the aggravation of the over-all situation had led a group of United States oil executives to submit a private memorandum to Mr. Nixon last September urging the preservation of American interests as a basis for the United States policy in the region.

The September meeting of oil executives was reportedly held in Beirut, Lebanon. Subsequent meetings were held in Beirut in October, informants said, and a session on Oct. 29 was attended by Mr. Rockefeller.

According to authoritative sources, Mr. Rockefeller then met with President Abdel Gamal Nasser of the United Arab Republic in Cairo on Oct. 31, to discuss the Middle East political situation along with some of the Chase Manhattan Bank's projects in Egypt.

Official quarters said that Mr. Rockefeller reported to the Administration at the time that President Nasser hoped the United States, through a change in its policies, could help him to become freer of the growing Soviet influence. The Soviet Union supplies most of the United Arab Republic's military equipment. The United States has had no diplomatic relations with Cairo since the 1967 Middle East war.

Others who conferred with Mr. Nixon on Dec. 9 have had direct communication with Arab leaders as well. Mr. Anderson, for example, talked with President Nasser and King Hussein of Jordan in Cairo last March.

It was this direct experience in the Middle East that, in the judgment of the White House, qualified these industrialists to present their views to Mr. Nixon.

However, officials said that the views expressed by the visiting group to the President were not mentioned directly when the National Security Council met Dec. 10 to debate the Middle East policy.

Authoritative informants said that the United States oil industry is concerned

Exhibit 1— Concluded

over the danger of Arab terrorist attacks on American petroleum installations and over the possibility that the greater British and French sympathies for the Arab policies may in time result in the erosion of the American oil presence in the Middle East.

Exhibit 2

TENSOR CORPORATION SUPPLEMENT
Advertisement in The New York Times, *January 8, 1970*

TENSOR CORPORATION NO LONGER "HAS A FRIEND AT CHASE MANHATTAN"

An Open Letter to the American Public:

It would appear that our neighborhood banker, who goes to great pains to tell us that he is our friend, has a rather narrow (mercenary) definition of the word friendship.

As reported in the December 22 issue of The New York Times, David Rockefeller, president of The Chase Manhattan Bank, and John McCloy, its former president, have warned President Nixon that U.S. policies in the Middle East are resulting in a loss of political and economic influence in the Arab world.

One must wonder how much Chase Manhattan's considerable economic interests in the oil-rich region figured in the decision to urge a new policy which would mollify the Arabs. Certainly world conditions do not indicate that such a change is in order. Israel is a truly democratic state, a modern oasis surrounded by feudal baronies. With the support of cynical Communists countries, the Arab chieftains have attempted to destroy Israel. With the moral support and material help of Americans, Israel has survived, so far.

Now Mr. Rockefeller has apparently decided it is best to put his mouth where his money is. I feel that turnabout is fair play. Accordingly, Tensor's account is being withdrawn from the Chase.

Ours is not one of the corporate giants, and no doubt Chase Manhattan will carry on very nicely without Tensor's business. But if others—small depositors and giant corporations alike—join in this protest against a "dollar diplomacy" based on oil interests, our former friends at Chase may learn that free men do not live by oil alone.

Sincerely,
JAY MONROE,
President
Tensor Corporation

Exhibit 3

TENSOR CORPORATION SUPPLEMENT
Article from The New York Times, *January 9, 1970*

DAVID ROCKEFELLER SAYS HE SUPPORTS SECURITY OF ISRAEL

David Rockefeller, chairman of the Chase Manhattan Bank, said yesterday that the United States "must do all it can to safeguard the security and sovereign existence of Israel."

Mr. Rockefeller said that his interest in Middle East issues was "in seeing that hostilities are ended and peace is achieved—a peace directly negotiated between the parties involved and taking fully into account their legitimate aspirations."

His statement followed the publication in The New York Times yesterday of an advertisement signed by Jay Monroe, president of the Tensor Corporation, manufacturer of high intensity lamps, asserting that the corporation "no longer 'has a friend at Chase Manhattan.'" The advertisement cited a dispatch in The New York Times Dec. 22 reporting that Mr. Rockefeller had been among a group of business leaders who met with President Nixon and warned that the United States was losing influence in the Arab states because of policies the Arabs felt favored Israel.

A spokesman for the Chase Manhattan Bank said Mr. Rockefeller's statement was in answer to the dispatch and not to the advertisement.

Mr. Rockefeller said he had been convinced during a recent trip to the Middle East that more and more thoughtful Arabs "appear disposed to explore reasonable compromises."

He said that in the meeting with the President, he intended "merely to suggest that the United States encourage these more positive and conciliatory sentiments."

Reached by telephone, Mr. Monroe said he was not a Zionist but supported Israel's "democratic position in the Middle East." He said he had withdrawn an account with a $250,000 line of credit from the bank.

7. Heublein, Inc. (A)

WITH GROWTH in sales and profits since 1959 far outstripping the liquor industry's "Big Four," Heublein, Inc., producer of Smirnoff vodka and other liquor and food items, had moved up to become the

TABLE 1*

Industry Rank in 1965	Company	1964 Liquor Sales (Millions)	1965 Total Sales (Millions)	Total Sales Gain 1959–65 (Per Cent)	Profit Gain 1959–65 (Per Cent)
1....	Distillers Corporation	$718	$1,005	37%	52%
2....	Hiram Walker	498	530	28	46
3....	National Distillers	430	829	44	24
4....	Schenley Industries (est.)	390	461	0	33
5....	Heublein, Inc.	123	166	89	259

* Derived from various company annual reports.

fifth largest liquor company in the United States by 1965. (See Exhibits 1 and 2 for Heublein financial statistics.)

Mr. Hart, Heublein's president since 1960 and a former executive vice president of international marketing for the Colgate-Palmolive Company, commented on the company's business as follows:

> Although liquor products account for most of our sales at the present time, we consider ourselves in the consumer goods business, not the liquor business. Liquor is a consumer good just like toothpaste and is sold the same way.
> To be successful in this business, you need three things: a good product, distribution, and advertising. You must have a good product. If you don't, the consumer will find you out and you will not get any repeat purchases. You also need good distribution, so the consumer will be able to get your product easily and conveniently. Finally, you must have a good convincing story to tell the consumer about why he should buy your product and you tell it through advertising.

In 1965, Heublein's management had three long-range goals: (1) to make Smirnoff the number one liquor brand in the world; (2) to continue a sales growth of 10% a year through internal growth, acqui-

241

Exhibit 1

HEUBLEIN, INC. (A)

Consolidated Balance Sheets as of June 30

(Dollars in Thousands)

Assets

Current assets:	1955	1960	1963	1964	1965
Cash	$ 2,298	$ 3,925	$ 2,744	$ 3,357	$ 3,338
Time deposits	...	...	6,000	1,750	...
Marketable securities	9	4,883	1,000	...	4,048
Investment in whiskey certificates	...	593	1,069	150	...
Accounts and notes receivable	5,157	12,426	17,835	18,668	19,010
Inventories	5,825	8,269	9,127	13,347	16.323
Prepaid expenses	297	382	356	325	548
Total current assets	$13,586	$30,479	$38,130	$37,597	$43,267
Long-term assets:					
Property, plant and equipment— net	$ 3,254	$ 5,793	$ 6,363	$ 7,339	$ 7,502
Deferred charges, other assets and goodwill	223	416	1,068	3,659	5,383
Total long-term assets	$ 3,477	$ 6,209	$ 7,431	$10,998	$12,885
Total assets	$17,063	$36,688	$45,561	$48,595	$56,152

Liabilities and Stockholders' Equity

Current liabilities:					
Notes payable to banks	$ 2,000	...	...	...	...
Accounts payable	687	$ 1,933	$ 2,078	$ 2,417	$ 3,584
Federal income tax	531	2,857	3,607	4,129	4,701
Accrued liabilities	513	2,688	4,044	5,175	5,774
Cash dividends payable	98	299	733	721	986
Long-term debt due within one year	301	631	777	850	1,013
Total current liabilities	$ 4,129	$ 8,408	$11,239	$13,292	$16,059
Long-term liabilities:					
Long-term debt due after one year	$ 4,699	$ 5,388	$ 3,239	$ 2,416	$ 1,403
Deferred federal income tax	...	...	154	248	316
Minority interest	...	...	...	272	...
Total long-term liabilities	$ 4,699	$ 5,388	$ 3,393	$ 2,936	$ 1,719
Stockholders' equity	8,235	22,892	30,929	32,368	38,374
Total liabilities and stockholders' equity	$17,063	$36,688	$45,561	$48,595	$56,152

Source: Heublein records.

sitions, or both; and (3) to maintain Heublein's return on equity above 15%.

Some industry observers, however, predicted a more normal growth rate for Heublein over the coming years because of the increasing competition from the four largest distillers in the vodka and other nonwhiskey markets from which Heublein derived the majority of its sales.

Exhibit 2

HEUBLEIN, INC. (A)

Consolidated Statement of Income for Year Ending June 30
(Dollars in Thousands)

	1955	1956	1957	1958	1959	1960	1961	1962	1963	1964	1965
Net sales................	$37,222	$68,543	$82,064	$87,839	$87,647	$103,169	$108,281	$116,142	$121,995	$135,848	$165,595
Cost of sales*...........	29,503	53,219	63,234	67,231	67,276	78,028	80,419	85,793	89,500	99,575	121,503
Gross profit............	$ 7,719	$15,325	$18,830	$20,608	$20,372	$ 25,140	$ 27,862	$ 30,349	$ 32,495	$ 36,273	$ 44,092
Expenses:											
Selling and advertising.............	$ 4,650	$ 8,013	$10,617	$12,613	$12,710	$ 14,276	$ 16,089	$ 16,444	$ 18,271	$ 20,477	$ 24,551
Administrative and general.............	1,479	2,288	2,699	2,822	2,561	2,783	3,205	4,111	3,710	3,485	4,257
	$ 6,130	$10,301	$13,315	$15,434	$15,271	$ 17,060	$ 19,293	$ 20,555	$ 21,981	$ 23,962	$ 28,808
	$ 1,590	$ 5,024	$ 5,515	$ 5,176	$ 5,100	$ 8,080	$ 8,569	$ 9,794	$ 10,514	$ 12,312	$ 15,284
Other†...............	$ 189	$ 316	$ 407	$ 519	$ 638	$ 293	$ 168	$ 199	$ (339)	$ (18)	$ (112)
	1,401	4,708	5,109	4,654	4,462	7,788	8,401	9,595	10,852	12,330	15,397
State and federal income taxes..........	733	2,531	2,697	2,524	2,399	4,232	4,587	5,188	5,830	6,516	8,021
Net income............	$ 667	$ 2,177	$ 2,411	$ 2,130	$ 2,063	$ 3,556	$ 3,814	$ 4,407	$ 5,022	$ 5,814	$ 7,376

* Cost of sales includes federal excise taxes on the withdrawal of distilled spirits from bond. For the fiscal year 1965, these totalled $90 million.
† Interest income, interest expense, and miscellaneous.
Source: Heublein records.

THE LIQUOR INDUSTRY[1]

Product. Ten categories of liquor (distilled spirits, excluding beer and wine) were listed by the U.S. Department of Commerce in 1964. Of these, five were whiskeys and five were nonwhiskeys.

Whiskeys	*Nonwhiskeys*
Straight	Gin
Blended	Vodka
Bonded	Rum
Scotch (100% imported)	Brandy
Canadian (100% imported)	Other (cordials, aperitifs, bottled cocktails, etc.)

The labeling of liquor products within these categories was subject to federal standards, as follows:

TABLE 2

Product	*Requirements*
Straight whiskey.......	Aged not less than 24 months in new charred-oak barrels; distilled from not less than 51% of the designated grain (corn,* rye, or wheat).
Bonded whiskeys.......	Straight whiskeys; aged at least four years; bottled at 100 proof; the product of a single distiller, a single distillery, and a single season and year.
Blended whiskey........	A mixture of two or more straight whiskeys.
Scotch and Canadian....	Aged not less than 24 months,† straight or blended; if blended, then designated as such.
Gin....................	No aging requirement;‡ at least 80 proof; containing the juniper berry flavor; made by direct distillation of mash or redistillation of distilled spirits.
Vodka.................	No aging requirement;‡ no distinctive character, flavor, or taste; approved by the federal government;§ usually made by filtering grain neutral spirits through activated charcoal.
Rum...................	Produced from sugar cane; no federal requirements regarding method of production.
Brandy.................	Obtained solely from the fermented juice, mash, or wine of fruit; distilled at less than 190 proof.‖
Other..................	Requirements depend on the product type.

* Of the straight whiskeys, 98% were bourbons distilled from corn.
† Usually aged four or more years.
‡ Gin and vodka were unique among the distilled spirits since they required no aging. The principal distinction between gin and vodka was that the juniper berry flavor was added to grain neutral spirits to produce the former, while as many flavor-producing ingredients as possible were filtered out from grain neutral spirits to produce the latter.
§ Federal requirements complex, but essentially as stated above.
‖ Usually produced from white grapes and bottled at 80 proof or higher.

---

[1] Several terms in common use in the industry require definition:

Proof is a term used to specify the proportion of alcohol in a product. The proof

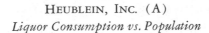

Exhibit 3

HEUBLEIN, INC. (A)

Liquor Consumption vs. Population

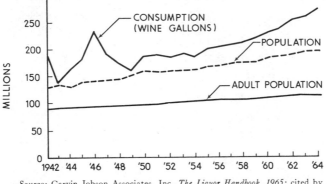

Source: Garvin Jobson Associates, Inc., *The Liquor Handbook, 1965;* cited by Glore Forgan, Wm. R. Staats Inc., in *Heublein, Inc.* (December, 1965).

Market. Between 1955 and 1964, U.S. consumption of distilled spirits increased from 199 million to 277 million wine gallons, or 39% (see Exhibit 3). By the latter year, some 60 million Americans—about 53% of the adult population—drank some sort of alcoholic beverage. These Americans spent about $6.5 billion for liquor, about one third of the amount spent for public elementary and secondary school education. Excise taxes[2] on these sales provided the federal government with about $2.5 billion in 1964, more than any other single source of revenue, except for personal and corporate income taxes. According to *Barron's,*[3] illegal distilling was increasing as a consequence of these taxes. In 1964, an estimated 50 million wine gallons of liquor was "bootlegged," representing about 18% of the 277 million wine gallons of legally produced liquor.

Rising sales of liquor could be attributed to various causes, including a rising population; increased personal discretionary income contributing to higher per capita consumption; changing social mores; the declining proportion of people in "dry" states; and changes in the population makeup by age groups.

number is equal to twice the per cent of alcohol (by volume) in the product. A *proof gallon* is any volume which contains the same amount of alcohol as a gallon of 100-proof spirits.

A *wine gallon* is a gallon by volume (regardless of proof). Thus, a gallon (five fifths) of 80-proof vodka would be one wine gallon but only 8/10 proof gallons.

[2] The federal excise tax on distilled spirits was $10.50 per proof gallon in 1965.

[3] Dana L. Thomas, "Flush of Success: New Competitive Spirit Has Given a Healthier Glow to the Distillers," *Barron's* (July 20, 1964), p. 3.

Exhibits 4, 5, 6, and 7 contain the best publicly available information on some of these trends. Mr. Edward Kelley, Heublein's executive vice president, cautioned that statistics about liquor consumption by demographic groups were not as dependable as for some other consumer

Exhibit 4

HEUBLEIN, INC. (A)

The Origins of Demand by Age Group

(Urban Family Expenditures for Alcoholic Beverages,* 1960–61)

SHARE OF MARKET PERCENT DISTRIBUTION

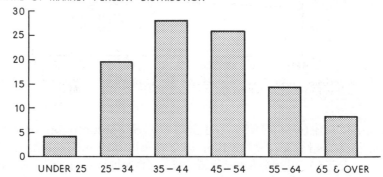

AVERAGE ANNUAL EXPENDITURES: DOLLARS

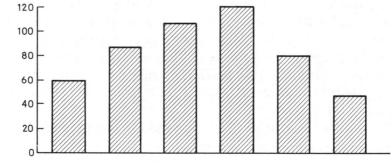

* Includes beer and wine.
    Source: Department of Labor; The Conference Board; cited by Glore Forgan, Wm. R. Staats Inc.,
in *Heublein, Inc.* (December, 1965).

goods. Mr. Kelley felt the growth in liquor consumption between 1955 and 1964 was primarily the result of the increase in per capita consumption, which appeared to be related to the growth in personal discretionary income, and the spread of drinking to more segments of the population and on more occasions, resulting from the trends of social living habits.

Predicting the future in relation to income and demographic changes, industry sources looked forward to an even faster growth in consumption from 1965 to 1970 than from 1955 to 1964: 4.5% or more a year, compared with 3.6%. Since the Bureau of the Census forecast that the 25 to 54 age groups would increase an average of nearly 17% between 1970 and 1980, many industry observers felt the picture beyond 1970 looked better than that between 1965 and 1970.

Market Changes. Demand for the various categories of liquor was changing as well as growing between 1955 and 1964 (see Exhibits 8, 9, 10, and 11). Thus there was a dramatic shift in consumer preference to straight whiskeys, imported whiskeys, and the nonwhiskeys, and away from the blended and bonded whiskeys. While some observers felt this represented a return to the pre-World War II relationship, which provided straight whiskeys with a slight edge over blended whiskeys, most industry sources felt the shift in consumption reflected a trend toward lightness in liquor taste. According to Roger Bensen:

The most probable reason [for the trend toward lightness] is that people drink mainly to satisfy social and status needs and for effect and not inherently for taste. The taste of many liquors is something which new drinkers find difficult to assimilate. Hence, they turn to various cocktails or mixed drinks to disguise the original flavor of the liquor product. And to complete the pattern, people achieve further fulfillment of social and status needs by using the newer, more current, more exotic liquors and cocktail formulations as a vehicle for their drinking.[4]

Exhibit 5

HEUBLEIN, INC. (A)

Total Population by Age

(Millions)

Year	Total	Under 15	15–19	20–24	25–34	35–44	45–54	55–64	65 and Over
1950	151.7	40.6	10.8	11.7	24.0	21.6	17.4	13.3	12.3
1960	180.7	56.1	13.4	11.1	22.9	24.2	20.6	15.6	16.7
1965	195.1	60.6	17.0	13.6	22.4	24.5	22.1	17.0	18.1
1970	211.4	65.7	18.9	17.1	25.2	23.0	23.4	18.5	19.6
1980	252.1	81.9	21.4	20.6	36.1	25.3	22.2	21.5	23.1

Per Cent Increase (Decrease)

1950–60	19.1	38.2	24.1	(5.1)	(4.6)	12.0	18.4	17.3	35.8
1960–65	8.0	8.0	26.9	22.5	(2.2)	1.2	7.3	9.0	8.4
1965–70	8.4	8.4	11.2	25.7	12.5	(6.1)	5.9	8.8	8.3
1970–80	19.3	24.7	13.2	20.5	44.8	10.0	(5.1)	16.2	17.9

Source: Department of Commerce, Bureau of the Census, figures updated as of July 9, 1964; cited by Glore Forgan, Wm. R. Staats Inc., in *Heublein, Inc.* (December, 1965).

---

[4] Roger Bensen, *Heublein, Inc.,* Investment Research Dept., Glore Forgan, Wm. R. Staats Inc. (December, 1965), p. 21.

Some of the most important of these changes are reflected in the following figures for distilled spirits entering trade channels:

TABLE 3*

Product Type	Volume (Millions of Wine Gallons)		Market Share (Per Cent)		Change in Volume (Per Cent)
	1955	1964	1955	1964	1955 to 1964
Whiskeys:					
Bonded	12.9	7.9	6.3%	2.8%	(39)%
Straight	46.1	69.6	22.7	24.3	51
Blend	81.5	74.7	40.0	26.1	(8)
Scotch	12.3	28.3	6.0	9.9	130
Canadian	9.2	17.2	4.5	6.0	87
Total all whiskey	161.5	197.9	79.5%	69.1%	22%
Nonwhiskeys:					
Gin	20.7	31.1	10.2	10.9	50
Vodka	7.0	28.1	3.4	9.8	302
Rum	2.7	5.9	1.3	2.1	119
Brandy	4.6	8.7	2.3	3.0	89
Other (cordials, etc.)	6.6	14.6	3.3	5.1	121
Total nonwhiskeys	41.8	88.4	20.5%	30.9%	111%
Total distilled spirits	203.3	286.3	100.0%	100.0%	41%

* For greater detail, see Exhibit 8.

According to many industry observers, one of the more important developments in the liquor industry between 1960 and 1965 was the growth of bottled cocktails. Although bottled cocktails had been on the market for over 50 years, they had shown little growth until 1960. In that year, Heublein, which had almost 100% of the market at that time, developed a new product formulation, package, and promotional campaign for its line of bottled cocktails. By 1965, volume had increased 100% to an estimated 1.9 million wine gallons, as Distillers Corporation, Hiram Walker, Schenley, and others entered the market. Nevertheless, Heublein, whose volume increased 60% during the period, still had 55% of the market in 1965. The convenience, low consumer price (only a few pennies more than comparable drinks mixed at home), and trend toward lightness caused one liquor authority to predict that bottled cocktails might represent close to 10% of the industry's volume by 1975.

Bulk imports were also expected to be an area of potential future growth. Bulk imports consisted of Scotch or Canadian whiskeys that were imported in barrels rather than bottles. They were then reduced to

Exhibit 6

HEUBLEIN, INC. (A)

The Origins of Demand by Income Class

(Urban Family Expenditures for Alcoholic Beverages,* 1960–61)

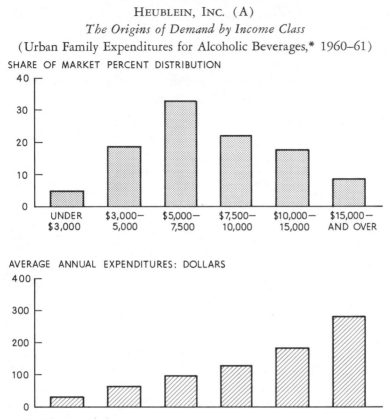

* Includes beer and wine.
Source: Department of Labor; The Conference Board; cited by Glore Forgan, Wm. R. Staats Inc., in *Heublein, Inc.* (December, 1965).

the desired proof by the addition of water and bottled in the United States. Since Scotch and Canadian whiskeys imported in bottles were taxed at a rate of $10.50 a proof gallon while the same whiskeys imported in barrels were taxed at a rate of $10.50 a wine gallon, bulk importing resulted in a tax saving of from $0.30 to $0.42 a fifth. This tax savings, coupled with lower transportation costs and reduced markups by the wholesaler and retailer, resulted in a price savings of as much as $1 per fifth to the consumer. Although the demand for bulk whiskeys increased during the early sixties, some bulk importers felt their gains were made primarily at the expense of American straight and blended whiskeys rather than the higher priced, bottled imported whiskeys.

Trends in Competition. Between 1955 and 1965, the majority of the companies in the liquor industry followed one of two broad strategies. Most of the medium-sized companies aggressively marketed their products in traditional ways. They did not increase, decrease, or change

Exhibit 7

HEUBLEIN, INC. (A)

Liquor Consumption

Wine Gallons

YEAR	TOTAL (Millions)	PER CAPITA	
		Total Pop.	Adults
1964	276.0	1.44	2.44
1963	259.0	1.38	2.32
1962	253.7	1.37	2.30
1961	241.5	1.33	2.21
1960	234.7	1.31	2.17
1959	225.5	1.28	2.12
1958	215.5	1.24	2.05
1957	212.1	1.25	2.03
1956	215.2	1.29	2.08
1955	199.6	1.22	1.95
1954	189.5	1.18	1.87
1953	194.7	1.23	1.94
1952	183.7	1.18	1.85
1951	193.8	1.26	1.97
1950	190.0	1.26	1.95
1949	169.6	1.14	1.76
1948	171.0	1.17	1.80
1947	181.7	1.27	1.94
1946	231.0	1.65	2.51
1945	190.1	1.44	2.23
1944	166.7	1.26	1.95
1943	145.5	1.09	1.68
1942	190.3	1.42	2.20
1941	158.2	1.19	1.85
1940	145.0	1.10	1.72
1939	134.7	1.03	1.62
1938	126.9	0.98	1.55
1937	135.4	1.05	1.67
1936	122.1	0.95	1.53
1935	89.7	0.70	1.14
1934	58.0	0.46	0.75

Source: Distilled Spirits Institute and U.S. Department of Commerce; cited by Gavin Jobson Associates, Inc., in *The Liquor Handbook, 1965.*

their product line, nor did they attempt to diversify out of the liquor business. None of these companies had a complete line of liquor products, and some had only one or two products. Several of these companies, however, experienced extremely rapid growth during this period. Their success could generally be attributed to having a leading product

Exhibit 8

HEUBLEIN, INC. (A)

Estimated Distilled Spirits Entering Trade Channels

Class and Type	1955 Gallons (Millions)	1955 Market Share (Per Cent)	1960 Gallons (Millions)	1960 Market Share (Per Cent)	1964 Gallons (Millions)	1964 Market Share (Per Cent)	Growth, 1964 from 1955 (Per Cent)
Domestic whiskey							
Bonded	12,869	6.3%	9,394	3.9%	7,911	2.8%	(38.5)%
Straight	44,838	22.1	58,939	24.6	68,802	24.0	53.5
Blend of straights	1,249	0.6	793	0.3	758	0.3	(39.2)
Blend of neutral spirits	81,494	40.0	74,074	31.0	74,731	26.1	(8.0)
Other	(449)	(0.2)	(119)	...	...	...	...
Total	140,001	68.9%	143,082	59.8%	152,203	53.2%	8.9%
Imported whiskey							
Scotch	12,284	6.0	20,585	8.6	28,249	9.9	130.5
Canadian	9,158	4.5	12,552	5.3	17,170	6.0	87.5
Other*	13	...	79	...	251	...	1,822.0
Total	21,455	10.6%	33,215	13.9%	45,670	16.0%	113.0
Total whiskey	161,457	79.5%	176,297	73.7%	197,873	69.2%	22.5%
Gin							
Domestic	20,447	10.1	22,001	9.2	28,963	10.1	41.5
Imported	291	0.2	1,149	0.5	2,167	0.8	645.0
Total	20,738	10.2%	23,150	9.7%	31,130	10.9%	50.0%
Vodka	6,968	3.4	19,406	8.1	28,130	9.8	304.0
Rum							
Puerto Rican, Virgin Islands	1,873	0.9	2,724	1.2	4,189	1.4	124.0
Other domestic	663	0.3	804	0.3	1,543	0.5	133.0
Total domestic	2,537	1.3%	3,528	1.5%	5,731	1.9%	126.0%
Imported	181	...	219	0.1	186	...	3.0
Brandies							
Domestic	3,726	1.8	5,300	2.2	7,575	2.6	103.0
Imported	893	0.4	1,163	0.5	1,113	0.4	24.5
Total	4,619	2.3%	6,463	2.7%	8,688	3.0%	88.0
Cordials and specialties							
Domestic	6,173	3.0	9,156	3.8	12,761	4.5	106.0
Imported	455	0.2	812	0.4	1,052	0.4	131.5
Total	6,629	3.3%	9,968	4.2%	13,813	4.9%	109.0%
Not elsewhere specified	178	...	342	...	750	0.3	320.0
Grand total	203,306	100.0%	239,373	100.0%	286,301	100.0%	41.0%
Total domestic	179,916	88.5	202,594	84.6	235,743	82.2	41.0
Total imported	23,390	11.5	36,779	15.4	50,559	17.7	121.0
Grand total	203,306	100.0%	239,373	100.0%	286,301	100.0%	41.0%

* Mainly Irish and Belgian.
Source: Distilled Spirits Institute: cited by Glore Forgan, Wm. R. Staats Inc., in *Heublein, Inc.* (December, 1965).

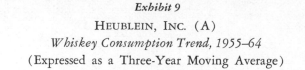

Exhibit 9

HEUBLEIN, INC. (A)

Whiskey Consumption Trend, 1955–64

(Expressed as a Three-Year Moving Average)

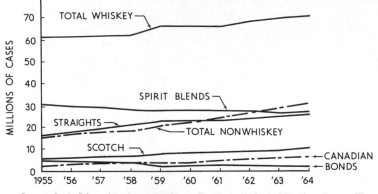

Source: Gavin Jobson Associates, *The Liquor Handbook*, *1965*; cited by Glore Forgan, Wm. R. Staats Inc., in *Heublein, Inc.* (December, 1965).

in one or two of the more rapidly growing segments of the liquor market.

The four major distillers also marketed their products in traditional ways. However, with the exception of Hiram Walker, each of these

Exhibit 10

HEUBLEIN, INC. (A)

Nonwhiskey Consumption Trend, 1955–64

(Expressed as a Three-Year Moving Average)

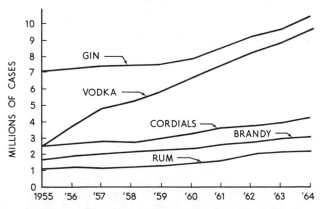

Source: Gavin Jobson Associates, *The Liquor Handbook*, *1965*; cited by Glore Forgan, Wm. R. Staats In *Heublein, Inc.* (December, 1965).

Exhibit 11

HEUBLEIN, INC. (A)

Projected 1968 Sales of Liquor

(Millions of Cases)

(Based on Extension of 1960–64 Sales)

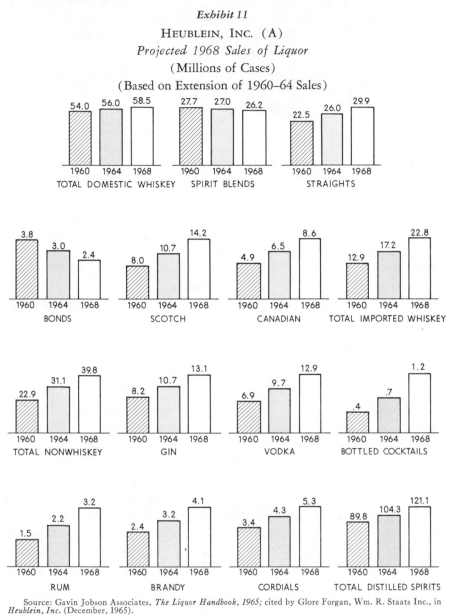

Source: Gavin Jobson Associates, *The Liquor Handbook, 1965;* cited by Glore Forgan, Wm. R. Staats Inc., in *Heublein, Inc.* (December, 1965).

companies attempted to diversify out of the liquor industry through acquisitions between 1955 and 1965. Even with this diversification, however, liquor accounted for the major portion of the sales of each of these companies in 1965. Moreover, with the possible exception of

National Distillers, the major distillers no longer seemed to be interested in further diversification outside of the liquor business in the middle 1960's. Rather they began to compete more vigorously in all segments of the liquor market during 1964 and 1965, particularly the more rapidly growing segments. This increased competition, coupled with the trend toward lightness, caused John Shaw of Equity Research Associates to predict that:

> Marketing efforts will become more consumer-oriented, stressing "appetite appeal" in much the same way as the food industry. Over all, advertising and promotional costs can be expected to trend higher, as brand competition remains intense.[5]

Thumbnail sketches of a few of the companies that have grown rapidly or that competed directly with Heublein are given below.

James B. Beam Distilling Company was a medium-sized liquor company that specialized in the production and marketing of premium Kentucky straight bourbon whiskey. Nearly 80% of Beam's $92 million sales in 1965 were derived from its Jim Beam brand, which was the second largest selling straight bourbon whiskey in the country. As a result of the expansion of the straight whiskey market, Beam was able to increase its profits by over 20% per year between 1953 and 1965.

Paddington Corporation[6] was the exclusive importer of J & B Rare Scotch whiskey, the number two brand of Scotch in 1964. Although J & B was Paddington's only product, the company sales and earnings growth were the highest in the industry between 1960 and 1964. In the latter year, Paddington earned 37.5% on its stockholders' equity, and gross sales reached over $125 million.

Distillers Corporation–Seagram's, Ltd., a Canadian-based corporation, was the largest worldwide producer and marketer of distilled spirits in 1965. Although 80% of Seagram's $897 million in 1964 gross sales came from whiskeys, the company also had a complete line of the nonwhiskeys. The breadth of its product line allowed Seagram's to take advantage of changing consumer preferences. Seagram's VO, for example, was the major recipient of the growing demand for Canadian

---

[5] John Shaw, "Trends in the Liquor Industry," *Equity Research Associates* (August 30, 1965), p. 6.

[6] Paddington Corporation was acquired by Liggett & Myers Tobacco Company in April, 1966. L & M also acquired Star Industries, a wholesale liquor distributor, liquor importer, and owner of 40% of Paddington's voting securities, at the same time. In 1964, Star's net sales (sales less federal and state excise taxes) were $82 million. During the same year, L & M had net sales of $293 million and total assets of $401 million.

whiskey. However, the company also changed old products or introduced new products in response to changing consumer preferences.
When sales of Calvert Reserve had declined for over seven consecutive
years, Seagram's replaced it with a restyled "soft whiskey," Calvert
Extra, in the spring of 1963, and experienced an immediate sales gain of
over 17%. In 1964, Seagram's withdrew Lord Calvert, a premium
blended whiskey, and replaced it with Canadian Lord Calvert, a moderately priced Canadian whiskey bottled in the U.S., to take advantage of
the trend toward bulk imports. In addition, Seagram's introduced nine
new liquor products between 1961 and 1964 to capitalize on the trend
toward lightness. Among these were two Scotches (100 Pipers and
Passport) and four liqueurs as well as a gin, a vodka, the first Hawaiian
rum, and a line of Calvert bottled cocktails.

Schenley, the fourth largest liquor company in 1964 with gross sales
of $406 million, had one of the lowest growth rates in the liquor
industry between 1955 and 1964. The company's gross sales decreased
about 3% during that period, even though Schenley had three of the
top 10 straight whiskey brands and had made several nonliquor acquisitions. However, in 1964, Schenley acquired Buckingham, the importer
of Cutty Sark, the number one brand of Scotch, and introduced a line of
bottled cocktails. As a result of these actions, several industry observers
were predicting a turn around at Schenley by 1967.

Methods of Distribution. Distribution of liquor took two basic
forms at the beginning of 1966. In 18 "control states," a state-regulated
agency was responsible for the distribution and sale of distilled spirits.
In these states, the marketer usually sold the product to the state agency
at the national wholesaler price and allowed the state to distribute the
products as it saw fit. These states often had laws which restricted the
type of point of promotion advertising that a company could undertake.
In the other 32 states, called "open states," distribution was accomplished through wholesalers who redistributed the product to the retailers who sold the product to the ultimate consumer. From 1958 to 1964,
the number of these independent wholesalers declined almost 43%, so
there were only 2,305 wholesalers left in 1964 who were licensed by
the Federal Alcohol Administration to deal in distilled spirits. This
trend, which was similar to that in other consumer product industries,
was primarily caused, according to industry observers, by a serious profit
squeeze on the wholesaler as his costs of operation increased while the
retail prices of inexpensive liquors declined because of intense competi-

tion—a situation which was aggravated by the spread of private labels. While distillers had not felt the effects of this squeeze by 1964, there was a feeling among some industry observers that distillers might have to lower their prices to wholesalers or lose lower volume lines if the trend continued.

Cost Structure. The cost of producing liquor products, excluding federal and state taxes on the raw materials, was relatively low compared to the retail selling prices. For example, high-quality vodka reportedly cost about 61 cents a fifth to produce, and retailed at $5.75. Federal taxes on raw materials (assuming an 80-proof product) were $1.68 per fifth. In addition, the costs of production, excluding federal and state taxes on raw materials, were often not much different for high-priced and low-priced liquors, even though they were often made by different processes. The different methods of production resulted in differences in taste and quality between the high-priced and low-priced liquors, however.

HEUBLEIN'S HISTORY

The House of Heublein was founded in 1859 in Hartford, Connecticut, by Andrew Heublein, a painter and weaver by trade. At that time, the House of Heublein was a combination restaurant, cafe, and small hotel. By 1875, Andrew's two sons, Gilbert and Lewis, were running the business. They branched out by conducting a wholesale wine business in addition to expanding the original operations. In 1892, through a combination of fortuitous circumstances, Heublein invented the bottled cocktail. From this time until the start of national prohibition, Heublein's principal business was the production and sale of distilled spirits.

In 1907, Heublein began importing Brand's A-1 steak sauce and later, when World War I disrupted the importation, acquired the manufacturing rights to the product in the United States. When prohibition forced Heublein to close down its liquor plant in 1920, the company transferred key personnel to food operations. Until the repeal of prohibition in 1933, A-1 steak sauce was Heublein's principal product.

In 1939, John Martin, Heublein's president and one of the company's principal stockholders, acquired the rights to Smirnoff vodka from Mr. Rudolph Kunett. Although Heublein sold only 6,000 cases of Smirnoff that year, a carefully planned promotional campaign, which was put into operation immediately after World War II, aided in boosting the sales of Smirnoff to over one million cases per year by 1954. As the vodka market expanded, Heublein introduced Relska vodka in 1953 and Popov in 1961 to have entries in the middle-price and low-price segments of the market.

Although Smirnoff's remained Heublein's principal product from 1959, when it accounted for over 67% of sales, to 1965, when it accounted for 51% of sales, Heublein began to diversify its product line and to expand its international operations in the former year.

Heublein used both internal growth and acquisitions to broaden its product line. In 1960, Heublein began a campaign to increase the sales of its bottled cocktails by introducing new kinds of cocktails and promoting the entire line more heavily. As Heublein's sales began to increase, other distillers, principally Distillers Corporation, began to market their own cocktails. By 1965, bottled cocktails sales exceeded 850,000 cases a year, more than double the 1960 sales. At that time, Heublein still claimed 55% of the market.

In 1961, Heublein made two acquisitions which strengthened its specialty food line. Timely Brands, which manufactured and marketed a complete line of ready-to-use, home dessert decorating products, including Cake-Mate icing and gels, was acquired in June. In July, Heublein acquired Escoffier, Ltd., of London, England, makers of 23 famed gourmet sauces and specialties.

Heublein made two more acquisitions during this period, both of which were designed to broaden and strengthen Heublein's liquor line. In April, 1964, Heublein acquired Arrow Liquors Corporation for an estimated cost of $5.7 million. Arrow's principal products were its line of cordials, including Arrow Peppermint Schnapps, Arrow Blackberry Brandy, and its domestically bottled, bulk-imported Scotch, McMaster's. According to Mr. Edward Kelley, the three principal reasons for the Arrow acquisition were that Heublein expected the cordial and Scotch markets to grow in the future, that Arrow had products that were among the leaders in these markets in the control states, and that Arrow had a small but extremely competent management.

In January, 1965, Heublein acquired Vintage Wines for approximately $2.2 million. Vintage, whose sales were about $4 million at the time of the acquisition, was integrated with the Heublein Liquor Division. Vintage's principal product was Lancers Vin Rose, an imported Portuguese wine that accounted for about 50% of the company's sales.

The expansion which occurred in Heublein's international operations consisted primarily of the establishment of franchise operations in 21 additional foreign countries. This raised the number of such operations from 11 in 1959 to 32 in 1965.

HEUBLEIN'S PRESENT OPERATIONS

Financial Situation. During the 1965 fiscal year, Heublein earned $7.4 million on sales of $166 million, which represented about a 19% return on stockholders' equity. Between 1959 and 1965, Heublein's sales growth, profit growth, and return on equity far exceeded the average of the four major distillers (see Table 1). In addition, even though Heublein was spending nearly twice as much (as a percentage

Exhibit 12

HEUBLEIN, INC. (A)

Heublein Sales Mix for Selected Years

Year	Smirnoff Vodka	Other Vodka	Total Vodka	Other Alcoholic Beverages	Food	Total
1965.........	51%	11%	62%	30%	8%	100%
1964.........	58	12	70	21	9	100
1963.........	62	12	74	16	10	100
1962.........	63	11	74	16	10	100
1961.........	64	11	75	19	6	100
1960.........	67	9	76	18	6	100
1955.........	61	2	63	32	5	100
1950.........	27	...	27	63	10	100

Source: Heublein records.

of sales) on advertising as the average of the four major distillers, and had increased the company's dividend payout ratio to 50% of earnings, the company had a cash flow of $8.6 million in 1965, about 22% on equity, which compared favorably to the 9% average of the four major distillers.

Product Line. At the end of 1965, Heublein was marketing well over 50 products through its four divisions. While vodka was the company's principal product, accounting for 62% of 1965 sales, the company's product base had been broadened considerably since 1960 by acquisitions, internal growth, and new marketing agreements (see Exhibit 12 for sales-mix trends). Heublein's product-line strategy was to market high-quality consumer products which provided the high margins necessary to support intensive advertising. Heublein aimed its promotions of these products at the growing, prosperous, young adult market. The company was also interested in phasing out some of its less profitable lines whenever possible.

The liquor products division accounted for over 80% of Heublein's 1965 sales. Its principal product was Smirnoff vodka, the fourth largest selling liquor brand in the United States in 1965, with estimated annual sales of 2.3 million cases. Company officials expected that Smirnoff, with its faster rate of growth, would move ahead of the third place brand (Canadian Club: 2.4 million cases) and second place brand (Seagram's VO: 2.5 million cases) within three years.

In 1965, Smirnoff had 23% of the total vodka market and outsold the second place vodka brand by over four to one. In addition, Smirnoff was the only premium-priced vodka on the market in 1965, since Wolfschmidt, formerly another premium-priced vodka, had lowered its wholesale price in 1964 in an effort to stimulate sales. After considering this action, Mr. Hart decided the appropriate response was to raise Smirnoff's wholesale price $1 per case and to put the additional revenue into advertising. Although Wolfschmidt's sales more than doubled, this increase appeared to come from the middle-priced segment of the vodka market, since Smirnoff's sales also increased 4% over the previous year and was running over 10% ahead in 1966. Smirnoff also appeared to be immune to the spread of the hundreds of private label vodkas, since company officials felt that these products obtained their sales from the 15% to 30% of the vodka market that was price conscious.

As a result, many industry observers expected Smirnoff to dominate the vodka market well into the future, particularly since Smirnoff could, on the basis of its sales volume, afford to spend $7 million to $8 million on advertising, while its closest rival could afford to spend only $2 million before putting the brand into the red.[7,8]

Relska, a medium-priced vodka, and Popov, a low-priced vodka, were produced and sold primarily to give Heublein's distributors a full line of vodka products. They accounted for 11% of company sales in 1965. They were cheaper to produce than Smirnoff but were not as smooth to the taste, according to company officials.

Heublein bottled cocktails sold an estimated 500,000 cases in 1965,

---

[7] Roger D. Bensen, *Heublein, Inc.,* Glore Forgan, Wm. R. Staats Inc. (December, 1965), p. 25.

[8] In 1963, according to the *Liquor Handbook,* Heublein spent $1.4 million to advertise Smirnoff, while total advertising for all other vodka brands during the same year was $1.2 million.

about 55% of the bottled cocktail market. Nevertheless, Heublein was beginning to receive competition from the national distilling companies, particularly Distillers Corporation, whose United States subsidiary, Seagram's, was marketing a similar line. Mr. Hart, however, welcomed this competition. He commented to the Los Angeles Society of Security Analysts in 1965:

> We believe the idea of bottled cocktails has not been completely sold to the American public. We were therefore delighted when we learned that one of the major companies in the liquor industry was introducing a new line of cocktails and that there would be heavy expenditures in advertising and merchandising to promote their usage to the public.[9]
>
> We are of the opinion that, as the cocktail market expands, our share will decrease, but Heublein cocktails will continue to be the leader, and that our sales will show remarkable increases.

Mr. Hart explained to the case writer that distribution was one of the principal reasons Heublein would keep its number one position:

> We secured distribution in 1960 when the other companies weren't too interested in cocktails. Since a distributor will usually carry only two or three lines, this means that he will have Heublein and Calvert or Heublein and Schenley: in other words, Heublein and somebody else. . . . In addition to being first, Heublein's wide line will also help us get and maintain distribution.

In 1965, Heublein's bottled cocktail line included Manhattans, Vodka Sours, Extra Dry Martinis, Gin Sours, Whiskey Sours, Side Cars, Vodka Martinis, Daiquiris, Old Fashioneds, and Stingers.

During 1964, the liquor products division reintroduced Milshire gin. For years, Milshire had been a regional gin selling about 100,000 cases a year. However, in 1963 the promotional budget was deemed sufficient to devote some real attention to Milshire. To prepare for this, the old inventory was sold off, the product was reformulated, and the package was redesigned. The principal difference in the product was that its botanical and aromatic content was lowered since it was filtered through activated charcoal in a process similar to that used to make Smirnoff. The net effect of this was to make the gin "lighter." Sales for 1964 increased to 150,000 cases, a significant jump, but still very far behind the 2.1 million cases of Gordon's, the leading brand.

In 1966, Heublein reached an agreement with Tequila Cuervo S. A. to be the exclusive U.S. marketer of Jose Cuervo and Matador tequilas and a cordial based on the same spirit. Heublein planned to market

---

[9] Heublein spent $2 million advertising its line of bottled cocktails in 1965. Seagram's spent $1.5 million advertising its Calvert line the same year.

these products on a nationwide basis through the liquor products division.

The liquor products division also marketed Harvey's sherries, ports, and table wines; Bell's Scotches; Gilbey's Canadian whiskeys; Byrrh aperitif wine; and the products of Vintage Wines, Inc.

The Arrow division accounted for about 10% of Heublein's sales in 1965. The division's principal products were Arrow cordials, liqueurs, and brandies, and McMaster's Scotch. Arrow's distribution system was particularly strong in the control states. In addition, Arrow's distribution in the open states was strengthened in 1965, when Heublein

Exhibit 13

HEUBLEIN, INC. (A)

Advertising Expenditures of Major Liquor Companies for 1965

Company	Advertising (Millions)	Sales (Millions)	Advertising as a Percent of Sales
Distillers Corp. Seagram's Ltd.	$43,750	$762,520	5.7%
Schenley Industries	23,100	380,200	6.1
National Distillers & Chemical Corp.	19,668	810,900	2.4
Hiram Walker	17,750	498,174	3.6
Heublein, Inc.	17,495	165,522	10.6

Source: *Advertising Age* (January 3, 1966), p. 46.

discontinued the production of its line of Heublein cordials and substituted the Arrow line.

Although the sales of the food division more than doubled between 1961 and 1965, it accounted for only 8% of the company's 1965 sales. Nevertheless, A-1 steak sauce was the company's number two profit producer in 1965, second only to Smirnoff vodka. Other food products included Cake-Mate icings and gels, Escoffier sauces, Grey-Poupon Mustard, and Maltex and Maypo cereals. In 1965, Heublein reached an agreement with the Costal Valley Canning Company of California to distribute and market Snap-E-Tom Tomato Cocktail. Snap-E-Tom was a tomato juice flavored with onion and chili pepper juices. It was designed for the pre-meal juice and the cocktail mixer markets, both of which had high profit margins.

Marketing. The case writer felt that Heublein's unique advertising and promotion policies and campaigns set Heublein apart from the other liquor companies (see Exhibit 13 for the advertising expenditures of various liquor companies). Heublein considered liquor to be a branded consumer product, and viewed itself as a marketer of high-quality consumer products rather than as a liquor company. As a result, Heublein developed intensive advertising campaigns to sell its products for the growing, affluent young adult market, since it believed it was easier to get a new customer in this market than to get a 40-year-old Scotch drinker to switch to vodka. Because of the importance attached to advertising, Heublein spent 10.6% of sales for advertising in 1965, nearly double the 5.7% of Distillers Corporation.

In addition, Heublein was an aggressive innovator among liquor industry advertisers. In the 1950's, industry self-regulation prohibited depicting a woman in an advertisement for a liquor product. In 1958, Heublein advised the Distilled Spirits Institute that it believed this ban on the portrayal of women was "obsolete, hopelessly prudish, and downright bad business." Finally the DSI agreed and Heublein became the first liquor company to portray women in its ads under the new DSI self-regulation, an advertising practice later followed by nearly every major distiller. Heublein also pioneered a change in DSI regulations to permit liquor advertising in Sunday supplements. At the end of 1965, Heublein was pushing for the use of liquor advertisements on radio and TV similar to beer and wine advertisements.

Another unique feature of Heublein's marketing was the promotions it used. These were designed to appeal to the young adult group and used celebrities and offbeat approaches to gain attention (see Exhibit 14). An example of this approach was the Smirnoff Mule promotion launched in May, 1965. The promotion, Heublein's largest for a single drink, was designed to catch the discotheque popularity on the upswing. The total investment was about $2 million for advertising, merchandising, and sales promotion. *The New York Times* commented that:

> Included in the Smirnoff advertising mix are a drink, called the Smirnoff Mule; a song and dance, called simply The Mule; a recording called Skitch Plays "The Mule"; a copper-colored metal mug in which to drink the Smirnoff Mule; and a recent phenomenon called the discotheque . . . the Gumbinner-North Company [Heublein's advertising agency] has recruited such vodka salesmen as Skitch Henderson, Carmen McRae, and Killer Joe Piro to put it over. . . . In addition to Smirnoff ads, The Mule will be featured in local advertising by the 7-Up people.[10]

Distribution.   Heublein sold its products directly to state liquor control boards in the 18 control states and to approximately 235 whole-

---

[10] Walter Carlson, "Advertising: Smirnoff Harnesses the Mule," *The New York Times* (June 27, 1965).

Exhibit 14

HEUBLEIN, INC. (A)

Smirnoff Mule Ad

THE SMIRNOFF MULE—SKITCH HENDERSON MADE IT A SONG. 'KILLER JOE' PIRO MADE IT A DANCE.

NEW DRINK...SMIRNOFF® MULE
It swings!

Taste the new party favorite that's sweeping the country, the swingingest drink since Smirnoff invented vodka. It's the Smirnoff Mule, made with Smirnoff and 7-Up®. Just pour a jigger of Smirnoff over ice. Add juice of ¼ lime. Fill Mule mug or glass with 7-Up to your taste. *Delicious!* Only smooth, flawless Smirnoff, filtered through 14,000 pounds of activated charcoal, blends so perfectly with 7-Up. That's why the fuel for your Mule must be Smirnoff! *It leaves you breathless.*®

SMIRNOFF VODKA 80 AND 100 PROOF. DISTILLED FROM GRAIN. STE. PIERRE SMIRNOFF FLS. (DIVISION OF HEUBLEIN). HARTFORD, CONN.

sale distributors in the 32 open states and the District of Columbia. Food products were sold through food brokers and wholesalers. It was Heublein's policy to strive to create mutually profitable relationships with its distributors. For example, one of the reasons for the creation of

Popov vodka was to give Heublein's distributors a low-priced vodka brand to sell.

International Operations.   At the end of 1965, Heublein was involved in three types of overseas activities. The largest and most important was its licensing operation. Distillers in 32 foreign countries were licensed to manufacture and market Smirnoff vodka. Among the countries in which Heublein had such franchises were Austria, Denmark, Greece, Ireland, New Zealand, South Africa, and Spain. When selecting a franchise holder, Heublein looked for a local distiller who had good production facilities and who was a good marketer in his country. Heublein felt this policy allowed it to get established faster than if Heublein tried to set up its own plant. Heublein also felt it improved relations with the local government.

Under these franchise agreements, the distiller produced the neutral spirits in the best way possible in his country. To maintain quality control, however, Heublein installed and owned the copper filtration units and shipped the charcoal to these locations from Hartford. This was done at cost. The contracts called for a license fee (about 10% of sales) and also stipulated that certain amounts be spent by the franchisee for advertising. Usually, during the first three or four years, Heublein would add its 10% license fee to these advertising funds in order to help build up the business. Plans were under way at the end of 1965 to begin operations in six more countries, including Ecuador, India, and Nigeria.

Heublein also exported Smirnoff, primarily to military bases overseas. In addition, Heublein opened an operation in Freeport, Jamaica, in 1965, to produce Smirnoff and other Heublein liquor products, and to market these products to customers such as ships' chandlers and diplomatic agencies who could purchase tax-free liquor.

Between 1961 and 1965, Heublein's export sales increased 99%, royalties from licenses 145%, and profits from international operations 458%. In 1965, net export sales stood at $1.2 million, and profits before taxes from international operations, including license fees, were $880,000.

Production.   At the end of 1965, Heublein owned and operated three plants throughout the United States, with an annual capacity of 20 million wine gallons for all product lines, and was building a plant in Detroit to replace the old Arrow plant. This plant was to cost $4.5 million and to have an annual capacity of 5.5 million wine gallons. When completed, this plant would give Heublein a total annual capacity of 25.5 million wine gallons. All these plants were highly automated.

Heublein had about 975 employees in 1965, of whom slightly less than half were hourly employees. In 1965, labor costs were only 3% of the total cost of sales.

Heublein did not produce the grain neutral spirits for its gin and vodka production, but rather purchased these requirements on contract and the open market from four distillers. Heublein maintained facilities in the Midwest for the storage of 8 million proof gallons, however, in case none of these suppliers could meet Heublein's stringent quality requirements. At 1965 consumption rates, this represented about a one-year supply.

According to Heublein, even the high-quality grain neutral spirits it received from its suppliers contained too many impurities for direct use in Smirnoff. The first step in Smirnoff production was, therefore, to redistill these grain neutral spirits. At the end of the redistillation, the alcohol was 192 proof. It was then blended with distilled water to reduce the mixture to 80 proof. This mixture was then filtered slowly through 10 copper tanks which contained over 14,000 pounds of activated charcoal. The filtering process required eight hours. According to company officials, it was during this process that the vodka became smooth and mellow and acquired its mild but distinctive taste. The only remaining step was to bottle the finished product, since vodka required no aging.

Heublein also redistilled the grain neutral spirits used in the production of its charcoal-filtered Milshire gin. However, the company did not redistill the liquors (purchased on the open market) used in the production of Heublein cocktails.

Most of the food products were manufactured at Hartford or at the plant in Burlington, Vermont. Heublein insisted on the same high-quality standards in the purchase of raw materials and production of its food products that it required in its liquor production.

8. Heublein, Inc. (B)

HAVING ACQUIRED four companies during the past six years (both Timely Brands and Escoffier, Ltd., in 1960—manufacturers and marketers of specialty food products; Arrow Liquors Corporation in 1964; and Vintage Wines in 1965),[1] Heublein's management at the end of 1965 expressed continued interest in further acquisitions.

The kinds of companies being sought were not just profitable financial deals, but rather firms in which Heublein's management believed it could improve operations. Heublein's acquisition policies were explained more fully by Mr. Ralph Hart, Heublein's president, in a 1965 presentation before the Los Angeles Society of Security Analysts:

> Frankly, we take a long hard look at any potential acquisition. We ask ourselves: "Will the new product or company we acquire have a potential at least equal to existing Heublein products, in order not to dilute present equity? Will new products lend themselves to our channels of distribution and marketing techniques? Will these products have sufficient gross margin to allow for our type of distribution, advertising, and merchandising?"

THE PROPOSED HAMM ACQUISITION

Early in the fall of 1965, Heublein's top management was seriously considering the possible acquisition of the Theo. Hamm Brewing Company. They were particularly interested because they felt Hamm's could profit immensely from what they felt was Heublein's major strength—the ability to market a consumer product extremely well. If the acquisition were consummated, Heublein would become the first company to engage in the production and sale of both beer and liquor.

Under the proposed agreement Heublein would acquire all of the outstanding shares of Hamm's common in exchange for 420,032 shares of Heublein's 5% preferred, and 200,031 shares of Heublein's 5% convertible preferred. Both preferreds had a par value of $100; the latter was convertible into three shares of Heublein common, subject to certain provisions against dilution of earnings. Although Hamm's stock was held by a family group and did not have a market price, Heublein's board estimated that the aggregate fair value was in excess of $62

---

[1] For further particulars, see Heublein, Inc. (A).

million, or book value (see Exhibit 1). The proposed agreement stipulated that each class of preferred would have the right to elect one member to Heublein's board. In addition, it was provided that the $25 million of securities indicated on the Theo. Hamm Brewing Company consolidated balance sheet as of 9/30/65 would be liquidated and used to buy out dissident Hamm's stockholders prior to the acquisition by Heublein. This would have the effect of reducing Hamm's working capital and stockholder equity before the purchase by about $25 million.

Exhibit 1

HEUBLEIN, INC. (B)

Theo. Hamm Brewing Company Consolidated Balance Sheets
(Dollars in Thousands)

	Nov. 30, 1964	Sept. 30, 1965
Current assets:		
Cash..	$ 3,475	$ 3,153
Certificates of deposit.............................	2,000	500
Commercial paper and marketable securities (at cost)*...	26,560	24,044
Accounts receivable (net).........................	5,452	7,959
Inventories...................................	5,352	6,479
Prepaid expenses...............................	898	891
Total current assets.......................	$43,737	$43,027
Investments and other assets.......................	6,467	6,536
Property, plant, and equipment (net)...................	26,381	26,930
	$76,585	$76,493
Current liabilities:		
Trade accounts payable............................	$ 2,639	$ 2,926
Salaries and wages...............................	1,207	1,304
Customers' deposits..............................	932	1,151
Miscellaneous accounts payable and accrued expenses....	470	1,301
Taxes other than taxes on income.....................	2,038	2,299
Federal and state taxes on income....................	2,657	2,559
Dividends payable...............................	1,538	660
Sinking fund deposits due in one year.................	100	100
Total current liabilities.....................	$11,580	$12,302
Eight per cent debenture bonds......................	1,400	1,400
Stockholders' equity		
Capital stock..................................	55,083	26,432
Capital surplus.................................	. . .	26,273
Earned surplus.................................	8,521	10,086
	$76,585	$76,493

* The market value of these securities was $28.1 million in 1964 and $25.7 million in 1965.
Source: Heublein acquisition study.

Hamm's History and Competitive Position.   Hamm's was a family-owned brewing company. During the five years preceding the proposed acquisition, sales and profits had remained relatively stable (see Exhibits 2 and 3). However, since industry sales had increased slightly more

Exhibit 2

HEUBLEIN, INC. (B)

Theo. Hamm Brewing Company Consolidated Statement of Income

(Dollars in Thousands)

	Years Ended November 30					Ten Months Ended September 30 (Unaudited)	
	1960	1961	1962	1963	1964	1964	1965§
Revenues:							
Sales less allowances	$119,881	$115,874	$114,885	$119,584	$124,233	$106,109	$109,449
Interest	161	240	270	575	958	748	941
Dividends	81	62	50	51	61	58	42
Other	283	95	175	196	351	301	359
	$120,407	$116,272	$115,380	$120,405	$125,602	$107,217	$110,791
Costs and expenses:							
Cost of goods sold*	89,843	86,314	86,595	90,878	95,388	81,004	84,597
Selling, delivery, advertising, general and administrative expenses	16,263	17,065	16,200	18,534	21,423	18,196	19,026
Interest:							
Long-term debt	235	164	120	120	120	100	100
Other	8	159	2	16	13	12	...
	$106,349	$103,702	$102,918	$109,548	$116,945	$99,312	$103,723
Earnings before taxes on income	$14,057	$12,570	$12,462	$10,857	$8,657	$7,905	$7,068
Taxes on income:							
Federal	6,750	6,150	6,100	5,100	3,900	3,550	3,000
State	450	400	400	275	300	275	225
	$7,200	$6,550	$6,500	$5,375	$4,200	$3,825	$3,225
Net earnings (excluding the operations of the Eastern division and related distributing subsidiaries)	$6,857	$6,020	$5,962	$5,482	$4,457	$4,080	$3,843
Loss on operations of Eastern division and related distributing subsidiaries less applicable income tax benefits†	1,092	1,717	2,124	1,408	...	...	...
Net earnings	$5,765	$4,303	$3,838	$4,074	$4,457	$4,080	$3,843
Preferred stock dividend requirements	210	210	210	210	210	175	142
Earnings applicable to common stock	$5,555	$4,093	$3,628	$3,864	$4,247	$3,905	$3,701
Per common share (dollars) earnings applicable to:							
Common stock‡	$2.14	$1.57	$1.40	$1.49	$1.63	$1.50	$1.40
Cash dividends declared	...	...	0.40	0.95	1.25	0.50	0.75

* Cost of goods sold includes federal and state excise taxes of between $32 and $38 million for each of the above periods.
† In 1960, the company acquired brewing facilities in Baltimore, Maryland, which were sold in 1963 for $6 million, the approximate net carrying amount of the facilities. Applicable income tax benefits ranging between $1.2 and $2.1 million have been netted against loss on operations of Eastern division and related distributing subsidiaries for the years 1960–63 inclusive.
‡ Earnings applicable to common stock are based on the number of shares outstanding at the end of each period as adjusted for the recapitalization during the year ended November 30, 1961.
§ Earnings for the 10 months ended September 30, 1965, were adversely affected by nonrecurring legal and centennial expenses aggregating approximately $400,000.
Source: Heublein acquisition study.

Exhibit 3

HEUBLEIN, INC. (B)

Heublein, Inc., and Theo. Hamm Brewing Company
Pro Forma Combined Statement of Income
(Dollars in Thousands)

	June 30, 1960 / Nov. 30, 1960	June 30, 1961 / Nov. 30, 1961	June 30, 1962 / Nov. 30, 1962	June 30, 1963 / Nov. 30, 1963	June 30, 1964 / Nov. 30, 1964	Ten months to Sept. 30, 1965
Heublein						
Hamm						
Net sales	$223,050	$224,156	$231,027	$241,579	$260,082	$249,056
Cost of sales	$167,872	$166,732	$172,389	$180,378	$194,963	$187,059
Selling, general and administrative expenses	33,323	36,359	36,755	40,515	45,385	43,164
Other income (deductions):						
Interest and dividend income	352	417	444	865	1,287	1,217
Interest expense	(560)	(595)	(363)	(344)	(342)	(215)
Miscellaneous—net	198	85	93	503	308	320
	$ (10)	$ (93)	$ 174	$ 1,024	$ 1,253	$ 1,322
Income before income taxes	$ 21,845	$ 20,972	$ 22,057	$ 21,710	$ 20,987	$ 20,155
Provision for income taxes	11,432	11,137	11,688	11,205	10,716	9,966
Net income before loss on discontinued operations of Hamm	$ 10,413	$ 9,835	$ 10,369	$ 10,505	$ 10,271	$ 10,189
Loss on discontinued operations of Hamm, less applicable income tax benefits	1,092	1,717	2,124	1,408	. . .	. . .
Net income	$ 9,321	$ 8,118	$ 8,245	$ 9,097	$ 10,271	$ 10,189
Deduct pro forma adjustments:						
Interest and dividend income	219	275	290	591	981	950
Interest expense	1,209	983	975	501	122	85
Income taxes	(738)	(638)	(652)	(549)	(496)	(418)
	$ 690	$ 620	$ 613	$ 543	$ 607	$ 617
Pro forma net income	$ 8,631	$ 7,498	$ 7,632	$ 8,554	$ 9,664	$ 9,572
Preferred dividend requirements:						
Heublein:						
5% preferred stock	$ 2,100	$ 2,100	$ 2,100	$ 2,100	$ 2,100	$ 1,750
5% convertible preferred stock	1,000	1,000	1,000	1,000	1,000	833
	$ 3,100	$ 3,100	$ 3,100	$ 3,100	$ 3,100	$ 2,583
Pro forma earnings applicable to common stock	$ 5,531	$ 4,398	$ 4,532	$ 5,454	$ 6,564	$ 6,989
Pro forma earnings per share (dollars):						
Assuming no conversion of convertible preferred stock	$ 1.15	$ .91	$ .93	$ 1.12	$ 1.37	$ 1.43
Assuming full conversion of convertible preferred stock	1.21	1.00	1.01	1.18	1.40	1.43
Actual Heublein earnings per share*	0.74	0.79	0.91	1.03	1.21	1.30

* Heublein shares outstanding in June of 1965, 4.9 million; approximate market price/share in 1965 (to September) $26–$27

Source: Heublein acquisition study.

than 11% during this period, Hamm's market share had declined from 4.5% to 3.7%. In addition, Hamm's return on sales had lagged behind the industry leaders (see Exhibits 4, 5, and 6).

Exhibit 4

HEUBLEIN, INC. (B)

Beer: Larger Markets, Tougher Competition*

The bigger it gets, the rougher it gets. That sums up the brewing industry, which has just had its best year ever. But no one brewer had an easy time of it, and the competition will get even stiffer in the years ahead.

by Kenneth Ford, Managing Editor

No one in the brewing industry had anything but kind words last week for the nation's growing number of young adults.

Not only were they quaffing their share of brew and more besides, but even more significant, they appeared willing to cast aside some old-fashioned concepts about beer being a "blue-collar" drink.

For the nation's 190 brewers (four fewer than the year before) the moral was that patience pays off. All during the long, dry decade of the Fifties the industry watched total consumption lag behind population growth and per capita consumption remain static at a low level. Brewers pinned their hopes on the vast crop of war babies of the Forties, hoping that when they reached drinking age they would set off a beer boom, but also fearing they might move from the innocence of Coke to the decadence of Martinis in one easy step.

They didn't. When the 1963 figures were totaled up at this time last year, there were clear signs that the brewing industry was on the move at last. No one outside the industry realized how fast it was moving until the 1964 totals came in last month.

The results: total sales (consumption) climbed to 98.5-million barrels, up five per cent from 1963's 93.8-million barrels. Per capita consumption, the more meaningful measure of marketing effectiveness, jumped to 15.7 gallons, up 2.6 per cent from 1963's 15.3 gallons. Both gains were the best year-to-year increase posted by the industry since 1947.

It is a certainty that the industry will cross the 100-million barrel barrier in 1965. The only question is whether it will reach 101-million or 102-million barrels. No one will be unhappy if it doesn't go that high—the industry's most optimistic forecasters hadn't expected it to reach the 100-million barrel level until 1967.

But though the overall industry outlook is sudsy, neither leaders nor laggards are finding it easy selling.

Competition has never been fiercer. The nation's top ten brewers have staked out 57.7 per cent share of the total market, selling 56.6-million barrels of that 98.5 million total. The next 14 ranking brewers take 25.4 per cent of the total, or 25-million barrels. All together, the top 24 brewers, each doing better than one-million barrels apiece, account for 82.9 per cent of total sales, some 81.6-million barrels.

---

* *Printers' Ink* (Feb. 12, 1965). Reproduced by permission.

Exhibit 4—Continued

But even what would be a normally respectable gain was not enough to hold the previous year's position, much less advance, in the top 24 standings.

LOSSES AND GAINS

Carling dropped in 1964 from fourth to fifth; Hamm from seventh to eighth; Rheingold from tenth to 11th; Lucky Lager from 13th to 16th; Pearl from 17th to 18th; Narragansett from 19th to 21st and Jackson from 23rd to 24th. Yet five had made sales gains—Carling's posted a 1.7 per cent increase; Rheingold a 3.1 per cent increase; Pearl a 5.4 per cent increase; Narragansett a 2.8 per cent increase; and Jackson a 2.2 per cent increase.

The leading brewers had set such a blistering pace that merely running to keep up just wasn't fast enough.

First-place Anheuser-Busch (Budweiser–Busch Bavarian–Michelob) achieved a 10.1 per cent gain that carried it across the ten-million-barrel level, an industry record, and gave it a 10.5 per cent share of the total market. A–B phenomenal performance was the culmination of marketing programs set in motion as long as a decade ago. Basically, these concentrated on development of marketing executives, achieving the best possible communication with its 900 wholesalers throughout the country and expanding plants into growing markets. (Its new Houston brewery will be ready next year.)

Though A–B is one of the heaviest advertisers in the industry, it makes only evolutionary changes in its advertising program from year to year. "Where There's Life There's Bud" (1963) became "That Bud, that's beer" (1964) and now becomes "It's Worth It, It's Budweiser" (1965).

Expansion-minded Schlitz, eyeing the heavier-beer-drinking Canadian market (per capita consumption 16.4 gallons) tried to migrate north by buying control of Canada's Labatt Brewing, but found itself ensnarled in antitrust actions and other legal complications. The time and attention it had to devote to these were reflected in only a 5.3 per cent gain, in contrast to 1963's 13 per cent gain.

Another 11.6 per cent gain like the one Pabst made last year might well knock Schlitz out of second-place. And fast-rising Falstaff is a factor that Schlitz and Pabst marketing executives both must reckon with in the year ahead.

Falstaff surprised everyone by clipping Carling out of fourth place in the brewing industry. Carling had made sixteen consecutive sales gains that brought it up from 19th in the industry and was generally conceded to be the brewer to watch. Controlled by Canadian entrepreneur E. P. Taylor, its marketing strategy is based on two rules: build plants where the markets are growing (it now has nine in the U.S.) and advertise heavily.

But it was Falstaff's ambition and innovation that carried it ahead. It markets only one brand of beer, Falstaff, in 32 states westward from Indiana. These states have 45 per cent of the nation's population but consume less than 45 per cent of total beer production.

A COMPETITOR TO RESPECT

"If we were in the other 18 states, we'd be selling 10.5-million barrels instead of 5.8-million," says George Holtman, vice president, advertising. Holtman's

Exhibit 4—Continued

boast is not idle. That Falstaff is a competitor to respect is attested to by Hamm's decline of 2.5 per cent. Both collided competitively in the Midwest generally and the Chicago market in particular. Falstaff began moving into Chicago three years ago and the 1964 figures reflect its arrival. Similarly, it began moving into the West Coast in recent years where traditional beer sales patterns are changing, too. Lucky Lager, long the leading West Coast brand, slumped 15.1 per cent, dropping below the two-million barrel level under the impact of competition from Falstaff and other interloping brewers. Among them: the Schlitz–Burgemeister brand team, Falstaff, Budweiser, and Carling. The latter is going to build its own brewery in the San Francisco area, which should make conditions in the important California market (it accounts for about 7.5 per cent of total consumption alone) even more competitive.

But the moral is not that the big bad national brands come in and knock off the poor little locals. Washington-based Olympia, strong in the Northwest, and Denver-based Coors both are making significant progress on the West Coast. Olympia scored a 22.1 per cent increase, and Coors, long the strong man of the Rocky Mountain empire, boosted advertising budgets by 11 per cent and barged into California. Result: a 12 per cent sales increase.

In the big New York market it was a locally-based brewer that led the pack—Brooklyn's F&M Schaefer Brewing. Schaefer soared to 4,250,000 barrels up 10.1 per cent, while Newark-based Ballantine dropped 3.9 per cent and Rheingold, up 3.1 per cent, slipped out of the top ten and found its claim to being top brand in the New York metropolitan area under severe pressure.

Ballantine, long handled by the Wm. Esty Co., is now looking for a new advertising agency. Rheingold, sold by the Liebmann family to Pepsi-Cola United Bottlers, switched agencies again. In recent years it has gone from Foote Cone & Belding to J. Walter Thompson, back to FCB, and is now at Doyle Dane Bernbach. Rheingold, under the aegis of its new management, reportedly was moving ahead at year's end behind a barrage of television and radio spots.

COMPETITION KEEN IN EAST, TOO

Throughout the East, competition was similarly strong. Philadelphia-based Schmidt (Schmidt–Prior–Valley Forge) gained 13.3 per cent, Baltimore-based National climbed 21.5 per cent, and Manhattan-based Ruppert, strong in New England, moved ahead 22.5 per cent. Rochester-based Genessee (up 20.2 per cent) cemented its already strong position in upstate New York.

One result of this fierce competition was increased ad budgets. With most brewers offering what economists call "poorly differentiated products"—i.e., sameness—images were the most important function in marketing. Most brewers in *Printers' Ink's* annual marketing survey, of course, declined to give data on ad expenditures, though a few admitted increases ranging from four to six per cent. However, the industry operates on a so-much-per-barrel basis in its ad budgeting. *Printers' Ink's* study of beer advertising expenditures (October 2, 1964, page 25) found the industry average was 96-cents a barrel for the four measured media. This would put total spending in a 98.5-million barrel year at $94.4-million in those media. This, however, is only about one-third of total expenditures. Big chunks of money go for "rights" to broadcast sports events, a

Exhibit 4—Continued

staple of beer marketing. For instance, Schlitz, now building a new brewery in Texas, paid out $5.3-million for rights to the Houston Colts games.

"It's all part of becoming a new resident of the area," a Schlitz spokesman explained. "We want to get known fast and this is how you do it."

So important are sports sponsorships that they significantly influence marketing strategy. For example, Schmidt's bought the old Standard Beverage plant in Cleveland from Schaefer (which then bought the old Gunther plant in Baltimore from Hamm). Schmidt originally intended to use the Cleveland brewery to supply its markets in Western Pennsylvania and Western New York state and had no immediate intention of entering the northeastern Ohio market. But the opportunity arose to buy a participation in radio-sponsorship of the Cleveland Browns' games. Schmidt's bought it and entered the market immediately.

CAN U.S. COMPETE ABROAD?

For the past few years, American brewers have enviously watched the success of imported European beers in the U.S. The European imports sell less than one per cent of the total sold in the U.S. but their profit margins are far better than the domestic brewers achieve on a unit basis. Would the same not hold true for U.S. and Canadian beers overseas? It is also a way to rise above the cannibalistic competition in the U.S. The other way is to increase the beer consumption of the American drinker. Though 1964's 3.3 per cent increase in per capita consumption was the best in recent years, the industry lags far behind the high of 18.7 gallons set in 1945 or even the postwar 18.4 gallons quaffed in 1947.

New products may help. Schlitz, Pabst and National are now strongly promoting malt liquor brands. A–B's Michelob and Hamm's Waldech in the super-premium class are upgrading beer's image and adding a new group of customers.

But it is a packaging development that may be of the most far-reaching significance. This is the home keg or draft beer that fits neatly into the family refrigerator. In the consumption battle, beer's increase in share must come from soft drinks, coffee, tea, and such—not merely from population growth or competitors' customers.

In the decade ending in 1963, beer consumption increased only 12 per cent while the population grew 19 per cent. Soft drinks shot up 48 per cent, soluble coffee 158, and tea 20 per cent.

The confirmed beer drinker guzzles about six quarts a week on a yearly averaged-out basis. That's about two and a half 12-ounce cans at a time.

What the industry must attract is the glass-at-a-time sipper. That's not much at a time, but there are an awful lot of them and enough sips by enough people can boost beer back near the 20 gallons per capita consumption level of pre-World War I days.

It will take a revolution in American beer-drinking patterns to do it, but it could happen.

BEER: A REVOLUTION IN DRINKING?

Beer's flat consumption curve may get the upward kick it needs from the new refrigerator keg that the man in the picture is "pulling."

Exhibit 4—Continued

Some brewers privately hail it as the most significant development in beer marketing in the postwar era. They think a keg of draft beer in the family refrigerator can't help but cause a gusty increase in per capita consumption.

Units like the one above have been in test markets for more than two years now, and indications are that a rush into this type of packaging is about to begin. Nine brewers now offer draft beer in one of three such packaging variations; more than a dozen others are negotiating with a leading supplier.

There are two basic types of kegs being used, the more elaborate, made by Reynolds Metals and Alcoa, utilize carbon dioxide to shoot the beer out; the other, made by National Can, utilizes squeeze-bulb-generated air pressure.

Falstaff, Hamm and National are using the Reynolds unit, called the "Tapper." Schlitz is now testing the Alcoa unit in eight markets. It's called the Home Keg.

Atlantic Lederbrau, Sterling Brew, Koch Brewing, Gettelman (owned by Miller's), Standard Rochester and National (using both) are marketing in National Can's Home Tap.

There are important differences in the units. Reynolds' Tapper holds $2\frac{1}{4}$ gallons, measures nine inches by $11\frac{1}{2}$ inches so that it will fit in 98 per cent of existing refrigerators, weighs seven pounds empty and 26 pounds full, contains the equivalent of 24 12-ounce cans, and will keep draft beer flavor-fresh for three weeks under refrigeration.

The Alcoa unit, being tested by Schlitz, differs from the Reynolds unit in two ways—the carbon dioxide mechanism, and size. The Alcoa unit holds only 144 ounces but Schlitz is packing two to a carton so the consumer buys the same amount of beer as in the Reynolds unit. Because of quirks in state liquor laws, the Reynolds size is illegal in a few states. Falstaff is now testing a $3\frac{1}{8}$-gallon size in Louisville that will meet such objections.

National Can's Home Tap, which holds one gallon, also fits snugly on the refrigerator shelf.

Because the Tapper carries a four-dollar deposit, Falstaff pioneered in extensive testing the Reynolds unit in Springfield, Ill.; Fort Wayne, Ind.; Tulsa, Okla.; Detroit; and Chicago. The beer itself is comparable in price to a case of 24 cans, making the initial outlay between eight and nine dollars, but the second-time cost is between four and five dollars.

Falstaff found that the average Tapper buyer was male and relatively prosperous. "These results tie in exactly with our predictions of what the beer drinker of coming years will be like," says Alvin Griesedieck, Jr., vice president, marketing. "Our projections show that although he will continue to be married, he will have a higher level of education, be a professional man or in the service industries, live in suburbia, and enjoy a higher income."

Griesedieck is enthusiastic about its potential. It should, he says, create "a revolution in beer-drinking habits." Others agree. Schlitz president Robert Uihlein, Jr., views the potential of draft beer in the home as "outstanding."

And that's what beer needs most.

Exhibit 5

HEUBLEIN, INC. (B)

Hamm and Industry Sales

(In Millions of Barrels)

	Brewing Industry, Tax-Paid Only*	Hamm's Beer Sales, Tax-Paid Only	Tax-Paid Hamm's Sales as % of Tax-Paid Industry Sales
1955..............	85.0	3.1	3.6
1956..............	85.0	3.3	3.9
1957..............	84.4	3.4	4.0
1958..............	84.4	3.4	4.0
1959..............	87.6	3.5	4.0
1960..............	87.9	4.0	4.5
1961..............	89.0	3.7	4.1
1962..............	91.2	3.7	4.0
1963..............	93.8	3.8	4.1
1964..............	98.6	3.7	3.7

* The data given with respect to the brewing industry represent tax-paid withdrawals of malt beverages as reported by the Internal Revenue Service.
Source: U.S. Treasury Department data.

Hamm's sold three brands of beer at the end of 1965: Waldech (premium price), Hamm's (premium and popular price), and Buckhorn (lower price). The 1964 sales breakdown among these brands had been 17,800 barrels[2] for Waldech, 3,624,700 barrels for Hamm's, and 57,800 barrels for Buckhorn, for a total of 3,700,300 barrels. In addition, Hamm's had produced some beer for sale to the F.&M. Schaefer Brewing Company under the Gunther brand in 1964.

In 1965, Hamm's beer was sold in 31 states and the District of

Exhibit 6

HEUBLEIN, INC. (B)

Returns on 1964 Sales of Leading Brewers

	Total Revenues (000)	Pretax Net (000)	Profit Margin (Per Cent)	Barrels Sold (000)	Pretax Returns/ Barrel
Anheuser-Busch.......	$491,384	$39,312	8.00%	10,235	$3.84
Schlitz..............	311,394	28,277	9.08	8,266	3.42
Pabst...............	227,610	20,421	8.97	7,444	2.74
Falstaff.............	211,943	13,604	6.42	5,815	2.33
Hamm..............	125,602	8,657	6.89	3,719	2.33

Source: Company annual reports.

---

[2] A barrel was equivalent to 31 U.S. gallons.

Columbia. Most sales, however, were made in the midwestern, western, and southwestern parts of the United States. Hamm's relied exclusively on 479 independent wholesalers for its distribution, most of whom carried other brands of beer. Although any of these wholesalers could terminate his relationship with Hamm's at will, none of them accounted for more than 2.5% of Hamm's 1964 sales.

According to some industry observers, Hamm's four breweries were one of its principal assets. Three of these were owned outright, while the fourth was leased. The location and annual productive capacity of each of these plants was as follows:

Location	Annual Productive Capacity (barrels)
St. Paul, Minnesota	2,550,000
San Francisco, California	1,000,000
Los Angeles, California	500,000
Houston, Texas (leased)	450,000
	4,500,000

According to industry estimates, the cost of replacing Hamm's 1965 capacity would be about $135 million, or more than double the proposed purchase price. This estimate was based on the industry rule of thumb which set the costs of new plant construction at $30 to $35 per barrel at the end of 1965.

Like Heublein, Hamm's purchased most of the raw materials needed for its production—malt, barley, hops, and corn grits—from various independent suppliers. About one fourth of the malt and hops requirements were met by wholly owned subsidiaries, however.

The Brewing Industry. At the end of 1964, the beer market was approximately the same size as the distilled spirits market, or about $6.4

Exhibit 7

HEUBLEIN, INC. (B)

Alcoholic Beverages—Consumer Expenditures, 1942–64

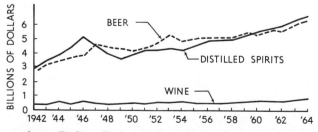

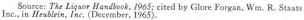

Source: *The Liquor Handbook, 1965;* cited by Glore Forgan, Wm. R. Staats Inc., in *Heublein, Inc.* (December, 1965).

Exhibit 8

HEUBLEIN, INC. (B)

Indexes of Per Capita Beer Consumption, 1940–64

INDEX: 1940 = 100

Source: United States Brewers Association; cited by Glore Forgan, Wm.
R. Staats Inc., in *Heublein, Inc.* (December, 1965).

billion a year (see Exhibit 7). In addition, from 1960 to 1964, the beer
market had grown at approximately the same annual rate as the liquor
market, i.e., at about 2.5%. Per capita beer consumption had increased
moderately during the period (see Exhibit 8).

Since people began consuming beer at a younger age than liquor,
industry observers expected beer consumption to increase as much as, if
not more than, liquor consumption through 1970. Most of this increase
was expected to be in the sale of packaged beer, since the sale of draught
beer had decreased from 22% of total beer sales in 1955 to 19% in
1964.

The same observers felt that brand loyalty was not as strong for beer
as for liquor. Nevertheless, the economies of high-volume production
and the use of high dollar advertising seemed to be causing a gradual
concentration of the beer industry, for the number of breweries operated
in the United States decreased from 329 to 211 between 1953 and
1963. Moreover, the percentage of sales accounted for by the largest
brewing companies had recently been increasing (see Exhibits 4, 9, and
10).

Exhibit 9

HEUBLEIN, INC. (B)

Market Share of Major Brewers

(Per Cent)

	1964	1963	1962	1961	1960	1959	1958	1957	1956	1955	1954	1953	1952	1951
Top 25...	83.7%	82.2%	79.9%	77.4%	75.1%	73.8%	70.5%	69.2%	67.5%	64.3%	62.1%	61.3%	60.2%	57.5%
Top 10...	57.7	56.8	55.0	52.8	51.4	50.0	45.9	45.2	44.4	42.7	40.8	40.1	40.8	39.2

Source: Research Company of America.

Exhibit 10

HEUBLEIN, INC. (B)

Advertising Expenditures of Major Brewers in 1965

Company	Advertising (000)	Sales (000)	Advertising Per Cent of Sales
Jos. Schlitz Brewing Co..........	$34,200	$311,375	11.0%
Anheuser-Busch, Inc.............	32,500	491,384	6.6
Pabst Brewing Co..............	15,900	227,610	7.0
Carling Brewing Co............	15,500	412,306	3.8
Falstaff Brewing Corp...........	15,000	211,943	7.0

Source: *Advertising Age* (January 3, 1966), p. 46.

THE PROPOSED WIDE LINE ACQUISITION[3]

At the same time as the purchase of Hamm was being evaluated, several other possible acquisitions were being considered. One of these was the Wide Line Soft Drink Company, which in 1963 had total assets of $15.5 million (see Exhibit 11). Although Heublein's management felt that Wide Line could benefit from Heublein's ability to market

Exhibit 11

HEUBLEIN, INC. (B)

Wide Line Soft Drink Company

1963 Balance Sheet for Year Ending December 31

(Dollars in Millions)

Current assets:

Cash...............................	$ 0.7
Accounts receivable (net)............	3.6
Inventories........................	3.3
Short-term bonds...................	0.6
Other............................	0.2
Total current assets..............	$ 8.4
Property, plant, and equipment (net)....	6.6
Other assets.......................	0.5
Total assets....................	$15.5

Current liabilites:

Bank notes.........................	$ 1.3
Notes payable......................	0.5
Current portion long-term debt.......	0.2
Accounts payable...................	2.6
Federal and state income taxes........	0.5
Other taxes........................	0.1
Total current liabilities..........	$ 5.2
Long-term debt......................	2.4
Customer deposit liability..............	1.2
Deferred federal and state income taxes..	0.4
Stockholders' equity	
Common stock.....................	1.3
Capital surplus....................	2.7
Retained earnings..................	2.3
Total liabilities and equity......	$15.5

Source: 1963 Wide Line Soft Drink Company annual report.

---

[3] For purposes of security, the name, geographic location, and certain income statement figures of the company have been changed. The description of the industry and other aspects of the company's operations (e.g., market share, product line, etc.) are accurate.

consumer products, management nonetheless entertained some reservations. The most significant of these related to Wide Line's relatively weak competitive position. While Wide Line—with sales of $26 million in 1964—was among the top eight soft drink manufacturers in the country, its 2% to 3% market share was far below Coca-Cola's 31% and Pepsi-Cola's 23%. Also significant was the fact that Coca-Cola, Pepsi-Cola, and Seven-Up were three of the most experienced marketers of consumer goods in the country. In addition, while Wide Line's sales

Exhibit 12

HEUBLEIN, INC. (B)

Wide Line Soft Drink Company

Income Statements for Year Ended December 31

(Dollars in Millions)

	1959	1960	1961	1962	1963
Net sales	$18.6	$21.7	$21.9	$24.4	$26.0
Cost of goods sold	13.5	15.3	15.2	17.0	18.9
Gross profit on sales	$ 5.1	$ 6.4	$ 6.7	$ 7.4	$ 7.1
Selling, general and administrative expenses	3.1	3.7	4.0	4.7	4.2
Advertising	1.4	1.6	1.6	1.7	2.0
	$ 4.5	$ 5.3	$ 5.7	$ 6.4	$ 6.2
Income from operations	0.6	1.2	1.0	1.0	0.9
Other income (charges)	0.0	0.1	0.0	0.0	0.0
Federal taxes	0.3	0.5	0.5	0.5	0.4
Net income	$ 0.3	$ 0.6	$ 0.5	$ 0.5	$ 0.5

Source: Various Wide Line Soft Drink Company annual reports.

had increased 40% between 1959 and 1963, profits had remained relatively steady (see Exhibit 12). Moreover, profits represented only a 2% return on sales, even though Wide Line was spending only half of the industry average (as a percentage of sales) for advertising and promotion.

The Wide Line Company. Wide Line manufactured carbonated beverage concentrates which it sold to franchised bottlers in the United States and foreign countries under its own brand names. During 1964, sales of Wide Line soft drinks by these franchise holders exceeded 45 million cases. Under these franchise agreements, Wide Line's franchise holders had to maintain certain quality conditions in their bottling operations, and were required to spend certain minimum amounts for advertising.[4] They were, however, allowed to produce carbonated beverages in addition to those sold under Wide Line's trademarks.

---

[4] Usually 30% of the cost of the concentrate. Half of the amount spent by the franchise holder, up to 50% of the concentrate cost, would be refunded by Wide Line.

In addition to its sales to franchised bottlers, Wide Line also sold concentrates to private-label bottlers, to the dairy and ice cream industries, and to the fountain trade as syrups.

Wide Line also bottled and sold carbonated beverages under its own brand name in the south central region of the country. Wide Line entered the bottling business in 1962 when it acquired its largest franchise holder. This operation, now the bottling division, used about 20% of the Wide Line's concentrate production. The bottling division not only produced carbonated beverages under Wide Line's trademarks, which it sold to independent distributors who redistributed these beverages to various retail outlets such as chain stores, drug stores, and hotels, but also produced a lower cost beverage, which it sold directly to chain stores, independent supermarkets, and cooperative food stores. In addition, the bottling division produced beverages under private-label brands to meet the demand for a low-priced product.

Wide Line's product line was one of the most complete in the industry. The company produced 24 different flavors, including the basic four: cola, lemon-lime, orange, and root beer. Ten of these flavors were also produced in low-calorie form. Although no figures were available, it was the case writer's judgment that low-calorie flavors accounted for about 20% of Wide Line's total concentrate sales.

Wide Line maintained its executive offices and concentrate manufacturing facility in El Paso, Texas. It also maintained sales offices and cold storage facilities in California, New York, and Toronto, Canada. The bottling division owned or leased plants with a total of 20 bottling lines in seven cities spread throughout the south central region.

The Soft Drink Industry.   Soft drink sales increased 27% between 1955 and 1964, from 1.5 billion cases in the former year to over 1.9 billion in the latter (see Exhibit 13). Over one third of this increase resulted from the increase in per capita consumption from 218 bottles a person in 1955 to 240 bottles in 1964. The most important industry trend during this period was the increasing importance of low-calorie soft drinks. These beverages increased their market share from less than 2% in 1955 to 10% in 1964, and estimates of future growth ranged from a plateau of 10% (predicted by Coca-Cola) to a forecast of 35% by 1970 (predicted by Pepsi-Cola and Canada Dry). While the market positions of the four major soft drink manufacturers—Coca-Cola, Pepsi-Cola, Royal Crown, and Seven-Up—had not changed much between 1955 and 1964, Royal Crown had advanced slightly as its Diet-Rite Cola captured 40% of the low-calorie market (see Exhibit 14). There

Exhibit 13

HEUBLEIN, INC. (B)

Soft-Drink Market

COMPANY	CASES (Millions)		MARKET SHARE (Per Cent)	
	1963	*1964*	*1963*	*1964*
Coca-Cola..............	560	600	31%	31%
Pepsi-Cola.............	420	440	23½	23
Royal Crown...........	185	200	10	10
Seven-Up..............	160	165	9	9
Canada Dry............	145	155	8	8
Beverages Int'l.........	55	60	3	3
Dr. Pepper............	55	55	3	2½
Cott.................	35	35	2	2
Squirt................	18	20	1	1
Shasta................	15	20	1	1
No-Cal...............	10	10	½	½
No Grape.............	10	10	½	½
All others.............	133	160	7½	8½
Grand total........	1,801	1,930	100%	100%

Source: *Printers' Ink* (April 9, 1965), p. 22.

was some concern among the industry leaders that the private-label brands, which were sold primarily on a price basis, might try to use low-calorie drinks to increase their market share still further, since low-calorie drinks provided a greater opportunity for price cutting than regular soft drinks because of their lower cost. The increased volume of low-calorie soft drinks was also partially responsible for the growing

Exhibit 14

HEUBLEIN, INC. (B)

Soft-Drink Market by Company and Flavors (1964)

COMPANY	COLA MARKET		LEMON-LIME		DIET SOFT DRINKS	
	Per Cent	Cases (Millions)	Per Cent	Cases (Millions)	Per Cent	Cases (Millions)
Coca-Cola............	44%	530	21%	65	20%	38
Pepsi-Cola............	33	400	11	35	20	38
Royal Crown.........	15	180	2	6	41	77
Seven-Up.............	...	...	50	155	included in all others	
All Others...........	8	100	16	50	19	37
Total..........	100%	1,210	100%	311	100%	190

Source: *Printers' Ink* (April 9, 1965), p. 23.

Exhibit 15

HEUBLEIN, INC. (B)

Soft-Drink Market by Flavors

Flavor	1964	1963	1958
Cola.................	62%	60%	53%
Lemon-lime...........	16	15	10
Orange................	8	9	5
Root beer.............	4	5	3
Other.................	10	11	29
Grand Total......100%	100%	100%	100%

Source: *Printers' Ink* (April 9, 1965), p. 23.

importance of the two basic flavors: cola and lemon-lime (see Exhibit 15).

Although adequate distribution was a crucial factor in soft drink sales, the primary selling tool used by most national carbonated beverage companies and their franchised bottlers was advertising. During 1964 these companies and their bottlers spent about $200 million on promotion. According to an industry rule of thumb, companies should spend about 10 cents per case on advertising. A comparison of actual and estimated advertising expenses for 1964 is contained in Table 1:

TABLE 1

Company	Rule-of-Thumb Estimate (Millions)	Actual Expenditure (Millions)
Coca-Cola.....................	$60.0	$59.0
Pepsi-Cola....................	44.0	35.0
Royal Crown..................	20.0	24.0
Seven-Up.....................	16.5	12.0

In this advertising, most of the companies developed themes which they repeated for several years. For example, Coca-Cola developed, "Things Go Better with Coke." Soft drink companies also used special advertising and promotional campaigns to attract additional sales during the summer sales peak.

In 1964, industry sales were divided into four categories: the take-home business, 66%; the vending of soft drinks in cups, bottles, and cans, 15%; fountain sales, 10%; and bottles in nonvending coolers, which accounted for the remaining 9% of sales.

According to *Printers' Ink,* "Bold advertising strategies, new or revitalized products, new packages, and fast action characterize the carbonated-beverage industry. This decade and the next will see a continuation of changing consumer tastes and consequent changes in the soft-drink industry itself."[5]

---

[5] "Battle of the Brands: Soft Drinks," *Printers' Ink* (April 9, 1965), p. 26.

9. CML Group, Inc.

IN EARLY JANUARY, 1971, John Morgan, general manager of Hood Sailmakers, Inc., the world's largest and most prestigious manufacturer of sails for big ocean racing yachts, was trying to make a final decision on whether to recommend to Hood's board of directors that $314,000 be requested for the establishment of a sailcloth weaving mill in Ireland. Hood had been a wholly owned subsidiary of the CML Group since February of 1970 but still operated with its own board of directors.[1] The project, even if recommended, would require approval by CML Group management, however, because of its size and nature. Hood was but one of the four recent acquisitions in the "leisure time" field which made up the CML Group, a company which had attained an annual sales volume of over $11 million in its first year and a half of operations.

In Mr. Morgan's opinion, several factors favored the investment. It represented a 13% after-tax return (based on cash flow) for the division, substantially better than Hood was making on its present asset base. Perhaps more importantly, both Ted Hood, founder and current president of the division, and his father, R. S. Hood, an influential Hood board member and general manager of the Hood cloth manufacturing operation, were in favor of the project, as they both felt that it would significantly enhance the long-run competitive position of the company and was therefore an important strategic move.

Mr. Morgan recognized that going ahead with the investment presented certain difficulties, however, and that several of these were of particular concern to CML corporate management. Most significant was Hood's sales and profits slump during fiscal 1970, when earnings had dropped about 30% from their peak year level. Though profitability was considerably better in the current year, sales had not risen appreciably above the prior year. As Hood had doubled its weaving capacity in 1968, only about 50% of existing weaving capacity was currently being utilized. Under such circumstances, corporate manage-

---

[1] Hood's board included five members, three chosen by the Hood family and two by CML.

ment's reluctance to invest in substantially increased capacity for Hood was understandable, especially in view of opportunities to invest in other divisions. Corporate management also questioned Hood's ability to take on a major new commitment in light of the many pressing issues already demanding management time and energy. Secrecy surrounding Hood's unique weaving process presented a further problem. All Hood sailcloth was currently woven in the very closely guarded Marblehead facility. A second mill naturally increased Hood's risk of exposure. Finally, uncertainties such as future tariff levels, fluctuation in domestic demand, and possible competitive moves and reactions complicated the economic analysis.

Since Mr. Morgan had joined Hood as general manager only nine months earlier and had no prior experience in the industry, he recognized that he was still in a transition period with regard to learning an entirely new business and establishing his own position within the company. Several factors made it important to come to some decision on the Irish project fairly soon, however. Although the Industrial Development Authority (IDA) of the Irish government had agreed to supply as a nonrepayable grant $266,000 of the $580,000 total funds required, Hood had already requested several extensions of the original deadline for purchasing land and commencing construction. While Mr. Morgan felt that a further extension could probably be obtained, he sensed that an increasingly wide credibility gap was developing on the part of IDA over Hood's real intentions in Ireland. In addition, preliminary planning for the Irish facility, which had already cost Hood about $20,000 since early 1969, was currently being funded by Hood at the rate of $1,000 per month in retainer fees and travel expenses. Further delay was therefore both risky and expensive.

CML Group Development

In May, 1969, Charles Leighton, Robert Tod, and Sam Frederick[2] resigned from the Willard Coporation, a large diversified manufactur-

[2] *Charles Leighton* (36 in 1971); M.B.A., Harvard Business School, 1960; product line manager, Mine Safety Appliances Corporation, 1963–64; instructor in management of new enterprises at the Harvard Business School, 1964–65; Group vice president, Willard Corporation Leisure Time Group, 1965–69.

Robert Tod (32); M.B.A., Harvard Business School, 1967; project engineer, Hooker Chemical, January–September, 1967; Group operations manager, Willard Corporation Leisure Time Group, 1967–69.

Sam Frederick (36); M.B.A., Columbia, 1962; accounting with Arthur Andersen & Co., 1962–68; Group controller, Willard Corporation Leisure Time Group, 1968–69.

ing company which had grown largely by acquisition, in order to establish their own company in the leisure time field.

Mr. Leighton had joined Willard in 1965 as group officer in charge of three divisions (a jewelry manufacturer and two boat manufacturers) with total sales of $7 million per year. Throughout the next four years internal growth and six acquisitions had raised the sales of the renamed "Leisure Time Group" to about $70 million; profits grew at about 25% per year during this period. By the time Mr. Leighton and his colleagues left the Willard Corporation in 1969 their group was one of the largest, most profitable, and most rapidly growing groups in the company, which then had sales of several hundred million dollars.

In the spring of 1969 Mr. Leighton described the original objectives of CML as follows in a short pamphlet prepared for prospective investors:[3]

We want to build an organization devoted to self-expression and individual creativity for profit. Basically, we intend to use the skills demonstrated by our success at Willard to build our own diversified company in the leisure time field. Our plan is to acquire quality companies and to operate them on a decentralized basis so that chief executives of acquired companies retain full authority for management of their businesses, with us at the corporate level providing supplementary assistance in the form of long-range planning help, marketing and manufacturing consultation, accounting, and, most importantly, strong financial control and support. We are looking for companies with top-quality product lines and excellent trade names in businesses where management experience and creativity are more important to success than bricks and mortar. Companies we'll be interested in will generally have been founded by men with great creativity from a product standpoint, but who basically dislike the administrative burdens of running a growing business. A key element of our strategy is therefore to provide administrative assistance to these companies, thereby freeing up more of an owner-manager's time for the really creative things he's most interested in. Another key aspect is motivation. We plan to acquire companies only on an earn-out basis so that the owner-manager is fully motivated to realize the growth and profit potential which we feel are in the business when we buy it.

From a financial standpoint our objectives are the following: growth in corporate earnings per share of at least 20% per year, a pretax return on CML's investment in acquired companies of at least 20%, and a 12½% annual profit growth of acquired companies.

With these objectives in mind CML's co-founders established the new company in early June, 1969. Two million dollars of outside equity

---

[3] See Exhibit 1 for further discussion of objectives appearing in CML's first annual report.

funds were raised in just 10 days by selling 50% of the company to 18 large investors.[4] The best known of these was a major national foundation which invested $400,000 in the company, choosing CML Group for one of its first attempts to invest in new ventures. The four co-founders paid a total of $40,000 for the remaining 50% of the equity.[5] Mr. Leighton described as follows the relative ease with which outside equity funds were obtained despite the unfavorable economic climate prevailing at the time:

> At that time, we hadn't made any attempt yet to negotiate with prospective acquisitions, so we couldn't talk specific companies to financial backers. Despite this, we felt we had several things to offer. First, we represented a team whose combined skills balanced out any individual weaknesses. I've always maintained that covering yourself on weaknesses is far more important than having outstanding but spotty strengths. Second, we had a very good four-year track record at Willard. Third, we had a concept of management which we had spelled out in detail in a recent *Harvard Business Review* article and which had already proved itself at Willard. Finally, we had two very influential men behind us. One was my father-in-law, Dan Smith,[6] who provided invaluable advice and experience. Homer Luther was the other. At 29 he was already an extremely successful and influential investment manager. I had met him in 1964 while he was an M.B.A. student at Harvard. We got to know each other as a result of a Creative Marketing study he made of the product line I handled at Mine Safety Appliances. We had kept in touch off and on since then, and after we decided to leave Willard we called him, since he had told me that if we ever needed money we should come to him. His introductions to potential investors and his assistance in general were invaluable. Dan Smith and Homer also became substantial investors in CML, and both are very active directors of the company.

Exhibit 1

CML GROUP, INC.
Excerpt from a Letter to the Stockholders, July 30, 1970

TO OUR STOCKHOLDERS:

A little over a year ago, the CML Group, Inc., was founded on the premise that a variety of new skills will be needed for business success in the 1970's. The ability to provide an environment which would encourage creative product development and innovative marketing will become a key success factor. Our previous business experience led us to believe that the orientation of business toward individual creativity could attract imaginative entrepreneurs and result

---

[4] A total of 800 shares of convertible preference stock (convertible on a 1 for 1 basis) and 3,200 shares of common stock were sold to outside investors for $500 per share. As no investment banking fees were paid, total cost of the issue was only $364.

[5] A total of 4,000 shares of common stock were sold to the four co-founders at $10 per share.

[6] Dan T. Smith, Professor Emeritus of Finance, Harvard Business School.

Exhibit 1—Continued

in a high rate of profitable growth. Of course, financial control, production and the other customary management skills will remain critical to the success of any business.

The "leisure-time" industry is the best candidate for the implementation of this theory because it contains a number of very creative people who founded companies with interesting products. As a result of increasing discretionary income in all levels of society, this industry also has a high growth rate. It was decided to group several of these companies into one corporation emphasizing performance and quality.

Widespread equity ownership among the managers of the companies would provide strong motivation for capital growth and act as a measure of their common success. The creative leaders could become even more productive by delegating their administrative burdens and financial problems to qualified persons. An active corporate management team would be able to introduce modern control systems and other management tools to support long-term growth. The diversity of experience and skills of the CML management team would be an advantage in this effort. Accordingly, the CML Group was incorporated in June of 1969.

The principal objectives of the Group were established at the outset as follows:

> First of all, the Group would seek several outstanding "leisure-time" companies to provide a base for business operations. At the same time, the Group would keep itself in a strong financial position. Bank relationships would be developed and lines of credit established. A pattern would be established for the integration of new members into the Group; this would include the strengthening of autonomous management whenever necessary and the introduction of an extensive, but easily administered control system.
>
> Secondly, the Group would begin immediately to prepare itself for a public offering of its stock at the most favorable opportunity in the next few years. Improved marketability of the Group's common stock would provide a better tool for use in attracting additional companies and employees and would improve the original subscribers' return on their capital investment. The Group determined that a high rate growth in sales and profits of each company after joining the Group would be the most important factor in valuing the Group's stock at the time of public sale. Also important would be a record of making prudent acquisitions.
>
> Ultimately and most importantly, the Group would begin to build for the long term. The desired environment would be developed slowly to ensure that creativity and innovation became permanent characteristics of the Group. The best management teams take time to form, particularly when business practices are considered a complement to innovation and art rather than the dominant force. The control systems would have to be structured so that the effect of changes within and without the business could easily be assessed and recognized.

Source: A letter to the stockholders appearing in CML Group, Inc.'s, July 31, 1970, annual report.

ACQUIRED BUSINESSES

Exhibit 2 shows CML's balance sheet as of July 31, 1969, shortly after registration of the new company and before any acquisitions had been made, and as of July 31, 1970, following one year of operations. During its first year CML acquired four companies and reported fiscal 1970 sales of approximately $11 million (see Exhibit 3 for the first year's operating results). Terms of purchase for acquired companies appear in Exhibit 4. A brief account of each acquired company follows.

Boston Whaler, Inc. Boston Whaler, CML's largest division, was estimated to be the tenth largest U.S. manufacturer of outboard boats. CML's 1970 annual report described this division as follows:

The first company to join the CML Group was Boston Whaler, Inc., of Rockland, Massachusetts, in September, 1969. Their principal product is the Boston Whaler outboard motor boat. A 30% interest in Boston Whaler Bearcat, Inc., manufacturer of nonpolluting 4-cycle outboard engines, was acquired at the same time. Dick Fisher, the chairman of Boston Whaler, has been instrumental in the founding of several companies requiring a high level of technical skill. The creativity and innovative talents of Mr. Fisher made this company particularly attractive as the first member of the Group.

The Boston Whaler meets the high quality criteria of the Group. [A well-known consumer report] has rated Boston Whaler as the most outstanding outboard boat produced in the United States. The boats are easily identified by their distinctive and functional shape and a well-regarded trademark. Boston Whalers are made of a monolithic casting of plastic foam with a smooth molded fiberglass "crust" on both sides. This construction causes the Boston Whaler to be extremely durable, and unsinkable. No other boat manufacturing company has developed the technical skills needed to build a comparable product.

An asset with long-term growth implications is the Boston Whaler marketing organization. There are eight sales representatives whose principal products are the Boston Whaler and Bearcat engines. More than 700 dealers are located throughout the world. The dealers are known to be the most reputable in the industry. Obviously, other products can be sold through this system as they are developed or acquired by Boston Whaler.

During the current fiscal year, Boston Whaler has introduced a new product, the "Outrage," a larger outboard boat with a new and distinctive hull configuration. A patent application is pending to cover the boat design. It is expected that the boat will have a pronounced effect on the design of larger outboard boats.

Major programs now under way in cost savings, manufacturing efficiency, and overhead reductions are expected to improve profitability to a level in excess of all previous years.

Despite modest volume and profit declines during 1970, Boston Whaler's long-term sales growth was expected to run somewhat above

Exhibit 2

CML GROUP, INC.

Consolidated Balance Sheet as of July 31, 1969 and 1970

(Thousands of Dollars)

Assets	1969	1970
Current assets		
Cash	$ 242	$ 731
Short-term commercial paper	1,787	—
Net receivables	—	1,217
Inventories	—	2,433
Prepaid expenses	14	109
Total current assets	$2,042	$4,490
Property, plant, and equipment (net)	3	2,143
Investments and other assets		
Investments	—	876
Excess of cost over net book value of acquisitions	—	1,959
Other assets	7	137
Total assets	$2,052	$9,604
Liabilities and Stockholders' Equity		
Total current liabilities	$ 14	$2,545
Long-term debt	—	3,424
Subordinated convertible debenture	—	498
Stockholders' equity*		
Preference stock (par value $.10)	1	1
Common stock (par value $.10)	1	1
Capital in excess of par	2,038	2,771
Retained earnings	(2)	364
Total equity	$2,038	$3,137
Total liabilities and equity	$2,052	$9,604

* Stockholders' equity information:

SOURCE OF EQUITY	NUMBER OF SHARES OUTSTANDING		
	Convertible Preference	Common	
	Nonfounders	Non-founders	Founders
Sold during June 1969	800 (Series A)	3,200	4,000
Exchanged to acquire Boston Whaler	1,000 (Series B)		
Exchanged to acquire Hood Sailmakers	4,600 (Series C)		
Sold during summer of 1970		920	
Total outstanding as of 7-31-70	6,400	4,120	4,000

Series A ranks on a parity with common stock with respect to voting and dividend privileges. May be converted by holder into common stock at any time on a share-for-share basis. May be redeemed by CML any time after September 30, 1971, at the original selling price ($500 per share).

Series B ranks on a parity with common stock with respect to voting privileges. Receives a preferential annual dividend of $10 per share. See footnote in Exhibit 4 for conversion privileges.

Series C ranks on a parity with common shares with respect to voting and dividend privileges. See footnote in Exhibit 4 for conversion privileges.

Source: Company records for 1969; annual report for 1970. Errors are due to rounding.

Exhibit 3

CML GROUP, INC.

Consolidated Statement of Income and Retained Earnings
for the Year Ended July 31, 1970

(Thousands of Dollars)

Net sales......................................		$11,109
Less costs and expenses		
Cost of goods sold..............................	$7,943	
General, selling, and administrative.................	2,553	10,496
Income from operations........................		613
Interest expense (net)...............................		190
Income before income taxes.....................		423
Provision for income taxes*.........................		217
Net income ($21.25 per share)†.................		206
Deficit, beginning of year...........................		(2)
Retained earnings of pooled companies................		161
Retained earnings, end of year......................		$ 365

    * Represents a reserve against future income tax payments. No income taxes were paid in 1970. Income for tax purposes had been reduced to zero as a result of:
    a) A tax loss carry-forward in connection with a relatively minor portion of one subsidiary's business spun off at the time of acquisition.
    b) Amortization charges in connection with certain assets revalued for tax purposes at the time of acquisition.
    † The annual report comments as follows upon earnings per share: Net income per common share and common equivalent share is based on the 9,675 weighted average number of shares outstanding. For purposes of computing net income per share, the convertible preference shares —Series A, B, and C—are considered to be common stock equivalents. The weighted average number of common and common equivalent shares assume conversion of the Series A on a share-for-share basis and the Series B and C on the basis of the number of shares issuable at the last sales price of common stock and the current level of income affecting the conversion rate of these securities.
    The 7% subordinated convertible debentures and stock options are not included in the net income per share computations, as their effect is not dilutive.
    Source: 1970 annual report.

the 8% average for the industry. In addition, significant profit increases at current sales levels were expected reasonably quickly through improving margins. These had consistently run well under half the level of Willard's outboard runabout divisions of equivalent size, which CML management knew well from their previous experience.

Carroll Reed Ski Shops. This division was described as follows in CML's 1970 annual report:

The [Carroll Reed] Ski Shops, which joined the Group in October, 1969, are a series of retail stores and a national mail-order business headquartered in North Conway, New Hampshire.

The business was founded by Carroll Reed in 1936 to service the burgeoning ski areas in northern New England. Mr. Reed's creative merchandising skills are the principal reason for the store's development into one of the country's best-known ski shops. The company has become known for its extremely high quality merchandise, excellent service, and unique "country store" style that appeals to both men and women.

In the early spring, an Executive Vice President [and General Manager] was employed by Mr. Reed. The new individual has had significant merchandising experience and will be of value in the day-to-day management of the business.

Exhibit 4

CML GROUP, INC.

Terms of Payment for Companies Acquired

Accounting Treatment	Acquisition Date	Name of Company	Original Payment in Shares of CML Stock		Original Payment in Cash and Notes (000s of Dollars)		Additional Earn-Out (000s of Dollars)	
			Common	Convertible Preference	Cash	Notes	Minimum	Maximum
Pooling..........	9/30/69	Boston Whaler	250	1,000			$ 500*	$2,975*
Pooling..........	2/25/70	Hood Sailmakers	400	4,600			1,600†	5,000†
Purchase.........	10/1/70	Carroll Reed			$700	$ 600		400‡
Purchase.........	5/1/70	Mason & Sullivan			450	1,050		1,100‡

* Represents conversion value of 1,000 shares of convertible preference stock. Conversion value is contingent upon the earnings of Boston Whaler, Inc, for the period beginning 8/1/69 and ending 7/31/74, and on the market price of CML's common stock at the time of conversion.

† Represents conversion value of 4,600 shares of convertible preference stock. Conversion value is contingent upon the earnings of Hood Sailmakers, Inc., for the period beginning 8/1/70 and ending 7/31/75, and on the market price of CML's common stock at the time of conversion.

‡ Additional cash amount payable through 1974 contingent upon achievement of certain earnings by the purchased company.

Source: 1970 annual report.

This new management depth will better allow Mr. Reed to concentrate on the future expansion of the business. The Group believes that the company employees are a major asset who provide an excellent foundation for future growth.

During the fiscal year, the mail-order handling systems were substantially improved by the construction of a 6,000 square foot addition in North Conway for order processing and additional storage space. The order processing was improved by introducing computerized equipment on a limited basis. A new ski shop of approximately 4,000 square feet is about to open in Simsbury, Connecticut, as the first in a planned program of store expansion.

Three residents of the northern New England area have been elected to the Board of Directors of Carroll Reed Ski Shops, Inc. and participate actively in the long-term planning for the business. They are Tom Corcoran [M.B.A., Harvard Business School, 1959], a former Olympic skier and President of Waterville Valley ski area; Malcolm McNair, Professor Emeritus of Retailing at Harvard Business School, and Leon Gorman, President of L. L. Bean, Inc. in Freeport, Maine.

Growth opportunities exist for Carroll Reed Ski Shops in the gradual expansion of the retail store business. The mail-order business can be further expanded without significant addition of facilities or personnel. Carroll Reed Ski Shops also provides a vantage point to study several fast-growing sectors of the leisure time industry.

Mr. Reed had played a leading role as one of the early pioneers in recreational skiing in this country and had opened the first U.S. ski lift and school, headed by world-famous Hans Schneider, in Jackson, New Hampshire, in the early 1930's. Several years later he sold his interest in the ski area and founded Carroll Reed Ski Shops (CRSS) in nearby North Conway. Not long after joining CML Mr. Reed described CRSS's success over the years to the case writer, as follows:

When my wife and I began this business in 1936 we had no idea it would ever grow to what it has become. We simply did not want to go back to Boston, liked the Conway area very much, and felt we could make a living here in this kind of business by treating customers well so that they would stop in and buy something from us the next time they passed through the area. I feel that many of our customers have come to feel a personal closeness to Kay and me and like the way we do business, and that this is what has brought them back over the years. It's this personal touch, a certain integrity in what we stand for in each transaction, that gives us something special to offer. This is the main basis on which we are able to compete with large city stores selling much the same type of merchandise as we do.

During the summer of 1970 Mr. Tod made the following observations about CRSS:

Carroll Reed has a number of important strengths. Most important are its reputation, based upon the quality and style of the items sold; its interesting, well-laid-out store in North Conway, which accounts for nearly half of total sales; its masculine image, despite the fact that 70% of all merchandise sold is for women; and the courteous, service-oriented manner of its retail people. They have unusually capable people with exceptionally high employee morale compared to others in their industry.

Carroll Reed's mailing list for catalogue sales, which account for about half of total sales, is another valuable asset. Average order size is nearly four times that of the mail-order industry as a whole, and about double that for small specialty houses like Carroll Reed. Another strength is Carroll's wide delegation of buying responsibility to six buyers. In most operations of their size, the top man tries to do all the buying himself.

The division's primary weakness, however, is its geographical dependence on one region—North Conway. This is alleviated somewhat by a couple of factors. Catalogue sales reach a customer group scattered across the country. Even retail sales are not confined to North Conway residents. Because of its location as both a winter and summer resort, North Conway draws large numbers throughout the year from all over New England and Middle Atlantic states. Partly as a result of these factors their product line has shifted significantly from almost 100% ski equipment in the early years to an increasing percentage of primarily women's fashion sportswear, and now less than one third of their volume is ski related.

Another weakness is their dependence on one retail outlet for selling marked-down merchandise from the catalog business. This problem is particularly pressing because of the current push to expand catalogue sales. Retail outlets are needed to dispose of unsold merchandise at the end of the catalogue season. The current procedure is to turn much of this over to the discount basement of a large downtown Boston department store at about 17% of Carroll Reed's retail price.[7]

Mr. Tod felt there were several additional areas of CRSS's operation in need of some strengthening, including internal controls (such as inventory and catalog order processing) and market knowledge in the mail-order area. He thought that an expansion of mail-order sales was CRSS's greatest opportunity for profit growth. The second major retail store, which was being planned for Simsbury, Connecticut, would provide both a non–New Hampshire retail outlet and an additional retail outlet for the resulting increase in markdowns.

Mason & Sullivan Company. CML's 1970 annual report described this division as follows:

The projected growth rate for the hobby sector is among the highest of the "leisure time" market because of early retirement and a renewed interest in hand work. The Group entered one of the fastest growing segments of the industry

---

[7] Approximately 10% (at retail valuation) of total sales were made at markdown prices.

when Mason & Sullivan of Osterville, Massachusetts, joined in June. This business sells clocks, barometers, and music boxes in kit form and by mail.

The founder, Ed Lebo, purchases the working parts of the various items in Europe. Wood, metal trim, and other parts are purchased from numerous suppliers in the New England area. Because the designs are largely antique reproductions with hand-crafted movements, there is virtually no model obsolescence.

The company has two unique assets. It has a high quality reputation among woodworking hobbyists throughout the United States and Canada; it also has established relationships with craftsmen-suppliers in Austria, Germany, Switzerland, and England.

Shortly after Mason & Sullivan joined the Group, the former chief executive of a large mail-order house was employed as Vice President and General Manager to assist in the day-to-day operations of the business. Efforts are being made to introduce control and information systems to support future profitable growth.

Mr. Lebo plans to expand the product line to include other related items.

Hood Sailmakers, Inc. By any index, Hood was clearly the leading supplier of sails for large ocean yachts (over 40 feet in length), commanding over 50% of the U.S. market. Exhibit 5 shows the text of a *Yachting* magazine article describing the company and its products.

Exhibit 5

CML GROUP, INC.
A Reprint from Yachting, *September 1970*
TED HOOD: SAILMAKER TO THE TWELVES
By B. D. Burrill

"They are the ultimate teaching and testing ground as far as we're concerned. A Twelve is under sail as much in three months as the average cruising boat in five years." Speaking was Frederick E. "Ted" Hood, the 43-year-old Marblehead, Mass., sailmaker who has made more sails for 12-Meter yachts than any man alive. And perhaps no man in the years since 1958, with the possible exception of Olin Stephens, has contributed more to keeping the America's Cup firmly bolted in the New York YC's trophy room than this genius of boat speed. During these years a small sailmaking operation that started in 1950 has grown into one of the world's largest, to a great extent as a result of the success his 12-Meter sails have enjoyed.

Ted Hood's involvement with the America's Cup and 12-Meter boats began in 1958 when he served in the cockpit of *Vim* during her brilliant bid to become the Cup defender. He served as an advisor to skipper Bus Mosbacher on sail trim and tactics, and generally made himself useful where help was needed. One day, when working on a coffee grinder, he somehow managed to loosen the bolted-down winch—Ted would be a good man aboard any boat on the basis of his physical strength alone.

Hood got his chance to make sails for *Vim* after her owner, the late Capt. Jack Matthews, had seen the sails he produced for the 5.5-Meter *Quixotic,* a

Exhibit 5—Continued

Ray Hunt design built and sailed by Ted, which narrowly missed becoming the 1956 U.S. Olympic representative. In spite of a DSQ in the next to last race, *Quixotic* had only to beat one boat in the final race to win the trials. Well up in the fleet on the final leg, the main halyard shackle unaccountably opened, the sail came down, and she finished last. So Ted's first experience with Meter boats wasn't very happy. But he also made sails for *Easterner* and *Weatherly* in 1958 and two famous red-top spinnakers borrowed from *Vim,* "Big Harry" and "Little Harry," were used by *Columbia* in her successful defense of the Cup.

In 1962 Ted designed and made just about everything except the hull and winches for *Nefertiti* which was the last boat eliminated in the trials by *Weatherly,* which had Bus Mosbacher at the helm. All of the Twelves, including the Australian challenger *Gretel,* used Hood sails that summer. *Gretel,* in fact, used a mainsail made in 1957 for *Vim* in the race she won over *Weatherly* in '62. This would seem ultimate proof of a theory which Ted still believes strongly, particularly with respect to mainsails, that good sails get better with age if they receive proper care. A Dacron sail develops a certain "set" much like the old cotton sails. After a few years the fabric has settled down and stretch is gone.

One anecdote of the '62 campaign bears repeating. Just before the final trial races between *Weatherly* and *Nefertiti,* Ted Hood spent a whole day, at Mosbacher's request, on the rival Twelve making sure her sails were the best possible. Some sails even went off to Marblehead for recutting and were rushed back in time to be used against him. Some of *Nefy's* crew felt this hurt their chances, but it's a mark of the man that he only wanted to win over the best possible boat, and he'd rather have been beaten by *Weatherly* than the Aussies. Hood now doubts that he'd ever again have the time to get involved in designing and campaigning a Twelve, business being what it is.

Not long after the '62 defense, the New York YC's Trustees passed a resolution interpreting the Cup's Deed of Gift to mean that challengers not only had to be designed and built in the challenging country but that gear and sails should come from there too. This has effectively cut off the challenging nations from Hood sails but they continue to order them from Marblehead as yardsticks. Many of the early pictures of the French trial horse *Chancegger* showed a lovely Hood main with one lower panel of a distinctly different color. Obviously the section had been removed for testing the Hood-woven cloth which continues to be one of the secrets of any Hood sail.

Hood sailmakers now have lofts in Canada, England, France, Australia and New Zealand. And while a challenging Twelve from any one of these countries would be allowed to have sails made at the local Hood loft, they cannot use the fabric produced in Marblehead. Largely due to the great success of the English loft, there is a plan afoot to weave Hood cloth in Ireland. If this ever reaches fulfillment, the sail gap will almost certainly be narrowed.

Back in 1964, with future challenges in mind, the Australians sent their top sailmaker, the late Joe Pearce, to spend a year with Hood, and he became a top assistant. With Ted preoccupied by a second unsuccessful attempt with *Nef-*

Exhibit 5—Continued

ertiti, Pearce became the man who dealt with the sails for the defender, *Constellation,* during the trials. Pearce may have learned quite a bit about the cut, but said his boss, "we didn't tell him much about the cloth."

Following this, and until his untimely death, Joe Pearce became the Hood sailmaker in Australia. He made *Dame Pattie's* sails in 1967 but by mutual agreement there was no communication with Marblehead on the subject of 12-Meter sails. The same arrangement applies with Peter Cole, the present Aussie Hood sailmaker, who has supplied the motive power for *Gretel II.* The Hood loft in France, newest of the foreign operations, has not been involved in Baron Bich's undertaking.

Although nearly all of the technical improvements and lessons learned are applicable to Hood's normal business of making sails for cruising/racing yachts, there are some special problems and differences in making sails for the Twelves. To begin with, a 12-Meter has a ¾ foretriangle rig (the maximum allowable under the rule) while most boats today have masthead rigs. Mainsails must be fitted to masts and booms that are designed to bend to a far greater degree than on any cruising boat. Spinnakers are not made to the maximum size the 12-Meter rule permits—experience has shown time and again that shape is more important than sheer size when it comes to making a Twelve go downwind. Nevertheless, a maximum 'chute is made every Cup summer just to be sure that the theory still holds.

In preparing for a Cup summer, the Hood loft is looking for ways to make their sails lighter, smoother and stronger. The Twelves put tremendous strains on their sails and it is essential that they be strong and durable. But still, to save weight, less provision is made to prevent chafing than in a normal sail. As to the weight of sailcloth, there is continuous research into ways of making it lighter but still strong enough to retain its shape-holding ability. This work comes under the supervision of Ted's father, Steadman, known to everybody as "The Professor," who has done much over the years to insure the success of his son's business. The Professor's research is continuous and he says that progress is slow. But the following table on mainsail cloth weights used by the Twelves would seem to belie this claim:

Year	Weight
1958	14-oz.
1962	12-oz.
1964	10-oz.
1967	7.5-oz.
1970	6.9-oz. (or slightly less)

One characteristic of every U.S. defender since 1958 has been a tendency to hobby-horse less than her rival in the seas off Newport. While hull design is all important in this respect, there is little doubt that lightweight sails—weight saved up high where it really counts—have also contributed significantly to this advantage.

Exhibit 5—Continued

One recent development of Hood research that has reached a sufficiently advanced stage to be used on 12-Meter sails this summer is the Hood Ring, a replacement for the large hand-worked grommets in the corners of sails. Hood Rings have proved to be almost twice as strong as the best hand-sewn equivalent even though they are considerably lighter in weight. Hood Rings are inserted by special high-pressure hydraulic tooling and now there is virtually no handwork in a typical Hood clew since roping has also been eliminated.

Other new wrinkles in 12-Meter sails this season include Cunningham holes for draft control in both genoas and mainsails. The latter have Cunninghams along the foot as well as the luff. When this was written, experimental zippers (two of them, side-by-side) seemed to have proved their worth as a further means of draft control along the luffs of mainsails. Hood and others have been using foot zippers on mainsails for many years. This year's lightest polypropylene spinnaker cloth is even lighter than *Intrepid*'s much talked-about Floater of '67, but The Professor won't say by how much. Mainsail headboards are now made of titanium for the ultimate in strength without weight.

Valiant and *Heritage* have the recently developed Hood Sea Stay, a hollow grooved rod in which the genoa luff is hoisted. This item eliminates hanks as well as the space between headstay and sail, thereby significantly reducing turbulence at the leading edge.

In perfecting 12-Meter sails, spinnakers and jibs are recut often. There has been a definite trend among U.S. Cup sailors toward working for perfection with the sails at hand rather than ordering one after another and trying to decide which of the lot is best, as was popular until 1964. *Intrepid,* for example, went through the entire '67 campaign with only two mainsails in her inventory. Hood has had great luck in making mainsails right the first time and thus virtually eliminating recutting. The 7.5-oz. main *Intrepid* used most only had one seam let out near the head. *Valiant's* first Hood main had not been touched, at least through the Preliminary Trials. Ted points out that owners often will get him out to look at sails believing they need to be recut when what is really needed may be a proper knowledge of how to adjust luff and sheet tension or how tight to carry a leech line. Hood personnel spend long hours discussing and demonstrating adjustment techniques to 12-Meter crews.

The problem is trying to find enough time to satisfy everybody. There can be little doubt that over the long haul Ted Hood's success in making 12-Meter sails has meant much to his business, even though it is now quite a small part of the total. But one of the ironies of a Cup summer for Hood is that much less other work comes in. Many owners apparently feel that the loft will be too busy with the Twelves to pay much attention to them. This is not true—a 12-Meter sail goes through the same manufacturing process as any other. But what is certainly true is that what started as a bedroom sail repair business during college years would never have grown to be the international enterprise it is today had Ted Hood not become sailmaker to the Twelves.

Source: Article appearing in the September, 1970, issue of *Yachting* magazine.

Some of the reasons behind the company's success were discussed in CML's 1970 Annual Report:

In every major ocean race of recent years, the winning boats (including *Intrepid* in the recent America's Cup Race) have consistently used Hood Sails. When Hood Sailmakers of Marblehead, Massachusetts joined the Group in February [1970], the Group became a very important factor in the marine accessories segment of the "leisure time" industry.

The business was started by Ted Hood as a hobby when he was a boy. Now there are sail lofts in Massachusetts, California, Canada, England, France, New Zealand, and Australia. The company weaves and finishes its own cloth in mills in Massachusetts, and, as such, it is the only fully integrated sailmaker in the world. Hood Yacht Systems, a division of Hood Sailmakers, manufactures masts, rigging, and specialty marine hardware.

The principal asset of the company is its technological and inventive skill. No other sailcloth maker has the technical ability to make such light yet strong cloth without the use of plastic resins. These innovative skills have also been applied in the design of sails and the manufacture of specialty marine hardware.

During the year, an entirely new style of sailcloth was introduced for use in the America's Cup. The company also began to extrude its own fibers for use in its "Floater" spinnaker cloths. The "Sea Stay" style of rod rigging became commercially available. Sail lofts were opened in France and California. A new [Executive] Vice President and General Manager was employed to give additional depth in administration and production management.

Additional lofts are planned in the United States and substantial sales growth is expected in the foreign markets. New marine accessory products are being developed for Hood Yacht Systems.

Competition for Hood came mainly from dozens of small local manufacturers which generally had strong market coverage in particular regions of the country only. Hood in fact had itself been established in the late 1930's as a strictly local loft supplying the Marblehead market. Over the years it had grown both nationally and internationally to its current position of preeminence. Mr. Morgan, the new division general manager, described the company's success as follows:

Hood's success can be attributed to a couple of factors. The most important of course is Ted Hood himself. Ted is a soft-spoken, modest kind of guy with an amazing knowledge of sailing and racing. He exudes confidence. What an ocean racer wants most from a sailmaker Ted Hood can supply in abundance . . . expert consultation in sail design and individual help in getting the best out of sails once they're made. Since the CML merger much of Ted's administrative load has been reduced and he now spends much more of his time testing new designs and out working with customers. Not only is this the kind of thing he enjoys most, but it's where Ted's time is most valuable to the company.

Hood Sailcloth is also a key competitive factor. Hood has a real product edge as the only U.S. sailmaker with its own weaving capability. In a very closely guarded process here in Marblehead we produce a tight-weave cloth of unusual lightness and strength. In fact, many in racing circles attribute *Intrepid's* victory over Australia's *Gretel* in the 1970 America's Cup Race at least in part to the fact that *Intrepid's* sails [using Hood cloth] weighed about half those of *Gretel.*

Hood sails were sold by five salaried salesmen and Mr. Hood himself through a variety of channels: direct to sailors (about half) and to dealers, naval architects, yacht builders, and the federal government. Hood competed only slightly in areas other than the large yacht market.

CML's Operating Philosophy and Policies

Hood's Irish investment was being considered in the context of an intricate set of relationships between CML and its divisions. According to Mr. Leighton, these relationships typically began taking shape even prior to acquisition itself and were strongly affected by personal factors:

It would have been very difficult to have acquired any of our companies without our personal interest in their products. Bob Tod, for instance, is a great hydroplane enthusiast and for a time even held the U.S. Class B hydroplane speed record. This, together with our outboard boat experience at Willard, made it much easier to approach Dick Fisher about joining us. My own sailing background gave us some immediate rapport with Ted Hood. Ted and I had even competed once in the 1956 New England Men's Sailing Championships. I had come in second behind Ted, who went on to win the U.S. Men's Championships that year. All of us in the group are skiers, so Carroll Reed's business was not completely foreign to us. Learning Carroll Reed's mail-order business in turn provided a background for rapport with Ed Lebo when we first approached him about selling Mason & Sullivan.

Mr. Leighton considered preacquisition discussions to be extremely important because they provided an opportunity for both parties to get to know each other. This involved both discovering the owner-manager's underlying needs and aspirations and outlining clearly for him what joining CML would mean in terms of policies, procedures, authority and responsibility relationships, management changes, etc. This "foundation building" period was considered of prime importance because it paved the way for changes to be made after acquisition. According to Mr. Leighton, only by letting an owner-manager know beforehand what changes to expect could a transition be made smoothly. He commented:

Most companies in our industry can benefit substantially from association with a larger, more sophisticated firm such as CML. We can provide capital and management know-how usually not available to a small company. We provide a vehicle for taking a small company public at favorable values and minimum expense. We can also provide a valuable environment for the top man in these companies. The independent businessman typically feels alone and would like someone to recognize his achievements and exchange ideas. His board of directors (if he has one) usually is not made up of professional managers who can give real guidance. He has no one to turn to for advice on a continuing basis. Therefore, he is typically a very lonely man under extreme pressure from long hours, and surrounded by subordinates he may not wish to confide in. About the only persons around to motivate and console him are his wife, banker, and accountant, and they may not be close enough to the business to do this effectively.

Countering this strong need for association is, of course, an equally strong need for autonomy. This creates an antagonism of forces which inevitably causes an owner anxiety during early stages of discussion with us. He has normally spent years building up his business and wants to make sure he'll remain in control after acquisition. Our big initial job is to subdue these anxieties. For this reason we deliberately don't talk price or even ask for financial statements during early contacts. Instead, we try to get to know his business, his problems, his personality. We explain to him in detail what life will be like with us and exactly what changes in his operation he can expect. The whole emphasis is one of building up trust and understanding. At some point along the way he inevitably brings out his financial statements to show us. As a result of our emphasis on mutual understanding, we are less apt to get involved in a bidding match than if we were to negotiate mainly on a price basis.

According to Mr. Leighton, the acquisition process itself had varied considerably among companies acquired so far:

One of our companies first came to us about joining CML. Another I had heard might be available. I simply phoned the president and set up a meeting to talk. For a third company we had to make overtures over a number of months before we finally got anywhere. Another acquisition came to us in an interesting way. Last spring an acquaintance of mine and the former president of a medium-sized mail-order company phoned to say that he had a company he wanted to buy personally, but that the purchase price was above his financial means, and he wondered whether CML might like to buy it in partnership with him. We liked the company so much we bought it outright and put him in as general manager, with the former owner's concurrence of course. This route is one we may use more frequently both for hiring new managers and acquiring new companies. I had a very qualified fellow in here not long ago who said he wanted to work for us. I told him we simply didn't have an opening at present, but that if he could bring us an attractive company we might acquire it and with the owner's approval put him in as general manager with attractive financial alternatives. He's working on one right now.

THE CORPORATE OFFICE

In January, 1971, CML's corporate office consisted of four officers. Mr. Leighton, chairman of the board, focused mainly on relationships external to operations, concentrating primarily on new acquisitions, investor relations, and the raising of new capital. Mr. Tod, president, spent an estimated 90% of his time working directly with divisions and was the corporate officer immediately responsible for operations. Mr. Chaffee,[8] treasurer, worked closely with divisional controllers in preparing accounting statements and various management studies such as cost-volume relationships, product mix contribution analyses, etc. He also handled companywide cash control, auditor relations, tax form preparation and corporate office accounting. Management felt that the existing four-man corporate staff was sufficient to handle expected growth for the next three or four years, with perhaps the addition of a financial controller to share some of Mr. Chaffee's current responsibilities.

Since July, 1970, borrowing and cash receipts for the entire corporation had been consolidated at the corporate level. Divisions could therefore no longer borrow on their own or build up their own cash balances; all funds passed through central CML accounts. Each division paid (or received) interest on funds received from (or advanced to) CML. Apart from interest payments there were no corporate charges.

FINANCIAL CONTROL

Mr. Tod commented as follows on the company's philosophy regarding divisional autonomy:

We want to give divisions their heads and let them make their own decisions within the broad policy constraints set at the corporate level. This much autonomy is workable only in the presence of complete, accurate, timely information on operations. Such data come in several forms. Prior to the beginning of our fiscal year each division submits three forecasts: monthly profit and loss for each of the following 12 months, end-of-month balance sheets for each of the following 12 months, and an annual capital budget showing forecasted expenditures by month. As the year proceeds, forecasts are compared on a monthly basis with actual operating figures.

In addition to strictly accounting data we receive a number of key indicators from divisions on a monthly basis. These are vital measures of each

---

[8] Philip Chaffee (32): B.S., University of Vermont, 1962; Financial Management Program, 1962–65, and then traveling audit staff, 1965–67, of the General Electric Company; Manager of corporate auditing, ITEK Corporation, 1968–70. Mr. Chaffee had joined CML as controller in June, 1970, and had assumed Mr. Fredericks's duties as treasurer upon the latter's resignation in December, 1970.

division's performance. For instance, from one division I get catalogue and retail sales and open-to-buy figures. For another I get bookings (orders), shipments, and discount levels for both dealer and direct sales, while another supplies order backlog, production, and inventory figures in addition to about six or eight others. For one division I look hardest at advertising response figures. Any variances are discussed in detail at regular meetings with division managements. Meetings are summarized in memo form and then sent back to divisions. If divisions don't agree with opinions or decisions stated in these memos they are supposed to let me know right away. With this system I feel we have about as tight a control system as we could get without our actually making the decisions ourselves.

Part of the reason for the emphasis on close control, Mr. Tod explained, stemmed from a desire to avoid an experience CML management had had at Willard. One of their divisions which had been reporting adequate profits for several years had suddenly shown considerable red ink following an examination of inventories which had precipitated large writedowns. This situation had come as a complete surprise to both group and division management, and in management's opinion was simply the result of inadequate controls.

Mr. Leighton offered the following comments on operating control:

We have two main operating policies: "No closets to hide in" and "No surprises." Together they spell full decentralization of operations *except for* financial information flows. If things go wrong in a division, division management has nowhere to hide because we've given them complete authority and responsibility for their operations. On the other hand, if things go well they take the bows. We don't want surprises either good or bad from divisions, and we try to ensure this by getting complete and frequent information on operations.

Division controllers were considered an important link in providing information flow from divisions to the corporate level, and CML had inherited what corporate management considered to be experienced men within three of the acquired companies. (The fourth required only a part-time bookkeeper.) Two of these men were CPAs, while the third was an M.B.A. from the Tuck School at Dartmouth. All had extensive backgrounds in either public or corporate accounting.

DIVISIONAL GENERAL MANAGERS

Another important ingredient to CML's operating strategy was the division general manager. Professionally trained, experienced general managers had been hired to complement all four division presidents, partially relieving them of administrative duties and thereby giving them more time to do what they were best at. While several of the general managers hired so far were still quite new to the company, Mr. Tod felt that they were already proving to be valuable additions to the divisions.[9] He stated that one of the most significant ways in which CML could benefit an acquired company was by recruiting for it people who would not normally be attracted to small companies, which often offered little opportunity for equity participation and promotion. Compensation of general managers was tied to earnings growth formulas similar to those of owner-managers, and involved liberal cash bonus and stock option possibilities based on performance. The relationship of a division general manager to an owner-manager was determined partly by this congruence of compensation interests, partly by the fact that each general manager had been selected by the owner-manager of the division involved from among several candidates prescreened by CML management, and partly by the understanding that the owner-manager ultimately had final say on all decisions affecting a division and in fact could fire the general manager if it became apparent that the two could not work together. All these arrangements had, of course, been discussed at length with owner-managers during the "foundation setting" stage preceding acquisition. All four general managers hired so far were still with the company in January, 1971.

Financial controls and other influences ushered in by CML appeared to have caused some changes within acquired companies. Middle management personnel from various divisions described some of these as follows:

It's not at all like it used to be around here. [The owner-manager] had always been an easygoing guy running the business pretty much on a day-to-day

---

[9] *Fred Snow* (35), executive vice president and general manager of Carroll Reed Ski Shops since March, 1970; A.B., Babson College, 1958; salesman, sales manager, promotions manager, and marketing vice president of Fieldcrest Company, 1959–70.

John Morgan (33), executive vice president and general manager of Hood Sailmakers, Inc. since April, 1970; Princeton, electrical engineering, 1959; M.B.A., Harvard, 1966; prior to joining Hood, had had a number of technical and management positions at General Electric Company over a 10-year period.

Bob Lavery (49), vice president and general manager of Mason & Sullivan Company since July, 1970; B.S., Kansas State College, 1940; 25 years' experience in catalog sales, first with Montgomery Ward and more recently with a successful medium-sized mail-order firm where he had been president since 1961.

Dave Wilson (33), vice president and general manager of Boston Whaler, Inc. since January, 1971; Cambridge, England, chemical engineering, 1961; M.B.A., Harvard, 1968; had worked for six years as a process engineer with a major U.S. chemical company, and since 1968 as president of a Canadian manufacturing concern where he had achieved profitable operations of the company for the first time since 1960.

basis. I liked this myself. It suited my style. Unfortunately, all this is changing now. Things are becoming much more systematic and "big business" around here. We're feeling this most in cost reduction and in sales promotion, but every one is feeling it to a certain extent. I don't think this will cause people to quit, though. Most of the workers are very unskilled and easy to train, so they aren't likely to do much better elsewhere. Most of the management people are like me. They've come here because they love [boating, sailing, skiing] and will stick it out because they love the sport.

.   .   .   .

[The new general manager] is a good man. We had about nine different men around here doing his job before he came. He made a tenth, but because he has just a little more finesse plus the authority of the job behind him things have been running much more smoothly around here since he came. I'm not sure, though, that any of the other nine couldn't have done just as well if they had been given the position.

.   .   .   .

I think people are happier and things are running more smoothly since we joined CML. Previously, it was hard to get big decisions made. Problems would frequently just float along without ever being resolved. This was frustrating. [The new general manager] is the kind of guy who looks at the facts and comes to a decision on them. This has made life easier for all of us.

MR. TOD'S ROLE

An additional important corporate link with divisions was provided by Mr. Tod himself. Mr. Tod tried to visit each division at least once every two weeks, and to spend not less than 50% of his time physically on site with division personnel. These visits enabled him to participate on an ongoing basis in divisional developments. According to Mr. Tod, discussion during these visits ranged over every aspect of a division's business: pricing policy, marketing strategy, expansion requirements, personnel problems, production scheduling, and so on. He stated:

It's hard to generalize about this relationship because it's so different in each specific instance. How I deal with a division depends upon the division involved, its key man, its employees, its particular problems, and so forth. One division president, for instance, is constantly after me to spend more time with him and his people. Until recently another division has been quite reluctant to seek any help.

There do seem to be certain patterns, however. When a new division first comes on board, Charlie and I try to schedule a luncheon for all its employees at which we introduce ourselves and discuss CML and our plans for the division. We deliberately wait two or three weeks after original announcement of the acquisition before having this luncheon in order to let division personnel get used to the idea prior to meeting us. During this period, we intentionally stay away from the division; this helps convey the impression that we don't intend to meddle too much in divisional operations. Before the luncheon meeting, Charlie and I try to learn as much as we can about the 12 or 15 key people in the division. We feel this is useful for getting to know a new division better and for establishing relationships with its key people.

While the above described the usual procedure, not every acquisition had had an initiation luncheon. One division president had objected to the custom so no luncheon had been held for that division.

Because, in principle, divisions operated relatively autonomously, Mr. Tod felt his influence upon operations was based less on exerting direct authority than on the confidence and respect he inspired as a manager. He commented on this situation to the case writer as follows:

The influence I can exert comes in preparation, really. I must have intimate knowledge of the business of each division, and must have the numbers involved in any particular situation at my fingertips. This means doing my homework. Otherwise, division people won't listen. They may pay lip service, but they'll make their own decisions in the final analysis. Of course, if they do, they'll have to live with them.

I have to be able to understand our divisions' businesses as well as division presidents themselves in order to do my job. I think I will be able to continue to do this as we expand the number of divisions. Keep in mind that all our divisions are in the leisure time industry and in many ways aren't really that different from one another. Our two mail-order businesses have a number of similarities, for example. The same is true, though to a lesser extent, of our two marine divisions.

I realize I have to walk a fine line most of the time between supervisor and boss, consultant and advisor. The key to this role of course is working with people, and the key to that is flexibility . . . listening to people, getting to know their capabilities, and correctly evaluating their judgments. All this of course requires intimate knowledge of the facts of specific situations. Again, doing your homework is essential!

When asked to comment upon the kinds of divisional situations he became involved in, apart from those involving routine financial control, Mr. Tod replied that these could be best classified according to the role he played in the development or solution of each. He saw himself playing several roles, but primarily those of:
1. Management consultant.
2. Management recruiter.
3. Participant in key decisions.
Mr. Tod described several situations as examples of each.

1. Management Consultant. This role typically involved the collection and analysis of information in such a way that it shed light on some important aspect of a division's operation. Mr. Tod described several instances in which he had played this role.

CONSUMER ANALYSIS. Dick Fisher, himself an avid fisherman, had deliberately designed the Boston Whaler for the fisherman's every need. As a result, the product combined the general advantages of stability, maneuverability, unsinkability, safety, and performance with specific fishing-oriented features such as a built-in bait box and a rack for fishing rods. Given this background and orientation, the company naturally directed advertising toward fishermen. Soon after acquisition Mr. Tod began to question whether such an orientation was really justified, however. He commented on this situation as follows:

> Working closely with the Boston Whaler sales organization during the months following acquisition, I came increasingly to feel that a significant percentage of Whaler owners were using the boat for family and recreational in addition to strictly fishing purposes. If this were true, I felt that Boston Whaler advertising copy should reflect the fact. One problem was that there wasn't really much product-in-use data available within the division. During my visits there I had plenty of opportunity to discuss my feelings, though, and suggested from time to time that a customer survey might be made to get a better feel for who bought Whalers and just how the boats were used. It took a while before anything happened, but gradually people began to get interested. During this period I spent quite a lot of time with the division advertising manager talking about what information might be helpful and how it might be obtained. After a while he began putting together a questionnaire, and we discussed this and revised it several times. Finally, by September [1970] a completed questionnaire was mailed out to about 400 customers. Responses have shown a significant family recreational clientele, and recent ad copy is already beginning to reflect this.

WINTER CATALOGUE PROGRAM. Mail order catalogs of one division had traditionally been published and mailed twice a year. The winter catalog consisted of 32 pages; the spring catalog, typically a less ambitious project, contained 24 pages. Each had a total mailing of several hundred thousand copies.

A review of catalog sales in past years had convinced Mr. Tod that an expansion of the spring catalog, in terms of pages, items, or mailings, or any combination of the three, could add to profits substantially. To demonstrate this he reconstructed from divisional accounting data a detailed analysis of the company's catalog experience to date, showing how past changes in pages, items, and mailings had affected volume, tying in enough cost data to provide estimates of profitability. This analysis indicated an optimum mix consisting of a 10% increase in total items offered, an increase in the number of pages from 24 to 32, and a continuance of mailings at their former level.

Getting the division to implement this increase was another matter, however. Mr. Tod commented:

Division personnel just didn't feel there was enough time to produce the eight additional pages before the deadline for mailings. It took a little pushing on our part to get this through, but eventually the division made it. I was able to help a little on a bottleneck situation involving page layout. By setting up a very simple PERT chart with deadlines for the various activities involved, I was able to persuade division personnel to farm out certain layout functions. As it turned out, by following the PERT chart, the catalogue was completed three days before the mailing deadline. Partly as a result of the page increase, profits from the 1970 Spring Catalogue were about $50,000 higher than the previous year.

The division president had the following to say about this situation:

I didn't feel we were geared up at the time to handle the increased volume. One reason I sold to CML was to get their professional help in solving some of our internal systems problems like order processing and inventory control. We haven't had too much help on this so far, however. The increase in catalogue volume before straightening out these problems inevitably caused some foul-ups with customers. I'm a little afraid that this kind of thing may undercut some of the goodwill and close personal contact with customers we've worked so hard to build over the years.

2. Management Recruitor.   A second corporate role vis-à-vis divisions in which Mr. Leighton and Mr. Tod appeared to be equally active was that of management recruiter. Mr. Leighton described this role as follows:

In talking with prospective acquisitions we typically find that the presidents really don't enjoy what they're doing. They have to be concerned with banking relations, accounting, marketing, production, and sales, but what they really want to do is develop more and better products.

To reduce the administrative load on division presidents, CML had helped recruit general managers for all four divisions, leaving the final hiring decision in the hands of division presidents themselves.

Mr. Leighton added:

We try to get division presidents to hire a man who will complement them. Generally, we try to get an M.B.A. who's been out and gotten six or seven years experience. We would rather go out and pay someone in his early 30's a lot of money because he has tremendous potential and good background than to get someone with less experience more cheaply or someone with more experience but with less potential.

We want the man that every company wants. We spend as much time trying to meet and recruit a man as we do a company. For example, we went night and day after John Morgan.

Mr. Morgan had graduated from Princeton in 1959 with a degree in electrical engineering and had joined the General Electric Company shortly afterwards. He worked there until 1964 in a number of technical and supervisory positions, including foreman of shop operations and project supervisor for the transfer of products from U.S. to European factories. Mr. Morgan then entered the Harvard Business School, graduating as a Baker Scholar with High Distinction in 1966. Following graduation Mr. Morgan returned to G.E., where he subsequently held positions as manager of business planning, manager of marketing administration (both at the division level), and finally as manager of resource planning for a $600 million product group. He resigned in the spring of 1970 to become general manager of Hood Sailmakers.

Mr. Leighton commented as follows on the process of recruiting a Hood general manager:

We had heard some very good things about John from his professors at Harvard. The feedback we got about his work at G.E. was also excellent. We heard that he was considered one of their most able young men. We decided that if he was that good, we would like him to join our team, so we went after him.

Mr. Morgan offered the following remarks on this situation:

I really hadn't been thinking of leaving G.E. when Bob and Charlie approached me. I had recently been promoted for the third time since leaving the Business School in 1966. I was getting all the right signals from higher management, and I felt I was on the way up.

I think what really appealed to me in CML's offer was the opportunity to build something on my own. Financially I'm at about the same level as at G.E. Of course there's a possibility of building some equity here, but the risks are great also. Over the long run G.E. probably offered about as good an opportunity for building a personal estate. What I couldn't resist about the Hood offer was the excitement of working in a small operation where I could really influence the future of the company.

3. Participant in Key Decisions. A third important role played by corporate management was that of participant in key decisions facing divisions. Mr. Tod offered the following as an example of the kind of decision he typically became involved in.

PRODUCTION CUTBACK. During the third quarter of fiscal 1970 Mr. Tod and one division president had held quite different opinions over what constituted a wise production level for the division. Each side claimed a good case for its position. Division management argued that sales for January and February had been well ahead of forecast, indicating that another good year was in the making. Corporate management feared that trends in the general economy might significantly reduce fourth-quarter shipments and was urging sizable production cutbacks. Mr. Tod was unsuccessful in getting division management to accept his view, however, and production continued at high levels throughout the first three quarters.

Mr. Tod noted:

I made my voice heard, but I couldn't convince anyone to follow me. In fact, I'm not sure whether if I'd been in the division's shoes I would have cut production myself, given the demoralizing impact this has on a division if high sales eventually materialize. From our standpoint, however, the risk of over-production seemed sizable, and we were advocating a path of prudence.

As it turned out, an unexpected stock market slide caused May and June sales to drop well below forecast. Inventories rose substantially as a result, requiring much more CML financing than originally budgeted. The division became dependent on us because it had to ask for additional financing to carry inventory. This puts us in a good position to exert our influence. At our urging, the division is reducing next year's forecast well below the level originally planned. In addition, it is making contingency plans to cover a further sales drop next year, and is cutting overhead substantially.

HOOD'S IRISH PROJECT

Corporate management's involvement in Hood's Irish weaving mill project constituted yet a further example of its role as participant in key decisions facing divisions.

Hood's organization had grown rapidly in recent years. As recently as early 1967 production facilities had been limited to one weaving and one sail-making facility, both located at Marblehead, and all sales (already 30% foreign in 1967) had been made by Mr. Hood and three sales consultants working out of Marblehead. To reduce tariff expenses on sails shipped abroad and to give better service to foreign customers, Hood had begun setting up foreign lofts, first in England (1967) and later in France, New Zealand, Australia, and Canada. In the United States a West Coast loft had been opened during this period, and the Marblehead weaving capacity had been nearly doubled. This expansion had naturally been accompanied by an increase in the number of Hood employees, from a total of about 165 in 1967, all located in Marblehead, to approximately 300 by 1971, 175 in the United States and 125 abroad. The organization had also become increasingly complex, as evidenced by Mr. Morgan's sketch appearing as Exhibit 6.

The concept of a European-based weaving mill had originated in 1968 with the manager of the newly established English loft, which paid a 20% tariff on all sailcloth imported from Marblehead. Hood's interest in a European mill naturally increased with the opening of additional foreign lofts in 1968 and 1969, since duties on the sailcloth

Exhibit 6

CML GROUP, INC.
Organization Chart of Hood Sailmakers, Inc.

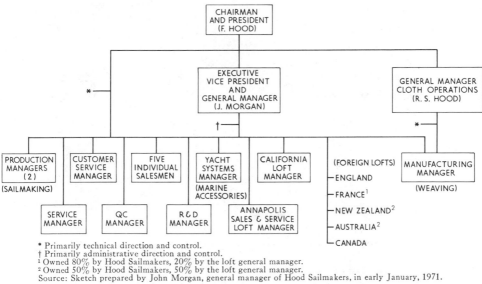

* Primarily technical direction and control.
† Primarily administrative direction and control.
[1] Owned 80% by Hood Sailmakers, 20% by the loft general manager.
[2] Owned 50% by Hood Sailmakers, 50% by the loft general manager.
Source: Sketch prepared by John Morgan, general manager of Hood Sailmakers, in early January, 1971.

they imported ranged as high as 35% in France and 31% in Australia. The ad valorem value of cloth represented approximately 25% of the final selling price of Hood sails; import tariffs therefore constituted a significant percentage of each foreign sales dollar: from 5% in England to more than 8% in Australia and France.

Because of increasing pressure from the managers of foreign lofts, Mr. Hood in early 1969 hired a brother-in-law of the English loft manager to begin site studies for a European mill. The desirability of an Irish site soon became evident because Ireland's inclusion in the British Commonwealth permitted tariff-free export to all Commonwealth countries, because the Irish government offered to underwrite 50% of capital costs for the new facility and to waive all tax on profits earned in Ireland, and because of low labor rates in Ireland. By August, 1970, the Irish Development Authority (IDA) had agreed to fund $266,000

Exhibit 7

CML GROUP, INC.

Capital Requirements for Irish Weaving Mill
(Thousands of Dollars)

	Total Cost	SOURCES OF FUNDS	
		IDA Grant	CML
Land	$ 8.4	$ 4.2	$ 4.2
Building	216.0	108.0	108.0
Equipment	329.6	154.1	175.5
Working capital (net)*	26.0	0	26.0
Total funds required	$580.0	$266.3	$313.7

After-Tax Cash Flow Savings Resulting from Transferring to Ireland all Weaving of Cloth Sold Outside the United States
(Thousands of Dollars)

	1971	1972	1973	1974	1975
Cash flow increase					
Resulting from decreases in:					
Tariffs	$ 16	$ 18	$ 20	$ 23	$ 27
Variable costs of manufacture	56	63	65	83	96
U.S. corporation profit taxes	74	85	87	110	128
Subtotal	$146	$166	$172	$216	$251
Cash flow decrease					
Resulting from an increase in:					
Fixed cost of manufacture†	98	97	96	96	96
Net cash flow increase					
(net cash flow savings)	$ 48	$ 69	$ 76	$120	$155

Discounted Cash Flow Return on $314,000 Investment = 13%

* Net of working capital freed in the United States as a result of moving a portion of the weaving operation to Ireland.
† Excludes depreciation.
Source: Company records.

of the total $554,000 fixed capital required by the project, and quotes for the necessary equipment were already being solicited.

As shown in detail in Exhibit 7, the project called for a total investment of $580,000. Mr. Morgan calculated that the cash flow savings resulting from the new mill (shown in the lower half of Exhibit 7) represented a 13% after tax return on CML's $314,000 investment in the project. Cash flow savings were expected in three areas:

1. Elimination of tariffs on cloth currently woven in Marblehead and shipped to lofts in Commonwealth countries.
2. A reduction in variable cost of manufacture arising mainly from lower labor rates in Ireland.
3. A reduction in U.S. corporate profits tax arising because the Marblehead mill would suffer a significant loss of contribution margin (approximtaely 40%) as a result of moving production to Ireland. The resulting reduction in profits reported in the United States would reduce U.S. taxes on corporate profits.

The only recurring cash outflow resulting from the investment arose from an increase in fixed manufacturing expenses. While no reduction in Marblehead's fixed expenses was expected despite the 40% reduction in through-put, Ireland would itself incur $98,000 of additional fixed costs (after depreciation).

Mr. Morgan offered the following comments on the Irish project:

From my standpoint, the big advantage of the project is strictly financial . . . the 13% after tax return it represents for us. There are minor strategic advantages, of course. The investment will protect our positions in England and France, where duties have pushed prices about as high as they can go. If duties should go even higher, which we feel could happen, we might be pushed out of these markets if we are still shipping cloth from Marblehead.

Hood's board of directors was scheduled to meet on January 15 to decide on a recommendation with regard to the Irish investment. Mr. Tod saw three alternatives open to the board: (1) dropping the project outright, (2) going ahead with it full speed, or (3) delaying it until Hood's domestic market improved. The more he considered the many factors involved, the more he came to favor the third alternative. First, cash inflows were relatively small during early years of the project. They would therefore not significantly contribute to the earnings track record CML hoped to establish prior to going public in 1972. Second, the tax status of profits earned in Ireland raised a complex set of questions including (1) whether or not future investors would be evaluating CML's earnings on a before-tax or an after-tax basis, (2) future cash needs in Europe providing a use for profits earned abroad, (3) difficulties and costs associated with eventual repatriation of profits earned abroad, and (4) possible legal complications arising from the fact that earn-out for former Hood owners was based on before-tax rather than after-tax profits. Third, Hood was showing a somewhat lower return on the funds currently being advanced by CML[10] than some of the other divisions of the company. Therefore, while Hood profits had improved somewhat in recent months, the division had not yet entirely demonstrated an ability to achieve its full profit potential. Fourth, the continued slump in domestic sales had reduced Hood's Marblehead operation to 50% of capacity. This made a sizable investment in additional capacity difficult to justify. Fifth, and most important, Hood management was already spread extremely thin over a great number of activities and did not appear to have the time and energy at present to take on a major new commitment.

There were of course disadvantages to delay. The IDA grant might be lost. Hood funds and management energy would be expended just maintaining status quo on the project. The Hoods themselves, concerned with the long-run competitive advantages of the investment and eager to get under way, might be disappointed.

Mr. Tod commented on his position as follows:

I just feel we can get a quicker pay-out by putting our money in other areas . . . expanding one company's product line, for instance, or improving another company's sales organization.

Mr. Leighton offered the following comments:

I think over the long run it makes sense for Hood to begin weaving abroad. It's a question of timing, really. With sales down, plus an overcapacity situation, I'm afraid of what the Irish investment will do to Hood's current profit picture. In addition, I wonder whether at this point in time Hood has enough management time and energy to take on something like this. A start-up situation is never easy.

Achievements to Date: Future Problems and Opportunities

Hood's Irish investment was under consideration just 18 months after the formation of CML and 15 months since its first acquisition in September, 1969. Mr. Leighton had the following to say about CML's achievements to date and the problems and opportunities facing the company in the months to come:

Progress so far has been excellent. Three out of four companies will show significant profit increases this year over last—20% or more. In the case of one division profits will fall somewhat, but mainly because we are deliberately scheduling manufacturing below break-even in order to work off excess inven-

---

[10] Totaling $800,000 in early January, 1971.

tory built up last year. Fiscal '72 should bring a big profit increase for this division.

As for further acquisitions, the biggest constraint at this point is pressure on Bob Tod. Right now, for instance, we are looking at three companies as possible acquisitions this spring. All are out of state and only one is in New England. This is quite different from our existing divisions which are all easily accessible from Boston. The big question on further acquisitions becomes how many companies one man can handle at once. This depends, of course, on how spread out they are geographically, and on the quality of division management. If our divisions can more or less run themselves, we can spread Bob a lot thinner. The real key to further growth then becomes the development of good management teams within divisions, and this in turn depends heavily on the quality of people we can bring into CML Group companies. As a matter of fact, after acquiring our fourth company last July we completely stopped all acquisition search and spent six months just looking for people. Now that general managers have been installed in all divisions and we've got four really good division management teams, we're back looking at acquisitions again.

There are other ways of easing the pressure on Bob, of course. One would be to limit acquisitions to businesses very similar to existing divisions. This would reduce the learning effort required at our level. Another would be to eventually develop several Bob Tods as group vice presidents for our three main areas: marine, sporting equipment and related accessories, and hobby crafts. An advantage of this would be the increased promotion opportunities it would open to new employees now being brought into the company. A disadvantage is that it would necessarily reduce the tremendous fun and personal involvement we are now having with our companies. How we go on this is a personal decision we'll have to make at some point. A third possibility would be to bring new companies in under existing divisions.

A long-term objective is to take CML public sometime after the fall of 1972. This would provide the three full years of audited operations required by the SEC. We'd like a major "quality" brokerage firm to handle the public offering and want a large enough offering in our shares to provide for after-market trading. To achieve this we feel we will need from $750,000 to $1 million in after-tax profits.

As far as we're concerned, the current economic downturn couldn't have been timed better. It has pushed us to trim dead weight in divisions to a point where they are now lean and hungry. When the economy finally turns around we should be in a position to show attractive internal earnings increases. This of course is the real key to the long-run success of CML Group: our ability to show earnings per share increases through internal growth rather than through newly acquired earnings. Stated another way, we believe that our future success will depend far more on our ability to successfully manage than on our ability to successfully acquire.

PART II
Administration

THE CASES IN PART II of this book focus more directly on the problems of designing and managing an administrative organization than do the cases presented in Part I. Consequently, the educational objective of the following sections is to extend the range of skills stressed in Part I by presenting case problems which focus class discussion on (1) those instruments of management that a general manager can use in implementing a plan of action, (2) the alternate ways of structuring decision-making within administrative subunits, and (3) administrative problems at the level of the individual manager which result from attempts to effect change.

In Section 3, for example, the principal issue raised is how best to gear a firm's organizational structure and systems of measurement and reward to overall corporate strategy. The student is asked to confront such basic questions as: How many administrative subunits should a given company have? How should these subunits be structured internally? How should their performance be measured and their managers rewarded? How should the various parts of the company be related as a whole? These questions are posed by a series of cases which progresses from simple to relatively complex situations. The cases on Midway Foods Corporation and the Rose Company deal with essentially single-product companies. In contrast, the subsequent cases deal with increasingly more diverse enterprises.

The cases in Section 4 present situations which for the most part assume both corporate strategy and structure as given. These cases focus, therefore, upon selected general management problems such as introducing a new planning and control system into Blow-Mold Packers, Inc.; establishing control over costs, operating procedures, and deteriorating personnel relations at Precision Controls, Inc., and Business Machines Corporation; and developing a total system which fits the particular industry and value system of the Rugby Portland Cement Company Ltd.

The cases in Section 5 are complicated and comprehensive, offering the opportunity for students to combine the analytical approaches of Part I and Part II and to explore the general management problems of conglomerates.

The situations and problems presented in Sections 3 through 5 are difficult, and the process of developing a useful set of recommendations for these cases may at times be frustrating. The challenge is in coming to understand how the general manager can influence the accomplishment of corporate purpose through the selective use of the management instruments available to him. The following cases have been designed and selected for this book with that goal in mind.

In preparing these cases, the student should still begin his analysis by summarizing what he believes the current corporate plan or strategy of the company is. This will provide the necessary base for a detailed analysis of the various alternatives that are available to top management in implementing its chosen strategy. In addition, careful attention should be paid to the principal tasks suggested by a given strategic plan. The student should think about alternate ways of organizing these tasks and controlling their performance. As part of this analysis, thought should also be given to the question of who should be making the important decisions in the organization and how the work of these key decision makers can be coordinated. And, of course, most organizational recommendations must reflect the administrative inheritance of the enterprise in question. Therefore, careful attention to corporate history, values, and administrative practices should be another part of thorough case preparation.

Section 3
Designing the
Administrative Organization

1. Midway Foods Corporation (A)

IN FEBRUARY, 1958, Midway Foods Corporation produced three principal items: two packaged food products and its Midway brand of candy bar. In addition it had purchased from Sherwood & Co., Ltd., of England its Robin Hood brand of candy bar for resale in the American market. Since candy sales accounted for most of Midway's volume, the company was basically a competitor in the candy subdivision of the food industry. And since both bars utilized chocolate as a principal ingredient, in a more direct sense Midway was a competitor in the chocolate-bar segment of the candy industry.

The Candy Industry

In 1957 total candy sales in the United States were over $1 billion (Exhibit 1), with package goods (plain and fancy) accounting for 35.9%; bulk chocolates, 16.7%, chocolate bars, 33.9%; and other candies, 13.5%. While package goods (particularly plain goods) had taken an increasing market share since the war, chocolate bars had accounted for a decreasing share until 1957. Total dollar sales of the candy industry had grown less than 5% between 1947 and 1956, and chocolate-bar sales had declined 30% during the same period from the all-time peak of $486 million (Exhibit 2).

In terms of structure, the candy industry was characterized by a spectrum from the very large integrated manufacturers such as Hershey Chocolate Corporation (1956 sales, $148 million) to a multitude of one-man operations, with the average company having about 45 employees. Many of the companies specialized in either bar goods, bulk candies, or package goods. Other companies such as Hershey and Nestle supplied the industry with chocolate items such as coatings and syrups and also manufactured bar and bulk candies. The number of companies in the industry had declined steadily since the all-time high in 1919, as indicated by the following figures:

	Number of
	Candy
Year	*Manufacturers*
1919	3,149
1933	2,218
1947	1,686
1954	1,434

Data on some of the better-known chocolate-bar manufacturers are presented in Exhibits 3 and 4.

The chocolate candy bars being sold in 1957 had a number of characteristics, some intrinsic, others the result of competitive conditions in the industry. Intrinsically the chocolate bar was a nonessential, low-priced food item which tended to have a seasonal sales pattern (with a summer decline due to the effect of heat upon the constituent ingredients of chocolate). As a result of industry practices, chocolate bars tended to be a packaged food item which was mass produced for wide distribution at a fixed retail price under an advertised brand name. While the bars varied in size and price from penny goods to a one-pound bar, Midway executives estimated that over 60% of dollar sales

Exhibit 1

MIDWAY FOODS CORPORATION (A)

U.S. Production of Candy and per Capita Consumption

	VOLUME		MANUFACTURERS' SALES VALUE		
	Total Pounds (in millions)	Per Capita Pounds	Total Dollars (in millions)	Per Capita Dollars	Average Value per Pound in Cents
1957	2,769	16.3	$1,062	$6.25	38.4¢
1956	2,625	15.8	1,005	6.05	38.3
1955	2,542	15.5	965	5.88	38.0
1954	2,606	16.1	977	6.04	37.5
1953	2,718	17.1	996	6.24	36.6
1952	2,705	17.3	986	6.28	36.4
1951	2,669	17.3	965	6.25	36.2
1950	2,784	18.4	924	6.09	33.2
1949	2,594	17.3	875	5.88	33.7
1948	2,673	18.2	1,001	6.84	37.5
1947	2,603	18.1	956	6.57	36.7
1946	2,438	17.3	687	4.84	28.2
1945	2,562	18.7	620	4.47	24.2
1944	2,804	20.5	658	4.81	23.5
1943	2,561	19.0	575	4.26	22.4
1942	2,519	18.7	490	3.64	19.5
1941	2,536	19.0	403	3.05	15.9
1940	2,225	16.9	336	2.55	15.1
1939	2,050	15.7	308	2.36	15.0

Source: U.S. Department of Commerce.

were in 5-cent bars, with 10-cent bars probably accounting for another 20%. Bar candy was distributed through brokers to an estimated 20,000 jobbers, and ultimately to more than 1,000,000 retail outlets.

While chocolate bars were probably more competitive with one another than with other products, such as box chocolates, bulk candies, or nonchocolate bars, their postwar sales decline was closely linked with the fortunes of the candy industry, an industry which for years had been lethargic, slow to change, and not quite able to grow in step with the expanding population. The story of this industry's decline, and the reversal of the decline in the 1950's, tells much of the competitive characteristics of the candy industry and of the problems and opportunities facing a chocolate-bar manufacturer.

LONG-TERM DECLINE

While in 1941 the American public had spent .42% of its disposable income for candy, in 1954 it spent only .38%, and in 1956 only .35%. In addition, candy consumption had shown an absolute decline

Exhibit 2

MIDWAY FOODS CORPORATION (A)
Industry Candy Sales by Major Types
(Dollars in Thousands)

	SALES	PACKAGE GOODS (PLAIN AND FANCY)		BULK CHOCOLATES		CHOCOLATE BARS		OTHER 1¢, 5¢ AND 10¢ GOODS	
		Sales	Percent	Sales	Percent	Sales	Percent	Sales	Percent
1957	$1,062,000	$381,258	35.9	$177,354	16.7	$360,018	33.9	$143,370	13.5
1956	1,005,000	359,790	35.8	171,855	17.1	338,685	33.7	134,670	13.4
1955	965,000	305,905	31.7	169,840	17.6	334,855	34.7	154,400	16.0
1954	977,000	289,192	29.6	174,883	17.9	356,605	36.5	156,320	16.0
1953	996,000	288,840	29.0	176,292	17.7	384,456	38.6	146,412	14.7
1952	986,000	277,066	28.1	178,466	18.1	378,624	38.4	151,844	15.4
1951	965,000	241,250	25.0	188,175	19.5	383,105	39.7	152,470	15.8
1950	924,000	209,748	22.7	188,496	20.4	396,396	42.9	129,360	14.0
1949	875,000	186,375	21.3	170,625	19.5	387,625	44.3	130,375	14.9
1948	1,001,000	206,206	20.6	181,181	18.1	478,478	47.8	135,135	13.5
1947	956,100	160,608	16.8	199,804	20.9	485,648	50.8	109,940	11.5
1946	687,000	100,302	14.6	135,339	19.7	366,858	53.4	84,501	12.3
1945	620,000	88,040	14.2	119,660	19.3	332,940	53.7	79,360	12.8
1944	658,000	76,986	11.7	136,206	20.7	346,108	52.6	98,700	15.0
1943	575,000	55,775	9.7	138,575	24.1	274,850	47.8	105,800	14.4
1942	490,000	53,410	10.9	143,570	29.3	203,840	41.6	89,180	18.2
1941	403,224	44,355	11.0	128,628	31.9	153,225	38.0	77,016	19.1
1940	336,000	33,936	10.1	111,552	33.2	124,992	37.2	65,520	19.5
1939	308,000	31,724	10.3	105,028	34.1	108,416	35.2	62,832	20.4

Source: U.S. Department of Commerce. Percentages prepared by Harvard Business School staff.

on a per-capita basis from 18.1 pounds in 1947 to a low of 15.5 pounds in 1955, a 14% decline in 8 years (Exhibit 1). Worst hit were chocolate-bar sales, declining from one half of total candy sales in 1947 to one-third in 1956, with dollar volume showing a 30% decline during the same period (Exhibit 2).

The period from 1919 to 1950 could be characterized as one of decline, in which narrow profit margins (except during the war) squeezed

Exhibit 3

MIDWAY FOODS CORPORATION (A)
Data for Selected Candy Manufacturers, 1956
(Dollars in Thousands)

COMPANY	CANDY BRAND NAME	ESTIMATED TOTAL COMPANY SALES*	ADVERTISING EXPENDITURES		
			Television	Other	Total
Midway Foods Corporation	Midway	$ 6,700†	$ 380	—	$ 380
	Robin Hood				
Food Manufacturers, Inc.	M & M	28,000	760	—	760
Hershey Chocolate Corp.	Hershey bars	148,000	–0–	–0–	–0–
Mars, Inc.	Mars	60,000	1,666	$67	1,733
	Marsettes				
	Three Musketeers				
	Milky Way				
New England Confectionery					
Company	Necco	18,500	170	—	170
	Sky bar				
Peter Paul, Inc.	Mounds	25,000	1,551	7	1,558
	Almond Joy				
Sweets Company of America	Tootsie Rolls	19,000	2,144	—	2,144

* Sales of all products, not just candy bars.
† Fiscal year, March, 1956–March, 1957.
Source: Estimates prepared by the Dearborn Advertising Agency, Inc.

out more and more competitors. These were also years when there were few successful new brands and little to catch the eye in the way of new advertising or packaging. One Midway executive commented: "In the chocolate-bar business things were in low gear. One indication is that most of the brands dated from the 1920's or earlier, and some had been household words since the turn of the century."

NEW VITALITY

Latterly the candy industry began to come to life again, and by 1956 the results could be seen in a small increase in per capita consumption (in pounds), reversing a trend which had been almost continuous

Exhibit 4

MIDWAY FOODS CORPORATION (A)
Sales Results for Selected Manufacturers
(Dollars in Millions)

Year	Midway	General Candy*	Hershey	New England Confectionery	Sweets	Food Manufacturers
1947	—	—	$120	—	—	—
1948	—	$9.0	168	—	$10.1	$ 4.2
1949	—	7.6	142	—	7.7	3.1
1950	$ .5	9.0	149	—	8.8	5.5
1951	1.3	8.9	154	—	9.8	9.7
1952	2.3	8.1	152	—	11.1	14.6
1953	3.3	7.7	150	$15.9	12.5	16.8
1954	3.6	7.4	159	15.8	15.7	17.6
1955	5.2	6.6	151	17.0	16.0	20.8
1956	6.7	6.4	148	18.5	18.9	28.5

* Includes Williamson Candy Company, a subsidiary, manufacturer of O Henry bars.
Sources: Moody's *Industrials*, Midway records, and, for Food Manufacturers, Inc. (M & M), Midway estimates

since 1944. Per capita consumption increased again in 1957 (Exhibit 1) and was expected to continue its climb in 1958. In addition, in 1957 the decline in the percentage of disposable income being spent for candy was finally halted, and the first substantial increase in 10 years was expected in 1958. The new vitality was also marked by an increase in chocolate-bar sales and by chocolate bars' taking a slightly larger share of the candy market, reversing, at least temporarily, a trend of some 12 years' standing (Exhibit 2).

OTHER TRENDS

The 1956–57 upturn in the industry could be ascribed mainly to increased marketing activities, including advertising, promotion, and distribution. Probably the most significant change in candy marketing was the increasing utilization of television advertising to support sales of nationally distributed brand-name candy bars. A number of the larger, "more progressive" firms had enjoyed dramatic sales increases in conjunction with television advertising campaigns, while other companies had failed to increase sales or even lost ground (Exhibits 3 and 4).

A second industry development was the rapidly increasing importance of the supermarket. Not only did supermarkets account for over 30% of candy sales in 1956; some of the big chains manufactured their own candy. In its 1958 candy industry analysis, Standard & Poor noted that Kroger, Safeway, and A & P were estimated to manufacture over 35%

of their requirements, while the average for all chains was estimated at 25%, with two-thirds of this 25% being made in their own factories and the remaining third made by others for the chains' private labels.

A third development was the increasing difficulty of securing wide distribution for new products. This resulted partly from the direct competition of the supermarkets and their reluctance to take shelf space for other than "own-name" brands, partly from the proliferation of sizes and packages of a single brand (such as 5-cent, 10-cent, 25-cent, one-half pound, and pound Hershey bars), and partly from the widening distribution of national brands which created more competition for shelf space in all stores. For some brands it was becoming a problem even to maintain distribution. One approach followed by some makers of little-known brands was to "buy" distribution, by contributing to supermarket advertising budgets, giving substantial discounts on the merchandise, or "doing favors" for the manager or purchasing director. And it was not unknown for food companies to do this type of thing in order to retain existing shelf space for items already being carried.

A similar, and probably even more competitive, situation existed in regard to securing vending-machine sales. Industry spokesmen estimated that there were approximately four million candy-vending machines in use and that vending-machine sales were between 5% and 10% of candy-bar sales. Since sales to a single vending company could be quite sizable, competition was intense for these outlets; industry informants stated that it was common for a company to buy increased distribution in order to expand sales or to buy another year's distribution for the identical outlets.

Finally, there appeared to be an industry trend toward the 10-cent candy bar. In 1956 over 60% of candy-bar sales were nickel bars, but dime bars accounted for 23%. And while the American market was described by Midway management as "still basically a 5-cent bar market," several bars, such as Peter Paul's Mounds and Almond Joy, had successfully gone from 5 cents to 10 cents and others were in the process. This trend was due primarily to rising raw material costs in an industry where it was not uncommon for the cost of the raw materials to equal 50% of the wholesale price of the item. The bars which had remained at 5 cents had often done so by reducing size or by adopting synthetic substitutes, or both. Rising labor costs were a secondary consideration, since candy bars were typically produced on automatic or semiautomatic forming and packaging equipment.

Two developments of a primarily internal nature were also apparent:

Exhibit 5

MIDWAY FOODS CORPORATION (A)
Average Cocoa Prices (Accra at New York)
(Cents per Pound)

A. AVERAGE MONTHLY PRICES

	1956	1957	1958
January	29.7¢	23.6¢	42.1¢
February	27.6	22.8	46.2
March	26.4	22.7	
April	26.5	25.6	
May	26.0	26.7	
June	27.1	30.6	
July	28.7	30.3	
August	28.4	32.0	
September	22.9	34.9	
October	26.0	35.4	
November	27.1	41.6	
December	26.2	40.8	
Average	27.3¢	30.6¢	

B. AVERAGE YEARLY PRICES

Year	Price	Year	Price	Year	Price
1957	30.6¢	1951	35.3¢	1945	9.0¢
1956	27.3	1950	32.1	1944	9.0
1955	37.3	1949	21.6	1943	9.1
1954	57.8	1948	39.6	1942	9.1
1953	37.1	1947	34.8	1941	7.6
1952	35.6	1946	12.0	1940	5.1

Source: *New York Journal of Commerce.*

factory automation and the previously mentioned proliferation of items under a single brand name. While Standard & Poor's 1958 candy industry survey indicated that labor costs were roughly 15% of wholesale value, it stated that there was a trend toward equipment with higher operating speeds and toward more fully automated production lines. The inceased number of items was a response to the need for more "supermarket items" and to the desire to obtain more shelf space and eye appeal from the larger displays.

Significantly, three major industry characteristics appeared to have remained unchanged despite the renewed industry vigor. First, it was still difficult and uncommon for new brands to be launched successfully. Industry spokesmen stated that only three new brands had been launched successfully since World War II, one of which was the Midway brand. Management also stated that a number of unsuccessful attempts had been made by major companies. A second holdover was the volatile market for commodities, particularly chocolate (see Exhibit 5). Finally, the number of competitors continued to decline, primarily because of the growing need for marketing skill and for greater financial resources to stay alive in the increasingly competitive industry.

Midway Foods

During 1949 Midway Foods had gone into bankruptcy. When the present management purchased it, there had been no shipments for over eight months. At that time Midway occupied a decrepit factory building on Maxwell Street, a location immediately adjacent to Chicago's "flea market" where residents and peddlers sold or traded everything from fish and fur coats to buggy whips and rebuilt lawnmowers. Midway manufactured several food products under less than ideal conditions in a plant where it was extremely difficult to maintain even minimal sanitation standards. Its products were distributed in Cook County and surrounding areas through jobbers to a limited number of small retail accounts, and its Midway bar was known to local wholesalers for its poor quality, poor appearance, and a price fully equal to that of competing products. Because of the characteristics of its products, and also because the previous management had "robbed the trade" during the war when rationing made that possible, Midway enjoyed singularly bad relations with the trade.

In the 1956–57 season, sales had passed the $6 million mark (Exhibit 6) and were expected to exceed $7 million in 1957–58. The brand had been successfully launched throughout the Midwest and had achieved some distribution on a nationwide basis. In the words of one industry source, "Midway not only has the goodwill of the trade, they have its respect." The company had moved to a five-story plant in Cicero, Illinois, increased employment to 100 people, and increased output of the Midway bar by more than 5,000%. The Midway bar was still below average in size but had been considerably improved qualitywise so that it became average in the market. The product line had been reduced by the discontinuance of all but two of the packaged food items, and a second candy bar had been added—the Robin Hood bar.

INTERNAL AND EXTERNAL PRESSURES

Midway's rapid growth had been achieved despite such internal pressures as limited initial funds and no subsequent additions of outside

Exhibit 6

MIDWAY FOODS CORPORATION (A)
Total Sales by Months, 1950–58

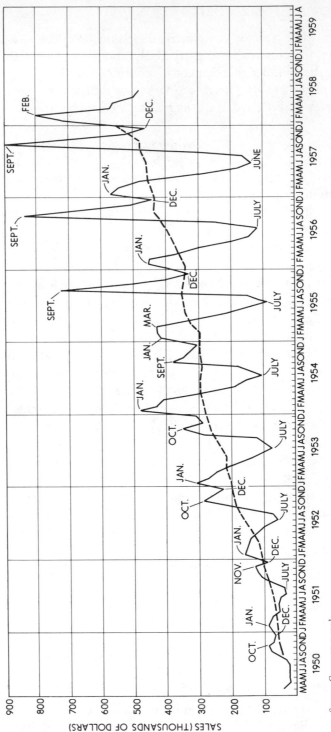

Source: Company records.

capital, a low profit margin, and a product of no more than average quality. Management summarized external pressures as follows: (1) distribution: (a) the need to fight for shelf space and new outlets, and (b) the need to rebuild distribution each fall with the return of cool weather; (2) the need to develop new markets: (a) to forestall competitors with "me too" brands copied after Midway or Robin Hood, and (b) to make Midway and Robin Hood "national" brands so they could some day reap the advertising savings of network television; (3) the need to develop markets as rapidly as possible because the industry was headed toward "advertising maturity" and with each passing year it would become more expensive to open new markets; (4) the need to maximize the efficiency of marketing expenditures since large competitors had larger marketing budgets but lower relative marketing costs (i.e., these costs were a smaller percentage of sales); and finally (5) the need to do fairly well in the commodities market in order to offer profitably a product not too much smaller than those of competitors. While these competitive pressures will be considered in more detail in this and subsequent cases, a passing note on the commodities market may help clarify the degree of pressure under which Midway operated.

Cocoa, the basic raw material in chocolate, had an especially volatile price, and there was no way to hedge completely against the wide price swings. Chocolate came from cocoa beans, a crop subject to wide production fluctuations and with a stable and generally rising demand. Furthermore, it took seven years for new cocoa trees to come into production (15 years to reach full production), and drought and disease could sharply reduce supply in a matter of months or weeks. From February, 1957, to February, 1958, the price of cocoa rose 100% due mainly to a poor crop in Ghana, where a decrease in supply combined with an inelastic demand caused a sharp increase in price (see Exhibit 5 above). Since candy bars had a fixed price, the increased cost of cocoa had to be absorbed by (1) reducing the size of the bar, (2) using synthetic substitutes, (3) changing the bar by using another raw material, or (4) reducing profits or taking a loss. While most manufacturers cut the size of the bar, profits of almost all declined sharply for the year. Midway's management noted:

We can make or lose more in the commodities market than we can running the business. Roughly 50% of our sales price of a Midway bar goes for chocolate, so a few cents a pound on the several million pounds we use can mean the difference between profit and loss for a year. Fortunately, we have done well in it for the last five years, but our turn to be wrong will probably come.

While Midway employed a purchasing agent, decisions on all commodity purchases were made by the president.[1]

CORPORATE CHARACTERISTICS

During his months of field exploration the researcher listed a number of factors which seemed to him to be dominant in Midway operations.

One characteristic appeared to be management's adherence to its explicitly formulated concept of corporate purpose. While the long-range target was "to become one of the major companies in the American candy industry," there were four shorter-range purposes or missions. First, management wanted the company to achieve "scope," a size at which the Midway line would be an important one with its brokers, at which the company could support a certain minimum selling organization, and at which it could begin to achieve efficient use of television advertising. To implement this purpose, it was early company policy to aim for growth rather than profits and to plow all available funds into additional advertising to achieve increased sales. Second, Midway aimed to sell only nationally branded food with "no one-shot deals, no subcontracting, and no unbranded items." Third, the company aimed to be a marketing company—a company that relied on its marketing skills for survival and growth and one that would not take on any activities "for corollary reasons." People at all levels in the various departments seemed to understand and accept this concept of corporate purpose. Finally, the company wanted to accomplish these things without outside equity capital. Midway was privately held and intended to remain that way at least for the foreseeable future.

A second characteristic was management's readiness to take very sizable risks. Management stated that in order to go national as rapidly as possible the company had to spread its resources thin. "The risks in doing this are great, but so are the rewards," said Mr. Clark Kramer, president of Midway. To implement rapid expansion on limited resources, the marketing department prepared a budget which "has no fat in it for contingencies," as Mr. Kramer said. "If the marketing vice president[2] thinks we can get by on $4,000 for TV in Atlanta, that's all he asks for. If it rains, or the TV program is a flop, he has to come back for some more money. I understand the risks involved and concur 100%

---

[1] Clark Kramer president of Midway Foods.

[2] Hal Reiss, marketing vice president.

in doing it this way. Any other way and we couldn't have grown the way we have."

A third characteristic was management's willingness and ability to make changes within the company and, in a more limited way, its initiative in influencing its competitive environment. This process of adaptation involved both destruction of existing systems and creation of new ones. Four examples, three internal and one external, were apparent to the researcher:

Internally, one example of this process was (1) the discarding of conventional record keeping in favor of punched-card data processing. Each sales invoice coming to the company was represented on a punched card, and subsequent accounting and statistical reports were prepared from the cards. (2) The manufacturing department had become adept at tearing down and rebuilding old machines for higher speed and more automated operation. (3) Finally, the company's organization had undergone considerable change, and numerous "less adaptable" people had been let go in the process.

Externally, as part of its influence on its environment, Midway had been instrumental in destroying the conventional concept of a candy broker. Management had insisted that brokers employ detail men to call on retail outlets. In the first years, Midway paid part of the cost of these men. While not new in the food industry, permanent detail men were almost nonexistent in the candy industry prior to 1953. In the succeeding years Midway had "persuaded" its brokers to hire detail men and had replaced brokers who would not be persuaded. By 1957 other candy companies were beginning to follow suit, and brokers all across the country were beginning to recognize the need to hire detail men in order to remain competitive.

A fourth factor, more difficult to define, was a group of characteristics descriptive of the people who made up the management of Midway. Youth (the average age of the four top executives was 39.8 years), drive, hard work and long hours, quick thinking and decisive actions, willingness to experiment, and, finally, *esprit de corps* seemed to characterize the personnel of Midway. One of the vice presidents said: "Even the clerks can tell this company is going places—one of them comes in at 4 A.M. during the rush season to see that things are ready to go out when the trucks arrive."

Finally, on a more technical level, corporate marketing strategy appeared to be clearly defined, and defined in terms which suited the company's position in the industry.

CORPORATE MARKETING STRATEGY

In overall terms, as mentioned previously, Midway's marketing strategy was to grow as rapidly as limited funds would permit. On the technical level, the company had three major but interrelated objectives. First, management sought to have the Midway line become the No. 1 line with each broker who handled it. To be the broker's No. 1 line was to be *his* most profitable line. The marketing vice president said:

We have built this business around the idea that we won't make money until our brokers do. When they make money on our line, it makes our business important to them. That makes them more receptive to our ideas—it gives us leverage. It means we get better service, especially in the fall when we need to rebuild our distribution. Also a strong distribution organization means our limited advertising budget goes further—we can go thin and still get some impact.

Second, management sought to develop its markets, not to "skim the cream." Midway used television advertising to help stimulate demand, with the eventual aim of having the Midway bar achieve a sales level somewhere near its "potential" in each market.

Third, management sought to create a distinct brand image for an ordinary product. Advertising strategy was built around an image and a basic copy "platform" which the company and its advertising agency had developed. On several occasions the researcher heard children repeating the Midway advertising message to their parents while they inspected the candy display in a supermarket.

MARKET DEVELOPMENT

Of these three only Midway's concept of and reasons for market development appear to need further description at this point. As stated previously, management used television advertising to develop a market up to its potential for the Midway type of bar. Since the company did not have enough money to do this in more than a handful of markets at one time, it had the option of "going thin" in a larger number of markets or of proceeding more slowly in a few new markets and "doing the job right."

The choice was an urgent one for two reasons. First, as the industry headed toward advertising maturity it would become increasingly expensive to open new markets; hence there was a need for speed—i.e., for going thin in order to open as many new markets as cheaply as possible. A second factor, that of potential competition from a "me

too" bar, was more difficult to evaluate. A large competitor with re-
sources adequate to support a large and sustained advertising campaign
for a "me too" product could outadvertise a small company such as
Midway and take away markets which had been only lightly developed.
A small competitor, on the other hand, might be forestalled from trying.
Summing up the alternatives, management stated it could:

A. Saturate a few markets.
   1. The conventional way of marketing, called "doing the job
      right."
   2. Tends to make each market profitable in a minimum length
      of time.
   3. Slow expansion from a solid base (the developed markets).
   4. Low short-run risk from competitors.
   5. High long-run cost, because of slow pace.
   6. High long-run risk if competitor takes rest of country un-
      contested and then uses those markets as base for advertising
      battle.
B. Go thin in more markets.
   1. Short-run risk from failure to generate satisfactory advertising
      impact.
   2. Short-run risk of being wiped out by competitor who out-
      advertises in all markets and takes them away, or takes a
      lion's share.
   3. Tends to leave each market on low-profit basis for many years
      —until well developed.
   4. Gets more markets going more quickly.
   5. Makes use of *time*—begins impact and slowly increases.
   6. Low long-run cost if not wiped out by challenge of major
      competitor. Gets markets going before total candy advertising
      reaches maturity.
   7. Low long-run risk because national market developed in mini-
      mum time and direct competition forestalled.

With these alternatives, the company had chosen the second, prefer-
ring the higher short-run risks in order to try to establish the staple,
national brands. To implement this overall strategy, management selected additional new markets each year from among the more than
200 American television markets. The new markets were selected on
the basis of two major and two lesser criteria:

First, management generally began television advertising in a market where distribution was already strong. This practice tended to maximize the payback on the advertising investment and also permitted small initial campaigns. Strong distribution in a city might allow two or three spot commercials a week to yield an appreciable sales increase, perhaps 25% or more.

Second, markets were originally selected in a concentric pattern spreading out from Chicago. Since transportation costs were a significant cost item, markets "close to home" tended to be the most profitable.

Of lesser importance as guidelines were commencement of advertising in a market in order to give a broker a lift or to boost the significance of the Midway line and thus allow the company to have better leverage to secure improved service throughout a broker's territory. (Twenty-five brokerage organizations serviced the 48 states.)

Finally, some markets were opened because they were "key cities," ones that had prestige value because they contained the headquarters of important chain stores. "Philadelphia is one such market," said Mr. Kramer. "Three big chains have headquarters there, and for them if you aren't in Philadelphia you aren't in the U.S."

A VISIT TO MIDWAY

Leaving Chicago's Midway airport, the researcher took a bus north along Cicero Avenue, the heart of Cicero, a once-famous Chicago suburb situated on the "near west side." The bus passed several miles of combined residential and industrial buildings, including the Hawthorne plant of the Western Electric company, "automobile row," and several partially completed urban clearance and renewal projects. The researcher got off the bus, walked west through a "run-down" semi-industrial neighborhood which adjoined a slum area known as one of Cicero's toughest, turned a corner and saw the familiar picture of a Midway bar, freshly painted on a high wooden fence. The fence enclosed a yard at one side of the factory, an old five-story building with a sign painted high on one wall reading, "Home of MIDWAY Foods." The researcher walked into the yard, passed the parked cars, the loading dock, a shed used for storage of old machines and miscellaneous junk, and through the main entrance into the shipping room. On the far side of the shipping room he waited for the only elevator to come down and the freight to be unloaded, and then he and a messenger rode to the fifth floor.

The elevator opened upon a long, narrow hallway which was partially blocked by a receptionist's desk and which led into the general office area. The researcher said good morning to the president's secretary, an attractive brunette whose desk was at the end of the hall. To his right were desks, filing cabinets, and the partitioned offices of two of the vice presidents; on his left was the president's office. After a few minutes' conversation with the secretary the researcher knocked on the president's door and went in. Mr. Kramer looked up from his work and said, "Good morning, come on in."

The researcher put his papers on Mr. Kramer's desk, took off his coat, and sat down to enjoy the comforts of the spacious, air-conditioned office, which was in striking contrast with the remainder of the plant and its surrounding environment. In addition to the window air conditioner, the well-appointed office contained a sofa, rug, and several chairs; a TV set; and a long, ultramodern desk behind which sat Mr. Kramer in his swivel chair.

"What would you like to talk about today?" Mr. Kramer asked.

"First I'd like a little background on some of the changes during the past seven years, and then I have some questions about money—about why there seems to be so little of it."

"Suppose I take them in that order. Midway is an old company which prospered during the war and then went down hill into bankruptcy. It wasn't a going business when I bought it—a low-quality product, a small group of unskilled factory people, very poor trade relations, and a local distribution organization.

"We feel we have come quite a way since then. Sales have gone from about zero to over $6 million on Midway alone. We now have an adequate plant instead of the run-down one on Maxwell Street. And we have a second candy line, the Robin Hood brand which we market for Sherwood & Co. On that brand alone there has been considerable growth, over 150% since we became their marketing agents two years ago.

"A lot has changed. Milt Lombard[3] has the factory in shape and running with reasonable efficiency. It's not like Maxwell Street where we used to have to set up the end of the production line in the street each day—and where Milt was sleeping in the factory when we went to operating a third shift. We now have national distribution on the Midway brand, and we are becoming one of the major television advertisers in our industry. Also, just this month we have added an administrative vice president[4] to help us modernize our paper work and

---

[3] Milt Lombard, manufacturing vice president.

[4] Ben Nagle, administrative vice president.

to increase our emphasis on profits. Hiring him was part of our plan to shift from 'phase one' to 'phase two.' "

"What do you mean, 'phase one' and 'phase two'?" the researcher asked.

"Phase one was growth. For the past seven years we have had one major objective, scope. We have been trying to expand sales, to achieve national scope. We weren't so interested in profits, because profits on small volume don't mean very much. In fact, going for scope has tended to keep our profits small; we have invested most of our gross margin in additional advertising.

"But now we are large enough to begin aiming for profits. We are calling it phase two of our development, and it will be to expand more slowly and begin to reap the profits of our advertising investments. We need the profits for two reasons: (1) we have to add to our capital resources in order to continue our expansion, and (2) we want to be sure we can run an $8 million business at a profit before we become an $80 million business."

"Does this shift mean you are going to be trying to operate at reduced risk from now on?"

"Exactly. Beginning with the 1958–59 season we will be aiming for a more conservative approach. Thus far we have gone all out to increase sales and have taken the risks because we had to in order to achieve the necessary scope. And if something went wrong, we were small enough so that I could make up for it by not drawing salary or some such thing. Now we have reached a size where that is no longer the case."

"What about financial resources? One of the things I have heard most often here is 'We are short of money. If we just had some more money, we could do this and that.' And as far as I can tell, you really are short of money. How does it happen that you haven't raised more?"

"There are a lot of reasons," Mr. Kramer replied. "I think there are 50 reasons anyway, so how many do you want?"

"Well, let's just start in and see."

"First, let me explain something about our present resources. We are able to extend our working capital substantially through the use of suppliers' credit. In fact, we are able to stay in business because we have developed good credit relations with our suppliers. We also raise working capital on a seasonal basis from our bank.

"One way to raise additional money would be by selling stock. Our reason for not doing so is that we would have to give up too much of the equity in addition to other intangibles. We have grown a lot, but we haven't made the kind of profits an underwriter would like to see. And you couldn't price stock at what we would want for it.

"So we could sell stock, but it would be very costly. We have managed to grow from zero to $6 million over the last seven years by stretching our money, so maybe we can go for a couple more years."

"What about something like a private placement with a more sophisticated investing group?"

"We might try that some day. We have thought about it. There is even a possibility of selling the business and pocketing a capital gain. But that's not my goal.

"I don't regard this business as a way to make a couple of million in cash—as some people might. I think of it as a means to an end for our top-management group, and not as an end in itself. Without getting involved in my own personal goals, let's say we want the business to provide us a comfortable living—as an example—and also a chance to do things."

"I see," the researcher said. "What about selling bonds or getting a term loan?"

"Well," Mr. Kramer replied, "as it is we borrow as much seasonally as the banks are willing to let us have. And as far as borrowing money to put into bricks and mortar, it would increase the risk in our business a lot. Right now, if sales don't go as well as we had planned we can tighten our belt and squeeze through somehow. But when you have to repay bank loans on bricks and mortar at the same time, you can lose the whole business."

"Doesn't this shortage of money mean that you miss out on some profitable opportunities?" asked the researcher.

"Yes, it's an ever-present problem," agreed Mr. Kramer.

"There's one other thing that has sort of been understood in our discussion thus far—it's implicit in what I've been saying. That is, we want to make a distinction between capital money and operating money. I don't want to borrow long-term or sell stock to get operating money. These sources should be used for capital money—for things where you expect a payback over a number of years, like a factory or a new manufacturing process."

"What about advertising? I've heard you speak of this as an *investment,* something that has a payout over time."

"We think of it that way," explained Mr. Kramer, "but no accountant would. Advertising money is operating money and has to come from profits. In operating we have to assure ourselves that we are covering our costs and making a profit—our operations have to be self-liquidating.

"Advertising is like another ingredient in the product, like packaging or raw materials or anything else in this particular respect. We want the product to be self-liquidating, so it would be no different to be borrowing for advertising, or ingredients, or salesmen's salaries. It's axiomatic that advertising money must come from sales."

"Is that literally true?" asked the researcher. "I thought advertising had a carry-forward—that Midway could terminate it and still have a carry-forward in sales for a year or two. In that sense, then, it would be like an investment, especially when you are opening new markets. You expect to invest before you get the sales return, don't you?"

"Yes, but it would be like investing in a Canadian mining stock instead of AT&T. There is a tremendous difference in the risk. With advertising you can't figure the uncertainties, why it works well in Atlanta and not in New Orleans. So even though we have to miss out on some sales opportunities, or maybe have to leave an opening for a competitor, from an overall corporate point of view the risk of borrowing to invest in something like that is just too great for us.

"And there's another aspect to this. Since we want to grow rapidly, we spread our advertising money thinner than we might if we were a big, rich company trying to develop the same markets. And while spreading thin gets the markets started and over time produces the results on less money, it doesn't give you the short-run payback that saturating each market with advertising would. So we don't get the short-run profits the way Procter and Gamble could, and we have to keep in mind that we need to invest some of our money where the payback will be quickest. While advertising in a new market might pay off over the years to come, we have a number of projects available which would pay off in a year or even less. So, really, we are limited in the number of investments we can handle, limited both financially and by the lack of depth in our organization.

.   .   .   .

"One other thing; to achieve growth with real stability we must diversify both within the candy industry and out into the food field. We want to begin this when we have a good opportunity, and also when we have achieved more depth in our organization."

GROWTH AND CHANGE

Midway's growth from $0 to over $6 million in sales had been accompanied by a number of changes in organization and personnel, and change continued to be a significant feature of the period during which the company was under study by the case researcher. As shown by the chronology table (Exhibit 7) the number of executives had increased, administrative jobs and titles had changed, and personnel had been moved around from one company level to another. In the process, numerous "less adaptable" persons had been released.

During the study, most of Midway's executive officers were moved from the factory to a downtown office location. Job shifts were continued and creation of a new administrative position was taken under consideration. The researcher was also informed by company executives

Exhibit 7

MIDWAY FOODS CORPORATION (A)

Chronology, February, 1950–January, 1958

1950	February	Company begins operations
	May	Hal Reiss, future marketing vice president, joins company
1951	June	Andy Kallal, sales vice president, joins company
	August	Milt Lombard, future manufacturing vice president, becomes consultant to Midway
1952	February	Milt Lombard joins company
1953	September	Otto Lehman, future director of R&D, joins company
	December	Midway leases Cicero plant
1954	August	Production begins in new plant
1955		IBM equipment is introduced
1956		Midway becomes marketing agent for the Robin Hood bar manufactured by Sherwood & Co., Ltd.
1957	September	Advertising begins on Robin Hood in seven cities
1958	January	Ben Nagle, administrative vice president, joins company

of shifts in policy emphasis, of changes in executive interpersonal relations, and of an opportunity to acquire a competing candy company. [See Midway Foods (B₁)]

As of mid-1959, Midway's executive organization was composed of the following personnel:

Mr. Clark Kramer	President
Mr. Hal Reiss	Marketing vice president
Mr. Andy Kallal	Sales vice president
Mr. Milt Lombard	Manufacturing vice president
Mr. Otto Lehman	Head of Research and Development
Mr. Ben Nagle	Administrative vice president

ORGANIZATION OF CASE MATERIAL

The Midway Foods material is presented as a series. Midway (A) deals with industry opportunities and competitive characteristics, company resources, and major company goals. Midway (B) deals with a profit opportunity: should Midway buy out a competitor? Midway (C) describes the four functional departments, including their missions, methods of operation, operating problems, and the personal and management philosophy of the executive responsible for each department. Midway (D) presents a number of incidents where these managers are working with one another and with the president.

2. Midway Foods Corporation (B₁)

MAIN LINE, an old and well-known firm in the industry, manufactured and sold two major brands of candy which had been marketed for over 40 years under the nationally known brand names of *William Penn* and *Liberty Bell*. Following World War II, Main Line had been one of the larger firms in the industry, but in the postwar years sales had declined about 75% under a series of absentee managements. By 1957 Main Line was reported to be operating in the red, with its loss for the year expected to be in excess of $300,000. For more than two years successive owners had been trying to sell the company; it had become known in the industry as a "loser that is up for sale again."

In the first week of February, 1958, Midway was considering the purchase of Main Line Foods, Inc. The negotiations between Midway and Conglomerated Holding Corporation, owner of Main Line, still had four principal issues to resolve: (1) the payment schedule, (2) the amount of the down payment, (3) skepticism on the part of Conglomerated that Midway's management could turn a "loser" into a profitable company, and (4) uncertainty on the part of Midway's management as to whether it could, in fact, turn the business around in as short time as it hoped it could.

PROGRESS OF THE NEGOTIATIONS

In December, 1957, Midway heard through a third party that Main Line was again for sale. Midway approached Conglomerated about possible purchase, saying "We have no money, but if you are still interested, so are we." A short time later the president of Conglomerated asked Midway to submit a plan of what it might do with Main Line in view of this fact. Midway asked for an opportunity to inspect the plant before submitting the plan, and as a result Midway management was given permission to visit Main Line's Philadelphia plant, inspect its operations and records, and receive pertinent financial data for previous years. Midway would then submit proposals for a deal and also a plan

341

Exhibit 1

MIDWAY FOODS CORPORATION (B$_1$)
General Information on Main Line Foods, Inc.

In November, 1955, Conglomerated had sold Main Line to In and Out Corporation for $1,375,000. In and Out Corporation was a holding company widely known for its buying and selling of companies. In and Out Corporation's 1955 annual report contained the following comments about its acquisition of Main Line.

In November, In and Out acquired Main Line Foods, Inc. Main Line is one of the best-known manufacturers in its industry, producing William Penn, Liberty Bell, Skimmer, and other nationally known brands. The company's main plant is in Philadelphia.

. . . .

Your management is pleased with the progress made in strengthening its business. However, we consider it only the beginning of a more profitable program. Our aim is to diversify our operations by acquiring additional companies so that eventually no more than 5% of our income is derived from any one type of business.

The 1956 annual report of In and Out Corporation contained the following information:

Sale of Subsidiary: Subject to possible cancellation by the purchaser as set forth below, on December 28, 1956, In and Out Corporation sold its investment in Main Line to High Finance Consultants, Inc., for $1,200,000, the purchase price to be payable in successive monthly installments of $20,000 each, without interest. . . . The sale is subject to [certain requirements]. Due to the fact that these requirements may not be met, it is possible that the beneficial interest in Main Line may be revested in the corporation during 1957.

The 1957 Annual Report of In and Out Corporation stated:

A number of unprofitable operations which we felt had no future prospects were eliminated. Main Line Corporation, A.B.C. Corporation, and X.Y.Z. Corporation were disposed of. . . .

In a note to its financial statements, In and Out Corporation explained that the sale to High Finance Consultants, Inc., had fallen through because of the latter's failure to meet its obligations. Since In and Out Corporation was unwilling to meet these obligations, Main Line had been returned to Conglomerated. In and Out Corporation had lost over $600,000 on the transactions.

Source: Annual reports, the In and Out Corporation.

of operations. On January 5, Mr. Ben Nagle[1] obtained the publicly available information in Exhibit 1.

On January 8, Mr. Clark Kramer,[2] Mr. Hal Reiss,[3] and Mr. Nagle went to Philadelphia. When they arrived at the factory, however, they

---

[1] Administrative vice president of Midway Foods.

[2] President of Midway Foods.

[3] Marketing vice president of Midway Foods.

Exhibit 2

MIDWAY FOODS CORPORATION (B₁)
Summary of Observations on Philadelphia Trip

1. Main Line's factory is ultramodern and in good repair. It could use a coat of paint to brighten it up.
2. The operations are at a small fraction of plant capacity, probably less than 30% of one-shift capacity. Two production lines are in use four days a week, and factory workers are on a four-day week.
3. The product line contains several items which require considerable setup time. Because of their small volume, these items are very expensive to produce. One product is being sold for less than direct cost.
4. Because of differences in product ingredients, Midway items cannot economically be manufactured on Main Line's equipment. Lack of space prevents manufacturing Main Line's products in Chicago. Therefore, until Main Line is owned outright, it would not make sense to combine the two operations.
5. Management of the factory is sloppy. People are not working hard. Production runs are short, thus maximizing setup time. The manager knows little of what goes on in the plant.
6. Main Line does not have a union.
7. Inventory is high. But the inventory is primarily in raw materials for the low-volume items. If they were to be discontinued, almost all the inventory could be sold. This inventory is probably salable at 75% or more of book value. Main Line has almost no inventory on hand for its two major items.

Source: Company records.

were given only a quick tour of the plant and were not allowed to inspect company records or to interview employees. A summary of management's observations on the Philadelphia trip is contained in Exhibit 2. After returning to Chicago the Midway executives learned that a misunderstanding had developed between Conglomerated and Main Line, for which Conglomerated's president apologized. He promised that financial statements would be forwarded posthaste.

After receiving Main Line's financial statements, Midway's top management held a Saturday–Sunday (January 11–12) meeting at Mr. Kramer's home. Management reviewed the information contained in Exhibits 3–6 and then drew up a statement of basic objectives and bargaining strategy (Exhibit 7), a projected profit and loss statement (Exhibit 8), and a projected cash flow statement (Exhibit 9). By Sunday, four alternative purchase proposals had been drafted, two of which became the basis of subsequent discussions.

Exhibit 3

MIDWAY FOODS CORPORATION (B₁)

Main Line Foods, Inc., Summary Profit and Loss Statements 1946–57, and Boxes Billed 1946–55

(Figures in Thousands)

	Yr. End. 12/31 1946	Yr. End. 12/31 1947	Yr. End. 12/31 1948	Yr. End. 12/31 1949	Yr. End. 12/31 1950	Yr. End. 12/31 1951	Yr. End. 12/31 1952	Yr. End. 12/31 1953	Yr. End. 12/31 1954	9 Mo. End. 9/30 1955	Yr. End. 12/31 1956	10 Mo. End. 10/31 1957
Net sales	$6,982	$9,310	$5,422	$2,555	$3,386	$3,599	$3,530	$3,546	$3,310	$2,499	$2,359	$1,902
Cost of goods sold	5,362	6,722	4,021	2,046	2,341	2,536	2,473	2,492	2,334	1,730	1,832	1,607
Gross profit	$1,620	$2,588	$1,401	$ 509	$1,045	$1,063	$1,057	$1,054	$ 976	$ 769	$ 527	$ 295
Net profit (loss) before tax	667	1,119	(661)	(69)	412	363	255	185	191	215	(181)*	(231)
Boxes billed:												
Liberty Bell	3,172	4,463	2,939	n.a.	n.a.	n.a.	1,440	3,249	3,328	2,752	n.a.	1,980
William Penn	7,412	7,704	4,219	n.a.	n.a.	n.a.	631	1,102	979	551	n.a.	442
Other	—	118	—	—	—	—	136	247	189	174	n.a.	251‡
Total	10,584	12,285	7,158	n.a.	4,610	4,756	2,207	4,598	4,496	3,477	n.a.	2,673

* After interest on factor's loan of $71,000.
† After interest charges.
‡ Includes 136,000 Skimmer brand and 115,000 of seven other brands.
Source: Main Line records.

Exhibit 4

MIDWAY FOODS CORPORATION (B₁)
Main Line Foods, Inc., Profit and Loss Statement,
October and November 1957 and 10 Months Ended October 31, 1957
(Dollars in Thousands) *

	October†	%	November	%	10 Months Ended October 31‡	%
Gross sales	$257.1	101.57	$207.4	101.14	$1,948.1	102.41
Returns and allowances	.8	}1.57	1.1	}1.14	11.9	}2.41
Free boxes	3.2		1.2		33.9	
Net sales	$253.2	100.00	$205.1	100.00	$1,902.3	100.00
Cost of goods sold	216.4	85.49	190.5	92.96	1,607.2	84.49
Gross profit	$ 36.7	14.51	$ 14.6	7.04	$ 295.1	15.51
Expenses						
Cash discount	4.8	1.88	3.5	1.69	32.0	1.68
Selling	25.1	9.91	20.7	10.11	202.2	10.63
Administrative	11.4	4.51	8.1	3.96	110.1	5.79
Freight and warehouse	17.4	6.88	13.1	6.38	135.2	7.11
Total expense	$ 58.7	23.18	$ 45.4	22.14	$ 479.5	25.21
Operating loss	$ 21.9	8.67	$ 30.9	15.10	$ 184.5	9.70
Other income						
Purchase discount	$ 1.3	}.55	$ 1.5	}.77	$ 6.8	.36
Bad debt recoveries	.1		.1		.4	.02
Miscellaneous	—	—	—	—	.3	.02
Total other income	$ 1.4	.55	$ 1.6	.77	$ 7.5	.40
Nonoperating expense	—	—	—	—	5.0	.26
Loss before interest charges	$ 20.6	8.12	$ 29.3	14.33	$ 181.9	9.56
Interest charges						
Notes payable and mortgage	—	—	—	—	29.6	1.55
Factoring and material loan	.3	.13	.4	.21	19.5	1.03
Total interest charges	$ .3	.13	$ .4	.21	$ 49.1	2.53
Net loss	$ 20.9	8.25	$ 29.7	14.54	$ 231.0	12.14

* Dollar figures fail to add exactly due to rounding.
† For breakdown of factory direct labor costs, October, 1957, see accompanying schedule (Exhibit 5).
‡ For breakdown of selling expense, 1–10, 1957, see accompanying schedule (Exhibit 5).
Source: Main Line records.

MAJOR PROBLEMS

The Payment Schedule. Midway insisted on a payment schedule which would permit purchase of Main Line out of the latter's anticipated future earnings. Midway made it clear that its own tight financial position made any other form of payment impossible. As a result, several payment schedules were discussed, with Midway favoring gradually rising payments spread over a 10-year period. Conglomerated expressed interest in a shorter repayment period, with the payments tapering off toward the end.

Exhibit 5

MIDWAY FOODS CORPORATION (B₁)
Main Line Foods, Inc., Selling Expenses and Factory Direct Labor,
Selected Periods, 1957

A. SELLING EXPENSES, 10 MONTHS ENDED OCTOBER 31, 1957

Salaries and wages		$ 28,238
Salesmen's salaries and expenses		20,729
Commissions		67,465
Samples and free goods		42,954
Advertising		
Magazine	$1,505	
Outdoor	312	
Point of sale	4,055	5,872
Entertainment and conventions		4,135
Travel		5,951
Miscellaneous		26,901
Total		$202,245

B. FACTORY DIRECT LABOR, OCTOBER, 1957

Item	Actual Labor	Standard Labor	Excess over Standard
William Penn	$ 5,151	$ 2,978	$ 2,174
Liberty Bell	18,015	12,764	5,251
Haverford	302	85	217
Esther Williamson	547	256	291
Skimmer	6,451	2,236	4,215
	$30,455	$18,318	$12,148

Source: Main Line records.

Working Capital Guarantee. Since Main Line was losing about $20,000 per month, Conglomerated had loaned $300,000 to Main Line for additional working capital. Conglomerated insisted that any sale agreement contain Midway's guarantee that Main Line's working capital would go no lower than $244,000. In the event that Midway was unable to fulfill its obligations, it would be required to reimburse Main Line to bring working capital up to the $244,000 figure. Although Midway had originally declined to be bound by such a guarantee, in January it provisionally agreed to do so in return for a 50% reduction in the down payment, from $100,000 to $50,000.

The Down Payment. Midway attempted to find the $50,000 needed for the down payment. The money was not available from company funds and could not be secured from either Midway's or Main Line's banking connections or from any of Midway's major suppliers.

Exhibit 6

MIDWAY FOODS CORPORATION (B₁)

Main Line Foods, Inc., Balance Sheet as of October 31, 1957

Assets

Current assets
Cash	$ 16,349
Accounts receivable (net)*	132,628
Inventories	
Raw materials	63,754
Packaging materials	114,643
Finished goods	138,311
Supplies	14,480
Total inventories	$ 331,187
Federal income tax refund	6,012
Deposits and freight claims	2,960
Total current assets	$ 489,136

Fixed assets
Land	67,921
Buildings (cost less reserves of $23,126)	460,814
Machinery, equip., fur., etc. (cost less reserves of $104,319)	830,988
Total fixed assets (cost less reserves of $127,445)	$1,336,597
Prepaid and deferred charges	21,190
Goodwill	50,000
Total assets	$1,896,922

Liabilities

Current liabilities
Accounts payable	$ 42,772
Notes payable, bank loan*	65,179
Notes payable, other†	150,000
Accrued payrolls	10,130
Commissions	9,911
Taxes, real estate, and property	13,886
Taxes, unemployment and withholding	11,810
Miscellaneous	17,177
Total current liabilities	$ 320,846
Mortgage payable†	1,149,072

Net worth
Common stock	1,000
Capital surplus	777,478
Earned surplus	(351,473)
Total net worth	$ 427,005
Total liabilities and net worth	$1,896,922

* A total of $76,681 in accounts receivable was pledged as collateral for a bank loan of $65,179.
† Owed to Conglomerated Holding Corp.
Note: Figures fail to add exactly due to rounding.
Source: Main Line records.

Subsequently, however, a Midway customer agreed to provide the required cash and to accept repayment through a purchase discount.

Purchase Price. The purchase price had not been a major issue from Conglomerated's point of view, as long as it was not less than

Exhibit 7

MIDWAY FOODS CORPORATION (B₁)

Guidelines for Negotiations

Objectives

1. Do not permit the purchase of Main Line to endanger the financial safety of Midway. Purchase only through the medium of a paper corporation to be owned jointly by Midway and Conglomerated and to be dissolved after Main Line has been paid for.
2. Minimize or eliminate the down payment.
3. Try to spread out payments so they can be met entirely from future earnings of Main Line.
4. Obtain full operating control of Main Line, subject only to cancellation for failure to meet obligations as specified in sale contract. Such operating authority to include right to discharge personnel and to discontinue all but the two major brands.

Negotiating Strategy

1. Conduct the negotiations in such a way that the principals for Conglomerated have a good opportunity to appraise how Midway manages its affairs, but do not show Midway financial statements.
2. Depend upon the word of Conglomerated's principals. They have been honest and fair in their negotiations to date and appear to be earnestly seeking a mutually satisfactory deal.
3. Depend upon Conglomerated's good judgment as Midway's No. 1 asset. Main Line is losing money at a rapid pace and must be disposed of shortly or Conglomerated's loan of $300,000 for working capital will be down the drain.
4. Conglomerated is delaying publication of its annual report because it wants to state in the annual report that Main Line has been disposed of for an amount in excess of its book value to Conglomerated.

Source: Company records.

book value, since (1) Conglomerated would receive at most only a $50,000 cash payment and the remainder from future earnings, and (2) Conglomerated's security in the deal rested upon Midway's ability to turn a loser into a profitable company in order to generate these future earnings.[4] Conglomerated's major concern, therefore, was not the exact amount of the sale price but the likelihood that Midway would actually make money on Main Line rather than "dumping it back in Conglomerated's lap." As seen in Exhibit 1, Main Line had been "revested" with Conglomerated following a previously unfulfilled sales

---

[4] Conglomerated Holding held Main Line Foods on its books at a value of $1,325,000.

Exhibit 8

MIDWAY FOODS CORPORATION (B₁)

Pro Forma Profit and Loss Statement for Main Line Foods, Inc.,
March, 1958, to March, 1959

(Dollars in Thousands)

PROJECTED OPERATIONS FOR SALES VOLUMES OF $2,100* AND $2,300

	Dollars	%	Dollars	%
Net sales				
Liberty Bell	$1,700.0	82.6%	—	—
William Penn	400.0	18.4	—	—
Total net sales	$2,100.0	100.0	$2,300.0	100.0%
Less manufacturing expense				
Raw materials	$1,176.0	56.0	$1,288.0	56.0
Factory labor	407.0	19.3	407.0	17.7
Traffic†	147.0	7.0	161.0	7.0
Commissions†	105.0	5.0	115.0	5.0
Selling	67.0	3.2	67.0	3.0
General and administrative	35.5	1.7	35.5	1.5
Total manufacturing expense	1,937.5	92.2	2,073.5	90.2
Gross profit	$ 162.5	7.8	$ 226.5	9.8

Overhead			
Nonoperative costs			
Depreciation	$ 60.0		
Taxes	16.0		
General insurance	4.6	$ 80.6	
Minimum operating expense			
Steam and air conditioning	$ 19.0		
Steam super	7.5		
Water and electricity	16.0		
Oil and coal	9.5		
Miscellaneous	8.0	60.0	
		$ 140.6	
Margin for error—15%		21.0	
Amount which must be generated in gross profit		$ 161.6	

* "Conservative" or "worst that can happen" estimate of sales.
† Fixed percentage of volume.
Source: Company records.

contract. The purchase price was not a major issue for Midway since the amount would, in any event, have to come from future earnings.

MIDWAY'S CORPORATE OBJECTIVES

The possible acquisition of Main Line would, in the opinion of the researcher, be consistent with some of Midway's corporate objectives and inconsistent with some others.

The acquisition of two new brands would be consistent with Midway's phase-one objective of growth. It would add over $2 million to

Exhibit 9

MIDWAY FOODS CORPORATION (B₁)

Pro Forma Projection of Working Capital before Payments on Principal
for Main Line Foods, Inc., January, 1958, to February, 1960

(Dollars in Thousands)

	Sales	Profit (Loss) Before Advertising	EOM Working Capital	Advertising Expenditure	Profit After Advertising	EOM Working Capital After Advertising
1958						
January................	$ 200.0	$(25.0)	$100.0*	—	—	—
February...............	200.0	(20.0)	80.0	—	—	—
March.................	200.0†	(15.0)	65.0	—	—	—
April..................	225.0	(5.0)	60.0	—	—	—
May...................	250.0	5.0	65.0	—	—	—
June..................	250.0	10.0	75.0	—	—	—
July...................	225.0	10.0	85.0	—	—	—
August................	200.0	(3.0)	82.0	—	—	—
September.............	250.0	15.0	97.0	—	—	—
October...............	250.0	15.0	112.0	—	—	—
November.............	200.0	(1.0)	111.0	—	—	—
December.............	200.0	(1.0)	110.0			
Total 1958...........	$2,650.0	$(9.0)				
1959						
January................	$ 250.0	$ 15.0	$125.0	$ 0.0	$ 15.0	$125.0
February...............	250.0	15.0	140.0	0.0	15.0	140.0
March.................	240.0	13.0	153.0	10.0	3.0	143.0
April..................	270.0	20.0	173.0	10.0	10.0	153.0
May...................	300.0	30.0	203.0	10.0	20.0	173.0
June..................	300.0	30.0	233.0	10.0	20.0	193.0
July...................	270.0	20.0	253.0	10.0	10.0	203.0
August................	240.0	13.0	266.0	10.0	3.0	206.0
September.............	300.0	30.0	296.0	0.0	30.0	236.0
October...............	300.0	30.0	326.0	0.0	30.0	266.0
November.............	240.0	13.0	339.0	0.0	13.0	299.0
December.............	240.0	13.0	352.0	0.0	13.0	312.0
Total 1959...........	$3,200.0	$242.0		60.0	$182.0	
1960						
January................	$ 300.0	$ 30.0	$382.0	$ 0.0	$ 30.0	$332.0
February...............	300.0	30.0	412.0	0.0	30.0	362.0

* Sources of initial $100,000 working capital: $25,000 brokers' commissions; $60,000 suppliers' additional dating; $15,000 Midway loan. In addition to the projected figures shown, working capital would increase by $300,000 at time of purchase because Conglomerated had agreed to convert its $300,000 short-term loan into long-term debt.

† Sales estimates henceforth on most probable basis.

Source: Company records.

annual sales in staple brand-name items, items which would depend for future growth upon Midway's marketing skills. Also it would fit in with the objective of diversification in the candy industry and was particularly suitable because the Liberty Bell candy bar did not contain chocolate and sold well in warm weather. Liberty Bell would, in management's words, "act as a balance wheel."

However, the two brands would require substantial advertising expenditures (1) to halt their sales decline and (2) to become more profitable by regaining loss volume. While both brands were nationally known, distribution was spotty, with approximately 70% of William Penn sales concentrated in the six-state New England area. Reintroducing this brand on a national basis would be (in management's opinion) only slightly less difficult than introducing a new brand. For either to become a truly national brand would require (in the researcher's opinion) some diversion of funds from either (1) the advertising budget for the Midway brand or (2) profits, thus delaying the accumulation of a profit backlog. Therefore if Midway were to try to develop either brand (or both) through advertising, it would in some measure compromise the new phase-two objective of consolidation for profits.

More difficult to assess was the strain on the manufacturing department. Since no new money for machinery could be appropriated, Main Line would have to use present equipment (which was in good condition, according to Mr. Kramer, and was *not,* according to Mr. Milt Lombard),[5] until its own profits had generated an adequate cash reserve. In the meantime the manufacturing department would have to cut costs sharply without spending money for equipment. Since the two manufacturing operations could not be integrated economically, the manufacturing department would have to supervise both plants, and do so without a significant increase in supervisory personnel. This would strain an implicit corporate objective of trying to get away from continual "crises."

Commenting on the risk involved in the Main Line acquisition, management stated:

There is nothing to lose provided we are careful not to allow the working capital to be depleted below the allowable $244,000. They are willing to change the $300,000 loan to a long-term note, which means we would start off with almost $400,000 in working capital. If we couldn't turn it around before it got down to $244,000, we could simply say. "We're sorry, fellows. We tried our best, but couldn't make it. Now you can have it back."

In another sense there would be some risk in taking time and effort away from running our own business. And of course we would be risking our $50,000 down payment.

---

[5] Manufacturing vice president of Midway Foods.

On February 4, with time running out, Midway's management knew that (1) it would have to make its final decision on the basis of existing information (Exhibits 1–6); (2) the monthly losses being suffered by Main Line were so large that sale of the company would probably be completed in the very near future, if not to Midway then to another purchaser; and (3) if its offer were accepted, immediate action to eliminate the continuing losses would be needed.

3. Midway Foods Corporation (C₁)

THIS CASE describes Midway's four departments—marketing, manufacturing, R&D, and administrative—as they operated following the Main Line acquisition. Data are presented on the functions, resources, and operating problems of each department; on how each department was managed; and on how each manager saw himself. With these data one can begin to understand better the relationship of one department to another and gain some appreciation for the president's task of co-ordinating these four organizations. In addition, this material is essential for the understanding of subsequent cases where the reader watches the three vice presidents interacting and watches the president[1] work with this top-management team.

The Marketing Department

The marketing department had two principal missions: (1) to sell staple brand-name food items to the national market, and (2) to develop individual markets so that a brand reached a significant level of sales in each market. Even though it was possible to have a small volume of sales in a market, Midway was aiming to exploit the potential of each market so that a directly competitive item could not come in, gain consumer acceptance, and eventually replace the Midway items in most or all outlets in the market. To implement its objectives, Midway invested money in consumer advertising in order to win basic consumer acceptance for each of its brands or, as the marketing vice president[2] called it, to "carve out a consumer franchise in a market for each brand."

The basic problem facing the department was how to build four staple national brands at the same time, within the limitations of Midway's tight financial position, and as rapidly as possible. Mr. Hal Reiss,

---

[1] Clark Kramer, president of Midway Foods.
[2] Hal Reiss, marketing vice president.

the marketing vice president, stated, "Because our industry is heading toward advertising maturity, with each year that passes it becomes more difficult and more expensive to establish a new brand" (see Exhibit 1).

PRODUCT LINE

Midway sold four major brands of candy and two branded food items. Each brand of candy was somewhat different from any competitive piece; none was a "me too" brand. Each was sold in several forms, varying from one-cent items to economy boxes or one-pound bars. However, each brand had one basic piece which accounted for over 50% of sales. All four lines had seasonal sales variations, with the cool-weather brands virtually disappearing from the shelves during the summer months. The three Midway-manufactured brands (Robin Hood was manufactured by Sherwood & Co. of Nottingham, England) were of average quality for their price class. All four brands were made with natural rather than the less expensive synthetic ingredients and were packaged in average-quality wrappers. Three were of average size, while the Midway bar was of less than average weight for its price class. Data on the four brands are shown in Table 1.

TABLE 1

Brand Name	Retail Price	Size (Weight)	Best Season	Relative Sales Rank
Midway	5¢	small	cool weather	1
William Penn	5¢	average	cool weather	4
Liberty Bell	5¢	average	warm weather	2
Robin Hood	10¢	*	cool weather	3

* No closely competitive product on the market.

PRICING

Retail prices on all four brands had been constant for years, though the company was trying to upgrade the Midway and William Penn bars from 5-cent to 10-cent items. This effort had met with limited success, management stated, since the American candy-bar market was still "basically a 5-cent market." Midway's prices to customers were equal to the industry leaders' prices and slightly higher than those of some of its smaller competitors. Management stated its wholesale prices were "at the top; they can't go higher."

Exhibit 1

MIDWAY FOODS CORPORATION (C_1)
Sales and Advertising Data for Selected Candy Manufacturers

Company	Candy Brand Names	Estimated 1958 Sales	Advertising Expenditures	Per Cent Advertising to Sales	Sales* Costs	Per Cent Sales Cost to Sales
Midway Foods..........	Midway Robin Hood William Penn Liberty Bell	$10,000,000	$ 780,000	7.8%	$ 500,000	5%
Gold Medal Candy Co.....	Bonomo's Turkish Taffy	2,000,000	155,000	7.7	100,000	5
Chunky Chocolate Corp.....	Chunky	6,000,000	350,000	5.7	300,000	5
Food Manufacturers, Inc.....	M & M	40,000,000	2,500,000	6.2	400,000	1
Quaker City Confectionery Co.....	Good & Plenty	4,000,000	335,000	8.4	200,000	5
Hershey Chocolate Corp.....	Hershey bars Hersheyettes	164,000,000†	—0—	—0—	No estimate	—
Mars, Inc.....	Mars Marsettes Three Musketeers Milky Way	70,000,000	2,000,000	2.9	840,000	1.2
New England Confectionery Co.....	Necco Sky Bar	20,000,000	750,000	3.8	600,000	3
Peter Paul, Inc.....	Mounds Almond Joy	45,000,000	1,600,000	3.5	1,125,000	2.5
Sweets Company of America.....	Tootsie Roll	24,000,000	1,500,000	6.2	600,000	2.5

* Includes only brokers' commissions or cost of direct distribution. Does not include promotion or advertising costs.
† Approximately $40–$60 million of this was in bulk chocolate and chocolate coatings.
Source: Midway estimates.

DISTRIBUTION

Midway products were distributed through 25 brokerage organizations to over 10,000 jobbers and chain-store accounts. Brokers received a 5% commission on all sales in their territory (there were no "house accounts") and in addition were eligible for progressively rising bonuses for sales in excess of the quota on each brand. The 5% "sales cost," as Midway called it, compared with 1½%–2% for the large companies that sold direct and 2%–3½% for the major manufacturers who sold through brokers. "Only the small fry pay 5%, and that's for only one reason—they have to pay it in order to get distribution at all. We are just now getting big enough to be a borderline case," said Mr. Reiss, the marketing vice president.

Probably the most significant aspect of Midway's distribution system was the company's insistence that brokers employ detail men[3] to cover retail and chain accounts. Brokers were expected to use the detail men to widen distribution and to secure a rapid increase in distribution each fall for the three cool-weather bars. The importance of fall distribution can be seen from the figures for Chicago in Table 2.

TABLE 2

Month	Per cent of Retailers with Midway on Hand as Detail Men Arrived	Per cent of Retailers with Midway on Hand After Call by Detail Men
August...................	6	7
September...............	35	60
December...............	65	80
March...................	82	91

"That's been one of the big problems with this business, we have to rebuild distribution each fall. It's almost like starting up a new business," Mr. Reiss said. Through extensive use of detail men, Midway believed it had secured much better than average distribution in the candy industry. Mr. Reiss also stated that such high distribution had allowed the company to develop markets more cheaply than if it had tried to rely on advertising to stimulate demand and pull the product through.

The researcher learned from one of the company's brokers that Midway's extensive use of detail men had helped create an industry trend. "Midway had a hard time convincing brokers to use detail men for a

---

[3] Salesmen who called on customers.

long time, but now people can see it's paying off and other companies are starting to do the same thing. Midway knows what goes on at the retail level," the broker continued. "They know what makes a product tick and how to develop a market. I'd say Midway was exceptional in the industry in this respect."

PROMOTION

Midway used a wide assortment of promotional activities to increase distribution and stimulate retail sales. Promotional devices included dealer discounts in the fall, combination deals, free merchandise, contributions to chain-account advertising campaigns, contests where consumers (particularly children) could win prizes, and occasionally special sales where retail prices were reduced for a short time. The company was regarded as among the most active in the industry in the promotion area.

ADVERTISING

Television advertising was the company's most important marketing activity. About half of the marketing budget was devoted to consumer advertising, all of which was spent for local or regional television commercials. The commercials included filmed cartoons, spot announcements, and straight "hard sell" commercials done live by local announcers.

All advertising was planned on the basis of local TV markets, and the amount devoted to each brand in a particular market generally depended on its anticipated sales within that market. For example, Robin Hood sales were high in Green Bay, Wisconsin, and were supported by advertising in that market, but William Penn sales in that area were negligible, and this line was not advertised there.

Midway's advertising was planned and put into operation by the Dearborn agency, a Chicago advertising firm noted for its overall marketing abilities. The agency, working closely with President Kramer and Mr. Reiss, developed a marketing plan each year for each brand. This plan included overall objectives as well as market-by-market projections and expenditures. Midway's management set limits on the advertising budget based on corporate financial and manufacturing considerations, played a major part in determining marketing strategy, and exercised final review over the plans; but the agency was responsible for development of a full marketing (not just advertising) plan and for the execution of the advertising part of the plan.

THE SALES PLAN

The marketing department developed an annual plan (a document of approximately 40 pages) which covered all phases of corporate sales activity. The plan included:

1. Corporate sales goals by brand.
2. The overall advertising plan.
3. Goals and plans for each regional territory (four in all).
4. Goals for each broker (25 in all).

It also contained a review of the progress (and disappointments) in each category for the current year. Exhibit 2 contains a sample page for one of Midway's brokers.

The overall marketing plan was based not on broker's territories but on TV market areas. Thus, while the New England broker's territory included six states, the company's marketing plans were based upon separate marketing programs for Augusta, Portland, Boston, Providence,

Exhibit 2

MIDWAY FOODS CORPORATION (C_1)
Marketing Department Goals for Broker No. 10

Sales Objectives—1958–59

  (a) Organize broader missionary operation by addition of more men.
  (b) Widen sales to independent supermarkets of package items through drop shipments or warehouse withdrawals.
  (c) Reinstate item No. 108 with Family Tea Chain.
  (d) Obtain wider distribution on Liberty Bell and Robin Hood.
  (e) Commence building William Penn sales.
  (f) Continue further expansion of item No. 104 sales through retail outlets.
  (g) Sell Hi Lo [chain stores].
  (h) Increase sales to prominent vending machine operators.
  (i) Obtain greater effectiveness from advertising contracts by arranging regular schedule of promotions.
  (j) Widen distribution among vendors on all brands by taking advantage of special promotion scheduled in late September.
  (k) Arrange to make *regular* calls on all syndicate stores.

All of us at Midway are ready to help in any way we can to assist you in reaching the goals we have set.

Our Regional Sales Managers, or Andy Kallal, Hal Reiss, or Larry Rosen will work with you at various intervals, giving you whatever sales or promotion assistance you might require.

Our objectives are reasonable—the planning is sound—the successful execution of these plans is in your hands.

Source: Company records.

Worcester, and New Haven. "TV has become so important in this industry that conventional marketing areas don't mean a thing," said Mr. Reiss.

MARKETING INFORMATION

The marketing department had three important sources of information: field personnel, customer orders, and the IBM reports. Midway's three regional sales managers spent almost all their time supervising and assisting the brokers, generally with matters relating to problems at the retail level. They were thus close to the sources of basic information and sent in informal memos or called long distance as the occasion arose.

Customer orders arrived in a pile on the marketing vice president's desk each morning, and both he and the field sales manager[4] looked through them for sales to key accounts and repeat orders. From these clues the two men said they could tell how special promotions were going and how a new advertising campaign was doing. The IBM section sent the department a *daily sales report* including sales received up to the previous day (grouped by each broker's territory), sales for the month and year to date, and the sales target through the end of the month. In addition, each month the IBM section sent a sales breakdown by TV market areas and by individual customers.

With this high-speed information, the department was able to spot trouble in a matter of days. For example "if we spot something in New Haven as we go over the invoices in the morning, we'll call the New England broker and have him fly in from Boston the same afternoon or the next day to find out the cause and correct it."

DEPARTMENTAL ORGANIZATION

The marketing department had two vice presidents, Mr. Andy Kallal and Mr. Reiss. Its organization was a mixture of specialization by job function, by customer and region served, and by the abilities of the people involved. Departmental duties were of two principal types— field work "with the trade," and staff work in the home office. While Mr. Reiss, marketing vice president, was responsible for direction of both, in practice he directed activities in the home office, and Mr. Kallal, sales vice president, worked in the field along with the three regional managers.

---

[4] Larry Rosen, field sales manager.

The field personnel operated under objectives and policies set forth in the marketing plan yet had considerable autonomy within these limits. Said one of the regional men, "I've been offered several jobs at over $2,000 more a year in salary, but I'm not interested. This job gives me real freedom to travel, to work out deals and promotions, and to try my own ways of doing some things. I'm training brokers to sell our way; the office gives me all the information and help I need and lets me do things my way as long as I get the results."

Andy Kallal. Mr. Kallal spent nine months of the year on the road, two on vacation, and one in the home offices. Describing his work, he said:

I'm Midway's ambassador to the trade. I've been selling to the trade for over 35 years and I know almost every jobber and broker in the business—over 10,000 of them, anyway. I'm known as the "postcard kid" because when I go on vacation to Europe I send a couple thousand postcards to brokers and business friends all over the country. I'm traveling almost all the time. It's a way of life, and I enjoy it. I guess there's no real difference between myself and a regional man except that I've known the accounts longer.

When I first came here, the most difficult job was to get the good will of the trade. The former owner had a lot of claims out against him, had been making a lousy product, and had robbed the trade during the second World War because he could get away with it. He had a very poor reputation. So we picked up all the claims and paid them on the spot—never questioned them, even though we had no legal obligation to pay them. Then we set out to build a good reputation in the trade and to build a strong, loyal broker organization.

We've built our distribution around the idea that the trade could live without us but we couldn't live without the trade. We've been like a department store—you know, the customer is always right. We've been 100% honest with our brokers and have built a reputation for two things: (1) when we say something, our word is good, and (2) they can't lose money on our line. If they get flooded and have spoilage, or anything like that, and they ask for help, we give it. And on taking back goods from retailers we make good 100% while many others may pay half or even less. In these respects we are quite different from most of our competitors.

Another thing that has helped this company make the progress it has is what you might call the feeling of being a big family. We're informal, not stuffy. We welcome suggestions from the trade, and they know we understand their problems. There's a lot of that atmosphere within the company, too—of welcoming suggestions and giving help. When Hal Reiss came here, he didn't know marketing—but I could tell he had it in him. So I've tried to help and teach him in any way I could. With him I don't have to any more, because he has a real feel for what is going on. But we still pass ideas back and forth and keep in close touch. And we're known for it in the trade—as a company that lets suggestions go up the line as well as down.

Hal Reiss. Company executives described Mr. Reiss to the researcher as

> . . . the genius of the marketing department. He's a hard worker and a quick thinker—sometimes even a little brash. But when he says sales of William Penn will be up in New Haven next month, you can depend on it. Also he's young and still pretty idealistic. He sometimes talks tough, but underneath he's pretty soft-hearted and inclined to be moved by other people's feelings.

Mr. Reiss described himself as a person for whom work itself was not the goal.

> I don't feel that I'm working hard because I have to, or because there is nothing better to do. Work isn't the goal; I'm interested in creating or building something. I'd like to see Midway become one of the big boys of the industry—for us to have $100 million in sales some day. You might say I'm out to prove something.
>
> I'm not working just to get a bigger salary. Some people seem to want to store up a lot of money and then retire to Florida and sit under a palm tree and drink lemonade. I'd like to sit under a palm tree, too, sometimes, but I'm not working so I can retire with security. Security seems to be the goal of a lot of people, but I'm not sure it's worth having or possible to have.
>
> I'm somewhat of an idealist, and sometimes I'm almost like a conscience here. I have a strong conscience myself; somtimes people tell me I should relax and stop fighting the problem. But I just don't go along with some of our American business values, even though they are accepted practices. Take expense accounts. Some companies send people to Florida for field trips during the winter, or to California for an industry convention or show. It's business and pleasure, all on the expense account. People tell me it's the American way, but to me it seems morally wrong. Saying "no" to these junkets makes me the conscience here, and that is not a pleasant role. But I'm here to work, not to relax on an expense account. I want to pay for my own vacations and then really have a chance to relax—to take three weeks or so and really unwind. Actually, I haven't had that kind of a vacation since I've been here—but I'll take one before too long, I hope.
>
> The way I work is to think quickly, to get to the nub of the problem in a hurry. And I tend to expect others to do the same. If there's one thing I don't like it's mediocrity, or stupidity frosted over with glib terminology. I tend to think logically and to reason with the specific problem at hand. I jump on people who talk in generalities or who take a lot of words to say nothing.

Mr. Reiss was graduated from the University of Illinois in 1949 with a major in journalism and minors in history and English. He was active on the school newspaper, "but marriage and a family looked grim on journalism pay." Following graduation, Mr. Reiss worked for 18 months as a clerk in a freight-forwarding agency and then contacted an employment agency for other leads. He noted:

The agency gave me Midway to try, so I came over and talked to Clark. I was interested because of the challenge. Also I wanted a growth situation, not one where I would be working on a bottom layer of middle management. This seemed to be what I was looking for—partly because Clark's philosophy and mine are pretty similar.

Basically, the job is what I hoped it would be, a real challenge and the chance to build something. But like anything, I guess, there are some times when it gets me down. Sometimes the long hours, the evening work, and the weekend meetings just get me. I tend to be impatient with lengthy deliberations, though not as much as I used to be. I'm learning to be more patient and to accept what can't be changed. It's particularly true with my relationship toward Milt.[5] I'm learning I can't sell the stuff unless he can make it, and even though we still argue a good deal, ours is becoming a close friendship.

My job here is to direct the marketing program. We are basically a marketing company; we process manufactured raw materials into an end product, package it, and sell it. There isn't much room to live by being good in manufacturing, so we have almost been forced to rely on marketing.

I divide my time here between planning, operating, and developing my department. Operating still takes too much of my time—I'm always dropping the planning to run over and operate. My staff people are young and inexperienced, so I have to do a lot of the pencil work as well as the planning and forecasting.

The most difficult part of my job is turning our overall strategy into successful market-by-market programs that will deliver the sales. You see, there's one thing you have to remember about Midway: we don't have even one brand that has nationwide acceptance. Each brand has a few good markets, and for historical reasons not more than two brands are really developed in any particular major market. We have Robin Hood well developed in Green Bay and Grand Rapids; Midway in Chicago, Cleveland, and Des Moines; Willian Penn in New England but nowhere else; and Liberty Bell doing fairly well in a lot of places. What this adds up to is a crazy quilt. You have to have a different marketing program for each TV area, and it has to be geared to the local conditions. It's turned out this way because we were expanding Midway concentrically from Chicago, and then we added three other brands that were selling with no planned pattern at all.

So the situation is a crazy quilt, and it makes this a real challenge. We are trying to expand rapidly, to develop national brands that have consumer acceptance and can be defended against potential competitors with a "me too" product that is heavily advertised. And with our No. 1 brand we are trying to put across a smaller-than-average bar and to get the job done before the candy industry reaches advertising maturity. So we are trying to grow rapidly with very little money; to do it we have to take risks and be opportunistic. We have to get the most growth for our money. It means putting together a plan that has no "fat" in it, no excess for safety or contingencies. If I think $2,000 in advertising will do the job, that's all I ask for, even though I may have to admit

---

[5] Milt Lombard, manufacturing vice president.

I was wrong and come back halfway through the season and ask for another $300. A regular marketing man would get $3,000 to do the job—and he would deliver the sales. But to my way of thinking he's no "hero"—he has wasted $700.

Getting more specific, we try to make the marketing program in each market fit the strength of our distribution organization, the amount we will need for deals and promotions, what our advertising dollars will buy for us, and what competitive conditions are. Take advertising. If you advertise Midway three afternoons a week on "Popeye," and it costs you $4,000 for the season, it may cost you only another $1,000 to get two more afternoons. You can save 20%–50% by buying TV time in quantity. So developing all four brands in each market would make some sense—we could really reap the advertising savings. But we don't have the money to do it, and, second, it would leave the rest of the country wide open.

We also use some of our advertising money to help strengthen sales of one line for a broker. It gives him a lift, gets more detail work on all our brands, and makes us a more important line for him. That gives us leverage, which is what we need to get service from him. But it means we can't get the advertising discounts, so our advertising costs would tend to be higher than those of competitors, particularly those of the big, well-established companies.

I hope someday to consolidate our markets and to be able to use network TV. Then we could reach an equivalent audience for 20%–30% less than the best local prices. Competition will be on network someday, and we'll need to have it to keep our four brands going."

The researcher asked Mr. Reiss how he operated his department.

Basically I'm trying to operate so my people will grow along with the company. I set high standards. I know they won't all be met, but at least people will know what I'm looking for. I expect a subordinate to have ideas and to have plans on what he wants to do and how. I may differ with him, and I'll explain why I think another way is better, but I don't penalize people for doing things their own way. What I want is results, and if a man has his own way, that's O.K.

Our regional men and brokers have quotas and also specific goals to reach in each market. I ask them to set a quota for themselves, partly to get their appraisal of a market and partly so I can appraise their motivation and judgment. I don't want them to promise pie in the sky, but neither do I want to see them aiming low to be sure of hitting it and getting a bonus.

We give each regional manager a discretionary fund to spend as he pleases. It's only $5,000, but it is important in a couple of ways. For one thing the way a man uses it helps me appraise his judgment. Second, it makes him a much more important part of the organization. The brokers look to him to use some of the money for promotions in their territory—so it helps the regional man get the broker's cooperation. And don't forget that it's the strength of our distribution that has let us grow rapidly on so little money.

All this field work is done within the general framework of corporate marketing objectives. We write these up and send them out to each broker and regional man. Each month we send him a rundown on how he is doing compared to the objectives (based on information from the IBM reports). At the end of the year we go over the plan and each unfulfilled objective with every man. We try to determine if we were unrealistic, if it was unavoidable, or if it was a lack of something on his part. It isn't done to crucify someone; we want our objectives and quotas to be realistic or they are worse than useless. We want each man to believe he can hit them, so it's important that we all understand *why* they weren't reached.

It's an important part of what has made this company tick. At first brokers were skeptical; they said Midway would be "like all the rest." Well, after a while they found that wasn't the case. We've built a reputation, and now when we tell a broker we are going to advertise in his territory and raise his quota from $5,000 to $50,000 he won't bat an eyelash.

The Manufacturing Department

The manufacturing department had a twofold mission: (1) to mass-produce acceptable merchandise as economically as possible, and (2) to expand production with a minimum expenditure for facilities and equipment. Even though production costs could have been reduced by the purchase of additional machinery ("We have had to pass up a number of them that would have paid off in less than a year.") it was company policy to use all available corporate funds for market development. "If we needed money to keep something from falling apart, we got it; otherwise the money has gone for additional advertising. We have had to settle for half a loaf here in the plant," said Mr. Milt Lombard, manufacturing vice president.

The major problem of the department was the continuing need for increased productivity to keep up with rising sales. "When I came here, we could produce 40,000 to 50,000 pieces a day. Now we can turn out 1.5 million if the occasion demands it," Mr. Lombard said. To accomplish this increase with the limited funds available while reducing manufacturing costs, the department had modified some standard equipment, rebuilt other machines which were bought as "junk," made some equipment of its own, learned to run the machinery safely at speeds considerably higher than "recommended," and developed detailed schedules and an hourly check or warning system to keep production under control on an hour-by-hour basis.

OPERATIONS

Manufacturing was basically a mass-production operation turning out upwards of a million pieces of candy per day in each plant when the plants were working on a three-shift basis. Manufacturing involved the blending and forming of liquid and solid raw materials, cooling or hardening, and packaging. Raw materials became finished goods in short order, as indicated by the normal maximum times below:

Event	Day
A. Raw material arrives at plant	1st day
B. Into manufacturing	2d day
C. Into finished goods warehouse	2d day
D. Out of warehouse	8–13th day

THE CHICAGO PLANT

Midway manufactured in Philadelphia and Chicago. The Chicago plant was a five-story converted bakery which the company leased for less than $30,000 per year. It was approximately 50 years old, had a single elevator (used for both freight and passengers), and was not as efficient as a one-story plant would be. ("We didn't especially want it, but it's a lot better than what we had on Maxwell Street and was about all we could afford at the time.") Manufacturing occupied the basement and three floors:

> 5: Offices
> 4: Empty*
> 3: Manufacturing
> 2: Processing and packaging
> 1: Finished goods
> Basement: Raw materials
>
> * R&D occupied about 30% of the area.

Raw materials traveled in liquid form by pipe and in solid form by freight elevator to the third floor for initial processing; materials then moved to the second floor by pipe for final forming and packaging operations, and down to the first floor by elevator as finished goods, boxed and ready for shipment. The operations themselves were carried on in cramped quarters, with conveyors running this way and that to the accompaniment of the banging and clacking of machinery.

EQUIPMENT

Midway's plant contained a variety of forming and packaging machines, some standard, some rebuilt for particular tasks, and others homemade or put together from "junk." According to Mr. Lombard, "This is one industry where an ability to develop your own special-purpose machinery is important. We are very lucky to have a man[6]

---

[6] Otto Lehman, manager of R&D and former plant manager.

who is a genius with equipment; he can make a machine do almost anything except talk."

While much of the machinery was not of the latest design and therefore not capable of highest speeds, the forming machines were particularly troublesome in terms of slow speed, a high reject rate, and lack of uniformity in output. Mr. Lombard noted:

Every piece of candy goes through those two machines; they are the heart of the manufacturing process, and one serious bottleneck. But our Midway candy bar has some unique forming problems because of its raw materials, and no one has been able to build a machine to do the job. People have asked as much as $100,000 to try, without giving any kind of guarantee, so we now have an R&D department that is going to try to build one. If we succeed, it will be a real breakthrough. We have a 16% reject rate as a result of those machines, not to mention a lot of wasted raw materials because we have to give over-weight [on two of the five sizes of bars] in order to avoid having merchandise returned by the state as underweight.

The researcher inquired if there were spare machines which would be used in case of a breakdown. "We can't afford them," said Mr. Lombard. "With our budget we can't even have a full complement of spare parts. We get $77,000 to heat the building, maintain it, buy spare parts, and make safety and quality-control improvements. If a machine runs into trouble, we just try our best to keep it running until the weekend."

PRODUCTION CONTROL

In order to operate within the guidelines set by management, the manufacturing department kept itself under tight control. There were three principal policies under which the department operated, the first pertaining to inventory, the second to flexibility, and the third to expenditures.

First, the department was not to build up a substantial finished goods inventory ahead of the fall season. Producing in advance raised costs, since the finished goods had to be stored in air-conditioned public warehouses and Midway had to borrow money to support the inventory. As a result the plant had only a one- to three-week inventory of finished goods on hand during the season. In addition, in 1958 factory start-up had been delayed from July 7 to July 23 owing to conditions in the commodities market. At that time the condition of the cocoa market was such that the spot price was higher than the future price (that is, prices were expected to decline), and in view of this unfavorable cost picture, Midway was attempting to wait until the very last possible moment to make a decision between the alternatives of cutting the weight of the 5¢ bar or providing a 10¢ bar only. Equipment and forms for a 10¢ bar were available, and one 5¢-size wrapping machine had been test-converted to 10¢ size in preparation for the possible choice of this alternative.

Second, production was to be flexible to respond to changes by the sales department in the desired product mix. The Chicago plant produced the Midway piece in over a dozen different forms made up of five different product sizes, and it had to change and reschedule the quantities to be produced and the amounts to be packaged in each way, as selling results caused changes in the sales forecast. These scheduling changes were translated into output within days or even hours during the season; otherwise one item would be overproduced for a period while another was out of stock. Failure to deliver an item in short supply meant that some selling efforts had been wasted, since, in management's opinion, lost sales could not be recaptured during the remainder of the season. "If A & P called Hal Reiss in the morning for a special, we would switch the packaging lines without shutting down, and turn the stuff out the same afternoon," said Mr. Lombard.

Third, the department was to maintain its production controls at minimum cost. For example, Mr. Lombard had asked for $12,000 to buy two heavy-duty in-the-line electronic check weighers that could weigh each piece as it moved along either of two conveyors; however, he had been allotted $6,000 to buy two smaller scales which subsequently proved unequal to the task. The smaller scales were guaranteed by one of the largest scale manufacturers in the country, and the manufacturer's engineering personnel were making frequent visits to Midway in an effort to get the equipment to work properly.

Production schedules were to be maintained without benefit of standby equipment (there was none) and with a minimum expense for staff assistance. (Except for a quality control man there was no staff prior to the Main Line acquisition.)

These policies gave rise to an assortment of departmental controls for (1) scheduling output, (2) spotting rejects, and (3) reporting to management.

1. Scheduling. Production scheduling at Midway was focused on two related problems: producing enough candy bars to keep up with demand for the product, and balancing production of each item with sales requirements. Both problems had been acute for the past eight years because the company had been scheduled at three-shift capacity on a five- or six-day week during the season. Also on more than one occasion the department had been asked to produce still more because sales were going "a little better than we had expected."

Historically, total sales had been limited by the ability of the factory to supply merchandise during the rush season. To meet peaks, factory output had been scheduled at 95% of "machine capacity," with equipment running at higher speeds than those recommended by the manufacturers. This practice left only a 5% slack (exclusive of weekends) for setups, breakdowns, maintenance, and any schedule modifications which might require additional setup time. When such delays did occur, machinery was run at still higher speeds for short periods so that production could get back on schedule. On one occasion in September Mr. Lombard said to the researcher:

This bearing on the forming machine is the key to how fast we can run the rest of the line. The machine is supposed to be operated at 44 rpm. We usually push it to 56 or 57, but today it is running at 63 so I come out now and then and put my hand on the bearing to check if it is overheating. We can't keep it going that fast very long, so we will slow it down and let it rest this afternoon.

As a result of schedules calling for maximum output, Mr. Lombard and Mr. Reiss met prior to the season to work out compromises in the sales forecast based in part on what the factory could produce. The discussions often took the form of Mr. Reiss's saying he could sell 30X and 40Y, while Mr. Lombard said the factory could produce 30X and 30Y or 20X and 50Y. The compromise was often achieved by sales' directing more selling efforts toward Y to permit higher total sales, while manufacturing made concessions such as promising production at an additional ½% of capacity. The two men had frequent meetings during the season. These sessions had been described as a running battle over such issues as "additional merchandise wrapped especially for Halloween promotions by big chain-store accounts." Other executives said "This seven-year running battle is part of the basic folklore of the company."

It was the researcher's judgment that the situation was due in part to the sometimes conflicting needs of the two departments and in part to the fact that Mr. Reiss and Mr. Lombard had different ways of thinking and working. The researcher learned that the two men were able to work out their problems despite these differences of opinion, that each had high respect for the other's knowledge and ability in his respective area, and that it was not uncommon for the two men and their families to get together socially in the evening.

Producing needed items at the right time was the second major scheduling problem. Production was scheduled in relation to a sales forecast prepared at the beginning of the season and revised as necessary during the course of the year. Upward revision of total sales for an item and advancement of shipment dates had been major problems in the past, because they often necessitated a scheduling change. When such changes required stopping one item to produce another, it increased setup time and tended to throw all items behind schedule. Mr. Lombard noted, "During the rush we are scheduled at near theoretical capacity, so there isn't much room to compensate for extra setup time. As a result, we have to run the plant so that we can turn on a dime. We have worked for flexibility to meet such contingencies."

2. Rejects. A second aspect of production control was the control and reuse of rejects. In 1959 one piece out of every six coming from the forming machines was rejected at some point before it was finally placed in a carton headed for the first floor. While the raw materials could be salvaged and reprocessed, some materials (such as wrapping stock) and labor were inevitably wasted, raising costs and reducing effective plant capacity correspondingly. The reject problem was almost entirely caused by the two forming machines, and, according to Mr. Lombard, the problem "won't be under satisfactory control until we either make basic changes in the forming equipment or modify our raw materials so the existing equipment can handle them."

To spot rejects, the company used two production-line check-weighing scales and two electric eyes, which weighed the product for size and looked for foreign substances. "Our existing methods aren't really controlling size or quality; they just keep notifying us that the problem still exists," said Mr. Lombard.

3. Hourly Production Report. A third element of production control was the hourly production report. This report contained hourly data on machine production and was used to determine whether a machine was falling below capacity. Since operations could slow down or rejects could climb without the supervisor's being aware of it, this report was considered a key to production control. (In the past there had been periods when the report was made every 15 minutes, and this was still done occasionally when production seemed to fall behind without a reasonable explanation.) It was reviewed by both the plant manager and the manufacturing vice president.

COST CONTROLS

In addition to production controls, the department maintained its own cost controls. They were generally prepared by Mr. Lombard, and the researcher noted that he kept them handy on his desk and sometimes referred to them while talking on the phone. The researcher also noted that the breakdown of cost figures which he prepared was more detailed than that maintained by the administrative department. When he asked Mr. Lombard about this, the latter replied: "Yes, they are more detailed. I need them to keep in close touch with our operations. It only takes me five minutes a day to keep these records, and since I'm an accountant by training these controls come naturally."

Minimizing Cash Outlay. As the researcher entered the manufacturing vice president's office one afternoon during the September "rush season," Mr. Milt Lombard, Mr. Otto Lehman (at that time, still plant manager), Mr. Mario Spumoni,[7] and a foreman were discussing the recently completed repairs on the loading platform which was located in the yard at one side of the building. The researcher asked Mr. Lombard about the discussion. He replied:

We were talking about the repair job. The loading platform needed some new cement along the front edge. The delivery trucks back up to it and break it down. We got some cement, and some of the boys mixed it up and did the repair work. The boys did a good job, but not what would be called a professional one.

You see, we got an estimate that a professional job would cost $500. Well, the money isn't in the budget. We might have gotten it by having a conference and saying we had to have it, but it wasn't worth the time it would take for the three of us to discuss it. So we got someone to tell us how to mix the cement and did the job with plant labor. We got it done for about $150; in my way of thinking we saved $350.

Yet management criticized us for the job. You see, management inspects the plant and picks up things that aren't right. Management pointed out that it wasn't perfectly even along the front edge. I'm not sure you could tell just at a glance, but it wasn't—not the way a professional would make it by setting up a guide string. So it was criticized, and that is as it should be. But I feel pretty good when management doesn't find anything more serious; it means the important things are going all right. The boys are going out now to try to even up the front of the cement.

LABOR FORCE

Midway employed an unskilled and semiskilled labor force, drawn mainly from recent immigrant and minority groups, to operate the

---

[7] Mario Spumoni, foreman of the first shift, became plant manager when Mr. Lehman became manager of R&D, in November, 1958.

factory. The work force varied from a skeleton group during the summer to over 100 workers when the Chicago plant was operating three shifts. The employees were unionized and received wages which management said were slightly below the average for other Chicago food manufacturers. Mr. Kramer handled most of the negotiating and said the company had received favorable treatment because the union leaders had some understanding of how difficult it was for a small company to survive in the industry.

Mr. Lombard described the union as "tough, but neither corrupt nor pigheaded." As the company continued to grow, he expected its wages would have to be brought into line. The Main Line plant in Philadelphia was not unionized, and there the workers received more than the "going wage."

ORGANIZATION

Mr. Lombard, in commenting on his organization, said:

Every problem seems to come to me except how to turn on a light switch. It isn't that the men are stupid; they find a fresh viewpoint helpful. And I haven't been as successful in passing on my knowledge as I should. It's part of the problem of not having the money to afford a strong, competent staff. Otto, for example, is a brilliant tool and die maker, not a trained administrator; and his replacement is really being promoted before he is fully ready. On the other hand, we don't have anyone in the department who has had formal engineering training, and I wasn't allotted enough money to hire a really high-caliber staff man. The one I hired after we acquired Main Line is as good as I could get for $5,000. It means our organization is somewhat thin and that I have to do a lot more detail work than vice presidents do in textbooks."

The comments of Mr. Otto Lehman, the R&D department manager, who until recently had been plant manager, appeared to the researcher to illustrate the way the manufacturing organization operated. When the researcher approached Mr. Lehman's desk, he found Mr. Lehman and Mr. Spumoni, the newly appointed plant manager, discussing a document.

Mr. Lehman greeted the researcher, "Sit down and have some coffee. Mario and I are just going over the hourly production report. He's taken over my job in the plant, and I'm showing him some of the things to look for on the report."

When the researcher inquired whether he could observe and take notes, Mr. Lehman replied,

Sure, go ahead, and I'll check them over for grammar and spelling [smiles]. And another thing, change some of my words around so those folks won't know

I didn't get to the eighth grade. O.K.? Now this is what we call our hourly production report. If a machine is running slow or rejects are becoming high, this report calls it to our attention within an hour or two instead of after eight hours. It's pretty easy for production to drop and for us to lose a lot of boxes of candy in a day.

This report keeps us on our toes. There is a human tendency to fall off, especially when spring rolls around and sales drop. We can see the inventory increasing downstairs so we know the summer cutback is coming. That means there is less pressure on each of us to produce. So keeping on our toes now means we keep up to snuff and we can lay off the third shift maybe a day or a week sooner. And the second shift, too. This makes a lot of difference in Milt's manufacturing budget.

Another thing about it is we need repetitious checking and supervision in production. We have to check for the same little things each day. Well, we look each hour at the figures, and sometimes we don't do it too carefully. We miss things just because we have seen them the hour before. Milt is really good at this, though. He backs us up with another check of figures and he finds what we have missed. It's good to have someone backing us up and keeping us on our toes.

Milt Lombard. Associates described Mr. Lombard as "the company philosopher," a man who sometimes repeated a proverb or gave a lengthy example to illustrate a point. "Also he's a little old-fashioned on things like employee relations techniques, not up on the latest concepts." He was described as a "damn fine production man. He makes that beat-up equipment produce and keeps on cutting costs while he is at it. He's a factory man—a real vest-pocket operator. He has his sleeves rolled up and carries his cost sheets in his pockets. He doesn't go much for formal memos, but he writes more now than he used to."

Mr. Lombard described himself as

. . . the old man around here, even though 46 doesn't really feel very old. In some ways I'm old-fashioned for this company. I'm still a Maxwell Street man, you could say—an operating man, not an office executive with a lot of ideas and terminology. Even with our new offices I spend at least three days a week in one plant or the other. Not that I wouldn't like to be an office executive—my organization just doesn't have the depth to make it practical.

I think I'm something of a realist, too, someone who doesn't kid himself along. I try to face facts, not to let sentiment or idealism obscure them. I believe I'm the only person here who would just as soon see us expand a little more slowly so we have time to grow into our new responsibilities. I know I can handle them, but I also know there is an increasing amount to learn as we get bigger and more complex. I'm not completely convinced that we are mature enough to successfully operate a company that will be as large as this one expects to be in the next few years.

Actually, my formal training was in accounting, so I'm not just a nuts and bolts man. Even though I get only a small percentage of the money I request, I keep track of my costs, do the cost accounting work on special orders and the payback figuring on the machines I hope some day to get. While I haven't been to school to brush up on the new techniques in this field, keeping track of the numbers comes naturally.

My objectives here are to continue to strengthen the department, to continue to grow as an administrator, and to do both without getting an ulcer. This is a job where the person has to produce; if he doesn't, he'll be out on his ear. Midway is too small to be able to find sinecures for people who no longer are producing; we can't afford such luxuries here, and I'd be the first to admit it.

Another objective here is to run this plant as effectively as possible on the money I'm given. I have a reputation that means a lot to me, one that began when I was plant superintendent for IFM.[8] And I won't run my department by using up all the money and asking for more. Once I get my budget allocation, I find a way to operate the plant within that figure. It means we don't have any frills here; in fact, we have only the bare essentials. And the amount of money we have to operate on is so small that, when management asks us to brighten up the walls with a new coat of paint, $500 is damn hard to squeeze out of our funds.

More immediately, I'd like to install bulk sugar-handling equipment in Philly. Our sugar supplier has offered to loan us the money to buy and install the equipment, to charge us no interest, and to take their payback from the 15 cents per hundred pounds they will save from not having to put it in bags and deliver it that way. We figure it can be paid back in about three years, and from then on we will get the 15-cent saving, which will amount to over $6,000 a year. In addition, I estimate it will save us $4,000 or more a year in handling costs inside the plant. We can begin to pocket this savings as soon as management approves the transaction. I've had the request in for over six months, but management is investigating.

Another goal has been to cut the direct labor costs at Philly by 55%. The plant manager we originally hired made progress, and direct labor came down about 35%. But I thought these costs should still be about 20% less, and over the months the figures have tended to back up this judgment. Direct labor costs fluctuated quite a bit, and on my trips out there I wasn't able to find any reasons for this except that he didn't seem to be leading—he was lazy. A month after we hired him, I recommended that he be fired; but it wasn't until November [after Mr. Kramer had made a trip to Philadelphia] that management concurred. I fired the manager in January after the rush season here was over; that was so we could spare Mario to run the plant in Philly.

Mario and I went out together, and I stayed 10 days until he got used to it. I told him that a 20% reduction in costs was the goal. Volume was rising, and as you can see from these figures the costs dropped 23%. We built some inventory, but then the company ran short of money, so we had to cut the work force and cut production. But now the people have the pace. It's like marching an army, a matter of rhythm or pace. Now we have eased off some, and with

---

[8] Illinois Food Manufacturing Company.

the reduced volume costs are running about 3% higher than they were when we attained our best percentage.

It's pretty good progress considering that the people have been working there 15–30 years; a new rhythm isn't easy to get used to. But I think we'll get it back down an extra 3% before too long.

Sending Mario out there has left me with no plant manager, so Otto is helping out again. We have been working together for 24 years, and he's one man I couldn't afford to lose. Also, since there really isn't a plant manager, the three foremen are getting a lot of responsibility, and it will be sink or swim. I'm spending more time in the plant as a result. I don't expect trouble to show up until May, really, because it takes about three months for a plant that has been under tight rein to begin to slip. Meanwhile Clark and I are looking for a new man to run the Main Line plant.

Mr. Lombard was graduated from Purdue with a B.A. in accounting in 1935. Following graduation he found employment in Chicago as a voucher register clerk for IFM at $15 a week. In 1938, during a strike, he became IFM's personnel director, and in 1941 when the plant superintendent received a commission in the Army, he became acting plant manager. In 1949 he left IFM to become part owner and president of a small company in Milwaukee. In 1950, on a buying trip to Chicago, he stopped by to congratulate Mr. Kramer on his purchase of Midway. Then, as Mr. Lombard noted,

. . . my monthly buying trip became a consulting trip as well. My business was only going so-so when Clark stopped by in Milwaukee one time, had dinner at the house, and asked me to come to work. The offer was attractive; Chicago is a better place to make a buck than Milwaukee, so I sold out and came to work here.

The job has turned out basically as I had hoped. It is showing a good income in a growing company. But I still have some of the entrepreneur in me, I guess, and sometimes wish I were in business for myself. Also the long hours have sometimes gotten me; I'm still in good health, but I hope the hours won't be this long in another five or ten years.

My job here, as I see it, has been to mechanize the factory to get acceptable efficiency, and to run the plant on a minimum of money. When I came here, a lot of the operations were done by hand, and the factory was on a one-shift basis. In six months we were running three shifts, with two shifts on Saturday, and were turning out more candy with fewer people per shift. We were such a small outfit that everyone had to fill in on jobs to get things done. I slept in the office in those days.

I've operated the plant without much in the way of formalities; we don't use job titles or formal memos down here. We've developed a way of talking to each other, and when we want something done in a hurry we find that short cuss words are very handy. They aren't intended to cuss someone out so much as to convey a meaning—like a form of shorthand.

The plant isn't all that I'd like it to be, and neither is our organization. The organization is partly one I inherited. As you can tell from those organization charts you drew up, some people had to be moved downward until they found a level of work they could handle [see Exhibits 3, 4, and 5]. But I feel this has been done without ruining them as people, and if they ever show more interest

Exhibit 3

MIDWAY FOODS CORPORATION (C₁)
Organization Chart, 1951–52

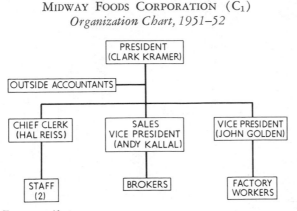

Source: Clark Kramer, president.

Exhibit 4

MIDWAY FOODS CORPORATION (C₁)
Organization Chart, 1955–56

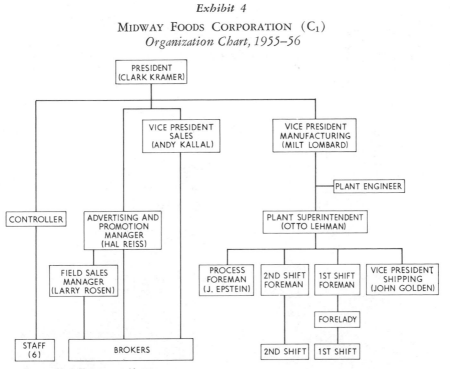

Source: Clark Kramer, president.

Exhibit 5

MIDWAY FOODS CORPORATION (C₁)

Organization Chart, 1958–59

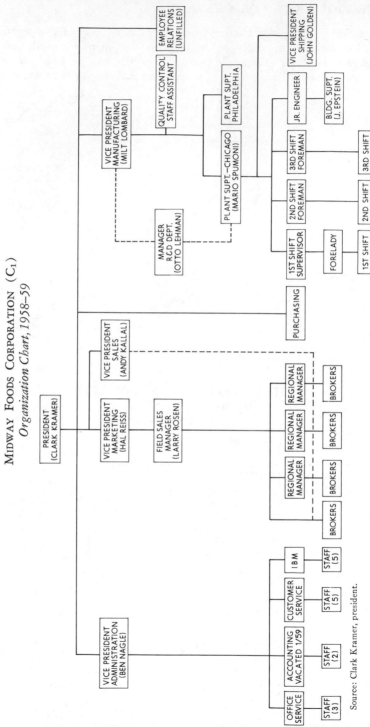

Source: Clark Kramer, president.

or spark I'd be the first to give them more responsibility. And, despite what people sometimes say about our organization, I think we have at least made the best of the people we had. You may have noticed that people last longer in this department.

The R&D Department

The R&D department had one major mission, to develop new forming equipment in time for the 1960–61 season. The department also was responsible for machinery repairs and for several less important development projects.

R&D had been established in November, 1958, when Mr. Otto Lehman, plant manager, was made R&D manager, reporting directly to the president. Of this, Mr. Lehman noted:

Myself—well, really Milt and I—thought we weren't quite ready for the change yet. There were too many things to take care of in the factory. But Clark had wanted to have something like this for a couple of years, and in November he decided the time had come. He said he wanted the two of us to begin working on this on our own, as I recall his words—that we could do better than outsiders and the time had come to try.

As to how it was to be set up, I don't know whether to say I was made head of R&D or not. I don't know how to put it without hurting anyone, and I don't know if Milt knew about it before I did or not.

When the change occurred, Mr. Lehman no longer had formal responsibility for the plant, but he, Mr. Lombard, and Mario Spumoni worked out an "informal understanding" that Mr. Lehman would continue to help out in the plant until Mario got used to the new job. The informal agreement was extended when the Philadelphia plant manager was fired in January and Mario went to Philadelphia to run the Main Line operation. During the same period, Mr. Lehman hired four mechanics, brought in some old equipment from Philadelphia and some from the shed out back, bought steel, and began development work on the fourth floor. He divided his time between the two departments.

OTTO LEHMAN

Mr. Lehman had worked at Illinois Food Manufacturing Company (IFM) in equipment development and as a foreman for 18 years. He said:

Then I went into the candy business for myself. It was a small operation, and it kept getting smaller—I was "kaput" in two years. Next I came to Midway as a mechanical supervisor, doing repairs, rebuilding, and also supervising some production.

I came to this country in 1930, when I was 19. I had just finished four years as an apprentice tool and die maker at General Electric in Berlin. I had been working on special jobs at G.E., building large transformers for Russia and China. I had a contract to work for them here, but when I got here they couldn't squeeze me in, so I was doing odd jobs for a few years before I got into food manufacturing.

When asked what he enjoyed most about his work, Mr. Lehman replied:

Making things work better. When someone comes up with an idea on how to simplify something or make it work better, I try it out after hours. I even tried building a bandage-wrapping machine at home. I wasn't able to sell it, but I converted it, and now it wraps Midway candy bars. It's the one that was presented to Clark one Christmas. We put a big red bow on it and put it next to a Christmas tree. He got quite a kick out of it.

The hardest part of my work these first few months has been finding good mechanics. It took over two months to find these four. I didn't sleep—I was looking and worrying all the time. Even though I tried to be careful, I'm going to have to let two of them go. They don't have it—and you know what, they are Europeans. I understand they have cut the apprentice time from four years to three over there. Of course, another problem is we don't want to pay the top price. We have to pay below our own top union rate to avoid problems with the older people in the plant, so at these wages you are taking some chances.

One day the researcher was talking with Mr. Lehman about the R&D budget when an incident took place involving a question of which department would be charged for a $2 iron pipe. Mr. Lehman said:

I've just turned in my first budget. It goes to Clark for approval and then to the administration department. We are now an independent department with our own money. I've hired four mechanics, brought in the stuff, and we have this whole floor to ourselves. [R&D was using about 30% of the space on the fourth floor.] Our money comes straight from Clark; we don't have to squeeze it out of Milt's budget any more. We even have our own account number, just like General Motors, number 641.

The telephone rang and Otto answered. "Hello . . . To us, Mario, to R&D? . . . O.K., I'll sign it, we can put it in R&D . . . the account number? It's number 641 . . . O.K., bring it up and I'll sign it."

Turning back to the researcher, Mr. Lehman continued:

Boy, we are like outsiders—like working for the bakery across the street. That was a call about a hunk of pipe. When we set up here on the fourth floor, we carried up some machines and tools and a couple of pieces of pipe. That was the factory saying they needed a pipe. They want us to pay for it with

R&D money since we had taken some of theirs when we moved up here. It's only $2, he says, hardly worth walking up here for. But Milt is up to his neck on his budget, and Mario knows I'm not on mine. Milt's boys know how tight that budget is, so they are trying to shift some of it on to us.

A few minutes later Mario Spumoni entered with a piece of paper. Mr. Lehman greeted him and signed the paper. "O.K., but don't use No. 641 as a bank [smiles]. And don't try to charge us for the floor or the windows." Mario smiled and left. "Having our own account really makes a difference," Mr. Lehman resumed. "It's meant I could hire mechanics, and get steel and parts as I needed them."

The Administrative Department

The administrative department had a threefold mission: (1) to help Midway establish and "stick to" an annual profit goal, (2) to help set standards for the items appearing on the P & L statement, and (3) to systematize the flow of information or "paperwork." Mr. Ben Nagle, administrative vice president, stated:

As I see it, I represent phase two here—that is going for more profits. To accomplish it, we are going to have to set standards, such as a $16\frac{1}{2}\%$ cost for marketing. That hits right at the guts of things. In the past our marketing costs have varied from 17% to 23%, and no one ever really thought about the variations. This causes problems, but so does setting standards. I want them to be on the tight side and I want us to shoot for a high-profit target. We've gone a step in that direction by setting the $16\frac{1}{2}\%$ target for marketing; it's going to mean a head-on clash when we get to the budget meetings. Any change like this is bound to be uncomfortable. It's basic. This company has been marketing-oriented, and we want it to become profit-oriented.

The administrative department's operating responsibilities included three principal staff services: (1) financial affairs, (2) record keeping, and (3) preparation of information for use by the other two departments. These services were performed by a department of 20 people functionally organized as customer service, accounting, and IBM sections. These three groups were basically engaged in processing information; customer services and IBM dealt primarily with externally generated information, while accounting dealt with internally generated data.

EXTERNAL INFORMATION

The principal source of external information was the customer order, a document made out by the broker and mailed in after each sale.

These invoices indicated each sale by customer, broker, TV market area, quantity and type of product, and terms granted or merchandise credits allowed. From these invoices IBM punched cards were prepared, with each card representing one order. In addition to being used for billing, accounts receivable, and payment of commissions, the IBM cards were the source of six major reports:

1. Daily sales summary by broker's territory.
2. Summary of accounts receivable.
3. Aging schedule of accounts receivable.
4. Analysis of credits allowed to customers by reason of allowance of credit.
5. Monthly analysis of sales by customer.
6. Monthly analysis of sales by TV market area.

The department processed manually all incoming freight bills and supplier invoices. Both were scheduled for IBM processing in the near future. IBM processing of freight bills was expected to be of considerable significance in management's judgment for two reasons: First, it would reduce the costs of paying freight bills and of keeping records of transportation costs. Second, and more important, it would permit analysis of transportation costs and might indicate either the need for different shipping policies or the need to relocate some of the company's 12 warehouses.

INTERNAL INFORMATION

Principal sources of internally generated information included company accounting records, operating information from the three departments, and pro forma forecasts. These sources were used in four major reports:

1. Monthly P & L statement.
2. Monthly balance sheet.
3. Annual budget, projected and actual.
4. Weekly cash forecasts.

Of these, only No. 4 appears to need amplification. The cash position of the company was so tight during the busy season that cash requirements and sources were forecast for each ensuing week and sometimes were prepared for each day of the week. These reports were prepared on a standard form called the "thumbnail financial report," a report which went directly to the president during the busy season.

The administrative department did not maintain any cost accounting records by product; factory costs were grouped by type of expenditure.

Thus, the administrative department knew whether the manufacturing department was staying within its budget, but it could not determine by product how the money was being spent. Although the manufacturing department kept more detailed records, it controlled its costs basically through attention to machine output and total labor cost. The labor cost was related to sales value of output, and this percentage became the rough efficiency index. Changes in product mix and volume affected it significantly, and both the manufacturing and administrative vice presidents said that it was only a rough indicator. "Better cost accounting is something we'll need as we grow," Mr. Nagle said. "But right now we can keep things under control without it. And there isn't much need to do anything about it in the immediate future, because when the manufacturing department says it can do the job on $X that's all they use. Somehow they get the job done."

THE "FREDDY"[9] REPORT

The Freddy report was a document which had evolved in response to an important operating problem—the inadequate control of shipments of finished goods. The control problem resulted from the need to keep up to 44 items in stock in each of 12 warehouses (1) where planning helped mitigate occasional shortages and (2) where truckload shipments made an important difference in transportation costs.

To mitigate the problem, Mr. Nagle had "pulled together" internal and external information in such a way that the IBM section could turn out a Freddy report every day. The report listed the following information for each warehouse:

1. Opening inventory balance on each item.
2. Deliveries to the warehouse.
3. Shipments from the warehouse.
4. Closing balance on hand.
5. Goods in transit to the warehouse.
6. Firm's orders for future delivery in the next two weeks.
7. Orders for future delivery beyond two weeks.

For the two factory warehouses the Freddy report contained additional information, including the amount added to inventory as a result of the previous day's production. There was also a summary sheet showing the overall position of the 12 warehouses.

This report was generally credited with having drastically reduced

---

[9] So called because the administrative vice president once asked "Where's Freddy?"

the confusion and arguments which had accompanied the disposition of merchandise. A separate copy of the report was sent each morning to each vice president, who used it in planning the operations of his own department.

SPECIAL REPORTS

In addition to the regular reports the administrative department prepared numerous special reports based on detailed investigations of company records. For instance, when Mr. Kramer inquired about usage of typing paper in the office, long-distance phone calls, or expense account breakdowns, the department worked up a special report which was prepared each month until Mr. Kramer and Mr. Nagle were satisfied that the matter was under control. The detailed reports were then discontinued. Mr. Nagle stated, however, that it was not uncommon for Mr. Kramer to look through reports or operating statements, to ask why a particular figure was high, and to ask for an investigation.

DEPARTMENTAL ORGANIZATION

The administrative department was organized into four sections, each of which was directed by a manager who reported directly to Mr. Nagle. The four managers were comparatively young men (average age 25), and for all four it was the first opportunity at full responsibility for a section.

Prior to Mr. Nagle's arrival, administrative services had been directed by a controller, who resigned about a month after Mr. Nagle was hired because, Mr. Nagle said, "his wife thought my appointment would limit his vistas too much." Subsequently, Mr. Nagle had hired another man, Joe Rivers, to fill some of the controller's duties. Mr. Nagle had trained Mr. Rivers for the controller's post, but promotion had been blocked by the opposition of the other two vice presidents. Subsequently, Mr. Rivers had been encouraged to resign, which he did in early 1959.

BEN NAGLE

Mr. Nagle was described by his associates in the organization as "a quick thinker; a good man with numbers, systems, and procedures; and the man who brought order out of chaos by whipping up the Freddy report." He was also described as "the professional administrator," the man who quotes "standard operating procedure in cases like this," talks about "new vistas," and uses all the modern management terminology. He was described as "good with reports and memos," but someone who "can bury the important things in a smokescreen when he wants to."

Mr. Nagle described himself as a "school-trained administrator." While he had an accounting degree and a C.P.A., he wasn't "a conventional accountant, just looking at the numbers. Sales are important, and without them controls don't mean anything—you're out of business. It takes the big picture to be a good administrative man, not just the numbers," he said.

Mr. Nagle described himself on another occasion as "a guy who sees what has to be done and goes after it; a guy who has respect for Machiavellian philosophy. I'm not sentimental about things; if someone has to be canned, that's just the way the ball bounces. I get it done and over with—none of this beating around the bush or putting people off in a corner so they won't be in the way."

Mr. Nagle also noted that he planned his day. "I try to schedule appointments from 10 to 11:30 in the morning, for instance. I place my phone calls from about 9:30 to 10. Studies show that you only connect on about 50% of your phone calls and that the other half call back in around two hours—after the man has finished a conference or appointment. Then I try not to schedule any meetings from 11:15 to 12 so I'll be free to take the return phone calls." On another occasion Mr. Nagle noted that he also planned his day to be able to spend his evenings at home with his family. "I'm a family man with a wife and two fine children. I like to spend the evenings with them, so when the work piles up I get here at 6 or 6:30 in the morning to catch up."

Mr. Nagle was graduated from the City College of New York in 1941 with a B.B.A. in accounting. Subsequently he passed his C.P.A. exam but shortly thereafter was inducted into the Army, sent to a special statistics program at the Harvard Business School, commissioned a second lieutenant, and sent to an air base as a mess officer. Later he worked in operations and finally in personnel. Following the war he became the controller of a publishing company and in 1953, after a year of inactivity due to illness, became the treasurer of Consumer Products, Inc., a company manufacturing proprietary medicines. He served as treasurer for three years, and then the president of Consumer Products recommended him to Mr. Kramer. He joined Midway in January, 1958.

Mr. Nagle described his jobs in the company as (1) "streamlining the office setup—the records and reports," and (2) "adding new emphasis to the bottom line of the P & L. I start a budget from the bottom line of the P & L, not the top, the way sales people do."

Mr. Nagle further noted:

Getting agreement on the figure for that bottom line is the toughest part; once you get agreement, the rest is easier because things have to fit. You work your way up the P & L and something has to give. We aren't in full agreement here on what the bottom figure should be—I'm on the high side—but we have agreed on a general area. Even with this general agreement, I expect a head-on clash when we get down to brass tacks in the budget meetings. It's going to be hard to stick to the profit goal when it means cutting expenses a lot, so there will be a slowdown.

As for the way I operate, I spend the biggest percentage of my time training people. I try to let a person know what the purpose of his job is and how it fits into the company. In fact I'm sometimes criticized for spending so much time discussing policy with my subordinates.

This was particularly true when I started in here, because there were no systems or anything. I had to introduce the new systems and to untrain and retrain the people. That takes a lot of time and discussion, because people are basically unwilling to change. Besides, some of the things they were doing were according to methods they had invented, so they had a pride of authorship. Those were the toughest to unconvince. As a result, we had some personnel turnover; some were fired, others quit. Not everything is accepted yet, so I'm still spending a good deal of time on it, but I think it's worth it. You see, these people are clerical. They expect to know what goes on. With manufacturing it's different; the people expect to be told what to do. Am I talking like a textbook? Bear in mind I have had professional training—these were things I learned. They had come to me through education rather than experience.

Asked what he enjoyed most about his work at Midway, Mr. Nagle replied after a long pause:

Basically, I like the feeling of wrapping something up and getting it completed. Planning and forecasting are the kinds of work I like most, and if they work out I really feel good. I feel even better if they work out without my being there.

The hardest part of my work? You know the answer to that one. The hardest part is always the interrelationships with fellow executives—the executive climate. This is always the hardest for *staff* people. Line people have plans, expansion, and output to work with. Staff is nothing tangible—purely advice. Well, my job is basically staff—pure staff.

So relationships are the hardest part, and I think anyone would be a jerk to discuss it with an outsider. He would be naïve to commit it to print. Realistically I can't say things here are like a family picnic—things are always changing, and change is always irritating to someone. With no changes maybe we could have a happy fraternity, and everyone would be satisfied with the status quo. But when you change, or try to cut the costs of doing business, something has to give. And that makes the climate uncomfortable.

The goals for this department? First, to get the department to run smoothly, without periods of stress. This one hasn't yet been attained. Second, to integrate Midway and Main Line. This is about accomplished. We have converted their administrative system to ours and are now running everything from here on IBM.

We don't have any dollar goals, really. We haven't yet reached that stage of thinking—the department is still in the metamorphosis stage. The goal has been to do a good job. We need more time to get a reporting system and to develop things to a point where the people would understand the dollar goals. Right now, they would just be a blur of figures.

We do have a dollar goal in one sense. We want to buy a 305 RAMAC unit for the IBM system, but we can't unless we can show Clark Kramer how it will save money. It rents for $24,000 a year, and we have to show more than that in *savings*, not just in new statistics. So far our IBM manager has figured $18,000. He is spending a couple of hours a day reading and studying about the equipment and getting a lot of help from the IBM people. They would like to see a company as small as ours make a success of the RAMAC.

4. Midway Foods Corporation (C₂)

"THE IDEA IN PHASE TWO is to boost profits," Mr. Ben Nagle[1] explained. "To do that we must bring more of the sales revenue through to the bottom line of the P & L, hopefully another 3%, and in any event at least 2½%. The question, however, is how do we do it. We have to trim expenses somewhere; and my job is to keep the heat on until we figure a way."

"Ben is trying to squeeze more profits from our sales dollar," Mr. Hal Reiss[2] stated, adding:

It's one of the main reasons Clark hired an administrative VP—to increase the pressure for profits. But in spite of these evening and weekend meetings, we still haven't found an acceptable way.

In a crude sense you can think of the problem as dividing a pie—the sales revenue pie—since capital expenditures are of very little significance for us. As of now expenses and taxes take almost the whole of it, 99+%. We need to expand the profit slice to about 3%–4% to have a healthy business, but this increase in profits will have to come from a decrease in some other item or items. In a rough and ready way, the problem is shown in the chart on page 387.

Not much can be done about raw material costs unless we reduce product size still more—we are substandard now by about 15%, we have had amazing luck in our cocoa purchases, and still we use 50% of revenues for raw materials.

Manufacturing looks like a good target, but some 17% goes for direct manufacturing costs, such as salaries, social security, and so on, 5% goes for shipping the product, and fixed charges take roughly another 2% at our present volume. Milt has only $77,000 a year to heat and maintain our main plant—how do you cut that?

Most of our thought has gone into trimming marketing. Roughly 8%–10% of sales has gone for advertising, 5% goes for brokers commissions, and the 4%–6% has gone for sales promotion and administration. The advertising has been the key to our growth, and we don't want to cut it much below 8% because we would not only slow our growth, but also we would lose some of the consumer franchise we now have. We can only spread our advertising so thin without losing drastically in consumer impact.

Our broker costs are high—very high—and our leading competitors have a big advantage on us here. But we have built our distribution on working closely

---

[1] Administrative vice president.

[2] Marketing vice president.

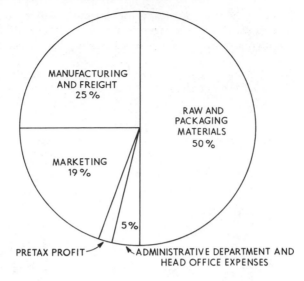

MANUFACTURING
AND FREIGHT
25%

RAW AND
PACKAGING
MATERIALS
50%

MARKETING
19%

5%

PRETAX PROFIT   ADMINISTRATIVE DEPARTMENT AND
                       HEAD OFFICE EXPENSES

with our brokers, insisting that they have detail men and so on. If we cut the commissions we will lose some brokers—some of our biggest and best ones, we think, and distribution will suffer. In addition, those who remain may give us less service because they will wonder when the day will be coming for Midway to try to cut the commissions again.

Our selling costs aren't out of line, given the need to fight for supermarket shelf space for four little-known brands. We have to have quite a bit of co-op money and additional funds for specials with individual supermarkets in order to build and hold distribution. Promotion costs are particularly high this year as we try to build three new brands, and probably should remain that way until we have established William Penn and Liberty Bell on a much broader front. After all the advertising won't pay off unless we can get the goods on the shelves, and that is just where the promotion money goes.

Maybe we should wait a while longer before moving to new downtown offices and save the $30,000 per year in unnecessary overhead—or cut executive salaries?"

"This cost cutting drive is a real 'merry-go-round,' " Mr. Milt Lombard[3] noted. He added:

Everyone is looking at everyone else. Personally, it's no threat—if they give me less money I'll get along on whatever I have to work with. But production will suffer, and we already run behind in the peak season because we have such antiquated equipment on the one hand, and management won't let us build inventory in advance on the other.

---

[3] Manufacturing vice president.

"Personally, I don't think we are ready for downtown offices and the extra overhead. Sometimes we forget how recently we were a Maxwell Street operation, and how we used to work at the machines or wrap bars if necessary to get the goods out.

"But basically it's management's problem to allocate the funds, and I'll live with the result however it gets decided."

5. Midway Foods Corporation (D₂)

AT THE GENERAL MANAGEMENT meeting of February 14, 1959, the discussion turned to Item No. 2 of the agenda, "title and salary review." The first person to be considered was Mr. Sam Painter, a member of the administrative department.

Midway management stated that Sam had been a controversial employee; some of his attitudes had been resented by fellow employees and by the executive group. Sam was 26 years old and had a high school diploma. Prior to employment at Midway he had been a dental tech-

Exhibit 1

MIDWAY FOODS CORPORATION (D₂)
Salary and Bonuses for Sam Painter

Year	Month	Weekly Pay	Bonuses
1956........................	July	$ 60	
	December		$ 30
1957........................	February	65	
	August	70	
	December		200
1958........................	January	75	
	March	80	
	April	90	
	August	100	100*
	December		325
1959........................	February	120	

* Three members of the administrative department received $100 bonuses in connection with installation of the Freddy report.
Source: Company records.

nician. After six months with Midway, Sam had gone into the Army. Upon his release in 1956 he rejoined Midway at a salary of $60 a week. Changes in his salary since 1956 are shown in Exhibit 1.

KRAMER:[1] Now let's go on to Item No. 2.

NAGLE:[2] Well, this subject has been on a few agendas, but I think it

---

[1] Clark Kramer, president of Midway Foods.
[2] Ben Nagle, administrative vice president.

now becomes more pointed. When Joe Rivers[3] left, Hal[4] made a suggestion that Joe not be replaced, that the job be abandoned, and that the various people who had reported to Joe report to me. Some months ago, we decided not to have a controller for the time being. We also agreed that this group would review any promotions of people who report directly to a vice president. [With the departure of Joe Rivers, Sam Painter reported directly to Mr. Nagle.] We agreed we should all review these people because their positions must, of necessity, become bigger and broader. And I would like to have a sense of direction on the staff we now have. Now I've taken one of these jobs which seems to be a debatable one—that's Sam Painter's—and let me read to you a job description which I prepared for background.

Sam Painter reports to the administrative vice president and at present he supervises one accounts receivable clerk, one credit cleark, three customer service clerks, and one warehouse inventory clerk. His basic functions are: responsibility for the proper administration of accounts receivable, cash receipts, credit limits, customer order processing, customer claims, freight claims on customer-into-warehouse shipments, warehouse inventory control, and intra-warehouse shipments.

Basically, he delegates responsibility and commensurate authority within a section for the effective execution of the foregoing functions. He is supposed to train and develop personnel under his jurisdiction for the assumption of more responsible duties.

His specific duties are as follows:
1. *Credit and collection.* Determines credit limits for new accounts, assumes responsibility for prompt collection of accounts receivable, and prepares monthly aging reports of overdue accounts receivable.
2. *Customer order processing.* He is responsible for seeing that the customers' orders and inquiries are promptly and efficiently processed. . . .

REISS: Is this . . . do we have to go through this, Ben, with each one of these guys?

NAGLE: Yes, yes!

REISS: I don't think this is the function of this meeting.

NAGLE: Well, people ought to know what he does.

REISS: Fine. Whatever you want him to do, let him go ahead and do it, but I don't think we ought to be burdened with job descriptions in a meeting.

NAGLE: I was asked to prepare job descriptions. I'm doing what I was asked to do.

---

[3] Joe Rivers had been employed in the administrative department as Mr. Nagle's assistant. He had been encouraged to resign three months previously.

[4] Hal Reiss, marketing vice president.

REISS: [to Mr. Kramer] Do you feel that this is the proper function of a meeting?

KRAMER: Did I ask you to prepare them?

NAGLE: Yes, sir.

KRAMER: Did I ask you to read them at the meeting?

NAGLE: You said to bring them in.

KRAMER: Yes, but I don't recall that I wanted them read, Ben. I don't know about the other fellows, but I can't digest it. I think it's not important, really.

NAGLE: I don't think you can discuss the scope of a man without knowing what he does.

REISS: What do you want to do with these people, Ben?

NAGLE: I want to know what management wants me to do with them.

REISS: Well, you're management. What do you want to do?

NAGLE: Well, to be specific, in my opinion Sam Painter has been a controversial personality for some time. The job he now performs is a responsible job. He has neither title nor proper salary for the job. The job calls for a title.

REISS: Of what?

NAGLE: Of something.

REISS: What?

NAGLE: As a "customer service supervisor," for instance, and "credit manager."

REISS: Why should the title be such a long one?

NAGLE: Well, he had to start in as credit manager.

REISS: Customer service supervisor would certainly cover credit.

KRAMER: Well, that's easy, Ben. If you want him to sign as credit manager, he can sign as credit manager, but his title doesn't have to be a hyphenated eight-word spread.

REISS: I understand customer service as covering all those areas.

KRAMER: How does he sign letters now?

NAGLE: Well, "customer service," except. . . .

KRAMER: Then it would be very simple to have him sign letters "Sam Painter, Customer Service Manager," wouldn't it?

NAGLE: Except that with the salary he's getting. . . .

KRAMER: But mechanically it would be very simple. . . .

NAGLE: Well, letters of collection would be more normal if they had "credit manager."

REISS: I kind of like the term customer service manager, Ben, instead of credit manager. When you really think of it, credit is one of the customer services. It's much more inclusive and I don't think it hits the customer quite so hard.

KRAMER: Not so much stigma to it.

REISS: That's right.

LOMBARD:[5] How old is this Sam?

REISS: I'd say about 26. Do you want to go into this, "When I was 26. . . ."

LOMBARD: No, I'm more concerned with the title in relation to what you

---

[5] Milt Lombard, manufacturing vice president.

think of his maturity. He may be doing the job. I have a fellow running Cicero now who is the acting plant manager.

NAGLE: I think—do you want my opinion? I think on an objective basis he does a very competent job, gets his work done, and is capable of growth. The only objection to him is what I would call on a subjective basis. His social attitudes might not be what we'd like; he might not be a type of personality we'd like to live with intimately. But a fact is a fact: he does a good job, and the question is do we want to live only with people we love or sometimes must there be someone in the pile that we don't love?

REISS: To add to what Ben says, I have found that among our outside people he is considered to be extremely valuable; he answers almost all their needs, does it promptly, and does it efficiently. And a lot of the correspondence that used to come into the sales department, well, about 90% of it, is now directed to Painter, which would certainly indicate the kind of confidence customers have in him.

KRAMER: What is he getting paid?

NAGLE: One other thing here. In the past two weeks I've had an opportunity to get down to the grass roots. I think he's done a very commendable job in the last six months in the area of human relations. The people who are subordinate to him, I think, are beginning to like him. He gets along with them. Six months ago the chronic complaint was that he was supercilious, was a wise little acre; but the people like him now, I've found.

KRAMER: You mean in two weeks you've suddenly changed from one opinion to another?

NAGLE: Me? No. I say I've had a chance to dig down and find out about this. People at his own level and at other department levels are not so antagonistic towards him as they were six months ago.

REISS: More important, I think almost everyone in the place that works with him respects his ability. I have a great deal of respect for his ability. One of the reasons people who work with him may dislike him is that he's a perfectionist. He demands good work from people. He has a great many personality problems; the prime one is his basic insecurity. I don't think we want to get into this at this particular juncture. The problem up for discussion is, does Sam Painter deserve the title of customer service manager and the salary increase that goes with it? Is it that much of a promotion?

KRAMER: Milt, what's your opinion? Are you close enough to it to have any feeling?

LOMBARD: I don't have much to do with Sam. That's why I asked the question about his age and what you fellows think about his maturity. Is he mature enough to carry that title, whatever that title means? Will a promotion help him now, or will it hinder him? These are things you fellows can better. . . .

NAGLE: Well, that's what we're here for. He's wearing the robe. Shall we give him the mantle now? This is the problem we're going to be faced with right along with the development of a corporation with comparatively young executives. You're not going to hire 40-year-old guys for those kinds of jobs, or 35-year-old guys. This is going to be our pattern in the future. They're going to be around 25 and 27. Because of our age, we're not going to hire mature people.

REISS: Well, Sam's problem is a personality problem. He walks around as if he's the cock of the walk, and in the terminology of the street I think he could be classified as a wise guy, a punk.

NAGLE: Right.

LOMBARD: This is the point.

REISS: Wait a minute, Milt.

LOMBARD: I don't want to call him that because I don't have much to do with him.

REISS: You call a spade a spade.

LOMBARD: All right.

REISS: He tends to be arrogant, but when you pin it down it's his attitude rather than fact. Now I believe that you can change attitudes. I believe that people change with responsibility; they grow as they get additional responsibility. I believe that the guy should be rewarded for the work that he does. And if he can't overcome this, it isn't going to hurt him any more as customer service manager at a hundred and a quarter a week than it did as customer service department at a hundred a week. But if he can't overcome this, he's got to understand that this is as far as he goes.

KRAMER: I think that's not too significant from my point of view. What I'm interested in doesn't concern his present title or the title he will get at this meeting or the salary he will be raised to. I'm much more concerned with what type of man he is. I agree that as far as I know Sam is a real "hot shot." We just stumbled onto a really good man. He's a real worker, he's intelligent, and he's interested. There are only two things I have against Sam. Number one, I think he's an arrogant young punk. Number two, I don't like his views on segregation. Now, I can live in perfect happiness with a customer service manager who believes in segregation, but I could not live in happiness or work in happiness with a department head that believed in segregation. I just don't think that this conforms enough with my own personal philosophy about life. And in case you're concerned here, I don't want to make a big thing over this, but I want us to think about this. Now, Sam is relatively young, it's true. I agree with you, Hal, that I think he can be changed. He was brought up in a blighted area and his background contains all the things that you would think would lead a guy to be just what Sam has become. So it's no surprise that he's become this. I think if we work with him we have a pretty good chance of getting him to understand some things, and to have a much healthier attitude toward life in general and business in particular. I'm in favor of taking this step, incidentally. But I would be very much against the next step unless Sam shows a distinct and specific change.

[Heated discussion]

REISS: I think we've blown this up out of all proportion.

KRAMER: Well, perhaps it seems that way, but it's important to me, Hal, because the Midway organization is very near and dear to me, and I'm concerned about the type of people in it. I say that being a great worker, an intelligent man, is not sufficient to cover up all things.

REISS: Clark, when you were 19—let's say your emotional development and maturation processes were at 19 what his will be at 27 or 28—when you were 19, did you ever get the urge to throw down to your seniors a provocation idea just to gain the center of attention?

KRAMER: I'm sure I must have, but I don't believe this is the case with Sam. I don't think we should discuss Sam's views on segregation or the reasons therefor. I've said that I believe he has these views.

REISS: But. . . .

KRAMER: We can discuss it later. But I also said that, if these are his true views, and if he doesn't change them, I don't think I can live at peace with him in the company. And if he goes further, as he will expect to go, and as we will expect him to go, then he must change his views. I don't believe in everyone in the company conforming to my views on everything or even anything except a few things, such as Mother, God, Country, and Integration, for example, and a few others. These I believe in as being the basic principles under which our country has existed and will exist. And if I don't believe in these things, then what's the use of it all, you see? And I don't want anybody in our company who is an opponent of what I consider to be these basic truths.

.   .   .   .

REISS: All I'm saying is that this is part of Sam, this attitude of challenging accepted ideas, challenging his superiors, challenging people with whom he works. We've either got to knock this attitude out of him or he's done in our company.

KRAMER: Let's not question the worth of his being provocative and stimulating and so forth. I'm merely trying to peer into the man to find out what is really there, and I'm saying that, as willing as I am to go along with this step, this is as far as I can go; and if it comes up again, as it surely will, and I feel that he has not changed basically and truly in this regard, you have my promise that he'll not go any further in our company.

NAGLE: What shall we call him, customer service manager or supervisor? Makes a big difference if you're going to start handing out manager or supervisor titles.

REISS: Well, which do you want?

NAGLE: I think supervisor is. . . .

REISS: Is supervisor higher or lower?

NAGLE: Lower.

REISS: Lower. O.K.

KRAMER: I personally prefer manager. I don't feel strongly about either one, but it's a better word, I think.

NAGLE: You mean as manager, then we'll call him. . . . It doesn't make any difference, the title.

KRAMER: Customer service manager is a title everybody understands, and so forth.

REISS: One more thing, while we're at it. What sort of salary bracket is this job? I don't see the need of going through this routine any time a man wants to be promoted within grade. . . .

KRAMER: Hal, we have agreed—at one of our first meetings we agreed—that any man that was being promoted in various departments into a position of being manager would be discussed at this meeting because all of us will have to live with him, and all of us have opinions about him; and in the absence of any formal job evaluation program the best way to evaluate these people would be just the four of us sitting around talking about them.

REISS: Well, then, suppose Ben wants to give him $10 in two more months. Does he come back to the group again for this?

KRAMER: No. That's not the point.

NAGLE: I don't want to create another Joe Rivers situation.

KRAMER: That's one thing I'm thinking about.

[Mr. B. Nagle proposed a 25% pay increase for Sam, from $100 a week to $125. After discussion it was agreed that a $20 boost immediately with another $5 in six months would seem more appropriate.]

During the morning of April 7, 1959, Mr. Reiss had had a long talk with the field sales manager, Mr. Larry Rosen, about the latter's status in the marketing department. Mr. Reiss had recently been officially promoted to marketing vice president, leaving vacant the title of sales manager. Mr. Rosen had expressed a wish to be promoted to fill this vacancy, while recognizing that his duties would probably remain unchanged.

Mr. Rosen was 44. He had joined Midway at the time it acquired the Robin Hood line. He had previously worked for the importing company which distributed that product. His duties were one-third field sales work, one-third supervising the regional men, and one-third assisting in departmental sales forecasting and analysis. About one-third of his time was spent on the road.

SEGMENT OF GENERAL MANAGEMENT MEETING (APRIL 7, 8:30 P.M.)

REISS: I would like to clear up one other thing. I had a discussion with Larry Rosen today and I want you people to know what happened in case it comes up in the future when I am not around. I had a very frank discussion with him about where he stands in the department. I heard via the grapevine that he was concerned about not being given the title of sales manager. I told him I didn't think he was ready for it, that he just wasn't putting in the initiative, drive, and spirit to do the job. He took it pretty hard, but I told him it was for his own good because, if anything should happen to me, I was sure that

Clark would go outside the company to get himself a marketing man. This is something he has to face up to.

NAGLE: I think you are making a mistake, Hal.

REISS: How?

NAGLE: I think sales manager and field sales manager are synonymous. It's really important to him, so why not let him have the title?

REISS: No, Ben, this is the only way I have of making him aware of his shortcomings. The discussion today was to clear the air. I don't want to kid him along.

KRAMER: Yes, I think this is important. Our idea is, it is the responsibility of the person to prove he is worth the job *before* he gets the title. I don't want people to get sucked along in the vacuum. We want demonstrated ability.

NAGLE: The theory today is that you sell fringe benefits, that you give out desks and titles and rugs.

KRAMER: I disagree. I don't want him going around the country with the title when he is not up to it. If he can't work for it and is down in morale for not being promoted, then he is not our kind of man and I would just as soon that he would leave.

NAGLE: What does the title mean?

REISS: It means he is assistant to the marketing manager, the No. 2 man in the whole department.

KRAMER: Yes, and do you think we could work with Larry as marketing manager if Hal was not here? It is out of the question.

NAGLE: O.K., then, leave it field sales manager, but I think it is a mistake.

REISS: I just wanted to inform all of you so you will understand my position.

6. Midway Foods Corporation (D₃)

On Saturday morning, February 28, 1959, Midway moved its main offices from Cicero to the Prudential building in downtown Chicago. The executives and several of the office people came in the morning of the move to help arrange furniture and filing cabinets that had been brought in the night before from Cicero. Workmen were still painting doors, woodwork, and trim as the desks and bookcases went into place. Potted plants and other gifts from suppliers and friends were scattered here and there, and a bundle of congratulatory letters and telegrams was on the president's desk.[1] At 11:30 A.M., while the moving in was still in progress, two executives from the Dearborn Advertising Agency arrived for an important meeting.

FIRST VISIT TO THE NEW OFFICES

Early that same morning the researcher had walked east to Michigan Avenue, turned north and looked at the window displays of some of Chicago's finest shops, and stopped to look across the street at the bronze lions poised in front of the Art Institute. Crossing Michigan Avenue, he walked through Grant Park and past Buckingham fountain. Noting that the meeting with the agency would soon be under way, he walked on through the park, now and then looking up at the Prudential building, Chicago's newest and most handsome office building. At the north end of the park he walked across the plaza, in through the glass door, past the impressive control panels for the Otis "autotronic" elevators, stepped into one marked "express," and pushed the button marked "34." At the 34th floor he walked down a corridor to a door where a workman was just stenciling in the final letters—Midway Foods Corporation. Inside he was greeted by the stir of movement as desks and cabinets were being carried into place. Mr. Reiss[2] looked up and said, "Good morning; pretty nice, don't you think? C'mon, I'll show

---

[1] Clark Kramer, president of Midway Foods.
[2] Hal Reiss, marketing vice president.

you the offices." "This is beautiful," said the researcher. "Quite a change from the top floor at Cicero."

"Watch the wet paint," Mr. Reiss continued. "This one is mine; what do you think of the blue wall and the four windows? [Smiles] With four windows facing Grant Park I won't need a resumé or any references—I can just tell people I'm a four-window executive. We are going to set part of this room up like a conference area. Clark thought it might even be a good idea to have a separate room for conferences, but I suggested using this part of my office, and also using part of his for the same purpose. Next door is Milt's[3] office—you can go through here; it's so we can open this door and annoy each other. It will be great to be able to chew him out without having to walk down two flights into the factory. And [smiles] maybe the new offices will let him see the light. I'm going to kid him about it first thing Monday when he comes in. Oh, here are the boys from the agency." Mr. Reiss greeted Bill and Ed, two executives from the Dearborn agency, and then Mr. Kramer emerged from his office to extend his greetings.

KRAMER: Well, what do you think of it?

ED: It's great! The view of the skyline and Grant Park is magnificent.

BILL: This is better than State Street. It's a big jump from Cicero to Michigan Avenue, and in one hop!

ED: Maybe you can rent us a room or a back office. This is beautiful.

KRAMER: This is the paprika room. [Room has one bright-red wall.] Let me show you the other offices. [Men leave room.] This is Ben's[4] office—the gold room. This is Milt's—the green room. This is Hal's—the blue room.

REISS: Notice the four windows, men? I've just been explaining here that I've really made it now. With the four windows, I won't need a resumé any more.

BILL: You said it. This is a great spot. [Mr. Kramer shows Bill and Ed through the rest of the offices. Then all return to his office.]

KRAMER: I think this new location has paid off already. It got the agency here early [smiles]. That's the first time they have ever been ahead of schedule on anything.

Mr. Kramer, Mr. Reiss, the two executives from the agency, and the researcher went into Mr. Kramer's office for a meeting. On several subsequent occasions the researcher asked the four executives about the reasons for and significance of the move to the new offices. A summary of their observations follows:

---

[3] Milt Lombard, manufacturing vice president.

[4] Ben Nagle, administrative vice president.

EXECUTIVES' COMMENTS ABOUT THE NEW OFFICES

Clark Kramer, president:

Moving downtown was pretty significant, and we had thought and talked about it quite a bit before we actually moved. You see, after we were on our way to digesting the Main Line acquisition, we realized that we could run a plant without having our offices in the same building. And if we could do it for one factory, why not for two? We wanted to move downtown to save travel time; Ben, Hal, and I were using a lot of time driving in from Cicero to see advertising, legal, and financial people. Somehow we couldn't get them to come out to Cicero very often; we had to come in to see them, and not the other way around. Now that's all changed; the first day we moved in was a sign of things to come—with the agency people coming to our offices.

Being in the Prudential building adds something when suppliers or customers drop in—at least, we think it makes some difference. And also it's more convenient for us to get to work. Milt and I can catch the train in from Highland Park and take the "El" across town, where we used to spend 45 minutes or an hour driving in. And it puts the office within walking distance for Hal.

Milt Lombard, manufacturing vice president:

The new offices are pretty nice, even though they don't mean as much to me as they do to the others. I'm here two days a week, and Monday, Wednesday, and Friday I'm out at the plant. And this shade of green on the wall is going to make me ill, I think. I told Clark I'd like a green wall, but not this bilious green. As soon as I get a chance I'm going to have it repainted a softer shade.

As far as the significance of moving downtown goes, I see it a little differently from some of the others. To me it represents more overhead; the rent for these offices is equal to what we pay for the five-story building in Cicero. I can't help feeling that there are things we need more than to cut down on travel time, but then maybe this is all part of "going national."

Ben Nagle, administrative vice president:

The new offices move us right into the heart of things. We are close to the pulse of the financial and advertising districts; even though they are over on La Salle Street, just being nearby gives this place a different atmosphere. Another thing, at our old offices we used to look out on a run-down neighborhood; it didn't give you the inspiration of Grant Park or the surf on the lake. And we used to watch the trucks backing in to load up with merchandise. A good bit of executive time was lost just watching those trucks load.

Hal Reiss, marketing vice president:

The new offices are significant for a number of reasons. For one thing the move is a symbol of going national, of moving out of Cicero and into the business community. It will save on travel time, and some of us were wasting a good bit of time driving back and forth between Cicero and downtown.

And it will allow Larry[5] to have an office of his own. We shared the same office in Cicero, and it meant I heard everything he said on the phone. Sometimes I couldn't help interrupting him or picking up the phone myself. Well, that wasn't fair to him; it didn't give him a chance to prove himself. So now he has a separate office and the chance to do his work the way he wants to. But it also means he's no longer in my office, and he has grey tile on his floor while all the VP's have white. It's not the way I would have made it—I don't go much for these status symbols. It's my belief that if someone can't tell that you know what you are talking about unless he sees a rug on your floor, or lamps and end tables, or how many windows you have, then I don't want to spend my time talking to him anyway. I kid the people at the agency about this, and also Clark. But it seems to be another one of those things where I'm the one that is not going along with the system.

But coming back to the office move, I'd say the most significant thing about it was something symbolic in another way. I used to be a freight-forwarding clerk and before that just a kid from the wrong side of town. And to a greater or lesser degree the same is true for all of us. Being down here symbolizes one kind of thing we have tried to build from selling candy bars—acceptability or approval of the world around us. It's something I've aimed at since I was a kid. Now that I'm up on the 34th floor I am beginning to realize there's a lot more to it than that. It's one of those things that, if you want it, you can never get enough of it. You could always want more approval from others, or to be more important so people would say, "There goes the vice president of so-and-so," as you walk by. Well, I'm beginning to realize that's not really what I want, but I'd be kidding both of us if I denied that I got a kick out of it. But what I've learned from this move is that there are still other things that are more important—a good evening of conversation, for instance, and a chance to trade ideas with people who really think. It's renewed my interest in trying my hand at teaching in a business school on a part-time basis.

---

[5] Larry Rosen, field sales manager.

7. The Rose Company

MR. JAMES PIERCE had recently received word of his appointment as plant manager of Plant X, one of the older established units of the Rose Company. As such, Mr. Pierce was to be responsible for the management and administration at Plant X of all functions and personnel except sales.

Both top management and Mr. Pierce realized that there were several unique features about his new assignment. Mr. Pierce decided to assess his new situation and relationships before undertaking his assignment. He was personally acquainted with the home office executives, but had met few of the plant personnel. This case contains some of his reflections regarding the new assignment.

The Rose Company conducted marketing activities throughout the United States and in certain foreign countries. These activities were directed from the home office by a vice-president in charge of sales.

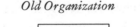

Exhibit 1

THE ROSE COMPANY

Old Organization

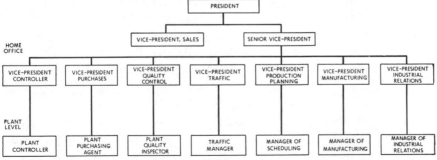

Manufacturing operations and certain other departments were under the supervision and control of a senior vice-president. These are shown in Exhibit 1. For many years the company had operated a highly centralized functional type of manufacturing organization. There was no general manager at any plant; each of the departments in a plant reported on a line basis to its functional counterpart at the home office. For instance, the industrial-relations manager of a particular plant reported to the vice-president in charge of industrial relations at the home office, the plant controller to the vice-president and controller, and so on.

Mr. Pierce stated that in the opinion of the top management the record of Plant X had not been satisfactory for several years. The board had recently approved the erection of a new plant in a different part of the city and the use of new methods of production. Lower costs of processing and a reduced manpower requirement at the new plant were expected. Reduction of costs and improved quality of products were needed to maintain competitive leadership and gain some slight product advantage. The proposed combination of methods of manufacturing and mixing materials had not been tried elsewhere in the company. Some features would be entirely new to employees.

According to Mr. Pierce the top management of the Rose Company was beginning to question the advisability of the central control of manufacturing operations. The officers decided to test the value of a decentralized operation in connection with Plant X. They apparently believed that a general management representative in Plant X was needed if the new experiment in manufacturing methods and the required rebuilding of the organization were to succeed.

Prior to the new assignment Mr. Pierce had been an accounting executive in the controller's department of the company. From independent sources the case writer learned that Mr. Pierce had demonstrated analytical ability and general administrative capacity. He was generally liked by people. From top management's point of view he had an essential toughness described as an ability to see anything important through. By some he was regarded as the company's efficiency expert. Others thought he was a perfectionist and aggressive in reaching the goals that had been set. Mr. Pierce was aware of these opinions about his personal behavior.

Mr. Pierce summarized his problem in part as follows: "I am going into a situation involving a large number of changes. I will have a new plant—new methods and processes—but most of all I will be dealing with a set of changed relationships. Heretofore all the heads of departments in the plant reported to their functional counterparts in the home office. Now they will report to me. I am a complete stranger and in addition this is my first assignment in a major 'line' job. The men will know this.

"When I was called into the senior vice-president's office to be informed of my new assignment he asked me to talk with each of the functional members of his staff. The vice-presidents in charge of production planning, manufacturing, and industrial relations said they were going to issue all headquarters instructions to me as plant manager and they were going to cut off their connections with their counterparts in my plant. The other home office executives admitted their functional counterparts would report to me in line capacity. They should obey my orders and I would be responsible for their pay and promotion. But these executives proposed to follow the common practice of many companies of maintaining a dotted line or functional relationship with these men. I realize that these two different patterns of home office–plant relationships will create real administrative problems for me."

Exhibit 2 shows the organization relationships as defined in these conferences.

Exhibit 2

THE ROSE COMPANY

New Organization

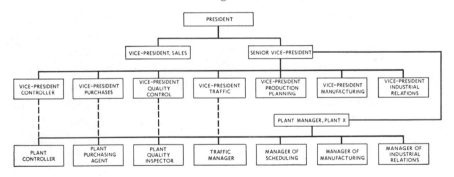

8. The Larger Company (A)

THE PHONE RANG, and highly indignant words blared: "Masters, what do you mean by submitting a report to all the executives without first talking it over with the division manager!"

Masters replied, "My men made every effort to see him. They never got past his secretary. He instructed her to have them talk to the works manager."

"I don't believe a word of it. Vining is up in arms. He says the report is vindictive. What are you trying to do—embarrass the division manager? I don't believe your men ever tried to see Vining and I question the veracity of their statements!" The phone on the other end was hung up with a bang.

Masters said to himself, "Gunn must be hot under the collar or he wouldn't have called me when I was away from my own office, visiting another plant."

The next day Masters' office received Gunn's letter confirming this telephone conversation and demanding an explanation. A week later Masters received a letter from Gunn's superior, a Mr. Jordan, stating, "I have read the aforementioned report and discussed it with Mr. Gunn. He has advised me that the report is essentially untrue, inaccurate, and overstated. I am not satisfied to have such wide differences of opinion and have scheduled a meeting to be held in my office on —————. I would appreciate it if you would be present."

In light of the phone call and the two letters, Mr. Masters decided to reassess all events leading to this climax.

.   .   .   .

The cast of characters is as shown in Exhibit 1. The Larger Company had an elaborate organizational structure as a result of its scale of operation. At the headquarters office of the corporation the president had a group of staff vice-presidents in charge of functions. Mr. Masters was a staff department head reporting to the vice-president, manufacturing. The headquarters staff departments assisted in policy formulation and made staff studies for the operating organization when requested. Members of such departments were encouraged to offer ideas for the good

Exhibit 1

THE LARGER COMPANY (A)

Organization Chart

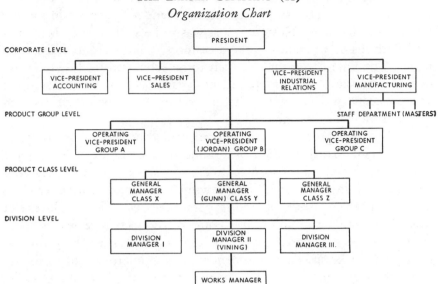

of the company. Their proposals were considered by a management committee consisting of the vice-presidents at the headquarters level and the operating vice-presidents in charge of product groups. Mr. Jordan of this case was the operating vice-president, Product Group "B."

Under the product groups there were general managers of product classes. They supervised the division managers, who were in charge of the sales and manufacturing operations of one or more plants. Mr. Gunn was general manager of Product Class "Y." One of the four division managers under him was Mr. Vining of Division II.

• • • • • • • • • • • • • • • • •

Two years before this incident occurred, Mr. Masters' staff department proposed to the management committee, with the approval of the vice-president, manufacturing, that representatives of Mr. Masters' office join with representatives of the vice-president, accounting to make studies in each plant of the procedures for and actual practices regarding expense control. The suggestion was approved, and enthusiastically endorsed by the general managers. They sent a letter through channels to each division manager advising that periodically a team of two men would visit each plant to make a comprehensive analysis of expense-control practices and systems.

After a visit these field representatives of headquarters were to prepare a report giving findings and recommendations. They were to discuss it with the appropriate division manager and his staff. Thus they would be able to incorporate any specific plans of action set in motion by division managers. Next, a report was to be submitted to Mr. Masters. Both his department and the accounting office were to make comments. The final document was then to be submitted to the vice-president, accounting; the vice-president, manufacturing; the operating vice-president, product group; the general manager, product class; and the division manager concerned.

This general procedure had worked smoothly within the company until general manager Gunn of Product Class "Y" exploded. In the first plant studied, the two team members spent approximately four weeks examining documents, interviewing line management, interrogating industrial engineers, observing operations, etc. The employees of this plant were very co-operative. Some of the facts revealed by them could have been embarrassing to the division manager. The team was enabled to make specific recommendations for improvement to the division manager. His reception of the report was good. According to him, the study had given an opportunity to review his situation and get his house in order. He intended to implement the recommendations unless they were changed in the review process at the higher level. Sixteen other plants were visited with reasonably good acceptance of the work of the team.

. . . .

In his review of the Division II situation, Mr. Masters found that the team had observed all the required organization routines. Mr. Sawyer, representing Mr. Masters, had a master's degree in industrial engineering and had twelve years with the company. Mr. Peters, from the accounting office, had served that department for thirty years. Both men had shown ability to gain confidences and to use them discreetly. They were considered straightforward, conscientious, and unobtrusive in their work. In Division II the team obtained from plant personnel considerable information which pointed up a number of practices and procedures requiring improvement. In the opinion of the team members, the operating organization at the lower levels sincerely wanted to make these changes. The team thought that there was some resistance at some level within the division to these suggestions and, in fact, to any from headquarters.

While the study was in process, Mr. Sawyer advised Mr. Masters about the possible impact of the information which was being collected.

Mr. Masters emphasized the necessity to report to the division manager, and Mr. Sawyer promised that he and Mr. Peters would do so.

The team made several efforts to see the division manager, but his secretary informed them that he was busy. They questioned the secretary closely to learn if the manager had knowledge of the procedural requirement that he and his staff go over the report with the team. She replied that he knew the requirements, but was too busy to discuss a headquarters program. He would ask his assistant, the works manager, and several staff members to go over it, and what they approved would be all right with him. Eventually this meeting was held.

The members of the local management staff took a very reasonable attitude; they admitted the bad situation portrayed in the analysis and offered their assurances that immediate steps would be taken towards improvement. The team members thought that the local management staff was glad to have their problem brought out in the open, and were delighted to have the suggestions of the headquarters representatives.

.   .   .   .

When Mr. Masters reviewed the report, both team members expressed their complete dissatisfaction with the brush-off they got from the division manager. Masters took this as a cue to question them extensively concerning their findings and recommendations. In view of the sensitive character of the situation and the possible controversy that it might create, he was reluctant to distribute the report. It was the consensus of the remainder of the staff and the representatives of the accounting office that the usual transmittal letter should be prepared, and distribution made. Mr. Masters signed this letter and took no other action until the telephone call came from Mr. Gunn.

9. The Larger Company (B)

Mr. JORDAN, operating vice-president, Product Group "B" of the Larger Company, called a meeting to review the report submitted by Mr. Masters' staff department and the accounting office. Mr. Jordan, Mr. Gunn, Mr. Masters, the vice-president, accounting and the vice-president, manufacturing attended. In a very constructive, two-hour meeting, the report was evaluated and many conclusions were confirmed.

Division manager Vining was not present. Mr. Jordan had not invited him because he wanted to keep "heat" out of the meeting. Mr. Jordan regarded Mr. Vining as an "individual operator" who on more than one occasion had shown definite disrespect for headquarters' functions and programs.

There was some heat in the meeting, nevertheless. Mr. Gunn stated that Mr. Masters should have discussed the report with him. Thus he might have had an opportunity to take executive action at his level. When a division manager failed to consider a report the superior should have a chance even though the formal procedure did not provide for it. Mr. Gunn said that Mr. Masters should have known that. Mr. Gunn also read a letter that had been prepared by Mr. Vining. It generally and categorically denied most of the statements in the report that were unsatisfactory to him. The vice-president, accounting and Mr. Masters, however, had certain information and supplementary reports which seemed to discount the effectiveness of the letter of rebuttal.

Before too much time elapsed, Mr. Jordan turned the discussion into ways of bringing about improvement in the future. "Where there was so much smoke," he observed, "there might be some fire." He suggested that men of higher rank review the work of the two team members; this would serve either to confirm or modify their findings. This step seemed advisable in order to assuage the feelings of the local division manager.

The meeting ended on a very harmonious note. Mr. Jordan asked Mr. Gunn to see Mr. Vining. "He needs to understand and appreciate that he has a responsibility to find time to review and comment on the type of reports being made by team members."

Mr. Masters was pleased by the results of the meeting and the follow-up actions. Mr. Gunn must have talked with Mr. Vining. Whatever was said may have contributed to better working relationships. Plant co-operation immediately improved. The division manager cleared any obstacles interfering with the success of the program. His influence was particularly noticeable in its effect on the behavior of the line supervisory organization. According to Mr. Masters, co-operation rather than resistance was now encouraged. The home office team became the advisory team it was intended to be.

In reviewing this experience Mr. Masters said, "There was bound to be some form of blow-up because Vining had the reputation of thinking he did not have to conform to company-wide programs unless it was to his advantage. Further, he was more rugged in nature than Gunn. On many occasions Gunn was inclined to support Vining. There has been a very definite change in this respect during the latter part of this year."

10. Westinghouse Electric Corporation (A)

THE WESTINGHOUSE ELECTRIC CORPORATION, with headquarters in Pittsburgh, Pennsylvania, had long been one of the largest and most diversified corporations in the United States. In terms of the annual *Fortune* survey of the 500 largest United States industrial corporations, Westinghouse ranked 17th in sales ($2.3 billion) and 24th in total assets employed ($1.6 billion) for 1964. The company had about 64 plant locations in the United States, sales offices throughout the country, and employed about 115,000 people in 1964. In addition to its domestic operations, Westinghouse also had investments in about 35 foreign countries and had over 150 foreign licensees.

Westinghouse was generally classified as an electrical equipment manufacturer, and produced a wide range of industrial and consumer equipment for the generation, transmission, distribution, control, and utilization of electric power. Some measure of the diversity of its operations can be inferred from the following comments in a *Time* article:

> Any company that makes both reactors for nuclear submarines and $1.25 magnets for extracting wire and nails from cows' stomachs has some claim to diversity—and Westinghouse Electric claims to be the world's most diversified company. The oldest electronics firm and the second biggest producer of electrical equipment (after General Electric) in the U.S., Westinghouse makes 8,000 different products in 300,000 variations. The company's 59 divisions with their 64 plants spread through 20 states, daily confront almost every American with some Westinghouse product, from 6,000 types of light bulbs to the output of five TV and seven radio stations.[1]

A more complete listing of Westinghouse products and facilities as of 1964 is shown in Exhibit 1. Of the product groups shown, the Electric Utility group had been the largest in terms of sales, followed by the Industrial and the Atomic, Defense & Space groups.

Single divisions ranged in size from about $5 million to well over $100 million in sales, and had from 500 to 5,000 employees. If listed as independent companies, all of the product groups listed as well as

---

[1] *Time* (October 30, 1964), p. 97.

many of the divisions would have been included in the *Fortune* list of the 500 largest U.S. industrial companies.

The great diversity of the products and services offered by Westinghouse is shown in somewhat more detail in Exhibit 2, which is a reproduction of several pages selected from a booklet entitled "The World of Westinghouse." It was stated in the booklet that the list of over 1,300 products was constantly growing and changing, and it was emphasized that multiplying the products listed by "ratings, sizes, styles, enclosures, colors, combinations, and all the other variables which fit them to specific needs" would explode the list into one of thousands and thousands of items.

Exhibit 1

WESTINGHOUSE ELECTRIC CORPORATION (A)

Westinghouse Divisions and Products

ATOMIC, DEFENSE AND SPACE

AEROSPACE ELECTRICAL DIVISION, Lima, Ohio
Electric power systems, generators, motors, control apparatus, thermoelectric devices, power conditioning and conversion equipment, and support equipment for military and commercial aircraft, missiles and spacecraft.

ASTRONUCLEAR LABORATORY, Large, Pa.
Nuclear power for space and other advanced applications; specialized equipment for space applications.

ATOMIC EQUIPMENT DIVISION, Cheswick, Pa.
Main coolant pumps, valves, control rod drive mechanisms, and other specialized apparatus for nuclear reactors; pumps for controlled circulation boilers; thermoelectric cooling devices for military applications.

ATOMIC FUEL DIVISION, Cheswick, Pa.
Nuclear reactor cores and core components for Naval applications.

BETTIS ATOMIC POWER LABORATORY, Pittsburgh, Pa.
Government-owned facility operated by Westinghouse for the Atomic Energy Commission. Development of nuclear reactors for Naval propulsion and electric power generation under contracts with U.S. Government.

DEFENSE AND SPACE CENTER:
Aerospace Division, Baltimore, Md.
Aerospace systems, equipment and associated support items: reconnaissance; detection, surveillance and weapon control; navigation; data handling and display; missile launch, guidance and control; space vehicle guidance and control; communications; com-

ATOMIC, DEFENSE AND SPACE (CONTINUED)

mand and control; instrumentation; scientific satellites and space vehicles; advanced weapons and electronic warfare.
Surface Division, Baltimore, Md.
Ground, ship and mobile surface systems, equipment and associated support items: surveillance; detection and weapon control; navigation; data handling and display; command and control; communication; instrumentation; satellite control; tracking and discrimination; anti-missile protection; advanced weapons and electronic warfare.
Underseas Division, Baltimore, Md.
Underwater systems, equipment and associated support items: torpedoes, mines and advanced weapons; mine, weapon and CW countermeasures; surveillance; sonar detection; data handling and display; instrumentation; oceanographic systems and equipment; manned submersibles.
Systems Operations, Baltimore, Md.
Management, design and integration of major defense and space systems and systems involving resources and capabilities of several Westinghouse divisions.

PLANT APPARATUS DIVISION, Pittsburgh, Pa.
Procurement of reactor plant equipment for Naval applications.

SUNNYVALE DIVISIONS:
General Products Division, Sunnyvale, Calif.
Electrical, mechanical and shock mitigation components for missile and rocket programs; missile launching and handling equipment; wind tunnel equipment, including axial-flow compressors; special apparatus such as tele-

ATOMIC, DEFENSE AND SPACE (CONTINUED)

scope drives and mountings, centrifugal machines, shock machines and large hydraulic valves.

Marine Products Division, Sunnyvale, Calif. Equipment for marine applications, including propulsion, providing ship service electrical power, ship handling equipment such as anchor and cargo winch controls, automatic ship and engine room controls, marine condensers, air ejectors, and marine wet winding submersible motors.

CONSTRUCTION

AIR CONDITIONING DIVISION, Staunton, Va. Packaged air conditioning and heating equipment for residential, commercial and industrial applications; engineered air conditioning systems; heat pumps and electric heat systems for residential and commercial installations.

BRYANT ELECTRIC DIVISION, Bridgeport, Conn. Wiring devices; lampholders; fluorescent devices; outdoor fixtures for reflector backed lamps; circuit breaker load centers.

ELEVATOR DIVISION, Jersey City, N.J. Passenger, freight, and shipboard elevators; electric stairways; electric walks; security systems.

ENVIRONMENTAL SYSTEMS DIVISION, Grand Rapids, Mich. Micarta-clad doors; movable partitions and walls; controlled atmosphere work areas; clean rooms.

LAMP DIVISION, Bloomfield, N.J. Lamps of all types for all applications: incandescent; fluorescent; mercury; sealed-beam; reflector; miniature; medical; photographic; Christmas tree; flashlight; sun; heat.

LIGHTING DIVISION, Cleveland, Ohio Commercial, industrial, fluorescent and incandescent fixtures; fluorescent and mercury ballasts; flood, roadway, and marine lighting; lighting accessories; Sterilamp equipment.

STURTEVANT DIVISION, Hyde Park, Mass. Air distributing units; fans, blowers—general purpose and heavy duty; heaters; heating and cooling coils, steam and hot water; Precipitron air cleaners; dehumidifiers.

PRINTING DIVISION, Trafford, Pa. Nameplates, printed circuits, all forms of printing.

CONSUMER

AUTOMATIC MERCHANDISING DIVISION, East Springfield, Mass.

CONSUMER (CONTINUED)

Automatic beverage coolers for bottlers of Coca-Cola.

COLUMBUS APPLIANCE DIVISIONS:
Dishwasher & Specialty Products Division, Columbus, Ohio
Dishwashers; waste disposers; water coolers; water heaters.
Refrigerator Division, Columbus, Ohio
Refrigerators and freezers.
Room Air Conditioning Division, Columbus, Ohio
Air conditioners.

MANSFIELD APPLIANCE DIVISIONS:
Laundry Equipment Division, Mansfield, Ohio
Laundromat® automatic washers; dryers; dry cleaners.
Portable Appliance Division, Mansfield, Ohio
Electric housewares; bed coverings; fans; floor polishers; vacuum cleaners.
Range Division, Mansfield, Ohio
Ranges and ovens; kitchen cabinets.

THE C. A. OLSEN MANUFACTURING COMPANY, Elyria, Ohio
Residential heating and air conditioning; incinerators; unit heaters.

TELEVISION-RADIO DIVISION, Metuchen, N.J. Television receivers; radios, portable and consoles; high fidelity and stereo phonographs; tape recorders.

ELECTRIC UTILITY

ATOMIC POWER DIVISION, Pittsburgh, Pa. (Forest Hills)
Advanced concept development programs, atomic fuel, nuclear steam supply systems, turn-key nuclear power plants—for commercial atomic power installations.

EAST PITTSBURGH DIVISIONS:
Distribution Apparatus Division, Bloomington, Ind.
Capacitors; lightning arresters; fuse cutouts; surge protective devices; reclosers; sectionalizers; load pick-up switches.
Large Rotating Apparatus Division, East Pittsburgh, Pa.
Large generators, motors, motor-generator sets; electric couplings; frequency changer sets; synchronous condensers.
Power Circuit Breaker Division, Trafford, Pa.
High voltage power circuit breakers; condenser bushings, insulators; arc heaters.
Power Control Division, Research and Development Center, Pittsburgh, Pa. (Churchill)
Dispatching control; digital datalogers;

Exhibit 1—Continued

ELECTRIC UTILITY (CONTINUED)

load-frequency control; printed circuit modules; steam plant automation; steam plant computer systems; turbine control systems.
Switchgear Division, East Pittsburgh, Pa.
Assembled switchgear; high voltage fuses; network protectors; nuclear plant control; regulators; substations; generator synchronizers.

MEASUREMENTS DIVISIONS:

Meter Division, Raleigh, N.C.
Watthour, demand, recording meters and accessories; sockets and mountings.
Relay-Instrument Division, Newark, N.J.
Electrical measuring instruments of all types; protective relays and relaying systems.

STEAM DIVISIONS:

Heat Transfer Division, Lester, Pa.
Surface condensers, air ejectors, circulating and condensate pumps, priming ejectors, flash evaporators, water conversion plants—for installation on land; nuclear steam generators.
Large Turbine Division, Lester, Pa.
Large steam turbine generators—for installation on land.
Small Steam and Gas Turbine Division, Lester, Pa.
Gas turbines, small steam turbine generators, steam turbines for mechanical drive—for installation on land.

TRANSFORMER DIVISIONS:

Distribution Transformer Division, Sharon, Pa.
Dry and liquid immersed distribution transformers; current and potential instrument transformers; metering units.
Power Transformer Division, Sharon, Pa.
Power transformers; power regulators; reactors; self-contained unit substations.

ELECTRONIC COMPONENTS AND SPECIALTY PRODUCTS

ELECTRONIC TUBE DIVISION, Elmira, N.Y.
Electronic tubes of all kinds; power amplifiers, oscillators, pulse, rectifier, cathode ray tubes; television camera and picture tubes; miscellaneous special tubes—industrial and military.

INDUSTRIAL CERAMICS DIVISION, Derry, Pa.
Porcelain insulators; industrial ceramics.

MATERIALS MANUFACTURING DIVISION, Blairsville, Pa.
High temperature, permanent and soft magnetic alloys; nonfuel nuclear and refractory metals.

MICARTA DIVISIONS:

Decorative Micarta Division, Hampton, S.C.

ELECTRONIC COMPONENTS AND SPECIALTY PRODUCTS (CONTINUED)

Decorative Micarta sheets.
Industrial Micarta Division, Hampton, S.C.
Laminated fabricated plastics, Micarta shapes, sheets; insulating enamels and materials (Trafford, Pa.).

MOLECULAR ELECTRONICS DIVISION, Baltimore, Md., Newbury Park, Calif.
Epitaxial material; functional electronic blocks; integrated circuits.

NEW PRODUCTS TASK FORCE, Research and Development Center, Pittsburgh, Pa. (Churchill)
Cryogenic systems; scientific equipment (Edgewood Site); electronic capacitors (Irwin, Pa.)

SEMICONDUCTOR DIVISION, Youngwood, Pa.
Transistors; power rectifiers; diodes; solid state relays; thermoelectric devices; specialty devices.

SPECIALTY TRANSFORMER DIVISION, Greenville, Pa.
Cores; charging reactors; transducers; specialty transformers.

X-RAY DIVISION, Baltimore, Md.
Medical and industrial X-Ray apparatus, supplies and accessories; electro-medical products.

INDUSTRIAL

MOTOR DIVISIONS:

Motor and Gearing Division, Buffalo, N.Y.
Integral hp. motors for general industry and specific purpose applications; brakes; couplings; motocylinders; drives; gearing and gear motors; speed reducers.
Small Motor Division, Lima, Ohio
Small motors, general and special purpose for all types of domestic, appliance and industrial purposes.
Copper Wire Division, Buffalo, N.Y.
Copper and aluminum conductors.

CONTROL DIVISIONS:

General Control Division, Buffalo, N.Y.
Motor starters and controllers; special purpose control; control components; static control; pilot devices; power supplies.
Hagan Controls Corporation, Pittsburgh, Pa.
Control components; control devices; control systems for combustion, flow and level, pressure and differential pressure, temperature, and chemical systems.
Low Voltage Distribution Equipment Division, Pittsburgh, Pa.
Control centers; panelboards; switchboards; custom control assemblies; special switchgear; custom power centers; high voltage bus.

Exhibit 1—Continued

INDUSTRIAL (CONTINUED)

Standard Control Division, Beaver, Pa.
Controls for motors; starters, contactors, relays, pushbuttons; bus duct; circuit breakers; safety switches.

INDUSTRIAL EQUIPMENT AND SERVICE DIVISIONS:
Electric Service Division, Pittsburgh, Pa.
Field engineering; technical direction; installation and startup service; inspection and maintenance.
Homewood Division, Homewood, Pa.
Non-current apparatus and parts.
Industrial Electronics Division, Baltimore, Md.
Induction heating equipment; ultrasonic devices for cleaning and process equipment.
Repair Division, Pittsburgh, Pa.
Repair, rewind, rebuild, update, modernize electrical and mechanical apparatus, in the field or in one of 42 repair plants.
Transportation Equipment Division, East Pittsburgh, Pa.
Motors, generators, gearing and control for transit vehicles; transit expressway vehicles.
Westing-Arc Division, Buffalo, N.Y.
Electric arc welders, electrodes, accessories; brazing alloys.

INDUSTRIAL (CONTINUED)

INDUSTRIAL SYSTEMS DIVISIONS:
Computer Systems Division, Research and Development Center, Pittsburgh, Pa. (Churchill)
Digital computers.
Industry Systems Division, Research and Development Center, Pittsburgh, Pa. (Churchill)
Design and management for large scale systems; includes the Metals Industry Systems Department, the General Industries Systems Department and the Public Works Systems Department.
Systems Control Division, Buffalo, N.Y.
Mill and marine materials handling control systems; numerical control; packaged drives; power rectifiers; Semitron® rectifier equipment (East Pittsburgh).

THERMO KING CORPORATION, Minneapolis, Minn.
Air conditioning for automobiles, trucks, buses and other personnel vehicles. Refrigeration-heating for semi-trailers, trucks, van bodies and other produce carriers.

Source: "The World of Westinghouse," a company publication.

Exhibit 2

WESTINGHOUSE ELECTRIC CORPORATION (A)

Sample Listing of Westinghouse Products

Coolers, Portable, *Portable Appliance Division, Mansfield, Ohio*
Evaporative
Cores, *Specialty Transformer Division, Greenville, Pa.*
Cubex®
Hipersil®
Wescor®
Corona Detectors, *Distribution Apparatus Division, Bloomington, Ind.*
Couplings, Electric, *Large Rotating Apparatus Division, East Pittsburgh, Pa.*
Couplings, Flexible, *Motor and Gearing Division, Buffalo, N.Y.*
Cryogenic Systems, *Cryogenic Systems Department, Research and Development Center, Pittsburgh, Pa. (Churchill)*
Cryptographic Equipment, *Aerospace Division, Surface Division, Defense and Space Center, Baltimore, Md.*
Cutouts, Fuse, *Distribution Apparatus Division, Bloomington, Ind.*
Enclosed
Open

Data Processing and Display Equipment, Ground and Shipboard, *Surface Division, Defense and Space Center, Baltimore, Md.*
Data Processing Equipment, Airborne and Spaceborne, *Aerospace Division, Defense and Space Center, Baltimore, Md.*
Data Processing Systems, *Systems Operations, Defense and Space Center, Baltimore, Md.*
Data Transmission and Reception Equipment, Ground and Shipboard, *Surface Division, Defense and Space Center, Baltimore, Md.*
Decorative Micarta®, *Decorative Micarta Division, Hampton, S.C.*
Degaussing Equipment, Marine, *Marine Products Division, Sunnyvale, Calif.*
Dehumidifiers, *Dishwasher and Specialty Products Division, Columbus, Ohio*
Dehumidifiers, *Sturtevant Division, Hyde Park, Mass.*
Sprayed coil type
Digital Datalogers, *Power Control Division, Research and Development Center, Pittsburgh, Pa. (Churchill)*

Exhibit 2—Continued

Dishwashers, *Dishwasher and Specialty Products Division, Columbus, Ohio*
Built-in
Portable

Doors, Micarta-Clad, *Architectural System, Grand, Rapids, Mich.*

Drives, *Motor and Gearing Division, Buffalo, N.Y.*
Mechanical adjustable speed (Adjusti-Flow®)
Planer

Drives, Packaged, Electrical, Adjustable Speed, *Systems Control Division, Buffalo, N.Y.*

Dry Cleaners, Commercial, *Laundry Equipment Division, Mansfield, Ohio*

Dryers, *Laundry Equipment Division, Mansfield, Ohio*
Commercial
Domestic

Pushbuttons, *Standard Control Division, Beaver, Pa.*
Heavy duty
Oil tite
Standard duty

Radars, Airborne and Spaceborne, *Aerospace Division, Defense and Space Center, Baltimore, Md.*

Radars, Ground and Shipboard, *Surface Division, Defense and Space Center, Baltimore, Md.*

Radios, *Television-Radio Division, Metuhcen, N.J.*
Clock
AM, AM/FM, pushbutton
Portable
AM, AM/FM, transistor, shortwave
Table
AM, AM/FM, FM stereo
Transceivers

Ranges, Electric, *Range Division, Mansfield, Ohio*
Built-in
Cooking platforms
Electronic
Ovens
Free standing
Conventional
Eye-level ovens

Reactors, *Power Transformer Division, Sharon, Pa.*
Current limiting
CL, oil-immersed and dry type
MSP, dry type
Shunt, oil-immersed and dry type

Reactors, Charging, *Specialty Transformer Division, Greenville, Pa.*

Reactors, Saturable Core, *Distribution Transformer Division, Sharon, Pa.*

Reclosers, *Distribution Apparatus Division, Bloomington, Ind.*

Reconnaissance Equipment, Airborne and Spaceborne, *Aerospace Division, Defense and Space Center, Baltimore, Md.*

Reconnaissance Systems, *Systems Operations, Defense and Space Center, Baltimore, Md.*

Rectifier Assemblies, *Semiconductor Division, Youngwood, Pa.*
High voltage
Standard

Rectifier Diodes, Silicon, *Semiconductor Division, Youngwood, Pa.*
Controlled avalanche
Fast recovery
"O.E.M." line
Standard

Rectifier Equipment, Semitron®, *Rectifier Product Group (Systems Control), East Pittsburgh, Pa.*

Self-Lubricating Bearing Materials, *Materials Manufacturing Division, Blairsville, Pa.*

Service, Electric, *Electric Service Division, Pittsburgh, Pa.*
(Available at all Westinghouse sales locations)
Field engineering services
Inspection, maintenance and repair service
Starting service on apparatus and systems
Technical direction and advice

Service, Steam, *Steam Divisions Service Department, Lester, Pa.*
Complete installation service, maintenance service, repair service and modernization programs for all products marketed by the Steam Divisions, including generators, exciters and regulators sold with turbines and waterwheel generators marketed by Large Rotating Apparatus Division.

Silicon Rectifier, *Rectifier Product Group (Systems Control), East Pittsburgh, Pa.*
Subassemblies for replacing Ignitron tubes

Sockets and Mountings, Meter, *Meter Division, Raleigh, N.C.*

Sonar, *Underseas Division, Defense and Space Center, Baltimore, Md.*

Space Propulsion Concepts, *Astronuclear Laboratory, Large, Pa.*

Space Systems, *Systems Operations, Defense and Space Center, Baltimore, Md.*
Electrical
Mechanical

Specialty Devices, *Semiconductor Division, Youngwood, Pa.*

Exhibit 2—Continued

Speed Reducers, *Motor and Gearing Division, Buffalo, N.Y.*
  Helical
  Moduline®
  Shaft
  Worm gear
Spot Film Devices, X-Ray, *X-Ray Division, Baltimore, Md.*
Starters, Electric Motor, *Standard Control Division, Beaver, Pa.*
  Magnetic
  Manual
Steam Generators, Marine, *Marine Products Division, Sunnyvale Calif.*

Steam Generators, Nuclear, *Heat Transfer Division, Lester, Pa.*
Steam Plant Automation Systems, *Power Control Division, Research and Development Center, Pittsburgh, Pa. (Churchill)*
Steam Plant Performance Computer Systems, *Power Control Division, Research and Development Center, Pittsburgh, Pa. (Churchill)*
Steam Turbine Generators, Land, *Large Turbine Division, Lester, Pa.*
  20,000 to 1,000,000 kw
Steam Turbine Generators, Land, *Small Steam and Gas Turbine Division, Lester, Pa.*
  20 to 15,625 kw

Source: "The World of Westinghouse," a company publication.

11. Westinghouse Electric Corporation (B₁)

ASSUME that you are the general manager of a product group with total sales of about $400 million in 1964. (See Exhibit 1, Westinghouse (A), for brief descriptions of typical product groups and divisions.)

Assume that each division manager reports directly to you. Profit objectives are established each year by corporate officers for your group as a whole, and by you and your division managers for the divisions in your group. A full set of financial statements is prepared by each division in your group. Your performance, and the performance of the division manager, is evaluated to a considerable extent each year on performance with respect to the objectives established.

While attending a management seminar made up of division managers and group managers from a number of large, diversified companies, you have been asked to indicate the degree of delegation you feel is appropriate in your organization for a number of problem situations. The "Delegation Questionnaire"[1] is reproduced as Exhibit 1. In order to facilitate comparisons among companies, you also have been asked to assume, for your company, that:

1. Business conditions have been fairly good, and are expected to continue to be favorable;
2. All of your divisions have been profitable, although generally not as profitable as desired by corporate management;
3. Each division has had at least one major product line that has shown losses, but you stand a fairly good chance of meeting your profit goals for the group this year; and
4. You have held your job for some time, and each of the division managers in your group has been in his job at least three years.

---

[1] Source of delegation questionnaire and problem situation: Mr. William Nesbitt, Director, Organization Planning, Westinghouse Electric Corporation.

Exhibit 1 — WESTINGHOUSE ELECTRIC CORPORATION (B_1)
Delegation Questionnaire

As a group general manager you would expect your division managers to: Problem requiring action	SEE LEGEND BELOW FOR DETAILED EXPLANATION OF HEADINGS:					
	Take action		Advise you		Provide information	
	A	B	C	D	E	F
1. Hire a replacement for the division manager's secretary who is leaving.						
2. Authorize a temporary $50,000 increase in division raw material inventory in anticipation of a possible steel strike.						
3. Establish next month's manufacturing schedule for the division, at an increased level which will require the hiring of two additional people in the factory.						
4. Establish next month's manufacturing schedule, at a substantially higher level which will require the addition of 50 people in the factory.						
5. Pass final approval on the design of a new product, and authorize work to start on production tooling.						
6. Postpone the scheduled introduction of a new model by 45 days, and authorize a crash program estimated to cost $100,000 which will modify the design and permit incorporation of a recently developed design feature.						
7. Establish the list price of a major product line, which in the aggregate amounts to 30% of division volume.						
8. Increase the price of an existing product line by 4%, to attempt to recover cost increases that have taken place in material and labor; this will place the price above the competitive level.						
9. One product line has an extremely seasonal pattern, with all sales occurring in the summer. Authorize the production schedule for the year, which will create a $6 million shipping stock of this product at the time of its peak selling season.						
10. Make a change in the division inventory standards, which will reduce field shipping stocks but increase factory work-in-process inventory, maintaining the same total investment.						
11. Increase the investment in inventory on a different product by approximately $1 million, because the sales department feels that they can get more sales if they have greater product availability.						
12. Initiate a computer activity, estimated to cost $1 million for feasibility study and programming, and which will require a commitment for a computer that will ultimately cost $200,000 per year.						
13. Introduce a new system into the factory that is recognized to have a 20% chance of precipitating strong opposition, possibly leading to a strike on the part of the union.						
14. Change advertising program for the division, reducing magazine advertising, increasing direct mail and trade show promotional activities.						
15. Authorize the manager of manufacturing to increase the methods and industrial engineering activity and reduce the size of the quality control department, maintaining the same total manufacturing expense.						
16. Authorize the marketing manager to increase the number of salesmen in the field, reduce the number of manufacturing engineers by a corresponding amount to maintain the same total cost.						
17. Select the replacement for the manufacturing superintendent who will retire soon.						
18. Take the superintendent off the job for poor performance; replace him with another man now serving as a general foreman.						
19. Select the replacement for the general foreman position now open.						
20. Increase the number of general foremen positions in the division from four to six. Select the individuals to fill the new positions.						
21. Authorize an 8% salary increase for the manufacturing superintendent, allowed for in the budget and within the rate range for the job.						
22. Authorize an 8% salary increase for the division sales manager, allowed for in the budget and within the rate range.						
23. Authorize the factory to work overtime two Saturdays next month to reduce the backlog of overdue orders.						
24. Increase the job classification and rate range for the engineering manager, to reflect the growth of his department and the increased responsibility of his position.						
25. Authorize a change in job classification for the six general foremen positions, as a result of changes in their responsibility.						
26. Cancel two engineering development projects included in this year's program, and concentrate the $250,000 effort on a new development believed to have real commercial potential, identified as a result of research performed in the corporate research center.						

Explanation of Headings:
A. Take action without any contact with you.
B. Take action; mention the action taken later if he happens to see you.
C. Advise you in advance of the action he intends to take; act unless you tell him not to.
D. Advise you in advance of the action he would like to take; delay action until you give him approval.
E. Give you an analysis of the alternative actions possible, with their merits and disadvantages, supporting his choice of the one he recommends for your approval.
F. Give you as many facts about the case as possible so you can identify alternatives and select the action you want to be taken.

12. Westinghouse Electric Corporation (B₂)

ASSUME that you are the manager of a division with total sales of about $60 million in 1964. Your division is a part of a product group which accounted for about $400 million in sales in 1964. (See Exhibit 1, p. 411 for brief descriptions of typical product groups and divisions.)

Assume that you and all of the other division managers in your group report directly to the group general manager. Profit objectives are established each year by corporate officers for your group as a whole, and by you and your group general manager for your division. A full set of financial statements is prepared by each division in the group. Your performance, and the performance of your group general manager, is evaluated to a considerable extent each year on performance with respect to the objectives established.

While attending a management seminar made up of division managers and group general managers from a number of large, diversified companies, you have been asked to indicate the degree of delegation you feel is appropriate in your organization for a number of problem situations. The "Delegation Questionnaire"[1] is reproduced as Exhibit 1. In order to facilitate comparisons among companies, you also have been asked to assume, for your company, that:

1. Business conditions have been fairly good, and are expected to continue to be favorable;
2. All of the divisions in your group have been profitable, although generally not as profitable as desired by corporate management;
3. Each division, including yours, has had at least one major product line that has shown losses;
4. You feel that you have a reasonable chance of meeting your division profit goals for the year;
5. Your group general manager has said that the group will probably meet its profit goals for the year "if everyone comes through";
6. You have held your job for some time, and the group general manager as well as the other division managers have all been in their jobs for at least three years.

---

[1] Source of delegation questionnaire and problem situation: Mr. William Nesbitt, Director, Organization Planning, Westinghouse Electric Corporation.

Problem requiring action	Take action		Advise group manager		Inform group manager	
As a division manager, you would:	A	B	C	D	E	F
1. Hire a replacement for the division manager's secretary who is leaving.						
2. Authorize a temporary $50,000 increase in division raw material inventory in anticipation of a possible steel strike.						
3. Establish next month's manufacturing schedule for the division, at an increased level which will require the hiring of two additional people in the factory.						
4. Establish next month's manufacturing schedule, at a substantially higher level which will require the addition of 50 people in the factory.						
5. Pass final approval on the design of a new product, and authorize work to start on production tooling.						
6. Postpone the scheduled introduction of a new model by 45 days, and authorize a crash program estimated to cost $100,000 which will modify the design and permit incorporation of a recently developed design feature.						
7. Establish the list price of a major product line, which in the aggregate amounts to 30% of division volume.						
8. Increase the price of an existing product line by 4%, to attempt to recover cost increases that have taken place in material and labor; this will place the price above the competitive level.						
9. One product line has an extremely seasonal pattern, with all sales occurring in the summer. Authorize the production schedule for the year, which will create a $6 million shipping stock of this product at the time of its peak selling season.						
10. Make a change in the division inventory standards, which will reduce field shipping stocks but increase factory work-in-process inventory, maintaining the same total investment.						
11. Increase the investment in inventory on a different product by approximately $1 million, because the sales department feels that they can get more sales if they have greater product availability.						
12. Initiate a computer activity, estimated to cost $1 million for feasibility study and programming, and which will require a commitment for a computer that will ultimately cost $200,000 per year.						
13. Introduce a new system into the factory that is recognized to have a 20% chance of precipitating strong opposition, possibly leading to a strike on the part of the union.						
14. Change advertising program for the division, reducing magazine advertising, increasing direct mail and trade show promotional activities.						
15. Authorize the manager of manufacturing to increase the methods and industrial engineering activity and reduce the size of the quality control department, maintaining the same total manufacturing expense.						
16. Authorize the marketing manager to increase the number of salesmen in the field, reduce the number of manufacturing engineers by a corresponding amount to maintain the same total cost.						
17. Select the replacement for the manufacturing superintendent who will retire soon.						
18. Take the superintendent off the job for poor performance; replace him with another man now serving as a general foreman.						
19. Select the replacement for the general foreman position now open.						
20. Increase the number of general foremen positions in the division from four to six. Select the individuals to fill the new positions.						
21. Authorize an 8% salary increase for the manufacturing superintendent, allowed for in the budget and within the rate range for the job.						
22. Authorize an 8% salary increase for the division sales manager, allowed for in the budget and within the rate range.						
23. Authorize the factory to work overtime two Saturdays next month to reduce the backlog of overdue orders.						
24. Increase the job classification and rate range for the engineering manager, to reflect the growth of his department and the increased responsibility of his position.						
25. Authorize a change in job classification for the six general foremen positions, as a result of changes in their responsibility.						
26. Cancel two engineering development projects included in this year's program, and concentrate the $250,000 effort on a new development believed to have real commercial potential, identified as a result of research performed in the corporate research center.						

Explanation of Headings:

A. Take action without contacting group general manager.

B. Take action; mention action later if you happen to see the group general manager.

C. Advise group general manager in advance of action you intend to take; act unless he tells you not to.

D. Advise group general manager in advance of action you would like to take; delay action until he gives you approval.

E. Give the group general manager an analysis of the alternative actions possible, with their merits and disadvantages, supporting your choice of the one you recommend for his approval.

F. Give the group general manager as many facts about the case as possible so that he can identify alternatives and select the action he wants taken.

13. Robbins, Inc.

In December, 1966, Mr. Robert Kurtz became the new general manager of Robbins, Inc., a firm operating in the electrical equipment field. In 1966, it was estimated, Robbins' sales were $100 million and the enterprise employed over 2,500 people.

Robbins, Inc., had recently been purchased by a group of wealthy investors. In view of their other varied business interests, the investing group planned to operate Robbins as a separate, independent company. Mr. Kurtz was given complete responsibility for the direction of Robbins' affairs. He had achieved an excellent reputation among industrialists as a manager capable of dealing with difficult business problems, and the investors had agreed that he was to have a free hand to make whatever changes he thought necessary to improve the company's "obviously unsatisfactory" profit performance.

Robbins manufactured and sold electrical equipment for industrial and consumer use. Its industrial products included a wide variety of standard and specialty motors. The company had achieved an excellent reputation for engineering design work. Over the years its legal staff had built up an imposing number of patents protecting improvements created by company engineers. In the consumer products line, the firm manufactured and sold a line of small "traffic" household appliances for the American and export markets.

In recent years company sales had increased substantially but profits had gradually declined to a point where only a very small profit was anticipated for 1966. While industrial products had been extremely profitable in early postwar years, the competitive situation had changed substantially in the early 1960's. Consumer appliance operations varied from early losses to small profit contributions in 1964 through 1966. Robbins was encountering increasing competition for its appliances from full-line companies, e.g., Sunbeam. Despite this, Mr. Kurtz believed that in the long run the consumer appliance area would become the most important and profitable part of the firm's business. He hoped to add new appliance items as rapidly as production and marketing facilities permitted.

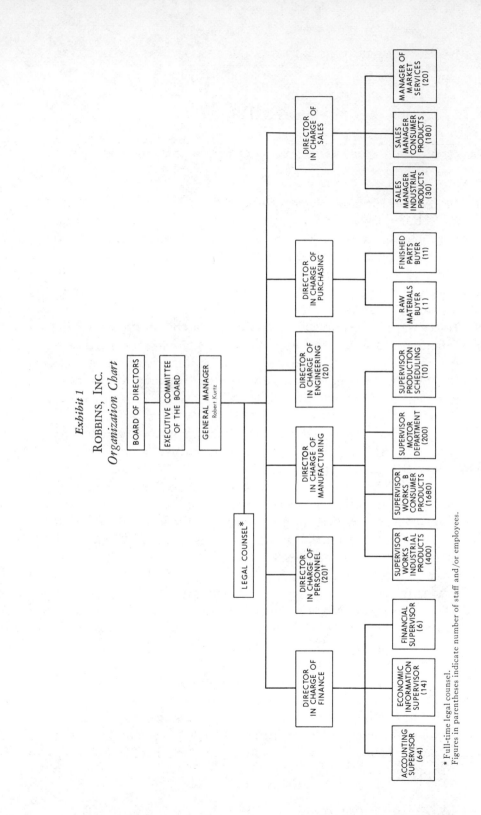

Exhibit 1

ROBBINS, INC.
Organization Chart

BOARD OF DIRECTORS

EXECUTIVE COMMITTEE OF THE BOARD

GENERAL MANAGER
Robert Kurtz

LEGAL COUNSEL*

DIRECTOR IN CHARGE OF FINANCE
- ACCOUNTING SUPERVISOR (64)
- ECONOMIC INFORMATION SUPERVISOR (14)
- FINANCIAL SUPERVISOR (6)

DIRECTOR IN CHARGE OF PERSONNEL (20)†

DIRECTOR IN CHARGE OF MANUFACTURING
- SUPERVISOR WORKS A INDUSTRIAL PRODUCTS (400)
- SUPERVISOR WORKS B CONSUMER PRODUCTS (1680)
- SUPERVISOR MOTOR DEPARTMENT (200)
- SUPERVISOR PRODUCTION SCHEDULING (10)

DIRECTOR IN CHARGE OF ENGINEERING (20)

DIRECTOR IN CHARGE OF PURCHASING
- RAW MATERIALS BUYER (11)
- FINISHED PARTS BUYER (11)

DIRECTOR IN CHARGE OF SALES
- SALES MANAGER INDUSTRIAL PRODUCTS (30)
- SALES MANAGER CONSUMER PRODUCTS (180)
- MANAGER OF MARKET SERVICES (20)

* Full-time legal counsel.
Figures in parentheses indicate number of staff and/or employees.

In the manufacture of these products, Robbins purchased substantial quantities of two raw materials ($16 million in 1966). These raw materials were subject to substantial price fluctuations and it was important for Robbins to buy at "the right time and price."

The new owners of Robbins requested that Mr. Kurtz prepare salary recommendations, for board consideration, in December, 1966. His recommendations were to cover the top 20 executives in the company including himself. Knowing the backgrounds of the new owners, Mr. Kurtz knew he would have to be able to defend his assignments of salary to specific jobs. He also knew that the new owners had been critical of the "haphazard way" in which salary payments had been made by the former general manager.

To carry out this assignment, Mr. Kurtz asked the member of the personnel department in charge of the executive payroll for the amount paid in salaries to the top 20 managers of the firm in the year 1966. This sum amounted to $860,000. He excluded individual bonus payments and incidental privileges such as company-furnished cars. Bonus payments for the Robbins management group had declined steadily during the past four years, and salary payments were now the important element in the firm's compensation program.

He then prepared to assign funds from this "common pool" to individual jobs in the organization. Mr. Kurtz realized that, after he had determined an ideal salary structure, he would have to modify his assignments on the basis of historical precedent as well as other factors. But he believed that the process of allocating the total salary fund to individual jobs, without prejudice of past history, would help him in thinking through the factors that should influence salary payments.

Exhibit 1 charts the organization of Robbins, Inc.

Section 4
Managing the Administrative Organization

1. Blow-Mold Packers, Inc.

SEVEN MONTHS after taking his MBA degree with distinction at Stanford University, Mr. Harold Finer, CPA, decided to quit the academic world and to accept a standing invitation to join Blow-Mold Packers, Inc. (BMP), a fast-growing firm with some $36 million sales in the blow-molded plastic container business.[1] Finer's title would be that of assistant to the president, and his assignment, staff direction of the acquisition program on which BMP had recently embarked.

In joining BMP in January, 1970, Finer was entering a firm with which he already felt himself familiar. As a second-year student, he had considered writing his research report on the company and had wound up exploring a business opportunity in which BMP's president was personally interested (the sale of inexpensive teaching machines). Then, on graduation, while deciding what to do next, Finer had spent some time with BMP at the president's invitation. "I accepted his offer," Finer said, "and for a month he paid my expenses while I wandered around listening and seeing what was happening."

At this time (June, 1969), BMP included four divisions in the East, Midwest, and West, all in the same line of business. The Western Division, with an old plant at San Jose, California, and a new one just about to start at nearby Sunnyvale, was the original BMP; the other three divisions (Mid-America, Eastern, and Blowco) were formerly independent, smaller concerns which had been acquired in 1967 and 1968. In an industry where transportation charges were a significant element in costs, the geographic dispersal provided by these widely separated plants was believed to give BMP a cost advantage and hence also a long-term sales advantage. In 1971, two of the acquired divisions were still being run by their original managements, and all were being run on a decentralized profit-center basis. Characteristically, both the divisional and the headquarters line executives had grown up with and in the industry. (See Exhibit 1 for a profile of top management personnel.)

---

[1] Disguised industry.

Exhibit 1

BLOW-MOLD PACKERS, INC.
Management Personnel Data

Title	Name	Age	Education	Previous Job Experience
President	Leo Hauptman	45	BS chemistry, Reed College	Research chemist—Gigantic Chemical Co. Vice president Research—National Resin Co. Founder—BMP
Executive vice president and division manager, Eastern Division	Frank Silone	41	High School	Mechanic—Mid-America Plastics Co. Founder-president—Eastern Blow-Molding Co.
Division Manager, Mid-America	J. E. Gardner	58	BS, ME, University of Kansas	Salesman Vice president—Mid-America Plastics Co. President—Mid-America Plastics Co.
Division Manager, Blowco	Frederick Winn	45	BA, Occidental College	Treasurer and Vice president—Blowco
Division Manager, Western	Donald Ferenzi	40	BA, CPA, City College, Los Angeles	Associate—Smith & Wesson, Certified Public Accountants Controller—BMP Treasurer—BMP
Vice president, R&D	Robert Quant	39	BS chemistry, University of Kansas	Chemist—Mid-America Packaging Vice president—Eastern-Molding Corp.
Treasurer	Harold Finer	30	MBA, Stanford University	Associate—Mitch, Lynch & Smith, Certified Public Accountants Director—Corporate Development, BMP

Source: Case writer's interviews.

At headquarters, reporting to BMP's president and founder, Mr. Leo Hauptman, age 45, were a few line executives and a newly hired staff. The exact role the staff should play had not yet been decided when Finer visited the company in the summer of 1969. As his contribution to solving this problem, Finer had suggested that each staff man should define his own objectives. "I noted that the new professionals had no specific tasks, and to compound this, everyone reported to Leo," Finer said. "We had no system of responsibility. After some discussions with me, Leo decided to get each of the corporate staff people to write up his own program of action, stating his priorities, problems, and a time-table. This led to BMP's 'red book' of goals."

While Finer saw some organizational problems during his first month's stay at BMP, looking back on this period as of April, 1971, he said, "What I saw then was success!"

Past growth in sales and profits of roughly 50% a year from 1961 through 1969 had permitted BMP to make acquisitions through exchange of stock on a favorable basis. Although the first three companies acquired had brought dispersal rather than diversification, by 1969 BMP's president felt the time was ripe for invasion of new fields. Hence, at the time Finer joined the company, the search for acquisition prospects took him far away from blow molding. Examined were concerns in such diverse lines as baby foods, soap, wigs, and even plastic credit cards. Commenting on these prospects, Finer later said, "I was apprehensive of certain of the possible purchases on the grounds that there seemed little match between our company and the prospective acquisition, but it was difficult not to find Leo's enthusiasm contagious —even in the case of his most far-out ideas." As things turned out, however, none of them was purchased.

Midway through fiscal 1970, it became clear that BMP would not continue to enjoy the growth in sales and profits which had previously made financing acquisitions through exchange of stock both easy and profitable. (See Exhibits 2 and 3 for relevant financial statements.) Instead, sales appeared to be headed to a level 30% below budget, and profits to a level 35% below. Although Finer continued to look at a few prospects, he later explained, "I became unhappy selling something we didn't have. I knew we didn't have the professional management which I was trying to sell to the companies we were trying to acquire, and I was very unhappy trying to sell it. I decided that my attention should go elsewhere."

In line with this thinking, Finer began to spend his time increasingly in the treasurer's office on control problems. This was an area in which, as a CPA, Finer felt he could be of some help.

As fiscal 1970 soured, changes in organization were effected. Among the first were the creation of the post of executive vice president to coordinate manufacturing policies and the departure of the recently hired corporate sales manager, after his proposals for implementing sales centralization struck other managers as "unrealistic." As the fiscal year drew to its disappointing close in September, several additional changes were made. The corporate staff was disbanded, with 5 of 12 members leaving the company, and 5, apart from Finer and a man in R&D, moving to divisional line positions. The company's treasurer, Mr. Don

Exhibit 2

BLOW-MOLD PACKERS, INC.
Consolidated Balance Sheet as of September 30, 1970
(Dollars in Thousands)

Assets

Current:

Cash and marketable securities	$ 965.6
Accounts receivable (net)	3,817.1
Inventories at lower of cost or market	2,274.5
Other	150.9
Total current assets	$ 7,208.1

Fixed:

Gross fixed assets	$ 7,107.8
Less: accumulated depreciation, etc.	1,649.8
Net fixed assets	$ 5,458.0

Other:

Patents and copyrights (net)	6.4
Other	151.3
Total other assets	$ 157.7
Total assets	$12,823.8

Liabilities

Current:

Accounts payable	$ 2,428.4
Accruals, including taxes payable	357.2
Current portion of long-term debt	202.6
Total current liabilities	$ 2,988.4
Deferred federal income taxes	55.5
Long-term debt (less current portion)	3,439.6
Contingent deferred credit	104.8
Total	$ 3,599.9

Stockholders' equity

Common stock	71.2
Capital in excess of par value and paid-in surplus	4,410.8
Retained earnings	1,753.5
Total stockholders' equity	$ 6,235.5
Total liabilities and stockholders' equity	$12,823.8

Source: Company records.

Ferenzi, was reassigned to head the Western Division, where shake-down problems with the new Sunnyvale plant were causing continued cost and output problems. Into the vacated treasurer's position stepped Hal Finer. "I became treasurer," he said, "because Leo asked me to step in on Don Ferenzi's departure to the Western Division. I had a long-standing interest in control, so I thought I would try it."

Seven months after assuming his new post, against a backdrop of continued declines, Finer raised the issue of implementing the control proposals which he had previously put forward during his first half-

Exhibit 3

BLOW-MOLD PACKERS, INC.
Comparative Consolidated Statement of
Earnings for Years Ending September 30
(Dollars in Thousands)

	1970	1969	1968
Net Sales	$33,210.8	$36,640.4	$27,012.8
Cost of goods sold	30,557.0	33,432.3	24,452.4
Selling, general, and administrative expenses	1,569.1	1,437.5	1,279.5
	$32,126.1	$34,869.8	$25,731.9
Operating income	$ 1,084.7	$ 1,770.6	$ 1,280.9
Other income	39.2	28.2	55.1
	$ 1,123.9	$ 1,798.8	$ 1,336.0
Other deductions	147.8	97.0	59.6
	$ 976.1	$ 1,701.8	$ 1,276.4
Special items*	115.4	—	—
Income before federal income taxes	$ 860.7	$ 1,701.8	$ 1,276.4
Federal income taxes	235.1	764.5	585.5
Net earnings	$ 625.6	$ 937.3	$ 690.9

PERCENTAGE BREAKDOWN

Net Sales	100.0%	100.0%	100.0%
Cost of goods sold	92.0	91.3	90.5
Selling, general, and administrative expenses	4.7	3.9	4.8
	96.7	95.2	95.3
Operating income	3.3	4.8	4.7
Other income	0.1	0.1	0.2
	3.4	4.9	4.9
Other deductions	0.5	0.3	0.2
	2.9	4.6	4.7
Special items*	0.3	—	—
Income before federal income taxes	2.6	4.6	4.7
Federal income taxes	0.7	2.1	2.2
Net earnings	1.9	2.5	2.5

* Start-up costs on new plant plus loss on abandonment of old equipment.
Source: Company records.

year in office. In a memorandum titled, "Some Notes on BMP's Strategy and the Treasurer's Program," he drew attention to the fact that no action had yet been taken on 16 of some 40 suggestions which he and the president had made following their joint budget review of the four divisions early in fiscal 1971. Under the heading, "Taking It Seriously," Finer wrote as follows:

A management control system cannot work unless managers take it seriously. Essentially, this means that the president and his senior colleagues must find that the management control reports are useful and that they must then use these reports and the budget reviews as an important source of information as to what is happening in the company. . . . Top management's belief in the system must be made evident if other individuals are to be motivated to act in the way intended by the system.

Translating these rather philosophical observations into an actual record of our recent budget review only highlights the point at issue: viz. [the number of Presidential] requests for action as of the OCT./NOV. Budget Review in 1970 on which no action had been reported as of APRIL 1971—some six months later.[2]

In the pages that follow, data are provided regarding the environment in which Finer was trying to get his program implemented, as well as on this program itself. These data bear on BMP's leadership and organization, company activities, industry trends, the treasurer's program and its implementation in Finer's first six months, Finer's assessment of what had been accomplished to date and why progress had not been greater, and the steps that he proposed to be taken next.

BMP'S LEADERSHIP AND ORGANIZATION

After founding his company in 1959, Mr. Hauptman indicated he had run it as a one-man show for a number of years. Later, he said, he had come to see the need for a more participative leadership style:

. . . When the company was started, it was purposely designed to function in an autocratic way. There was only one stockholder: me. There was no question about who was going to make a decision. I was answerable to no one but myself. This helped a lot during the early period. I'm sure that if someone had come and asked me why I made a particular decision, I might have thought twice and never accomplished anything.

During this period, the organization was completely subservient. I was able to handle all the tasks that involved decisions. Finally, it outgrew me, and we had to bring in some heavyweights. . . . Don Ferenzi, who is now over at Western, was one of the first such men that we brought in. He had his CPA so we couldn't call him a bookkeeper, and thus was born the controller's office.

From there on it has been one hell of a climb to get this group of characters to evolve into an organization. For a long time our only organization was me, meeting with someone else to solve a crisis.

Finally, after I joined the YPO[3] and got some managerial ideas, we decided to have a meeting and set down some objectives and goals for the company. Twelve of us went away and formulated some goals. At the second corporate meeting we had a psychologist who helped us to discuss our two-person rela-

---

[2] A following passage of the treasurer's "Notes" went on to summarize these neglected items. Eight were suggestions to the Western Division, and are reproduced below as part of the Appendix.

[3] The Young Presidents' Organization, a group whose activities included conducting short-session management training programs.

tionships and the problems of delegation. Soon after that meeting we went public. . . . [Pointing to his attire] That's when I got my vest.

Besides the YPO, there were other influences on the evolution of the president's role-concept and the company structure. Mr. Hauptman continued his account of these as follows:

At the end of 1967 we started our program of acquisition, buying firms in the Midwest and East. Of course, the pattern of purchases we made gave us instant delegation of many responsibilities. But it hasn't solved many of our management problems. . . .

Then, too, Du Pont, as it does with many of its smaller customers, tried to help us to set up a rational set of procedures. Du Pont's help led us to develop our "red book" of organizational problems and goals.

I would say that throughout this period, our aim was to develop an organization like General Motors. That is, an organization with decentralized plants, centralized control, and creativity. General Motors's Sloan captures for me the essence of being a great manager.

.   .   .   .

I honestly believe Sloan had the proper approach: decentralized manufacturing, but with centralized centers for finance, research, sales, and technical services.[4]

President Hauptman went on to describe his own recent effort, in line with the General Motors model he admired, to run the several divisions of his company with the aid of a central headquarters staff. He also gave his views on why this scheme had failed:

Finally, something happened. I got on the kick of building a centralized corporate staff. We got personnel, sales, materials management, engineering, and corporate development staff people in here. You might even say we developed "instant corporitis."

What should have happened was for me to get all of those guys into a room and tell them what they were going to do. Instead, some of our old line people complained that superimposing a corporate staff would cause us to lose talent and versatility in our line divisions. The result was that we went on a decentralized basis with the staff acting as consultants.

Basically, the structure which we were working toward was sound. But we had a few unfortunate things happen. First, there were a few guys on the staff who weren't congruent with corporate goals. They thought that the jungle warfare of office politics was the way to succeed. They were wrong. They are gone. Second, on top of the mismatch of people, we tried to do too much too fast. We had 14 or 15 highly paid and talented people running around without a true sense of direction. With the move to Sunnyvale and the new-plant problem there, we had to cut our goals down.

---

[4] See Alfred P. Sloan, *My Years with General Motors* (Garden City, N.Y.: Doubleday & Co., Inc., 1964.)

As to people in his company and his own role in relation to them, Mr. Hauptman's comments included the following:

One of my main jobs is to protect the values of the organization.

Our managers must develop the desire to learn. I think we have an interesting thing going here with our company!

Our business requires creativity in sales and R&D.

We have to get cross fertilization through sharing of ideas and through crisscrossing people in the organization.

Young guys have survived rather well in our organization; maybe they are more willing to listen than the older experts!

Having personal help such as Hal Finer is useful. They run interference for me. They serve up material for me to make decisions.

I think Hal is more concerned than I am that I get on with it and make a decision about the organization. I have to see how I think the organization should be five years hence.

I think one of the terrible things about myself is my desire for involvement. I have to develop an impersonal approach eventually. I must develop a regularity and a rhythm.

One of our major tasks currently is to get the right kind of information. We are developing an MIS[5] and we will get the information!

You ask about rewards. In my opinion, once top management understands the information they will be getting, the information itself will be a major reward! It will be an important scorecard in the game.

Or course, we will have to come up with an incentive pay scheme. Probably we will have to provide some form of stock incentive.

The real question is, can we both make money and make people a little bit happier?

Managerial Responses. Interviews with management personnel elicited many comments on BMP's organizational environment. Speaking of the president, Finer indicated that his strength lay in creativity rather than in decision implementation through his organization.

I would say that Leo Hauptman, the president, is an intellectual who is capable of dealing with the problems of business at a high level of abstraction. He has a fantastic ability to conceptualize and to visualize new products and new applications. He knows philosophically where he wishes to go, and this is vitally important. But in some sense he tries to wave a magic wand when it comes to implementing the detailed programs necessary to achieve his basic goals through the organization. For example, it is his policy to have a fresh flower

---

[5] Management information system.

on each secretary's desk each Monday morning. With the same type of motion which he makes to have this rather mundane task accomplished, he indicates that he wants to have responsibility accounting. The intentions are often widely separated from the implementation.

There is in the company a lack of systematic relationships. Almost all of the communications are informal and many of them obscure completely the nominal lines of authority.

As to the corporate staff, Finer furnished the following account of why it was hired and how:

About two years ago, Leo thought that he had the solution to some of the problems of the growth of the company. His solution was to "hire a corporate staff." He wanted to staff this organization with systems people. He hired these people out of a belief that the organization would be professionalized. He hoped that the professional education of the staff personnel would help by breathing into the organization some systematic relationships which were desirable in the old organization, but not obtainable.

It is interesting to note that the professionals were all interviewed by psychologists and not by line managers. Leo is oriented toward defining the individual rather than the problems. He doesn't want people around whom he can't understand as people.

Reporting his own early views on the corporate staff, Finer said he had seen it as a difficult assignment for both Leo and the professionals:

There was some question as to how professional were the professionals; there was the problem of bringing 12 staff people in on top of an already unsystematic organization and there was therefore the increasingly worrisome query as to whether the transition could ever be consummated from entrepreneurial to professional. Thus the corporate staff could not possibly learn enough about the business to cope with the old-timers in the organization, and there was not enough of a management information system to give them the formal and numerical tools with which they could work.

Finer believed further that the effort to create a corporate staff, while not wrong in any absolute sense, could have been premature, in view of the importance of the growth and development of the line managers, whose role in the company was critical. In a memorandum drafted by Finer at the president's request and finalized and signed by the president under the title, "Ending 1970–1971 Strategy," this point was put as follows:

The failure of the corporate staff was in my opinion not a failure of concept so much as an overly ambitious *top* management program in circumstances where the company's *middle* management had not been adequately and formally developed at the corporate and divisional level. Thus the creation of the corporate staff was fated to be a premature attempt to bring centralization into being at a time when no systematic and detailed internal procedure for sales or manufacturing financial reporting was available, and at a time when the critical manufacturing problems of efficiency and quality were largely occurring within the local plant (and even line) organization.

While this experience does not diminish my belief in a long-term program to develop a corporate staff. . . . I do believe that at the present time we must emphasize internal management growth within . . . our existing corporate and divisional organization in circumstances where the facts indicate that this is where the problems are.

The idea that inexperience was a problem in the line as well as in the staff was also expressed by BMP's executive vice president, Frank Silone. This officer, who had entered the company through the recently acquired Eastern Division of which he had been the founder-president, had the following to say:

We have got to find the right people to fill the boxes on the organization chart with a minimum amount of confusion. . . . It is unfortunate, but many of the people in responsible positions just don't know their own inadequacies. For example, we have supervisors who just don't know anything about the equipment. When something breaks down, they make sure that they are nowhere around so their own ignorance will not be exposed.

The managers just don't get involved. They let the decisions be left too far down in the organization. Our old corporate staff was unsuccessful because we had mechanical engineers who never had practical experience.

As to the staff, Silone believed that its members had not only been too inexperienced, they had also had a "wrong" conception of their role:

The old staff failed, but not because the divisions were unwilling to co-operate. There has never been a hesitancy among the general managers to work together with the staff people. I have heard that there was. This is foolish. The general managers have too much to do, and they don't have enough staff people within their own groups to accomplish the tasks.

What did happen was that we got staff groups who were inexperienced, ineffective, and hired for the wrong purpose. Starting with this base, the staff people came in to work on areas that had low priority. The general managers just didn't have time to support them. Unless they were going to work in areas that were important to the line people, they should just forget it.

Staff is a supporting function. They should do the things that the line managers don't have time to do or can't do for themselves.

Another headquarters executive expressed the view that what was needed throughout BMP was better communication and direction:

Direction from a staff and from a corporate point of view has been almost negligible. In my experience, I have found that you can't have an organization without objectives, directives, reports, and instructions. There has to be communication, both up and down. The failure has been that no one person was available to monitor the organization and make sure that it was given direction.

BMP'S ACTIVITIES

Blow Molding. Blow molding was one of the most recent developments in plastic technology. Using a technique borrowed from the glass industry, the blow molders had developed a relatively inexpensive method of fabricating lightweight, inexpensive bottles, which could be lithographed directly or labeled with gummed labels. The major volume application for blow molding was initially detergent and bleach bottles, but new equipment had been developed to make possible larger products such as automobile gasoline tanks, beer kegs, oil drums, etc. In addition, new formulations for the plastics had been developed, and these had been approved by the Food and Drug Administration (FDA) for use in food and drug containers. Other technical advances, such as the development of a clear, see-through plastic, had allowed the industry to compete successfully for some cosmetic business and other products where it was deemed desirable to have the contents visible.

The actual process of blow molding consists of blowing a thin balloon of molten thermoplastic material against the inside walls of a female mold and chilling it to a rigid solid. This technique offers extremely high production rates and low unit costs.

A typical line producing 32-oz. detergent containers could produce over 10,000 bottles per shift, with four persons employed directly in the fabrication of the bottles. Such an installation would require an investment of from $100,000 to $150,000. Industry sources indicated that additional lines could be added at a slightly lower cost owing to the overlapping of auxiliary equipment. In a completely automated operation such as BMP's, however, where all equipment was tied to a single blow molding machine, capital investment in the factory was roughly proportional to the number of lines required.

BMP was believed to be among the largest of the approximately 250 independent blow molders in the United States. In addition to this group of independents, however, there were approximately 330 blow molding plants which were integrated into the end user's operation, and another 50 blow molders which were owned by large manufacturers of resins.

The independent blow molders such as BMP were equipped to perform a variety of services for their customers. In addition to producing the package, BMP would accept contracts to fill the containers with the end product. In most cases BMP had to label the bottles produced either with paper labels, lithography, or therimage; to store the packages until needed by the marketer; and to make final shipment.

In some special cases where contamination danger was high or a particularly unusual resin was used, the customer supplied the resins employed in fabricating the bottles. In most cases, however, BMP assumed all responsibility for the purchase of raw materials. In addition, in those cases where BMP filled the bottles, it often purchased the materials for and compounded the customer's product. In either event, materials costs represented a high proportion of BMP's sales dollar, as was generally true in blow molding. On the average, BMP realized only 20% more sales income than it paid out in materials charges. With this breakdown of the company's sales dollar in mind, one executive stated, "We are really just a $7 million business. The other $29 million we take into sales is just dollars which we trade between our customers and our suppliers."

Product Lines. The bottles which BMP produced were originally almost all for household items such as detergents and bleaches. Later the company had taken advantage of new formulations to develop clear plastic bottles for shampoos, etc. With the acquisition of the Blowco Company, BMP had become an important supplier to pharmaceutical houses, its lightweight containers taking over a large share of the market for aspirin and stomach-pill bottles, etc. Because some Blowco customers supplied their own resins, materials costs were not so high a portion of total costs as they were in other BMP divisions. Gross margins, too, needed to be higher than in other divisions, to compensate for higher handling costs on the very large number of very small bottles, extra quality controls, and, in some cases, filling of the containers by Blowco.

Sales. In terms of both product applications and customers, BMP's sales were highly concentrated. Thus the five highest-volume applications (bottles for like products of several customers) accounted for two thirds of BMP's sales, with two applications alone accounting for one half. Similarly, the top 10 customers accounted for 45.6% of sales, with the top 3 accounting for 24.1%. The loss of one important customer who had purchased his own blow molding machines had been an important factor in the profit decline of 1970.

In an attempt to mitigate the risk of losing a large account, BMP's president and division managers were actively engaged in maintaining relationships with large current customers and in seeking new ones. For fiscal 1971, BMP had developed five new accounts which were budgeted to yield 16% of sales.

Besides seeking to attract new customers for established applications, BMP also sought to develop new applications and find customers to adopt them. Mr. Hauptman's personal record was a particularly strong one in this area. In the past his new product-application ideas had led to some of BMP's strongest sellers. Company-developed new applications were budgeted to yield 5.6% of total unit sales in 1971. Thus new customers and new applications were expected to contribute almost one fifth of sales in fiscal 1971.

Purchasing and Materials Management.   Although materials costs were passed on, BMP had always sought to make effective use of its considerable purchasing power. Executives claimed and Finer agreed that the purchasing function was well handled, and that every possible advantage was being achieved through present procedures. Besides effective buying, BMP required effective inventory controls. From a sales standpoint it was critical for the company to have on hand materials for prompt delivery of rush orders.

Inventory and shipping requirements in turn placed a premium on efficient warehousing and materials handling. Overheads and indirect labor connected with this function were a charge on BMP and were grouped together as the materials management expense ($570,000 for the first six months of fiscal 1971).

Manufacturing.   Among its four divisions BMP had six plants. These varied from one another in terms of product lines, facilities, and machinery, and so far no effort had been made to standardize their operations. Even within a single plant, variations in the yield of finished goods from raw materials were an important factor. Different resins employed affected yields considerably. In addition, heat, air pressure, and machine speed played important roles. More manageable, but important nonetheless, were operator errors, maintenance, and mechanical downtime.

In addition to other differences, BMP's divisions in fiscal 1971 had different ratios of capacity to sales. Thus, in the first half of the year two of the divisions were looking for more volume. One was oversold. And one, Western, was in the position of having actual sales in excess of rated capacity during the first quarter, while budgeted sales for the year as a whole would be insufficient to fill up the plant—should planned improvements in efficiency actually be achieved. At the end of the second quarter, however, Western's capacity expansion program was lagging behind schedule.

Western's first-half problem with capacity was associated with a problem of high costs. Both problems were, in turn, associated with the new plant at Sunnyvale which had been opened late in 1969. As to why this plant was still having trouble, Finer laid some blame on the way its design was planned. He said:

> Leo believes in people. He let all of those who were potentially involved with the Sunnyvale plant help to design it. The result was that nobody was responsible. Many now are asking, "Who put the lines in an 'S' shape? Why did the costs jump so far?" We don't know the answers to these questions.

Although Western's cost problem at Sunnyvale attracted the most executive attention, Finer emphasized that this was not the only significant cost problem BMP had. Both direct labor and overheads were rising as a percentage of sales in other plants as well. Finer saw this upward movement as an important problem for a company performing a service function for large cost-conscious customers in an industry which, he felt, was becoming increasingly competitive.

INDUSTRY TRENDS

BMP's analysis of industry trends as of early 1971 was expressed in a report drafted by Finer and finalized by the president as part of a policy memorandum entitled, "Ending 1970–1971 Corporate Strategy." In part, this went as follows:

> Whilst the demand for our products is increasing and whilst there is evidence for a growing acceptance of the custom molder's role, competition and consolidation amongst the various molders over the last few years have begun to rationalize a new structure for our industry in which only the most efficient will survive.

THE TREASURER'S PROGRAM

On assuming office, Finer realized that his approach to control was going to be different from that of his predecessor, Mr. Ferenzi, who was now head of the Western Division. At least through the "good" year of 1969, Mr. Ferenzi had focused most of his attention on materials costs, since these were some 80% of the total. Mr. Ferenzi had also argued that BMP had no need for a standard cost system, or for cost records on the basis of which the relative efficiency of different line layouts and machines could be compared. Nor did Mr. Ferenzi believe it was worthwhile to try to keep track of the estimated profitability of different applications and package types and sizes. It was more important, he argued, to establish BMP in new fields as they developed than to seek to concentrate company efforts on fields with the highest current estimated payoff.

As far as imposing controls on the divisions was concerned, Mr. Ferenzi had collected reports on the basis of which, he believed, unfavorable trends could be spotted and help given. These reports were not standardized, he said, nor were divisional managers evaluated on the basis of their profit performance. Mr. Ferenzi was sure, however, that divisional managers acted like entrepreneurs and attempted to maximize profit.

In line with his belief that "only the most efficient" would survive as the blow molding industry was "rationalized," Finer had concluded that BMP's old system of controls would no longer suffice for 1971. In his previously cited "Notes," he informed the organization that these accounts "revealed very little about the performance of our factory managers" and "even less [about] our account executives." Furthermore, while the "old system was analytical to the extent that it revealed the profits by plant on a relative basis," any comparison that might be made was "subject to the obligation of the reader to exercise some judgment as to the impact of product mix on plant revenues and costs."

Finer's own program, in contrast with his predecessor's, called for measuring individual performance by a system of "responsibility accounting," for detailed budgets and budget reviews, for collection of additional data on variables "critical to the business," for an "integrated system of reports" designed to help implement the above objectives, and—as a longer-run goal—for development of standard costs, first on a product[6] and then on a process[7] basis.

Responsibility Accounting. The principle of holding executives accountable for their level of performance was one that Finer wished to see applied throughout the company, at least as far down as divisional departmental managers (e.g., divisional managers for sales, production, quality control, engineering, maintenance, etc.). What responsibility accounting was and why it was important, Finer explained to other members of the organization in his previously cited "Notes" as follows:

---

[6] All costs associated with the production of a particular size and shape of container.

[7] Costs collected by type of production activity, i.e., compounding, molding, labeling, etc. These would be useful in understanding the economics of the various parts of the production process.

For management control purposes, a responsibility accounting system is nothing more or less than a way of defining the job assigned to each manager in our organization by providing him with an explicit listing of all the costs and/or revenues for which he is responsible. . . . Each individual manager then knows precisely what his boss expects of him, and, more importantly, knows that . . . superlative efforts on his part will not pass unnoticed. . . .

Holding managers accountable, Finer continued, meant measuring their performance against some yardstick. Since nothing in BMP's old system of accounts adequately served this purpose, this yardstick would at first have to be a manager's best estimate of what he could accomplish. Speaking informally of this approach, Finer said, "It's not analytical, but it seeks to record the promises which the managers make when they take over, and to see how they perform with regard to those promises." In his "Notes" he wrote, "The recommendation proposed here is . . . that a yardstick of good performance be for the time being the achievement of budgeted goals. A corollary of this policy is that managers who consistently fail to meet their promises must be replaced."

Budgets and Budget Reviews. As Finer envisioned his control system, the "promises" the managers made as to what they hoped to achieve would be pulled together into divisional and corporate budgets. Both the targets set and the actual performance against target would be subject to periodic review. Finer would, of course, have a role in this process, along with the president.

Collection of Additional Data. Besides collecting prime financial data for the operating budget and budget reviews, Finer envisioned integrating these data into statistics on critical variables. These variables Finer listed as follows:

1. Manufacturing capacity adjusted for standard downtime versus scheduled production.
2. Standard contribution by line hour by product and plant versus overhead by line hour by plant.
3. Standard contribution by account executive, product (old/new), and customer (old/new).
4. Aged finished goods, raw material, and accounts receivable/payable statistics.

An Integrated System of Accounts. In line with his plans to initiate in BMP such new departures as responsibility accounting, numerical goals, and collection of more detailed data on variables critical to the business, Finer decided that one of his high-priority tasks was to prepare an integrated set of report forms on which managers would be asked to enter the kinds of information required. What would be in these reports, who would fill them out, and where they would be routed were among the issues to be decided.

Standard Costs. Over the longer run, Finer knew he would not be satisfied with a budget that featured estimates based on "promises" from each manager reflecting what each "believed" he could accomplish. Finer thus looked forward to developing "analytical" standards, by which he meant standards derived from analysis of past experience. In line with this intention, standard costs would be developed in two phases, with "first priority" being given to the development of direct labor and direct material job costs, and "second priority" to process costs. To communicate to others in the company why such changes were needed in the accounting system, Finer included in his "Notes" the explanation reproduced as Exhibit 4.

Exhibit 4

BLOW-MOLD PACKERS, INC.
Excerpts from the Treasurer's "Notes" Pertaining to the Need for an Analytical Standard Cost System

. . . The present policy of the treasurer's department . . . has as its aim the establishment of an analytical system of accounting which will yield a formal schedule of standard costs and/or standard revenues for each of our managerial centers of responsibility and for each of our products—and which will in this way supplement the system of responsibility accounting by adding to it such financial and statistical data as will help our managers to analyze their performance as well as communicate it.

I. *First Priority—Job Costing:*

The earliest priority of this program is to set up an accounting system which will determine and allocate the actual usage of raw materials and direct labor by job and which will in this way:
  1. Verify our *actual* raw material process costs on a monthly basis.
  2. Refine the yardstick of good performance for 90% of our costs by:
      a) Enabling and encouraging operating improvements to be made (and demonstrated) on a job-by-job basis.
      b) Allowing valid comparisons of costs to be made on a product-by-product basis as between different plants and different time periods.
      c) Raising questions as to precisely where material wastage and poor labor utilization are occurring on particular products.
  3. Refine the yardstick of good performance for all our account executives [salesmen] by creating a formal schedule of standard contribution dollars based on standard material and labor costs. In this way the company can

Exhibit 4—Continued

break away from its overreliance on the fabricating fee concept (which in any event is contaminated with material price and usage variances) and instead reinforce the responsibility accounting concept which formalizes the separation between the sales (contribution) and the production (cost) functions.

4. Refine the sales strategy of the company by relating it to a formal monthly statement of product (as well as account executive) profitability.

II. *Second Priority—Process Costing:*

The second priority of this program is to correlate such a body of financial and statistical data as will enable us to understand how costs behave as a process (as opposed to a job) and how process inputs can be optimally related to process outputs. This program seeks to help our managers discover the relationships that lie behind economic variables and, for example, seeks to show:

1. How our "fixed" costs vary with output or investment decisions.
2. How standards of improvement can be created for our overhead cost centers.
3. How savings can be created *and traced* as a result of capital investment programs.
4. How the optimum use can be made of our productive capacity through rational sales contracts based on the financial history of given products and given customers.

Source: Treasurer's files.

IMPLEMENTATION OF THE TREASURER'S PROGRAM

Looking back in April, 1971, Finer recalled that he had first gone to work, informally and unofficially, in the treasurer's office during June of the previous year. "By September," he added, "I had a clear idea of what I wanted." Thus, when Finer became treasurer himself, he was able to move quickly to implement several parts of his program. Indeed, he had already been able, in spite of "some resistance," to get the idea of responsibility accounting accepted.

Finer's first official recommendation, made in October, 1970, pertained to his goal of setting up a new integrated system of reports. Readied for presentation to the board when it convened for its December meeting was a 30-page black notebook, containing forms for the different reports that Finer saw as needed by various levels: i.e., by the board itself, by the president, by the executive vice president, by the general manager and by the departmental managers of the divisions. Accompanying these forms was a short introduction explaining the various purposes they served and a one-page diagram indicating where the data would be filled in and where each of the reports would be routed.

Besides for the first time introducing forms on which department heads in each division would record their budgeted and later their actual costs and revenues (if any), Finer made some changes in the operating statements used internally for purposes of control by the corporation and each of its divisions. These changes reflected Finer's conviction that "fabricating fees"—especially as computed in the past (i.e., sales less materials at net)—had received undue attention as measures of divisional performance. For one thing, Finer believed that divisions should be charged with materials not at *net* but at *gross* (the reason being that any trade discounts received were really a function of the whole corporation's size and ability to pay). For another thing, Finer believed that the important measure to watch was not just the fabricating fee, but the fabricating fee *minus* the direct labor costs apt to be incurred in making up each order. To the resulting figure, which he hoped to see used as an important measure of performance, Finer gave the title, "contribution from sales." In essence, the changes he proposed would affect divisional statements as follows:

Old	*New*
Sales	Sales
— Materials costs (net)	— Materials costs (gross)
= Fabricating fee	= Fabricating fee
— Direct labor costs	— Budgeted direct labor†
— Overheads	= Contribution from sales
— Corporate charges*	
= Profit before taxes	— Direct labor variance
	— Overheads
	= Profit before taxes

* No corporate charges would appear under the new setup, since cash discounts and other income would be set against the cost of the headquarters group.

† Figures would reflect management's estimates until standard costs could be developed on an analytical basis.

In addition to affecting the divisional reports by as much as $300,000, the proposed changes emphasized the importance of account executives by breaking out profitability by account executive as well as by plant. As Finer put it, "Plants do not generate sales; we must control the salesmen."

After the new report forms were devised, Finer's next major project, carried out in October and November, was his first divisional budget review. In company with Mr. Hauptman he called on each general manager to examine and discuss each division's forecast for 1971. On returning from these trips, Finer drafted and the president finalized and signed a letter to each manager, summarizing the conclusions reached.

Besides being sent to the officers concerned, these letters were also bound in a black notebook for presentation to the board in December.

In each instance, these letters of review began with the assurance that any comments made, including any that would appear "critical," were made "in good faith" and with the "sole intent" of helping the manager "improve his role." There followed a review of the figures which the manager had submitted. Here attention was directed to any special problems which might reduce the profit below forecasted figures (e.g., inadequate sales in one division, inadequate capacity in another, the impact of downtime and quality control problems on predicted labor costs in a third). Following this analytical section, there came a section headed "Specific Actions to be Taken." Included in this were four to nine proposals per division, of which some comprised subsidiary steps. Winding up each letter was a group of exhibits. Most of these pertained to each division's problems and the actions recommended especially for it, but also included in each letter were the budgeted operating statements that had been presented by all four divisions. (Excerpts from the budget reviews of October–November, 1970, are presented in the Appendix.)

The objective on which Finer indicated he had made least headway during his first six months in office was his project of developing standard job and process costs upon an analytical basis. In connection with this purpose, forms had been developed on which managers were asked to record their current cost estimates and their actual costs in detail, so that variances could be analyzed and more realistic standards developed. Managers, however, saw these forms—at least in their initial versions—as calling for more work than the information on them was worth. One divisional accountant put this point as follows:

We are now on our third cost accounting program since Hal Finer became treasurer. We are gradually coming to an agreement and getting the program down to a level where there is a balance between the usefulness of the information and the time consumed in preparing it. Three months ago I couldn't handle all of the numbers we were supposed to be collecting. For each job we were being asked to collect far more information than we were capable of using. The detail which we were being asked to gather was far too great. No one could use it for every job. The materials quantity usage variances were not useful to me here, and no one in the factory knew how to use them. . . .

Another divisional executive, a manufacturing manager, indicated that he still believed that "feel" and a few figures were the only feasible guides to efficient operations in the kinds of business done by his plant:

I don't find the new system particularly useful yet. As it becomes firmly entrenched and we develop some history and information, I am sure that it will be more useful to me. Right now I rely mainly on some of the numbers and estimates which I have collected to tell me how efficiently we are doing our job. I have been in the industry a long time. Experience plus a few numbers are still the best guide.

The problem of this plant is that we make such a wide range of sizes that it is difficult to set numerical standards. Speed can vary all over the lot. You really have to sense the rhythm of the plant to know if things are slacking off or if they are running properly.

Lack of understanding and cooperation was also a problem, Finer indicated, in making the best use of a relatively high-cost computer ($100,000 a year) that had been installed at the beginning of 1970 in the Western Division to account by skid for the actual movement of Western's materials. Western's general manager, Mr. Ferenzi, "does not know if he wants the computer with all its detail by location and skid," Finer said. Partly for this reason, data inputs into the computer were incomplete. On material used, for example, "The fact was that 30% of the pallet tickets were not getting up to the data-processing center." Under these circumstances, Finer continued, Mr. Ferenzi had decided to take the computer off calculating actual material costs altogether. "Instead, the decision was made to use the computer to calculate theoretical costs based on theoretical usage per the product bill of material. Right now it is just in the process of making these unreal pro formas."

Pursuing the computer issue further in his "Notes," Finer summarized his position as follows:

. . . viewed historically Sunnyvale has become an increasingly worrisome force for those of us who are trying to create a corporatewide system of direct material and labor job costing.

The focus of our present problem centers on Sunnyvale's computer installation, and no doubt there is currently a feeling going around that the treasurer has turned into a data addict who spends his nights kneeling before a programmed prayer wheel in his search to become the electronic-age administrator that he far from looks. Nonetheless, it is true that the computer represents the only viable way to create a job costing system at the Western Division, and it is also true that as yet Western's management has been unable to collect any accurate input for this system in spite of many detailed recommendations as to how this might be done. Put as briefly as possible . . . no progress has been made in correcting inaccurate inventories, maintaining accurate inventories, or in reconciling the various skid tickets which in total make up the material handling system and which in detail can provide the basis for a real-time actual materials cost system.

ASSESSMENT OF PROGRESS TO DATE

With April, 1971, came Finer's second budget review and the first review in which he could compare actual achievements for a six-month period with the budgeted promises that he had asked the division heads to make at the beginning of the current fiscal year. This time, Finer's "Treasurer's Report" assumed the form of an assessment of progress to date. Starting with a rundown on profit prospects for fiscal 1971 as a whole, the review went on to analyze where first-half cost and income factors were getting out of line, not only with the optimistic forecasts made six months before, but also with the record of past achievements. There followed a section on the revised forecasts for the second half of the year, and then a discussion of the implications of these data for BMP's sales and manufacturing policy makers.

As to profit prospects for 1971 as a whole, Finer pointed out that these now appeared headed toward being only $58,000 after taxes—a net reduction of over 90% from what had been expected six months earlier.

Already first-half pretax operating profits for the four operating divisions combined were $628,000 below budget. This variance Finer traced to four major causes: $190,000 represented "standard contribution \dollars" lost through the failure of BMP's manufacturing operations to provide capacity for budgeted volume; $152,000 represented "failure to achieve actual output at budgeted direct labor"; $211,000 represented failure to control overhead costs; and the remaining $74,000 was a variance caused by "failure of BMP corporate sales to deliver budgeted volume where manufacturing capacity was available." One of the graphs in the back of the report (see Exhibit 5) indicated in which divisions these four variances arose. Except in the case of inadequate sales volume, the Western Division proved the major source of unfavorable actual-to-budgeted performance, with the Mid-America Division also making significant additions to variances due to lack of direct labor and overhead controls.

Comparisons of divisional performance in 1971 with 1968 showed

Exhibit 5

BLOW-MOLD PACKERS, INC.
First-Half Variance Analysis, Divisional Performance,
Six Months Ending March 31, 1971

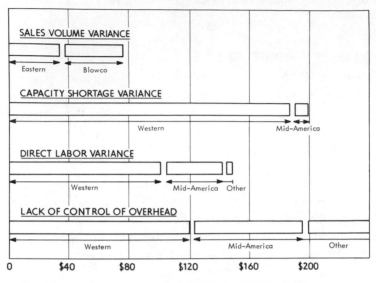

Source: Treasurer's report at the termination of the first half of fiscal 1971.

just how far the divisions had slipped since BMP's last really good year (see Table 1).

Back of these long-term profit declines lay the same difficulties in each division that the variance analyses had shown. Rising overheads were the most at fault in Western and Mid-America, while lower contribution from sales at Eastern reflected mainly a "sales famine." (For a graph of these relationships, see Exhibit 6. For detailed divisional operating statements for the first six months of 1971, see Exhibit 7.)

As to the division heads' revised forecasts for the last six months of

TABLE 1

Year	Western	Mid-America	Eastern	Blowco	Total
1968 pretax profit............	$ 448	$197	$259	$165	$1,069
1971 pretax budgeted profit (loss)....	(920)	47	44	205	(624)
Gap* 1968–71.....................	($1,368)	($150)	($215)	$ 40	($1,693)

* Based on 1971 first-half actual results plus estimated second-half figures; excludes corporate income in both cases.

Exhibit 6

BLOW-MOLD PACKERS, INC.
Historical Analysis—Contribution and Overhead Trends, 1968–71

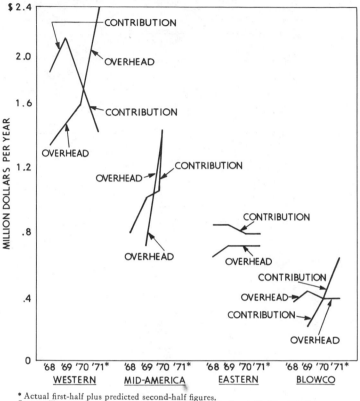

* Actual first-half plus predicted second-half figures.
Source: Treasurer's report as of the termination of the first half of fiscal 1971.

1971, Finer indicated he had made "an attempt to examine the validity of the operating assumptions" which lay behind the newly submitted figures. In this connection he pointed out that "Western has forecast an increase in monthly production rates exceeding, by over 50%, its best output performance of the current fiscal year, and at the same time has forecasted halting its long history of rapidly rising overhead costs." At Blowco, he noted, "Increases in overheads . . . are expected to halt in spite of declining excess capacity." Eastern and Mid-America, in contrast, were not at this time found to be expecting favorable reversals of past trends.

As to the implications of these data for sales and manufacturing

Exhibit 7

BLOW-MOLD PACKERS, INC.

Internal Operating Data, First Half of Fiscal 1971
(Dollars in Thousands)

	Western	Per Cent	Mid-America	Per Cent	Eastern	Per Cent	Blowco	Per Cent	Total	Per Cent
Sales.................	$5,730	100.0	$7,150	100.0	$3,161	100.0	$941	100.0	$16,982	100.0
Materials costs (gross)......	4,638	81.0	6,000	83.9	2,565	81.1	498	52.9	13,701	80.7
Fabricating fee.......	$1,092	19.0	$1,150	16.1	$ 596	18.9	$443	47.1	$ 3,281	19.3
Standard direct labor......	501	8.7	422	5.9	125	4.0	144	15.3	1,192	7.0
Sales expenses.........	65	1.1	52	0.7	48	1.5	21	2.2	185	1.1
Contribution from sales.......	$ 526	9.2	$ 676	9.5	$ 423	13.4	$278	29.6	$ 1,904	11.2
Operating expenses:*										
Manufacturing (including direct labor variance)†	722	12.6	434	6.1	247	7.8	135	14.3	1,539	9.1
Materials management.......	256	4.5	191	2.7	94	3.0	29	3.1	570	3.3
Administrative (plant).......	143	2.5	50	0.7	71	2.2	30	3.1	293	1.7
Total operating expense.......	$1,121	19.6	$ 675	9.5	$ 412	13.0	$194	20.5	$ 2,402	14.1
Operating income (loss).......	(593)	(10.4)	—	—	11	0.4	83	8.9	(498)	(2.9)
Other income (loss) (net)......	—	—	2	0.03	(27)	(0.9)	5	0.5	21	0.1
Divisional income (loss).......	$ (593)	(10.4)	$ 2	0.03	$ (16)	(0.5)	$ 88	9.4	$ (519)	(3.0)
Corporate income.......									375	2.2
Pretax income.......									$ (144)	(0.8)
Provision for taxes (refund).......									90	0.5
Profit (loss) after tax.......									$ (54)	(0.3)

* Included in operating expense were the following costs per division:

	Western	Mid-America	Eastern	Blowco
Indirect and labor..............	$332	$264	$140	$77
Other manufacturing............	566	169	169	82

† Total direct labor variance = $152,100.

Note: Figures fail to add due to rounding.

Source: Treasurer's report at the termination of the first half of fiscal 1971.

policy makers, Finer argued that not industry trends, but BMP's own decisions seemed to be the root of the company's troubles:

Although it is true that the packaging industry and specifically blow molding is getting more competitive, the preceding analysis shows that it is also true that BMP's deteriorating financial position is due as much to BMP's own decisions as it is to any decisions that have been made in the outside world. Thus, while on the one hand, fabricating fees have generally held up, on the other hand, contribution dollars have fallen due to increased direct labor costs in the West, and pretax division costs have risen due to dramatic increases in Western's and Mid-America's overhead burden.

To underscore the point that the company must now take remedial actions, Finer then pointed to the break-even charts which he had prepared for the two divisions where excess overhead charges were a problem. If present cost-income assumptions were valid, Mid-America could do very little better than break even, even if it operated at 100% of its capacity. And Western would need to generate 40% more sales volume than its present contracts to achieve this same result. With expected losses at Western more than wiping out expected divisional profits elsewhere, BMP in 1971 would be dependent on its extradivisional or "corporate" income for the small profit that, overall, the company expected to show.

IMPEDIMENTS TO PROGRESS

At about the same time as Finer wrote his midyear "Treasurer's Report," he wrote his previously quoted "Some Notes on BMP's Strategy and the Treasurer's Program." Here he posed the question why, in view of the profit decline that had started more than 12 months earlier, so little had been done to implement his past proposals for improving control.

Two answers came to mind: management's propensity for not "taking it seriously" and management's propensity to "blame it all on Sunnyvale." Finer called on top managers to set an example that would evidence its belief in controls. And he called on top managers to recognize also that BMP's problems went beyond a single plant:

It is an easy and understandable feeling for BMP's top managers to become preoccupied with the dangers of Sunnyvale and to ascribe all their and our difficulties to this division's lack of success. And it is certainly true that Sunnyvale represents a critical step in the development of our company and a precipitous height from which to fall should this investment become mismanaged. At the same time it must be pointed out that the disappointing financial results of the company are due to a number of factors which are quite independent of Sunnyvale's management—and which include, amongst other trends:

1. Rapidly rising overhead costs at our Mid-America Division.
2. Lack of either a sales strategy or a retrenchment program for our Eastern Division.
3. Insufficient emphasis on cost control at our Blowco Division.
4. Rapidly falling contribution from our sales volume dollar.

The selective degree of inattention which is given to these problems is a dysfunctional force for the company and a demoralizing influence on the efforts of the treasurer's department to establish companywide policies with regard to cost and revenue controls.

PROPOSED STEPS

Both for BMP as an organization and for himself as treasurer, Finer in his "Treasurer's Report" and his "Notes" came up with several proposals as to what should be done next.

For the corporation, Finer's "Report" prescribed as follows:

1. Controls must be more stringently created and applied to BMP's present level of overhead expenditure ($5.5 million *budgeted* in 1971 versus $3.1 million actual 1968), and in this context it is recommended that as a first step no increase in overhead expenditure should be allowed without the authorization of either the president or the treasurer.
2. A decision must be made with regard to consolidating and expanding BMP's Mid-America Division, which is the fastest sales growth division in the company. The increased pretax operating profit potential of this division is substantial (up to $812,000 per annum at present fabricating fee rates, *if* manufacturing capacity here can be planned to equal expected sales levels).
3. Corporate sales must be given the priority responsibility of selling BMP's capacity on the East Coast. A 35% increase in unit sales produced by this division at current fabricating fee levels would add in excess of $312,000 to the pretax income of this division.
4. A definitive and integrated plan must be prepared for the president by corporate sales and Western's operating management to make some sense out of Sunnyvale.

For himself as treasurer, Finer set the following "goals for 1971":

1. To enforce the responsibility accounting system.
2. To establish direct material and labor job costing throughout the company.
3. To improve the budgetary process through the data supplied by 1 and 2.

As further elaborated in his "Notes," Finer's program of action was as follows:

It is the treasurer's belief that the president must increasingly be able to insist that the budgetary process is effectively carried out and that budgetary instructions are complied with, regardless of the rank or position of those involved. In addition it is the treasurer's position that the president will shortly have to lay down a policy with regard to the implementation of the various forms of analytical accounting that have been described in the preceding pages.

This program of action proposed by the treasurer's department is in support of these objectives and is as follows:

1. Use the May meeting to impress our managers that responsibility accounting and the budgetary process are to be taken seriously.
2. Hire a professional accountant to examine and report on monthly variances wherever and whenever they occur.
3. Use the May meeting to push for managerial programs which will aim to overcome Sunnyvale and non-Sunnyvale weaknesses alike.
4. Use James Albee . . . to implement a corporatewide system for direct material and labor job costing *once* direction has been given by the president as to the nature of the program he requires here.
5. Conduct a financial budget review in August and September, 1971, in preparation for the presentation of the fiscal 1972 budget to the president and the board of directors.

This has perhaps been yet another overelaborate attempt to state my belief that we must now set about strengthening our divisional management teams and strengthening the relationship and understanding between them and a simplified corporate organization which is geared toward financial control as the only viable prelude to greater manufacturing cost reductions, more profitable utilization of our plant capacities, and lusher incentives to those managers who can demonstrate performance excelling standard.

Though prescription is admittedly not the best method of working with others, it is the contention of this writer that we have yet to demonstrate that we can handle more complex approaches to the problem of administration.

Appendix: Blow-Mold Packers, Inc.

EXCERPTS FROM THE 1971 BUDGET REVIEW LETTERS OF OCTOBER AND NOVEMBER 1970

(Drafted by Harold Finer, finalized and signed by Leo Hauptman) To Mr. Fredrick Winn, General Manager, Blowco, Inc.

I. *Review of 1971 Budget Submitted by Blowco, Inc.*

1. *General Comments*

Exhibit A, attached . . . shows that Blowco fully expects to be the Company's second most profitable division in 1971. Specifically, the Blowco budget commits your division to a 100% increase in unit volume . . . with . . . little or no change in indirect expense forecasted. . . . The remainder of this section is directed toward examining the credibility of what is, at first sight, a most ambitious program.

2. *Sales Forecasts*
   a) *Specific drop-outs and vulnerabilities*
     . . . detailed examination of Blowco's sales forecasts reveals certain specific weaknesses in your unit volume program:
       Of the total units forecast, some 20% already looked bad or doubtful.

       Of the remaining units, some 32% are attributable to the sale of . . . a product class still subject to technical and market uncertainties.

       . . . Orders for [the second most important product] have been canceled for the first quarter and . . . this whole program may yet suffer serious delay.
   b) *Lack of overall sales program*
     . . . There is in fact . . . a wide gap between Blowco's list of call priorities and what it, as a division:
       Is able to achieve with the marketing resources budgeted for it— i.e., no increase in selling expenses in spite of a 100% increase in volume now forecasted . . . and
       Has been able to achieve (and is forecasting) in terms of profits and production capabilities for our regular lines.
     These gaps add an atmosphere of incredibility to an already sparsely laid out framework for both future marketing strategy and individual account-call and follow-up procedures.
3. *Production*

Lack of overall production program
Apart from the peaks and valleys indicated by your production plans for fiscal 1971, there seems to be a fundamental lack of production planning at Blowco—a lack of demand for systematic high levels of production at an optimum product mix.

To Mr. J. E. Gardner, General Manager, Mid-America.

I. *Review of 1971 Budget Submitted by Mid-America*
  1. *General Comments*
     . . . Mid-America expects to be the Company's least profitable division . . . in spite of the fact that volume is forecast to increase substantially and . . . that Mid-America can truly be said to have the most favorable product mix of any division in the Company. In view of the seriousness of this fact . . . I intend to devote much of the following . . . notes to examine exactly what is amiss at your division.

  5. *Budgetary Practices*

     As we discussed at the last Executive Operating Committee meeting, a budget is a commitment, and as such, it is neither optimistic nor pessimistic—rather, it is a realistic promise. . . . In this connection I was disappointed to learn that:

> Your departmental budgets were not examined by you in sufficient detail to insure that each manager involved was committed to a plan congruent with the best interests of the company.

.   .   .   .

> Your production capacity (which was overstated) does not in fact match with your sales program, and that quite apart from production capacity your real constraint may well prove to be warehouse space—an item which was not even referred to in your budget.

To Mr. Frank Silone, General Manager, Eastern Division.

I. *Review of 1971 Budget Submitted by Eastern*

1. *General Comments*

. . . shows clearly that . . . Eastern is committed to improve its profit picture. . . . What . . . additionally throws credit on your shoulders are the facts that:

> You delegated the responsibility of preparing the budget. . . .
> Most of the numbers in the budget clearly emanated from the departmental managers who . . . generally took an active part in the budgetary process.
> Red-book objectives were prepared by each individual manager outlining a program of action for self and divisional improvement.
> Your budget contained realistic assumptions; and as such, could be contrasted with the budgets of the other divisions which have all been returned for numerical adjustments.

To Mr. Donald Ferenzi, General Manager, Western Division.

DEAR DON:

Subject: Western Division—Budget Review—28–30 November 1970

This memorandum stems from the discussions which we had last week and from some of the impressions that were reported to me by Frank Silone and Hal Finer. Although some of the comments which follow may appear critical, I would like to emphasize at once that this letter is written in good faith and that, in particular, I do not hold you responsible for the present condition of the Western Division. . . .

I. *Review of 1971 Budget Submitted by the Western Division*

1. *General Comments*

. . . the Western Division presented a budget which reflected its commitment to be the most profitable division in the company. The remainder of this section of these notes is directed towards examining the validity of this commitment.

2. *Production*

The briefest inspection of the Sunnyvale Plant highlights the critical production problems of your division and the impact that these problems are likely to have on your financial results. Summarily, these problems may be listed as:

a) Lack of line running time.
b) Lack of organization.
c) Lack of quality control effectiveness.
d) A carryover of the San Jose housekeeping and safety culture.

a) *Lack of Line Running Time*

. . . To be specific, in your Sunnyvale plant your current rate of line downtime is presently creating direct labor costs per thousand units of 80% above budget.

In your older plant, direct labor costs are currently costing 17% above budget.

. . . The numerical impact of this situation is likely to add $284,000 to your direct labor costs—thereby . . . making your division the lowest instead of the highest contributor to corporate profits.

b) *Lack of Organization*

. . . During our budget review you have seriously questioned the abilities of your

Assistant general manager	Warehouse manager
Quality control manager	M&E manager
Materials management manager	Resin manager
and your controller	

Quite apart from whether or not your feelings are justified, whilst these feelings exist . . . they inhibit the establishment of an organization to cope with your two-plant operation and . . . they also inhibit any rational attempt to analyze your indirect labor budget in terms of those responsible for its increase by $70,000. . . .

c) *Lack of Quality Control Effectiveness*

. . . During the course of our budget review, it became apparent that your division is currently suffering from an outbreak of quality control problems. . . . Perhaps even more disturbing . . . is the fact that there appears to be no systematic reporting procedure . . . by which you, as general manager, can estimate [the] physical and financial effects. . . .

3. *Sales*

Of the unit sales increase forecast for the Western Division, 150% of the total were contributed by account executives outside of the Division, leaving lost ground to be accounted for.

Finally, it should be noted that this lack of marketing aggressiveness arises in circumstances when 1970 was a poor year . . . and where our new Sunnyvale plant may well be at 56% of capacity in the fourth quarter . . . with its extremely high-cost overhead burden.

II. *Specific Action to Be Taken*

Don, as I have already indicated, I am trying to use this budget review, not as a destructive tool but as a constructive method of helping myself (and, I hope, you) to become a better manager. The following decisions are made for this reason only. . . . Specifically, I want you to see to it that:

a) You become familiar with the economic and managerial assumptions that lie behind every material figure in your budget by the time of the next budget review.

b) Frank Silone is brought into an active role in order to help you stabilize the manufacturing organization within your division.

c) You change your Sunnyvale direct labor budget figures to read their current actual rate in the first quarter, $2 less in the second, $2 less in the third, and $2 less in the fourth quarter—which will still be $2 above your present budget. Needless to say, I expect you to at least keep your manufacturing performance within these limits.*

d) You submit a written report to Frank Silone and myself by January 1st recommending the form of organization you propose to adopt at San Jose and at Sunnyvale, and justifying the $70,000 increase in indirect labor charges that your division had budgeted for the coming year.*

e) You prepare a written report to Frank Silone and myself by the end of the second quarter listing the merits and weaknesses of each key manager under your control. Each report should only be presented after discussing its contents with the individual manager concerned, and each report should be accompanied by a recommendation with regard to the manager's eligibility for future promotion and responsibility.*

At the risk of going into too much detail—but at the same time because I believe this topic is of the utmost importance, I will go further and suggest that you:

Spend between one and two hours a week with each of your key managers—using this time both to understand his point of view and to review specific situations which have arisen in his department during the course of the week.

Hold weekly staff meetings along the lines of your memorandum of November 15th.

Make no personnel changes without discussing them with Frank Silone and me.

Keep notes with regard to both the individual and the group meetings which you hold with your managers.

f) You prepare a written report to Frank Silone and myself by the end of the second quarter showing your plans for the line at San Jose and giving economic justification for either transferring it to Sunnyvale or for the dual operation which will result from leaving it at San Jose. In the meantime, please see to it that the San Jose offices and quality control laboratory are cleaned up by the end of the current calendar year.*

g) You create systematic records which account for the financial impact of ineffective quality control. In this regard, I shall want to see quality control statistics on a monthly basis along the lines requested by Mark Simon in connection with his responsibility accounting program.*

h) You appoint a manager who will be responsible for housekeeping and safety procedures and who will have the authority to see that they are implemented.* In this connection, the manager appointed should:

Study our existing safety and housekeeping rules.*

Distribute the DuPont Safety Manual to key managers.*

Devise some kind of competition and prize system which will encourage *all* our employees to participate fully in the program.*

j) You prepare a written report to Frank Silone and myself with regard to this up-coming Union negotiations.*

Whilst you are helping Frank Silone and me in this way, I will try to breathe some new life into our sales program. . . . In the meantime, I want to sincerely thank you for volunteering to help the company in a role which I know will mean plenty of personal anguish for you.

> With kindest personal regards,
> LEO HAUPTMAN

---

* Starred entries denote actions that Finer stated were not yet implemented at the time of his second budget review during April, 1971.

2. Precision Controls, Inc.

In December, 1962, Steven Dietrich, chief executive officer of Precision Controls, Inc., of Los Gatos, California, believed that the biggest problem facing the company was its overhead cost structure. Since 1954 the company had added to its original product line, which consisted of relatively simple electro-mechanical controls, increasingly complex electronic control devices and aerospace components which created additional engineering and technical work. In commenting on the situation, Mr. Dietrich said:

I suspect that the overhead costs in some areas are high, but I want to prove it. Our overhead has inceased to six or seven times direct labor on many of our items. Overhead is hard to control for several reasons. One is that we have $10 million in sales, and for our company the area between $10 and $15 million is an awkward one. We are big enough to need a good accounting facility, standard practices and systems, a relatively strong management group, and other assets of a modern corporation, but these same overhead items, by and large, are capable of handling a much higher level of sales. It takes more overhead now that we are out of the little business stage, but our company needs about $15 million in sales to make the overhead pay.

Another reason is that standard cost accounting is no help in allocating costs among our product lines because it uses overall percentages for allocation. Our 28 product lines are in various stages of development, and we are sure that some of the newer products are taking more of the development and engineering time than the older products, but we just don't know what they really cost. Last July I asked our new controller, Harold Dickenson, to make a complete review of the 28 product lines and determine exact costs for each. We will have his results soon and then we will have facts instead of guesses to evaluate our operation.

The following discussion of the Precision Controls company deals with (1) the operations of the company prior to the accounting review, (2) the details of the accounting review, and (3) the management decisions made following the accounting review.

See Exhibits 1 and 2 for financial data for the years 1952–62.

OPERATIONS OF THE COMPANY PRIOR TO THE ACCOUNTING REVIEW

History. Precision Controls, Inc., had been organized in 1936 by Paul Nelson, a Stanford University professor, and three students to exploit their patented electro-mechanical control devices. The company originally was located in the Palo Alto, California, home of Mr. Nelson, but prior to 1940 it moved to leased quarters in Los Gatos, 20 miles south of Palo Alto. World War II provided a great impetus to the young company. Precision Controls' products were readily adaptable for use in military applications, and the company devoted all its efforts to war production, principally for use in military airplanes. During the war, sales increased to approximately $6 million.

In 1946 Precision Controls, like many other California firms associated with the aircraft industry, faced the problem of adjusting to the peacetime economy. Although the company had developed an engineering and manufacturing proficiency in the mass production of high-quality control devices during the war, it lacked products geared to the lower quality mass commercial market. Early in the postwar period the original owners brought in Steven Dietrich as executive vice president to manage the company during the transition period. Mr. Dietrich had previously been an executive with a major industrial company specializing in electric equipment for civilian and military uses. Under his administration the company began to develop its commercial market. The original products were adapted to a variety of commercial uses and a lower priced control device was added to the product line to give a broader product coverage. During these changes the company did not lower its quality standards but continued to concentrate on quality controls for both the commercial and military markets. It also built a strong distribution system, composed largely of manufacturers' representatives, to handle its products nationally.

With the outbreak of the Korean War the company was prepared to provide quality instruments to the government on short notice for military requirements. Although most of the government work called for aircraft applications of the original electro-mechanical product line, the company also developed several completely electronic control devices for military use. In 1954 Precision Controls hired a market research firm to investigate the company's market. The consultants forecast an eventual decline in the aircraft control applications, which then represented 90% of the company's business. Following the Korean War the company again emphasized commercial applications and concentrated on refining and adapting its electronic controls to the civilian economy. The electronic controls subsequently developed into the company's Division No. 2 products. Precision Controls also began to build a direct sales organization in order to reach the more technically oriented electronic control market.

Exhibit 1

PRECISION CONTROLS, INC.

Income Statements for the Years 1952 to 1962

(Dollars in Thousands)

	1952	1953	1954	1955	1956	1957	1958	1959	1960	1961	1962
Net sales	$6,662	$5,895	$5,680	$7,067	$8,371	$8,923	$8,333	$10,028	$9,715	$10,280	$10,348
Cost of sales	3,313	3,179	2,912	3,379	5,152	5,794	5,369	5,912	5,990	6,451	5,562
Gross profit	$3,349	$2,716	$2,768	$3,688	$3,219	$3,129	$2,964	$ 4,116	$3,725	$ 3,829	$ 4,786
Selling, administrative and general expenses	2,101	1,972	2,030	2,427	2,249	2,587	2,616	2,962	3,043	3,014	4,242
Operating income	$1,248	$ 744	$ 738	$1,261	$ 970	$ 542	$ 348	$ 1,154	$ 682	$ 815	$ 544
Other income	73	68	72	51	86	97	67	24	54	88	146
Other expense (interest)	351	221	261	353	301	218	64	46	56	52	251
Profit before taxes	$ 970	$ 591	$ 549	$ 959	$ 755	$ 421	$ 351	$ 1,132	$ 680	$ 851	$ 439
Taxes	539	208	60	282	299	200	198	622	367	467	237
Net income	$ 431	$ 383	$ 489	$ 677	$ 456	$ 221	$ 153	$ 510	$ 313	$ 384	$ 202

Exhibit 2

PRECISION CONTROLS, INC.

Balance Sheets for the Years Ending December 31, 1952 to 1962

(Dollars in Thousands)

	1952	1953	1954	1955	1956	1957	1958	1959	1960	1961	1962
Cash	$253	$218	$279	$179	$332	$272	$346	$383	$304	$316	$318
U.S. Treasury notes	...	87	38	101	...	...	248	977	977	749	749
Accounts receivable	347	460	447	641	728	707	820	1,117	907	1,166	1,346
Inventory	667	617	585	836	1,072	1,072	1,230	1,527	1,273	1,326	1,588
Prepaid expenses	26	31	30	30	38	41	57	53	108	66	130
Total current assets	$1,293	$1,413	$1,379	$1,787	$2,170	$2,092	$2,701	$4,057	$3,569	$3,623	$3,382
Investment in subsidiary companies	715	794	1,204	1,708	290	330	213	168	211	245	200
Real estate not used	...	...	...	...	41	...	...	...	...	...	...
Net fixed assets	399	422	417	520	616	717	549	596	537	666	1,108
Due from Precision Real Estate Co.	...	...	...	...	...	...	...	...	...	456	475
Patent rights	...	...	...	...	...	...	41	37	30	25	9
Total assets	$2,407	$2,629	$3,000	$4,015	$3,117	$3,139	$3,504	$4,858	$4,347	$5,015	$5,174
Notes payable	...	...	...	...	$375	$375	...	$85	$85	$85	$250
Current installment of long-term debt	...	...	...	...	...	...	...	...	...	...	...
Accounts payable	$102	$59	$83	$177	140	122	$210	335	233	274	220
Payroll taxes payable	40	41	35	44	61	71	135	154	105	110	85
Accrued expenses	301	226	246	282	252	197	191	275	150	250	157
Due to subsidiaries	...	...	...	...	...	...	...	...	...	22	...
Other reserves	...	...	...	...	...	...	...	...	...	...	99
Federal and state taxes due	223	168	69	268	288	163	223	609	181	418	233
Total current liabilities	$666	$494	$433	$771	$1,116	$928	$759	$1,458	$754	$1,159	$1,129
Long-term debt	...	...	...	...	...	...	752	918	836	752	666
Capital stock	375	375	375	375	375	375	375	375	375	375	375
Earned surplus	1,366	1,760	2,192	2,869	1,626*	1,836	1,618	2,107	2,382	2,729	3,004
Total liabilities	$2,407	$2,629	$3,000	$4,015	$3,117	$3,139	$3,504	$4,858	$4,347	$5,015	$5,174

* Investment in subsidiary charged off to surplus.

In 1957–58 the company asked another consulting firm to review Precision Controls and recommend plans for the future direction of the company. The consultants approved of the expansion in the electronic controls field and recommended the development of a broader line of industrial products. They also recommended that the company develop precision components for aerospace applications but that it not endeavor to undertake complete aerospace control systems. The recommendations were never fully adopted, for the company continued to specialize in the measurement and control of only one environmental factor; but the company did hire a new vice president of engineering who directed the company's engineering efforts toward the government's aerospace requirements. This aerospace and systems research work continued as the company's Division No. 3 after the vice president left the company in 1960. During the late 1950's the development of the Division No. 2 and Division No. 3 products took most of Precision's engineering time. The owners believed that investment in the engineering department was an investment in the firm's future growth and at times sacrificed current profit to develop new products.

The company's expanded activities also required additional space. In 1957 Precision Controls leased a three-story building (Plant No. 2) in San Jose, five miles from its original plant. In 1962 it built a modern, climate-controlled, dust-free, two-story plant to replace the four-story frame building that it had leased since 1940 and used as a main plant. The company hoped eventually to expand the new building and consolidate the operations which were presently located in various leased buildings in the area.

Ownership. By 1962 the ownership of the company was divided fairly evenly among five officers: Lester Clark (chairman of the board), Steven Dietrich (president), Paul Nelson (treasurer), John Hurley (director of engineering), and Bill Cole (secretary). Although only Steven Dietrich was active on a full-time basis, each of the owners had an office in the company's main plant and maintained a close interest in company affairs. Mr. Clark visited the office weekly and served as a consultant to the other officers. As one of the company's founders he had a thorough knowledge of the company's technology and through several businessmen's associations he had contacts and a breadth of business experience that were of great value. Mr. Hurley also operated on a part-time basis and provided extensive experience and engineering ability. Mr. Nelson had invented the original product and maintained an active interest in the technical and financial activities of the company. Mr. Cole was on the faculty of a local university and also acted as an engineering consultant. The four semiactive owners had extensive outside interests which required much of their attention. All of the owners were in their early 50's, except Mr. Nelson, who was 65.

The five owners also comprised the board of directors, which met weekly to review the activities of the company. Although the board discussed the full range of company business, including insurance programs, major personnel decisions, and tax and financial policy, Mr. Dietrich described the main interest of the directors as technical rather than economic. "The members of the board are sympathetic to research and have had a lot of fun blazing trails." Although the members of the board reviewed the policies of the company, they left the actual operations to Mr. Dietrich.

Top-Management Organization.   The five men who reported directly to Mr. Dietrich were Harold Dickenson (controller), Jim Moore (vice president of manufacturing), John Stykes (vice president of engineering), Don Hudson (vice president of sales), and Joe Morrell (director of labor relations).

Harold Dickenson had joined the company in 1950. He had previously graduated from college with an accounting degree and had worked for 10 years in the manufacturing department of another company. Until his promotion to controller in 1962 he had been sales service manager. Part of his duties as sales service manager had included preparation of sales forecasts. He had also reviewed the profit from engineering projects suggested by the sales department and had earned a reputation as an advocate of better cost control.

Jim Moore was described by Mr. Dietrich as a "very good man who followed me here. We had worked together prior to joining Precision Controls." Jim supervised, through the division managers, the manufacture of the electro-mechanical controls (Division 1) at the company's new plant and the electronic controls (Division 2) at the company's plant No. 2. Two thirds of the Division 3 products were produced in the facilities of the other divisions and also came under his manufacturing supervision.

John Stykes, vice president of engineering, worked under the supervision of Steven Dietrich in all operating matters; in formulating technical policies and appraising technical approaches to problems he also worked closely with John Hurley. Mr. Stykes had graduated from college with an engineering science degree and had taught for several years before joining Precision Controls in 1950. His department provided engineering support for Divisions 1 and 2 and also operated a separate research group which investigated new product possibilities.

Don Hudson, vice president of sales, had joined Precision Controls in 1953 after graduating from the engineering and business schools of Stanford University. His department provided a direct sales effort for the more complex control devices manufactured in Divisions 2 and 3 and supervised the manufacturers' representatives in the commercial market.

Joe Morrell, the labor relations director, was past retirement age. In addition to acting as director of labor relations he supervised the company's credit department. Mr. Dietrich explained that Joe Morrell's long experience in both fields and the staffing behind him in anticipation of retirement made it possible for him to bridge both functions with considerable effectiveness.

Mr. Dietrich described his direction of subordinates as informal and based to a high degree upon delegation. Each department head was responsible for developing a capital budget and controlling costs within his department, but capital and departmental budgets were consolidated on a companywide basis and were reviewed by the board of directors. In general, the ratio of capital expenditures to depreciation charges was used as a measure of the adequacy of the maintenance of the existing facilities with additional expenditures authorized by the board of directors for economic, technical, or growth reasons where the value of the individual piece of equipment could be proven.

Mr. Dietrich met weekly with his five subordinates and the assistant treasurer as a "Planning Committee." He described the objectives and limitations of the committee as follows:

It is the job of the operating department heads to operate within general policies as laid down by the board of directors or communicated by general management. Committees sometimes can be effective in decision making, but I feel that the real value of these meetings has been to provide a regular reporting session in which we are forced to consider problems of the company as a whole. In return, operating heads are given an opportunity to voice their opinions, to learn more intimately the problems of their associates, and also jointly to arrive at certain guidelines of mutual operation. Effective decisions, however, I believe, are most often handled directly by the line and staff organization functioning with assigned duties and responsibilities and with what I hope is reasonable guidance from the top.

Obviously, in a technical company many matters of a technical nature come to the foreground during planning committee meetings, representing problems or opportunities for the company. However, the meetings are also a vehicle for examining our monthly statements, reviewing business activity in terms of incoming orders, comparing expenditures with budgets, and reviewing person-

nel matters and the host of general problems which come up to any management. Many hours have also been spent over many years in trying to foresee the
future and to modulate the company's policies in terms of changing times.

One officer pointed out that the name "planning committee" for this
group was actually a misnomer. Prior to its formation Mr. Dietrich had
held staff meetings which were attended by department heads and their
subordinates. The new planning committee had been established as a
means of reducing attendance at the staff meetings without hurting the
feelings of the individuals who were excluded rather than to signify a
different purpose. Meetings of the entire staff had been discontinued.

Divisional Organization.   Although the top-management positions
were divided along functional lines, the production and engineering
efforts were separated into three product divisions. Mr. Dietrich explained the divisional organization as follows:

> When we divided the company into divisions, it was as an expedient for
> controlling the operations. We didn't really create the divisions separately; we
> just divided up what we already had. The divisions identify the different kinds of
> businesses that we are in and vary across the spectrum. The industrial products
> of Division 1 require the least engineering time and are the most stable. The
> electronic products of Division 2 require more engineering, and the exotic
> products of Division 3 require the highest engineering content and the fastest
> reaction time. In Division 1, material cost is extremely low as compared with
> Division 2 and often Division 3. Our first effort to get a handle on our costs was
> by identifying these kinds of businesses, segregating them, and treating them as
> separate businesses in manufacturing and operating areas, including engineering.

Exhibits 3, 4, and 5 describe the product lines of the three divisions,
Exhibit 6 indicates the total 1962 company sales and costs by division,
and Exhibits 7, 8, and 9 indicate the sales and cost by product line for
each division as determined by the accounting review.

Division 1.   The electro-mechanical control devices of Division 1
comprised the original products of the company and were based largely
upon the same patented applications developed by the original inventors. They were sold to a wide range of industrial users. The customers
who purchased from this division were basically of two types: the
industrial user, who bought small quantities at the time of installation
of equipment or for replacement, and the original equipment manufacturer, who bought large quantities on a price basis for inclusion in a
variety of equipment ranging from small appliances to aircraft. Prices
varied by quantity purchased to allow the company to compete for the
large quantity business and still cover the cost of the more expensive
small orders.

Exhibit 3

PRECISION CONTROLS, INC.

Product Lines in Division 1

	PRODUCT LINE										
	1	2	3	4	5	6	7	8	9	10	11
Date of introduction......	1936	1948	1949	1946	1951	1955	1954	1954	1954	1936	Various
Approximate price........	$10	$15	$15	$1.75	$13.50	$30	$3.75	$50	$11	$10	(see below)
Type of purchaser......	O.E.M. Commercial	Government	Commercial	O.E.M.	Commercial	Aircraft	Military Electronics	O.E.M. Commercial	Commercial	Commercial	
Type of distribution......	Mfg. Reps.	Direct	Mfg. Reps. & Direct	Mfg. Reps.	Mfg. Reps.	Direct Sales	Mfg. Reps.	Mfg. Reps.	Mfg. Reps.	Mfg. Reps.	
Company evaluation....	Stable	Declining	Stable	Stable	Stable	Declining	Declining	Growing	Stable	Stable	

Comments:

Product #1—The company's original product reaches a wide market and has enjoyed stable sales for many years. The company has patent protection on this product and is presently suing one of the two small competitors that make similar products for patent infringement.

Product #2—A run-out product being used only for replacement parts.

Product #3—Limited by design features to this stable volume. The company is designing a new product which will eventually replace this one. This product has undergone almost yearly major engineering changes over the past 12 years.

Product #4—A low-price but quality instrument which differs from the regular line of more complex products. It is needed to maintain a full line.

Product #5—A special unit of very high quality with a constant limited demand. Competitors sell only low-quality units at one-fourth the price.

Product #6—A special unit designed for aircraft which are no longer manufactured. The company sells only replacement units.

Product #7—A product with wide industrial application which is expected to remain stable for one year and then decline because of changes in industrial design requirements. The company's design efforts with Product 8 and other instruments have contributed to the decline of this product.

Product #8—A widely used product with good growth potential which has just been completely redesigned by the company. The company expects sales of about $600,000 in 1963 without the excessive development, tooling and manufacturing costs of 1962.

Product #9—A special product with limited stable sales.

Product #10—A part used exclusively with Product #1.

Product #11—Includes a variety of replacement parts for other products and sales in foreign countries through licensing agreements.

Exhibit 4

PRECISION CONTROLS, INC.

Product Lines in Division 2

	PRODUCT LINE					
	1	2	3	4	5	6
Date of introduction....................	1959	1959	1960	1961	1961	Various (see below)
Approximate price......	$45	$165	$100	$125	$2,000 & up	
Type of purchaser........	Commercial	Commercial	Aircraft-Military	Commercial	Commercial	
Type of distributor.......	Mfg. Reps.	Mfg. Reps.	Direct	Mfg. Reps.	Mfg. Reps.	
Company evaluation.......	Growing	Growing	Dead	Growing	Declining	

Product #1—The company executives believe that a $1.5 million market exists for this product and its recent modifications and that the company can capture most of that market because of its superior distribution system even though it is competing with a number of electronic firms and enjoys no patent protection. The company expects a 30% growth in 1963.
Product #2—Although not a mass market item the company expects a growth of about 20% in 1963.
Product #3—This item was developed for an aircraft firm which had difficulty selling its planes. No more will probably be sold.
Product #4—Used with Product #1 and should enjoy the same growth potential.
Product #5—This is a system made up of components from the other products in Division 2. It is declining and will probably be replaced by Division 1 products.
Product #6—Composed of parts and miscellaneous sales.

Exhibit 5

PRECISION CONTROLS, INC.
Product Lines in Division 3

	PRODUCT LINE										
	1	2	3	4	5	6	7	8	9	10	11
Date of introduction	1961	1946	1958	1953	1960	1959	1958	1958	1954	1957	
Approximate price	...	$9	$105	$130	$150	$12	$1–$120	$30,000–$50,000	$220	$1–$200	Various (see below)
Type of purchaser	Government	Aircraft	Aircraft	Aircraft	Aircraft	Various	Various	Commercial	Aircraft	Government	
Type of distribution	Direct	Direct	Direct	Direct	Direct	...	...	Mfg. Reps. & Dir.	Direct	Direct	
Company evaluation	Stable	Declining	Uncertain Slight Growth	Static or Declining	Declining Rapidly	Growing	See Below	Growing	Static	Fluctuating	

Product #1—This account represents cost plus fixed fee contracts. About half of this is an open service contract which the company will keep in 1963 but intends eventually to drop because it has not led to the hoped for new products. The other half represents research contracts in the company's area of interest. The company has contracted for equivalent work in 1963.

Product #2—A replacement item which will be needed as long as present aircraft fly. The company has a strong patent position.

Product #3—A combination of instruments replacing Product #2 in newer planes. The company has some patent protection.

Product #4—A high-quality product for a small but competitive market.

Product #5—A product designed primarily for one aircraft manufacturer. Since planes did not sell well a 75% decline is expected in 1963.

Product #6—A component part of Product #5 and of Division #2 products. Although a competitive item, cost problems have been "solved," and the company expects a 33% increase in 1963.

Product #7—This represents sales through cross licensing agreements. The company is turning this business over to its representative and in the future will receive a commission from their efforts.

Product #8—A promising item in the "investment stage." This item represents complete control systems installed and serviced by Precision Controls in large industrial plants. The company hopes for $450,000 sales in 1963 and an eventual market of $700,000 per year with $300,000 additional service contract income. The manufacturers' representatives are finding prospective customers, with sales handled by company salesmen.

Product #9—An item designed for aircraft. Only replacement parts are sold.

Product #10—Replacement parts for aircraft control systems not developed by the company.

Product #11—Represents other small parts sold and engineering service performed.

Exhibit 6

PRECISION CONTROLS, INC.

Sales & Costs by Division—1962

(Dollars in Thousands)

	Division 1	Division 2	Division 3	Total
Sales....................................	$6,050	$1,200	$3,098	$10,348
Costs directly applicable to products:				
Materials.............................	$ 730	$ 368	$ 820	$ 1,918
Direct labor..........................	392	132	208	732
Commissions.........................	446	102	106	654
Other................................	168	22	54	244
Indirect production expense.............	786	80	344	1,210
Division period costs...................	502	202	712	1,416
Corporate period costs:				
Building.............................	314	60	200	574
Engineering..........................	198	184	234	616
General administrative................	300	58	128	486
Selling..............................	424	116	314	854
Total allocated costs...............	$4,260	$1,324	$3,120	$ 8,704
Income after allocated cost................	$1,790	$ (124)	$ (22)	$ 1,644
Nonassignable costs.....................	884	144	356	1,384
Income after total cost..................	$ 906	$ (268)	$ (378)	$ 260
Add:				
Volume variance (to adjust direct costing to accrual basis)................	174	41	69	284
Income per books....................	$1,080	$ (227)	$ (309)	$ 544

Employment Breakdown 12/31/62:	Total	*Production Workers*
Division 1	283	173
Division 2	53	29
Division 3	51	16
Corporate building	38	
Corporate engineering & research	75	
Corporate administration	54	
Corporate selling	77	
	631	

Each of the 11 product lines mechanically measured the same environmental factor. Most of the instruments were also equipped to activate electronic controls when indicated by the mechanical measurements. The product lines ranged widely in size and complexity, depending upon the purpose of their application. Although the price and quality of the instruments generally were higher than those of similar instruments used in mass consumer applications, the Division 1 products had a wide range of industrial uses. They could be varied to serve the purpose of the individual industrial customer by changing the calibration and mountings to fit a particular application. In any single month the company might produce 1,000 different models for 8,000

Exhibit 7

PRECISION CONTROLS, INC.

Division 1 Profit & Loss Statement by Product Line—1962

(Dollars in Thousands)

	PRODUCT LINE											TOTAL
	1	2	3	4	5	6	7	8	9	10	11	
Sales	$3,296	$96	$562	$224	$342	$44	$670	$264	$314	$52	$186	$6,050
Direct product expenses:												
Material cost	$265	$10	$33	$37	$38	$8	$63	$76	$125	$4	$71	$730
Labor cost	190	6	34	22	24	2	54	22	22	4	12	392
Commissions	257	2	34	17	31	1	42	27	28	5	2	446
Other	90	4	11	8	7	1	9	3	3	1	31	168
Total direct product expense	$802	$22	$112	$84	$100	$12	$168	$128	$178	$14	$116	$1,736
Division production expense	359	16	80	40	52	8	99	58	60	8	6	786
Division period costs	176	19	62	20	34	7	52	68	48	6	10	502
Total direct and division costs	$1,337	$57	$254	$144	$186	$27	$319	$254	$286	$28	$132	$3,024
Income contribution after total direct and division costs	$1,959	$39	$308	$80	$156	$17	$351	$10	$28	$24	$54	$3,026
Corporate period costs:												
Building	$147	$6	$28	$14	$24	$3	$40	$29	$18	$3	$2	$314
Engineering	71	4	14	6	4	4	8	70	14		3	198
Selling	206	5	32	16	17	3	54	35	31	8	17	424
Administrative	158	5	22	12	15	2	30	14	19	5	18	300
Total corporate period costs	$582	$20	$96	$48	$60	$12	$132	$148	$82	$16	$40	$1,236
Income contribution after corporate costs	$1,377	$19	$212	$32	$96	$5	$219	($138)	($54)	$8	$14	$1,790
Nonproduct assignable costs ($884,000) net of volume variance to adjust direct costing to books	390	11	46	28	30	2	67	26	41	11	58	710
Operating profit by product per books	$987	$8	$166	$4	$66	$3	$152	($164)	($95)	($3)	($44)	$1,080

Exhibit 8

PRECISION CONTROLS, INC.
Division 2 Profit & Loss Statement by Product Line—1962
(Dollars in Thousands)

	PRODUCT LINE						TOTAL
	1	2	3	4	5	6	
Sales.........................	$567	$270	$6	$136	$137	$84	$1,200
Direct product expenses:							
Materials cost...........	$162	$ 86	$2	$ 42	$ 50	$26	$ 368
Labor cost..............	80	24	...	12	14	2	132
Commissions............	53	28	...	14	6	1	102
Other...................	12	4	...	2	3	1	22
Total direct product expense.........	$307	$142	$2	$ 70	$ 73	$30	$ 624
Division production expense..........	48	18	1	8	3	2	80
Division period costs................	116	44	1	22	11	8	202
Total direct and division costs......	$471	$204	$4	$100	$ 87	$40	$ 906
Income contribution after total direct and division cost...	$ 96	$ 66	$2	$ 36	$ 50	$44	$ 294
Corporate period costs:							
Building................	$ 37	$ 11	$0	$ 6	$ 4	$ 2	$ 60
Engineering............	96	18	2	27	34	7	184
Selling.................	43	37	...	26	2	8	116
Administration..........	28	12	...	5	4	9	58
Total corporate period costs......	$204	$ 78	$2	$ 64	$ 44	$26	$ 418
Income contribution after corporate costs.......	($108)	($ 12)	$0	($ 28)	$ 6	$18	($ 124)
Nonproduct assignable costs ($144,000) net of volume variance to adjust direct costing to books........	36	22	...	11	4	30	103
Operating profit by product per books......	($144)	($ 34)	$0	($ 39)	$ 2	($12)	($ 227)

Exhibit 9

PRECISION CONTROLS, INC.
Division 3 Profit & Loss Statement by Product Line—1962
(Dollars in Thousands)

	PRODUCT LINE											TOTAL
---	1	2	3	4	5	6	7	8	9	10	11	
Sales	$274	$767	$777	$240	$138	$437	$88	$199	$26	$102	$50	$3,098
Direct product expenses:												
Materials cost	$ 84	$115	$179	$ 45	$ 46	$151	$62	$ 66	$14	$ 52	$ 6	$ 820
Labor cost	58	49	45	18	8	18	..	4	2	..	6	208
Commissions	..	23	18	3	2	40	3	15	1	1	..	106
Other	9	29	7	3	1	3	..	1	..	..	1	54
Total direct product expense	$151	$216	$249	$ 69	$ 57	$212	$65	$ 86	$17	$ 53	$13	$1,188
Division production expense	8	106	136	37	7	29	1	7	1	3	9	344
Division period costs	55	73	228	50	26	72	8	172	6	18	4	712
Total direct and division costs	$214	$395	$613	$156	$ 90	$313	$74	$265	$24	$ 74	$26	$2,244
Income contribution after total direct and division cost	$ 60	$372	$164	$ 84	$ 48	$124	$14	($ 66)	$ 2	$ 28	$24	$ 854
Corporate period costs:												
Building	$ 6	$ 45	$ 73	$ 14	$ 6	$ 14	$..	$ 37	$ 2	$ 2	$ 1	$ 200
Engineering	2	25	93	4	22	34	5	36	13	..	..	234
Selling	21	27	151	8	12	44	..	32	2	5	12	314
Administration	11	24	32	8	4	26	1	7	1	5	9	128
Total corporate period costs	$ 40	$121	$349	$ 34	$ 44	$118	$ 6	$112	$18	$ 12	$22	$ 876
Income contribution after corporate costs	$ 20	$251	($185)	$ 50	$ 4	$ 6	$ 8	($178)	($16)	$ 16	$ 2	($ 22)
Nonproduct assignable costs ($368,000) net of volume variance to adjust direct costing to books	13	46	70	13	9	72	6	17	2	11	28	287
Operating profit by product per books	$ 7	$205	($255)	$ 37	($ 5)	($ 66)	$ 2	($195)	($18)	$ 5	($26)	($ 309)

customers from its 11 product lines by varying the components and adding special parts.

All production in Division 1 took place in the company's main building. There were two major stages in the production process— manufacturing and final assembly. The first phase included receiving and storing stock metal, fabricating basic component parts, machining the parts to exact specifications, brazing parts to form subassemblies, painting, and storing the parts until required by the assembly departments on the second floor. The production control department established inventory levels for basic component parts. When a part reached the minimum inventory level it was scheduled for production and the required number cut from the raw stock and turned on the company's 12 automatic screw machines. Although the company's original product line was easily manufactured on the automatic screw machines, the more recent additions to the line and most of the Division 2 products were housed in casings that were more easily produced by die-casting techniques. The company lacked die-casting equipment and was considering investing $25,000 for this type of operation.

After the preliminary work had been completed, the parts were moved to the finishing department, where they were ground to exact specifications, drilled, and brazed together to form finished subassemblies. In the finishing department large production lots were completed on automatic equipment and small lots were finished by hand or semiautomatically. After the relocation of the equipment in the new plant, the department had an over-supply of machines, and workers could move from one machine to another rather than reset the same machine for the various operations; thus both overtime and setup time were temporarily minimized. The operations were highly automated; one punch press combined with an automatic feeder could produce a three months' supply of one small part in one shift. The company hoped to find additional uses for the feeder. At the present time, Mr. Moore stated, the department was working at about 60% of capacity; he did not anticipate a higher capacity in the machining or finishing department during 1963.

After the completion of the subassembly, the parts were placed in inventory until needed in the assembly area on the second floor. The company maintained a raw stock and semifinished inventory of about $1 million. Assembly of the finished products was scheduled by the production control department on the basis of sales orders and past sales experience. Production in the assembly area remained fairly stable;

where possible, the company produced its instruments for inventory and then calibrated them for individual customers as orders were received. Small orders could be processed quickly from finished stock inventory, but large modifications were scheduled into the regular production runs.

The assembly operation was divided into product line areas; the basic product line required about half of the available space. The company had devised numerous control devices of its own to aid in the manufacture and calibration of its products, with the result that the actual assembly process was not a highly skilled operation.

Division 2. Division 2 had been added to the company in 1955 after the company had entered the electrical control field. Products in the electrical division were designed to measure the same conditions as the products in Division 1 but electrically rather than electro-mechanically. The Division 2 products were therefore more complex and more easily adapted to use in extensive control systems.

Except for two parts produced in the main plant, all of the electrical products were manufactured in plant No. 2 which also housed the sales and accounting offices, Division 3, and the office of the executive vice president. The division's engineering department, however, was housed with the Division 1 engineering department in a small building adjacent to the main plant.

Whereas most of the Division 1 products were manufactured from stock, Division 2 was primarily an assembly operation. The division purchased the die-cast housing and the delicate sensing devices for its instruments and assembled them into the final product. While the Division 1 operation was done on an assembly-line basis, the Division 2 operation was on a job-order basis.

The company had encountered difficulty with one particularly sensitive purchased part which was a key component in most of the electronic devices. Much of the activity of the division had been spent in determining how to replace this part without having to recalibrate the instrument. The company finally succeeded in solving this engineering problem and in obtaining a small price reduction in the cost of the part.

Don Hudson, vice president of sales, worked closely with the Division 2 manager. He believed that in addition to a concern for the production and the quality of his items, the manager also understood the sales problems of the line and was of assistance in developing a coordinated marketing and manufacturing effort.

Division 3.   Division 3 could be more accurately described as an engineering capability than as a production division. The only production facility of the division was a small model shop. The "products" of the division included government development contracts, the end result of some of the company's extensive research work, and combinations of the company's more standard products for installation in control systems for military and industrial purposes.

The division consisted of three engineering groups and a manufacturing section plus additional units as required to service particular development contracts. The electro-mechanical and the electronic engineering groups within Division 3 (five engineers and four technicians each) were responsible for applying the company's technology and products in these areas to military and industrial control system applications. Although these groups occasionally re-engineered the standard products for their own use, the re-engineering of the standard products and the special engineering for products in the general industrial line were the responsibility of the Division 1 and 2 engineering sections.

The division's third engineering group, consisting of five engineers and three technicians, worked only on the division's product line No. 8. The company hoped that the development of a complete plantwide control system would eventually become a large outlet for the company's standard products and would also lead to a steady income from service contracts.

Engineering.   The company considered itself engineering oriented, and engineering activities were carried on throughout the organization. The sales and manufacturing staffs consisted largely of engineers. The engineering department, however, included only the activities under the direction of Mr. Stykes, the vice president of engineering. He supervised two groups of engineers. The first group concentrated on the engineering problems of Divisions 1 and 2 products, while the second concentrated on research.

While Mr. Stykes was described by his associates as a researcher and teacher, the chief engineer in charge of Divisions 1 and 2 engineering, Mr. Olson, was pictured as a strong-willed, "hard-nosed," highly competent engineer. Mr. Olson used weekly and monthly project reports to keep track of the engineering projects in his department. These included reports, by project, on the hours spent in engineering and design and reports on the costs of the model shop, the laboratory, and materials. An analysis of the project reports of the engineering department as a whole indicated that activity was evenly divided between support engineering for existing projects, engineering for major customer application, and engineering for adapting present products to new uses.

Mr. Dietrich believed that the company offered engineers several advantages that they could not get in other companies. It not only paid the going rate for engineering talent, but it also offered steady work that was not dependent on government contracts and the advantages of living in a pleasant suburban community.

Sales. Don Hudson, vice president of sales, controlled his department through four sales managers. Three of the sales managers were in charge, respectively, of aerospace programs, international sales, and market development. The fourth sales manager was responsible for the four regional sales managers, a service manager who ran the clerical staff and handled returned instruments, a warehouse manager responsible for shipping, and the four sales engineering teams at headquarters which supported the regional sales departments. Each of the sales engineering teams included a sales engineer and a customer service supervisor.

The four regional sales managers handled direct sales and maintained contacts with the manufacturers' representatives. The company also employed five salesmen; three worked under regional managers and two other salesmen operated out of the main office and covered industrial accounts in California.

The activities of the sales department varied greatly because of the wide range of products it handled. The company believed that one of its greatest assets was its manufacturers' representatives and had spent a great deal of time and effort in providing them with a variety of training courses, including a two-week course at the company plant, to indoctrinate them in the proper sales techniques for the company's products. The company arranged for the representatives to carry products complementary to Precision products so that they could present a more complete and attractive line to their customers. The company also had arrangements with special representatives to cover certain government installations and aircraft companies. The representatives, therefore, in addition to handling the bulk of the commercial sales, sold the other lines of the company, sometimes with the aid of the company salesmen.

The company set up its direct selling organization in the late 1950's because it believed that the representatives did not reach the market which it hoped to enter with its more complex electronic and aerospace equipment. The regional managers and the regional salesmen concentrated their efforts upon locating and selling large accounts in their regions. In selling the services of Division 3 the salesmen usually found the customer and then relied upon the engineers of the division to complete the sale.

Building. In 1954 the company began planning for the new building which a management consulting firm had recommended as part of the company's growth program. The plans were postponed in 1956–57 when the predicted profits failed to materialize and the company underwent some personnel cutbacks, and again delayed in 1958 by the recession. In 1961 the plans were revised and the modern, two-story, atmosphere-controlled building was built in early 1962. The move to the new plant was made during the company's two-week shutdown period in July, 1962. Little new machinery was purchased, since the company had continually modernized its equipment following the Korean War.

The new building was a source of pride to both the executives and the employees of the company. The actual plans, developed over a period of eight years, were designed to overcome the problems that had become evident during 20 years of operating in a four-story plant originally designed as a shoe factory. Although the final decisions had been made by the board of directors, many of the suggestions for the building came from Jim Moore, and he was pleased with the manufacturing engineering in the new building. The company's former plant had required substantial movement of products, which resulted in inefficient operation, particularly in processing the large government orders. As much of this inefficiency as possible had been eliminated in the new plant through the detailed planning efforts of the manufacturing engineering department.

The 106,000-square-foot building was specifically designed to allow an even work flow and to accommodate the special requirements of the firm. It was well lighted, spacious, dust free, climate controlled and contained special, closely controlled work areas for highly sensitive operations. All painting and "dirty" operations were confined to one end of the building; the air conditioning was designed to take air toward the dust rather than away from it. Additional features included automatic shoe cleaners at the entrances, hydraulically operated loading platforms that rose to the height of any truck bed, and a roof sprinkling system to increase the effectiveness of the air conditioning in the summer.

One officer described the building as "an extension of the direction in which we were going." By this he meant that the production line techniques were designed to produce efficiently a large number of high-quality precision electro-mechanical components, while some of the climatically controlled rooms were designed to do the most complicated of electronic subassembly work. The building could be expanded as the requirements of the electronics division warranted; with a small addition and two-shift operation the plant could employ 1,000 production workers. The company did not, however, plan an expansion in the next five years.

The planned capacity of the new building had been based upon the company's sales plus an additional margin based upon the forecast growth of each product line. Mr. Dietrich explained that the move to the new building had resulted in a consolidation of equipment and overcapacity in some departments.

Production in the old building was utter confusion and highly inefficient. When we laid everything out in the new plant, we had more machine tools and other equipment than we needed. We realize that some of the departments are out of balance and have more capacity than is necessary, but we would get very little for the extra equipment if we sold it. We plan to bring the plant into balance through our capital purchasing and replacement policies. We have always done a good job of replacing our equipment and keeping our operations modern so we are not planning on getting rid of anything useful but we are only buying those things that we require. With the eventual growth in sales things will come into balance.

Original estimates of the savings to be gained by producing in the new building were $260,000, but as of the end of 1962 it was doubtful that these savings would be fully realized. Material handling savings had been offset by higher power costs and a 250% rent increase paid to an affiliated company on a sale-leaseback basis. It was hoped that savings would increase to the expected level when work was completed on the office area of the building. In December, 1962, the manufacturing offices and the offices of four of the owners had been moved to the new building. Eventually the company hoped to transfer all headquarters operations to the new plant.

Adjacent to the new plant was a new engineering building housing the engineering staffs of Divisions 1 and 2. Since 1957 the company had also leased three stories of a building five miles away (plant No. 2) where were housed the operations of Division 3, the sales and accounting offices, the vice president of engineering, and the president, who "wanted to be close to the inputs of the operation." He believed that his presence influenced the sales department to hold down its demands on the engineering and production departments. As of December, 1962, the third floor of this building was unoccupied.

THE PRODUCT COST ANALYSIS

In January, 1963, Mr. Dietrich received the results of the detailed product cost analysis prepared by Mr. Dickenson. The results covered the year 1962 and broke down the cost figures into their elements by division and product line according to the company's responsibility accounting and direct costing systems (see Exhibits 6, 7, 8, and 9). In commenting upon the results Mr. Dietrich said:

> The traditional accounting allocates overhead costs by using overall ratios. When you have to multiply labor and material by high rates, it's a problem to identify and get at actual overhead costs. I never believed the accounting results. I knew by feel that certain areas were making money and that we were losing our shirt in others, but we never could get beyond the accounting to identify costs.
>
> Now we have an allocation of costs by time and effort expended that will show the true distortion of our overhead. I can go to the board with facts rather than conjectures.

Mr. Dickenson went on to explain further the importance of the accounting review as follows:

> Under our regular cost accounting procedures we were generating a great deal of cost accounting information, but only about half of the cost could be directly assigned to products. We have a responsibility accounting system which charges salary and the indirect costs of each individual to his superior's account and then distributes the cost to the products, usually on the basis of direct labor dollars. Since we introduced the system, a number of changes have occurred that have tended to distort the results of the monthly product line accounting statements. When the system was initiated, all the company's products bore about the same ratio of labor costs to total costs, and the total company overhead as compared with the labor cost was a relatively low 2½ to 1. Since then the company has started to develop products with differing proportions of direct labor cost and with a great deal more engineering and other overhead cost attached. In 1962 the allocated charges had increased to 8.2 times the direct labor and showed signs of increasing even more; therefore any distortions that we used to have are magnified many times over.

Mr. Dickenson also believed that the use of the same overhead formula in evaluating new products resulted in a distortion of the statements. New product proposals were evaluated on the basis of direct cost plus eight times labor cost compared with the probable sales at the price the market would bear. In selection, those products with low labor costs and with purchased rather than manufactured parts were more attractive regardless of actual overhead costs.

In order to achieve a more realistic picture of the actual costs by product line, Mr. Dickenson began an intensive investigation of the allocated costs. This involved examining in detail all cost records, surveying plant capabilities, and questioning those contributing to the indirect charges to determine the actual projects worked on during the year. Under this procedure many costs which had been allocated were determined exactly and others that had to be allocated were done on more justifiable grounds. In total, 86% of the company's expenses were associated with particular product lines.

EXPLANATION OF ACCOUNTING REVIEW

The results of the accounting review are presented in Exhibits 6, 7, 8, and 9. The accounts for Divisions 1 and 2 were kept on the same basis. The actual manufacturing costs associated with Division 3 were incurred largely in the other two divisions and transferred to Division 3; minor amounts of special items were incurred in the Division 3 model shop. Various company executives gave the following explanations of the accounting entries.

Sales. The sales figure represented the shipments made by the company during the accounting period as a result of orders received by both the company salesmen and the manufacturers' representatives. The representatives carried practically no inventory of company products.

Material Cost. This cost represented the standard cost of the material used during the period. Material variances were minor and were included with the other direct expenses. The quality of materials used during production affected the material cost more than did the quantities consumed. Because of the mechanical nature of the products in Division 1, a wide variety of purchased and manufactured parts with exacting specifications were needed. Decisions to make or buy a part were made by the engineering department during the design of the product.

Direct Labor Cost. Direct labor was entered at the standard costs determined by the manufacturing department. The company considered these standards realistic. The executives were very conscious of direct labor costs and sought to use labor with the greatest possible efficiency. Robert Moore, the manufacturing vice president, believed that some room for improvement still remained in obtaining the maximum productivity from the direct labor.

Commissions. Commissions included only the commissions paid to the 33 manufacturers' representatives throughout the country. Company salesmen were paid on a salary basis and the cost of direct sales and assistance to the manufacturers' representatives was included as part of selling expense. The company was completely satisfied with its representatives. They were encouraged to carry a full line of noncompetitive control devices for sale to industrial users and received the same commission on the Precision Controls products as on other control instruments. The sales department maintained that the representatives' only complaint was that the company had confined its products to one area of the control field.

Other Direct Expenses. This account contained other miscellaneous costs which could be directly assigned to a specific product line, including small amounts of material variance, employee benefits for direct labor personnel, and outside costs associated with the development and production of specific lines.

Indirect Production Expense. This account included costs incurred by the production departments as well as the cost of providing auxiliary services for the production departments. Sixty per cent of this expense was associated directly with production and included the difference between standard and actual direct labor, manufacturing supplies, perishable tools, setup time, overtime premiums, and salaries through the assistant foreman level. These charges were distributed to the product lines on the basis of direct labor costs in the various departments.

The 40% of indirect production expense not associated with the departments consisted of the supplies and salaries of those directly engaged in supporting the departments. The quality control inspectors and toolmakers accounted for most of this cost. Quality control personnel entered into every phase of the company's operations. When bar stock was received, it was checked before storage; when a machine was set up, the first piece of the run and as many more pieces as necessary were inspected. In addition, statistical samples of parts were made to insure quality. Special climate-controlled areas were available for testing, and certain delicate calibrations were made by the quality control personnel. Other charges in this account included stock clerks and shipping clerks and a customer return section. Very few of the instruments were returned, and in half of the cases the return was due to the customer's failure to properly install or read the instrument. In these cases the manufacturers' representative sent an engineer to instruct the customer in the proper use of the instrument.

Division Period Costs.   One fourth of this account represented depreciation, the salaries of factory superintendents and the expense of operating the offices of the division managers. Division managers attempted to coordinate manufacturing and selling operations. Another 16% represented the cost of the methods engineers in the manufacturing engineering department. The remainder represented the salaries and clerical costs of the quality control department, the tool engineering department, factory supervision, and production control (including time study). Management hoped that Division 2 manufacturing cost would decrease with greater volume.

Corporate Period Costs.

1. BUILDING.   Building expenses were allocated to departments on the basis of square feet of floor space used and then were allocated to products according to the historical record of work done. An additional $300,000 charge representing unused space and cafeteria area was designated as "nonassignable cost," of which $175,000 was a nonrecurring item representing the expense of moving into the new building and continuing rental payments on the original four-story, wooden-frame "firetrap" occupied since 1940. This lease expired at the end of 1962.

2. ENGINEERING.   For purposes of product accounting the engineering account included only the engineering activities which were directly associated with the division product lines. The operations of the research department ($190,000) and $98,000 of other engineering work not related to present products were considered nonassignable costs.

Most requests for engineering projects were initiated by the sales department to meet the special requirements of a potential customer. An analysis of the engineering investment during 1958 and 1959 in Division 1 and the sales returns during the period 1958 through 1960 is set out in Table 1.

A similar analysis of engineering expense on Division 2 projects indicated that no sales were made on $130,000 of investment and that the gross profit on other investments had not always reached the estimate.

Following this analysis in early 1961 the company adopted a policy of rejecting customer projects with less than a 10 to 1 return on engineering investment and of rejecting work for Division 2 in excess of $3,000 unless other considerations warranted the investment. Because of the difficulty of estimating the prospective sales of an engineer-

TABLE 1

DIVISION 1 PROJECTS

	Projects with Less than a 10 to 1 Return on Engineering Investment	Projects with a More than 10 to 1 Return on Engineering Investment	Total
Sales (1958 through 1960)............	$284,000	$1,003,000	$1,287,000
Cost (material + labor + 2½ times labor)........................	137,000	440,000	577,000
Gross profit.......................	$147,000	$ 563,000	$ 710,000
Engineering investment..............	127,000	16,000	143,000
Average return	1.16 to 1	35.10 to 1	4.97 to 1

TABLE 2

DIVISION 2 PROJECTS

PROJECT	DEVELOPMENT COST	GROSS PROFIT		RETURN
		Estimated	Actual	
A................	$ 652	$ 8,140	$*	0 to 1
B................	11,971	113,400	1,935†	0.2 to 1
C................	13,679	160,000	86,376	6.3 to 1
D................	227	31,000	276	1.2 to 1
E................	331	10,000	4,870	14.7 to 1
F................	1,744	2,700	1,807	1.1 to 1
G................	425	6,700	3,180	7.5 to 1

* $3,000 on order.
† $144,000 on open order.

ing idea and the company's desire to develop products in the electronics area, this policy had not been strictly enforced.

3. SELLING.   The sales department cost figures were developed from the individual reports of department members.

Nonassignable Cost. $1,384,000 of costs could not be assigned to individual products. This amount was composed of the items listed in Table 3.

TABLE 3

NONASSIGNABLE COST

Nonrecurring building cost.............$	175,000
Unassigned space, including cafeteria....	125,000
Research department...................	190,000
Other engineering activities............	98,000
Space advertising.....................	200,000
Other sales activities..................	49,000
Personnel department..................	96,000
Executive after partial distribution of the planning committee............	390,000
Other................................	61,000
Total................................$	$1,384,000

MANAGEMENT DECISIONS FOLLOWING THE ACCOUNTING REVIEW

After receiving the final results of the accounting analysis in January, 1963, Mr. Dietrich used the report as the basis for making significant changes in the operation of the company. He commented:

Once I had the facts on which to base a decision, I went through a reappraisal of the objectives of the company. My personal and corporate desire is to make this a flourishing company. I want to see us in a good solid business position with sound products. The owners have not yet reached a decision on the eventual future of the company but we realize, of course, that a good earnings and growth record will give us more flexibility no matter what we do.

When I had the figures, I went to the board with a cost reduction program and they agreed to it unanimously. The first thing that we did was to knock the hell out of the blue-sky stuff. We eliminated all research and development on items which would not be in production within a reasonable period of time. We had some research with a five- to 10-year payout and nothing for a market but hope. We also eliminated most of our central research staff.

We defined the area where we are successful and hope to concentrate on the electronics and electro-mechanical area and drop the exotic research. We also are limiting our government work. We have done too much engineering on missiles that were canceled after three firings. We have no complaints about the government, but it's a lot of cost and bother to put up with over 40 renegotiation audits. It's hard for us to drop some of the things that we have brought along. Some of our special work is unique and has a lot of people connected with defense activities excited, but it's just not close enough to our main interest.

A third thing that we are going to do is establish new criteria for projects coming in. We are going to be real tough on input. The sales department will have to make an assessment of the opportunity of each project. Then the sales, engineering, and manufacturing people will get together periodically and go over the projects. They should be able to decide on the spot the value of 80% of the projects on a go, no-go basis. The rest will have to have a detailed analysis. We want a return in two years.

We are always looking for weak spots in our operations. Now that we have started on the overhead problem we hope to continue by putting our new accounting procedures on IBM and furnishing the top management with a continuity of effective operating data. Eventually some relaxing of the cutbacks will have to be done but we hope to establish a ratio of overhead to volume and keep within that limit. That should keep our overhead in line with our growth. We also want to start thinking about probing new market areas in depth with our products.

As far as the future is concerned we want to grow to keep up with the economy and we want that growth to be at a profit and on a strong economic footing. I am hoping for a growth of 15% next year, with a gross profit on sales of 10%. Eventually we should have a gross profit of 15% to 18% and a net profit of 7% to 8%. We are looking for a heavy growth in the electronics area of Division 2. The commercial products of Division 1 will also increase, but our more exotic products will become stable or decline. One thing that will help us is the government's emphasis upon conventional weapons and new airplanes. Ten years ago a consultant forecast a decline in aviation business, so we shifted from 90% aviation to 80% commercial; but the recent emphasis on conventional weapons makes the aviation business look good. We are close to the aviation industry and can project sales five years in advance through the experimentation and production stage to the spare parts market; this market now looks promising. We also expect a rapid growth in our commercial market, but new commercial markets are hard to define and forecast. We are now aiming at certain specific markets in the commercial field.

Budgeted Cutbacks. The actual budgeted cutbacks in the 1963 operations of the company involved a two-phase reduction. In the first phase, begun in the fall of 1962, the department heads voluntarily made cuts in their operations and personnel. Following the board of directors' review of the accounting study, a second arbitrary cut of $150,000 each was made in the projected budget of the sales and engineering departments. Although the department heads were allowed to make the cuts as they pleased within their departments, they were told of the directors' general decision to eliminate the exotic ventures from the budget. The total voluntary and compulsory cuts by department follow:

TABLE 4

TOTAL DEPARTMENT CUTS

Manufacturing	$180,000
Sales	150,000
Accounting	70,000
Engineering	175,000
	$575,000

In January, 1962, the company had 725 employees. During 1962 it reduced its employment to 631, largely through the improvement in manufacturing methods in the new building and a reduction in the accounting department. Phase two of the cutback further reduced employment to 600 by eliminating higher priced positions in the engineering and sales departments. After the cuts had been made, the various department heads commented on the new policy and its effect upon the future operations of the company.

Engineering. John Stykes commented:

Understanding the significance of the cutback requires an understanding of the company itself. This is a technically oriented company in a peculiar sort of way. Mr. Nelson, the treasurer, originated the product. The other four owners are extremely creative engineers. They are so creative that their creativity cannot help but spread beyond the company's area of interest. Technically we have almost an academic climate. The owners have tried to resist the technical enthusiasm but have never been able to resist it 100%. It's a cliche in this company that our activities are spread too thin and the criticism starts with engineering. A director will talk to an engineer at lunch about a problem and sometime later the engineer will put a new gadget on the director's desk. They will be fascinated by it and have difficulty understanding why everyone won't want it, but the sales people won't know what to do with it because it doesn't fit into the product line.

The owners are all close to the company, and each has his special interest. These interests have created ambivalence. Emotionally, the owners want to try new, exotic things that cost money, but when they do they are brought up short by the P.&L. figures. That's why the cuts in the engineering budget don't hurt the department and may have made it stronger. The morale certainly has improved, for the people in the department know that at last the owners have made a decision. Even some of the people who left were happy to see the decision.

We made the biggest cut in the research and development department. Over the years this department has developed from a director's interest facility into a very sophisticated engineering operation. Most of its original work was in the glamour areas like aircraft and other big deals that the directors and the organization were interested in. When it looked as though the aircraft market was declining, the company brought in a new vice president of engineering who urged the company to "get exotic." Under his direction the research department increased its aerospace efforts and developed a strong scientific capability. In 1960 he resigned and we were left with a crippled industrial effort. We kidded ourselves along and tried to develop products out of this work, but we were going in all directions at once.

Now we are concentrating again on the industrial line. The engineering department has eliminated the exotic research, and that allows the other departments the opportunity to eliminate the personnel that had been established to handle these items. That doesn't mean that we have stopped all of our research and development, but we are concentrating on the items that are close to the production stage for commercial sale. We are quite encouraged about three items in particular.

The first of these is a new low-cost controller which is an attempt to extend the electronic products into the low-price field—low for us, that is. [Included in Product Line 1, Division 2.] It will still not be as low as some of the competitive controls, but it will be a low-price quality control that will be the Ford of our line. It should be ready for production in four months, and the sales people think that it will sell about 10,000 units per month.

Another product that we are working on is a special application for the textile industry that should be ready for production in about 10 months. We are also working on a new concept for the electro-mechanical line that will change the original concept of the product and make it more adaptable to a wider range of business applications. The preliminary work has been completed, to a large extent, and we have added one adaptation of it to the product line.

While we terminated most of the R.&D. people, we did hire a new research engineer with a lot of practical experience and some patents in our area of control instruments. Whereas many of our new controls call for die-casting which we cannot do ourselves, his interest is in the type of control that can be made on our screw machines. He is doing work now in a new area which we hope to develop.

In selecting the areas for engineering we are now much more under the guidance of the sales department. That's why my office is here with the sales people rather than in the engineering department. We and the manufacturing people make an estimate of the cost of developing an application and the sales people give us practically all of our guidance. Most of our present work is for a particular industry that the sales people have selected, such as the packaging industry, the textile industry, or the frozen food industry. We used to have a new products committee composed of the chief engineers, the division managers, the sales coordinators, and the top people from sales and engineering, but that was stopped last December when we shifted emphasis to increasing sales for our present products.

The elimination of the nonessentials in the engineering department has not solved all of our problems. Probably the biggest problem in the company is making Division 3 work. The new approach has placed the financial responsibility for developing its products in the hands of the division instead of spreading it among the total activities of the company, which is an improvement, but the division still has not shown the ability to sell its service and product. The sales department is still separate from the activities of the division, and the service must be sold by the division engineers.

Another problem is product direction, which has a psychological effect upon the engineers in the department. An engineer likes to work on something that is important and that has a chance of development. The directors have always been good about talking to the engineers and keeping them interested in the projects, but the directors have never talked about where the company was going. There is an iron curtain there that you just can't talk about. The directors give no indication about the possibility of going public or selling out. If the company stays as it is, there are great advantages to the engineers. Although the wages are a little lower than those paid by the electronics firms in the city, this is a better place to work and has a friendly atmosphere. We are the highest paying industry in a small town where all the people have roots and are a part of the community. We are not a high-pressure business like some of the government contract firms where the people have to put in seven days a week. Maybe this is not the kind of place that can keep highly skilled engineers who are extremely ambitious in terms of technical competence or business success, but we offer decent employment and a sense of being wanted.

Sales. In discussing the reductions in the sales department, Don Hudson, vice president of sales, said that the reduction in his budget had eliminated the development of future programs for the company. His statement was:

The biggest cut came in our market development section. The market development section includes the advertising, product planning, market research, and sales analysis functions. We kept our advertising man and gave him the job that was formerly handled by a technical publicity agency. We eliminated the product planning section and the sales analysis section, and for the time being we are also doing without the market research section, but I hope to fill that position as soon as I can get the money. Basically we have taken the attitude that we have five years of product direction mapped out for us and we are concentrating on selling our present products.

We had been using advance promotion for our new products; we are eliminating most of that and all aerospace advertising. We also have cut out all of the aircraft advertising, have reduced the aircraft section of the home office to one man, and have dropped the sales engineer in Los Angeles who worked with the aircraft industry. The only thing that we are going to do for the aircraft industry is shoot for the big jobs instead of trying to cover the whole field.

One of the other things that we have done to cut expenses is to eliminate the home office training program that we offered to the representatives' salesmen. We are substituting a correspondence course which will allow the salesmen to learn about the products at home. It will take a little time to get it organized, but it will be just as good and will cost a lot less when we get it established. Most of the actual sales force has been maintained. We did have three regional salesmen working with the aircraft industry, but now we have only two. We retained the four regional managers, the two manufacturers' representatives that were on a retainer, and the two local salesmen.

We are still looking for a sales increase during 1963 of about 10% in dollar sales and about 20% in orders received. We can make a fairly good prediction of the amount of the present products that will sell during the year from the number of orders on hand at the beginning of the year. Over the years our sales have been running at the rate of about four times the beginning orders, and we expect that some of the newer products will increase the amount of orders during the year. Division 1 products have doubled over the past five years and we expect them to double in the *next* five years. We have developed a new product that we are not ready to produce that differs radically from our original concept of measurement, and this should provide an increase in sales. It will replace line 3 in Division 1 but will have more growth potential. Since design and testing have not yet been completed, we will not have it field tested until 1964 and in general use until 1966.

I am predicting a 25% yearly increase in the Division 2 products, particularly because of a new product that we will soon bring onto the market. We expect to have production of 10,000 units per month at a sales price of about $15 each. This will in part replace product No. 1 in the electronics line. It will be a quality electronics instrument at a low price. It will be the Ford of our line, but the competition will still undersell us with lower quality.

In Division 3 we are also picking up some new contracts in our area of interest and will pick up sales with our present products, even though we have dropped some of the ideas that we were working on. Much of the market research work was done for the systems line (product No. 8) of Division 3, and although we have stopped our market research work, I hope to be able to start this program again soon.

A big part of the change in the procedures in the last few months is the new policy of increased justification of the engineering work that we do. After dropping the market research group, we have had a difficult time predicting the future of some of the applications that we work on, and I am doing most of it now although it is a very loose thing. I hope as soon as possible to get some help in the market research area.We in the past have been looking for particular markets and trying to develop one market, such as the food packing market. We are now using a factor of 10 times investment in two years to determine which projects to try. Each of the directors also has his own interest in certain markets, and we have tried to fit them in if we could. Mr. Clark is particularly interested in the scientific market for control equipment; Paul Nelson invented the original product and is interested in improving and applying it to more varied industries; John Hurley is interested in systems; Bill Cole is interested in the food industry; and Steve Dietrich has always been fascinated with aircraft. When we cut out the aircraft work, it cut a piece out of Steve.

Our biggest problem is deciding just what our market should be. I think that we should concentrate on our own specialized type of controls from the appliance market up to but not including complete process instrumentation. I feel that our market should include components for complete process systems but that we should not go into the completed systems. Some of the others want to go further to include the smallest appliances, the complete systems, or to expand into the full range of controls.

Manufacturing.   Jim Moore, the manufacturing vice president, took his own steps to reduce the overhead in his department during the first phase of the overhead reduction program. He eliminated the division managers for Divisions 1 and 2 and took over the operations of the divisions himself. He reduced the staff personnel and expected that once the plant was running on a normal basis more efficient operations would permit still further reductions.

Mr. Moore made the following comments on the problems facing the company:

This has always been a most exciting company to work for. We have had our fingers in so many pies and they all have looked so delicious that we have had difficulty deciding which one we are going to sit down and eat. It is difficult to drop any line because almost all of them are promising.

I think that we should charge more for some of the things that we are doing. As a manufacturing man I have a horror about work stoppage, and some of our controls are vital to the operation of a plant. The sales people don't understand this or they would put the price where it belongs—sky high. If we are control experts, let's get paid for it, because we are already taking the risk of a failure. Lately, however, we have done a better job of pricing. We have set a price on small quantities which reflects the additional cost of handling the small order and have established a $20 minimum for them. We also have improved our pricing on special orders.

I think that we need on a companywide basis a sound plan for increasing profit. We should have an overall plan for the company. As far as my own problems are concerned, my immediate problem is the 1963 program. We are trying to reduce cost on a day-to-day basis. We are constantly reviewing our processes and looking for better methods, and we are making economic evaluations of tooling cost and of other manufacturing operations to determine if we should use special tooling. On the die-cast control instruments that you saw we used metal fabricated parts for many years because we didn't have the confidence in ourselves to go ahead and spend the $25,000 necessary to make the parts for less.

Of course we could use volume, but we have just about given up hoping for that rare product which would give us large volume operations. We are concentrating on doing our present work more simply. We have intoduced argon arc welding which allows us to weld without flux, thus producing a better quality instrument at reduced cost. We are also trying to eliminate the secondary operations from the lathes so that the whole operation can be performed at one time. We are standardizing our finishes to reduce the cost of the painting department. Another thing that we are working on is productivity. If the coffee break is supposed to be 10 minutes, we are trying to get it down to 10 minutes. We are trying to get the people to work right up until 3:30 and to move faster on the job. This is mostly a problem of discipline; we have never been really rough around here, so it's a matter of disciplining children. First you tell them, and then when you have to, you punish them.

Accounting. Mr. Dickenson was pleased with the results of his work in implementing the budget changes, and he explained:

I think that the directors now have confidence in the figures. We have been talking about cost for a long time around here, but mostly in generalized terms. Our recent approach of furnishing more detailed data has proven very effective. I know the company can be more profitable on a long-term as well as short-term basis and can obtain a better growth rate with proper controls. Now the question is: Can they keep it up, or when we get a little money in the bank will we go right back to where we were? We had a cutback in 1959, and you can see how effective it was, but look at what happened in the next two years when we relaxed.

The real problem was one of realism. In seeking growth, we tried to carry on too many good things. Meanwhile our government business changed to lower volume orders with higher engineering costs. For commercial work we had to engineer each product individually. About $1 million of our sales each year were re-engineered. Now that we have the necessary information we are trying to be more selective and use better evaluation before taking on projects. When we look at each thing that we are doing, we can decide to reduce cost, increase price, or get out.

As far as next year is concerned, I think that we will definitely be more profitable by the amount that we have cut the budget. Once we set a budgeted figure, we are pretty good at living up to it. But I think that the sales figures that some of the others are talking about are overly optimistic. Remember that I have been making the sales forecast for the past 10 years, and I have never been more than 5% off and usually am much closer than that. My budget, which is based upon products now in production plus the one item that we know will be added, is for $10,973,000 in 1963, with $6,075,000 in Division 1, $1,335,000 in Division 2, and $3,563,000 in Division 3.

3. Business Machines Corporation

IN MARCH, 1963, Stewart P. Saunders had been president of the Business Machines Corporation (BMC) of Trenton, New Jersey, for 19 months. In that time he had restored profitability to the near-bankrupt firm, revamped the executive organization, and made plans for future expansion of the company's operations.

The June 30, 1961, annual report of the BMC indicated a net loss of $986,566 for fiscal 1961 and a negative earned surplus account of $2,929,102. The company had suffered increasing losses in each of the previous four years. Its principal stockholder had tried three different chief executives during that time but still was not satisfied with the results. On September 1, 1961, he hired Stewart Saunders, president of a hospital supply firm and an executive with a reputation for "reviving sick dogs," and gave him complete freedom to revive the company. Between September 1, 1961, and July 30, 1962, the top management of BMC experienced a 100% turnover and lower management experienced extensive changes in personnel. The fiscal year ended June 30, 1962, was the first profitable year of operation since 1957. (See Exhibit 1.)

Although the rejuvenation continued during the last half of 1962 and early 1963, it did not sustain the rate of the previous fiscal year. Mr. Saunders explained that in March, 1963, the company had reached the point it should have reached in September, 1962. He attributed the setback to several unusual occurrences. First, the distributor sales had proved disappointing; second, the company had had a great deal of trouble with a government contract; and finally, in February, 1963, the company was struck by the local union. These developments had diverted much of Mr. Saunders' attention from his primary task of building an organization capable of rapid and profitable growth.

PRODUCT AND COMPETITION

BMC sold three different types of recording equipment: commercial office dictating equipment (70% of sales), long-playing tape recorders (20%), and government contracted equipment (10%). The company

493

Exhibit 1

BUSINESS MACHINES CORPORATION

Statement of Income and Earned Surplus for the Fiscal Years Ending June 30
(Thousands of Dollars)

	1956	1957	1958	1959	1960	1961	1962
Sales and service contracts......	n.a.	n.a.	$3,016	$4,038	$ 4,192	$ 4,037	$ 5,278
Operating costs...............	n.a.	n.a.	3,341	4,284	4,868	4,809	4,779
Depreciation..................	$ 51	$ 57	91	96	112	133	124
Operating profit (loss)........	$ (13)	$ 349	$ (416)	$ (342)	$ (788)	$ (905)	$ 375
Interest expense...............	30	31	71	99	35	82	114
Federal income taxes..........	...	2	(1)	...	...	...	...
Net profit (loss)..............	$ (43)	$ 316	$ (486)	$ (441)	$ (823)	$ (987)	$ 261
Retained earnings at beginning of year...................	(88)	(136)	207	(279)	(725)	(1,548)	(2,929)
Adjustment (primarily the writeoff of patents and development expense)........	(5)	27	...	(5)	...	(394)	(92)
Retained earnings at end of year......................	$(136)	$ 207	$ (279)	$ (725)	$(1,548)	$(2,929)	$(2,760)

n.a. = Not available.
Source: Published reports.

competed with three well-established firms (Dictaphone, Gray, and McGraw-Edison) and one newcomer (IBM) for sales in the office dictation market. Dictaphone, the largest and most competitive of the established companies with 50% of the total market, was BMC's major source of competition. Financial difficulties had made the Gray Company a strong price competitor in competitive bidding, but BMC's executives felt that the BMC Model 7 had basic design advantages over both the Gray Audograph and the McGraw-Edison Ediphone. In December, 1960, IBM entered the office equipment dictating field by purchasing the Pierce Recorder Company and introducing an all-transistorized magnetic belt recording machine. This equipment was distributed by the IBM typewriter salesmen throughout the country. The Ediphone with 15% of the market was second to Dictaphone, with the other companies and foreign competitors sharing the remainder of the market about equally.

Each company offered a full line of dictating and transcribing equipment with accessories. Each company claimed that certain features of its own machine made it superior to those of its competitors. IBM claimed that its magnetic belt could be used "thousands of times" by erasing the message and recording again. The magnetic belt held 14 minutes of recording time. BMC claimed that its equipment had been designed as a total communications system and therefore had advantages over its competitors. Part of this system was the BMC Model 7, which provided a microphone and controls at the executive's desk and the machine next to his secretary's desk to relieve the executive of the bother of servicing the machine. The BMC machine could also be used to record conferences. Mr. Saunders believed that BMC made sales in about 95% of the cases where it demonstrated its equipment in competition with other manufacturers. The machines of each company were competitively priced and sold nationally through a branch or a distributor's sales-service organization.

BMC's 24-hour transverse tape recorder had been developed during the late 1950's for governmental use. Not until 1962 did the company seek to sell its equipment in the commercial market on a large scale. The tape recorder could hold 24 hours of continuous recording on a wide magnetic tape. A time index was preprinted on the tape. The widest application so far had been the use of tape recording devices to replace court recorders. This system was accepted by the Alaska courts and was also used in some courts of lower jurisdiction which previously had not been courts of record. The advantage of this system was that it gave an exact reproduction of the proceedings which did not need to be transcribed unless a case was appealed. The system also had been used successfully in police dispatching offices and was accepted by the FCC as a method of recording radio broadcasts for FCC monitoring. The tape units were also used as component parts of many airplane and communication systems products.

The company had no competitors in the transverse tape recording field who could exactly duplicate the performance of its equipment. Many other companies did have available combinations of more conventional equipment which would provide the same service. However, their equipment was more bulky and did not provide a continuous tape record. BMC intended to equip its plant with a 24-hour recorder and microphones at convenient locations throughout the plant so that workmen could record their starting and stopping times on various job orders. If this system of production control proved successful, BMC felt that it would reduce its own production control costs and would also provide a marketable service to other industrial firms.

Most of the company's government contract work had been done for the Federal Aviation Agency. This work consisted mainly of one large contract for 100 30-channel recorders. These recorders would ultimately be used by airport control towers to record the conversations between the control towers and the pilots in airplanes. Each unit could record 30 conversations at a time.

The FAA contract had been a major source of difficulty for the company. It had been negotiated prior to Mr. Saunders' arrival and called for the completion of the units in February, 1962. In the fall of 1961 it became evident that the company was behind schedule in developing the project, and new engineers were brought in to assist in the development. The technical problems of the contract were not solved until the summer of 1962. During the fall of 1962 the FAA tried to cancel the contract and found fault with the company for failure to follow its specifications. Mr. Saunders spent much of his time in Washington arguing about the specifications and working to retain the contract. He pointed out that some of the minor flaws were the fault of the FAA-approved supplier, that the circuits called for in the specifications were the wrong ones for the unit, and that the government did not need delivery until April, 1963.

Through these efforts the contract was maintained. The company had completed its first unit in March, 1963, and it was undergoing acceptance testing. The company anticipated the delivery of 12 units by April.

Although most of the company's engineering effort between September, 1961, and March, 1963, had been devoted to the FAA project, the company had also been able to improve the design of its basic commercial unit and introduce several new items to the market. One of these items was a combination recorder and slide film projector for use in sales presentations. In the fall of 1961 Mr. Saunders entered into an agreement with a Japanese manufacturer to create BMC of Japan, an affiliate company 50% owned by the American company. The affiliate company produced a small portable dictating and transcribing unit designed for sale through the regular BMC sales outlets. As of March, 1963, sales of these other items were negligible.

HISTORY

1940–1961. The Business Machines Corporation had been incorporated in New Jersey in 1940 to exploit the patents of an inventor, Mr. Rollins. The company's original office dictating machine, marketed in 1940, was a drastic innovation in the dictating equipment field. The BMC machine recorded electronically on a plastic disc while its two competitors, Dictaphone and Edison, recorded acoustically on wax cylinders. Subsequently both competitors started to make electronic equipment, although they continued to use wax cylinders.

During World War II BMC devoted extensive effort to military contracts and the dictating line was not pushed. Following the war the company continued with its original line until 1949, at which time it introduced an improved lightweight machine, "The Century," with a metal, instead of wood, frame and an improved indexing system. This redesigned machine was in response to new machines offered by the Gray Manufacturing Company in 1947 and by Dictaphone and Edison in 1948.

Although improvements had been made in the machine periodically and accessories added, no drastic changes were made between 1949 and 1960. By 1960 profits had vanished and management considered a new line of equipment necessary. The company quickly designed the "System 660" to replace its then current line and scheduled it for production in July. In July, 1960, the company stopped producing the Century and started setting up for the new line, but production problems delayed the final introduction of the line until October. During the summer of 1960 salesmen had no machines to sell and became increasingly dissatisfied. Several large distributors gave notice of canceling their distribution contracts.

By the fall of 1960 the company was producing at a maximum capacity of 2,000 units per month to refill the channels of distribution. By early 1961 it became apparent that the new machine had basic design problems, particularly in the bearing and motor board system. Rework rose sharply and sales declined. In March of 1961 sales were so low that 40% to 50% of the production force had to be laid off.

Between 1949 and 1960 BMC's competitors had improved their products but none had brought out a completely revised product line. The design failures in the 1960 BMC model were caused by a multitude of small problems throughout the system rather than a single major problem. Therefore customers made frequent calls for service and the cost of service calls and rework mounted. Before the problem was solved, the company had replaced parts on every machine produced in the fall of 1960. In July, 1961, an additional 10% of the original production force was laid off because of further declining orders.

September, 1961–June, 1962. On assuming the presidency in September, 1961, Mr. Saunders soon found that the company faced serious problems in all areas of its operations and insufficient managerial talent to cope with them. The first 10 months of his efforts were devoted to working on the most serious of these problems and finding capable men for top-management positions.

He believed that the basic problem of the company was the "attitude of the people." Prior managements had created a "rough union situation" where workers were paid for 100% of a measured day's work while producing at only 30% efficiency. Manufacturing overhead was 360% of standard direct costs. Although the company had a great deal of excess capacity because of declining sales, the company still purchased many component parts for its machines. A defeatist attitude pervaded the sales organization. Because of past design problems the servicemen were overworked and the salesmen found it difficult to sell machines. The engineering department's concern with the BMC machine had placed it behind on several important government contracts. In addition, Mr. Saunders believed that the company was incurring excessive costs through overstaffed office personnel and overvalued auditors and patent attorneys.

Mr. Saunders' first action was to take charge of all check-signing and purchase-order approval in order to control expenses. He also replaced the manufacturing manager in the hope of bringing more efficiency to that operation and personally controlled all hiring within the firm. In November, 1961, it became apparent to Mr. Saunders that neither the

Exhibit 2

BUSINESS MACHINES CORPORATION
Sales and Profit by Quarter
(Thousands of Dollars)

	Sales	Profit (Loss)
Fiscal Year Ending June 30, 1961		
First quarter	$ 840	$(128)
Second quarter	866	(216)
Third quarter	1,236	(304)
Fourth quarter	1,095	(339)
Total	$4,037	$(987)
Fiscal Year Ending June 30, 1962		
First quarter	$ 930	$(165)
Second quarter	1,262	(47)
Third quarter	1,604	118
Fourth quarter	1,482	355
Total	$5,278	$ 261
Fiscal Year Ending June 30, 1963		
First quarter	$1,064	$ 34
Second quarter	1,210	46
January, 1963	306	(33)

Source: Company quarterly reports.

new manufacturing manager nor the general sales manager was achieving the results that he expected. He replaced the new manufacturing manager and personally assumed control of sales. At the same time he hired Allen Parker as director of research and development and charged him with the task of improving the company's engineering capabilities. Through an industrial psychologist and other business contacts he sought other managerial personnel to improve the quality of his own staff while concerning himself primarily with sales and overall corporate problems. In late 1961 he negotiated an arrangement with a Japanese firm for the production and foreign distribution of a lightweight transistorized portable dictating machine. This machine was to be sold through the BMC distribution channels in the United States and through the company's distribution channels in 63 foreign countries.

In February, 1962, Mr. Saunders hired George Shea to accelerate his program of returning the manufacture of component parts to the BMC factory and to handle all the company's purchasing. By June of 1962, the company had purchased equipment to do its own metal stamping, cutting, and screw turning.

In the summer of 1962, Mr. Saunders completed his management reorganization by hiring a new controller (June), a new director of employee relations (July), and a new manufacturing manager (August). In recruiting management and engineering talent the company offered generous salaries. The financial data during this period showed a steady increase in sales and profit (see Exhibit 2).

July, 1962–March, 1963. During the fiscal year 1963 the company continued its development with a permanent top-management organization. Although sales and profits continued to increase, the rate established in 1962 slackened. Some of the trends in labor efficiency registered during the 1962 fiscal year reversed themselves. The company operated under the continued threat of a strike. It sustained a six-day wildcat strike in December, 1961, and a brief strike upon expiration of the contract in July, 1962; it operated without a contract until November. After a labor contract had been obtained and labor efficiency restored, the union again went out on strike in February, 1963. The distributor organization also failed to live up to its previous sales record. The company had to continue to drop established distributors and institute sales branches. Furthermore the FAA contract problems continued to plague the company's engineering staff and took time from other projects. The company had anticipated that the fiscal year 1963 would be a period of cash shortage; this forecast proved accurate. Prior

Exhibit 3

BUSINESS MACHINES CORPORATION

Balance Sheets for the Fiscal Years Ending June 30, 1956, to 1962, and January 31, 1963

(Thousands of Dollars)

	1956	1957	1958	1959	1960	1961	1962	January 31 1963
Assets								
Current assets:								
Cash	$ 167	$ 247	$ 111	$ 100	$ 188	$ 68	$ 92	$ (131)
Receivables (net)	393	467	572	739	952	782	1,224	1,329
Inventories	754	1,265	1,080	1,161	1,787	1,479	2,255	2,540
Prepayments	32	44	31	30	40	33	28	21
Total current assets	$1,346	$2,023	$1,794	$2,030	$2,967	$2,362	$3,599	$3,759
Property, plant and equipment	$ 457	$ 652	$1,359	$1,494	$1,672	$1,586	$1,661	$1,726
Reserve for depreciation	175	203	244	341	411	418	523	598
Net property	$ 282	$ 449	$1,115	$1,153	$1,261	$1,168	$1,138	$1,128
Construction in progress		556	51	57	71	92		
Patents (net)	43	45						
Deferred charges and development expense		107	256	380	398	2		
Tax claims	14	25						
Total assets	$1,685	$3,205	$3,216	$3,620	$4,697	$3,624	$4,737	$4,887
Liabilities								
Current liabilities:								
5½% demand notes payable to bank							$ 701	$1,200
5% convertible notes payable June 1, 1963							120	120
5½% convertible subordinated notes payable June 9, 1963							500	500
5½% convertible subordinated notes payable November 10, 1963								750
Current installment of mortgage and of notes prior to 1961	$ 15	$ 746	$ 251	$ 730	$ 330	$ 30	$ 26	26
Accounts payable and accrued liabilities	656	711	819	945	1,221	867	850	443
Customer service contracts prepaid						242	291	316
Total current liabilities	$ 671	$1,457	$1,070	$1,675	$1,551	$1,139	$2,488	$3,355

Long-term debt:								
6% mortgage note payable August 7, 1968	…	…	275	245	215	185	159	145
5% convertible notes payable June 1, 1963	…	…	700	125	125	125	…	…
5½% convertible subordinated notes payable June 9, 1963	…	…	…	…	500	500	750	…
5½% convertible subordinated note payable November 10, 1963	…	…	…	…	…	750	200	200
5½% convertible subordinated note payable September 15, 1964	…	…	…	…	…	…	…	…
Other notes payable	363	228	137	163	…	…	200	200
Stockholders' equity:								
Common stock	715	1,204	1,204	1,515	2,022	2,022	2,053	2,053
Paid-in surplus	72	109	109	622	1,832	1,832	1,847	1,847
Earned surplus (deficit)	(136)	207	(279)	(725)	(1,548)	(2,929)	(2,760)	(2,713)
Total liabilities	$1,685	$3,205	$3,216	$3,620	$4,697	$3,624	$4,737	$4,887

Notes to the 1962 financial statements:

1. *Demand notes payable*
The 5½% demand notes payable to bank are secured by an assignment of accounts receivable. Subsequent to June 30, 1962, the company borrowed $1 million from a bank under a revolving credit agreement which provides, among other things, for loans up to $1 million for 90 days at 5½% at any time until October 1, 1963. The proceeds of this borrowing have been used to repay outstanding 5½% demand notes and for working capital purposes. (The unsecured loan limit is $1,200,000.)

2. *Patents*
Prior to July 1, 1961, the company followed the policy, for financial statement purposes, of amortizing patent costs over the life of the respective patents. Effective as of July 1, 1961, the company adopted the policy of expensing patent costs as incurred and charged to earned surplus (deficit) the unamortized patent costs at June 30, 1961, amounting to $91,905. This change in policy had no significant effect on the company's financial statements.

3. *Long-term debt*
The notes due June 1, 1963 (included under current liabilities) are convertible into 10,000 shares of common stock at the rate of one share for each $12 of principal amount. The notes due June 9, 1963 (included under current liabilities), November 10, 1963, and September 15, 1964, are subordinated to bank loans and are convertible into 131,817 shares of common stock at the rate of one share for each $11 of principal amount. A total of 141,817 shares of authorized common stock is reserved for the conversion of notes.

4. *Restricted stock option plan*
At June 30, 1962, 44,200 shares of common stock were reserved under options granted to directors, officers, and employees, and 23,800 additional shares were reserved for future grant. Option prices (not less than the fair market price of the stock at dates of grant) range from $9.25 to $19 per share. During the year ended June 30, 1962, options were granted for the purchase of 33,700 shares. Options were exercised during the year for the purchase of 7,500 shares aggregating $41,250.

5. *Federal income taxes*
The company and its subsidiary have a tax loss carryover of approximately $2,476,000 which, under present law, may be applied against future earnings for federal income tax purposes. Unless utilized, a loss carryover of $123,000 will expire on June 30, 1963, $517,000 on June 30, 1964, $915,000 on June 30, 1965, and $921,000 on June 30, 1966.

6. *Contingent liabilities*
The company is contingently liable on assigned retail time payment sales contracts of approximately $151,000. The company is involved in certain legal proceedings in which various claims and counterclaims have been filed. In the opinion of management, claims asserted against the company, if sustained, would have no material effect on the consolidated financial position of the company.

Source: Published reports and company records.

to 1961 the company had made extensive use of convertible notes to finance its losses. A total of $1,320,000 in convertible notes was due for redemption or conversion in June and November, 1963 (see Exhibit 3 for details). During 1962 the company had issued $200,000 in convertible debentures and secured additional working capital by assigning the company's receivables. In January, 1963, the company used the limit of its $1,200,000 line of credit. Through inventory reduction during the strike, however, the company was able to pay back $59,000 by March, 1963. Mr. Saunders expected the convertible debentures to be converted to stock rather than redeemed in cash because the stock price in March, 1963, was $19 per share while the conversion amounts were between $11 and $12 per share. The company's immediate objective was to clean up the subordinated notes so that it could finance future operations through loans and retained earnings.

ORGANIZATION

In late October, 1962, Mr. Saunders said:

I told the board of directors at their last meeting that for the first time I'm beginning to feel enthusiastic about the future of the company. I explained that I meant I had finally found the people that I think can do the job. It will take three or four months before we have eliminated the past problems and can start thinking about current problems, but now we have the organization that can do it. We have a new man by the name of Peter Sharp as manufacturing manager. He is doing a magnificent job. Also we have a new personnel manager, and he is doing an excellent job. Basically, I am still filling the general sales manager's spot, but within the past three weeks I have hired a fellow by the name of Sam Caldwell, who was one of IBM's better regional managers, and he is now field sales manager until he becomes acquainted with the product, with our organization, and with our problems. In engineering, Allen Parker is a fine engineer and administrator but a little weak on follow-through. He doesn't like unpleasantness, no one does; so in those areas I usually have to take over instead of his carrying through as he should. Now that I know his weakness I can watch him. Mike Spadone, our controller, is also coming along nicely.

None of them is on his own as yet. That's why the other two manufacturing managers didn't last; they wanted to take on the full responsibility too soon. I look at successful management like an amoeba. I know what I want and am sure of what is going to be successful. When a new man comes, I take over most of his problems myself and then give him more of the problems as he becomes familiar with the job. I figure that I know the problems better than a new man does, so I give him in writing a list of goals that I want him to carry out when he first gets here. Then, as he gets to know the job, we can revise and change the objectives. Eventually I can pretty much forget about watching him. He will carry out his department objectives and I know he will keep me informed on major problems.

I manage the men here individually. Frankly, I don't believe in meetings. I think they are a waste of time and I think they are just another reason for people. to excuse their responsibilities. I give them a goal and an objective and I expect them to meet it; if they have any problems with their counterpart in another department, I expect them to work them out jointly or come to me. I don't believe in this meeting business or this committee business. I think this is the one thing that has wrecked American companies more than anything else in the last 25 years.

Production. All production was carried on in the company's five-year-old plant at Trenton, New Jersey. The company planned, however, to transfer all production of commercial items to Florida by the spring of 1964. After the production workers showed a marked increase in productivity during the spring of 1962, plans were abandoned to close down and sell the Trenton plant and a revised expansion program was initiated which contemplated the production of government orders and of newly acquired products at Trenton.

The manufacturing operation was divided into three departments. A machining and metalworking department cut the frame for the machine and did machining operations on component parts. The assembly department assembled the commercial machines on an assembly-line basis. The third department was the military department where government equipment was assembled on a job-order basis. The assembly and military departments required no special skill. The company, however, had encountered problems in hiring skilled machinists for the metalworking department because of the announced move to Florida. The severe layoff in July of 1961 had eliminated all employees with less than eight years' seniority.

Upon taking over the manufacturing operations in September, 1961, Mr. Saunders noted two particularly costly deficiencies. First, the company was purchasing many parts which it could manufacture while at the same time it had excess capacity in its own operations. The company was also getting extremely low productivity from its production workers as compared with the measured daywork system used in the plant.[1] Productivity for the major department was at 30% of the rated stand-

---

[1] The measured daywork plan, according to the union contract, measured each employee's daily production against a 100% efficiency rate defined as "the number of production units of consistently required quality which may reasonably be expected from an experienced, first-class operator working at normal and reasonable speed." Standards were set by the employer but subject to the grievance procedure, including final arbitration by a mutually acceptable engineering firm. During the spring of 1962 the company hired an outside engineering firm to review the standards. Their report indicated that the BMC work pace was 50% to 60% of the work pace of other Trenton area plants.

ard; the company had retained its 40 overhead personnel after reducing the work force to half of the original 300 workers in July, 1961.

In the fall of 1961, Mr. Saunders reduced the overhead production personnel from 40 to 6 and brought in a new manufacturing manager to improve productivity and to bring some of the subassembly work back into the plant. When the new man failed to show satisfactory progress he was replaced. Although his replacement made some improvements in the methods and added a shear to the machining department so that the company could cut its own metal frames from stock instead of buying finished metal, he also proved unsatisfactory and in the spring of 1962 was fired. Mr. Saunders took over the production supervision until August, 1962, when he hired Peter Sharp as manufacturing manager.

Under Mr. Saunders' direction productivity in the manufacturing department increased sharply, rising by July to about 92% of the measured daywork standard. Mr. Saunders believed that much of this was done simply by enforcing the union contract. Under the contract the pay of a worker was determined by the percentage of a measured day's work performed. Workers who continually performed below their pay scale were subject to pay cuts or dismissal. When a few workers were dismissed and others cut, the productivity increased. Manufacturing overhead decreased from 360% of standard direct costs to 150% by June, 1962.

Quality control also had been a major production problem. In the fall of 1961, 75% of all units in the commercial line were rejected at final inspection. To remedy this problem the company eliminated the union inspectors and substituted quality assurance engineers to inspect parts on a sample basis during production and on a 100% basis after assembly. It also enforced the provisions of the union contract which called for payment only on the basis of acceptable units produced.

Mr. Saunders also assigned his purchasing agent to investigate several ideas for bringing operations into the plant. The improvements made during the spring included winding the coils for the company's motors, purchasing a centerless grinder and doing the grinding of shafts in the plant, changing the work methods so that the dual winding machine could wind two coils at once, and rearranging the machines so that one man could attend three machines instead of one. During this time he managed the manufacturing operations through daily production meetings with the production control supervisor and the purchasing agent. At these meetings they discussed the day's production, analyzed the results of the previous day and the efficiency reports from accounting, and determined the improvements that could be made in the operations.

In July, 1962, Mr. Saunders believed that the operations had improved to a point where the manufacturing operation could be turned over to another man. Production had increased from 400 to 1,000 units per month without an increase in personnel. Through a placement service he met Peter Sharp, an engineer with 16 years' experience in manufacturing, and hired him to run the operation. Before hiring him, however, Mr. Saunders fired all of the company's production foremen in order to give Mr. Sharp a fresh start and ease the personnel problems.

Mr. Sharp began directing the production activities in September, 1962. He earned the respect of Mr. Saunders through the improvements that he made in the housekeeping and material flow in the plant. Between October, 1962, and January, 1963, however, the efficiency of the workers declined from 90% to 60%. Mr. Saunders told Mr. Sharp of his displeasure with the results and told him to enforce the contract and improve the efficiency. This Mr. Sharp did and the efficiency improved during January (see Exhibit 4).

While the plant was on strike during February, Mr. Sharp, at the

Exhibit 4

BUSINESS MACHINES CORPORATION

*Weekly Worker Efficiency Reports for the Period
October, 1962, to February, 1963*

WEEK ENDING	PER CENT OF MEASURED DAYWORK EFFICIENCY	
	Assembly Department	Machine Department
October 12, 1962.............	91%	87%
October 19, 1962.............	89	91
October 26, 1962.............	81	93
November 2, 1962............	78	103
November 9, 1962............	74	102
November 16, 1962...........	73	93
November 23, 1962...........	73	93
November 30, 1962...........	71	76
December 7, 1962.............	74	90
December 14, 1962............	75	86
December 21, 1962............	75	85
December 28, 1962............	Christmas shutdown	..
January 4, 1963...............	61	66
January 11, 1963..............	69	85
January 18, 1963..............	72	91
January 25, 1963..............	74	104
February 1, 1963..............	78	92

Source: Company records.

insistence of Mr. Saunders, rescheduled the operations of the assembly department and devised a method of reducing the assembly line workers from 10 to 5. Through this and other methods improvements he was able to eliminate about 25 production jobs.

Mr. Saunders was very pleased with Mr. Sharp's progress in the company. In March, 1963, he said: "Peter Sharp has probably come along faster than any of the others. His final lesson in how bad things really were came during the strike when he found that he could cut the production line in half."

Labor Relations. Since 1954, all production workers had been members of the International Brotherhood of Electrical Workers (IBEW). Wages and working conditions were collectively bargained biannually; the most recent contract expired on July 15, 1962. The union contract contained many provisions which were not enforced by management prior to the arrival of Mr. Saunders. The director of labor relations had modified the contract through numerous private agreements with the union officials; these agreements were never reduced to writing. Mr. Saunders' attempts to increase productivity in the fall of 1961 contradicted some of the private agreements but did not violate the contract. During the fall of 1961, the union members became increasingly resentful of management's policies and initiated a large number of grievances against management's actions. The resentment culminated in a wildcat strike in December, allegedly in protest of management's replacement of the union inspectors with quality assurance engineers. Management asserted that it had upgraded the jobs beyond the union's jurisdiction and the union agreed to return to work and settle the issue during the July negotiations. The union officials disclaimed all responsibility for the strike.

Mr. Saunders believed that labor relations had been one of the basic problems of the company before his arrival.

Management sat back on its dignity and let the union run the company. The union contract was never enforced. The contract calls for the workers to be paid on the basis of their percentage of production as compared with a measured day's work. They were not making production but they were still getting the top pay. A lot of the fault rests with the personnel manager, who was straddling the fence. He wasn't enforcing management's part of the contract and was making secret agreements with the union. I got rid of him and brought in Joe Ventrella as personnel manager. Joe's problem now is to win the respect of the union. So far he has done a pretty good job.

During the contract negotiations, management sought to eliminate from the contract a number of provisions which it felt were economically unreasonable. Mr. Saunders believed that the former management had engaged in "a giveaway program" by including in the contract such provisions as a day off with pay for the death of a relative as far removed as second cousin; a bumping plan whereby a man could not be furloughed for half a day without changing job assignments throughout the plant; and a vacation payment plan which provided payment on a sliding scale up to 8% of a year's pay for a worker with 20 years' seniority. Mr. Saunders also believed that overall wage scales were too high, particularly in light of the fact that the production workers were not meeting the efficiency rates required by the measured daywork plan.

No settlement was reached on July 15. After a brief walkout, both parties agreed to extend the contract until October 31, 1962, to allow more time for negotiations. During the negotiations Mr. Saunders announced the company's intention to move its plant to Florida. The union became more militant and, as one executive said, took the attitude that "We'll break you before you go."

Management was represented at the negotiations by Joe Ventrella Peter Sharp, Allen Parker, and Mike Spadone. Stu Saunders did not participate because he believed that the management actions should be ratified outside the negotiating room just as the union committee decisions had to be ratified by the membership before they became final. In commenting on the negotiations Joe Ventrella said: "I probably would have given in sooner, but Stu wouldn't give an inch; finally the union gave in. Whenever we sit down with the union, they get emotional and bring out a long list of grievances that should go through the grievance procedure. We are taking a strict interpretation on all grievances and Stu isn't giving an inch, so they will all go to arbitration."

An agreement was reached in October, without a strike, in which management offered an improved insurance program and no wage decreases. The union agreed to reduce vacation benefits, allow temporary furlough without regard to seniority, reduce the time off for death of a relative, accept management's jurisdiction over inspectors, and accept the new engineering standards for work performed. Several grievances still pending were compromised. Mr. Saunders was generally pleased with the outcome of the negotiations.

Just before the conclusion of the negotiations in late October, 1962, Mr. Saunders announced that because of the increased productivity in the plant during the spring and summer the company intended to continue the operation of the Trenton facility even if the commercial operations were moved to Florida. The union asked for and received a letter of intent to this effect as part of the agreement. As Mr. Saunders said: "The productivity has shown a good increase lately; that's why we decided to stay in Trenton. If the workers here will just behave themselves, we have no intention of leaving" (see Exhibit 5).

In January, 1963, labor relations deteriorated. The union threatened several times a week to strike over various issues. During the first week in February, management furloughed two girls in the machine department without regard to seniority because there was no work available for them. Management claimed that the action was covered by the contract because the only place where they could go was the assembly department, where they could be furloughed without regard to seniority under the new contract. Instead of taking the issue through the grievance procedure, the international representative went to Joe Ventrella and demanded that the two girls be reinstated with pay or the company would have a strike.

When management would not concede, the union struck, claiming that no contract was in effect since the international union had not yet approved the October agreement and had not yet returned signed copies to the company. Management had a copy of the agreement signed by the local officers and claimed that this was sufficient evidence of a contract.

During the strike and the subsequent mediation, the union centered its attacks upon Mr. Saunders personally. In a letter to the company's directors it claimed that Mr. Saunders was the cause of the strike and that the union would not return to work until the "cause was removed." During the mediation Mr. Saunders decided to let the other officers of the company handle the negotiations, but the union requested that Mr. Saunders come to the session since he had the ultimate decision in the company and because many of the grievances were directed at him personally. In a final session lasting from the early evening to 6 A.M. Mr. Saunders had an opportunity to answer the union charges.

Each time the international representative made a charge that was untrue, I pointed out that he was a liar. When the industry representative asked me to let them finish, I did, but I took notes and refuted each statement. They said that they wouldn't come back to work while I was here. Well, I told them that I didn't want them back. Look at the efficiency figures and you can see that they have been on a slowdown between October and January (see Exhibit 4). They were smart about it; it was a gradual slowdown, the kind that is hard to detect. The police caught two of them stealing machines, and we had them arrested. I then had a security check on the employees and found that 30% of them had

Exhibit 5
BUSINESS MACHINES CORPORATION
Newspaper Article, October 25, 1962

BMC MAY REMAIN, EXPAND HERE

President Says Decision Hinges on Production, Tax Adjustment

Trenton—There is a strong possibility today that the Business Machines Corp., instead of closing its Hollins Street plant as announced some months ago, may remain here and expand its operations.

Stewart P. Saunders, president and chief executive officer of BMC, made this disclosure Wedenesday night in a talk before the Society for the Advancement of Management at Anthony's Restaurant.

Continuation of Trenton operations, he said, depends on the present quality of work and an adjustment of taxes, described by Saunders as "high."

BMC is now building a plant near Winter Gardens, Fla. Removal there will cut $400,000 in labor costs, eliminate union problems, eliminate sales and property taxes, and place production nearer the center of sales, saving on transportation, Saunders said. The Florida plant will be used when ready. The question is how much can be salvaged at Trenton.

"BMC found its people in New Jersey were not energetic," Saunders said. "A one hundred per cent (workday) turned out to be no more than three and a half to four hours of work a day," according to consultants.

The president said quality in Trenton was so poor that the firm had to spend $300,000 to $400,000 annually in field branches rebuilding units before they could be delivered to customers.

"We employed a consultant and found that 56% of BMC's market was located in the Midwest, Southwest and West," he continued. "The freight on a unit to the West cost $2.93."

Then came wildcat strikes, grievances and a second strike, Saunders said, and earlier this year the firm made its decision to move to Florida.

"We planned to close and sell our Trenton plant," he continued, "but since we started planning the move to Florida, quality and production have gone up here. . . . If this improvement trend continues and we can get reduction in present high taxes, we may even expand in Trenton."

Saunders said Florida, like many southern states, would build a plant for an incoming firm, and move it free. Combined with this is a work force that is paid $1 to $1.50 an hour less than in New Jersey. "They make it very difficult for you to walk away," he added.

In answer to a question, however, Saunders said he didn't expect this "honeymoon" to last more than 10 years, to the time when workers would be demanding wages equal to the North. "But in 10 years you save $5 million," he remarked.

BMC, which manufactures and sells communications systems, monitors, and office dictating equipment, is moving to Winter Gardens, Fla. It also has a Japanese branch.

Exhibit 5—Continued

Blames Management

Saunders joined the firm in September, 1961, and feels some of the present problems were caused by former management. "I feel management gave in to demands to the point of bankruptcy," he said. "I blame management as much as I do the people."

"In Florida," Saunders continued, "people are unspoiled. They are not used to getting as much as they can for as little as they are able to do."

He said freight costs would be $75,000 higher because of the move, but that $400,000 would be saved in labor costs.

In answer to a question on whether his firm would be unionized in Florida, Saunders said, "Not if I can help it."

One member of the audience who said he lived in Trenton took issue with Saunders' statement that taxes in the town were too high.

"Taxes for BMC are too high," Saunders replied. He had noted earlier that they totalled $38,000 annually, and added that, combined with state taxes, it was too much.

Saunders said he hoped to get a tax reduction from the town, but had received no commitment from town officials.

police records. I did some more checking and found that a lot of them came from another local company after they had driven it into bankruptcy. We finally reached an agreement on callback; we would have carte blanche to call back the people that we needed for the first 30 days after the strike was over, and for 60 days after that we could call back on a job-seniority basis rather than on a plantwide seniority basis. With three weeks of strike and a slow callback we should be able to get rid of the troublemakers. We also won the right to keep the people that we hired during the strike. With the 15 or so that we hired and the total jobs in the plant cut to about 100, there won't be any room for all of the 128 who went out on strike. I'm not trying to break the union—I just don't want them to run the manufacturing department.

Purchasing and Material Control. One of the areas which Mr. Saunders found particularly perplexing was purchasing. Upon joining BMC he learned that the company contracted extensively for the manufacture of parts while its own manufacturing facilities were operating at only a portion of normal capacity. He immediately started pulling back as many as possible of these manufacturing operations. He questioned the ability and motives of the purchasing agent and felt that he should approve all further purchase orders himself.

In January, 1962, he fired the purchasing agent and replaced him with George Shea. Mr. Shea, a 1945 graduate of Tufts, had taken the

General Electric value analysis course for purchasing agents. He had worked for several large companies and had joined BMC after meeting Mr. Saunders through a mutual friend.

During the spring and summer of 1962, Mr. Shea and one girl handled all purchasing for the company, a drastic reduction from the four-man department. He at first thought that another purchasing agent would have to be hired but finally accustomed himself to the new situation. Mr. Shea was given the authority to release purchase orders without Mr. Saunders' approval.

The basic purchasing guide was the weekly inventory report. This was a tab listing of inventory along with the company's estimated requirements in the next two-month period and the amount of inventory over or under requirements. The basis for the requirements was the company's authorized manufacturing schedule developed from sales estimates and approved by Mr. Saunders. The inventory over or under figure was only a purchasing estimate; Mr. Shea also considered lead time, economic order size, etc., before placing orders. Although inventory had been reduced during early 1962 through closer supervision, he felt that further reduction could be obtained through a "maximum-minimum" inventory system for small parts; he was developing the figures necessary to control such a system.

Mr. Shea felt that the company "has had a lot of bad suppliers," and he had devoted much of his time to developing more dependable and less costly sources. In general this change resulted in manufacturing many of the parts which had previously been purchased and in reducing the number of suppliers for other items to the two or three best sources.

In addition to his regular duties Mr. Shea also investigated capital purchases suggested by Mr. Saunders. The purchase of the 10-foot shear in the fall of 1961 had cost $8,000 but had allowed the company to buy sheet steel at $300 a month instead of cut metal at $1,400 per month. Both Mr. Saunders and Mr. Shea believed that similar savings could be made through additional capital purchases. With this in mind Mr. Shea had visited several suppliers to look over their heat-treating equipment. He also believed that the coil-winding, metal-finishing, and thread-grinding operations could be brought into the plant as well as the manufacture of some other electrical components. These suggestions were eventually adopted.

The company not only absorbed a great deal of overhead by making rather than buying its parts, but also achieved better control over inventory and scheduling. By consolidating its remaining sources it had achieved a closer relationship with the suppliers and reduced problems of poor heat treating, plating, and grinding. This had proved particularly troublesome on government work which had stricter specifications.

In the fall of 1962, Mr. Saunders expanded Mr. Shea's duties to cover all material control within the company. In November Mr. Saunders explained his duties as "purchasing, materials control, receiving, shipping, stores—the whole gamut of materials. We were going through a shifting period here and it was a question of developing him to the point where he could take over. This was the plan all along, although I don't think he knew it—in fact, I know he didn't."

During the winter Mr. Shea had a chance to put his ideas into operation and did so to the satisfaction of Mr. Saunders. In March, 1963, Mr. Saunders reported that "George has developed more than anyone else. He has done wonders. Nothing is too hard for him to tackle. He handled inventory control while we were in a tight cash position, in addition to purchasing. He could develop into a good operations manager. He has the internal drive and is quick to get things done."

Engineering.   Allen Parker, an electrical engineer in his early 40's, joined BMC in October, 1961, after 14 years with a major competitor. He was promoted from director of research and development to vice president in charge of engineering in February, 1962, because of his initiative in introducing improvements into the development engineering section; these improvements included project accounts, time scheduling for research projects, and periodic progress reports. As vice president and No. 2 man in the organization, his expanded duties involved the supervision of five departments: research and development, quality assurance, production control, manufacturing-engineering, and technical publications. Upon assuming these responsibilities it was understood that he would be relieved of some of them as soon as other competent executives could be developed within the company. Consequently, the responsibility for production control was transferred to Mr. Shea and the responsibility for manufacturing-engineering to Mr. Sharp in September, 1962.

In October, 1962, Mr. Parker believed that the engineering department had survived its most critical period.

When I arrived last fall we were behind on the FAA contract; it wasn't until February that I realized how far behind we were. It wasn't until this summer that we finally worked out all of the problems on the job. It took almost all of our engineering staff to get the job done. Now we can start thinking about other projects for the engineers. Our engineering staff is still developing. We had about 20 development engineers when I first came here; we have replaced most of them and built up our engineering staff to about 32. Our budget calls for 50, so we are still looking for good engineers.

Most of my time is spent hiring new engineers and looking for development contracts to fill this plant when our commercial work is moved to Florida. Now I am gone about 40% of the time and as we get closer to the move I expect to be away practically all the time.

Mr. Saunders, although not an engineer, maintained an interest in engineering, suggested topics to be worked on, and even took home machines and tore them apart in an effort to find easier methods.

I've started something new here; each month the project manager and the director of engineering meet with me to report on progress on the projects during the month. I'm doing this for three reasons: first, to be sure that they are getting the right direction in the engineering area, because, by and large, the engineers are not very good managers; second, to acquaint myself with the progress that is being made; and third, to serve as a morale builder for the project group to get a hearing with me and tell me what they have accomplished. This is the third month we have done it.

Bob Carter, director of research and development, attended these meetings in the fall of 1962. He had joined the company in November, 1961, and had succeeded Mr. Parker as director. Mr. Carter said that he was having a problem getting the right people to fill out his engineering department.

It's hard to pick up the right people at the salary offered. We feel that the salaries are high but we're not willing to pay for experience outside of our interests. Also the Florida move is not helping. It hasn't cost us any men because these men want to stay around for the experience, but besides wanting the challenge and money, engineers want to stay put. I don't know what will happen when we move to Florida, or who will go. I have a lot of ties here and a new home.

During the winter of 1962 Bob Carter left the company and was not replaced. Mr. Saunders took over the direction of the research and development engineering department himself because he had become increasingly displeased with the progress that Allen Parker was making with the company. Mr. Parker's failure to follow through on the problems of the FAA contract disappointed Mr. Saunders.

I don't know what happened to Allen, but after I made him a vice president he seemed to sit back and relax. I don't know if it's the weight of the problems or the lack of cash or what, but he doesn't seem to be challenge-motivated.

Yesterday morning I asked him to see about $4,000 that the FAA owes us and he said that he would. When I asked him about it today, he hadn't done anything. Allen just does not follow through. The thing that he seems to like to do is sell to government agencies. I am going to give him a chance to do that; if he doesn't make the grade, I will have to get rid of him. Right now he is not producing for the dollars being spent.

Accounting. Mike Spadone, controller and treasurer, joined BMC in May, 1962. After graduating from college in 1950, he worked with a CPA firm and an electronics company before answering an ad in *The Wall Street Journal* and learning about BMC.

Mr. Spadone was high in his praise for Mr. Saunders.

He is a really dynamic person who knows where he wants to go and is going to get there. In the accounting area he knows what he wants. He was an internal auditor for Continental Can for many years and knows as much about accounting as anything else. When I arrived, I received a letter telling me all the things that he wanted done in this department. The goals included reporting balance sheet figures and P.&L. figures by the 15th of the month, installing budgets and new inventory procedures, reducing manpower, and projecting levels for receivables and payables. Before I came here the accounting was not very sophisticated. All we really had were the standard P.&L. accounts and a very loose cost accounting system. We have introduced better sales analysis and responsibility accounting in sales and have revised the reports. We also have made the cost accounting reports more specific. Stu Saunders is very interested in the labor efficiency report and the internal statements. He receives these daily and uses them to control operations.

We have made a lot of progress in the accounting department but we have been hampered by the turnover in personnel. Almost all of the people in accounting are new; five of the six tab people are new since May. One girl in cost accounting has been here 20 years, but the rest are new. Only a few of the other girls have been here more than three years. Our future plans will have to wait until some of these people come along.

There are a lot of things that we want to do in the future. We hope to get an organizational chart set up soon. We also want to get the complete statements out in eight days, whereas now we take 30 to 35 days to get them out. There are a lot of other things that should be done, too, such as putting accounts payable on tab, devising better inventory control and production control programs, developing economic order quantities, and improving the standards.

As of March, 1963, Mr. Saunders was generally pleased with Mike Spadone's progress but conceded that he too was weak on follow through. "During the strike the timekeeper refused to work on the production line, so we fired him. I told Mike Spadone and Peter Sharp that this was a good time to put in our new production control system which will replace the timekeeper with a 24-hour tape recorder. When the strike was over, they wanted to hire a new timekeeper but I wouldn't let them. They have to learn to use their problems as opportunities."

Mr. Spadone also made cash projections and kept Mr. Saunders advised of the company's cash position. In financial matters Mr. Saunders relied upon the treasurer's figures but made all decisions himself.

In reviewing the cash position of the company in March, 1963, Mr. Saunders said the past year had been very tight. "The worst came in January. We have a $1,200,000 line of credit with a New York bank and in January we had to use all of it. The strike actually helped the cash position. Because of the labor problems, we have had to keep a four-month inventory of finished machines, but when the strike came it freed a lot of money that was in inventory. Since then we have been able to repay $59,000 of the loan. We should be able to get $300,000 to $400,000 from the FAA for April deliveries. The total due on the contract is $600,000, which will ease the cash situation considerably. With that and better purchasing and inventory control we should be past the worst of our cash problems."

In the past the company had used convertible debentures and factored receivables to finance its operations. The company expected that the increasing profitability of the company would reduce the convertible debt. In September, 1962, it negotiated a $1,200,000 unsecured line of credit and ceased its receivables financing.

Sales.   As general sales manager, Mr. Saunders spent 60% of his time on sales problems. A major source of concern was the ineffectiveness of the distributors.

The distributor organization has not developed well; in fact, we are closing out our distributors because they just aren't doing the job for us. I don't think this is a good distributor product; unless you give away too much of the profit to the distributor, he isn't interested. We have closed out our distributors in Des Moines, Flint, Rochester, and Syracuse. We have bought out one in New York and are closing Akron. We are putting our own branches in all of these areas; we have opened new branches in Philadelphia, Washington, and Sacramento and will open branches in Florida soon. As far as I'm concerned, if the distributor does the job we won't throw him out. But many of them just aren't doing the job. We set quotas for each sales area based upon the area's sales potential as established by the Office Machine Equipment Institute. In many areas the distributors not only aren't meeting their quotas but aren't making any sales at all.

We have had some problems with the product, but our big problem is convincing the sales organization that the company is behind them. I find that by and large the BMC sales organization has always had a crutch as to why they couldn't sell. First, they couldn't sell because of design difficulties. That's now behind us. Then, they couldn't sell because we weren't giving them enough machines. Well, that's behind us, too. I don't know what the latest excuse is, but we are not accepting excuses any more.

Once we have developed a strong sales organization, we will look for new products that can be sold by the same people. Primarily, we are interested in office equipment but are also considering other items in the electronics field. We have offers all the time from people who want to come in with us. What we are looking for is something like a dry photocopy process which would increase our sales without much increase in overhead. It will take two years to really build the sales force, but I hope that in three or four months the sales organization will be in shape so that we can start thinking about diversification.

Branch Sales Operations. Mr. Saunders believed that successful sales branches were vital to the overall success of the firm and spent a majority of his time visiting sales offices and recruiting new branch managers. In December, 1962, he reorganized the Boston office of the company and installed Dick Frankel as branch manager. By February the Boston office led all branches in sales. Dick had left the company in September, 1961, and had returned as a salesman in the Trenton office when he heard of Mr. Saunders' accomplishments. The following paraphrased comments by Dick Frankel indicate some of the changes that Mr. Saunders had accomplished in the branch offices:

Mr. Saunders has made some real changes in the sales organization. I think his biggest change has been giving the sales department strong leadership and confidence in the company. He also gives the sales offices more direction through his review of the results and his letters. Before, the branch managers used to get only a profit and loss statement. Since my background is in marketing, I couldn't tell if the results were good or bad. Now we not only have the P.&L. but he also gives us specific goals and objectives for each of the accounts. We have a budget and a forecast of sales to strive for and each month we get a P.&L. which shows not only the amount of each account but the percentage that each account should be of total sales. I get a monthly letter from him reviewing my accounts and questioning me on items that may be out of line. Of course he evaluates by results; when the results are not good, he can really put the pressure on you.

We now have production backing us up, which we didn't before. I used to phone in a rush order and get promised a machine only to have it arrive late because of production problems or some shipping clerk who would refuse to work five minutes overtime to get it out. Saunders is a production man and has made some real changes there.

Another improvement is simplified reporting. We used to have to report our transactions daily. Now we report weekly and get back a tab run that we can use to make up our monthly reports. This lets me spend more time out of the office. I'm afraid, though, that Sam Caldwell has just come up with another report comparing forecast and actual sales that will take us about four hours a month to fill out. I could give this to my girl to fill out, but she is new and I don't feel that this should be general office information.

Another thing that I like is that I have complete freedom in running the office. I do the hiring, firing, training, and the management of expenses. I can do what I want as long as I produce results. I think that most of the people now selling are out to prove something. Stu has gotten rid of the ones who sat back waiting for the business to come to them, even though many of them were good salesmen. The men we have now are more eager. It's not just a matter of energy; it's a matter of desire to do a job right. I sometimes come in early and work until 11 o'clock, and so do the others.

I think it's necessary to have that desire to sell BMC products. Our salesmen have to be creative sellers who are able to meet the arguments of our competitors. One of the arguments that competitors use is that we are a small company with P.&L. problems while the others are long-established firms. Now we are better on that count. Another is that they give better service. They can't say that in Boston anymore because we have a very good service department, but a company like Dictaphone or IBM is bound to have more facilities in some parts of the country because of its size. Finally they talk about their design features. I'm sure that we have the best all-around design on the market, but its features have to be sold. The big feature of our equipment is that it is the easiest operating system on the market and has been designed to save the time of the high-priced executive rather than that of the office girls. Our system is easy to load, has accurate backspacing and identification of corrections, and returns quickly and simply to the place where it stopped recording. The equipment is so simple that the executive can operate it with one hand without looking. The actual recording is serviced by the secretary at her desk, so the executive never has to take discs to her; she can change discs and start typing at her convenience.

The new salesmen are always concerned about the price of the equipment. All the companies are within $5 of each other at around $400, except IBM which I think is about 5% higher. But the big feature in selling dictating equipment is not the initial investment but the savings in time for the executive. The salesmen have to be creative to put this across. Of course, if it's a big account that we want to get into, we will go low with a competitive bid and hope to get back to list price with future business.

Another reason that we have to be creative is that we can't sit back and wait for sales to come to us, like Dictaphone. Dictaphone has been established so long that the name has become generic in the business. When a Dictaphone salesman goes out, he has over $70 of advertising helping him. We are lucky to have $2 per salesman. We have to fight uphill for sales and we make sales in most of the competitive situations. The sales that we lose are the sales that we never hear about. We don't have the salesmen to cover the market like Dictaphone or IBM. Actually IBM helped us when they came in with their machine. The IBM salesmen get businessmen to think about dictating equipment, but most companies want to see several machines before they buy. The typewriter salesmen are not familiar enough with dictating equipment to sell it. About 60% of our business comes through leads from people who call us and ask for a demonstration. The other 40% we have to find ourselves.

The most important part of our selling effort is done before we see the customer. Right now we are making a telephone survey and a survey of some office buildings to find prospects. Even when a customer calls us we have to give some thought to his particular problems before we make a presentation.

In this office the new equipment has not been as much of a help in increasing sales as the changes in the management operations have been. Our sales increase has been mainly in the standard dictating line. We have sold few of the memoscribers (Japanese imported machine at half the price) because the quality is not so good as the regular equipment, it does not form a complete office system, and it takes as much of a salesman's effort to sell a $200 memoscriber as a $400 regular machine—and to a salesman working on commission that makes a big difference. The memoscriber is the type of thing that should be sold through Western Auto or a camera store to individuals; we look for most of our business in offices where we have a chance to sell more machines at a higher price. We haven't been selling the audio-visual system because we can't get production on it. When we do get it, I will have to go out and determine the best prospects and the best presentation for it. Right now with three men and a quota set for six we have all that we can do to keep up with the office dictating business.

I think that the company has taken care of the biggest problems that faced the sales force, but the things that remain to be done as far as I am concerned are in the area of training and motivating salesmen. The branch managers do all the training now. Even with only a skeleton force here I spend a lot of time in the field with the salesmen and I have put together three books full of information for training. As we add salesmen, training will become a problem.

Motivating the salesmen is another problem. We pay well at BMC, but salesmen work for more than money. Motivating salesmen is a matter of attention to every detail. You have to see that they have a pat on the back at the right time and that they keep up the pressure on sales. You have to see to it that they never lose faith in the product or the company and that they never work through fear. A salesman who has too many problems of his own can't concentrate on the customer's problems. In production a man can come to work after a fight with his wife and he will only produce 20 units instead of 30, but he is all right as long as he keeps his finger out of the machine; a salesman in the same circumstances, however, will produce nothing. That's why I didn't tell the salesmen about our strike until it was over and that's why I get irritated when things from the home office come in the mail or by telegram and the people in the office see them before I do.

PROPOSED MOVE TO FLORIDA

In December, 1961, one of the BMC stockholders tried to interest Mr. Saunders in moving his plant to Florida. The stockholder was building a completely new city in Florida and hoped to bring in light industry and attract workers to his homes. The stockholder had taken an interest in BMC because of its handling of the union problem and the turnaround in the profit picture and became determined to get BMC for his new city. The overcapacity at BMC and the value of the four-year-old plant combined with the problems of the workers' attitude at Trenton made the offer appealing. The stockholder offered to build a new plant and lease it to BMC on reasonable terms. Florida offered savings in labor costs of about $1.50 per hour. Mr. Saunders estimated that the total cost of the move would be $350,000 to $400,000. In addition, the company expected to incur about $75,000 per year of additional transportation costs but believed that the savings in labor costs would more than offset this.

Mr. Saunders announced his decision to retain the Trenton plant in October, 1962 (see Exhibit 5). "We planned to close and sell our Trenton plant, but since we started planning the move to Florida, quality and production here have gone up. If this improvement trend continues and we can get reduction in present high taxes, we may even expand in Trenton."

Only the commercial segment of the operations would move to Florida. The Trenton plant was to be used for expanded government work and to house other operations which the company hoped to acquire.

Groundbreaking for the Florida plant was expected in the summer of 1963 with the building to be completed in the spring of 1964.

What we plan to do is produce about a four months' supply of machines which we will store. Then we will produce probably five to six months' supply of parts needed to assemble machines here, ship the parts to Florida, and gradually start an assembly process there. In selecting people in Florida, we plan to do what RCA did. As I understand it, they actually set up the units to be assembled or the job to be performed and gave the prospective employee three or four hours to play with the material and watched him to see how he made out. If they thought he had an aptitude for the work, they would say fine, in three months you have a job; if not, they would just forget it. We will probably do something along this line, too. We will probably take all of the good supervisors with us or ask them to go with us. If there are any dogs in the group, no, we won't even invite them. We haven't specifically asked them yet, but most of them have come and said that they hope they are invited to go. Mr. Sharp will probably go down as overall manager of production. We haven't really decided about the other people. Some of the engineers will have to go and probably the personnel man.

THE FUTURE

Mr. Saunders believed that the company was still working on problems created by the past management and would continue to do so for the next several months. After that he believed that the only problems remaining would be

. . . the standard, everyday problems that occur in any other business. You will always have personnel problems, finding the right people for the right task. I don't mean at the top level; I mean at the foreman level and under. You will always find people who will function perfectly in the next three months as a foreman and then all of a sudden will fall apart. I don't foresee anything other than normal everyday problems facing us—mostly people.

I have no intention of leaving the company after our present problems are overcome. I took a cut in pay to come here but was given a sizable stock option, so I intend to stick around and see that the company grows.

So far we aren't looking for companies to acquire—they are coming to us. I wouldn't acquire anything that we couldn't move into our facilities and eliminate the duplicate administrative and overhead costs. Every one of these companies is in serious trouble because they have too much overhead; unless we could consolidate and eliminate overhead, I wouldn't even touch them at the moment. We aren't going to pick up anything that is going to upset our profit position. We've been on the loss side so long that this is detrimental to our selling efforts, so we're not going to slip back.

Mr. Saunders believed that the company's growth could be accomplished through retained earnings and, if necessary, cash supplied by the major stockholders. There were no limits to the size of company acquired so long as BMC would remain the "ultimate company." Acquisition plans were confined, however, to the electronics and office equipment fields.

With our present machine and modifications to it, we expect to expand our present business to about $12 to $15 million in annual sales in the next two years. My long-range plan is that in five years we will be worth at least $50 million through acquisitions as well as expansion of our present products, and in eight to 10 years I want to be well over $100 million.

4. Consolidated Drugs, Inc.

MR. RICHARD TRUCKS had been transferred to the Syracuse (New York) Division of Consolidated Drugs, Inc., in the first week of May, 1952. At this time he was appointed sales manager of the Syracuse wholesale drug division. Formerly he had been an assistant to the vice-president in charge of sales at the company's headquarters in New York.

At the month-end sales meeting on the last Friday of June, 1952, Mr. Asa Bush, a salesman in one of the division's rural territories, informed Mr. Trucks that he wished to retire at the end of July when he reached his sixty-fifth birthday. Mr. Trucks was surprised by Mr. Bush's announcement because he had been informed by the division manager, Mr. B. D. Burton, that Mr. Bush had requested and received a deferment of retirement until he reached his sixty-sixth birthday in July, 1953. The only explanation offered by Mr. Bush was that he had "changed his mind."

The retirement of Mr. Bush posed a problem for Mr. Trucks, in that he had to decide what to do about a successor to Mr. Bush's territory.

BACKGROUND OF THE SYRACUSE DIVISION

When Mr. Trucks became the divisional sales manager he was twenty-nine years old. He had joined Consolidated (as the firm was known in trade circles) as a sales trainee after his graduation from Stanford University in 1946. During the next two years he worked as a salesman. In the fall of 1948 the sales manager of the company made Mr. Trucks one of his assistants. In this capacity Mr. Trucks helped the sales manager to arrange special sales promotions for the lines of different manufacturers.

Mr. Trucks's predecessor, Mr. John K. Martin, had served as divisional sales manager for 15 years before his death in April. "J. K.," as Mr. Martin had been known, had worked as a salesman for the drug wholesale house that had been merged with Consolidated to become its Syracuse Division. Although Mr. Trucks had made Mr. Martin's acquaintance in the course of business, he had not known Mr. Martin well. The salesmen often expressed their admiration and affection for

Mr. Martin to the new sales manager. Several salesmen, in fact, made a point of telling Mr. Trucks that "Old J. K." knew every druggist in twelve counties by his first name. Mr. Martin had died of a heart attack while trout-fishing with the president of the Syracuse Pharmacists' Association. The Syracuse Division manager said that most of the druggists in town attended Mr. Martin's funeral.

The Syracuse Division of Consolidated was one of 25 wholesale drug houses in the United States owned by the firm. Each division acted as a functionally autonomous unit having its own warehouse, sales department, buying department, and accounting department. The divisional manager was responsible for the performance of the unit he managed. There were, however, line functions performed by the regional and national offices that pertained directly to the individual departments. A district sales manager, for instance, was associated with a regional office in Albany for the purpose of implementing marketing policies established by the central office in New York.

As a service wholesaler, the Syracuse Division sold to the retail drug trade a broad line of approximately 18,000 items. The line might well be described as consisting of everything sold through drugstores except fresh food, tobacco products, newspapers, and magazines. In the trading area of Syracuse, Consolidated competed with two other wholesalers; one of these carried substantially the same line of products; the other, a limited line of drug products.

The history of the Syracuse Division had been that of a profitable family-owned wholesale drug house before its merger with Consolidated in 1928. The division had operated profitably since that date with the exception of three years during the 1930's, although it had not shown a profit on sales equal to the average for the other wholesale drug divisions of Consolidated. Since 1945, the annual net sales of the division had risen each year. But since its competitors did not announce their sales figures, it was impossible to ascertain whether this increase in sales represented a change in the competitive situation or merely a general trend of business volume in the Syracuse trading area. Mr. Martin had been of the opinion that the increase had been at the expense of competitors. The district drug sales manager, however, maintained that, since the trend of increase was less than that of other divisions in the northern New York region, the Syracuse Division may have actually lost ground competitively. A new measuring technique for calculating the potential wholesale purchasing power of retail drugstores, which had been adopted shortly before Mr. Trucks's transfer, indicated that the share of the wholesale drug market controlled by the Syracuse Division was below the median and below the mean for Consolidated divisions.

Only a few of the employees working in 1952 for the Syracuse Division had also been employed by the predecessor company. Mr. Martin had been the only person in the executive echelon whose employment in the Syracuse Division antedated the merger. Most of the executives and salesmen currently active in the organization had come into the organization either between 1933 and 1941 or after the end of World War II. Two salesmen, however, Mr. Bush and Mr. John Jameson, had worked for the predecessor company before the merger.

Of those who were employed as executives or salesmen before World War II, only Mr. B. D. Burton, the division manager, had a college degree, which he had earned at a local Y.M.C.A. night school. All the young men employed since 1946 were university or pharmacy-college graduates. None of the younger men had been promoted when vacancies had occurred in the job of operations manager (who was in charge of the warehouse) and of merchandise manager (who supervised buying) in the Syracuse Division; however, two of the younger men had been promoted to similar positions in other divisions when vacancies had occurred.

THE SYRACUSE DIVISION SALES FORCE

From the time that Mr. Trucks took over Mr. Martin's duties he had devoted four days a week to the task of traveling through each sales territory with the salesmen who covered it. He had, however, made no changes in the practices or procedures of the sales force. The first occasion on which Mr. Trucks was required to make a decision of other than routine nature was when Mr. Bush asked to be retired.

When Mr. Trucks took charge of the Syracuse Division sales force, it consisted of nine salesmen and four trainees. Four of the salesmen, James Pepper, Michael Waller, Daniel Carmack, and Paul Smith, had joined the company under the sales training program for college graduates initiated in 1946. Concerning the other five salesmen, who had been with the company many years, Mr. Trucks was given the following information: Asa Bush and John Jameson were senior in terms of service to the others. John Dangler joined the company as a warehouse employee in 1928 when he was nineteen and became a salesman in 1933. Homer Babbidge came to Consolidated as a salesman in 1933 when the wholesale drug firm for which he had previously worked went out of business. In 1952 Mr. Babbidge, who was then forty-eight years old, had been a wholesale drug salesman for 28 years. Russell Means at the age of twenty-six came to Consolidated in 1938 after working as a missionary salesman for a manufacturer. Mr. Means served as an officer in the Army Medical Corps during the war and was discharged as a captain in hospital administration in 1945. He returned to Consolidated immediately after his discharge.

The four trainees had graduated from colleges the preceding June. When Mr. Trucks arrived in Syracuse, these men were in the last phase of their twelve months' training program. The trainees were spending much of their time traveling with the salesmen. Mr. Trucks, who now had the full responsibility for training these men, believed that Mr. Martin had hired four trainees to cover an anticipated turnover both among the salesmen and among the trainees themselves, as well as to implement the New York head office's policy of getting more intensive coverage of each market area. The trainees, he understood, expected to receive territory assignments either in the Syracuse Division or elsewhere on the completion of their training period.

Mr. Trucks had not seen very much of the salesmen. His acquaintance with them had been formed at the sales meetings and in traveling with them through their territories.

Mr. Trucks judged that Homer Babbidge was an easygoing, even-tempered person. He seemed to be very popular with the other salesmen and with his customers. Mr. Babbidge was proud of his two sons, one of whom was in high school and the other married, with a son named after Mr. Babbidge. Mr. Trucks thought that the salesman liked him, because Babbidge had commented to him several times that his suggestions had been very helpful.

Asa Bush had not, in Mr. Trucks's opinion, been particularly friendly. Mr. Trucks had observed that Bush was well liked because of his good humor and friendly manner with everyone; however, Mr. Trucks had noticed that on a number of occasions Bush had intimated that his age and experience should cause the sales manager to defer to his judgment. Mr. Bush and his wife lived in the town of Oswego.

On June 4, 1952, Mr. Trucks had traveled with Mr. Bush, and they visited five of Mr. Bush's accounts. On a routine form for sales managers' reports on field work with salesmen, copies of which were filed with the district sales manager and the New York sales manager, Mr. Trucks made the following comments about Mr. Bush:

Points Requiring Attention: Not using merchandising equipment; not following weekly sales plan. Pharmaceutical business going to competitors because of lack of interest. Too much time spent on idle chatter. Only shows druggist what "he thinks they will buy." Tends to sell easy items instead of profitable ones.

Steps Taken for Correction: Explained shortcomings and demonstrated how larger, more profitable orders could be obtained by following sales plan—did just that by getting the biggest order ever written for Carthage account.

Remarks: Old-time "personality." Should do terrific volume if trained on new merchandising techniques.

On a similar form made out by J. K. Martin on the basis of working with Mr. Bush on March 3, 1952, the following comments were made:

Points Requiring Attention: Not getting pharmaceutical business. Not following promotion plans.

Steps Taken for Correction: Told him about these things.

Remarks: Bush made this territory—can sell anything he sets his mind to—a real drummer—very popular with his customers.

Daniel Carmack, twenty-nine years old, was the oldest of the group of salesmen who had passed through the formal sales training program. Mr. Trucks considered him earnest and conscientious. He had increased his sales each year. Although Mr. Trucks did not regard Carmack as being the "salesman type," he noted that Carmack had been fairly successful in the use of the merchandising techniques that Mr. Trucks was seeking to implement.

John Dangler handled a number of the big accounts in downtown Syracuse. Mr. Trucks believed that Dangler was an excellent salesman who considered himself "very smooth." Mr. Trucks had been surprised at the affront Dangler had taken when he had offered a few suggestions about the improvement of Dangler's selling technique. Mr. and Mrs. Dangler were good friends of the Burtons. The Danglers were social friends of merchandise and operations managers and their wives. Mr. Trucks suspected that Dangler had expected to be Mr. Martin's successor.

John Jameson seemed to Mr. Trucks to be an earnest and conscientious salesman. He had been amiable, though not cordial, toward Mr. Trucks. Mr. Trucks's report on calls on ten accounts on June 5, 1952, with Mr. Jameson contained the following statements.

Points Requiring Attention: Rushing calls. Gets want book and tries to sell case lots on wanted items. Carries all merchandising equipment but doesn't use it.

Steps Taken for Correction: Suggested change in routing; longer, better-planned calls; conducted presentation demonstration.

Remarks: Hardworking, conscientious, good salesman, but needs to be brought up to date on merchandising methods.

Mr. Martin's comments on observations of Mr. Jameson on March 4, 1952, reported on the same form, were as follows:

Points Requiring Attention: Uses the want book on the basis of most sales. Not pushing promotions.
Steps Taken for Correction: Discussed shortcomings.
Remarks: Jameson really knows how to sell—visits every customer each week. Hard worker—very loyal—even pushes goods with very low commission.

On the day Mr. Trucks had traveled with Jameson, the latter suggested that Mr. Trucks have dinner at the Jamesons' home. Mr. Trucks accepted the invitation, but at the end of the day Jameson took him to a restaurant in Watertown, explaining that he did not want to inconvenience his wife because his two daughters were home from college on vacation.

Russell Means had caused Mr. Trucks considerable concern. Means complained about sales management procedures, commission rates, the "lousy service of the warehouse people," and other such matters at sales meetings. Mr. Trucks believed that most of the complaints were founded in fact, but concluded that the matters were usually trivial, since the other salesmen did not complain about them. Mr. Trucks mentioned his difficulties with Means to Mr. Burton. Mr. Burton's comment was that Means had been very friendly with Mr. Martin. Means seemed to be quite popular with his customers.

James Pepper was, in Mr. Trucks's opinion, the most ambitious, aggressive, and argumentative salesman in the Syracuse Division. He had been employed by the company since his graduation from the University of Rochester in 1948, first as a trainee and then as a salesman. Pepper had substantially increased the sales volume of the territory assigned to him. He had persuaded Mr. Martin to assign him six inactive hospital accounts in July, 1950. Within six months Pepper made sales to these accounts in excess of $36,000. The other salesmen considered him "cocky" and a "big spender." Mr. Trucks thought his attitude was one of independence. If Pepper agreed with a sales plan, he worked hard to achieve its objectives, but if he did not agree, he did not cooperate at all. Mr. Trucks thought that he had been very successful in working with Pepper.

Paul Smith, who was twenty-four years old, impressed Mr. Trucks as being unsure of himself. Smith seemed to be confused and overworked. Mr. Trucks attributed this difficulty to Smith's trying to serve too many accounts in too large an area. Smith was very interested in Mr. Trucks's suggestions on improvement in his work. Mr. Trucks believed that he would improve in time with proper help. Smith had raised his sales to the point where he was on commission instead of salary in March, 1952.

Michael Waller, twenty-five years of age, was the only salesman who worked on a salary. His sales volume was not sufficient to sustain an income of $325 a month, which was the company minimum for salesmen with more than one year's experience Waller was very apologetic about being on a salary. Mr. Trucks believed that Waller's determination to "make good" would be realized because of the latter's conscientiousness. When he had been assigned the territory two years before, it had consisted largely of uncontacted accounts. The volume of sales had tripled in the meantime. Mr. Trucks felt that Waller appreciated all the help he was given and that in time Waller would be an excellent salesman.

Both Bush and Jameson earned about $2\frac{1}{8}\%$ of sales in commissions. The other salesmen all earned about $2\frac{1}{4}\%$ of sales as commissions, except Pepper and Carmack who earned about $2\frac{3}{8}\%$. Mr. Trucks said that expense accounts amounted to about $\frac{3}{4}\%$ of sales for both city and country salesmen. The differences in percentage rates of commissions were explained by Mr. Trucks in terms of the differential commissions set by the company. Higher commission rates were given on items the company wished to "push," such as pharmaceuticals and calendar promotion items.

The trainees were something of an unknown quantity to Mr. Trucks. He had training conferences with them in which he had thought they had performed rather poorly. He believed that Mr. Martin had neglected the training of the new men. All four of them seemed to be good prospects and were eager to be assigned territories, as they informed Mr. Trucks as often as possible.

The turnover of the Syracuse Division sales force had been very low among the prewar salesmen. Six of the sales-training program men had left the division since 1947. Two of these men had been promoted to department heads in other divisions, whereas four had left to work for manufacturers. Because manufacturers valued salesmen with wholesaling experience and competing wholesalers did not have training programs for young men, there were many opportunities for a salesman who desired to leave.

SALES MANAGEMENT

Since Mr. Trucks had become sales manager, he had devoted considerable thought to the problem of improving the sales performance of the Syracuse Division. He had accepted a transfer to the new job at the urging of Mr. Cameron Crow, the vice-president in charge of sales. Mr. Trucks was one of a dozen young men whom Mr. Crow had brought into the New York office since the end of World War II to work as assistants to the top sales executives. None of the young assistants had remained in the New York office for more than three years, for Mr. Crow made a policy of offering the young men field assignments so that they could "show their stuff." Mr. Trucks believed that the sales performance of the Syracuse Division could be bettered by an improved plan of sales management. He knew that the share of the Syracuse market for wholesale purchases of retail drugstores[1] held by Consolidated was only 19.5% as against a 48% share for some of the other divisions in their respective markets.

Mr. Crow, for whom Mr. Trucks worked immediately before his transfer, had focused his staff's attention upon the qualitative aspects of sales policy. Mr. Trucks had assisted Mr. Crow in implementing merchandising plans intended to utilize the salesmen's selling efforts in such a way as to minimize the handling cost of sales and maximize the gross margin.

The company encouraged the salesmen to use a threefold plan for increasing profitability:

1) Sales of larger average value per line of the order were encouraged because the cost of processing and filling each line of an order was practically constant;

2) Sales of larger total value were encouraged because the delivery cost for orders having a total weight between 20 and 100 pounds was practically constant;

3) Because some manufacturers offered margins considerably larger than others, sales of products carrying higher margins were encouraged. Salesmen's commissions varied with the margins available to Consolidated on the products they sold.

The executives of the company also sought to increase the effectiveness of Consolidated promotions by setting up a sales calendar. The sales calendar co-ordinated the activities of all Consolidated divisions so that during a given calendar period every account would be solicited for the sale of particular items yielding satisfactory profits. The type of activity represented by the sales calendar required that the salesmen in

---

[1] The potential wholesale sales for retail drugstores were calculated by the New York office market-analysis section. This market estimate, called the P.W.P.P. (potential wholesale purchasing power) was calculated for each county by adjusting retail drugstore sales to an estimate of the purchases of goods from wholesalers.

each division follow a pattern in selling to every individual account. The sales manager was responsible for co-ordinating the activities of his own salesmen.

The matter of selling patterns was largely the responsibility of the division sales manager. Mr. Trucks believed that his predecessor had never really accepted the changes that had taken place in the merchandising policy of the New York office.

Mr. Trucks had inherited from his predecessor a system of sales-department records which had been carefully maintained. The national offices required each division to keep uniform sales and market-analysis records. During the period of Mr. Trucks's work in the New York office, he had developed a familiarity with the various uses for these records.

The basis of the sales and market-analysis record was the division trading area. The limits of the trading area were determined by the economics of selling costs, and the factors on which the costs were based were transportation costs of delivery and salesmen's traveling expenses. Mr. Trucks knew from his own experience that delineation of trading areas was influenced by tradition, geographic conditions, the number of salesmen, the number of calls a salesman could make, the estimated market potential, competition, and agreements with adjacent Consolidated divisions. The Syracuse Division was bordered by the trading areas of Consolidated divisions located in Rochester and Albany on the east, south, and west; to the north was the Canadian border. A map of this division is included here in Exhibit 1.

Within the divisional trading area the market was broken into sales territories. Exhibit 2 includes data on salesmen's territory assignments; Exhibit 3 shows the salesmen's territories by counties; Exhibit 4 indicates estimated potential sales and sales by counties for various classification of customers. During the time since his arrival, Mr. Trucks had formed the opinion that the present salesmen's territories had been established without careful regard for the number of stores in the area, the sales potential, or the amount of traveling involved. Although Mr. Trucks had not yet studied any one territory carefully, he suspected all his salesmen of skimming the cream from many of their accounts because they did not have adequate time to do a thorough selling job in each store.

Mr. Trucks had been able to observe the performance records of other divisional sales managers while he worked in New York. He knew that some sales managers had achieved substantial improvements over the past performances of their divisions.

Exhibit 1

CONSOLIDATED DRUGS, INC.

Syracuse Division Trading Area

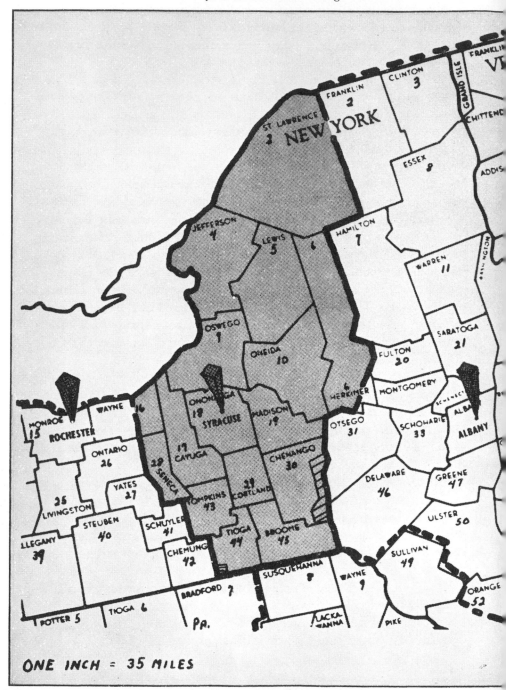

ONE INCH = 35 MILES

Exhibit 2

CONSOLIDATED DRUGS, INC.

Selected Data on Salesmen's Territory Assignments and Performance

Salesman	County	Sales, 1951*	Active Accounts	Estimated Potential†	Assigned Accounts‡
				(000)	
Babbidge	Chenango..................	$ 20,634	4	$ 189	15
	Tompkins..................	63,226	9	388	19
	Tioga.....................	39,839	4	161	11
	Broome....................	122,968	22	1,807	45
	Total.....................	246,667	39	2,545	90
Bush	Jefferson..................	81,162	16	371	20
	Lewis.....................	28,798	8	87	11
	Oswego...................	148,073	25	517	37
	Total.....................	258,033	49	965	68
Carmack	Onondaga.................	76,339	14	297	14
	Madison..................	86,950	12	417	19
	Cortland..................	46,005	6	146	11
	Total.....................	209,294	32	860	44
Dangler	Onondaga.................	252,051	33	743	44
	Total.....................	252,051	33	743	44
Jameson	St. Lawrence..............	136,058	25	364	32
	Jefferson..................	123,681	19	353	19
	Oswego...................	1,091	1	200	1
	Total.....................	260,830	45	737	52
Means	Onondaga.................	244,642	29	1,009	48
	Total.....................	244,642	29	1,009	48
Pepper	Onondaga.................	212,691	28	500	29
	Total.....................	212,691	28	500	29
Smith	Herkimer..................	48,530	10	312	19
	Oneida....................	113,607	46	1,053	85
	Total.....................	162,137	56	1,365	104
Waller	Wayne....................	22,675	4	103	5
	Cayuga...................	70,598	14	312	18
	Seneca....................	36,260	8	186	13
	Total.....................	129,533	26	601	36
	Hospitals, Syracuse (Pepper).......	$ 36,079			
	All others.....................	$ 8,595			
	House accounts.................	$ 76,622			
	Total division sales...........	$2,197,174			

* This figure includes sales to chain and independent drugstores, and to miscellaneous accounts but does not include sales to hospitals.

† No potential is calculated for hospitals or miscellaneous sales. Where a county is divided among several salesmen, the potential-sales figure for each salesman is obtained by allocating the county potential in proportion to the *number* of drugstore accounts in that county assigned to that salesman.

‡ Includes hospitals and other recognized drug outlets in the territory.

Source: Company records.

SALES TERRITORIES OF BUSH AND JAMESON

The territory that Mr. Bush covered included accounts scattered through small towns in four counties of the rural area northeast of Syracuse (see Exhibit 5). Mr. Bush had originally developed the accounts in the four-county area for the predecessor company. At the time

Exhibit 3

CONSOLIDATED DRUGS, INC.

Syracuse Division Salesmen's Territory Assignments,
by Counties

Code Number	County	Salesmen
1............	St. Lawrence	Jameson
4............	Jefferson	Bush, Jameson
5............	Lewis	Bush
6............	Herkimer	Smith
9............	Oswego	Bush, Jameson
10............	Oneida	Smith
16............	Wayne	Waller
17............	Cayuga	Waller
18............	Onondaga	Means, Dangler, Pepper, Carmack
19............	Madison	Carmack
28............	Seneca	Waller
29............	Cortland	Carmack
30............	Chenango	Babbidge
43............	Tompkins	Babbidge
44............	Tioga	Babbidge
45............	Broome	Babbidge

he undertook this task the competing service wholesaler already had established a mail-order business with the rural druggists in this area. Mr. Bush had taken to the road in a Model-T Ford in 1922 to build up the sales in all four counties. He had been hired specifically for this job because he was a native of the area and an experienced "drummer."

Five years later Mr. John Jameson, a friend of Mr. Bush, became a division salesman, and, at the suggestion of Mr. Bush, covered other accounts in the same four-county area. Mr. Jameson had been a salesman for a proprietary medicine firm before he joined the wholesale drug house. He was seven years younger than Mr. Bush. Since that time Mr. Jameson had serviced a number of accounts in the four-county area. The list of accounts that each of these men handled appears in Exhibits 6 and 7. Mr. Trucks noticed that the incomes which Messrs. Bush and Jameson had received from commissions were very stable over the years.

A VISIT FROM MR. JAMESON

On the Wednesday morning following the June sales meeting, Mr. Trucks saw Mr. Jameson come in the front door of the Syracuse Division offices. Although the salesman passed within 30 feet of Mr. Trucks' desk he did not appear to notice the sales manager. Mr. Jameson walked through the office area to the partitioned space where Mr. Burton's

Exhibit 4

CONSOLIDATED DRUGS, INC.

Selected Data on Sales and Sales Potentials, by Counties

| County | Code | Population | Per Cent | Chain and Independent Stores | | | | | | | | Hospitals | | | Miscellaneous |
				Sold	Inactive Accounts	Accounts Not Sold	Total	P.W.P.P. (in Thousands)	Per Cent Area P.W.P.P.	Sales (in Thousands)	Per Cent P.W.P.P.	Sold	Not Sold	Sales (in Thousands)	Sales (in Thousands)
St. Lawrence	1	99,400	7.0	19	2	5	26	$ 364	3.9	$ 107	29.4	2	4	$ 3	
Jefferson	4	86,700	6.1	26	8	..	34	724	7.8	201	27.8	2	2	2	
Lewis	5	22,800	1.6	8	..	..	8	87	0.0	29	33.1	..	1	..	
Herkimer	6	46,800	3.3	10	6	1	17	312	3.3	49	15.6	..	2	..	
Oswego	9	78,300	5.5	22	4	..	26	537	5.7	124	23.1	1	2	..	
Oneida	10	226,000	15.9	46	14	12	72	1,053	11.3	111	10.5	..	13	..	
Wayne	16	14,400	1.0	4	..	1	5	103	1.1	23	22.0	..	..	..	
Cayuga	17	71,100	5.0	12	4	..	16	312	3.3	56	17.9	2	..	2	
Onondaga	18	346,600	24.3	104	7	9	120	2,549	27.3	722	28.3	6	9	36	
Madison	19	47,000	3.3	12	2	3	17	417	4.5	87	20.9	..	2	..	
Seneca	28	29,700	2.1	6	1	3	10	186	2.0	28	15.1	2	1	2	
Cortland	29	37,700	2.6	6	2	1	9	146	1.6	46	31.5	..	2	..	
Chenango	30	39,900	2.8	4	2	6	12	189	2.0	21	10.9	..	3	..	
Tompkins	43	60,200	4.2	9	1	4	14	388	4.2	63	16.3	..	5	..	
Tioga	44	30,600	2.1	4	..	7	11	161	1.7	40	24.7	..	..	..	
Broome	45	187,800	13.2	22	2	13	37	1,807	19.4	115	6.3	..	8	..	
Total		1,425,000	100.0	314	55	65	434	$9,335	100.0						
Totals, 1951			..	..	..	..	..	..	..	$1,819	19.5	15	54	$45	$334
Totals, 1950			..	..	..	..	..	..	..	$1,659	18.6	..	..	$27	$ 256

Source: Company records.

Exhibit 5

CONSOLIDATED DRUGS, INC.

Counties Sold by Messrs. Bush and Jameson

Exhibit 6

CONSOLIDATED DRUGS, INC.

Accounts Sold by Asa Bush, by Counties, with 1951 Purchases

Jefferson County:		Oswego County:	
Adams Center, D*.........$	1,986	Caloose, D*.............$	684
(Alexandria Bay, D.......	10,192)	Central Square, D........	743
(Alexandria Bay, D.......	8,764)	Constantia, M...........	29
Bellville, D..............	1,165	Cleveland, M...........	156
(Carthage, D.............	33,903)	(Fulton, D..............	6,051)
Chaumont, D.............	336	(Fulton, D..............	9,817)
(Clayton, D.............	5,901)	(Fulton, D..............	11,116)
(Clayton, D.............	9,113)	(Fulton, D..............	15,396)
Deferiet, D..............	205	Hannibal, D.............	1,558
Dexter, D................	6,481	Hastings, M.............	1,539
Ellisburg, D..............	131	Lacona, M..............	185
LaFargeville, D...........	290	Mexico, D..............	6,371
Plessis, D................	490	Oswego, D..............	4,827
Redwood, M.............	60	(Oswego, D.............	8,307)
Rodman, D..............	1,787	(Oswego, D.............	9,641)
Sackets Harbor, D........	358	(Oswego, D.............	16,415)
		(Oswego, D.............	17,593)
County total...........$81,162		(Oswego, D.............	8,982)
		Oswego, H..............	6
Lewis County:		Parish, M...............	2,065
Beaver Falls, D*.........$	1,270	Phoenix, D..............	3,895
Croghan, D.............	8,199	(Pulaski, D.............	3,501)
Harrisville, D...........	6,172	(Pulaski, D.............	11,636)
Lowville, D..............	7,896	Sandy Creek, D..........	5,655
Lowville, D..............	1,438	West Monroe, D........	1,911
Lyons Falls, D...........	2,008		
Port Leyden, D..........	775		
Turin, M.................	1,040	County total.........$148,079	
County total..........$28,798			

Territory total........................$258,039

Increase over 1950......................   0.9%

*D: Independent Drugstore; C: Chain Drugstore; M: Miscellaneous Account; H: Hospital.
NOTE: Accounts in parentheses are those indicated by Mr. Jameson as the ones he wanted.
Source: Company records.

private office was located. Twenty minutes later Mr. Jameson emerged from the division manager's office and made his way to Mr. Trucks' desk.

"Hi there, young fellah!" he shouted as he approached.

"Howdy, Jack. Sit down and chat awhile," Mr. Trucks replied. "What got you out of bed so early?" he asked, knowing that the salesman must have risen at 6 o'clock to make the drive to Syracuse from his home in Watertown.

Mr. Jameson squeezed his bulky frame into the armchair next to the desk. "It's a shame Asa is retiring," he said. "I never thought he could stand to give it up. I never knew anyone who enjoyed selling as much

Exhibit 7

CONSOLIDATED DRUGS, INC.

Accounts Sold by John Jameson, by Counties, with 1951 Purchases

St. Lawrence County:		Jefferson County:	
Canton, D*	$ 13,080	Adams, C*	$ 1,049
Edwards, D	672	Carthage, C	1,176
Edwards, M	1,885	Evans Mills, D	1,229
Gouverneur, D	226	Philadelphia, D	2,101
Gouverneur, D	9,383	Watertown, D	16,782
Gouverneur, C	16,519	Watertown, D	2,632
Heuvelton, D	108	Watertown, D	4,889
Massena, D	11,259	Watertown, D	17,041
Massena, D	3,397	Watertown, D	10,262
Massena, C	2,448	Watertown, D	14,622
Massena, C	2,225	Watertown, D	21,249
Massena, H	38	Watertown, D	12,791
Madrid, D	1,432	Watertown, D	5,388
Morristown, D	2,731	Watertown, D	475
Norfolk, D	2,995	Watertown, D	6,282
Norwood, D	3,139	Watertown, C	2,019
Ogdensburg, D	8,090	Watertown, C	3,318
Ogdensburg, D	22,555	Watertown, M	378
Ogdensburg, D	7,203	Watertown, H	70
Ogdensburg, D	3,380	Watertown, H	2,009
Ogdensburg, M	149		
Ogdensburg, H	2,653	Total county	$125,760
Potsdam, D	15,444		
Potsdam, C	7,371	Oswego County:	
Rensselaer Falls, D	367	Pulaski, C	$ 1,091
Total county	$138,749		

Territory total........................$265,600
Increase over 1950......................　11.6%

*D: Independent Drugstore; C: Chain Drugstore; M: Miscellaneous Account; H: Hospital.
Source: Company records.

as Asa—'cept, maybe me." Mr. Jameson continued praising Mr. Bush and telling anecdotes which illustrated his point until Mr. Trucks began to wonder whether Mr. Jameson thought that the sales manager was biased in some way against the retiring salesman. Mr. Trucks recalled that he had made some critical remarks about Mr. Bush to Mr. Burton, but he could not recall any discussion of Mr. Bush's shortcomings with Mr. Bush himself or any of the other salesmen. Mr. Jameson ended his remarks by saying, "Old J. K., God rest his soul, always said that Asa was the best damn' wholesale drug salesman he had ever known."

There was a brief silence as Mr. Trucks did not realize that Mr. Jameson was finished. Finally Mr. Trucks said, "You know, Jack, I think we ought to have a testimonial dinner for Asa at the July sales meeting."

Mr. Jameson made no comment on Mr. Trucks's suggestion; instead, he went on to say, "None of these green trainees will ever be able to take Asa's place. Those druggists up there are old-timers. They would resent being high-pressured by some kid blown up to twice his size with college degrees. No sir! You've got to sell 'em right in those country stores."

Mr. Trucks did not believe that Mr. Jameson's opinion about the adaptability of the younger, college-educated salesman was justified by the evidence available. He recalled that several of these men in country territories had done better on their May sales quotas than either Mr. Bush or Mr. Jameson. He was proud of his self-restraint when he commented, "Selling in a country territory is certainly different."

"That's right, Dick. I wanted to make sure you understood these things before I told you." Mr. Jameson was nervously massaging his double chin between his thumb and forefinger.

Mr. Trucks looked at him with a quizzical expression. "Told me what?"

"I have just been talking to Mr. Burton. Well, I was talking to him about an understanding between Asa and me. We always agreed that if anything should happen to the other, or he should retire, or something—well, we agreed that the one who remained should get to take over his choice of the other's accounts. We told J. K. about this and he said, 'Boys, what's O.K. by you is O.K. by me. You two developed that territory and you deserve to be rewarded for it.' Well, yes sir, that's the way it was."

Without pausing, Mr. Jameson went on, "I just told Mr. Burton about it. He said that he remembered talking about the whole thing with J. K. 'Yes,' he said, 'Tell Trucks about it,' he said, 'Tell Trucks about it.' Asa and I went over his accounts on Sunday. I went over his list of accounts with him and checked the ones that I want. Here is the list with the accounts all checked off.[2] I already know nearly all the proprietors. You'll see that—"

"Wait a minute, Jack! Wait a minute!" Mr. Trucks interrupted. "You've lost me completely. In the first place, if there is any assignment of accounts to be made I'll do it. It will be done on a basis that is fair to the salesmen concerned and profitable to the company. You know that."

"Dick, I'm only asking for what is fair." Mr. Jameson's face was flushed. Mr. Trucks noticed that the man he had always believed to be

---

[2] Mr. Jameson's selected accounts are the accounts in parentheses in Exhibit 6.

deliberately confident and self-possessed was now so agitated that it was difficult for him to speak. "I don't want my territory chopped up and handed to some green kid!"

Mr. Trucks noticed that everybody in the office was now watching Mr. Jameson. "Calm down, Jack," he whispered to the salesman, indicating with a nod of his head that others were watching.

"Don't talk to me that way, you young squirt!" replied Mr. Jameson. "I don't care. A man with 25 years' service deserves some consideration!"

"You're absolutely right, Jack. You're absolutely right." As Mr. Trucks repeated his words Mr. Jameson settled back in his chair. The typewriters started clattering again.

"Now, first of all, Jack," queried Mr. Trucks, as he tried to return the conversation to a friendly basis, "where did you get the idea that your territory was going to be 'chopped up'?"

"You said so yourself. You said it at the very first sales meeting when you made that speech about how you were going to boost sales in Syracuse." Mr. Jameson emphasized his words by pounding on the side of the desk with his masonic ring.

Mr. Trucks reflected for a moment. He recalled giving a talk at his first sales meeting at the end of May entitled, "How We Can Do A Better Job for Consolidated." The speech was a restatement of the merchandising policy of the New York office. He had mentioned that getting more profitable business would require that a larger percentage of the total purchases of each account would have to come to Consolidated; that attaining a larger share of the business from each store would require more selling time in each store; and that greater concentration on each account would necessitate reorganization of the sales territories. He realized that his future plans did entail reorganization of the territories; he had not anticipated, however, any such reaction as Mr. Jameson's.

Finally, Mr. Trucks said, "I do plan to make some territorial changes —not right away—at least not until I have looked things over pretty darn carefully. Of course, you understand that our first duty is to make greater profits for the company. Some of our territories would be a great deal more profitable if they were organized and handled in a different manner."

"What are you going to do about Asa's territory?" asked Mr. Jameson.

"Well, I just haven't had a chance to study the situation yet," he replied. "If I could make the territory more profitable by reorganizing it,

I guess that is what they would expect me to do." Since Mr. Trucks had not yet looked over the information about the territory, he was anxious not to commit himself to any course of action relating to it.

"What about the promises the company made to me about letting me choose the accounts I want?" the salesman asked.

"You don't mean the company's promise; you mean Mr. Martin's promise," Mr. Trucks corrected him.

"Well, if Mr. Martin wasn't 'the company' I don't see how you figure that you are!" Mr. Jameson's face resumed its flush.

"O.K., Jack. How about giving me a chance to look over the situation. You know that I want to do the right thing. Let me go over your list of the accounts you want. In a few days I can talk intelligently about the matter." Mr. Trucks felt that there was no point in carrying on the discussion.

"All right, Dick," said Mr. Jameson, rising. The two men walked toward the front entrance of the office. As they reached the top of the steps leading to the front door, Mr. Jameson turned to the sales manager and offered his hand, "Look, Dick. I'm sorry I got so mad. You just can't imagine what this means to me. I know you'll see it my way when you know the whole story." Mr. Jameson's voice sounded strained.

Mr. Trucks watched the older man leave. He felt embarrassed at the realization that Mr. Jameson's parting words had been overheard by several manufacturers' representatives standing nearby.

A CONVERSATION WITH THE DIVISION MANAGER

Mr. Trucks decided to talk at once to Mr. Burton about his conversation with Mr. Jameson. He walked over to Mr. Burton's office. He hesitated in the doorway; Mr. Burton looked up and then indicated with a gesture that Mr. Trucks was to take a seat.

The sales manager sat down. He waited for Mr. Burton to speak. Mr. Burton was occupied for the moment with the problem of unwrapping a cigar. Mr. Trucks opened the conversation by saying, "Jack Jameson just stopped by to speak to me."

"Yeah?" said Mr. Burton, removing bitten flakes of tobacco from the end of his tongue.

"He said something about getting some of Asa Bush's accounts when Asa retires," Mr. Trucks said in a deliberately questioning manner.

"Yeah."

The sales manager continued, "Well, this idea of his was based on a promise that he said J. K. had made."

"Yeah. He told me that, too."

"Did Martin make such a promise?" Mr. Trucks inquired.

"Hell, I don't know. It sounds like him." He tilted back in his swivel chair.

"What shall I do about it?"

"Don't ask me; you're the sales manager." Mr. Burton paused, holding his cigar away from his lips as if he were about to speak. Just as Mr. Trucks was about to say something Mr. Burton lurched forward to flick the ashes from his cigar into his ash tray. "Look here, Dick. I don't want any morale problems around here. You're the first of the 'wonder boys' to be put in charge of a department in this division. I don't want you to do anything to mess up the morale. We never had any morale problems when Martin was alive. We don't want anything like that in this division."

Mr. Trucks was momentarily bewildered. He knew by the way that Mr. Burton used the phrase "wonder boys" that he was referring to the college men who had been brought into the Syracuse Division since the war.

Mr. Burton went on, "Why the devil did you tell the men that you were going to reassign the sales territories without even telling me?"

"But you were there when I said it."

"Said what?"

"Well, at my first sales meeting, that one of the ways we were going to get more business was to reorganize the sales territory," Mr. Trucks replied.

"I certainly don't remember anything like that. Dick, you gave a good inspirational talk, but I sure can't remember anything about reassigning territories."

"Actually, I just mentioned the reorganization of territories in passing," the sales manager smiled.

"I'll be damned. That sort of thing is always happening. Here everybody is frothing at the mouth about something that they think we are going to do and we haven't the slightest idea why they think we're going to do it. You know, the real reason Asa Bush asked to be retired instead of staying on as he planned was probably this fear of having his territory reorganized. Both he and Jameson know that their pension on retirement is based on their earnings in the last five years of active employment. Now that I think of it, three or four of the other salesmen have stopped in during the last couple of weeks to tell me what a fine job they were doing. They probably had this territory reassignment bogey on their minds."

Mr. Burton's cigar was no longer burning. He began groping under the papers on his desk for a match.

Mr. Trucks took advantage of this pause in the conversation. "Mr. Burton, I think there are some real advantages to be won by an adjustment of the sales territories. I think—"

"You still think that after today?" the division manager asked in a sarcastic tone.

"Why, yes! The profit we make on sales to an individual account is related closely to delivery expense. The larger the total proportion of the account's business we get, the more profit we make because the delivery expense remains more or less constant."

"Look, Dick. You college men always have everything all figured out with slide rules, but sometimes that doesn't count. Morale is the important thing. The salesmen won't stand for having their territories changed. I know that you have four trainees that you'd like to put out on territories. You put them out on parts of the territories belonging to some of the more experienced men—bam! God knows how many of our good salesmen would be left. Now, I've never had any trouble with sales force morale since I've been manager of this division. Old Martin, bless his soul, never let me down. He wasn't any damn' Ph.D., but, by golly, he could handle men. Don't get off on the wrong foot with the boys, Dick. With the labor situation in the warehouse being what it is, I've just got too much on my mind. I don't want you to be creating more problems than I can handle. How 'bout it, boy!"

Mr. Burton ground out his half-smoked cigar, looking steadily at Mr. Trucks.

Mr. Trucks was upset because the division manager had imputed to him a lack of concern for morale problems. He had always thought of himself as being very considerate of the thoughts and feelings of others. He realized that at the moment his foremost desire was to get away from Mr. Burton.

Mr. Trucks rose from his chair saying, "Mr. Burton, you can count on me. I know you are right about this morale business."

"Atta boy," said the division manager. "It does us a lot of good to talk like this once in awhile. Now, you see if you can make peace with the salesmen. I want you to handle everything yourself."

"Well, thanks a lot," said the sales manager, as he backed out of the office door.

As he walked through the office after talking with Mr. Burton, he saw two manufacturers' representatives with whom he had appointments already seated near the receptionist's desk. His schedule of appointments that day did not permit him to do more than gather the material pertaining to the Jameson and Bush territories.

MR. TRUCKS GOES HOME

Mr. Trucks left the office shortly after five o'clock to drive to his home in a suburb of Syracuse. It was a particularly hot and humid day. Pre–Fourth-of-July traffic lengthened the drive by nearly twenty minutes. When he finally turned into his own driveway, he felt as though his skin were caked with grime and perspiration. He got out of the car and walked around the house to the terrace in the rear. Nancy, his wife, was sewing in a deck chair under the awning.

"Hello, Dick. You're late," she said, looking up with a smile.

"I know it. Even the traffic was bad today." He dropped his coat on a glass-topped table and sprawled out full length on the glider. "Honestly, I'm so exhausted and dirty that I am disgusted with myself."

"Bad day?"

"Awful. You just can't imagine how discouraging it is trying to get this job organized. You would think that it would be obvious to everybody that what ails the Syracuse Division is the organization of the sales force," said Mr. Trucks, arranging a pillow under his head.

"I didn't realize that you thought anything was wrong with the Syracuse Division."

"Well, what I mean is that we get only 20% of the potential wholesale business. If I could organize the salesforce my way—well, God knows, maybe we could get 40% of the business. That is what the New York office watches for. The sales manager who increases his division's share of the market gets the promotions when they come along. I knew Mr. Crow transferred me to this division because he knew these possibilities existed."

"I don't understand. Is Mr. Crow still your boss, or is Mr. Burton?" asked his wife.

"Nancy, it's terribly discouraging. Mr. Burton is my boss, but I'll never get anywhere with Consolidated unless Mr. Crow and the other people in New York promote me."

"Don't you like Mr. Burton?"

"I had a run-in with him today."

"You didn't!" she said crossly as she laid her sewing aside.

Mr. Trucks had not anticipated this reaction. He gazed up at the awning as if he had not noticed his wife's intent expression. "We didn't argue particularly. He just—well, he doesn't know too much about sales management. He put his foot down on my plans to reorganize the territories."

"I can't understand why you would go and get yourself into a fight with your boss when you haven't been here even two months. We should never have bought this house!"

"Honestly, honey, I didn't have any fight. Everything is O.K. He just —well, do you want me to be a divisional sales manager all my life?"

She smiled and said nothing.

He continued, "I'm sorry you married such a grouch, but I just get plain mad when somebody calls me a 'wonder boy.'"

"You're tired," she said sympathetically. "Why don't you go up and take a shower while I feed the children. We can have a drink and then eat our dinner whenever we feel like it. It's only meat loaf anyway."

"That sounds wonderful," he said, raising himself from his prone position.

AN UNEXPECTED CALLER

Mr. Trucks had just stepped out of the shower when he heard his wife calling to him. "Dick, Jim Pepper is here to see you."

"Tell him I'll be down in just a minute. Give him a drink, Nancy."

As he dressed, Mr. Trucks wondered why the salesman had chosen the dinner hour to call. During the month since he had moved into his new home no salesman had ever dropped in uninvited.

When Mr. Trucks came downstairs, he found Mr. Pepper sitting on the living-room couch with a Tom Collins in his hand.

"Hello, Jim," said Mr. Trucks crossing the room with his right hand extended. "You look as if you had had a hot day. Why don't you take off your coat? If we go out to the terrace, you may get a chance to cool off."

"Thanks, Dick," the visitor said as he moved out to the terrace. "I'm sorry to come barging in this way, but I thought it was important."

"Well, what's on your mind?" said Mr. Trucks as he sat down.

Mr. Pepper started to speak but hesitated as Mrs. Trucks came out of the door with two glasses in her hand. She handed one glass to Mr. Trucks, then excused herself, saying, "I think I better see if the children are all right."

After she had disappeared into the house, Mr. Pepper said, "I heard about what happened at the office today, so I thought I'd come over to tell you that we stand 100% behind you."

Mr. Trucks was perplexed by Mr. Pepper's words. He realized that the incident to which the salesman referred was probably his meeting with Mr. Jameson. Mr. Trucks said, "I'm not sure what you mean, Jim."

"I heard that you and Jameson had it out this morning about changing the sales territories," Mr. Pepper replied.

Mr. Trucks smiled. Two thoughts entered his mind. He was amused at the proportions that the brief conversation of that morning had assumed in the minds of so many people; but, at the same time, he was curious as to how Mr. Pepper, who had presumably been in the field selling, had heard about the incident so soon. Without hesitation he asked, "Where did you hear about this, Jim?"

"Jack Dangler told me! He was down at the warehouse with Homer Babbidge when I stopped off to pick up a special narcotics order for a customer. They are all excited about this territory business. Dangler said Jameson came out to his house at lunch time and told him about it. Everybody figured that you were going to change the territories when you started traveling around with each of the boys, especially after what you said at your first sales meeting."

"Well, the reason I went on the road with each of the men, Jim," said Mr. Trucks, "was so that I could learn more about their selling problems and, at the same time, meet the customers."

Mr. Pepper smiled, "Sure, but when you started filling out a rating sheet on each account, I couldn't help thinking you had some reason for it."

Mr. Trucks realized that the salesman had spoken with irony in his voice, but he thought it was better to let the matter pass as if he had not noticed it. Since he was planning to use the information he had gathered for reorganization of the sales territories, he decided that he would be frank with Mr. Pepper in order to find out what the young salesman's reaction might be on the question of territorial changes. He said, "Jim, I've thought a lot about making some changes in the territories—"

Mr. Pepper interrupted him, "That's terrific. I'm sure glad to hear that. I don't like to speak ill of the dead, but old Martin really gave the trainees the short end of the stick when he put us on territories. He either gave a man a territory of uncontacted accounts so he beat his head against a stone wall until he finally quit, and that is just what happened to two guys who trained with me, or else he gave him a territory where somebody had to be replaced and where some of the best accounts had been handed over to one of the older salesmen. Well, I know for a fact that when I took over my territory from Rick Hunt, Jack Dangler and

Rusty Means got twelve of Hunt's best accounts. And, damn it, I got more sales out of what was left than Hunt ever did, but Dangler and Means' total sales didn't go up at all. It took me awhile, but, by golly, I had the laugh at every sales meeting when our monthly sales figures were announced."

"Is that right?" said Mr. Trucks.

"Damn' right! And I wasn't the only one. That's why those old duffers are so down on the four of us that have come with the division since the war. We've beaten them at their own game."

"Do you think that Waller and Carmack and Smith feel the same way?" asked Mr. Trucks.

"Think, hell! I know it! That's all we ever talk about. If you re-organize those territories and give us back the accounts that Martin took away, you'll see some real sales records. Take, for example, the Medical Arts Pharmacy out by Mercy Hospital. Jack Dangler got that one away from my territory and he calls there only once a week. If I could get that one back, I'd get in there three times a week and get five times as much business."

Mr. Trucks had to raise his hands in a gesture of protest. "Don't you have enough accounts already, Jim, to keep you busy?"

"Dick, I spend fifty hours a week on the road and I love it; but I know damn' well that if I put some of the time I spend in 'two-by-four' stores into some of those big juicy accounts like Medical Arts Pharmacy, I'd do even more business."

Mr. Trucks commented, "I'm not particularly anxious to argue the point now, but if you start putting your time into Medical Arts Pharmacy, what's going to happen to your sales to the 'two-by-four' stores?"

The salesman replied, "Those druggists all know me. They'd go right on buying."

Mr. Trucks did not agree with Mr. Pepper, and he thought that the salesman realized this.

After a moment of silence Mr. Pepper rose from his chair saying, "I'd better scoot home. My wife will be waiting for me with a rolling pin for being late so I'd better get out before your wife gets at me with a skillet." Mr. Pepper laughed heartily at his own joke.

The two men walked around the house to Mr. Pepper's car. As the salesman climbed into the car, he said, "Dick, don't forget what I said— Waller, Carmack, Smith, and I stand 100% behind you. You won't ever hear us talk about going over to a competitor!"

"Who's talking about that?" asked Mr. Trucks.

"Well," said Mr. Pepper as he started the motor and shifted into gear, "I don't want to tell tales out of school."

"Sure," Mr. Trucks said quickly. "I'm sorry I asked. So long, Jim. I'll see you soon."

Mr. Trucks watched the salesman back out of the driveway and drive away.

5. A Note on the Manufacture and Distribution of Portland Cement in the United Kingdom*

CEMENT MANUFACTURE

PORTLAND CEMENT was developed from an invention of a laborer in Leeds, England, in 1824. It was called "portland" cement because the concrete made from it resembled the well-known portland building stone in color and texture. Its manufacture is today a major world industry. World consumption has risen from 81 million tons in 1938 to 315 million in 1960 and is still rising.

Cement itself is manufactured from a closely controlled mixture of calcium carbonate, alumina, and silica. Calcium carbonate is found in various forms of limestone fairly liberally throughout the world. To be suitable for the manufacture of cement, the calcium carbonate content of the limestone must be relatively free from impurity. Soft chalk, which is very high in calcium carbonate, is found uniquely on either side of the English Channel toward the southern part of the North, Sea. Chalk is easier to process than hard limestone, and its availability accounts, in part, for the fact that nearly half of British production is located in southeastern England.

Alumina is found in some forms of clay or shale. A relatively small amount of sand supplies the silica requirements.

From 3,000 to 3,600 pounds of raw materials are required to make a ton of cement. These are quarried with large diesel or electric power shovels and conveyed to the works, which is normally placed nearby. There they are crushed and ground to a fine powder, and—in what is known as the "wet process"—mixed in strictly controlled proportions with water to form cement slurry. (Slurry normally contains about 40% water by weight.) The liquid state of the mixture is necessary to

* Much of the material included in this description was taken, with permission, from a paper "The Manufacture and Distribution of Cement" prepared by the Chairman of The Rugby Portland Cement Company Ltd., Rugby, England.

facilitate a perfectly homogeneous mixture of the raw materials and to permit rapid adjustment of the proportions by merely adding materials which quickly become uniformly dispersed throughout the liquid.

The slurry, when chemically correct, is fed to the kiln, which in a modern works is a large steel cylinder from 3 to 500 feet in length and 9 to 14 feet in diameter. It rotates at the rate of approximately once every 45 seconds, on a slightly inclined axis. The slurry is fed in at the higher end.

Near the lower end of the kiln is the burning zone, where fuel is injected into the kiln and fired to produce a temperature of about 2,500°F. Pulverized coal is the usual fuel in Britain, but oil and natural gas are used in other countries where these fuels are readily available. The water in the slurry is driven off as steam, together with the carbon dioxide content of the calcium carbonate and minor quantities of other gases. The remaining materials are fluxed in the intense heat and leave the kiln in the form of pea-sized nodules called cement clinker. The chemical part of the process, completed at this point, is closely controlled throughout by chemists who test the raw materials, the coal, and the slurry every hour, day and night.

Thereafter, the process is largely mechanical. The cement clinker is ground in large water-cooled mills to a predetermined fineness, and a small amount of calcium sulphate, or gypsum, is added in order to control the "setting time" of the resultant powder, now finished cement.

As it leaves the mills, the cement is weighed automatically and then pumped through pipes by compressed air to the large concrete silos in which it is stored. It remains in storage until it is withdrawn by mechanical means to the packing plant, where it is packed into paper sacks, which are automatically fitted, sealed, weighed and delivered by means of conveyors to the truck, the rail car, or the ship. It may be withdrawn from the silos into special bulk trucks which deliver it unpacked.

THE USES OF CEMENT

Cement is used as the binding agent in concrete and in mortar. Concrete, one of the world's primary construction materials, is composed of cement, sand, aggregate (clean gravel and stones), and water. Cement reacts chemically with the water and hardens within a few hours after mixing, binding the sand and gravel particles in a solid mass. Concrete can be used without reinforcing (as in highway pavements which contain only wire matting for temperature stresses), or it can be used with steel reinforcement, as in buildings and bridges.

STRUCTURE OF THE INDUSTRY IN THE UNITED KINGDOM—1960

The cement industry in the United Kingdom consists of nine financially independent groups, all of which have been members of the Cement Makers' Federation since its establishment in 1934.

The three largest interests held, in 1960, about 83% of the home market and have provided much of the leadership within the federation. Associated Portland Cement Manufacturers Limited is considerably the largest company, with about 62% of the United Kingdom market. The Tunnel Group has about 12.4%, and The Rugby Portland Cement Company Limited 7% of the United Kingdom market. Practically all the United Kingdom export trade is conducted by these three makers, which are also the only companies having manufacturing subsidiaries abroad.

The federation regulates the internal affairs of the industry and arranges an interchange of technical information and industry-wide statistics. By far its most important function, however, is establishing the basis of selling prices and conditions of sale, in order, it is asserted, that the costs of distribution—which average nearly 20% of delivered cost of cement—can be controlled. Membership is voluntary and voting power is proportionate, although not directly, to the previous year's home deliveries. Approval of any proposal, however, requires the concurrence of at least four of the nine members. The federation has no control over the production of any manufacturer, nor is it concerned with the export trade.

The British cement industry also maintains a large research and promotional organization, the Cement and Concrete Association, part of whose function is to increase the use and uses of concrete. Cement itself has no substitute; however, it is used only to form concrete, which is in competition with steel, brick, stone, tile, timber and many other materials.

The industry also organizes its conduct of labor relations. For more than 35 years it has operated a National Joint Industrial Council at which industry-wide wage rates and working conditions are set. The industry has never had a national strike or lock-out. Holidays with pay and profit-sharing plans were features of the industry for many years before World War II.

POSTWAR GROWTH OF THE INDUSTRY

The postwar progress made by the industry is shown in the following exhibit:

Exhibit 1

THE MANUFACTURE AND DISTRIBUTION OF
PORTLAND CEMENT IN THE UNITED KINGDOM

United Kingdom Cement Deliveries

(000 tons)

	Home	Export	Total
1961 (est.)	13,800	800	14,600
1960	12,463	1,000	13,463
1959	11,683	1,088	12,771
1958	10,675	1,145	11,820
1957	10,709	1,382	12,091
1956	11,275	1,600	12,875
1955	10,759	1,766	12,526
1954	10,079	1,769	11,848
1953	9,335	1,917	11,253
1952	9,147	2,055	11,202
1951	8,144	1,974	10,119
1946	5,479	1,095	6,574
1939	7,587	665	8,252

THE ECONOMICS OF THE INDUSTRY

Siting of the Plant. It is considered a matter of prime importance that cement plants be located as close as possible to raw material deposits. Adequate water supplies, fuel, and electricity, and access to road, rail, and water transport must also be available. Thorough technical investigation is required since both the physical and chemical properties of the raw materials will influence the design of many of the factory components.

Costs of Production. The manufacture of cement is a highly mechanized process and employs comparatively little labor. The capital investment is among the highest for any industry; it equals almost £20,-000 per man employed, which is over six times what it was before World War II. Depreciation is therefore a heavy charge, and will become progressively heavier as prewar plants are replaced.

Coal is the largest individual item in the cost of production. It takes approximately 800 pounds of coal, including the coal used to generate electricity, to make a ton of cement.

In general, industry production costs are distributed as follows:

Coal and power.............................45–50%
Direct labor...............................10–15%
Consumable equipment....................... 9–12%
Depreciation (installed cost).............. 9–12%

Indirect factory labor and other overheads (super-
    vision, testing, maintenance, cost accounting,
    etc.)....................................15–20%
Manufacture cost........................... 100%
Average haulage............................20–30% of Manufacture Cost
Sales expense.............................. 5– 8% "   "   "
General administrative overhead............10–15% "   "   "

Profit margins are not disclosed. It has been asserted that current prices allow profits only because the manufacturers are still using, in part, equipment installed in the late 1930's. As greater proportions of new, more expensive plant installations are brought into use, prices may rise to cover increased depreciation charges.

Leaders of the British cement industry have repeatedly stated that manufacture of cement in the United Kingdom has for years been conducted with the highest efficiency and one of the lowest unit costs of any producing country in the world.

Distribution. The distribution of cement to the site where it will be used is a more technical and complicated problem than at first sight appears, for it is not the cost of production at the place where the cement is made but the cost at the site where it will be used that is important. The geographical distribution of demand, which in itself varies quite considerably from year to year (and can be materially distorted at different times by large airport programs, road works, reservoirs and similar forms of construction using large quantities of cement) is not coincident with the geographical distribution of the works.

Most companies in the industry maintain a fleet of trucks for road delivery. Little goes by rail, owing to the costs of double-handling. Delivery in bulk (in special vehicles) has rapidly increased in recent years and now accounts for nearly 50% of the home trade.

PRICING AND THE ROLE OF THE CEMENT MAKERS' FEDERATION

The manufacturers feel that a joint policy of distribution and price can avoid the severe price competition which, in the early 1930's created difficulties for both producers and users. For example, a works near to a large consuming area might be able to supply only one-third of the demand in that area, leaving the remaining two-thirds to come from a much greater distance. If there were not a co-ordinated price policy, it has been said, a builder taking his supplies from the nearer works would pay one price, while his competitor would have to pay a higher price for cement coming from a more distant works. This would assertedly lead to endless complications in bidding for construction projects.

The federation's pricing arrangements, therefore, have the following objectives:

1. To sell and distribute cement throughout the country in the most efficient and economical manner commensurate with the interests of the country as a whole, of the users of cement, and of the manufacturers—in particular by:
   a) Encouraging the delivery in any particular area from the nearest works with the object of avoiding unnecessary and wasteful haulage.
   b) Eliminating depots (except where these perform useful functions) and delivering straight from works to construction sites.
   c) Providing a stable system of prices which takes into account the high proportion of the cost of transport in the price of cement and avoids disproportionate price differentials which would otherwise arise between various parts of the U.K.
2. To provide a price system giving sufficient stability to enable manufacturers individually and collectively to plan production in advance efficiently and economically, and individually to undertake the heavy expenditure required to meet increasing demand for cement.
3. To ensure during any temporary shortage of cement that prices remain at a reasonable level.
4. To eliminate unnecessary and expensive advertising.
5. To provide for standard forms of packages, bulk delivery and the like.
6. To arrange for the convenience of both manufacturers and buyers, standard conditions of supply and forms of quotation and contract.
7. To facilitate joint research and exchange of information to improve the standard and the potential utility of cement.[1]

To achieve these aims, the federation's present system provides for the same delivered price at the same point of delivery for all brands of cement, irrespective of the works from which the cement may come.

There are 48 cement works in the United Kingdom. (Cement works very near one another usually have the same base price.) There are 37 base prices, one for each location where cement is manufactured, and one for each cement importing center on the coast. These base prices are nearly the same at every factory, although there are slight variations made for the type of raw materials used, and the delivered

---

[1] Summarized from a policy statement of the federation.

price of fuel to the works. For the former, for instance, plants using chalk as their source of calcium carbonate have base prices about 5% lower than those using limestone, since all limestone crushing and grinding expenses are eliminated. In 1961, the base factory price (delivered within five miles of plant) of ordinary portland cement ranged from 111/6d. to 127/6d. per ton.

Radiating from each works is a series of concentric circles at four- or five-mile intervals, the circles from any particular works continuing until they meet the circles radiating from another works. The delivered price within each of these circles increases by 1/6d. for each circle. (See Exhibit 2.)

These price increments do not, in fact, cover actual transportation costs; therefore, manufacturers allow 10–15% of the base price plus the zone price increments for covering haulage costs. As a result, between 20 and 30 miles from a producing unit is considered the "breakeven" haulage distance, below which haulage costs are less than the allowance in the base price plus the incremental price increases, and above which the converse is true. The more efficiently a producer can operate his truck fleet, the greater will be his breakeven haulage distance.

The pricing scheme means that every buyer at a particular point will pay exactly the same price for his cement. It also means that there is every inducement for a manufacturer to save transport costs by selling as much of his production as possible within the circles controlled by his own works. The further he delivers cement from his own works, the more likely he is to run into the circles controlled by another works, where the price he will receive will begin to decrease. The federation asserts that the effect of this arrangement is to save as much as possible of the heavy transport costs and so maintain throughout the country, on the average, a lower level of prices than would otherwise be the case.

There exist standard merchant discounts. Retail building material suppliers are entitled to a merchant's discount, but they in turn must sell cement at the same prices, in the particular zones, which apply to the manufacturers. Thus, a buyer pays the same price whether he buys from a manufacturer or a merchant. Merchants play a major role in supplying small orders, since the minimum order normally accepted by a manufacturer is 6 tons. A relatively small percentage of industry sales is made directly to merchants for their own accounts, but much more cement is delivered to the customer "on site" at a merchant's order.

Exhibit 2

THE MANUFACTURE AND DISTRIBUTION OF PORTLAND CEMENT IN THE UNITED KINGDOM

Illustration of the Federation's Pricing Agreement

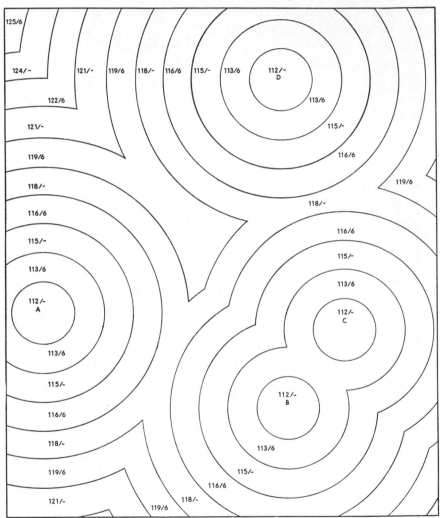

Sales price in shillings and pence per ton shown for each four- or five-mile zone.

THE RESTRICTIVE TRADE PRACTICES ACT

In 1956, England passed the Restrictive Trade Practices Act, which required that all trade agreements be registered with the Registrar of the Restrictive Practices Court. These agreements subsequently had to be justified before the Court, which would decide whether they were contrary to the public interest. On March 16, 1961, the Restrictive

Practices Court handed down its decision: it upheld the federation's price agreements with only minor modifications.

In essence, the federation argued that, because of its price-fixing agreement, U.K. cement manufacturers could operate with more certainty of profit than under free competition. Because of this greater security, they were willing to accept a lower return on investment and thus could sell cement appreciably lower than if prices had not been fixed.

Experts on both sides agreed that, in order to attract new capital into the industry, a net return on investment of at least 15% would have to be available. The federation proved that, in order to yield such a return, a new cement plant would have to price its cement at least 25 shillings per ton higher than the current average price. It also established that federation members were earning, on the average, less than 10% return on investment. The Court therefore concluded that, had the price-fixing arrangement not existed, the price of cement would have been "significantly" higher, and the public would have suffered accordingly. Thus the Court upheld the main price-fixing clause. It found that the industry was efficient and had acted with a sense of responsibility.

The presiding judge was concerned only that the price-fixing agreement should be as honorably administered in the future as had been true in the past. Thus he requested, and the federation agreed, that if at any future date the Registrar should wish to determine whether prices were still being kept at a fair level, the federation would cooperate fully by making cost and price data available for inspection.

The federation's practice of giving quantity discounts based on total annual purchases from *all* federation members was disallowed by the judge, on the grounds that it did not reflect true economies from volume sales.

The court also scrutinized, and upheld with one exception, minor agreements regarding terms of sale. In summing up his decision, Mr. Justice Diplock remarked:

In the result, therefore, the Respondents have satisfied us that the main price-fixing conditions, other than those providing for general rebates to large users and large merchants, are not contrary to the public interest, and that the ancillary restrictions, other than that relating to the prohibition upon the quotations and contracts for the supply of cement for periods exceeding twelve months, are also not contrary to the public interest. . . .[2]

---

[2] *Judgement in the Restrictive Practices Court on an Agreement between Members of the Cement Makers' Federation,* printed by the Cement and Concrete Association, 1961.

In commenting on the Court's decision, Sir Halford Reddish observed:

I am not being wise after the event if I say that the judgement accorded closely with our expectations, for we were confident throughout that a detailed examination of our arrangements would show conclusively that they were in the public interest. And the cement makers were not alone in their satisfaction with the outcome of the case. Over four thousand buyers of cement sent us replies to a questionnaire before the hearing: something like 97 per cent of them were strongly in favour of a continuation of the present system.[3]

---

[3] *Investors Chronicle,* March 24, 1961.

6. The Rugby Portland Cement Company Limited (A)

HISTORY, GROWTH, AND ORGANIZATION

THE RUGBY COMPANY began producing lime in the early nineteenth century at a works near Rugby, England. Cement manufacture, under the company's "Crown" Cement trade-mark began at the works in the 1820's, and thereafter became its principal product. In 1925, the company, which hitherto had been a partnership, became a private limited company with share capital of £100,000 owned by descendants of the previous partners. In 1929, Mr. (now Sir[1]) Halford Reddish, a young chartered accountant with a consulting practice, joined the board which previously had comprised only representatives of the two descendant branches of the original owners. Four years later, upon the death of the general manager, Mr. Reddish became managing director, and shortly afterward, chairman.

At that time, the cement industry was in the middle of a deep depression. Prices were at a very unprofitable level. In spite of this crisis, the chairman decided to expand and modernize the company's production facilities. Contrary to previous industry tradition, he also decided to operate the plant 52 weeks per year, thus ensuring steady employment for the workers. Despite the depression and difficulties of selling the increased output, a profit was realized at the end of the first year of the new management. A second manufacturing site was obtained when a nearby company went into receivership. Erection of a new factory at the second site plus the modernization and expansion of the Rugby works required substantial fresh capital. In 1935, the company became a public company with its shares quoted on The London Stock Exchange, and additional capital of £140,000 was introduced. Since that time, additional equity capital had been raised by occasional "rights" issues.

---

[1] In early 1958, Her Majesty Queen Elizabeth II knighted Mr. Halford Reddish for his public services.

In 1936, Rugby acquired a third site and erected its Rochester works. In 1939, another company was purchased and its facilities were combined with those at Rochester. In 1945, Rugby acquired another company, and although its production facilities were closed, Rugby used its brand name and distribution organization.

Rugby made major additions to its three plants in Great Britain after 1946.

During the immediate postwar years, export trade was very profitable, with unit margins several times those of the home market sales. The proportion of Rugby's deliveries accounted for by exports reached a maximum in 1951 and 1952 at about 43%. In 1961, however, Sir Halford Reddish said that in recent years export sales had become almost marginal because of the increased competition (much of it subsidized) from non-British manufacturers and the growth of cement industries in areas formerly importing cement. Rugby had itself established overseas subsidiaries and built manufacturing plants in Trinidad and western Australia. The former started production in 1954, and the latter in 1955. Both units were able to supply cement at substantially lower prices than existing imported cement and made useful contributions to Rugby's consolidated profits.

With a rapidly developing local market plus export trade in the eastern Caribbean, the Trinidad factory required the doubling of its capacity within less than five years of starting its operation. Management decided in 1961 to extend the Australian plant in the near future.

In highlighting Rugby's growth, Sir Halford said in 1961:

In 1933 we had the one not very modern works at Rugby and total net assets with a book value of £109,250. Today all our works at home and abroad are modern and up-to-date and the total net assets of the company at book values amount to £13,404,369. (The real value is probably in excess of £18,500,000.) Additional capital introduced from 1st January 1933 to 31st December 1960 amounted to £13,295,119. Here's how the money has been found.

Shareholders have subscribed for shares (including premiums and loan stock)...................	£ 5,890,863
by leaving profits in the company..............	5,666,076
And others (by minority interests in, or loans to, subsidiary companies) have found...........	1,738,180
	£13,295,119

Net profit before taxes rose from less than £4,000 to almost £1.8 million in the same period. Postwar growth produced 11 years of successively record deliveries from 1945 to 1956 and 16 years of successively record group profits, 1946–61 (see Exhibits 1–3).

Exhibit 1

THE RUGBY PORTLAND CEMENT COMPANY LIMITED (A)

Consolidated Balance Sheet Statements 1946 and 1951–61

(1,000's of £)

Assets	1946	1951	1952	1953	1954	1955	1956	1957	1958	1959	1960	1961*
Current Assets	576	1,847	1,982	2,616	3,836	4,211	4,521	4,195	4,692	6,744	7,597	
Fixed Assets (1937 Valuation or Cost If Subsequently Acquired)	1,673	3,271	3,591	3,876	6,171	7,861	8,613	9,309	9,487	9,809	10,627	
Less Accumulated Depreciation	436	987	1,125	1,261	1,562	1,635	1,969	2,306	2,601	3,008	3,456	
Net Fixed Assets	1,237	2,285	2,466	2,616	4,609	6,226	6,644	7,003	6,886	6,801	7,171	
Investment in Subsidiary Companies (Not Consolidated)	209	33	393	793	760	…	…	…	…	…	…	
Total Assets	2,022	4,165	4,841	6,025	9,205	10,437	11,165	11,198	11,578	13,545	14,768	

Liabilities and Net Worth	1946	1951	1952	1953	1954	1955	1956	1957	1958	1959	1960	1961*
Current Liabilities	367	1,355	814	776	1,327	1,498	1,759	1,292	1,190	1,191	1,364	
Debt Capital:												
4% Debenture	420	:	:	:	:	:	:	:	:	:	:	
Mortgage Loans	…	…	…	…	…	400	480	560	640	720	800	
4½% Unsecured Loan 1957-62	…	…	1,000	1,500	1,500	1,500	1,500	1,500	1,500	1,500	1,500	
Total Debt	420	…	1,000	1,500	1,500	1,900	1,980	2,060	2,140	2,220	2,300	
Share Capital:												
4% and 6% Preference Shares	325	825	825	825	825	825	825	825	825	825	825	
Ordinary Shares 5/ par	325	500	500	750	1,250	1,500	1,500	1,500	1,500	1,750	2,000	
"A" Shares 1/ par					50	50	50	50	50	50	50	
Capital Reserve	325	610	563	810	1,265	1,300	1,358	1,415	1,275	2,133	1,950	
Revenue Reserves:												
General Reserve	100	500	500	750	1,125	1,500	1,750	2,000	…	…	…	
Reserve for Future Taxation	…	249	408	504	352	390	320	303	350	1,000	1,217	
Reserve for Ordinary and "A" Share Dividend Payment (Net)		52	55	55	115	201	230	230	276	329	383	
Undistributed Profit	161	73	175	56	120	106	275	451	2,947	3,067	3,741	
Total Capital and Reserves	1,236	2,809	3,026	3,750	5,102	5,873	6,308	6,774	7,223	9,154	10,166	
Interest of Outside Shareholders in a Subsidiary Company					1,277	1,165	1,117	1,072	1,025	980	938	
Total Liabilities and Net Worth	2,022	4,165	4,841	6,025	9,205	10,437	11,165	11,198	11,578	13,545	14,768	
Net Working Capital	210	491	1,168	1,841	2,510	2,712	2,762	2,903	3,502	5,553	6,233	
Equity/Debt Ratio	2.9/1	no debt	3.0/1	2.5/1	3.4/1	3.1/1	3.2/1	3.3/1	3.4/1	4.1/1	4.4/1	

* Balance sheet information for 1961 not available.

Exhibit 2

THE RUGBY PORTLAND CEMENT COMPANY LIMITED (A)

Consolidated Profit and Loss Account 1946 and 1951–61

(1,000's of £)

	1946 £	1946 %	1951 £	1951 %	1952 £	1952 %	1953 £	1953 %	1954 £	1954 %	1955 £	1955 %	1956 £	1956 %	1957 £	1957 %	1958 £	1958 %	1959 £	1959 %	1960 £	1960 %	1961 £	1961 %
Consolidated trading profits	213		522		656		744		904		1,256		1,369		1,397		1,500		1,877		2,183		2,569	
Other income			19		20		24		27		39		65		51		52		57		99			
Less depreciation	79		124		142		136		210		270		340		342		381		443		506		550	
Net profit before taxes	134	100	417	100	534	100	633	100	721	100	1,025	100	1,093	100	1,106	100	1,171	100	1,491	100	1,777	100	2,019	100
Taxation—profits tax‡			100		102		125		62		115		109		135		60		45		88			
Income tax	39		150		255		300		313		325		255		235		260		475		550		776	
Total taxes	39	29	250	60	357	67	425	67	375	52	440	43	364	33	370	34	320	27	520	35	638	36	776	
Net profit after taxes	95		167		177		208		346		585		729		736		851		971		1,139		1,244	
Preference dividends	12	9	21	5	21	4	22	3	22	3	22	2	23	2	23	2	23	2	24	2	24	1	24	
Ordinary dividends (net)	22	16	52	12	55	10	55	9	115	16	172	17	194	18	194	18	230	20	268	18	306	17	306	
"A" share dividends (net)											29	3	36	3	36	3	46	4	61	4	77	4	77	
Retained in business	61	46	94	23	101	19	131	21	209	29	361	35	477	44	484	44	553	47	618	41	732	41	837	
Ordinary dividend per share (gross)	7½d		1/-d		1/-d		1/-d		1/-d		1/-d		1/1½d		1/1½d		1/3d		1/3d		1/3d		1/3d	
Capital distribution per share (gross)	3d		3d		3d		3d						1/3d		1/3d		1/6d		2/-d		2/6d		2/6d	
"A" share dividend per share (gross)											1/-d													
Net profit before taxes as return on total capital and reserves	10.85%		14.87%		17.65%		19.50%*		17.65%†		17.42%		17.30%		16.30%		16.20%		16.29%		17.48%			
Gross ordinary dividend as return on capital employed, i.e., ordinary plus disclosed reserves (less reserves credited to "A" shares)	4.36%		5.04%		4.54%		4.12%*		6.20%†		6.09%		6.36%		5.84%		6.06%		5.43%		5.56%			

* Excluding the £500,000 of additional capital introduced at end of 1953.

† Excluding the £1,000,000 of additional capital introduced at end of 1954.

‡ *Profits Tax* was the estimated liability for the year ending with the statement. *Income Tax* was the estimated liability for the subsequent two-year period. This procedure gives rise to the Reserve for Future Income Tax in the balance sheet. The estimated income tax for the future period is put into this reserve; and at the end of each year, the actual tax liability for the year is withdrawn from the reserve and put into current liabilities, from which the actual remittance is made.

Exhibit 3

THE RUGBY PORTLAND CEMENT COMPANY
LIMITED (A)

Indices of Deliveries, Profit, and Net Worth 1946–61
(Base: 1946 = 100)

Year	Deliveries*	Capital†	Profits
1946	100	100	100
1947	105	184‡	140
1948	138	203	195
1949	139	208	214
1950	155	219	262
1951	168	227	311
1952	208	245	398
1953	214	303§	473
1954	238	413‖	538
1955	302	475	765
1956	307	510	816
1957	294	548	825
1958	296	584	874
1959	319	741¶	1,113
1960	357	822	1,326
1961	388		

* These are total group deliveries, in tons, used as an index basing point.
† "Capital" here equals total equity capital, including reserves.
‡ In 1947, £1,000,000 of new capital was raised: £500,000 from new preference shares sold, and £500,000 from new common shares. Without this sale of shares, the index would have remained at 100.
§ In 1953, £500,000 of new common shares were sold. Without this sale, the index at the end of 1953 would have been 265.
¶ In 1954, £1,050,000 of new capital was raised, £50,000 by the sale of "A" shares, £1,000,000 by the sale of new common shares. Without this new capital, the index would have been 330 at the end of 1954.
‖ In 1959, £1,075,000 of new capital was raised through sale of common shares. Without this sale, the index would have been 655 at the end of 1959.

Late in 1961, a new kiln, with an annual capacity of 180,000 tons, was installed at the Southam works. After this addition, the five company works and their annual capacities in tons were:

Southam (England)	500,000
Rochester "	400,000
Rugby "	320,000
Trinidad	165,000
Australia	120,000

The company also maintained a chalk quarry at Totternhoe, some 48 miles from Rugby.

At the end of 1961, The Rugby Cement Company had about 1,600 employees in its three United Kingdom factories, other U.K. subsidiaries, overseas operations, and headquarters in Rugby, England. The headquarters was organized into seven functional departments: accounting, production, engineering, transportation, domestic sales, export sales, and legal. There was also a secretarial department. Above these departments was a small control and co-ordination group called the administration department. This group, consisting mostly of assistants to top management, directed and co-ordinated the activities of the functional departments and served as the intermediate link between subsidiary companies, which addressed all inquiries and reports to Sir Halford Reddish, who was the chairman of each, and to the headquarters staff departments.

The board of directors comprised seven members, three of whom were top executives in the company. These three were: Sir Halford Reddish, chairman and managing director; Mr. R. L. Evans, deputy managing director; and Mr. M. K. Smith, head of the legal department. Sir Halford and Mr. Evans worked closely with one another attempting to attain an interchangeability of talents. Sir Halford played a leading role in all major policy decisions, but was particularly concerned with financial management and public relations. Mr. Evans' background was also in accounting; he was considered the expert on accounting and technical phases of the operations. As second in command, he in effect headed the administration department. Mr. Smith generally confined himself to the company's legal matters and did not become involved in routine company operations.

Sir Halford, who served on the boards of three other corporations and on a number of semipublic councils, spent the greater part of each week in London. His days in Rugby included the weekend, and he normally met with Mr. Evans on Sunday morning to discuss current operations and problems, and also to do financial planning up to "two or three balance sheets ahead."

REASONS FOR GROWTH

Sir Halford felt that the company's growth and profitability were attributable to several interrelated activities.

1. *Emphasis on operating efficiency* was considered one of the most important of these activities. Sir Halford said that the key to lower unit costs when producing with expensive, continuous process equipment was keeping the plant operating as close to full capacity as possible and minimizing every element of operating and overhead costs. Therefore, avoiding down time, improving efficiency of men and machines, and fuel and power economies were all important. To accomplish these ends, Rugby employed an elaborate monthly cost reporting system which facilitated pin-pointing the items of excessive costs. The factory

managers were held responsible for costs under their control, and the chief engineer and production manager were continually watching fuel and power costs and working on means of increasing machine efficiency. Excess overtime, costly repairs, stores usage and factory staff costs were other items which attracted the attention of the central cost control department. One manager said: "We continually work on the weakest point reflected by the cost analyses."

The company's research on improvement of its manufacturing process produced several cost savings. The major outcome of such research was the recent development of a "wetting" agent for the slurry. Without affecting the chemical properties of the finished product, this agent produced the same "liquidity" and thus the same mixing and handling properties in a slurry containing only 35% water contrasted with 41% previously required. The smaller amount of water to vaporize meant appreciable fuel savings.

Worker efficiency was also a matter of continuous attention. Because of the expensive equipment and need to operate without stoppages, misconduct on the job, unexcused absences, and excessive tardiness were considered grounds for release. Such strictness was necessary because, for example, a kiln burner[1] could, through 10 minutes' neglect, permit many thousands of pounds' worth of damage to the equipment. Sir Halford said that his insistence that all employees "play the game according to the rules of the organization" was not only necessary for efficiency but was also a matter of loyalty. "But," he added, "I hold firmly to the view that loyalty should be two-way traffic. If the head of a business expects a man to be loyal to him, then I say that man has every right to expect the same loyalty from the head of the business."

Finally, emphasis was placed on clerical and procedural efficiency. Sir Halford said that greater use of mechanized accounting and invoicing, and continuous analysis and improvement of office procedures had slightly reduced the head office staff in the past few years. Periodic evaluation of the forms and paper work systems was conducted to eliminate unnecessary ones. "We have even had our competitor friends," he said, "come to look over our reporting and accounting systems. They are amazed by the fact that we get our data faster than they do with a proportionately smaller clerical staff."

2. *An effective sales organization* was the second contributing factor to growth and profits. Manufacturing savings effected by maintaining

---

[1] The kiln burner was the worker in charge of operating one or more kilns.

peak production were attainable only as long as the output could be sold. Mr. Yeatman, the general sales manager, remarked, "Since the industry sells on a common price arrangement, you don't sell cement by selling cheaper than the next man. You sell on delivery service, goodwill, product quality, and on contact with the customer. We like to think that we rate very high on all these counts. Selling cement is very much of a team effort, and we have a fine organization here, which naturally makes my job much easier." Under Mr. Yeatman were two area sales managers, one for midland sales and one for southern and export sales. Each manager had eight salesmen, most of whom worked from their homes. Three of the southern salesmen were located in the London office. The salesmen were paid entirely by salary, because, Mr. Yeatman said, "It's very difficult to say who's responsible for an individual sale. Most of our orders are sent in to one of our four offices: London, Birmingham, Rochester, or Rugby, rather than through the salesman. Our salesmen sell the company in general rather than the product; they are chiefly purveyors of goodwill."

Mr. Yeatman added that many customers bought from two or more manufacturers as a matter of policy. "I might mention," he added, "that all the U.K. cement manufacturers make cement which is so much higher in quality than standard British specifications that our customers have come to expect such quality from us. Accordingly, all manufacturers are constantly checking one another's product quality. Finally, since most large users have their own expert technical information on cement, we find ourselves giving technical advice only to an occasional small user. It's not an important tool in our sales kit."

3. *Overseas manufacture and other subsidiary activities* accounted for much of the company's growth and its increased profits in the past five years. Rugby was continually conducting site investigations and negotiations in search of new overseas opportunities for expansion.

4. *Transportation* of the U.K. cement sales was another reason for RPC's growth and profitability. Rugby's fleet had grown from 52 trucks in 1946 to 196 in 1961 (77 flat-bed trucks, 17 bulk tippers, and 102 pressurized bulk wagons)[2] plus extra trucks hired in the peak construction season. Rugby was proud of the efficiency of its fleet, the operating costs of which remained below the transportation allowance in the delivered price. During 1960, the fleet averaged less than 7% delays for

---

[2] Flat-bed trucks carried cement in bags; pressurized bulk wagons carried loose cement in large tanks which were slightly pressurized to remove the cement at the delivery site; bulk tippers were fully enclosed dump trucks which carried loose cement.

repair, less than 10% nonoperating idleness, and 6% on-the-job delays. Company officials believed that their truck fleet was one of the most efficient in the industry. The major reason for this efficiency, the directors believed, was the highly centralized scheduling of truck dispatches. Each day the central transportation department, working with the sales department, prepared schedules of the following day's dispatches of all trucks from each of the three works. Scheduling attempted to maximize the number of deliveries by each truck and to make as uniform as possible the work-load at the packing and loading plants.

5. *A philosophy of teamwork:* Sir Halford and the other directors of Rugby believed that the most important reason for the company's success was the achievement of company-wide teamwork through the chairman's human relations philosophy and application of profit-sharing and employee-shareholding plans. Rugby had no "personnel" department; development of teamwork was the job of managers at all levels within the firm. The impersonal term "personnel" and the word "welfare," with its connotation of charity, were banned from the Rugby vocabulary.

During the course of his career, Sir Halford had developed a philosophy of business as a team effort. A concrete expression of this philosophy was his introduction at Rugby of employee shareholding and profit-sharing plans. Commenting on the relationship between his philosophy and these plans, he said:

> I am convinced that no scheme of profit-sharing or employee shareholding can succeed unless it is built on a firm foundation of confidence within the business and of real esprit de corps, of a strong feeling on the part of all employees of pride in the company and its achievements. The goodwill of those working together in an industrial enterprise cannot be purchased for cash—of that I am sure. A scheme which is put in with the primary object of buying goodwill is almost certainly doomed to failure from the start. It may indeed not only do no good but may even do positive harm by creating suspicion, however ill-founded.[3]

Teamwork, commendable in any organization, was held to be doubly important in the cement industry where production in large units of continuous-process plant made it impossible to associate individual effort with specific product output. Mutual confidence was felt to be the basic ingredient of teamwork: the board's confidence that all employees would put forth a fair day's work, operate and maintain the plant in-

---

[3] Quotation from "This is Industrial Partnership," a pamphlet written by Sir Halford in 1955 explaining his philosophy and the profit-sharing and employee share-holding schemes of Rugby.

telligently, and follow the leadership of the company; the employees' confidence in the capability and integrity of the directors and that discipline "which is as fair as it is firm" will be maintained.

ESPRIT DE CORPS AND COMPANY POLICIES

The following paragraphs summarize the most important company policies which Sir Halford felt had established *esprit de corps* within Rugby.

1. Personal contact between top executives and operating people all over the world was relatively frequent. Sir Halford visited the Trinidad and Australian plants at least once a year, and someone from the central headquarters staff visited them, on an average, every two or three months. At home, Sir Halford not only delivered his annual "Message to My Fellow-Workers," but he always personally made presentations which were given to men with 25 years' service and again after 50 years' service. Such presentations were made in the presence of the recipients' colleagues, and Sir Halford usually gave a brief review of the recent progress of the company.

2. In his annual messages to the employees, he described recent developments within the company, emphasizing the co-operative roles played by employees and shareholders. He frequently discussed the importance of profits. The following is part of his message following the 1951 operations:

> I want now to say something about profits, because a lot of nonsense has been talked about profits in the last few years, often by politicians of all parties who have never been in industry and have no practical knowledge of industry.
>
> You and I know that profits are the reward and the measure of economy and efficiency, and are essential to the maintenance and expansion of a business. They are, in fact, the real and only bulwark behind our wages and salaries, for if this company ceases to make profits it can be only a comparatively short time before you and I are out.
>
> Let us recognize that it is up to every one of us in this team to go all out all the time, to give of our best, to maintain and increase our production with economy and efficiency, and, in turn, the profits of the company: first—and note that I put this first—because it is the job we are paid to do, and it is only common honesty to our shareholders to do it; and secondly in our own interests to safeguard our jobs for the future.

3. Another aspect of the teamwork was the "works committee" at each plant. Composed of the works manager, the works engineer, the safety officer, and five representatives elected from the factory work force, the committee met without exception each month with a senior

member of the headquarters staff in attendance. The committee discussed matters of particular interest to the works concerned, and suggestions for operational improvements. The head office staff took this opportunity to clarify and discuss newly announced changes in policy and other company developments such as the annual financial statements.

Late in 1961, an IMEDE[4] researcher had the opportunity to attend a works committee meeting at the Rochester works. Mr. R. L. Evans was the representative of top management in attendance. The committee chiefly discussed matters of plant safety and of amenities for the workers, such as a sink and hand towels for workers at a remote plant location. Mr. Halfden Lav, the Rochester works manager, said that this meeting was typical, especially insofar as it was primarily concerned with safety and working conditions. The researcher was impressed at the free and easy manner in which the workers entered into the discussions. Mr. Evans explained in great detail some minor points of company policy on tardiness and vacation time. Mr. Lav commented that the worker representatives occasionally brought up very minor points in the committee; "I think," he added, "that some men do this just to show that they are on their toes and doing a good job for their fellow-workers. We let them talk as long as they want to, and the result is that the committee functions very well, and in a very good spirit."

4. Another policy was that no one but Sir Halford had the authority to release people during slack periods. He had in fact never authorized a layoff. For instance, the rail strike in 1955 almost closed the Rochester factory as coal reserves ran low. As the shutdown date approached, Sir Halford announced that no one would be laid off, but that:

a) Some men would have to take their vacations during the shutdown.
b) Everyone would have to agree to do any job given him (at his usual pay rate) during the shutdown.

(Last minute settlement of the rail strike saved Rugby Cement from its contemplated shutdown.)

5. Since 1954, the company had offered its weekly paid employees the option of having their contract of employment determinable not by the usual one week's notice but by one month's notice by either side for employees having 10 years' service, two months for those having

---

[4] IMEDE is the abbreviation of l'Institut pour l'Etude des Méthodes de Direction de l'Entreprise at Lausanne, Switzerland.

15 years, and three months for those having 20 years. Of those to whom the offer applied, over 85% had accepted one of these options.

In commenting on the fact that 15% of the workers had not chosen to take one of these options, company officials said that some workmen preferred the independence of being able to leave on short notice. "Our employee turnover is, however, quite low," one executive pointed out. "If we set aside employees with less than two years of service, our average worker has been here about 13 years. We do find that some new employees, especially young men, are not prepared for the demanding work in a cement plant, and such men leave, usually within 12 months. Thus new employees should not be fairly included in our average turnover figure. Incidentally, taking total annual wages and bonuses as an indicator, the cement industry ranks in the top half-dozen British industries in terms of earnings."

6. The final key policy of the company was summarized by Sir Halford:

If there is to be a lively interest and pride in the company and its doings, then it is necessary that all employees be kept informed as far as possible about what is going on. . . .

We try as far as we can to ensure that everyone has an opportunity of reading on the company's notice boards a few hours *before* it appears in the newspapers any release issued to the Press. We do not think it right that a man should learn from the newspapers something which he could quite properly have heard at first hand within the company.[5]

Besides all of the aspects of teamwork within an organization, two other features of any profit-sharing or employee-shareholding plan were felt necessary by Sir Halford. The first was that any such scheme must be tailored to suit the circumstances of the company and the outlook, philosophy, and intention of its leader. The second feature was simplicity.

THE PROFIT-SHARING SCHEME

Sir Halford said that the Rugby profit-sharing scheme, inaugurated in 1935, was designed to emphasize two things:

a) That the efforts of the employees are the efforts of a team—that we are all working to one end.

b) The essential partnership which exists between the ordinary shareholders and the employees.[6]

---

[5] "This Is Industrial Partnership."

[6] *Ibid.*

In speeches both to shareholders and workers, Sir Halford referred to the partnership between capital and employees. He said that capital was nothing more than the "labour of yesterday—the production of yesterday which was surplus to the consumption of yesterday."

Fundamental to the partnership was the following bargain:

. . . the labour of today is guaranteed payment for its services and the profit is calculated only after the remuneration of that labour has been paid. Capital, therefore, takes the risk and in return takes such profit (or loss) as arises *after* the labour of today has been paid in full.

But to my mind this difference in the basis of their respective remuneration in no way destroys the conception of industrial enterprise as essentially a partnership between the labour of yesterday (capital) and the labour of today. Nor is it destroyed if the "bargain" is varied slightly by guaranteeing the greater part of labour's remuneration irrespective of profit or loss and by making an additional but smaller part of it dependent on the results of the enterprise as a whole.[7]

The employees' profit-sharing scheme provided for an annual bonus in excess of industry-negotiated wages (wage-earners) or contracted salary (staff) for all Rugby workers. Basic points of the scheme are summarized below:

1. To qualify for the profit-sharing bonus, an hourly or salaried employee must have completed, on December 31, twelve months' unbroken service to the satisfaction of the Directors.

2. For the purpose of calculating the bonus, each qualified employee is treated as if he held a certain number of ordinary shares in the company. A staff employee received two "notional shares" for each £1 of annual salary. An hourly worker received shares in proportion to his length of service. For example, a worker with one year's service had 250 "notional shares"; a worker with five years' service, 375; a worker with 20 years, 750; and a worker with 40 or more years had 1,250.

3. The bonus is calculated at the full rate per share of the gross dividend declared and paid to the ordinary shareholders for the financial year in question and is paid immediately after the Annual General Meeting. For example, in 1960 the ordinary dividend declared was 1*s*.3*d*. per share. Thus a worker with five years' service, holding 375 notional shares, would receive a bonus of (375 × 1/3*d*.) or £23/8/9.

4. Certified sickness or compulsory National Service are ignored in calculating the number of years of unbroken service.

5. Any employee who leaves or is under notice to leave prior to the date of payment forfeits his bonus.

6. The scheme confers no rights in respect of any capital distribution, or distributions other than those declared as dividends on the ordinary shares of the company out of profits.

---

[7] *Ibid.*

7. The scheme is subject to modification or withdrawal at any time at the discretion of the Directors.[8]

Sir Halford emphasized that the bonus was not automatic. In a very small number of cases each year, bonuses were withheld completely or in part because service was not "to the satisfaction of the directors." If a man's record for the year was questionable, including several unexplained tardinesses, for instance, it was submitted, without name, to the works committee of the factory. In all cases, the directors had abided by the committee's recommendation. Sir Halford said that withholding the bonus was not so much a penalty to the slack worker, but was necessary in fairness to those who gave 100% service during the year.

Summarizing, Sir Halford said:

I believe that this is important: the bonus must be something that is earned —not something which becomes a right. I also feel that the link with the ordinary shareholders' dividend is fundamental: if the dividend per share goes up, so does the bonus; if the dividend is reduced, the bonus falls too—which is as it should be.

THE "A" SHARE SCHEME

After the war, Sir Halford saw two factors that made the profit-sharing scheme inadequate in emphasizing the partnership between capital and labor. He felt that the twin virtues of hard work and thrift no longer assured a man of personal savings for his old age—*taxation* restricted savings and inflation *devalued* them. Unlike the ordinary shareholder's income which flowed from an asset whose market value reflected both the company's prosperity and inflationary pressures, the employee's profit-sharing bonus was not reflected in a realizable capital asset. Thus he did not have a "hedge" against inflation.

To supply this need, Sir Halford presented his "A" share plan, in late 1954, for approval by the ordinary shareholders. He said that the scheme was designed to do three things:

To give practical form to the unity of interest which I have always held to exist between the ordinary shareholders and the employees; to give a return to the ordinary shareholders on profits "ploughed back" in the past; and to give to every full-time employee the opportunity to have in his hands a capital asset readily realizable on death or retirement. It was received enthusiastically by shareholders and employees alike.[9]

---

[8] This explanation of the profit-sharing scheme contains only the major aspects. Full details are available in Sir Halford Reddish's booklet, "This Is Industrial Partnership."

[9] Explanation of "A" share plan summarized from "This Is Industrial Partnership."

One million "A" shares of 1*s.* each were created with the following conditions attached to them:

1. For any financial year after 31st December 1954 for which (*a*) the net profits before tax are not less than £900,000, and (*b*) the gross amount distributed as dividend to the ordinary shareholders is not less than £300,000, the holders of the "A" shares shall be entitled to an amount of £70,000 plus 20% of any excess of the said net profits over £900,000 (see Exhibit 4). However, (*i*) the amount attributable to the "A" shares shall not exceed 12½% of the net profits; and (*ii*) in the event of the issue of additional ordinary share capital by the company after 31st December 1954, otherwise than by way of a capitalization of reserves or undistributed profits, the said figure of £900,000 shall be increased by a sum equal to 6% of the proceeds or other consideration received by the company.[10]

2. Any amount atributable to the "A" shares as ascertained under (1) above may be distributed as dividend or carried forward in the books of the company to the credit of the "A" shares for subsequent distribution, as the Directors may decide.

3. The holders of "A" shares have no voting rights.

4. In a winding-up, the "A" shares may participate only insofar as the amount of their paid-in capital value and the "A" share credit carried forward on the company books, but no further participation in assets.

5. No further "A" shares shall be created without the sanction of an Extraordinary Resolution passed by the holders of the "A" shares.[11]

Half of the "A" shares were offered to the ordinary shareholers at par and half to the employees.

"All full-time employees of the company were included: this was not a get-rich-quick exercise for the favoured few," said Sir Halford.

Allocation to the employees was done by dividing all employees into groups according to remuneration, responsibility, and status within the company (length of service was not a factor). Those in the first group were offered 250 shares, followed by groups of 500, 750, 1,000, 1,500, 2,000, and so on. (Most factory production workers were in the first group, for example.) Over 90% of Rugby's employees had exercised their option and purchased the "A" shares.

Sir Halford was particularly concerned about two aspects of the scheme. About the first, he said:

I was anxious that there should be no element of a "gift" from one partner (the holders of the ordinary shares) to the other (the employees); and that the equity owned by the ordinary shares should be unimpaired. I was convinced that the holders of the ordinary shares could have no legitimate cause for complaint

---

[10] Because additional equity had been introduced since 1954, the "A" shares now began participating at net profits of £964,500.

[11] Explanation of "A" share plan summarized from "This Is Industrial Partnership."

if the profits were so substantially increased in the future and some comparatively small part of the increase went to the employees as a reward for their efforts.

The "A" shares should be worth no more than was paid for them when issued, so that the employees could feel that whatever increased value accrued thereafter was due to their teamwork, with, I do not forget, nor do I allow them to forget, the capital provided by their partners in the enterprise.[12]

This reason, and tax considerations (discussed later) dictated that the minimum profit level at which the "A" shares would start participating (£900,000) should be well above the profit levels when the "A" shares were issued.

The second aspect was that the main object of the scheme was to insure employees of a capital sum on death or retirement. Sir Halford foresaw that the "A" shares might have some speculative attraction to the general public and he did not want the employees to be tempted into selling and thus depriving themselves of retirement or death benefits from the plan. He also felt that anyone leaving the firm be required to sell his shares back at par and thus enable newcomers to participate. To accomplish these ends, Sir Halford designated that the shares allocated to the employees were held in their behalf by Staff Nominees Limited which was accountable to the employees for dividends declared and authorized to act in their behalf in all matters relating to the "A" shares. The following conditions applied:

1. Initially and whenever an employee moves upward to a new group, he is given the opportunity to buy his allocation of shares at par. Failing to do so, he is not given a subsequent opportunity.
2. "A" shares may be sold by the employee at any time *at par* to Staff Nominees Limited and *must* be sold any time he leaves the company.
3. An employee's share may be sold at market value (market price was established by quotation on The London Stock Exchange of the "A" shares allotted originally at par to the ordinary shareholders) *only* in the event of the employee's death while in the service of the company, or upon his reaching the age of 65 (55 for women).
4. Any dividend declared on the "A" shares is paid immediately to the employee.

Fifty thousand shares remained unallocated to the employees after the initial sale. The Directors felt that this block of shares and those shares which Staff Nominees Limited bought back, at par, from employees who left, would be sufficient to offer shares to new and promoted employees for the foreseeable future.

---

[12] *Ibid.*

In his message to his fellow-workers in the company following the 1958 operations, Sir Halford said the following about the "A" share plan:

. . . Quite often a man will say to me: "This 'A' share scheme of yours—tell me, has it increased production?" And I reply: "I haven't the slightest idea, but I shouldn't think so." So he says: "But surely that was the object. It's an incentive scheme, isn't it?" "On the contrary," I tell him, "I have always insisted that it should *not* be called an incentive scheme, because that to my mind would imply that we in Rugby Cement were not already doing our best, were not doing our duty in return for our wages and salaries. And that I will not have."

What our "A" share scheme does is to give to the employees the opportunity to build up capital available on retirement or on earlier death, and to promote the feeling that we are all one team working to the same end in partnership with our shareholders. The value of the "A" shares depends in the long run on the success of our efforts in making profits. And don't overlook the fact that half the "A" shares were issued, also at par, to the holders of our ordinary shares. They very rightly benefit too, as they have seen these 1s.0d. shares change hands on the Stock Exchange at prices up to 42s.0d.[13]

Apart from the capital aspect, the holding of "A" shares by the employees of the company, and also, of course, our "profit-sharing" schemes, give some reward for successful endeavour—which is surely right.

The Taxation Aspect.   For the company, the profit-sharing bonus was considered a wage bonus and therefore a before-tax expense. The "A" share dividends, however, were similar to ordinary dividends, being paid out of after-tax profits.

For the employees, the profit-sharing bonus was taxed as ordinary wage or salary income. Taxation of the employees in connection with "A" share distribution was a most difficult problem and one for which Sir Halford spent many hours in consultation with the Board of Inland Revenue.

The law held that if at the time of issue the value of the shares was greater than the amount the employees paid for them, the difference was taxable as a "benefit" arising from employment. The Rugby "A" share sale to its employees, however, had two characteristics which affected any ruling under this law:

1. "A" shares were not quoted on the market until two months after issue; thus it was a matter of discussion whether at time of issue they were worth more than the par value paid for them.
2. Employees were not free to sell their shares at market price except on retirement or death.

---

[13] In 1961, "A" shares were quoted on the stock exchange at up to 100 shillings per share.

Final agreement with the Inland Revenue was reached which assessed the value of the "A" shares at time of issue slightly above par.

Tax assessment for shares issued subsequently to newcomers or to promoted employees required a different arrangement with the Inland

Exhibit 4

THE RUGBY PORTLAND CEMENT COMPANY LIMITED (A)

Profit Participation of the "A" Shares
Graph of Participation "Formula"
and
Schedule of Gross Profits *before* Taxes

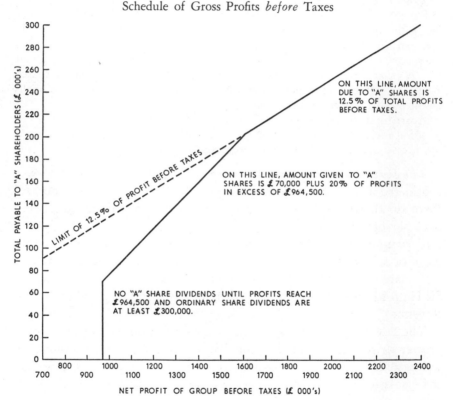

Revenue, since by that time a market value was established. Final agreement resulted in considering a variable fraction of the difference between current market value and par value as taxable income. The fraction varied inversely with the length of time between the recipient's age and 65 when he could realize the market price of the "A" shares. For instance, a 25-year-old newcomer receiving 500 "A" shares would have to consider as income, for income tax purposes, only 10% of the

Exhibit 4—Continued

THE RUGBY PORTLAND CEMENT COMPANY LIMITED (A)

Summary of Earnings and Gross Dividend Payments 1954–61

(1,000's of £)

Year	1954	1955	1956	1957	1958	1959	1960	1961
Profit before tax	721	1025	1093	1106	1171	1491	1777	2020
Gross ordinary dividend	200	300	338	338	375	437	500	500
Gross payable to "A" shares	..	95	109	111	124	179	222	252
Actual "A" share dividend	..	50	63	63	75	100	125	125
Difference carried forward as "A" share credit	..	45	46	48	49	79	97	127
Cumulative "A" share credit*	..	45	91	140	189	268	365	493

* The "A" share credit was contained in the Undistributed Profit account in the balance sheet. The directors considered this credit as a "dividend equalization reserve" to supply "A" dividends if they were not earned according to the formula (i.e., if pretax profits were below £964,500).

difference between market value and the price paid (one shilling per share), because he could not realize the market value for 40 years. On the other hand, a 50-year-old man receiving 500 "A" shares would have to consider 60% of the difference as taxable income, because he was much closer to realizing the gain. (The United Kingdom had no "capital gains" tax, but all dividends received by employees on their "A" shares up to retirement age were treated, for tax purposes, as "earned" income and therefore taxed at income-tax rates.)

Overseas. An employee profit-sharing plan, similar to that existing for Rugby workers in the United Kingdom, had been established for workers in the Trinidad and Australian plants. "A" shares were offered only to workers in the United Kingdom, including staff assigned temporarily to the overseas operations.

7. The Rugby Portland Cement Company Limited (B)

LATE IN 1961, an IMEDE[1] research team decided to attempt to expand the Rugby Portland Cement case by adding information on the ways in which various employees of the company viewed their jobs. To this purpose, an IMEDE researcher toured each of the company's three cement works in England; he also conducted interviews with a number of hourly paid workers and with a substantial number of middle- and top-management executives. This case includes excerpts from some of these interviews, as well as some of the researcher's impressions of what he saw.

VIEWS OF SOME RUGBY WORKMEN

Rugby's management was very co-operative in helping the researcher to interview some of the workmen. Although in theory it would have been useful to interview a rather large number of workers selected at random, this was not practicable for certain reasons:

1. There were limitations on the research time available for these interviews.
2. There was a chance that some men, if chosen at random, might:
    a) Not be able to articulate their views.
    b) Be less than wholly frank.
    c) Be unable to leave their work posts at the desired time.

Accordingly, Mr. R. L. Evans (deputy managing director) and Mr. Baker (works manager of the Rugby works) selected from the Rugby work force four workers who, they thought, would be articulate, honest, and as representative as possible of the general sentiments of the entire Rugby worker group. The researcher interviewed the four men separately, in an office at the Rugby plant; nobody else was present during the interviews. The names of the four men interviewed have been disguised.

---

[1] Once again, IMEDE is an abbreviation for l'Institut pour l'Etude des Méthodes de Direction de l'Entreprise at Lausanne, Switzerland.

INTERVIEW WITH MR. RYAN

Mr. Evans and Mr. Baker, in arranging the interviews, mentioned that Mr. Ryan should provide a highly entertaining and useful interview, that he was outspoken and highly articulate. Mr. Ryan, who had been working for the company since 1956, was an Irishman; he appeared to be about 40 years old. He worked in the transport department of the company as a truck driver and had been a member of the Rugby works committee for some time. The researcher asked each of the four men only one question to begin: what did the man think about working for the company, what were the bad points and the good points? Mr. Ryan began:

Well, I might tell you I'm an old union man, been a sort of union agitator all my working life. Before I came here I never held a job longer than eighteen months. I've been here almost six years now and I can tell you this, I'm going to stay here the rest of my life. And, mind you, I got a lot less to gain by staying here than most of the men. I have no A-shares, because you know you only get one chance to buy them A-shares, and when I had to buy them, I didn't have the money because my wife just had to have an operation. So now for the rest of my life I got to work here knowing that I'll never have no A-shares, and I think this is unfair, and I keep fighting to get me shares, and maybe I will and maybe I won't, but I'll stay on here no matter what.

And another thing is I'm a very bad timekeeper—sometimes it's my fault, and sometimes it was because I had to take my wife to the doctor and so I'd come in late, and so for three straight years I lost my profit-sharing bonus on account of being late so much. [Mr. Ryan had actually lost his bonus in two nonconsecutive years, management reported.] So you can see what I mean when I tell you that I got much less to gain by working here than the other men.

But even though there's lots of little things could be done, this is a wonderful place to work, and that's the Lord's own truth. I'm not saying anything to you I wouldn't say right to the Chairman's face if he asked me—I'm not a man to say what he doesn't mean.

You got to remember this: it's no good coming down to a cement works if you don't want to work hard. But they pay you good and, the main thing is, you always get treated fair. If you got a complaint, you can take it as high as you want, right up to the Chairman himself, but it's no good complaining unless you give 'em the facts. That's what they want to see: facts.

Another thing you ought to write down is this: in this company, I'm just as good as anybody, as good as the Chairman or Mr. Evans—that's what you won't get anywhere else. We all know this here, and we know you've got to work as a team. And I'll tell you this, I know the Chairman would let me buy my A-shares if he could, but you see he's got to be fair to the other workers too. But I do think that you get punished awful hard for being late. [Mr. Ryan's profit-sharing bonus would have amounted, in those years when he lost it, to about £30. His weekly wages were about £15.]

Over in Coventry, you know [about 15 miles away], in the car and airplane factories a man can make £30 a week while here he'll only make about £15, but we get the £15 for 52 weeks of the year, plus the profit-sharing, the A-shares, and lots of other benefits. The company buys up lots of clothes for us so we can get them cheaper. I once compared what I earned in a year with a friend of mine who works in Coventry for £29 a week, and you know what? I came out £48 ahead of him for the year, because those fellows are always getting laid off.

And let me tell you this: you'd never get a better firm to work for, no matter where you went; there isn't another company like this, at least none I've ever heard about.

You know, when I tell you we work hard here, you've got to remember that the Chairman doesn't ask us to to do anything he doesn't do himself. You know, he works eighteen hours a day, and when he come down sick recently and had to have that operation, his doctors told him to take it easy, and so he did—he only worked ten hours a day.

[Mr. Ryan then gave the researcher a very detailed description of what was involved in his truck-driving. He stressed that the equipment was the best obtainable, that the company paid much more attention to driver safety than to delivering a maximum daily tonnage of cement, that scrupulous care was taken at great expense, to be certain that the customer received all the cement he had been billed for.]

You see my truck out there? That truck, it's brand new, and it cost £10,000, and they expect me to take care of it like if it was my own, and I do. [The truck in fact cost slightly over £3,500.] And I know I've got 42 hours a week guaranteed, and more hours on weekends if I want to make extra money, and that's a hell of a nice thing for a truck driver. And as soon as I've driven 11 hours in a single day, even if I didn't get home with the truck by the time my 11 hours was up, the company would send out another lorry with two drivers to drive me and my truck home, that's how careful they are about the 11-hour rule. And you see them fine overalls we drivers got, and them jackets? Mr. Reddish, I believe, bought them for us out of his own pocket. That's just the kind of man he is. [In fact he didn't: they are provided by the company.]

I told you I used to be a union man, but I tell you this, if a union came in here now, it would hurt the workers—they'd get less pay, they couldn't touch anything they weren't supposed to. That's the kind of a union man I am today.

In summing up, and this is God's own truth, I think Sir Halford Reddish ought to be England's Prime Minister, and Mr. Evans ought to be the Secretary for Foreign Affairs.

INTERVIEW WITH MR. MASON

Mr. Mason was a foreman in the "raw plant," where the slurry was made. He had been working for the company about 14 years and appeared to be about 50. He began:

Well, wherever I went, I don't think I could better myself, that's what I'd say. The Chairman puts us in the picture about what's going on, he has more of a fatherly concern for us, I think. I've known the Chairman 30 years and if he says a thing he means it. He's put in some wonderful plans for the men, he has. For example, when my father died, we got about £1000 for his A-shares, and this was a big help, because I've got a sister who isn't very well, and this money pays for her. From the workman's point of view, if you want it, I find that they're very, very satisfied. I've got 30-odd men working for me, and I get all the points of view, so to speak, and I think I can say that they're all happy to be working here. Now, of course, there's some men as will always find something to complain about, you're going to have that anywhere, but in the main I think that the men like working here very much.

You're an American, so I'll put it in American: damn it all, we're on to a good thing here and we know it.

I've got a brother, a son, and two brothers-in-law working here, and my father before he died. They all came to work here after I did. Now do you think they'd have come if this wasn't a good place to work?

I do believe honestly, and I'm not handing you any bull, that we couldn't better ourselves. And you've got to remember this: Sir Halford will give any of his men a proper hearing anytime. And what's astonishing is that as the firm gets larger, the company seems to give us more attention, when you'd think it'd be the other way around.

Now you take your average Englishman, he's the biggest grumbler in the world, about anything at all. But you won't find much grumbling here. You'd have to kick them out to get the men here to leave.

INTERVIEW WITH MR. TOOT

Mr. Toot, who appeared to be about 50, had been with Rugby about seven years. The researcher received the distinct impression that Mr. Toot was temperamentally a sort of cynic who only grudgingly would admit that a workingman's life could be decent, although this impression was formed on the basis of very little evidence. Mr. Toot began:

Taken all around, I should say that this is a very good place to work. A workman here knows that he can go as high as he likes, if he has the ability. You get fair treatment here. I suppose that work here is 80% satisfactory. For the other 20%, it's hard to say what the objections might be. But one thing is, when a man first came to work here, he didn't get enough participation in the bonus system (the profit-sharing scheme), but they've changed that now.

If a man's willing to do an honest day's work, he'll generally be satisfied here. I suppose I could say this: the longer a man's been here, the more he wants to stay.

Now, you get some fellows, especially young ones, come in and they can't stick the work; it's too heavy or too hard for them. They usually leave, if they're this type, in 12–18 months. If a man sticks it a year or a year and a half, he'll probably stay here until he's through working.

This is a long-term policy job, so to say. It's good if you're thinking about your old age, because the company really takes care of you after you retire. I don't suppose you know this, but all the company's pensioners [retired workers] get a ton of coal from the company at Christmas. There's a Christmas party for the pensioners. And men like Mr. Evans and Mr. Baker visit the pensioners very regularly. The company doesn't just forget you when you've stopped working for them—they take care of you.

I suppose when I think of it, it's hard to say what kind of objections, you might say, a man could have to working here, if he's not just a casual laborer who doesn't care about doing an honest day's work, if he doesn't care about doing a good job. This is a good place to work.

INTERVIEW WITH MR. FORSTER

Mr. Forster had been working for Rugby for 48 years, and he worked in the quarry. He talked rather little, much less than the previous three men.

Well, I've been working here all my life, and that's a fact. It's hard work, and no doubt about it, but it's a wonderful company to work for. I was here, you know, when Sir Halford took over, and it was wonderful when he did. He promised us steady work, and we've had it ever since. Some of your casual lads, now, who come here looking for an easy day's work and high pay, they don't stay, but a real man, a man who doesn't mind work, he'll be happier here than anywhere else I've ever heard of.

RANDOM IMPRESSIONS OF THE RESEARCHER

In the course of his tour of the three different works, the researcher spent a great deal of time with Mr. R. L. Evans, who toured each plant with him, and with the works managers. The researcher was especially struck by two facts. First, Mr. Evans and the works managers appeared to know a great deal about the background of every company employee. The researcher was, while walking through the plant, introduced to one worker who had been a chef in Wyoming some years ago. Another worker was pointed out as having been (he was now 72) a good Rugby player in his youth. These and similar details were forthcoming quite frequently from Mr. Evans or the works managers. Second, the workers all said "hello" to Mr. Evans as he passed through the plant, and Mr. Evans would chat with them about their families and how things were going.

Another impression, although a difficult one to justify with explicit evidence, was that the various managers were more than superficially concerned with their workers and their lives. Words and phrases which often recurred in the four days of conversation included: "fair treatment," "decent work for a man," "take care of our men," "except them to work as part of a team." Workers and managers alike constantly referred to themselves as being part of a single team; they did so either implicitly or explicitly.

8. John Adams

You know, if there is one topic I think we should spend more time talking about somewhere in the Harvard Business School curriculum, it is "company atmosphere." It exists everywhere, obviously, but it certainly is hard to get a very good impression of what it will be like in a company you are considering going to work for. It turned out to be much more important to me than I had ever anticipated, and I really wish we had spent more time thinking about what it is, what influences it, how to recognize it early, and what the choices open to you are in learning to live with it. I sure ran into problems of this sort when I went to work for Accutronics right after I got my MBA in 1967.

JOHN ADAMS, Harvard Business School graduate of 1967, was discussing some of his experiences in his job of the preceding three years. Adams had resigned his position a few weeks before and was stopping over briefly in Boston to visit some old friends and classmates before proceeding to his new job in Florida.

SPRING, 1967

Adams' first contact with Accutronics had been on a job interview trip in the spring of 1967, shortly before his graduation from the Harvard Business School.

Accutronics was a Denver-based company which had started with the development and manufacture of specialized microwave and radar components and was trying to build up competence in highly sophisticated electromechanical systems for military and space applications as well. The company was strongly oriented toward research and technology. It had grown very rapidly from sales of a few million dollars in the early sixties, when it had been founded by a small group of businessmen and university scientists, to about $35 million per year in 1967.

In reviewing the impressions he had formed of Accutronics on this brief 1967 visit, Adams commented as follows:

I think what impressed me most about the company at that time was their strong commitment to growth and the emphasis they placed on individual ability and initiative in getting ahead. They really preached the virtues of competition. I must have been told a dozen times that they expected people to use their initiative and to take on responsibility for doing what needed to be done,

581

and that as soon as you showed that you could handle the job, you would get more to do. They all said that there was simply too much opportunity for growth and too much to get done to worry about whether you would be infringing on someone else's private domain. In fact, the president had stated publicly that they were strongly committed to their policy of rapid growth, partly because this was necessary to provide enough career opportunities for the caliber of people they wanted in their organization.

I was to go to work in a headquarters staff group which reported to the executive vice president, a fellow named Mike Butler. He was aggressive and forward and seemed to be a real go-getter. My first meeting with him was in his home, and he just about stood me up against a wall and fired questions at me. He wanted direct answers, too, not these "on the other hand" statements. He hit me with technical questions about radar sets, inertial guidance, what I expected to earn in five years, how many hours a week I would be willing to work, and so on. I don't think he expected me to know the answers to a lot of the technical questions; I think he was more interested in seeing how I responded to that sort of cross-examination. After awhile he called another vice president and told him—just as brusquely—that he had a good man at his house and arranged another interview for me.

Nobody was very specific as to exactly what I would be doing; they said they were much more interested in getting good men than fitting people in slots. Mike said the work at first would mostly be on special projects at headquarters and would also involve something he called "internal consulting," which meant working on problem areas in various parts of the company's operations. He said it would be an excellent chance to get around to various parts of the company and learn about their operations, and then after a few years to go out into one of the operating departments. He emphasized that they didn't want any career staff men, and that suited me fine.

The job met a number of the criteria that were important to me. It seemed like an environment in which I could get ahead, mostly on the basis of my own ability and level of effort and performance rather than on seniority or politics; in fact, Mike told me that the main reason they were able to make such good headway against the big companies was that they didn't waste their time with very many rules or procedures or in internal jockeying for position and bickering. I must admit that appealed to me, because I've been in organizations where it has been very different.

The company was also growing very fast, with no slowdown in sight. They all seemed to have a real drive to make Accutronics into a major industrial company rather than just something which would provide them with security and a comfortable income. It looked like a good chance to make use of both my engineering and business training, too—a real challenge to try to deal with both the scientific and commercial worlds within the company.

The salary offer was pretty good—$13,000, which was above the offers most of the fellows seemed to be getting[1]—but I did have a few higher offers else-

---

[1] Average starting salary in 1967 for Harvard MBA's with an engineering degree was actually $12,000 (placement bureau records).

where. It sounded like the kind of work I would really like, though, and I was sure that if I did a good job the advancement in both position and money would be enough to keep me happy. I thought it might even give me some experience which could be useful if I ever saved enough money to be able to strike out on my own some day, which is still a dim goal I have tucked away in the back of my mind.

Adams had financed his business school education by a combination of savings and student loans and had graduated in the top third of his class. He was characterized by several of his professors as being unusually mature and well balanced; one of the slightly older students with some working experience whom they could rely on for constructive and commonsense comments. According to several of his classmates, he was the sort of person that people found it easy to talk to and had been well liked and respected. One friend characterized him as ambitious and a hard worker, but also a "strong family man," and said that he tried to spend as much time with his wife and child as is possible while attending the Business School. Another spoke of him as having a strong competitive spirit, but with equally strong ideas about fair play and consideration for others. He was remembered as being active in section activities, particularly the intramural sports program.

Previous to attending the Harvard Business School, Adams had obtained a degree in electrical engineering at a western college, had worked for a large steel company for about a year, and had served as an officer in the Navy for two years. He had been active in sports while in high school and college, and had won several wrestling championships. He and his wife were both from the same medium-sized northwestern city.

FALL, 1967

In the fall of 1967, Adams wrote a few words to a classmate about his new job with Accutronics:

. . . As far as the job is concerned, things are going just great. I have worked on a number of interesting projects already and have learned a lot both about how the company works and about some problems I never gave much thought when I was at the B-School.

People certainly have a strong sense of identification with the company, as we used to call it so glibly, and I am beginning to see how it has come about. It does not come at all from what you could call a paternalistic attitude on the part of the company; it is completely different. I don't know what to call it; everyone is caught up in both the challenge and the reward of making the company grow. We have been doubling our sales every two or three years for a number of years, mostly through internal growth, and it looks like we will be able to keep that up for a while. There is no union out here, either; even the hourly employees seem to feel that they are a part of the team. The management tries to promote this feeling, of course, and they have done a good job of it.

They weren't fooling when they said the hours would be long! We don't get any overtime, of course, and I was amazed to find that people think nothing of working 60 hours a week regularly. I've worked over 80 hours a week for several weeks at a time, and if I had worked like that in the steel company I would have been carted off to the company headshrinker. Those hours are tough for the men with families, but I don't really mind it because this is such a dynamic and exciting place to be working. We have a congenial group in the department, and people seem willing to pitch in and get the job done. There are a number of us with MBA's in the department, and we all view this as a steppingstone for a better job out in the divisions.

One reason people work the way they do out here, I am sure, is that the officers themselves put in a fantastic work week. They built up the organization from nothing and it took a lot of work, and their level of effort just filters down in the organization. If your boss works long hours, you do too. Besides, I think most people feel they are in on the ground floor now, and that the rapid growth will generate enough promotions to make the present long hours worthwhile. . . .

One thing that was both surprising and rewarding was to find that the level of education of most of the management out here is so high. Most people in my office have MBA's from somewhere, and of course we have a lot of Ph.D.'s in the sciences around here. This makes the competition tougher, but it also makes it a much more rewarding place to work. I was also surprised at the number and quality of job applicants that we have. We seem to be getting the reputation of a growth company in a growth industry, and a surprising number of people from all over the country who want to change jobs for one reason or another seem to be attracted to our situation. Part of the reason for our popularity may also be the living conditions out here; we both have found them very pleasant.

FALL, 1968

Adams wrote as follows about his first year at Accutronics:

. . . Work is still exciting and worthwhile; the pace hasn't slowed down at all and I feel I have learned a lot during the last year. I am still working on a variety of projects, just like when I started, but there are enough different things coming up constantly so that it by no means resembles a routine. I don't report directly to Walter Gorman (the department head) any more, though. We have expanded in this area a lot, and during the year two people with some previous experience were hired in above me. I must be the only member of the class of 1967 who has been "demoted" twice already and still likes his job! The company is still growing like a weed, though, so there are bound to be lots of opportunities opening up, even though people are brought in from the outside to fill some of them.

Nobody has left the department to go elsewhere in the company yet, either, although the department is now about two and one-half years old. That worries me a bit, because I didn't come out here to be a staff man all my life. I think part of the reason may be that some of the operating divisions and departments seem to regard us as spies from a competitor rather than as someone working for the same company, but maybe this is natural. They have been used to doing things their own way, and besides, I guess we often do regard them as enemies in our efforts to justify the importance of our department by ferreting out inefficiencies and showing how we can save money for the company. You inevitably get involved in politics and see people doing some things in order to protect themselves or "get" somebody else, but I guess that happens everywhere.

Just like with any job there are some drawbacks, of course. We do work long hours, and not all of it is necessary. Walter tries to establish an atmosphere whereby you come in on Saturdays unless you have something special going on at home, rather than coming in only if there is something special going on at work. I think one of the ways he tried to do this was pretty funny. On a few Saturdays when I was not in he left a little note on my desk saying "see me." Each time when I talked with him on Monday morning, he said he got someone else to do it and implied I missed out on something worthwhile without saying what it was. I came in about 11 A.M. one Saturday and found a note on my desk, and so I went right over to ask about it. He was completely at a loss about it, because he had left it there only five minutes ago and there really was nothing that he wanted anyway! I still come in most Saturdays, though—it is simply expected, and most people do.

I now see that one of the reasons people work so hard is that there are a lot of what I would call "false crises," or deadlines which are shorter than they need to be just to get people to do more work. The president even stated at one of the regional management conferences that this was something he did deliberately in order to get more work out of his people, and I'm not so sure that I like that. But it does seem to accomplish his objective, even though people view it as something temporary.

I've gotten to understand the company a lot better during the past year, and I really give the management a great deal of credit for what they have been able to build up from virtually nothing. Lots of them are millionaires now, and the stock is still going up. I wish I had more money to put into it. And one of the most interesting things to me has been the insight you get into how the problems of a company change as it becomes larger, and how difficult it is for the management to change their behavior as the problems get too complicated to handle on the "personal" basis that worked so well during the earlier stages.

SUMMER, 1970

Back in Boston briefly while en route to his new job in Florida, Adams commented as follows about his recent career at Accutronics and his reasons for leaving:

I've now taken another job; I left Accutronics a few months ago. I had my ups and downs out there, but when I left things were going very well for me.

After my first year I was shifted around a lot. Our department sort of fell apart, mostly, I think, because of opposition from the divisions. I went through a great number of "reorganizations," but for the year before I left I was working as one of the two assistants to the operations vice president. I had several divisions assigned to me, and I was supposed to know everything that was going on in those divisions. Our total sales, by the way, were over the $100 million rate when I left, which will put us in *Fortune's* list of 500. Most of that was through internal growth, too, although we did buy several small companies.

I worked on all sorts of projects, and also sat in on a lot of top management meetings, including the monthly operating meetings involving the officers of the company and the division managers. Usually when my boss visited any of the divisions I was responsible for, I went along with him too.

It was great experience to see how things work at that level in such a large and dynamic company, and I wouldn't trade it for anything. I was making good money, too, and was well liked, I think, by the people I worked with. Several said to get in touch with them if I ever wanted to come back. They were certainly nice to me when I left, and I have a lot of friends there that I will call up and chat with if I ever get to Denver again.

I guess the main reason I left is that I just didn't like the atmosphere in the company as well as when I started. It seemed to me that too many people were spending too much of their time on things which had nothing to do with making a contribution to the company, and I didn't see how I could avoid it myself, even if only in self-defense. I saw too many people lose out because they didn't pay enough attention to the politics involved, and I just didn't find playing politics very satisfying. Besides, I don't think I'm very good at it.

I certainly was naive when I graduated from the Business School. I had been in the service and worked some before that, and I thought I knew how the world worked. When I went out to Accutronics I really thought that getting ahead would depend mostly on solving problems for the company better than anyone else, and one of the main reasons I went with them was that they seemed to be looking for someone with exactly my viewpoint. I now doubt that more than 10% of the reasons for promotions in most companies depend on this. I'm convinced that the surest way to go down the drain in most organizations is to spend your time solving problems better, rather than impressing the people who make the promotions.

I have never made any list to see what happened to the people who were sort of in my department, but it would be interesting to see what became of that group. There were several in the 25 to 35 age category in my general area at headquarters when I arrived, and we hired several more during the year. After the first year there were so many reorganizations that it would be impossible to keep track. As I remember it, this [Figure 1] would be the list of people, with a little bit on their backgrounds and what happened to them.

Don't let the title "staff assistant" worry you; it really doesn't describe either your work or your relative position in the department very well. It was just a catchall title that was used a lot in our department.

It scares me to look at what has happened to the relatively few men in my group who have stayed—without exception, I think it is fair to say that they

Figure 1

DEPARTMENT ROSTER

Name	Age in 1967	Education and Background	Brief Job Titles and Comments for 1967–70 Period
David Gordon*	27	MBA, Stanford	Staff assistant; left after one year
Andy Johnson*	27	MBA, Wharton	Staff assistant; left after 18 months
John Adams*	27	MBA, H.B.S.	Staff assistant; various Jobs; left after three years
Kirk Spencer*	28	MBA, H.B.S.	Staff assistant; left after 18 months
Frank Nolan	28	MBA, Stanford	Staff assistant; assistant to marketing vice president; left after four and one-half years
Gene Farrell	29	BA	Accounting staff; some supervisory (staff) positions
Bob Hartwell	31	BA	Systems and procedures work
Len Halstead	31	BA; CPA	Internal auditor
Ed Becker*	32	MBA Columbia, formerly planning director for a division of a large company	Staff assistant; out for six months with nervous breakdown
Lou DiSantis*	33	MBA, H.B.S., accounting and data-processing experience	Accounting systems specialist
Leo Hoyt	34	MBA, Michigan, former consultant	Staff assistant and internal consultant; left after three years
Ray Nelson	35	MBA, H.B.S., former budget manager for a division of a large company	Budget analyst, financial analyst, left after three years

* Indicates personnel added during 1967–68.

have given up. They have decent jobs, and they do whatever they are told, no matter how foolish it seems. Lou DiSantis is the example that I feel the worst about because he and I came to be good friends, and our wives also saw a lot of each other. He came to Accutronics because he hadn't liked the work atmosphere in the two large companies he had worked for and thought he would find something completely different out here. He enjoyed it for a while and really felt that he was contributing, but by now he has had to compromise so many times that he just doesn't have any spark any more.

The last time we talked about this he said he had concluded that the key is "to keep your nose clean, don't take a strong stand on anything, and just draw your check." He knows that much of what he is doing is wasted effort, but the only way to get along is to do it. I know he makes over $25,000, and he said if anyone ever found out what he *really* contributes to the company he would be fired for sure.

Mitchell, who was sort of in my department but whom I didn't put on the list because he is a lot older, is another example of the same thing. One time when I was talking to him about this and told him how dissatisfied I was because of the things we do which obviously bear no relation to the main task of the company, he said I was taking it much too seriously. "I don't give a damn what I do," he said, "I just do what they want me to and draw my paycheck. That's the only way to get along." Well, he is in a tough spot because of his age and lack of marketable experience, and he also has a large family. I don't really blame him, but I hope I never have to regard my job that way.

Maybe examples of some of the things that were going on will give you a better idea of why I left. The incident that stands out most vividly in my memory is something that happened about a year and a half ago. I was working for one of the corporate staff departments that reported to Walter Gorman, who in turn reported to Allen Lawson, one of the vice presidents at the time. Another department which also reported to Gorman did work which was related to ours, and I suppose these two departments could conceivably have been combined into one.

One day when George, our department head, was away on a trip, Fred, the head of the other department, called Andy[2] and me into his office. He closed the door, and then said that he was out to get George and wanted to know whether we were for or against him. If we were for him, he said we could help him undermine George, and if we were against him, he would take care of us when he got control of George's department anyway.

Well, we never talked about *that* in school. We both said we didn't want to get involved in such power politics and got out of there as fast as possible. Andy and I discussed it, of course, but couldn't really decide what to do about it, aside from hoping the problem would go away. But when George came back from his trip, I decided that the best thing to do would be to tell him what Fred was up to so that he would at least be on his guard. I said I wanted to tell him something off the record, and he assured me that it would be completely personal and confidential between the two of us.

So, I told him what had happened. Before I had even finished, he stalked out of the office and left me standing there. He went straight to Allen Lawson without even bothering to look for Walter Gorman, and inside of two minutes I was in Al's office. A few minutes later a company lawyer came in also. I was ordered to tell them the story, Andy was brought in separately for his version; Walter was called in, Fred was called in, then we were all called in, and so on. This went on for days, and it soon became apparent that Al Lawson was trying to minimize the whole thing. Andy and I must have been asked a dozen times if perhaps Fred had been kidding. We were all asked what everyone else said, what they said someone else said, and so on. It was a first-class mess, and Andy and I came out of it the worst. No action was taken against Fred, but Andy and I were clearly in Al's disfavor.

I had been at the company a little over a year at that time, and that was the first time I thought seriously about leaving. I'd be damned if I would quit under

---

[2] Andy Johnson, a co-worker. See department roster, Figure 1.

those circumstances, though; I never had been a quitter before and I didn't intend to quit then. What saved me was that I was picked up by Sam Merrill, who was the second in command in one of the divisions. I had worked with Sam on some projects previously, and we had gotten along fine. I worked for him about six months, and then his boss, the division manager, became the operations vice president, with responsibility for all of the company's operations. He took Sam along, and Sam took me along back to headquarters. This affair with Fred had blown over to some extent by then—Fred left the company a few months after it happened—but Al Lawson never did look me square in the eye again.

What really clinched it was when I found out, about a year after the incident, why Al had been so reluctant to have Fred placed in a bad light. I was told by a friend who left the company shortly after this had happened to Andy and me. It seems that Al had approached my friend with the suggestion that he act as an "informal source of information" for Al with respect to what was going on in Gorman's department, and my friend had turned it down. He suspected strongly that Fred had taken on the task, because "all of a sudden Fred's wife just couldn't keep from talking about how closely Al and her husband worked together." This would all have occurred shortly before our fiasco.

Another thing that I must admit made me feel both furious and very sad was when I found out that at least three people had asked Al Lawson, who was my "big boss" for a couple of years, if they could offer me a job in their divisions. I found this out when I went around to say goodbye to several of these people as I was leaving the company, and they mentioned that they were sorry I had never come to work with them. I never heard about the offers, even though two of them would have been clear promotions at the time.

There were other incidents, of course, which seemed important at the time but which are easy to forget. There were so many things going on that were directed at promoting the interests of some individual or department rather than the company interests. The great quantities of viewgraphs and reports that we generated were one example of this; most of them were never used for any purpose at all, and we knew it. Walter Gorman wanted them to impress Al Lawson, I guess, and I'm not sure why Al wanted them. Nobody that had any line authority paid the least bit of attention to them, as became completely clear during my last year when I was sitting in on operating meetings.

We even had cases of our computer people simulating results from the computer by using it as a typewriter. At one point the management became enchanted with the idea of putting the entire operations of the company on a computer. The computer systems people had serious doubts about the feasibility of the project in relation to the resources and time available, but they were given the task and a completely unrealistic deadline anyway. Rather than say it couldn't be done, they pretended to meet the deadline by working out most of the figures on a desk calculator and printing the results on the computer. What do you suppose that does to your sense of "professional responsibility"?

It sounds amazing, but during one period even quitting became a real challenge. At one point the management came very suspicious about the possibility of persons taking confidential information from the company, either of a technical or commercial nature. There were some cases of individuals quitting and starting up competing companies in certain of the specialties they had been working in, but I guess that happens generally in a high-technology industry such as ours where the right idea or process is sufficient to attract all the financial backing you might need. Denver is full of such companies, and I guess Boston is too. As far as I know there were never any instances of people misusing commercial information, though, as opposed to the technical know-how they acquired.

Anyway, when Andy quit he left his letter of resignation, saying he was giving the customary 30-days' notice, on Gorman's desk one evening. The next morning he was met by Gorman, Al Lawson, and the company legal counsel as he came to work, and the four of them went to his desk and went through it, item by item. He was allowed to keep his personal papers, and was then asked to leave immediately. They said they preferred not to have anyone working there who was not happy with the company and that there was no point working any longer once he had given his notice.

This pattern was repeated with several people. They all got their pay for the next 30 days, of course, so that was not an issue. But it certainly is not a very nice atmosphere under which to leave a company, and it really made you wonder as to what sort of a reference you could expect from them in the future.

I don't think that sort of treatment of those who left the company was done with any ill intent or malice towards the people involved. It just seemed to be the natural outgrowth of the strong team spirit that the management tried to foster in the company and which they believed in themselves. They *really* believed there was an "Accutronics type," and the reaction was that if you didn't like it there you weren't an Accutronics type after all and didn't belong in the company. The fault was always seen as being in the individual rather than the system. There is some value to that kind of an approach, but I think they carried it too far. There were some periodic surveys made by teams of outside consultants to determine what people liked and didn't like about the company, but most of the results I ever saw looked like they pertained to some other company.

I don't want to give the impression that what happened in my group is normal at the company, because I don't really know that much about the atmosphere in the other areas, although I know the politics were not confined to our area. I knew lots of people who were very strong in their support of the company, and it certainly had an excellent public image. There was a high turnover of professional personnel—around $2\frac{1}{2}\%$ per month—during the last year I was there, but part of that may have come from the fact that it looked like the growth would be slowing down to a more normal rate because of the leveling off of defense spending, and the opportunities in relation to the costs involved just wouldn't be as great as several years ago. Four of us from the Class of '67 went out there, though, mostly working in different areas, and I was the third to leave. I don't know if the fourth is still there or not.

Another thing that became obvious was that there was a big difference in the way people responded to what you might call the politics of the situation. I really think some people simply never realized what was going on. Of those who were aware of it, some "fought the system," some just accepted things the way they were, and some viewed it as a personal challenge and opportunity.

Frank Nolan was a wonderful example of the last type. He viewed it all as a big game and seemed to take genuine delight in finding out how things worked around the company so he could play the game better. He paid more attention to the informal things going on than anyone else that I knew of, and he also seemed to know more about what was going on in various parts of the company than anyone else. He always had a series of complicated explanations for what seemed like simple things, but in several cases I think he turned out to be right.

Just as an example of the kind of thing he paid attention to, I was told that when he first came with the company, which was a couple of years before I did, he made it a point to find out what colleges all of the top-management people had gone to, where they had first met, how they happened to join the company, what jobs they had had in the company, whom they seemed to be bringing along as proteges in the company, what social activities and clubs they were involved in, and so on. I guess information of that sort does help you to understand what is going on, but I have to admit that I don't like to think that those things are all that important, and I don't like to spend much of my time on them.

I became pretty good friends with Frank, and he was quite outspoken about a lot of things. We talked a lot about where the company was going and what the opportunities were likely to be for people like us within the company. He had been quite enthusiastic about the staff group that they were trying to build up, but after I had been there about six months he concluded that Walter Gorman, who was really his superior, was never going to make it into the top management ranks. Frank attached a great deal of importance to working for someone on the way up in the company, and at that point he just about quit working for Walter. He didn't try to make any formal moves, he just managed to get started on some projects for Carl Lund, the marketing vice president, who he thought was going to move up. He took to working Lund's hours, which were a little different from ours, and simply told Walter that he was "on an important and confidential project for Lund" when Walter came to him with work. There were sparks for a while, but after a while Frank started working for Lund full time.

Frank based his conclusions about Walter on a whole lot of things—the progress the department was making and the reception we were getting out in the divisions, the apparent lack of strong backing of Walter by Lawson, Butler, and the rest of the officers, the fact that Walter and his wife had been at the company for over two years but were not on close social terms with anyone of consequence in the company, and a difference in dress and appearance. Gorman did look a bit like a gambling casino operator, and Frank felt there was a significant "All-American" bias in the management. He also felt that what our department was trying to do would not be seen as being as important to the company as either research, production, or marketing skills during the next several years.

Frank was right about Walter, by the way. About six months after this Walter was "reorganized" into a less important job, and a while later he left the company.

Frank also had a way of trying to trade information so that he always came out a little bit ahead in the exchange. He seemed to collect bits of information from all over that might make some sense when put together. Whenever he would volunteer some information to you, you could be sure that the main reason was he thought you had something that he needed. In a way he was trying to place himself in the center of the wheel, with bits and pieces of information flowing back and forth along the spokes but with him in the center, putting things together.

Although Frank and I got along very well, I noticed that he always managed to cover up whatever he was working on whenever I came in his office. Nobody else did that, and we all used to joke about it a bit. Frank tried to maintain the impression that he was always working on something confidential and important.

It is easy to find fault with any company, I suppose, and I hope I am not being too critical of Accutronics. Many people seemed to like it, so maybe there is such a thing as an Accutronics type, and I'm not it.

I can't pass my experience off as "bad management" on the part of the company, because it has been an enormous success story. I give a great deal of credit to the group of about six or eight people who changed that company from an unknown with a few million dollars in sales in the early sixties to one of the outstanding growth companies of the past ten years, with a sales level which will bring it into the *Fortune* list of 500.

The growth may slow down, but they want to make it into a billion-dollar corporation in their lifetimes. They all started with nothing, they took big risks, they still work extremely hard, and it has paid off. Individually, they are worth anywhere from several million to over fifty million dollars in terms of the market value of their stock by now.

I am sure my viewpoint of what was happening in the company would be different if I were in their position, but I still think they overrate the value of their "modern management approach," which they honestly believe is 10 years ahead of the rest of industry, and underemphasize the part that several virtual monopolies which resulted from outstanding technical and production breakthroughs have played in their success. I think a lot of us were misled by this when we were evaluating the company as a place to work. I know I assumed for quite a while that any company with such an outstanding growth record *must* be "well-managed," but the longer I was there the more convinced I became that the growth was due more to several critical technical breakthroughs than to exceptional management skills or approaches.

The management group is unquestionably smart and hard-working, and they built up the company by competing fiercely against some of the giants of industry. I suppose this is probably why they seek aggressive and ambitious people and encourage competition within the company to the extent that they do. But you don't compete against Lockheed Electronics or General Dynamics or Litton when you come to work for Accutronics now; you compete against people within the company. It is people versus people, not companies versus companies, and I think that makes a big difference. I don't think that the kind of competitive behavior which paid off extremely well for the company is necessarily what you should encourage at lower levels within the company, because I really think it results in a lot of wasted effort. Also, some good people probably have left the company for just the reasons I did.

I think most of the things I didn't like were the results of our widespread pyramidal form of organization, and a basic management philosophy that the best man will be the one that climbs the pyramid, regardless of the environment or the nature of the competition. It is ironic that this was one of the things about the company that appealed to me in the first place. Their strong emphasis on competition and the "free enterprise" philosophy within the company made it seem like a place where I would have the greatest chance of getting ahead by my own abilities and work rather than by seniority or politics, and a place where I wouldn't be hemmed in by a lot of restrictions and formalized procedures.

I had lots of arguments about this with one of the personnel men that I knew quite well, and he was quite definite about the prevalence in top management of a strong belief that "the best man will get ahead, regardless of the environment." I kept asking him best man for *what,* and what about the need to cooperate within the company, to observe some kind of limits on the form of competition, and so on, but we never got anywhere. They oftentimes put several people or several departments on virtually the same tasks, for example, and made a practice of obscuring titles and responsibilities and then encouraging people to take on more responsibility if they could get away with it. They also did a great deal of reorganizing; the number of blue sheets that came around announcing changes in personnel or organizational structure was amazing.

I think that is just like offering a big prize to the winner of a boxing match and sending the referee home. You wouldn't have a boxing match following the Marquis of Queensberry rules for very long; you would have a street fight. Unless you restrict the grounds on which people are allowed to compete, I think that loose an approach to organization will lead to a lot of conflict and activities which are not good for the company and which may also be unpleasant for the people involved. I remember a quip of Harry Truman's with regard to the sometimes merciless criticism of public officials that "if you can't stand the heat, get out of the kitchen." Maybe that is what I'm doing.

I have just accepted a job with a much smaller and highly technical company in the Cape Kennedy area. They sought me out and gave me a substantial salary increase, but the money is not the main reason I quit. I was making $20,000 a year at Accutronics, which was above most of the people who were roughly in my category out there and which I suppose is above what most of my classmates are making now. I just didn't like working there any longer because of some of the things I've mentioned to you.

I'm looking forward to the new job, both because of the challenges involved in the business as well as the financial opportunities for me. I also think that this management will be likely to keep things in check a little more within the company than was the case out at Accutronics. It's a tough balance to maintain, though—aggressive company behavior but a cooperative and satisfying working atmosphere. If I were just graduating and job hunting again, I sure would pay more attention to factors like this. Unless you fit in with the atmosphere you find in the company, you will either have to change yourself, quit, or be unhappy about it.

Section 5
Follow-up and
Reappraisal

1. Aerosol Techniques, Inc.

IN JANUARY, 1966, Mr. Robert Meyer, a 1965 Harvard MBA, joined Aerosol Techniques, Inc., in Bridgeport, Connecticut, as director of corporate development. While his immediate concern was the evaluation of numerous acquisition proposals that ATI had received, Mr. Meyer was also responsible for appraising overall corporate strategy. Shortly after assuming his position, Mr. Meyer concluded that environmental trends might require a strategy change.

Founded in December, 1955, by Mr. H. R. Shepherd, a chemist and biologist with aerosol R.&D. experience dating back to the end of World War II, ATI was a "contract filler," or producer and packager of items marketed to consumers by others. With 1965 sales of $47 million, or about 22% of the total contract filling market, ATI was the largest contract filler of aerosol products in the United States. Yearly growth since 1960 had averaged 46% for sales and 65% for profits. (For financial statements, see Exhibits 1 and 2.)

From the start, ATI's policy had been to emphasize service and development research for new products. As a result, about 95% of 1965 dollar volume was made up of products that ATI had developed in its laboratories either alone or jointly with customers. Mr. Shepherd indicated that ATI did not want to have to compete on a price basis, or to compete with customers by marketing products under its own name. Thus ATI's name was not on any products packed for other firms.

In 1965 ATI was the only contract filler with plants in each major section of the country. These provided an economic advantage over other contract fillers because of the relatively high cost of transporting filled aerosol containers. Nevertheless, Mr. Meyer was worried about ATI's strategy of developing and manufacturing aerosol products for national marketers because of several trends that had developed between 1960 and 1965. Of these, he felt the most important were a general decline in prices and profit margins for filling operations and a tendency on the part of some national marketers to install their own aerosol filling lines as sales volume increased.

596

Exhibit 1

AEROSOL TECHNIQUES, INC.

Balance Sheets for Years Ended September 30, 1960, through 1965
(Dollars in Thousands)

	1960	1961	1962	1963	1964	1965
Current assets:						
Cash	$ 60	$ 449	$ 290	$ 359	$ 1,067	$ 1,433
Accounts receivable—net	461	832	1,279	3,373	4,924	6,566
Inventories—lower cost or market	465	238	468	2,136	2,329	3,098
Prepaid expenses	15	15	16	103	185	185
Miscellaneous	3	23	22	90	40	65
Total current assets	$1,005	$1,557	$2,076	$6,061	$ 8,544	$11,348
Fixed assets:						
Land	0	0	0	13	13	179
Buildings	0	0	0	362	365	880
Machinery and equipment	479	496	541	2,024	2,497	3,226
Other	134	144	154	308	384	1,429*
	$ 613	$ 640	$ 695	$2,707	$ 3,260	$ 5,715
Less: acc. dep. and amort.	175	240	307	1,377	1,556	1,805
Total fixed assets	$ 438	$ 401	$ 388	$1,330	$ 1,704	$ 3,909
Other assets	19	18	24	155	75	125
	$1,462	$1,976	$2,488	$7,546	$10,322	$15,383
Current liabilities:						
Notes payable	$ 0	$ 0	$ 0	$1,298	$ 1,500	$ 0
Accounts payable	596	527	758	2,480	2,842	4,151
Federal and state taxes payable	89	164	238	564	695	886
Other	179	209	200	388	396	1,318†
Total current liabilities	$ 864	$ 901	$1,196	$4,730	$ 5,434	$ 6,356
Long-term debt	217	98	34	241	200	3,152
Deferred federal taxes	36	43	47	53	55	60
Contingent deferred credit	0	0	0	355	257	184
Stockholders' equity:						
4% voting, cumulative, preferred	0	0	0	715	715	715
Common stock: 10¢ par value	30	43	44	61	76	78
Capital in excess of par value	20	20	20	20	20	20
Paid in surplus	0	421	456	131	2,083	2,179
Retained earnings	295	450	691	1,240	1,480	2,639
Total stockholders' equity	$ 345	$ 934	$1,211	$2,167	$ 4,375	$ 5,631
	$1,462	$1,976	$2,488	$7,546	$10,322	$15,383

* Incudes $934,000 for construction in progress.
† Includes $672,000 of current portion of long-term debt.
Source: ATI annual reports.

THE AEROSOL INDUSTRY

Aerosol Products. The term "aerosol product" was used to describe any product packed in an aerosol container. The total item consisted of a pressurized container, a propellant to supply the desired pressure, the usable product fill, and a cap-and-valve combination that controlled the release of the product and propellant. While almost any product

Exhibit 2

AEROSOL TECHNIQUES, INC.

Income Statements: 1960–65
(Dollars in Thousands)

	1960	1961	1962	1963	1964	1965
Net sales	$7,052	$7,734	$10,776	$21,327	$34,632	$46,975
Cost of goods sold, selling, administrative, and general expense	6,835	7,415	10,302	20,159	33,079	44,705
	$ 218	$ 319	$ 475	$ 1,169	$ 1,553	$ 2,270
Other income	10	12	24	66	222	36
	$ 228	$ 331	$ 498	$ 1,235	$ 1,775	$ 2,306
Other deductions	27	16	11	85	104	124
	$ 200	$ 315	$ 487	$ 1,150	$ 1,671	$ 2,182
Provision for federal income taxes	99	159	247	567	751	980
Net earnings	$ 101	$ 156	$ 240	$ 583	$ 920	$ 1,202

Source: ATI annual reports.

that was liquid or gaseous at ordinary temperatures could theoretically be packaged in an aerosol container, in actual practice it was often difficult to "marry" the product, the propellant, and the cap and valve into a workable combination. Nevertheless, by 1965 such diverse products as shaving cream, perfume, starch, furniture polish, hair sprays, and room deodorants were sold in aerosol containers.

Industry History and Growth. The first aerosol product was the "bugbomb," of which some 40 million units were produced for issue to servicemen during the last two years of World War II. When the war ended, the bomb was modified for civilian use.

While these first aerosols were high-pressure, refillable types which retailed for $3.98, myriad technical developments soon reduced both pressure and price. As a result, aerosol packaging spread to dozens of other products, as seen in Table 1.

According to industry sources, aerosol packaging would continue to spread to other fields in the future.

TABLE 1

	Year First Marketed in Aerosol Packages
Room deodorants, lacquers, mothproofers	1948
Hair sprays, paints, automobile waxes	1949
Shave lather	1950
Whipped cream	1951
Perfumes	1954
Starches	1955
Glass cleaners	1956
Furniture waxes and polishes	1959
All purpose cleaners, antiperspirants	1962

Also important to the rapid growth (about 17% a year between 1955 and 1964) of the aerosol market was the increasing penetration of aerosols as a packaging form in each of the above product areas. The percentage of room deodorants, shave lathers, and colognes packaged in aerosol containers increased from 0% in 1947 to 91%, 82%, and 64%, respectively, in 1964 (see Exhibit 3). Moreover, some products, such as hair sprays, were made possible by aerosol packaging.

Exhibit 3

AEROSOL TECHNIQUES, INC.

Percentage Penetration of Aerosols as a Packaging Form in Various Market Segments: 1951–64
(Per Cent of Dollar Volume)

	1951	1952	1953	1954	1955	1956	1957	1958	1959	1960	1961	1962	1963	1964
Insecticides	30%	32%	37%	37%	39%	38%	39%	42%	47%	47%	47%	47%	48%	44%
Room deodorants	0	0	40	44	58	56	67	73	82	79	85	89	91	91
Shave lathers	0	12	29	38	47	51	59	60	65	69	71	79	81	82
Colognes	0	0	0	13	33	45	48	51	57	58	62	64	66	64

Source: Eighth Annual Aerosol Market Report, 1964, prepared by Freon Products Division of Du Pont. Data supplied to Du Pont by *Drug Trade News* (New York).

In 1964, total sales of all aerosol-packaged products reached over 1.3 billion units. All but 6% of this total was made up of nonfood items, of which 46% were personal products, 30% household products, and 24% miscellaneous products (see Exhibit 4). Table 2 gives examples of the types of products included in each category:

TABLE 2

Personal Products	*Household Products*	*Miscellaneous Products*
Shave lathers	Room deodorants and disin-	Paints and coatings
Hair sprays and dressings	fectants	Insecticides
Medicinals	Cleaners (all types)	Automotive waxes
Colognes and perfumes	Household waxes and	Veterinarian and pet prod-
Personal deodorants	polishes	ucts
Other (shampoos, suntan	Starches	Industrial products
preparations, hand	Shoe and leather dressings	
lotions, etc.)		

Industry observers expected each of these major categories to grow at least 8% a year during the coming decade. Du Pont, for example, in a 1965 market report, forecast that between 1965 and 1967 sales of personal products would increase 14% a year, household products 12%, and all other nonfood products 10%.

Estimates of aerosol growth for foods were more uncertain.. While sales of nonfood aerosols had increased more than 19% a year between

Exhibit 4

AEROSOL TECHNIQUES, INC.

Du Pont Company Estimate of Aerosol Production (Nonfood Products Only)

(Millions of Units)

	1953	1954	1955	1956	1957	1958	1959	1960	1961	1962	1963	1964	1965
Personal products													
Shave lather	27.3	47.0	53.1	51.0	59.3	65.0	75.0	79.1	84.7	94.8	97.6	102.6	108.1
Hair sprays and dressings	16.1	34.5	55.8	83.4	95.6	112.1	88.7	120.9	152.5	245.6	294.0	314.0	337.0
Dental creams						23.0	11.8	5.8	3.1	3.1	3.0	3.0	3.2
Medicinals and pharmaceuticals	0.8	1.1	1.5	2.4	6.2	8.1	10.5	12.3	19.5	36.9	39.8	45.6	49.4
Colognes and perfumes	0.1	3.0	7.0	8.8	18.6	30.0	37.9	43.1	54.7	55.1	60.4	66.2	69.2
Other*	3.8	4.4	7.2	7.7	7.1	9.6	12.9	18.7	18.5	36.9	38.5	47.1	52.8
Total	48.1	90.0	124.6	153.3	186.8	247.8	236.8	279.9	333.0	472.4	533.3	578.5	619.7
Insecticides†	47.0	47.0	57.0	61.4	50.7	71.3	78.9	92.5	87.3	89.2	73.2	75.1	76.4
Household products													
Room deodorants	17.3	21.3	33.1	38.4	44.6	62.8	62.9	78.1	86.3	99.0	118.5	126.4	131.6
Snow	8.9	7.1	6.8	8.9	9.0	9.8	9.5	10.5	8.6	9.5	10.5	12.5	13.5
Glass cleaners				8.0	11.2	6.6	24.2	22.2	26.0	31.0	47.3	52.3	54.3
Shoe or leather dressings				1.5	4.3	7.7	14.1	16.6	7.3	4.7	8.9	11.1	13.0
Waxes and polishes (all types)							12.1	40.6	42.1	52.9	50.9	57.8	61.0
Starches								20.6	50.5	65.4	86.9	99.0	107.3
Other	2.3	3.1	8.2	16.4	8.3	11.6	25.4	10.5	15.7	18.6	11.8	13.2	14.8
Total	28.5	31.5	48.1	73.2	77.4	98.5	148.2	199.1	236.5	281.1	334.8	372.3	395.5
Coatings	13.0	13.1	14.7	22.5	43.0	50.0	63.2	77.1	95.6	110.3	137.9	158.4	174.5
Miscellaneous products													
Veterinarian and pet products	0.3	0.5	1.0	1.5	2.3	3.3	4.3	6.3	8.3	7.1	7.6	8.7	9.4
Automotive products‡											33.2	36.9	39.6
Other§	3.1	5.9	10.3	13.3	15.0	14.3	30.2	42.2	52.8	44.7	23.6	21.4	19.7
Total	3.4	6.4	11.3	14.8	17.3	17.6	34.5	48.5	61.1	51.8	64.4	67.2	71.0
Grand total	140.0	188.0	255.7	325.2	375.2	485.2	561.6	697.1	813.5	1004.8	1140.1	1251.3	1334.8

* OTHER PERSONAL PRODUCTS include shampoos, suntan preparations, personal deodorants, hand lotions, powders, depilatories, etc.
† INSECTICIDES include high-pressure and low-pressure products (including space, residual, and mothproofers).
‡ AUTOMOTIVE PRODUCTS included in other miscellaneous products prior to 1963.
§ OTHER MISCELLANEOUS PRODUCTS include antistatic sprays, industrial applications, fire extinguishers, etc.
Source: Eighth Annual Aerosol Market Report, 1964, prepared by the Freon Products Division of Du Pont, p. 24.

1955 and 1964, the sales of aerosol-packaged foods had increased less than 2% a year (see Exhibit 5). However, in 1963 and 1964, Du Pont gained approval from the Food and Drug Administration for two new tasteless propellants. According to some industry sources, these promised to overcome previous technical problems and to open the way to aerosol packaging of a wide variety of foods—from staples, such as peanut butter and cheese spread, to additives, such as vermouth. As a consequence, some industry sources were predicting in 1965 that the growth curve for food products would soon begin to resemble that of nonfood aerosols.

Exhibit 5

AEROSOL TECHNIQUES, INC.

Growth of the Food Aerosol Market
(Millions of Units)

Year	Sales	Year	Sales	Year	Sales
1951	43	1956	69	1961	58
1952	50	1957	75	1962	63
1953	56	1958	80	1963	67
1954	60	1959	79	1964	75
1955	64	1960	59	1965	100 (est.)

Source: Eighth Annual Aerosol Market Report, 1964, prepared by the Freon Products Division of Du Pont, p. 18.

Reasons for Aerosol Usage. According to a study by the Freon Products Division of Du Pont, there were three primary reasons for the use of aerosol packaging: (1) increased product effectiveness, (2) greater user convenience, and (3) time savings. The study noted that not all successful applications exhibited all three advantages; even where effectiveness was not improved, convenience alone was often enough to stimulate sales.

Nevertheless, aerosol packaging was relatively expensive (see Exhibits 6 and 7). Some observers felt that cost would restrict the use of aerosol packaging for products with low profit margins.

Industry Structure. During World War II, the Bridgeport Brass Company produced most of the bugbombs used by the armed services. After the war, this company continued to make bugbombs, which it sold through its regular sales force. Soon, however, Bridgeport, which had no product development activities, was forced out of the aerosol market by contract fillers, which carried on intensive product development programs. These contract fillers were small, regional companies which would purchase the cans from national firms such as American

Exhibit 6

AEROSOL TECHNIQUES, INC.

Cost Estimates for Various Aerosol Products

Product Type	Starch*	Hair Spray†	Shave Cream‡
Product fill......................	1.0¢	4.0¢	1.5¢
Propellant.......................	0.3	12.0§	0.1
Can‖	7.0	6.3	5.0
Valve...........................	3.0	2.6	3.0
Cap............................	0.5	1.0#	0.5
Carton**.......................	0.6	0.5	0.5
Direct labor.....................	1.0	1.0	1.0
Overhead........................	1.5	1.5	1.5
Profit (max.)....................	1.0	1.0	1.0
Factory price....................	15.9¢	29.9¢	14.1¢
Approx. retail price..............	39¢	$1–$1.20	$.79 to $1
Approx. retail price of comparable product (nonaerosol)...........	19¢ for 12 oz.	none available	$1 for 10 oz.

* 16 oz. size, for laundry use.
† 12 oz. size, alcohol-base, most "name brands."
‡ 6 oz. size, most "name brands."
§ Much more expensive than others shown because the product requires Freon as a propellant, which amounts to 70% of the weight of the contents. The propellants used in the other products shown are hydrocarbons and are only 4% of the weight of the contents. Water-based hair sprays, with somewhat different characteristics, are available; these entail a lower propellant cost.
‖ Printed cans; no separate labels.
More expensive only because usually fancier.
** Carton for a dozen cans.

Source: Estimates furnished by an industry source other than ATI. Estimates are for an established product with a volume per production run of about 25,000 units or more.

Exhibit 7

AEROSOL TECHNIQUES, INC.

Cost of a Typical Aerosol Food Product

(Food Product: Pancake Mix)

Cost	*Per Unit*
Direct labor...	$.04
Can (16 oz.)..	.09
Gas (nitrous oxide)..................................	.005
Valve and release....................................	.05
Product (pancake mix)................................	.04
Overhead (interest and depreciation)*.................	.01
Profit margin..	.015
Cost to marketer before distribution charges..............	$.250

* Assumes an investment of $300,000 for a line that produces 9.6 million units a year for eight years with indirect labor and storage costs of $50,000 a year.
Source: Harvard Business School student reports conducted for ATI.

Can Company, the propellants from firms such as Du Pont, and the caps and valves from small companies like themselves. They would then assemble these components, including the product fill, which they usually manufactured, into the final aerosol product. The contract fillers would then sell the finished product to marketing firms, which resold to retailers under their own brands. By 1950, at least 50 firms met the contract filler definition.

As the demand for aerosols grew, two changes occurred in industry structure. First, the contract fillers became larger through both internal growth and acquisition of other contract fillers. Second, some national marketers began to erect their own filling facilities since they felt their volume now warranted such a move. Such a marketer was called a "captive filler."

By 1964, output of nonfood aerosols was about evenly divided between captive and contract fillers (see Exhibit 8). Most industry observers felt a definite trend toward captive filling had not yet emerged among national marketers, however. While firms such as Colgate, S. C. Johnson, Alberto-Culver, Johnson & Johnson, Mennen, and Gillette had established their own filling lines, firms such as Procter & Gamble and Breck still relied on contract fillers. Moreover, most of the firms that had established their own filling lines still relied on contract fillers to supplement their own production during peak sales periods.

The difficulty of deciding between captive vs. contract filling was partly responsible for the lack of a definite trend. The economics of the decision required the marketing company to consider not only the cost of filling equipment and personnel, but also distribution costs, inventory costs (since the contract filler usually kept part of the inventory), and research and development costs (since many contract fillers developed new product formulations for the marketers). In addition, the marketing company had to consider noneconomic factors, such as the need for security in protecting the product formulation and the need for tight quality control.

One industry observer (not ATI) agreed that the issue of captive vs. contract filling was complex. He estimated, however, that a yearly volume of five million units in a standard product might be an "average break-even point" as far as the economics of the filling operation were involved. Although some companies used captive operations for as few as one million units a year, and others used contract fillers for annual volumes as high as 10 million, he felt that these companies were clear exceptions and were probably influenced by other-than-economic factors. He also thought that it was becoming easier for companies to set up their own filling operations since the necessary equipment could readily be purchased, and an increasing number of people with experience in aerosol filling operations were becoming available.

Other industry observers felt that many marketers would not go

Exhibit 8

AEROSOL TECHNIQUES, INC.

ATi's Share of the Contract Filled and Total
Aerosol Filling Markets: 1963–64 (Nonfood Products Only)

	PER CENT OF MARKET CONTRACT FILLED		ATI SHARE OF CONTRACT MARKET		ATI SHARE OF TOTAL MARKET	
	1963	1964	1963	1964	1963	1964
Household products:						
Room deodorants........	36.9%	22.1%	7.1%	17.0%	2.6%	3.7%
Cleaners...............	64.1	62.0	34.8	31.0	22.3	18.9
Waxes and polishes......	18.9	22.1	28.9	23.5	5.5	5.2
Starch.................	82.9	84.0	26.7	25.0	22.2	21.0
Shoe and leather dress-						
ings.................	86.9	96.1	1.3	3.9	1.1	3.8
Other.................	69.4	82.0	21.5	5.7	14.9	4.7
Personal products:						
Shave lather...........	23.0	37.0	7.1	1.6	1.6	.6
Hair spray............	60.0	61.0	30.9	35.1	18.6	21.4
Medicinals and pharma-						
ceuticals.............	63.0	68.8	13.9	21.4	8.8	15.0
Colognes and perfumes...	51.0	38.1	15.9	31.0	8.1	12.0
Other.................	36.1	38.9	29.3	3.2	10.5	1.3
Miscellaneous products:						
Insecticides...........	34.0	31.0	54.4	30.5	18.5	9.5
Coatings..............	52.0	41.0	4.5	4.3	2.4	2.0
Veterinarian and pet.....	96.3	77.5	3.9	1.4	3.8	1.1
Automotive and in-						
dustrial..............	59.0	70.3	14.6	8.8	8.6	6.4
Other.................	...	36.7	...	10.3	...	3.8
Total..............	51.1%	50.4%	22.0%	21.9%	11.2%	11.1%

Source: ATI marketing statistics.

captive because of the low profit margins on filling. They reasoned that such marketers would be far more interested in new marketing opportunities which promised high margins than in a production activity with a rapid rate of technological change. (For further discussion of the advantages of using a contract filler, see Exhibit 9).

Contract Fillers and Their Strategies. Although the aerosol filling industry had grown tremendously, it had nevertheless become increasingly competitive during the mid-60's as the 98 independent contract fillers fought for a large but limited supply of contracts. The intensity of competition was suggested by the fact that three contract fillers had been forced into bankruptcy in 1963, and Old Empire, Inc., of Clifton, New Jersey, one of the oldest and most respected names in aerosols, had also filed a bankruptcy petition.

On the other hand, several large companies entered the aerosol

Exhibit 9

AEROSOL TECHNIQUES, INC.
Advantages of Using a Contract Packager
by
A. S. Pero

1. *Research & Development Advantages*
   a. Can draw from lab personnel already experienced in aerosols.
   b. Developments by fillers, either directly or in cooperation with other suppliers, are available promptly to marketers.
   c. Prevents added load being placed on marketers' lab facilities.
   d. Reduces marketers' outlay for research and development.
2. *Production Advantages*
   a. Can select latest and best equipment available for particular job required.
   b. Two or more products can be run simultaneously.
   c. Contract packagers offer facilities to cope with seasonal demands, or unexpected market fluctuations either of higher or lower volume than anticipated.
   d. Personnel of long, varied, and impartial experience available for quality control.
   e. Marketer can ask, and often gets, tighter specifications on his product.
   f. Supplier problems are handled by the filler.
   g. Can eliminate or minimize labor-management problems.
3. *Service Advantages*
   a. Marketer can warehouse both raw and finished materials, often at no charge, on filler's premises.
   b. Filler's trucking facilities can be used for drop shipments, emergency services, etc.
   c. Marketer can draw on know-how and information sometimes not available within his own organization.
4. *Economic Advantages*
   a. No money outlay for equipment and maintenance, plant building or expansion, or personnel and training of same.
   b. A contract packager is actually a co-op manufacturer who divides his labor, overhead, etc., among a wide group of customers and products.
   c. Working capital is conserved on material purchased by filler until product is completed.
   d. Material purchases are often less, due to filler's volume buying.
   e. Lowest costs on final product can be obtained through competitive bidding.
   f. Use of strategically located fillers can offer substantially lower shipping costs when products are to be nationally distributed.

How high a volume of product must an aerosol marketer be turning out before it pays him to consider doing his own filling?

Actually product volume is relatively unimportant in itself. More important is to seriously study the overall advantages a good filler has to offer vs. the overall advantages of the marketer doing his own work. Once this is determined, a

Exhibit 9—Continued

further evaluation is needed on the aerosol product or products to be manufactured.

Is the product to be a low-profit, highly competitive one? In this case a larger volume will be needed to justify the total expenditure involved. Or is the product a high-profit one, in a noncompetitive line? In the latter, a lesser volume might justify doing one's own filling.

In general, a careful analysis of all factors involved by the marketer, in the light of his own capacities and business interests, should provide him with a satisfactory answer. A survey of the aerosol field today clearly indicates that most marketers have already decided it is to their advantage to have their aerosol lines produced by contract packages. The aerosol filling industry is today so competitive that the margin above direct labor is small enough to discourage not only the marketer's equipment plan, but also new competitive contract packagers as well.

Source: Article by A. S. Pero of the Fluid Chemical Co., Newark, N.J., *Aerosol Age* (June, 1975), p. 28.

business through acquisitions. Borden's, for example, in 1963 and 1964 acquired Krylon, an aerosol paint manufacturer, and Aerosol Brands, a general contract filler. During the same period, Corn Products Company bought Peterson Filling in order to package its products in aerosol containers.

In an article in *Aerosol Age,* the industry trade journal, Mr. H. R. Shepherd, president of ATI, discussed the future role of the independent contract filler as follows:

It is clear that in the future there will be only two types of contract fillers—first, the filler with national distribution and plants strategically distributed throughout the nation (or in several countries) which can adequately service a national or international marketing concern. The other type of successful contract filler will be the small filler, who can handle low volume runs of specialty products or products that are only beginning to be felt in the marketplace.[1]

Vim Laboratories exemplified the latter type of company. One of the few publicly owned fillers, Vim had annual sales only slightly above $1 million. Custom filling represented part of its business, but the company's own specialty line, which included insecticides, paints, room deodorants, shaving cream, Christmas snow, insect repellent, suntan lotion, and charcoal lighter, represented a significant portion of aerosol capacity.

George Barr & Company, which had been purchased by Pittsburgh

---

[1] H. R. Shepherd, "The Contract Filler's Role in Aerosol Product Development," *Aerosol Age* (December, 1963), p. 48.

Railways Company in 1962, was the second largest contract filler in the United States in 1965. Barr's 1962 sales had exceeded $15 million, but had not been reported separately since 1962. In May, 1965, the company unveiled a new filling plant in Piles, Illinois, which was described as "the largest aerosol filling plant in the world." Barr's apparent strategy was to become a "packaging consultant." With this objective in mind, Pittsburgh Railways in 1963 and 1964 had acquired Advance Packaging Company, a filler of nonaerosol packages and Aero Valve Corporation, a manufacturer of caps and valves for aerosol containers.

Power-Pak, Inc., of Bridgeport, Connecticut, was a medium-sized contract filler. In 1962, Power-Pak formed agreements with three other contract fillers—one English, one Canadian, and one midwestern domestic—under which Power-Pak licensed these companies to use some of Power-Pak's product formulations. Power-Pak also performed R.&D. activities for these firms for a fee. While Power-Pak did not see any direct increase in the sales of its own products, Mr. Edward Helfer, Power-Pak's president in 1962, felt that this arrangement might lead to a penetration in continental Europe, which was just beginning to experience an aerosol boom similar to that in the United States between 1955 and 1960.

Industry Suppliers. The four principal components of an aerosol product—containers, propellants, caps and valves, and product fill— were supplied by diverse groups of companies.

The market for propellants was dominated by five large chemical companies: Du Pont, Allied Chemical Corporation, Union Carbide, Pennsalt Chemicals Corporation, and Kaiser Aluminum & Chemical Corporation.

The market for aerosol containers was also dominated by large firms. Among the most important were Continental Can Company, Inc., American Can Company, Crown Cork & Seal Company, Inc., and National Can Corporation. Glass container manufacturers included Owens-Illinois Glass Company, Foster-Forbes Glass Company, and T.C. Wheaton Company.

Small companies, similar to many of the contract fillers, played an important part in the supply of caps and valves. The major supplier was Precision Valve Corporation, which had an estimated 50% of the market. The other half of the market was split among many suppliers.

The aerosol filler, contract or captive, usually produced the product fill. In the case of certain products, such as perfumes, however, the contract filler secured the product fill from the marketing company.

ATI HISTORY

Immediately after World War II, Mr. H. R. Shepherd joined the Bridgeport Brass Company as administrative assistant to the director of research. About a year later, he and three friends founded Connecticut Chemical Research Corporation. After eight years, Mr. Shepherd resigned to form his own company, Aerosol Techniques, Inc.

ATI was launched in 1955 with $20,000 capital invested by Mr. Shepherd, a $125,000 bank loan, and $600,000 in trade credit. Although contracts were obtained almost immediately to load hair sprays and colognes, ATI was $75,000 in the red after six months. At year's end, however, the company emerged with a modest profit of $5,000 on sales of $1.5 million. *Aerosol Age* reported as follows:

> During this stage of growth, Mr. Shepherd emphasized that the theme will be "give service—expand research—put profits into new equipment and technical development". . . . The company has started a research program with an eastern university on basic problems with aerosols. . . . A complete aerosol service center is a must for proper handling of customers in aerosol packaging, according to Mr. Shepherd.[2]

By 1960, sales had risen to $7.1 million and net profit to $101,000. Although hair sprays remained ATI's most important single product, the line had been expanded to include shaving creams, toothpaste, furniture polishes, and other items. In addition, R.&D. laboratories had been established. A continuing effort was being made to improve formulae for customers and to develop or adapt aerosol packaging to new products. Though product diversification and research had reduced ATI's dependence on a few major clients, three customers still accounted for almost 60% of sales in 1960.

Although ATI lost an account which contributed 13% of 1960 sales because the customer went captive, the addition of new products and growth of established lines pushed 1961 sales to a new high of $7.7 million. Early in 1961, ATI issued 130,000 shares to the public, representing a 30% interest in the company, at $4 per share. This financing helped to alleviate the financial pressures caused by the company's tremendous growth. Even though ATI had decided to retain all earnings and to conserve funds for working capital by leasing rather than purchasing facilities, creditors were supplying over three fourths of the firm's invested funds in 1960. In October, 1961, the stock was listed on the American Stock Exchange.

---

[2] *Aerosol Age* (July, 1956), p. 21.

In 1962, ATI's spectacular growth trend was resumed as sales reached $10.8 million and net income climbed to $240,000. In addition, ATI established a subsidiary, Aeroceuticals, Inc., to produce and market an assortment of ethical drugs which company R.&D. had developed for aerosol containers. Major reasons for this move were the high growth rate (over 40% per year between 1957 and 1962) of pharmaceuticals and the relatively high gross margin on these products.

In 1963, ATI moved into first place in the contract filling business with sales of $21.3 million and profits of $583,000, partly as a result of the acquisition of two contract fillers: Western Filling Corporation in Los Angeles, California, and Continental Filling Corporation in Danville, Illinois.

When acquired, Western had shown a rapid growth similar to ATI's. Sales had doubled between 1960 and 1962 from $2.3 million to $4.7 million, while earnings had increased from $19,000 to $278,000. The Western acquisition was basically an exchange of stock.

Continental's sales had fluctuated in the four years prior to the acquisition, dropping from $9.6 million in 1960 to $6.9 million in 1962, but recovering somewhat in 1963. Profits had declined continuously during the period, however, from $118,000 in 1960 to $5,000 in 1962 and then to a $27,000 loss in 1963. Because of this weaker record, the Continental acquisition was a cash and deferred payment agreement, even though Continental's capacity was somewhat greater than Western's: 40 million vs. 35 million units annually.

To finance these acquisitions, ATI negotiated a $1 million loan with its New York bank, and in November, 1964, offered 80,000 shares to the public at $18 per share.

In 1964, ATI acquired Armstrong Laboratories, Inc., of West Roxbury, Massachusetts, through an exchange of stock. Armstrong's sales had been $1.1 million in 1963, with profits of $52,000. Armstrong had already achieved a strong reputation as an aerosol producer specializing in pharmaceuticals and other close-tolerance filling operations. Armstrong had also opened a new building with advanced production and research facilities just prior to acquisition.

With this addition, ATI's sales increased to $34.6 million in 1964, with a net income of $920,000. This growth continued in 1965, with sales increasing to $47 million and profits to $1.2 million.

In December, 1962, and again in December, 1963, ATI declared 5% stock dividends.

ATI'S CURRENT OPERATIONS

Product Line. ATI's 1965 product line consisted of over 200 products manufactured for nearly 150 customers. The largest customer, however, accounted for over 45 million units, or nearly 17% of 1965 production. In addition, the top five customers accounted for about 50% of ATI's production, and the top 10 for slightly more than 75%.

By product class, ATI was concentrated in personal products, which represented nearly 65% of 1965 volume—hair sprays alone accounted for over 45%. Household products were next in importance, representing about 28%. Most of this was starches, which accounted for 15%.

John Thomson, corporate director of sales, indicated that ATI's product line strategy was to reduce the company's dependence on personal products by placing more emphasis on household products and pharmaceuticals. Nevertheless, Mr. Thomson indicated that ATI planned to continue its outstanding record in hair sprays and personal deodorants.

According to Mr. Thomson, coatings, paints, and food products represented special cases for ATI. While he felt that the market for coatings and paints would not grow as fast as other product categories, he indicated that they might become more important for ATI. However, he also indicated that if ATI decided to enter the coating and paint field at all, it would probably market as well as manufacture these products. This move would represent a major change in ATI's present strategy of not marketing products to end-use consumers.

In Mr. Thomson's opinion, food products represented a far more promising field for ATI. Up to 1965, ATI had not devoted much effort to this area because of the technical problems encountered in propellants and caps and valves. However, Mr. Thomson indicated that ATI would increase its effort in this direction as the food aerosol market developed—perhaps within three to seven years, he believed. ATI was also studying the possibilities of aerosols for the industrial cleaning and sanitation markets, Mr. Thomson said.

Marketing. ATI's sales objective was a volume of $100 million in contract manufacturing by 1969. To reach this goal, the company planned to broaden its line, particularly in the household products area, and to concentrate its selling efforts on national marketers in the continental United States. In this sales push, ATI planned to rely heavily on what it considered its two distinctive competences: low distribution costs resulting from having plants in the East and Midwest and on the

West Coast; and a continuing flow of new and improved products resulting from its R.&D.

Mr. Thomson felt that ATI would have to price more competitively if it expected to hold its large national accounts. However, he felt that a new plant which was being erected at Milford, Connecticut, would allow production economies which would keep ATI competitive for at least the next five years. In addition, Mr. Thomson felt that ATI might acquire or build a southern production facility which would permit lower prices because of reduced distribution costs.

In 1963, ATI started to develop a corporate marketing staff to coordinate sales activity and develop marketing plans. One of the staff's first jobs was to develop a yearly sales forecast. This was accomplished through account-by-account analyses by each ATI salesman, which were later combined at headquarters into a national sales forecast.

Throughout 1965, the corporate marketing staff was assisting ATI's salesmen with major presentations to national marketing companies. These presentations represented a relatively new development for the industry. They were made to old customers whom ATI hoped to retain by developing new products for them, and to prospective customers who were either existing or potential aerosol marketers. As a result of one of these presentations, ATI developed a complete program—product, package design, and advertising theme—for marketing an aerosol hair spray for the American Home Products Company. Even though American Home had never marketed a hair spray before, this new brand, Sudden Beauty, became one of the top four hair sprays in 1965.

At the end of 1965, ATI had two men on its corporate marketing staff, four divisional sales managers, and six field salesmen. In addition to helping make the major presentations, the salesmen served as a liaison between the customer's purchasing, research, and marketing groups and the ATI organization.

Research and Development. In late 1965, ATI formed a new corporation called the Aerosol Techniques Research Center, Inc. This division was building a new research center in Milford, Connecticut, which would eventually be staffed by 15 to 25 people, headed by Mr. Clarence Clapp, an ATI vice president formerly with Western Filling. At the same time, a new technical services department was formed under ATI vice president Fred Presant, who had worked in the aerosol industry for 18 years. Technical services encompassed all the operating division's customer service, quality control, and product development laboratories. In Mr. Clapp's opinion, the new research center, combined with the technical services department, would give ATI the best research and product development activity among all contract fillers.

While the technical services department worked hand in hand with ATI's customers to improve product formulations, the research center was to be devoted solely to the development of new or improved products and new or improved technology in the aerosol field. According to Mr. Clapp:

> The direction of the research and development effort at the research center will be determined to a large degree by the market research department. Market research will be involved at both the initial and final stages of most projects. This is necessary because the ultimate dependence of our success rests with the consumer.

This policy implied that most projects chosen were expected to become commercially feasible within one to three years. Nevertheless, Mr. Clapp said that ATI would still have some commitment to "blue sky" projects, provided the financial commitments were not too heavy. He also indicated that ATI would seek technical assistance from its suppliers as much as possible but, when necessary, would perform research in the areas of new containers, valves, and propellants. To help protect accomplishments, ATI planned to seek far more patents than in the past. Mr. Clapp indicated that, when patents were not obtainable, ATI would seek contractual agreements with its customers or utilize secrecy.

The importance of R.&D. to ATI's success up to 1965 is indicated by the company's record for new products and technical developments generated. These included the first personal deodorant, Right Guard; a patented water-based hair spray, which allowed cost savings of 10% to 30%; the first aerosol mouth freshener; the first dimethyl ether propellant system, which reduced costs because it was water soluble; and the first aerosol barbecue sauce. In conjunction with a leading can company, ATI developed the first three-piece high-pressure container, which reduced costs since less propellant was required. ATI also developed new formulations which became leading products in their respective markets, e.g., Sudden Beauty hair spray, Dust and Wax furniture polish, Perform aerosol starch, and Fuller's oven cleaner. In addition, ATI had a complete cross section of all types of aerosol products on the market in 1965, even though the company might not have been the original developer of some of these products.

Another indication of ATI's commitment to R.&D. was contained in Mr. Shepherd's exposition on "The Contract Filler's Role in Aerosol

Product Development," which appeared in the December, 1963, issue of *Aerosol Age:*

In order to know of the future and to predict, within reasonable bounds, what we [the contract fillers] should be doing, we must understand the past and recognize the trends that are already discernible . . . we must understand what are the distinctive competences of the filler today and what these will be in the future. How should they be shaped and guided in order to continue the development of the aerosol industry? In the application of the resources at the disposal of the contract filler, how and when should these resources be allocated? How should they be developed? When I write of "resources," I mean things such as men, money and materials. I also mean the fund of knowledge and experience of the contract filler and new technological changes which shall come from the contract filler. . . . I think we can expect to see a continual increase in the concentration of power in the hands of the marketing companies. We can expect to endure severe conditions of excess capacity and price competition among fillers. Because of these increasing economic pressures on marketers and contract fillers, there will be an even greater need for creative, new product and marketing concepts. In order to continue to play a role in the development of this industry, the contract filler must now begin to use effectively those distinctive competences and resources which he has developed over the years. These distinctive competences are first *creativity* and the *ability to innovate technologically*. The second distinctive competence . . . is that of the many years of experience in the organizations of the members of this industry. The next resource is that of having capacity to manufacture a wide spectrum of aerosol products. Next, those contract fillers who have moved toward putting facilities up in strategic locations, in this country and on the continent, have moved toward offering more complete servicing of both national and international markets in terms of distribution. Finally, one distinctive competence which is not universally held by contract fillers organizations is that of capably using new management techniques and tools.

Production. Aerosol products were manufactured in two basic ways in 1965. The slower but more accurate method was called cold filling. In this method, the propellant and product fill were liquefied by refrigeration and "poured" into the containers in carefully measured amounts. The cap and valve were then inserted by hand and sealed by machine, after which the filled containers were passed through a hot water bath to test for pressure leaks. Finally, labels were applied and the product was packaged for storage or shipment. The more rapid method was called pressure filling. In this method, the cap and valve were inserted in the container and then sealed at the same time a vacuum was created in the container. Next the product fill and propellant were injected through the valve into the empty container by the application of extremely high pressure. The filled container was then labeled and packaged for storage or shipment. In 1965, filling speeds of 200 cans per minute were considered high for aerosol production. However, speeds of 100 cans per minute had been considered high in 1960. Mr. Donald Schoonmaker, ATI's eastern division production manager, indicated that filling speeds might double again by 1970.

At the end of 1965, ATI had four plants with 21 filling lines located across the United States so as to insure national distribution at minimal cost. About 50% of ATI's equipment was new and 50% was relatively old. However, Mr. Schoonmaker said ATI's production efficiency was equal to or better than that of other contract fillers. Mr. Schoonmaker also felt that ATI had extremely good quality control, which he thought most contract fillers would be hard pressed to match. At this time, ATI's annual production capacity was about 390 million units.

Table 3 indicates the location and number of filling lines for each of ATI's four plants.

TABLE 3

Location	Number of Filling Lines	Approximate Annual Production Capacity (Millions of Units)	Warehouse Space (Thousand of Square Feet)
Bridgeport, Conn. (leased).........	6	150	150
Los Angeles, Calif. (leased).......	4	95	130
Danville, Ill. (owned).............	6	100	100
West Roxbury, Mass. (leased)......	5	45	30
Total.....................	21	390	410

The Bridgeport facility, a converted piano factory, also contained the company's executive offices and research laboratories.

In June, 1965, ATI began an expansion program designed to raise capacity to 430 million units by the end of 1966. This $4.2 million program included (1) a new building in Milford, Connecticut, to house the company's main offices and eastern division plant, replacing the overcrowded Bridgeport factory and offices; (2) a new research center, also located at Milford; (3) acquisition of a new building and property in Danville, Illinois, to double the facilities of the company's Continental Filling division; (4) addition of a production line and new warehouse area in Los Angeles to increase the capacity of the Western Filling division; and (5) completion of a new aerosol pharmaceutical development and filling installation at Armstrong Laboratories in West Roxbury.

All facilities were designed to permit the installation of additional lines in the future. Expenditures required to bring capacity into line with future sales targets were estimated as shown in Table 4.

TABLE 4

Fiscal Year	Target Sales (Millions of Units)	Production Capacity* (Millions of Units)	Capital Expenditures to Obtain Additional Capacity (Thousands of Dollars)
1967...............	330	467	$480
1968...............	400	497	490
1969...............	460	532	520

* Reserve capacity in excess of sales targets was required to handle emergency orders and seasonal fluctuations.

According to Mr. Schoonmaker, expansion would be aimed at meeting the needs of national marketers who had medium-volume, high-quality, high-margin products. He felt this policy would enable ATI to make better use of its distinctive competences in R.&D. instead of having to sell on a price basis, as was necessary on mass-produced standardized products.

Organization and Control. In late 1965, ATI had four operating divisions in addition to the corporate staff and the research and technical services divisions. The name, location, and general managers of these divisions are listed in Table 5.

TABLE 5

Division	Location	General Manager	Previous Position of General Manager
Eastern division.....	Bridgeport, Conn.	John Kossak	Plant manager, General Foods, and operated own company
Western division....	Los Angeles, Calif.	John Manara	President, Western Filling Company
Continental division.	Danville, Ill.	Chris Canaday	President, Continental Filling Company
Armstrong Laboratories division.....	West Roxbury, Mass.	Robert Armstrong, Jr.	President, Armstrong Laboratories

Each of these general managers was an ATI vice president. According to Mr. Rossetti, corporate treasurer, these general managers operated their divisions somewhat like independent entrepreneurs. For example, while the divisions sent monthly and quarterly profit reports to corporate headquarters, these reports were not standardized, and Mr.

Rossetti said the divisional general managers were not evaluated on the basis of these reports. Nevertheless, Mr. Rossetti felt that the divisional general managers tried to maximize profits. The primary purpose of the reports was to enable the corporate staff to assist the divisional general managers by uncovering unfavorable performance trends.

In 1965, ATI did not employ a standard cost system or accumulate actual costs in such a way that it could estimate the relative efficiency of its different pieces of equipment or the relative profitability of its different products. While Mr. Rossetti indicated that such estimates might be desirable in the future, he felt it more important for ATI to keep up with rapidly expanding new product areas than to allocate its resources on the basis of estimated profitability.

In addition, since materials accounted for 85% of the total cost of finished products, Mr. Rossetti felt that costs could be effectively controlled by having efficient, modern equipment, by having careful quality control to minimize rejects and insure proper filling operations, and by purchasing high-quality materials at competitive prices. In order to help control materials usage, ATI was installing an IBM 1401A computer at the end of 1965.

Financial Situation. To finance new fixed assets and increase working capital, ATI sold 80,000 shares of common stock to the public in October, 1965, at $22 a share. An additional $3 million was raised by the sale of 5½% 25-year secured notes of subsidiaries to an insurance company.

PROBLEMS AND ALTERNATIVES AT THE END OF 1965

An internal policy memorandum issued in December, 1965, stated:

> . . . ATI's position of leadership in the aerosol industry may not be sufficient to sustain ATI's objectives of $100 million in sales and 7% after taxes by 1969. This gap between our abilities and our goals has been brought about by factors underlying both the company's environment and the company's resources.

Environmental trends noted in this memorandum included the maturation of industry structure and aerosol technology, the increasingly heavy competition among contract fillers, the attendant threat to high-level profits, and the increasing power of the marketing companies. Mr. Shepherd commented as follows on these and other problems:

> Most of the problems ATI faces now—customers going captive and pressured profit margins—we faced 10 years ago, and in a sense, they're no more serious now than then. However, because of the trend toward competition on the basis of price, we are increasingly aware of the fact that ATI will have to become

more formalistic and number-oriented—a prospect I would dislike *if* it saps creativity. Thus, if the only thing I can do is beat a competitor's price, I don't feel that I'm contributing much—and more to the point—I don't feel that ATI is contributing. Our historical excellence is in creating profits for our customers through the kind of innovation which helped us to develop Right Guard for Gillette and, more recently, miniatures, a development which was written up in *The Wall Street Journal*.[3]

Again, this trend toward a more formalistic organization will have to be balanced with what I believe are my responsibilities to the people who make up our organization and its social and business interrelationships. Up until now our creativity has given us an opportunity to allow the people within our organization to find their own particular niche—even though this process takes time and in the short run uses up profits. However, in a really price competitive market there would be no time for slack, no time for learning, and no opportunity for personal change. I believe that, in the long run, such an atmosphere would be damaging to our organization and to the interests of the company. So it is for this reason, in addition to our natural desire to achieve economic success, that we are looking at other businesses where we can use the technical and organizational creativity that we have developed over the past ten years.

This doesn't mean that we plan to de-emphasize the aerosol business altogether. However, we are considering other businesses which we might enter to hedge against the threats we see in the aerosol business. Ten years from now I expect that the aerosol business might be like the can business today: efficient production, tight control, low margins, and no fun—except when creating new opportunities for new products through technical and marketing research.

In looking at other businesses, there are three things I consider important. First, we should get closer to the consumer, where price isn't the only reason for survival. This is where the real opportunity for product innovation lies. Second, the acquired company should have good management so that we can build on it, rather than being forced to decimate the company and start from scratch. Finally, I would like to have a "feel" for the business.

As a result of environmental trends and Mr. Shepherd's concern about the future nature of the aerosol business, considerable attention was being focused on the question of what economic opportunities were available to ATI.

Although the European aerosol market was expanding rapidly, ATI

---

[3] "Marketing Miniatures: Now Products Come in One-Use Packages," *The Wall Street Journal* (April 13, 1966):

Make way for the teeny-weeny economy size.

It contains one serving or application, and it's one of the hottest packaging concepts since the super-duper economy size. What's more, despite the increased cost per ounce the one-shot helping can prove to be a consumer's most economical buy.

. . . . . .

Many of the goods are sold in pressurized aerosol containers. Aerosol Techniques, Inc., for example, is about to start commercial production of a breath freshener in a small aerosol container—not one shot but much smaller than any previous models—and is testing small containers of an antiperspirant, a man's hair spray, and a nasal spray.

paid little attention to expanding its operations overseas. However, it was considering strategies that would allow continued success in the domestic aerosol business. At the end of 1965, it had three groups of Harvard Business School students working on projects related to forward or backward integration. One group was considering possible acquisitions of plastic cap-and-valve manufacturers, even though this industry appeared at first glance to suffer from strong price competition and from profit margins lower than for contract filling. Another student group was concerned about the future of the food aerosol business. The third was studying markets for other types of packaging services that ATI might provide.

Possible Forward Integration. Some members of management felt that ATI should begin marketing products to the end-use consumer in order to get the higher profit margins associated with this business. There was, however, considerable concern lest such action cause ATI to lose some of its present customers, who would not want their supplier as a competitor. On the other hand, there had been little reaction from these same customers when ATI took Sudden Beauty hair spray to American Home Products, Inc., a company that had never been in the hair spray business, and essentially established AHP as one of the country's leading hair spray marketers. ATI's management also wondered whether ATI had the financial and managerial resources to market a consumer product nationally.

Diversification Guidelines. The major focus of ATI's attention, however, was directed toward diversification out of the aerosol business. According to the December policy memorandum,

The need for an unconventional miracle is prompted by our objectives, by an assessment of the present economic progress of our aerosol business and by the question of whether ATI's strategy is viable for the next decade. . . . It is the contention of this paper that at least the following criteria must be met if a profitable diversification is to be achieved:
1. The company should promise a growth rate compatible with ATI's own rate of growth.
2. The company should promise a return on investment compatible with ATI's own R.O.I. performance.
3. The company's management should not retard the growth of our own management structure.
4. The company should be a company to which ATI should be able to contribute synergetically so that there will exist the best possible opportunity for reaching the above listed financial criteria. In this context ATI's distinctive competences have been suggested as:
  a. Nationwide manufacturing and management facilities;

    b. A capacity to direct technological innovation toward supplying consumer and/or industrial needs;

    c. A strong series of relationships with the chemical industry; and

    d. A strong series of relationships with the financial community.

5. The company should be a company which has the capacity to contribute an additional distinctive competence to ATI. Examples of the kind of contribution we have in mind are:

    a. A sales force for the sale of (say) industrial specialty chemicals;

    b. A technological niche in a nonaerosol packaging service so that ATI can be in a position to develop an integrated system of packaging services backed by nationwide manufacturing facilities, a nationwide sales force, unique packaging machinery of our own design, and a research facility specializing in formulation chemistry related to personal, household, pharmaceutical, and food products;

    c. The ability to manufacture nonaerosol personal products—e.g., specialty soap, eye makeup, lipsticks, etc.

6. The size of the company should be such as to make possible a noticeable contribution to ATI's earnings per share after taking into account the potential effect of a synergetic relationship. In this regard the generation of an incremental 10¢ per share in earnings would be considered by ATI to be a noticeable financial contribution.

Such opportunities could lie in industries as diverse as microencapsulation and radiation as well as in consumer and/or industrial packaging and/or product services, but what is most important for us to develop is a sense for the future and a technological and marketing ability to meet this challenge within the framework of the financial criteria listed above and our own resources.

The Quality Products Company. At the beginning of 1966, Mr. Meyer was engaged in the evaluation of over 20 possible acquisitions in light of the above guidelines for diversification. He indicated that the guidelines did not adequately emphasize the desire of ATI's management for developing an end-consumer marketing activity. According to Mr. Meyer:

ATI's management would like to reduce both the risks associated with being a one-product company and the risks associated with being solely a supplier to those companies which market a product to the end consumer. While Mr. Shepherd would prefer to serve industrial end customers, the real emphasis is to get closer to an end-use market where ATI can best exploit its distinctive creative and innovative talents and yet not prejudice its relations with its existing customers. In this connection, it will be an interesting task to identify the "legitimate" path between customer loyalty and new opportunities in those end-use markets suited to our strengths.

Presently we're not sure whether we should acquire several small companies or one large one. Having a family of small companies is certainly a situation which we have learned to live with in a constructive and profitable way. It is also true that having several associated companies might help us to solve some management problems if it becomes necessary to move toward more centralized management of our aerosol operations, since these associated companies might then provide a constructive way to utilize the talents of those of our present divisional managers who are experienced and gifted entrepreneurs. On the other hand, a large acquisition might be the essential step necessary to help us build a reputation of excellence in a new field and this strategy might have substantial appeal to the entrepreneur who looks forward to corporate size as a means of at long last achieving the institution of a stable enterprise.

Basically then, no acquisition is too big or too small. Rather different, and at first sight perhaps conflicting, criteria must be used to judge each individual case. Meanwhile, we are trying to use the time we have to test the assumption that we have the brains and feelings necessary for growth into a different and changing environment with a different and changing organization.

The Quality Products Company[4] was one of the more promising acquisition prospects that Mr. Meyer was considering. Quality Products was a small company in the women's hand lotion business. During the fiscal year ended December 30, 1965, Quality earned about $92,000 on sales of $2.3 million, which represented an increase of $28,000 in profits and $300,000 in sales from the 1964 fiscal year (see Exhibits 10 and 11).

Exhibit 10

AEROSOL TECHNIQUES, INC.

QUALITY PRODUCTS COMPANY

Income Statements

(Dollars in Thousands)

	1961	1962	1963	1964	9 months 1965
Income from sales	$1,258	$2,024	$1,890	$2,002	$1,744
Cost of sales	1,036	1,596	1,579	1,575	1,380
Gross profit	$ 222	$ 428	$ 311	$ 427	$ 364
Selling expenses	60	74	102	107	88
General and administrative	60	72	91	109	81
Other expenses	3	2	9	7	7
Total deductions	$ 123	$ 148	$ 202	$ 222	$ 176
Income before officers' salaries, profit sharing, and taxes	$ 100	$ 280	$ 109	$ 205	$ 188
Officers' salaries	58	58	58	61	60
Profit sharing	16	24	23	30	..
Federal and state income taxes	8	103	10	50	59
Net income	$ 17	$ 95	$ 19	$ 64	$ 69

Source: Quality Products annual reports.

---

[4] For reasons of security, ATI desired that the name of the company and the name of the industry be disguised. The basic characteristics of the company and of the industry (e.g., size, nature of competition, product-market characteristics, etc.) are not disguised, however.

Exhibit 11

AEROSOL TECHNIQUES, INC.

QUALITY PRODUCTS COMPANY

Balance Sheet for Year Ending December 31, 1965

Current assets:

Cash	$135
Treasury bonds	2
Accounts receivable	193
Inventory	357
Other	38
Total current assets	$275

Fixed assets (net):

Machinery and equipment	$122
Laboratory equipment	1
Furniture and fixtures	22
Leasehold improvements	34
Total fixed assets	$179
Other assets	46
Total assets	$950

Current liabilities:

Accounts payable and accrued expenses	$105
Notes payable to bank	225
Other	3
Taxes payable	72
Total current liabilities	$406
Deferred tax credit	11

Stockholders' equity:

Capital stock $25 par value	$ 94
Capital surplus	83
Retained earnings	356
Total stockholders' equity	$533
Total liabilities and stockholders' equity	$950

Source: Quality Products 1965 annual report.

Quality specialized in the manufacture of high-grade women's hand lotions, which it then sold to various prestige marketing companies which marketed the products under their own brands. Quality also manufactured hand lotion of normal quality, which it sold to various supermarkets on a private-brand basis. At the end of 1965, Quality was constructing a new plant in Philadelphia which would increase capacity from $2.5 million to $4 million and would make possible more efficient operations than the present three-building plant.

Quality's management felt that, as soon as the new plant had "shaken down," a minimum sales increase of $1.3 million could be expected on the basis of preliminary contacts it had made with potential customers. Quality's management also expected that demand for high-grade hand lotions would increase because of several trends: the increased wealth and general desire for luxury, the rapid growth of the fragrance market and the impact thereof on sales of higher priced hand lotions, and the public's increasing receptiveness to greater luxury in hand creams as a result of mass advertising by the larger manufacturers who were improving their lower priced, mass-marketed hand creams.

Mr. Meyer indicated that the proposed acquisition was not without risk, however. His primary concern was that almost 50% of Quality's 1965 sales came from one customer, and that this percentage was expected to increase to 75% after the new factory was in operation. Mr. Meyer felt that with Quality producing nearly 30% of this customer's requirements, representing $3 million in sales, there was some risk the customer might decide to manufacture for himself. Nevertheless, given the willingness of ATI's management to live with this kind of risk, which was common in the packaging industry, Mr. Meyer felt that the decision to acquire Quality would rest on the cost of the deal and the degree to which ATI's resources could help Quality to grow and to minimize its vulnerability to the decisions of its major customer.

Mr. Meyer also indicated that if ATI acquired Quality, it would probably try to purchase the high-grade hand cream division of one of the large national manufacturers that was located in the Midwest, giving ATI national coverage of this grade of hand cream business. He felt the chances of negotiating this purchase would be better than fifty-fifty, since the national manufacturer had not exhibited a deep interest in this division for over 15 years.

2. Devonian Electronic Components Ltd. (A)*

"I tell you, I will just not put up with any more of it—and you can tell them so from me. I'm sick and tired of being subjected to a day-to-day administration from 3,000 miles away and I've just about had enough. . . ."

The speaker was Henry Masterman, managing director of Devonian Electronic Components Ltd. (DECL), which was an English subsidiary of Newark Electronic Parts Corporation (NEPCO). His listener was Antony Ross, a young consultant who had been hired by the parent organization to study and report on the situation in the English subsidiary.

ROSS'S BACKGROUND

Ross was, in fact, an Englishman who had recently completed a two-year course of study at a school of business administration in the western part of the United States. He had gone to America with the intention of staying only the necessary two years, and towards the end of the second year he had begun to wonder how he could earn funds to pay his return passage. He had conceived the idea of offering his services as a consultant to a few small and medium-sized American firms in the electronics field who had newly started subsidiaries in England. He had a strong electronics background and he believed that some of these firms would be glad of the chance to have an impartial observer with a dual American-English background look at their English operations for a comparatively small fee.

Ross's efforts had met with mixed success. Some firms were anxious to employ him full-time in England, but not as a consultant. Others said they already had more information about their subsidiaries than they knew what to do with. However, there were a few who definitely were interested in his proposal. NEPCO was one of these.

---

* Copyright 1963 by l'Institut pour l'Étude des Méthodes de Direction de l'Entreprise (IMEDE), Lausanne, Switzerland. Reprinted by permission.

THE VISIT TO NEPCO

Ross had stopped in at NEPCO for a day on his way back across the States to obtain background information about the parent company. He felt it important to understand as thoroughly as possible the problems of the parent company and its attitude towards its subsidiary, so that his report could be tailored to those who would receive and perhaps act on it.

He found that NEPCO's product line consisted of a wide range of small, high-quality component parts for the electronics industry. Though most of these products were simple in themselves, they usually became extremely essential parts in large and very complex pieces of electronic apparatus. The number of different parts manufactured by NEPCO was large—perhaps three to four thousand—but they could be classified into four general groups: relays, switches, sockets, and connectors.

After walking through the plant and the stockroom, Ross had the impression that the majority of the parts required precise stamping and machining by fairly complex machines and skilled workers. In the stockroom, he saw hundreds of neatly labelled wooden boxes ranged on steel shelves, most of which contained parts of millimeter dimensions, varying one from another only in minute details. It was obvious that great attention was paid to quality. Ross learnt that NEPCO's customers rejected an average of between 1 percent and 2 percent of parts sent to them. This reject rate compared very favourably indeed with that obtained by any other manufacturer of similar parts. This quality, in fact, allowed NEPCO to remain very competitive even though its prices were, in general, somewhat above the industry average.

Ross inquired about NEPCO's selling organization and was told that the company sold either through manufacturers' representatives (who were allowed a commission of 8 percent) or through stocking distributors (who typically received a margin of 27 percent).[1] NEPCO's commissions and margins were above the industry norm and its delivery promises could definitely be relied upon. These two factors, plus the quality of NEPCO products, had caused sales over recent years to keep pace with the growth of the electronics industry as a whole. See Exhibit 1. NEPCO financial data for recent years are presented in Exhibit 2.

---

[1] A "stocking distributor" may be defined as a manufacturer's agent who carries inventory and holds title to the goods in his possession, in addition to performing the sales function.

Ross gained from the plant and the stockroom an impression of a well-organized and successful company, and this impression was confirmed by a tour around the offices. Since the company was situated in a part of suburban Newark that had experienced rapid growth, it had not been able to acquire surrounding land at a rate that allowed the physical expansion to match the growth in sales. As a result, there was a severe shortage of office space. Only the president had a private office. The remaining executives worked in groups in rooms that were noisy and overcrowded. However, despite these handicaps, there was a definite air of efficiency. The executives all seemed to have an ability to concentrate firmly on their own tasks while ignoring the lack of material comfort and quiet in their immediate environment. Exhibit 3 shows the NEPCO organization at the time of Ross's visit.

CONVERSATION WITH NEPCO EXECUTIVES

As his day at NEPCO drew to a close, Ross felt that, although he had not acquired as much information about the company as he would have liked, he had learnt the maximum possible in the seven or eight hours that had been available. It had been arranged for him to have dinner with the three leading NEPCO executives so that he could become acquainted with developments in the English subsidiary and be better aware of his mission in England. The three executives were the president, James Whidden; the executive vice-president, Al Nelson; and the sales manager, Sam Morey.

Ross had arranged to meet the executives in Mr. Whidden's office at about 6:30. When he arrived, he found them all still at their desks. No one suggested a drink before dinner, so the four of them went around the corner to the most convenient restaurant and took a corner table.

They had scarcely finished ordering before Al Nelson said, "Well, I guess I'd better give you a little background information on our English company. It is at present only a small operation with 16 employees, not including the three English directors. They have at the moment five machines and have attained a very reasonable rate of production. The company is situated in the county of Devonshire at a town called Okehampton, which is midway between Exeter and Plymouth— perhaps you know the place?"

Ross shook his head, "No, but I have a rough idea of the area."

"Well, no matter," Al Nelson continued, "the situation isn't important. The 16 employees of whom I spoke include one salesman, a couple of office staff, a quality control inspector, and 12 production workers."

"Who's in charge of all operations there?" Ross asked.

Al glanced at Sam Morey and Mr. Whidden before answering. "That's just the problem. We are at the moment looking for a man to fill the role of general manager, and this has caused us one hell of a lot of trouble so far."

"What about the directors?" asked Ross. "Isn't one of them a managing director?"

Mr. Whidden, who had been making some calculations on his paper napkin, now tore off the relevant part, put it in his pocket, and looked up. "I think you'd better explain the setup with the directors, Al, before we go any further."

Al nodded. "I should perhaps have begun at the beginning and told you how the company was started. About a year ago—in May, 1960, in fact—we decided to form an English subsidiary. After an exchange of correspondence with a cousin of Mr. Whidden who lives in England and with whom he has kept in touch over the years, it was decided that this man, by name Henry Masterman, should assist us in starting an English subsidiary. He therefore came over here and we discussed what should be done. When he went back to England, Henry looked around and purchased the buildings and property of a local slate-quarrying firm which had gone bankrupt. One of the conditions attached to his promise to help us was that our subsidiary had to be situated within easy distance of his home in Devonshire."

"Can I interrupt a moment," said Ross, "and get some further background on Mr. Masterman? What is his age and how much business experience has he had?"

Mr. Whidden answered the questions. "He will be 56 this winter. He's a mechanical engineer by training who served his apprenticeship with one of the largest engineering companies in Britain. For a long while now he has been engaged in business of his own which involves selling for various heavy engineering firms in the Exeter, Plymouth, and Bristol areas. But I think that he has pretty much retired from this, particularly in view of our requirements."

"He's an Englishman, I take it," said Ross.

"Yes, certainly."

"And you know him well, or only through meeting him on a few family occasions?" asked Ross.

"I knew him very well in the 1930's when he used to come to

America to stay with my family. Since the war we have kept in touch with one another fairly regularly, and I was delighted to have such a close contact, with excellent business experience, who could help me start a company in England."

Ross nodded. "I see. Go ahead, Al, I'm sorry to have interrupted you."

"Well," Al resumed, "English law requires that a company registered in England have a majority of English directors. Since Mr. Whidden and I wanted to be directors of this subsidiary, it was up to Henry to obtain another two and he chose two friends of his—Colonel Sykes, a retired army officer, and Anthony Paton-Jones, a lawyer who had handled a good deal of business for Henry in the past. Henry himself is, of course, managing director, and that is how things have stood since last year. We are now trying hard to find a general manager who can be a full-time employee and who has our fullest confidence, but we are having some real problems which we want you to help us solve."

Ross looked puzzled. "Isn't it just a simple matter of interviewing candidates? There must be many people who would jump at a job like that, and if you had real doubts about picking the right man, it would surely be worth your while in the long run for one of you to fly over to England to do the selection."

All three NEPCO executives laughed, somewhat mirthlessly. "That's what we thought," Al said, "but it just hasn't been that easy. We seem to be up against three fellow directors who are intent on keeping the company in their own pockets."

Ross looked surprised. "You mean that Mr. Masterman has turned out to be thoroughly untrustworthy as managing director?"

Al hesitated and glanced at Mr. Whidden, clearly not knowing what to say. The latter came to his help. "I certainly don't think one could call Henry untrustworthy in any dishonest sense. The real trouble seems to be that he has become too interested in the English company and seems to be in danger of throttling its growth by trying to control every detail of its operations himself."

"And the net result," Sam Morey put in, "is that we are finding it impossible to keep in that company anyone whose authority and control will rival, if not supersede, Masterman's own."

Ross frowned. "I'm afraid I still don't quite understand."

"Well," said Al, "two months ago, for instance, we thought that we had a very promising candidate for general manager, and the English directors seemed to agree. However, when they held a formal directors' meeting to decide the question, they suddenly turned round and went against him for no very good reasons that we could ascertain."

"Were any of you present at that meeting?" Ross asked.

Sam Morey nodded. "The meeting was planned to coincide with a trip I made to England to try and boost their sales. I was able to talk with Jones—that was the man's name—a good deal. In fact, I talked with him intensively over a period of two days, testing his ideas and his technical knowledge. I concluded that as a manager he might need a steadying influence from his superior from time to time, but that his grasp of the business from a technical standpoint was very good. I was amazed and upset at the meeting when all the directors voted against him."

"Have you no idea why they voted against Jones?" Ross queried.

Sam shook his head emphatically. "Very little. It seemed to me to be personal prejudice of some kind, or some other equally intangible reason."

"And then there was the Harvey incident," put in Mr. Whidden. "I myself went to England five months ago after a visit to Switzerland to buy some screw machines. Henry had had an assistant called Harvey doing the office work, but he had dismissed this assistant shortly before my arrival. When I looked over a lot of the work the man had done, it seemed to me to be very competent, and I judged him exactly the sort of assistant that Henry needed. In fact, I was so certain of Harvey's value that I tried to get him back in the company."

"Well, I must say, I find their behaviour very odd," said Ross, who was becoming more and more curious about the situation. "I take it, then, that you still have no general manager there and that Mr. Masterman is still exercising general control over all the company's operations."

"Exactly," said Al, "and since the company has been going nearly a year, you can understand why we are concerned. We would like you to try and find out why the directors are behaving as they are and to recommend what we might do about it."

"No easy assignment," laughed Ross, "particularly if two of you were unable to obtain satisfactory answers to your problems. Are you sure that I will be able to contribute enough at this point to make it worthwhile hiring me?"

"Quite frankly," said Mr. Whidden, "the whole situation is now so difficult that we are prepared to try anything, and we all feel that an outsider, even if he has not got our experience, might be able to see something which we ourselves have missed."

"Do you mind if I ask a few more questions?" said Ross. "I know that we haven't got the time to talk as thoroughly as I would wish, but I think that already I have a pretty good background, and a few more pieces of information will complete the picture."

"Sure, go right ahead," said Al. "We'll tell you anything you want to know."

"Well, let's see." Ross paused and consulted his notebook. "Do you receive any information regularly from Okehampton?"

"Certainly," answered Al. "We have a weekly report sent to us which gives full details of day-to-day production, details of all expenses, and information about sales. This report is compiled almost entirely by Norris, Harvey's successor, and I must admit that it is done well."

"What are you producing in England?"

"Mostly stampings, but also a few connectors. So far, we are limited by the number of machines and the knowledge of the men operating them."

"Are all the production workers English?"

"Yes, all the workers are, and this has caused something of a training problem. When we despatched the first machines, we sent over Bill Ryles, our production superintendent, for six weeks and he got production started. Since his return we have been very pleased with the results that have been obtained, both as to quality and quantity of production."

Ross was making notes. "How much has been sold so far?"

"Much less than we expected. You will be able to get the exact figures in England."

"Who is doing the selling?"

"Basically, only one man, Jack Turpin, whom we hired on Henry's recommendation and trained over here for six weeks. But Henry himself has also done some selling, and we have recently—perhaps two months ago—engaged the services of a stocking distributor in the London area."

Ross again consulted his notes. "Am I right in saying that the only NEPCO personnel who have visited England to date are Mr. Whidden, Sam, and Bill Ryles? You have not been yet, Al?"

Al shook his head. "And remember that Henry and Jack Turpin have each been over here—Henry for a few days and Jack for six weeks."

"Which of you is responsible at this end for attending to English matters?"

"It depends on the American situation. I guess all of us spend a moment or two with English stuff that needs attention. Who actually does it at any one time depends on who can manage to take time off his American work. We're pretty thin on the ground here, you know, and all of us are probably overworked."

"What were some of the reasons for starting an English company?"

"The usual things—we wanted a foothold in the Common Market area, and it seemed pretty likely that England would join. Also, we felt that we had quite enough know-how to make the English market and the European market in general sit up and take notice. We don't regret our decision."

At this point the conversation became more general and little was added to the information Ross had already gained. It was apparent that the Americans were very perplexed and Ross sympathised with them. During his two years in America, and particularly during the second year, Ross had come to understand very well the American belief that the average European businessman was intensely conservative, rather inflexible, disinclined to take risks, and, in general, rather a pale shadow of his vigorous, flexible, dynamic American counterpart. There was one point in the conversation when Al had said, half sarcastically and half apologetically, "I'm afraid we take the somewhat naïve view that we are in business to make a profit," and the other two NEPCO executives had smiled rather sadly, shaking their heads over the mysterious and unbusinesslike behaviour of the English directors. As Ross drove back to his hotel, he reflected that he would probably have to attempt to introduce as tactfully as possible some superior American methods into the thinking of the English directors.

.   .   .   .

ROSS GOES TO OKEHAMPTON

Some six weeks later, after the necessary exchange of correspondence with NEPCO and the subsidiary, Ross set out from London to pay a four-day visit to Devonian Electronic Components Ltd. The main road from London passed through Exeter and Ross noticed that Exeter was certainly not an industrial city, and indeed, was little more than a large market town. From naval service, Ross knew Plymouth, the other large city in the neighbourhood of DECL, to be an important naval dockyard with a number of shipbuilding firms but not much other industry. Okehampton itself was situated some 20 miles from Exeter and was the largest of a number of small towns and villages that were strung out along a valley. This valley, which was heavily wooded, formed the western border of Dartmoor, an extensive tract of wild and almost uninhabited moorland. Both Dartmoor and the Valleys which surrounded it had been made into a National Park, which meant that all further building and development within the area was subject to a strict examination (and perhaps prohibition) by a body of local town and county officials known as the National Park Planning Council.

As Ross slowly threaded his way through a herd of cows being driven along the road just outside Okehampton by a straw-sucking farmhand, he reflected that the surroundings in which NEPCO had placed their English subsidiary could hardly be more unlike their Newark environment. He wondered what the three NEPCO executives who had come to Okehampton had thought about it, and he remembered a remark by Sam Morey—"You mustn't expect miracles from the plant; it's not one of those gleaming white, well-ventilated, one-storey establishments that electronic firms build for themselves in California."

THE FIRST MEETING WITH MASTERMAN AND NORRIS

The following morning, Ross asked in one of the shops in the main street where he might find the DECL plant. He was directed down a narrow and muddy lane leading to three stone buildings which looked like farm buildings. On nearing them, Ross heard the sound of machinery and saw that two of them were apparently used to house machinery and inventory while the third had been made into an office with fluorescent lighting. As Ross approached the door of the office building, a tall man with untidy hair and thick-rimmed glasses flung open the door and strode out, shouting over his shoulder, "And you can tell Turpin from me that he's darn well going to work Saturday mornings in future."

He nearly bumped into Ross but stopped in time. There was a pause. "My name's Masterman and you're Ross, I suppose," he said, offering a hand perfunctorily. "You'd better come in here."

They returned through the door from which Masterman had just emerged and Ross saw that what he had assumed to be a single office had been partitioned into two rooms with a connecting door. They passed into the inner office and Ross noted that the outer office was occupied only by a secretary and several filing cabinets. In the inner office there were two desks: one of them was occupied by Norris whom Masterman introduced briefly; the other was an old roll-top desk, littered with piles of papers. Masterman gestured Ross to an upright wooden chair standing against the wall and sank into a swivel chair behind the roll-top desk.

"So you're studying NEPCO's subsidiary in Europe," he said. "Well, you can tell them from me that I'm fed up with them. I've no doubt that when you've finished you're going to write some sort of a report, and I think it damn well ought to tell the people in Newark that they haven't the first idea how to run a company. They query my judgement of people, they do nothing but complain about our expenses while pouring out money themselves, they refuse to do anything that we recommend because they think they know better, and now, to crown everything, they insist on telling me from 3,000 miles away who can and who cannot be fired."

Ross's surprise must have showed in his face, for Masterman continued, "I don't suppose you know anything about the latest development. It's typical of them, absolutely typical. A week ago I received a telephone call from Bill Ryles telling me that I was to dispose of six of the production workers, whom he named. As you can imagine, I was thunderstruck both because this action had been taken without my being consulted first in any way, and, even more, because they had presumed to know better than I who should be laid off if six people had to go. Two days later I received a letter from Ryles confirming the telephone call and adding that no new people were to be hired without NEPCO consent and that voluntary terminations should not be replaced. The letter ended"—and here Masterman picked up a piece of paper from his desk and began to read—" 'Of course, Henry, as you must realize, these actions are a must if DECL is ever going to become a self-sufficient and profitable venture. We sincerely hope that sales will soon become a reality and that the people you have let go will be back with us again.' "

Masterman snorted disgustedly and spread out his hands in a gesture of helplessness. "What could I do? I conferred with the production foreman and we both agreed that if anyone was to go it should be two troublemakers whom we wanted to get rid of anyway and who had not been named by NEPCO. I cabled NEPCO to advise them of this but received an answering cable this morning telling me to do exactly what I had been told to do originally. They must be mad!"

"Do the other two English directors know about this?" asked Ross.

"Well, as it happened, I was having a cocktail party up at my house last Saturday evening and Anthony Paton-Jones and Colonel Sykes, both of whom live about 100 miles away from here, were present. We had a directors' meeting on Sunday morning so that our formal protests could be registered in some Minutes."

Masterman again consulted the papers on his desk and thrust some typewritten pages in Ross's direction. Ross glanced at them and saw that they were the Minutes Masterman had referred to. Meanwhile, Masterman had looked at his watch, risen hurriedly to his feet and seized his briefcase. "I can't stop to talk to you all day," he said as he strode to the door. "I've got too much work to do in Plymouth. My time is precious—and that's something else that the Americans don't seem to realize. Norris will show you anything at all you want to see,"—he waved a hand round the office—"we have nothing to hide. See you tomorrow morning."

He slammed the door behind him and a few moments later the din of the machinery in the adjacent buildings was drowned by the roar of Masterman's red sports car, which had been parked in the yard. Ross, still trying to adjust himself to the events of the last few minutes, looked up in time to catch a look of amusement on Norris' face.

"I wouldn't have liked to have met Mr. Masterman for the first time this morning," he said, "—at least, not with these dismissals on his mind. He can be explosive at the best of times, but—" he broke off and looked at his watch—"I'll bet he makes Plymouth in even time this morning, and I wouldn't care to be driving the other way."

"Does he often go to Plymouth?" asked Ross.

Norris looked surprised. "Of course; that's where his office is. He has his own firm, you know, which is called Masterman Engineering Ltd. He does a lot of big selling, I believe. He's certainly got a lot of important contacts—he knows everyone in the county and an enormous range of important people in the rest of England. He's the sort of person I wouldn't be surprised to find in the Royal Box at Ascot. He had a very important job handling tank production in the war, I think."

Ross was beginning to feel that the NEPCO executives had painted a somewhat misleading picture of Masterman. "How often does he work here, then?" he asked Norris.

"Oh, an hour or two every morning and sometimes even more than that. I know he writes a lot of letters to NEPCO from his Plymouth office using his other secretary. Very often he comes back here in the evenings as well."

"Are you in charge at DECL whenever Mr. Masterman isn't here?"

"Yes, provided that Jack Turpin isn't here either. I've had no experience in this line of business at all, so I'm just not competent to deal with things that come up. If a decision is needed straight away on anything, I have a talk with Dowdell, the foreman, and we work something out. But if Jack Turpin is here we refer decisions to him because he's the only man in DECL who really knows what he's talking about as far as the DECL product line is concerned."

"Does he know more than Mr. Masterman?"

"Oh, yes, I think so. You see, Mr. Masterman's background is in heavy engineering and the stuff he sells in his business is worth thousands of pounds at a time. Jack's background is also heavy engineering, but at least he's had six weeks at NEPCO and a year or two selling to build up his knowledge."

Ross thought for a moment. "Do you mind if I have a look at one of your weekly reports?"

"Not at all. Here's the one that I sent off yesterday. I make them up every Monday."

A quick look at the report showed Ross that it was just as Al Nelson had described it, except that it was even more detailed than he had expected. Even the very smallest expenses had been listed. "Does NEPCO keep a very close check of all DECL expenses?"

Norris grinned. "Well, you heard what Mr. Masterman said. They certainly do a great deal of complaining about expenses one way or another. We have to get all expenses above the very smallest sums approved. For instance, we recently asked if we could hire a woman for four hours a week at 2/6 an hour to clean the offices. They refused our request. On the other hand, when Sam Morey came over, he had to spend three days in London talking to Thames Electronic Distributors Ltd. (TEDL), our distributor there. During this time, he stayed at the Savoy and we were later sent a bill for £101/3/6, which we paid and put on the weekly report. NEPCO was horrified, and not only was it insinuated that the expense was our fault, but we even had a letter from Sam Morey saying that he had added up his bill before he left and had purposely noted that it came to £99/12/6. The silly thing is that if they really wanted to save money, everyone around here could give them 101 good ways in which to do it."

Ross stood up. "I'd now like to take Mr. Masterman at his word and have a look through some of the office files, particularly the correspondence between DECL and NEPCO."

"Of course," answered Norris. "I'll move over to this table in the corner here and you can use my desk. And I'll try and answer any questions you may have."

.   .   .   .

ROSS OBTAINS FURTHER INFORMATION FROM THE DECL FILES

For the rest of the day, Ross concentrated on bringing to light factual information about the NEPCO-DECL situation. This was not easy. The only income statement and balance sheet to date had been prepared at the end of 1960 and were therefore seven months old. See Exhibit 4. Ross also guessed that there were substantial gaps in the correspondence file—probably because Masterman kept the most important letters in a personal file in his Plymouth office. Ross decided that someone of Masterman's apparent volatility probably wrote quite a few letters that he would not wish to leave lying around the DECL office.

Ross first of all looked through the Minutes, which Masterman had just given him. They were, as might be expected, strongly worded and concentrated on presenting the arguments against sacking any employees. It was argued that the dismissal of six employees was bound to give the firm a bad name in the community and that the action would have a serious long-run effect on the ability of DECL to attract skilled labour. It had been difficult enough to get the required labour in the first place; now that such labour had been trained for some months, it seemed ridiculous to run the great risk of losing those employees for good. It was also pointed out that the morale of those employees who remained would be badly upset at a time when a very willing and cheerful spirit had begun to establish itself in the plant. And the Minutes also noted that a layoff of half the work force would cause the entire valley to think that the firm was going bankrupt, no matter what denials were issued.

Ross spent some time thinking over these Minutes and the action that had caused them. He asked Norris for a list of the production workers and the dates of their employment by DECL. He found that the six who had been laid off were the six most recently employed.

Ross then turned his attention to establishing some sort of chronology of events since the foundation of DECL. It was then early July, 1961. DECL had been incorporated on September 14, 1960. September and October seemed to have been taken up with getting the buildings ready. During the previous fourteen months, Turpin, who had returned from his six weeks in Newark in July, 1959, had been making sales calls all round England trying to sell products which NEPCO had agreed, for the time being, to export from America. Bill Ryles had arrived with the first stamping machine in the first week of November, 1960, and had supervised its installation and the training of the first few workers. He had gone home in the third week in December in order to spend Christmas with his family, leaving behind him some enthusiastic workers and a second stamping machine which had arrived from America in the second week of December. On January 11, 1961, Ryles had written to Harvey from America saying, "We have lined up an ambitious program for DECL in 1961 and should have a minimum of eight stamping machines and molding presses to you by July 30." Ross gathered that this number had been confirmed by Sam Morey who, on his recent visit, had given the scheduled dates of dispatching from the States. However, since Morey's departure no machine had arrived, so that DECL had only five by the beginning of July.

Harvey had been dismissed in the first week of March, 1961, and Mr. Whidden had spent his few days in England in the second week of that month. The services of TEDL, the London distributor, were engaged at the end of March. The months of April and May were taken up with two problems: sales and the finding of a general manager. In the matter of sales, Ross found an Outline Marketing Plan that had been prepared by Al Nelson before Sam Morey's English visit during the first two weeks of May. See Exhibit 5. He also found a letter to Masterman from Al Nelson which showed NEPCO's feelings about sales at that time. The letter was dated April 3:

As you are fully aware, the major problem confronting DECL is the need for sales. The production capacity at Okehampton, even though limited, in fact exceeds the sales bookings which are being produced. In addition, you have a stock of products on the way to you from our United States plant for which we obviously need to get a turnover. Moreover, we have considerable capacity here at Newark which can support sales in your marketing territory. . . . We would appreciate at this time any comments which you, Turpin or TEDL would like to make on the Outline Marketing Plan and additional sales matters. . . .

With regard to the finding of a general manager, Ross gathered that Jones had been introduced to Mr. Masterman as a possible candidate and that the latter had been enthusiastic, at any rate at first, for there was a letter from him to Al Nelson, dated April 13, which said:

I want to make quite clear here and now that, whilst I have every confidence in Jones, the decision to hire him must be made by the Newark management rather than by the English directors.

It had obviously been agreed that the interests of all would be best served if the final decision regarding Jones were not made until Sam Morey's visit. In the month that had elapsed between the writing of this letter and the directors' meeting at which Jones had been turned down, it was clear that something had happened which had changed the minds of the English directors. The Minutes of the meeting afforded no clue.

The correspondence that had passed between NEPCO and DECL subsequent to Sam Morey's visit in the first and second weeks of May dealt with a number of issues. Sales were again a subject of much concern and a long letter had passed from Sam to Jack Turpin offering advice and instructions based on three days spent by Sam in making sales calls in England along with Jack. It appeared that there were several occasions when Jack's technical knowledge was badly needed in Okehampton, but NEPCO had steadfastly refused to allow him to spend one day a week in the DECL plant.

In the matter of finding a general manager, it was clear that the English directors wanted to advertise for one. At the same directors' meeting at which Jones had been turned down, it had, in fact, been agreed that the next step was to advertise for a general manager through the media normally employed in England for such purposes. However, a letter from Al Nelson dated June 11 firmly disallowed the expense of advertising on the grounds that advertising would simply attract malcontents and unsuitable people. Al suggested instead that DECL should work through a technical employment agency, as was the normal American practice. His suggestion had not been carried out because such agencies were rare in England, if not nonexistent. A stalemate therefore existed which, Ross felt, would only be broken by Turpin or Mr. Masterman coming across another possible candidate in the course of their everyday tasks.

In May and June, there was also a certain amount of correspondence on the subject of DECL's expenses. Ross found letters about the two or three matters Norris had referred to and in addition he saw that the NEPCO managers had complained about the £100 director's fee that Masterman had proposed should be offered to both Colonel Sykes and Paton-Jones. They had also queried the £20 spent on business entertainment by Mr. Masterman between January and May.

It was apparent to Ross, even after a very quick reading of the NEPCO-DECL correspondence, that by the middle of June, 1961, several important disagreements between the English and American managements had occurred. Since Ross himself had left America at the end of May, he read the letters sent from Newark during June with particular interest, for they afforded his only guide to the most recent thinking of the American management. He was particularly interested in the fact that Al Nelson had seized the opportunity, following a particularly indignant letter from Mr. Masterman, to set forth the American managers' thinking on most of the essential issues. This letter is reproduced in Exhibit 6, together with the substance of Mr. Masterman's reply. Ross noted that Al's letter had apparently done very little to calm the English directors even before they had been further upset by the NEPCO decision to lay off six of the production force.

A TOUR ROUND THE DECL PLANT AND A FURTHER TALK WITH MASTERMAN

On the morning of his second day at Okehampton, Ross had an opportunity to talk at some length with Mr. Masterman. The latter obviously felt he had been somewhat abrupt on the previous day, and seemed determined to atone. He showed Ross round the two production buildings and introduced him to Dowdell, the foreman, and Inman, the quality control inspector. From Inman, Ross was amazed to learn that DECL had not yet sold anything actually produced at Okehampton because NEPCO had not yet been satisfied with the quality of the parts produced.

"I just can't understand it," Inman said. "Each week we send them off a sample of what we have made during the week and always it comes back with a few minor criticisms but nothing else. They just don't realize that we are all working for the same cause. They don't give us any advice. They will never tell us which dimensions of a part are the critical ones, and, above all, they won't send us duplicates of the gauges they use to measure the various parts. As a result we are quite unable to check accurately almost all the features which they criticise and therefore we can do nothing except continue to send samples which raise the same criticisms." Inman added that DECL had received, three months earlier, the official approval of the Standards Department of the Ministry of Aviation. This approval was highly coveted, even by large electronics companies, because it influenced greatly, often decisively, a company's ability to obtain Government work. The fact that DECL's limited production staff had been able to obtain this approval had apparently not been appreciated fully by the NEPCO management.

Dowdell also had his problems. "Since Mr. Ryles left last December," he said, "we have been running these machines entirely on our own after only six weeks' training. Mind you, I'm not saying that this hasn't been a good thing in many ways because we have just had to become thoroughly familiar with the machines and the production process. Yet still aren't using the right oil, for instance, just because we can't get an analysis of the oil NEPCO are using. All they tell us is the make and type of oil they use and that's not much use because the oil company concerned doesn't make the stuff over here."

"What's the most serious production problem right now?" asked Ross.

Dowdell plunged his hand into the bin underneath the stamping tools. He brought up a handful of something that looked like metal chippings. "See these?" he said. "Mixed in with these chippings are the finished parts. In order to get any of these parts, we have to sort out each one of them by hand—and you can imagine what that means."

"But doesn't NEPCO do the same?" Ross asked.

"The hell they do. They'd have a six-year backlog if they did," answered Dowdell. "All we know is that they use some sort of centrifugal processes, but so far we haven't even gathered what these are, let alone had permission to use them."

"How many different types of parts have you been making?" said Ross.

"Not very many, so far, simply because we can't get the go-ahead to sell even the few we are making. Until we get these right, there's no point in trying any others, though, goodness knows, there's enough left to try. In some ways it's even a good thing that some of the men were laid off, though the layoff has ruined morale in the plant. But if we still had twelve men here, we'd have stampings coming out of the chimney next month."

Outside in the yard again, Masterman turned to Ross. "You see how it is? I'm not alone in my complaints. The interesting thing is that it seems to be impossible to make NEPCO understand that we're having these problems." Ross frowned. "Couldn't you even get the point across to Mr. Whidden or Sam Morey when they were actually here?"

Masterman snorted. "Well, Sam Morey was almost useless in the plant. All he did here was to go on a few sales calls with Jack Turpin and I gather that he hadn't got much idea of how to sell to an English customer. It's true that he promised to get Inman some gauges, but we've never heard any more about them. As for Jim Whidden,"—and here Masterman looked almost puzzled—"I always thought that I'd been pretty close to him and that we got on well together. But he only spent about half an hour in the plant and he didn't seem able to answer any of the technical questions the men wanted answered. He didn't even seem very interested in things."

While they were talking, they had been walking up the yard and away from the buildings. Ross noticed that there was a fair-sized rectangular field separating the DECL buildings from the nearest Okehampton houses. Masterman now waved a hand in the direction of this field.

"See that field?" he said. "Jim Whidden decided he wanted to buy that, just in case DECL had to expand. It belongs to a Mr. Simpson who lives in one of those houses over there. Simpson himself wants to build on this land, but since it's within the boundaries of the National Park, he can't do this without the permission of the National Park Planning Council. I used my influence to make sure he didn't get this permission and now we're negotiating to buy this land from a disgruntled Simpson for £1,500. I think that if we wanted to build on it we could get permission on the grounds that the addition to local industry would be good for the valley. I need hardly tell you that all this rather unpleasant manoeuvering on my part was unappreciated by NEPCO."

Ross felt at a loss for an appropriate comment and said the first thing that came into his head. "Maybe they'll add a bonus to your salary."

Masterman stopped dead. "What do you mean—'add a bonus'? They don't pay me a damn thing. I took on this because I was Jim's cousin and that's why I'm doing it now. Family loyalty may seem a lousy reason to you for putting up with all this, but it's the only one. Besides, I liked Jim and still do. Although he's done one thing which upset me a good deal, I reckon that a lot of their stupidity is not his fault."

Having said this, Masterman turned away and Ross sensed that there would not be much point in talking further that morning. Masterman's abruptness in speech and frank way of talking was extremely disconcerting to Ross after his two years of human relations courses at the business school. He wondered whether the Americans weren't a little scared of Masterman.

They walked back along the yard in silence and Masterman got into his sports car. He reached behind the seat and brought up a thick envelope. "I brought you the correspondence file for NEPCO that I keep at my office. For goodness sake, don't let it out of your sight. I'll be away tomorrow, so you can give it back to me on Thursday when I suggest you come and have dinner at my house up on the hill. I'm not married, but my housekeeper cooks a pretty good meal. See you then."

He thrust the package at Ross, let in the clutch, and roared away, spattering mud in all directions. Ross just stood there, nursing the envelope and trying to collect his thoughts.

A MEETING WITH TURPIN

In the end, Ross walked back to his hotel, ate lunch and then spent the afternoon looking through Masterman's file. It added very little to what he already knew except that it confirmed his impression of Masterman's volatility and abruptness. Most of his letters went straight to the point with considerable vigour and fluency and Ross felt that he would not have liked to have been on the receiving end of many of them. He guessed that the reason Masterman did not want them lying around at DECL was that there was clear evidence in the letters of the last two months of a growing feud between him and Turpin on the subject of the latter's working hours and general approach to his job. Ross found himself very curious to meet Turpin. On the previous day, Ross had taken advantage of Turpin's daily telephone call to DECL to arrange to see him. It happened that Turpin was selling in the West of England during the period of Ross's visit, so that it was convenient for him to call in at Okehampton. The two had arranged to meet on the evening of the following day and have a drink together.

Turpin arrived just as Ross was finishing his coffee after dinner and immediately suggested a tour of the various pubs in the valley. Three hours and a good few pints later, Ross sat down before he went to bed to make a few notes on the evening. He had found Turpin, who was about his own age, to be extremely easy-going and friendly. He also was a fine athlete. His wanderings with various athletic teams had led him all over England, so that even before he began selling on a national scale, he had a good knowledge of England and a very wide range of acquaintances. He knew someone in almost every large city in England with whom he could be sure of spending an interesting evening.

Turpin had few strong feelings about his job. His main complaint was that the Americans were inefficient in getting their products to England, no matter how much their letters implied the opposite. Even at that time, TEDL had not been provided with adequate promotional literature, let alone stocks, and, according to Turpin, were about to write a pretty strong letter of complaint to Newark. However, Turpin also stressed that much delay was involved in getting products through the British Customs and Ross gathered that Masterman was in the middle of a bitter feud with the chief Customs officer at Plymouth as a result. In general, the evening left Ross with the impression that Turpin would have been an excellent salesman for a company with an established product and reputation but that he was not imbued with the missionary zeal necessary to gain NEPCO products a firm foothold in the English market. He also noted that Turpin himself frankly admitted that his knowledge of the products and their uses was still fairly patchy because of his lack of background in the electronics field prior to his six weeks' indoctrination at Newark.

A VISIT TO THE DECL AUDITOR

On the Wednesday morning, his third day at Okehampton, Ross went to Plymouth to call on Mr. Williamson, DECL's auditor. Al Nelson had arranged for Ross to make this call and had assured Williamson that he was free to talk to Ross exactly as he would talk to Whidden himself. Ross found Williamson, who was a partner in the Plymouth office of one of the largest accounting firms in England, to be a deliberate, elderly, conservative man with a strong inclination to talk about his early days as an accountant with the British Army in India. He was, however, a man with many years' experience as an accountant and these years had given him a shrewdness and an insight into human nature that made his comments on the DECL-NEPCO situation invaluable to Ross. They talked for nearly three hours, for, although DECL was only a small client, Williamson had become more and more interested in their affairs. He was delighted to have a chance to vent his ideas freely without betraying any professional confidence.

In the course of the conversation Ross asked Williamson if he could tell him about Harvey's dismissal. Williamson nodded and smiled. "I think it's better you should ask me rather than Mr. Masterman about that." Then he slowly refilled his pipe and drew on it with satisfaction.

"Harvey's dismissal was just one of those things. There was no major cause—only a series of little ones. Harvey is one of those people who don't know their own limitations. He rather fancied himself as a production man and there were at least two or three occasions when he actually offered customers who called on the 'phone some parts which the plant has just not got the equipment to make. And he offered them at ridiculous prices, as well. Another thing was that he had a very peculiar way of keeping the books—not dishonest, you understand, but very difficult to follow, so that I had a lot of trouble in carrying out the audit. A third thing was that Harvey had many relatives in the valley and he kept trying to get them employment in the company. This annoyed Mr. Masterman very much and I always felt it was only a matter of time before Harvey would have to leave. In the end, he left just before Mr. Whidden came over. I understand that Mr. Whidden was surprised at Harvey's dismissal because NEPCO had always been satisfied with the presentation of any information they had requested from him. In fact, I also know that Mr. Whidden went to see Harvey behind Mr. Masterman's back to try and persuade him to come back. When Mr. Masterman found this out he was, understandably, terribly offended and very angry. I myself am surprised that Mr. Whidden could have done such a thing and even more surprised that the NEPCO management could have made exactly the same mistake later on in the Jones affair."

This opening was too good to miss and Ross had then asked Williamson to tell him what he knew about the whole Jones affair.

"Well," said Williamson, frowning a little in an effort to remember, "I think it was Turpin who first introduced Jones to Mr. Masterman. And—" he added, with a quick glance at Ross, "I don't think that was the best beginning possible. Jack has some pretty wild drinking companions and I am inclined to think Jones was one of them. Nevertheless, he got on well with Mr. Masterman and soon everyone, including Mr. Masterman, seemed to take his future employment at DECL very much for granted. Norris tells me that Jones was very often down at DECL looking around and suggesting changes and even on occasion giving orders. Pretty odd behaviour for a man who hadn't even been hired, if you ask me. Anyway, nothing happened for a long time until Sam Morey came over. He spent almost two whole days with Jones, during which time I suppose he satisfied himself as to Jones's technical abilities. When the directors' meeting came along, we all sat round the table to make an official decision about Jones, now that a representative of the NEPCO management was on the spot."

"Can I just interrupt a moment and ask why you yourself were there?" said Ross.

"Oh, yes. I forgot that. I always attend the DECL directors' meetings because Mr. Masterman likes official Minutes to be taken by a disinterested party. I've attended every one including the last one which was called in protest against the NEPCO decision to lay off men. I suppose you know all about that, by the way?"

Ross nodded and smiled. "I've heard almost too much."

Williamson shook his head sadly. "That was an unfortunate business." He paused. "Well, now where was I? Oh, yes, the directors' meeting. Well, we were all sitting there and Jones came in. He at once sat down and for nearly half an hour, without any prompting, told us how he would run DECL. The other two English directors had never met Jones before and I could see they were astonished by his attitude. The door had hardly closed behind him before they shook their heads and said they couldn't possibly agree to hiring a man who had so little idea of how to behave in an interview. Morey, who had seemed to expect Jones to behave like that, protested that his electronics knowledge was pretty sound and that was what mattered. I expected Mr. Masterman to put in a word for Jones, but instead he strongly agreed with Colonel Sykes and Mr. Paton-Jones. The meeting therefore turned Jones down and Morey immediately went out, shaking his head. We all saw him get into Jones's car and go off with him."

"Have you any idea why Mr. Masterman changed his mind?" asked Ross.

"Yes, indeed—because he then told the three of us who were left a rather surprising story. It turned out that he had asked Jones up to his house to have a drink one Saturday before lunch, just about the end of April. Jones had drunk so much that Masterman suggested that they should go in separate cars down to the hotel at Okehampton, where they had decided to have lunch. Mr. Masterman says that Jones had some narrow shaves with two brick walls and a bus on the way down but that he somehow arrived intact. However, they had no sooner finished their soup than Jones stood up and was violently ill all over the table. He left at once and Mr. Masterman did not see him from that time until the directors' meeting."

"I'm surprised that none of you knew at the meeting," said Ross. "I would have thought that the story would have been all round the valley by the middle of the afternoon."

"That's what I thought," said Williamson, "but I gather that the hotel keeper is a good friend of Mr. Masterman and that there was no one else in the dining-room at the time, so the incident could be hushed up to save Mr. Masterman embarrassment. I was also surprised that he hadn't told us before the meeting; his reason for not doing so was that he didn't want to bias our opinions."

"What did you yourself think of Jones?" asked Ross.

"I agreed with the directors. Jones's electronics knowledge may be all right but his character is clearly pretty wild," Williamson said.

"What happened to Morey after that?" Ross said.

Williamson shrugged his shoulders. "He was due to catch a train back to London that evening in order to make his plane. Mr. Masterman had arranged to drive him into Exeter, but when the time came to leave Okehampton, Morey had still not appeared. Mr. Masterman drove into Exeter all the same, thinking that Jones might have driven Morey to Exeter. This is, in fact, exactly what happened—Jones and Morey had spent the whole afternoon together and they only just got to the station in time to catch the train. Morey barely had time to say a hurried farewell to Mr. Masterman, who was so angry by this time that it was probably just as well. He knew perfectly well that Morey had probably promised Jones the job despite the directors' meeting and I think he was right. The funny thing is, though, that the NEPCO people did finally turn Jones down in a letter which they did not write until June 5, three or four weeks after the meeting."

Ross, who had seen the letter, nodded. "I take it that Mr. Masterman would add little to what you have already told me about the Harvey and Jones affairs?"

"I don't think he would. Anyhow, I would advise you not to talk to him about either subject because they are very sore points with him. Not that he wouldn't be perfectly frank with you, but I doubt if you would learn anything more and you would run the risk of annoying him personally."

The conversation had then passed onto the subject of Mr. Masterman, and Williamson confirmed that he had always found him to be a slightly frightening personality because of his propensity for saying exactly what he thought in a very blunt way. He added that he understood that Masterman was a fine salesman who had built up a very profitable business of his own. He gave Ross an introduction to the managing director of a large Plymouth engineering firm for which he knew Masterman had done a lot of selling.

After lunch, Ross had called on this man and learnt that for some years Masterman had sold over a million pounds' worth of equipment annually almost single-handed. He also learnt that this volume had dropped off very seriously in the past year, largely because of the time and emotional effort Masterman was devoting to Okehampton. The managing director had, in fact, said outright, "If you ask me, this work he's doing at Okehampton is ruining his business and his health. He doesn't say much to me about it, but I knew enough from various sources to write him a personal letter about four months ago to beg him to concentrate his efforts on his own business once again. After all, he's 55 and not a young man and he should think about providing for his retirement as best he can."

Finally, Williamson commented very favourably on Norris, whom he regarded as a man who knew his own limitations and kept within them. He said that Norris had formerly been a police officer in one of the villages in the Okehampton valley and that, after an early retirement, he had decided to undertake part-time work at DECL. Williamson's comment had been—"I reckon he got more work than he bargained for."

ROSS CALLS ON HARVEY

As Ross was driving back from Plymouth on the Wednesday afternoon, he tried to make up his mind whether to call on Harvey, who was still living and working in the Okehampton valley. He had in his pocket a copy of a letter Bill Ryles had written to Harvey to ask him if he would see Ross and talk to him about the DECL situation. In addition, he was well aware that one of the few specific instructions the NEPCO management had given him was to find out more about the Harvey incident. Ross doubted that he would be able to find out more than Mr. Whidden had done in his visit to Harvey, but at last he decided to make the call. He knew, however, that gossip in the valley travelled so thoroughly and so fast that there was a strong possibility that Mr. Masterman would hear about his visit and would regard it as a repetition of American subterfuge tactics. Ross therefore determined to tell Masterman frankly, when he saw him on Thursday evening, that he had called on Harvey simply to gather some more information about the administrative details of DECL's early days.

It turned out that the visit to Harvey was hardly worth the trouble. It seemed that Harvey was still on reasonable terms with Mr. Masterman; certainly he was not at all bitter about his dismissal and recognized that it had been largely because of an extended series of disagreements with his superior. He added nothing to what Ross already knew about the first few months of DECL's existence, and his only opinion about DECL was that the company would not succeed and this was why he had not considered going back there.

AN EVENING WITH MASTERMAN

On the Thursday, Ross's final day at Okehampton, he spent most of the time in going over the correspondence files once more, taking notes of critical passages in various letters so that he would be able to substantiate some of the opinions and judgements expressed in his report. In the evening, he drove up to Masterman's large stone country house, which was set in spacious grounds half way up a hill overlooking the entire valley. As he reached the end of the drive, he saw Masterman sitting in the evening sun on one of two garden chairs set on the flagged terrace in front of the house. Masterman suggested that Ross should join him in having a martini, and the two sat making small talk for a while. Ross decided that this was an appropriate moment to tell of his visit to Harvey. He tried to sound as casual as possible in telling Masterman both about the visit and his reasons for making it. As soon as he had uttered a couple of sentences, however, Ross realized he had made a bad mistake. Masterman hardly waited for him to finish before he sat bolt upright in his chair and said with an incredulous look—

"Do you mean you actually went to see Harvey without having the courtesy to tell me first? What kind of behaviour is that? I've come to expect that kind of thing from the Americans, but you—you've had an English education, and I think you've been a disgrace to it."

He paused, and Ross watched him without saying anything. It was obvious that Masterman was with difficulty controlling his mounting anger. Ross felt like a spectator listening to a nuclear test countdown.

"It's disgraceful, absolutely disgraceful. First Jim Whidden goes behind my back. Then Morey makes an ass of himself with Jones and now, to crown everything, they even pick out an Englishman to do their dirty work. You ought to be ashamed of yourself being a pawn in such a game. As for them, they're not even fit to manage a business. Perhaps this is the sort of sly, underhand way in which all business is carried on in the States; but, for goodness sake, people just don't behave like that here. They're a pack of ill-bred people." —Suddenly he broke off and looked at his watch; then he picked up his glass and slammed it down on the table, breaking the stem. "I know what I'll do," he roared, "I've a damn good mind to call them up here and now and tell them what I think of them. It'll be the middle of the afternoon there and it'll wake up Al Nelson. Damn good thing too. And I know what else I'll do. I'll play them at their own game. I'm perfectly sure that they always tape-record their transatlantic telephone conversations so I'll start doing it too. I'll put you on one 'phone, a tape-recorder on the second one, and I'll give them hell on the third. It'll be darn well worth the expense."

Ross felt a strong desire to walk out then and there, but he thought there was a possibility that the evening still could be salvaged if he encouraged Masterman's anger to take its course. "If you feel like that," he said, "why don't you telephone Newark?"

Masterman got up without another word and strode into the house. Ross heard him giving his housekeeper firm instructions about the tape-recorder. Then Masterman motioned him to the telephone in the hall and stomped off himself to the third 'phone upstairs. There was a pause while the transatlantic operator tried to get through to Newark. Then she told Masterman to go ahead. Ross winced and held the telephone away from his ear, hearing Masterman's voice booming all over the house. "Hello, HELLO. Is that you, Al? Well, I'm just calling you up to say that I think you people are a bunch of unethical, under-hand, dishonest businessmen, and I've got Antony Ross on one of my 'phones and a tape-recorder on the other to hear me say that. First of all you go behind my back to try and get Harvey back again, then Morey tries to play his own clever little game with Jones, then you do nothing but complain about our expenses, then you keep trying to tell me how to run a business that's under my nose, then you go ahead and sack six men without telling me and don't pay a hoot of attention to anything that I've got to say on the subject, and now, as if all that wasn't enough, Ross tells me that he's just been to see Harvey and I know damn well it was on your instructions. That's absolutely the final straw—for two pins I'd resign and let the company stew in its own juice."

There was a pause while Masterman drew breath. Al Nelson's slow drawl came over the wire—"Well, I'm certainly sorry you feel like that, Henry, and I'm sure you'll feel differently when you have time to think more about it."

"Think more, be damned!" snorted Masterman. "I know damn well that I think that kind of behaviour stinks and I'm surprised at you for condoning it. You've been a senior officer in the United States Army and you should know better. Well, you can take it from me that I'm just not going to stand any more of it. You people won't do anything I say. You persist in thinking you know better, and as a result you've done nothing that's been any help whatever. The sooner you all learn how to behave, the better."

Ross found it incredible that Al Nelson's voice could still keep its slow, imperturbable, southern drawl in the teeth of such an onslaught. "Well, Henry, I agree there have been mistakes, but I'm sure we can sort them out in a letter or two. You know that we'll do anything we can to help you and I'm sure you'll see it that way tomorrow morning."

"Well, all right," shouted Masterman upstairs, "I'll put the whole damn lot in a letter and see how you like it that way. I've already spent too much time and money talking to you now. Goodbye."

Ross heard the receiver being slammed down and he replaced his own with a sigh. Five seconds later the telephone rang.

"Hello, Okehampton. Your call cost five pounds, ten shillings," said the operator.

Ross heard Masterman reply, "That's all right, operator. It was worth it."

When Masterman came downstairs again he was a changed man. All his anger seemed to have evaporated and he even made a half-apology to Ross for his rudeness. By the end of the evening, he was actually expressing admiration for the way Al Nelson had withstood the blast.

The following morning, Ross called in at DECL just before leaving. Masterman again apologised to him for the previous evening and did his utmost to be pleasant. Nevertheless, Ross grimly reflected as he drove back to London that he was going to have a very difficult time writing his report. "The position I have to assume in no-man's-land," he muttered to himself, "is not an easy one from which to try to explain to both parties that war is hell."

Exhibit 1

NEPCO Sales and Other Relevant Data*

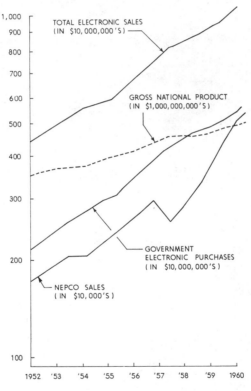

* Sales are plotted exponentially.
Source: *Fortune*, August, 1960; U.S. Government Statistics; NEPCO company records.

Exhibit 2

NEPCO Financial Information

(Figures in $000s)

I. Balance Sheets as of December 31*

	1954	1955	1956	1958	1959	1960	1961
Cash	97	39	43	262	434	589	727
Accounts Receivable	251	402	474	399	578	615	742
Notes Receivable		18	5	6			
Inventory	119	141	201	309	327	405	488
Securities				3	22	22	22
Fixed Assets	259	355	450	588	648	738	873
Depreciation†	139	163	205	328	378	451	538
Net	120	192	245	260	270	287	335
Investments				7	7	8	7
Prepayments	2	6	6	8	9	9	9
Total Assets	589	798	974	1254	1647	1935	2330
Accounts Payable	76	106	141	150	205	224	270
Notes Payable	26		134		132	150	180
Accruals	30	42	41	80	193	219	268
Taxes Payable		96	45	123			
Stock	19	19	19	19	19	19	19
Capital Surplus					6	6	6
Retained Earnings	438	535	594	882	1092	1317	1587
Total Liabilities	589	798	974	1254	1647	1935	2330

II. Sales

	1954	1955	1956	1958	1959	1960	1961
Sales	2070	2445	3000	3195	4490	4875	5850

III. Sources and Applications of Funds

Sources of Funds:§

	1955	1956	1958	1959	1960	1961
Earnings	99	59	288	210	225	270
Depreciation	36	45	123	64	73	87
Sale of Stock				6		

Applications of Funds:

	1955	1956	1958	1959	1960	1961
Fixed Assets	114	98	138	75	90	135
Working Capital	17	6	264	204	208	222
Investments, etc.	4	6	9	1		

* No balance sheet figures were available for 1957. The sources and applications of funds for 1958 are based on the two-year period.

† It was assumed that depreciation taken during any year would be approximately 10% of the total depreciable assets outstanding at the end of that year. This is believed to have been the case in recent years.

§ In establishing sources and applications of funds, it was assumed that all earnings are retained in the business. This is justified by the fact that taxes accrued in any given year bear a relationship to the amount of earnings transferred to the retained earnings account such as to indicate that these retained earnings were the sole after tax profits for the year.

Exhibit 3

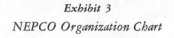

NEPCO Organization Chart

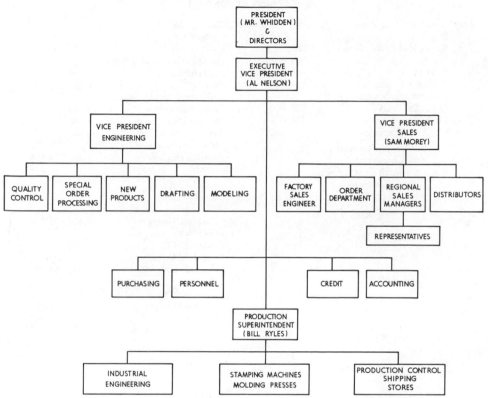

Exhibit 4

DECL Accounts for Period from 24th July 1960 to 31st December 1960
(Figures in Pounds)

I. Profit and Loss Account

Sales		1,416
Stores & Materials consumed	260	
Wages	995	
Salaries	1,061	
Travelling Expenses	589	
Directors' Expenses	94	
Other Expenses	979	
Depreciation	729	
Total Expenses		4,707
Net Loss on Trading		3,291
Add: Charges on Formation of Company		534
Total Loss transferred to Balance Sheet		3,825

II. Balance Sheet, December 31

Current Assets:		
Cash in hand	1,329	
Accounts Receivable & Pre-payments	3,746	
Stock	1,050	6,125
Fixed Assets (less Dep'n.):		
Land & Buildings	9,913	
Plant & Machinery	7,146	
Loose Tools & Eqp't.	601	
Office Equipment	239	
Motor Vehicles	1,205	19,104
Total Assets		25,229
Current Liabilities:		
Bank Overdraft	56	
Accounts Payable & Accrued Charges	7,430	7,486
Long-term Loans:		
From NEPCO	5,028	
From NEPCO of Canada Ltd.	13,940	18,968
Net Worth:		
Ordinary Shares (2/-)	2,600	
Less: Loss to date	3,825	(1,225)
Total Liabilities		25,229

Exhibit 5

Outline Marketing Plan for DECL Ltd.
(Prepared by Al Nelson, April 1961)

I. PURPOSE

The purpose of this Outline Marketing Plan for DECL is to serve as a basis for the development of *profitable* sales and marketing activity for the DECL organization.

II. BACKGROUND

Prior to June, 1959, NEPCO served the British and European markets by direct export to customers on the Continent. In June of 1959, arrangements were made with Masterman Engineering Ltd., of Plymouth, England, to act as NEPCO representatives in Great Britain. Mr. Jack Turpin was employed by Masterman Engineering Ltd. to act as a full time sales engineer on NEPCO's behalf. Mr. Turpin came to the United States for a period of approximately six weeks to receive training at the Newark factory. During the period July, 1959, through June, 1960, Masterman Engineering did missionary selling by calling on prospects throughout England. The results of these calls produced relatively few sales. The lack of success in this effort can be attributed to several factors. One of these factors was the relatively high price of imported NEPCO products as compared with products produced in Great Britain. Another significant factor was the nationalism expressed on the part of potential British customers. Simply stated the customer said, "We would like to buy from you if you manufacture in this country." Another important factor was insufficient management and administrative supervision on the part of Masterman Engineering and NEPCO. Still another was the narrow outlet for a broad line of products, with a limited number of distribution outlets for the line.

Exhibit 5—Continued

During the summer of 1960 the decision was made to manufacture in England. As a result of this decision, a manufacturing works was purchased at Okehampton. During the latter half of 1960, Mr. Bill Ryles, Manufacturing Engineer from NEPCO, spent a period of approximately six weeks during November and December in setting up the manufacturing facilities at Okehampton and effecting the transformation to electronic production. In March of 1961, there were four punch presses in place and actually turning out stampings of the same kind as manufactured in Newark. During March, 1961, Mr. James Whidden, President of NEPCO, went to Okehampton and further established the manufacturing facility at the British location. A revised price list for the British market was distributed in February, 1961.

III. MARKET

The market for electronic components in Europe as a whole is considerably smaller than that of the United States, due primarily to the smaller sums being expended for electronics by the various governments. However, the rate of future growth of the electronics industry in Europe appears to be greater than that in the United States. In 1961 it is estimated that the total market in countries outside the Communist bloc will be approximately the equivalent of two to three billion dollars. The population of the pro-Western countries is approximately 200 million, which exceeds the population of the United States. Past market research studies have indicated that there is a broad correlation between population and electronic potential in industrialized countries. On this basis the future growth of the electronics industry in Europe would appear to be well substantiated.

The electronics market in England is estimated to be between 5 percent and 10 percent of the U.S. market, that is, between 500 million and a billion U.S. dollars for all types of electronics. This market is strengthened by Commonwealth ties. If England is successful in becoming a member of the Common Market—and there are indications that she is thinking of joining—the future market potential for NEPCO products appears large enough to permit an economic manufacturing unit.

IV. MARKET STRATEGY

The market strategy for NEPCO products in a European environment should be based fundamentally on an engineering approach. Due to the technical nature of the product lines, the marketing focus should be directed primarily to the design engineering influences. Emphasis should be placed on the engineering characteristics and capabilities of NEPCO products in a wide variety of electronic applications.

The marketing strategy should include stress on the fact that products are "made in Britain and manufactured from a European source." The strategy should also include the concept of local availability through distributors.

The marketing image should be one that the products are competitive but the lines should be distinguished by their engineering advantages and quality rather than by price competition with existing national sources.

V. CHANNELS OF DISTRIBUTION

Initially it is conceived that NEPCO products should be made available directly from the DECL works in Okehampton and, as mentioned above, through modern electronic distributors in England and on the Continent.

The possibility of using manufacturers' agents should be considered. However, in such a consideration the problems of multi-layer channels, the availability of technically qualified manufacturers' agents, and adequate margins must be taken into account.

The channels used must also take cognisance of the physical size of territories, transportation, selling customs and techniques of the country concerned.

VI. SALES ORGANIZATION

The sales organization of DECL is conceived initially to consist of a Managing Director of DECL who has an appreciation of the essential sales function and one who is

Exhibit 5—Continued

capable of providing adequate sales engineering support to the sales force. There should be a minimum of one direct factory technical salesman capable of producing adequate sales to cover his own expenses and to produce total sales commensurate with the overall cost of maintaining this salesman on the DECL payroll.

Initially it is believed that a distributor in the London area should be utilized since the bulk of the electronics market in England is centered in the London area and since the works is located some way away from this area. One such distributor, Thames Electronic Distributors Ltd., has already been engaged as an authorized NEPCO distributor in England. It is desirable to add distributors at locations later to be determined, in order to provide better coverage through wider local availability and to avoid dependence on one or two distributors. The factory sales representative should be employed so as to provide support for the distributors, and inherent conflicts between the factory sales engineer and the distributor are to be avoided.

Manufacturers' agents, if used, should be integrated into the total marketing effort so as to support and not conflict with the factory sales organization or the distributor.

Several distributors are considered necessary in any one country or marketing territory.

VII. SALES TRAINING

Sales training has consisted of the orientation which was given to Mr. Jack Turpin when first employed in 1959, his subsequent field experience, and sales literature which has been provided to DECL. In addition, the personnel of DECL have provided training to members of TEDL.

Additional sales training is undoubtedly required to improve the sales ability of personnel already provided with earlier training. Moreover these sales people need further training in depth on established products, and training to make them effective in selling new products which are available. If additional salesmen are added by either the factory or distributors, initial training will, of course, be required for them.

Formal training sessions are needed as well as coaching on field calls.

VIII. ADVERTISING AND SALES PROMOTION

Due to the nature of NEPCO products, it is essential that sales promotion and advertising be carried out on a broad basis. The products are utilized in a wide variety of applications by almost every original equipment manufacturer in the electronics industry. Therefore it is necessary to provide for wide advertising coverage and extensive use of catalogues and product promotions. At the same time, it is essential that this advertising and sales promotion be backed up by competent sales engineering.

The advertising itself could well be directed initially towards getting catalogues into the hands of potential users. Concurrently it appears appropriate to conduct advertising campaigns to secure specific inquires on individual products.

In order to keep the cost of advertising within bounds it will probably be necessary to limit the amount of general exposure and corporate image type advertising. Different types of technical journals might well be used, and advertising should be directed towards the key buying influence, who appears to be the design engineer. The tabloid and general news-type advertising may have a certain usefulness in the earlier stages for announcement-type messages, but the overall advertising programme must be directed to the real buyer or buying influence.

In addition to trade journal advertising, direct mail advertising should be employed as a supplement. A definite and specific programme covering a definitive period should be prepared and executed. Emphasis necessarily should be placed initially on the most important types as outlined above. More detailed and extensive promotions, such as point of sale promotion, can be developed for the most part later.

IX. SALES STATISTICS

Continuing market research and sales data are needed to permit an intelligent and orderly marketing plan to materialize potential into sales.

Exhibit 5—Continued

In order to provide for standards and to measure performance, sales statistics by salesmen, by type of unit, by product, and by customer, must be developed and maintained current.

X. SPECIFIC MARKETING PLAN

Based on this marketing outline and further specific analysis of the DECL market, action is required to develop a specific marketing plan for the remainder of 1961 and for 1962 thereafter. This marketing plan is to be used to provide a clearly defined and orderly approach to securing the maximum possible sales at the earliest date in order to permit the DECL organization to operate on a profitable basis. The marketing plan so developed must also serve as a basis of measuring management and sales performance of those responsible for the profitability of DECL.

. . . .

Exhibit 6

Correspondence between Nelson and Masterman

June 22, 1961

DEAR HENRY:

After receiving your letter of June 14, Mr. Whidden, Bill Ryles, Sam Morey, and I each independently devoted careful thought and consideration to this particular letter. The reason is that we all feel that in one way or another the matters contained in this letter involve the very basic objectives and policies of DECL. There are certain fundamental factors on which there must be full agreement. It is essential that these fundamentals be clearly agreed upon by all of us, and, most importantly, carried out by all of us regardless of where we may be located physically. Therefore the purpose of this letter is to redefine and clarify the basic policies concerning the operation of DECL.

Authority and Responsibility

The ultimate authority for the control of DECL, like any company, rests with its owners. In turn the principal directors of the company have the responsibility for the prudent and profitable operation of the company and the Managing Director of the company has full responsibility to the Board of Directors for his performance. The matter of prerogatives is one which is fully appreciated, and there is no question that appropriate authority must be in the hands of the Managing Director. At the same time, the Managing Director is obligated to carry out the directives of the principal directors and to demonstrate sound judgement in the execution of the duties of Managing Director.

Financial Limitations

Certain financial limits necessarily have been placed on the authority of the Managing Director. The limitations to be complied with are:

a) Any expenditure involving capitalization requires prior written approval from the parent company;

b) Operating expense for labour and materials is to be restricted to that directly applicable to salable products.

It should be noted particularly that these financial limitations apply *before* the commitment of funds.

It is the intent of NEPCO that the DECL subsidiary must stand on its own two feet financially. It is our further intent to limit the subsidizing of DECL in the future to the export of a certain number of manufacturing machines and associated capital equipment and to the export of manufactured products from NEPCO stocks. Otherwise DECL is expected to be self-sufficient.

Exhibit 6—Continued

Management

The most important and most urgent need for DECL is a full-time general manager. This need has often been reiterated by all concerned, yet the fact remains that the position is not now filled, nor has it been for some months.

Distribution

The relationship between TEDL and DECL has apparently been subjected to varying interpretations. It is desired that TEDL act as a stocking distributor with its territory throughout the U.K. DECL has the responsibility for sales to other manufacturers, control of factory-distributor operations, and engineering services to all customers including the distributor. The factory salesman shall have the right and the responsibility to sell to anyone, but is expected also to coordinate (but not subordinate) his efforts with those of TEDL.

The matter of how Jack Turpin has been utilized has been a source of disagreement in the past. It is the desire of the parent company that a full-time salesman be utilized in actual direct sales and sales engineering support to customers. Jack Turpin was engaged for this purpose under the agreement made two years ago with Masterman Engineering Ltd. Since there have been virtually no sales, Jack Turpin must be maintained in a full-time selling capacity. It has been the observation of our personnel that Turpin will improve in his job. Unless there are some significant sales, DECL will never be able to stand on its own feet. Although it is fully expected that TEDL can do a good job of selling and that its promotions will be of assistance, the engineering level selling required in the electronics industry can only be done by Turpin to any real degree of success. Inquiries which are directed to the factory can be handled by other personnel in the office, particularly as these individuals gain experience. For detailed technical inquiries, information must be relayed by phone to Turpin who can then contact the customer concerned. By careful planning of his time and by at least occasional work on Saturdays during these early stages of the DECL enterprise, the several demands on Turpin can be handled simultaneously and do not appear excessive.

Absentee Control

It is desired that at the earliest practical time control from the parent be minimised. However, frankly, the controls which have been exercised from Newark have been instituted because of the severe financial demands created by the enterprise. Very honestly, the amount of money put into this venture has exceeded the amount originally conceived by a considerable sum. Furthermore, certain controls have been instituted because of the technical nature of the business and the experience required for operations in such a technical field. Moreover the Managing Director has had a tremendous problem in developing a business of this kind and magnitude in a relatively short period without the help of a general manager. This has placed a great burden on the Managing Director, and the controls instituted have been for the purpose of genuine help rather than for restrictions. What we must insist upon is that we maintain complete control until sufficient profits have been realised to warrant the change in the extent of controls.

Henry, in the somewhat formalised paragraphs above, we have provided you in a forthright manner those major factors in the operation of the business on which we feel there must be absolutely no basic disagreement. The agreement on these fundamentals must be complete, and, most importantly, they must be reflected in the day-to-day actions of all of us and in the results which are forthcoming from these actions. We know that you have done a tremendous amount of work in setting up this company, and you must appreciate that we have contributed a great deal of time and effort as well as really sizeable amounts of money. We simply are not in a position to continue the financial support of the operation at its current level. Accordingly, there must be increased sales on the one hand and reduced expenses, including reduction in payroll, on the other hand.

(*Signed*)
AL NELSON

Exhibit 6—Continued

Masterman's Reply

In his reply of June 27, Masterman made four main points:

1. That there were occasions when it was desirable for NEPCO management to seek his advice before they took action;

2. That he was doing exactly what NEPCO required both financially and as regards Turpin;

3. That he now did not think that Turpin would be able to generate the sales required by NEPCO, and that TEDL were very dissatisfied with the state of affairs presently existing because they had neither stocks nor selling material in adequate quantities;

4. That there was an urgent need to advertise for a general manager and that this was the only suitable approach.

3. Devonian Electronic Components Ltd. (B)*

ON HIS RETURN to London, Antony Ross spent some time thinking about the situation that had confronted him at Devonian Electronic Components Ltd. on his recent visit there as a consultant to the American parent organization, Newark Electronic Products Corporation. When he was satisfied that he had thought through the problems he wrote the report that follows.

CONFIDENTIAL REPORT TO MR. JAMES WHIDDEN

Subject: Visit to Okehampton plant, July 1 to July 6, 1961

1. *The Present Situation*

Before I begin the body of this report, I feel that I must emphasise that I have endeavoured to be as impartial as possible during my consulting assignment. The instructions which you gave me originally were broad enough to allow me to assume to some extent the responsibility of making the first steps towards improving your present difficulties. Unfortunately these first steps involve criticism of the actions of both sides over the last few months. If you at NEPCO are to accept these criticisms, it is essential that you should be convinced that I have made every possible effort to be unprejudiced.

I'm afraid that a situation has now developed where each side is strongly suspicious of the actions of the other and much resentment and misunderstanding are being generated. It might be useful to summarise briefly what I believe to be the main feelings of the English and American participants.

The feelings held by NEPCO at this point are ones of disappointment and frustration. Although a European subsidiary would only be able to tap a market far smaller than the American one, it was judged originally that a foothold in the European electronics market might be a useful and profitable thing to have. Since you had an apparently valuable contact in England in the form of Mr. Masterman, he was approached initially, I think, with the idea of his engaging a salesman who would ascertain the degree of enthusiasm in England for NEPCO products. This seemed a suitably cautious way in which to begin the project and although few sales were effected, it was felt (see the Outline Marketing Plan) that certain plainly discernible factors were responsible for this lack of sales, and that the most important of these factors could be obviated by manufacturing in

---

Britain. Therefore, DECL was formed under the managing directorship of an enthusiastic Mr. Masterman.

From that point on, it has seemed to the NEPCO management that they have done everything possible to make things easier for DECL and to ensure the success of the English operation. It is true that misunderstandings have occurred with regard to paperwork—in pricing, perhaps, or in the various order and inventory control forms—but these were only to be expected since sheer geographical separation made the starting of an English subsidiary a difficult and complicated business. In the matter of finances, NEPCO have poured a good deal more money into DECL than was originally expected; furthermore, the top people in NEPCO have devoted valuable time—devoted at the expense of the far larger American market—to DECL's problems and no fewer than three Atlantic trips have been made so far by the Americans alone, quite apart from the two made on the English side.

To all these efforts, the English response appears to be disappointing. In fact, there seems in England to be a very serious lack of response to NEPCO's point of view. It is even doubtful if the very urgent need for sales is appreciated fully enough, and the administration at Okehampton seems often to be lethargic or unpredictable in its actions, as well as to betray insufficient realisation of the rate at which money is disappearing into DECL. Furthermore, on top of the rather surprising dismissal of Harvey—who seemed to be a knowledgeable and efficient assistant to Mr. Masterman, there was the difficult Jones incident in which Mr. Masterman's enthusiasm changed almost overnight to inexplicable disapproval and his opinion along with those of the other two Masterman-appointed directors, became ranged against that of Sam Morey who had deliberately spent a good deal of time satisfying himself about the most important facet of any future general manager at DECL, namely, his technical ability.

By the end of June, therefore, the situation, if not yet desperate, was at any rate serious enough to take the drastic action of dismissing the six most recently hired employees in such a way as to impress upon the DECL administration NEPCO's determination to cut expenses firmly until such time as money should materialise from much needed sales.

.　　.　　.　　.　　.　　.　　.　　.　　.　　.　　.　　.

The feelings of those at DECL, on the other hand, are also, rather surprisingly, ones of frustration and a certain amount of righteous indignation. Caring little about the demands of the American market and with eyes only for the success of the English operation, they feel themselves thwarted time and again by the unwillingness of the Americans to look at the problems in the same light as that in which they are seen by those on the spot.

Up to the end of 1960, there was a considerable spirit of cooperation which made light of many of the problems which arose. But in the course of 1961, difficulties began to creep in which have slowly assumed more and more irritating proportions. As far as the actual production was concerned, the first problem was to get the initial machines installed and running; once this had been done, those in the plant began to learn more and more about the machines and their capabilities and there was a definite spirit of enthusiasm. Nevertheless problems have arisen which cannot be solved by enthusiasm alone: the finished pieces have still to be picked by hand from the chippings and this is an extremely slow and tedious business; then, no means other than straightforward drainage has been devised to separate the oil from the chippings and the finished pieces, and there is a good deal of wastage of oil at present because those at DECL feel that they still have not got the right oil for the machines; most important of all, it has so far proved impossible to perform with speed and accuracy all the measurements which are apparently necessary to maintain the quality of the smallest parts, simply because NEPCO cannot or will not get across exactly how and to what extent quality control is maintained in Newark on the parts concerned.

Nevertheless, these problems should not be overestimated, serious as they are, because there seems little doubt that in the plant itself there was, until recently, little dissatisfaction and much good morale. Such ill feeling as now exists among the DECL production workers towards NEPCO is caused by the recent dismissals, which have created a good deal of alarm and despondency.

Far more serious from the standpoint of the NEPCO–DECL relationship are the feelings of Mr. Masterman and the other two English directors and, to a lesser extent, the feelings of Norris. From their point of view, it seems the Americans are doing everything possible to make life difficult and a series of incidents, perhaps of small importance in themselves but very significant when looked at in retrospect, together with the recent dismissals as the final straw, has produced this feeling which is in so much contrast to what the NEPCO management itself thinks. The efforts to persuade Harvey to return to DECL after being dismissed; the dealings of Sam Morey with Jones after a directors' meeting had clearly turned Jones down; the constant letters about DECL expenses which often imply not only recklessness on the part of DECL but perhaps even dishonesty; the refusal to advertise for a General Manager despite the directors' advice; and, most important of all, the recent dismissals which were undertaken summarily and without the advice of the directors in England—all these things led to Mr. Masterman's outburst on the telephone the other day. By now, in fact, it seems almost incredible to the DECL management that the Americans, traditionally supposed to be very fine managers of business operations, can behave in such a way.

These two seriously conflicting points of view have caused a situation in which neither side really believes that the other knows what's best for the company, and the result has been some rather shaky administration of a comparatively simple operation. At the present time, morale at DECL is low and, far worse, sales are low as well. The machines have by now turned out hundreds of thousands of parts, not one of which has been sold because nobody seems to be sure whether these parts are of the required quality. TEDL, as you know, are contemplating sending a strongly worded letter of complaints which, as far as I can see, are justified. Finally, Mr. Masterman himself is rapidly beginning to feel that it is impossible to conduct the administration of the company in the teeth of the American insistence on management from 3,000 miles away; and meanwhile you at NEPCO appear to be getting steadily more concerned at the inability of your English counterparts to appreciate the true nature and urgency of the situation and you are unlikely to be satisfied with anything but sharply increased sales in the near future. In short, DECL looks at the moment to be anything but a promising venture.

2. *Analysis of the Problem Areas*

A. *Sales*. Naturally, I am not qualified to make many detailed remarks about your sales policy with DECL, but there are some observations which can and should be made on a general level. The lack of sales is clearly at the root of most of DECL's present problems and it is natural that a critical observer should review (as you at NEPCO must have done so often) the developments on the sales side to date, to try and see whether any serious mistakes were made which might yet be remedied.

One's first impression is that there has been inadequate American control and training in the very area where it is needed most. I wish I had some feel for the degree to which technical knowledge is required in order to sell NEPCO products. For it seems to me that it was a mistake to take Jack Turpin, who was not an electrical engineer by training, and expect him, after only a few weeks' indoctrination at NEPCO, to do selling work in England which was up to U.S. standards. For it meant that up to the engagement of TEDL, you were placing a good deal of responsibility for the success or failure of DECL on the shoulders of a single salesman in whom you could hardly have had the required confidence. Furthermore, you were handicapping this one salesman severely by requiring him to sell products manufactured 3,000 miles away and therefore subject to inevitable delays in passage across the Atlantic and through Customs. It may be unfounded, but I have an uneasy feeling that because the potential English market is only a small fraction of the American one, NEPCO, albeit subconsciously, regard it as an easy market to sell to by comparison with the American one and have therefore not devoted adequate time and thought to cracking it open. The tone of the letter from Al Nelson to Mr. Masterman (dated April 3, 1961) which deals with Sam Morey's forthcoming visit is definitely one of optimistic hope that Sam Morey's visit will prove to be something of a panacea to the sales problem.

In contrast to this optimism, I believe that the English market is not an easy one to enter. Not only do gentlemen's agreements and established contacts count for a great deal, but there is also widespread anti-American feeling which has to be countered. I think that only a salesman of high selling ability, considerable experience, and detailed knowledge of his sales line and its uses could be expected to generate enough volume to provide the necessary impetus for DECL.

This last comment brings me back to the subject of Jack Turpin: to judge from the variety of correspondence both to him and concerning him, I gather that NEPCO can hardly have the fullest confidence in his performance. There are constant reminders in the last half of 1960 that results are required urgently, there are even more reminders to this effect in the correspondence files for this year and, of course, there is Sam Morey's visit itself which was again followed by a long list of instructions and exhortations to Turpin. All this would seem to betray a high degree of worry about Turpin which was undoubtedly very justified. Yet on the other side of the question, the fact remains that Turpin is still employed, perhaps because you feel that you have too much invested in him already. It is entirely understandable that you should be keenly aware of the training and experience which Turpin has had selling NEPCO products; yet it must also be remembered that "sunk costs," so to speak, should not be taken into account if you think you can get a better salesman and if you need to do so.

There remains the subject of TEDL who, I understand both from Turpin and Mr. Masterman, are dissatisfied with the service they are getting from NEPCO. In fairness to Turpin, it must be said that if TEDL are feeling this kind of handicap even at this point, one wonders what kind of backing-up Jack Turpin has received over the last eighteen months.

In summary, I feel as strongly as I am able to feel without further information that NEPCO has devoted inadequate planning and effort to DECL's sales programme, at any rate until recently. I fully understand the reasons for this since I am well aware that the demands of the huge American market are incomparably more important to NEPCO. Nevertheless, I assume that at the time you decided to form DECL, you realised that a commitment would have to be made not only in terms of money but also in terms of the skill, knowledge and effort which have gone into building up NEPCO. In other words, a ten-day fire-fighting visit to England is not enough to solve DECL's sales problems, unless they are very superficial ones (which I don't believe they are). What was required—and what probably still is required despite TEDL's presence—is someone on the English side who is a skilful and knowledgeable electronics salesman and who has the trust and confidence of you at NEPCO. Such a person could have sat down at the beginning or the middle of last year and planned a strategy in detail, based on a first-hand and intelligent appraisal of the marketing problems. It is true that the problem of efficient supply would still have required drastic alteration. But at least it would have been flexible, in that it could have been controlled and altered by the man on the spot.

By contrast, as I have already stressed, NEPCO have a salesman in England in whom the officers do not seem to place much confidence and a stocking distributor who, despite the high commission he is being offered, does not seem to have accomplished very much to date. The whole sales effort has been rather patchily planned and controlled from America—and the Outline Marketing Plan is a good example of this patchiness, for it only vaguely states the problems involved in DECL's selling effort and it makes no attempt to give detailed recommendations on how to surmount these problems.

These are unpleasant comments to be faced at this stage of the operation and I would be only too glad if you could soundly refute them with evidence of a sales programme which, right from the start, was soundly conceived and executed. I suspect, however, that their substance cannot be refuted except on the grounds of NEPCO's overwhelming preoccupation with the American market. This is a preoccupation with which I completely sympathise, of course, but it is one which may yet prove disastrous for DECL.

B. Production. In this area also, I shall concentrate only on raising the major questions that my business school training prompts me to ask; for I certainly do not have the knowledge (or the experience) to make any detailed criticisms involving the machines themselves or the way they are being handled.

In the first place, I can't help wondering what would have happened if Jack Turpin had suddenly started acquiring floods of orders back in October or November of last year, and it had become necessary for NEPCO to get DECL producing as many different parts as possible to the required standards within a very short space of time. For under the present circumstances, it has been possible to run the production aspects of DECL on a comparatively leisurely timetable, and the lack of sales has covered up potentially serious shortcomings on the production side.

Here, again, the greatest lack at DECL is that of a man who is familiar with all the aspects of NEPCO's production. I say this for the following reasons:

1. When I was shown around the NEPCO plant, it was stressed that NEPCO manufactured thousands of different parts and that a great many of these parts were in frequent demand. As you know, DECL are at present manufacturing only a few different parts, and Sam Morey's letter to Jack Turpin of May 23 ordered him to concentrate first and foremost on selling the parts currently being produced by DECL. Now it may be that you decided to manufacture first at DECL those parts which you felt you had most chance of selling after you had made a study of the potential English market. I would guess, however, that the parts which are at present being made at DECL are those which are technologically the simplest to make and that this was the main determinant in choosing the parts to make.

   At any rate, it doesn't really make sense that DECL, nine months after starting production, should still be making only a very small number of the full parent company line. I am sure that even with DECL's present limited equipment, it would be possible to make a much wider range of parts and I suspect that the main reason why this has not been done is that no one at NEPCO now knows what the people at DECL are capable of or whether they can attain NEPCO standards in more than a few respects. Therefore, the easiest course is to let the DECL plant continue to pour forth stampings, etc., until the sales situation positively demands that it produce a much wider range of parts. This may well be a sensible decision, but I think it should be made by someone on the spot who knows a great deal more about the production setup both at NEPCO and at DECL than anyone on either side of the Atlantic appears to know at present.

2. Quality control is an aspect of the production process which is very important, of course, to NEPCO. It would therefore seem to be correspondingly important to have a high degree of coordination in this area between NEPCO and DECL. Yet at this point, no one seems sure whether the parts already made by DECL are fit to sell or not—and this is eight months after production has started. The problem is certainly not attributable to lack of competence at DECL as far as measuring is concerned, or even as far as the actual machining is concerned. Rather, the problem lies in the lack of adequate measuring tools and the lack of knowledge of the way NEPCO do it. Furthermore, there is no one, with the possible exception of Jack Turpin, at DECL who can say with authority which tolerances on a particular part are the vital ones to maintain. Here, again,

what is required is someone who knows *in detail* the situation on both sides of the Atlantic.

3. A number of technical problems crop up from day to day, I gather, which no one can answer satisfactorily. The separation of the oil from the chippings has been a problem for a long time, for instance, as you probably well know; as has also the matter of sorting the finished pieces. Many of the problems which come up can be solved over a period of time by the workers at DECL and they say that it is often excellent experience for them to have to do this; but there are problems also which no one at DECL can answer satisfactorily, even at this relatively uncomplicated stage in the Okehampton operation.

4. Finally, not only the production side but also the whole Okehampton operation would benefit from having someone on the spot who knew what was going to happen next and who could make sure that everyone understood what was happening and why it was happening. I refer not only to the dismissals (of which more later) but also to such letters as the one written by Bill Ryles to Harvey on January 11 of this year. In this letter, Ryles said: "We have lined up an ambitious programme for DECL in 1961 and should have a minimum of eight punch presses and molding machines to you by July 30th." Sam Morey on his visit confirmed this number and also the dates on which the machines would be despatched from the States. Yet the last machine was sent on April 15 and since then, not only have no more been despatched, but men have been laid off. You have, of course, a complete right to change your minds and make these latter decisions, but it would cause less doubt and consternation at DECL if someone were on hand to explain the reasons behind the decisions.

C. *General Administration.* Here we come to most of the problems which I think were bothering you when I was in Newark and also those aspects of the Okehampton situation which you felt required an outsider's point of view. For the most part, such comments as I have will concern Mr. Masterman directly or indirectly. Despite his relationship to you, I have decided that to be less than completely frank with regard to my own opinions would do you a disservice. Moreover, I believe that is in keeping with the spirit of my assignment from you.

It was unfortunate that the relationship between yourself and Mr. Masterman was such that he was the natural and obvious man to start up DECL. For Mr. Masterman—as he would now probably admit—is quite unsuited both by training and by temperament to doing the jobs that have been required of him over the last year. I know nothing at all about the decision to form DECL or what was said at the time. It may well be that at that time Mr. Masterman was both enthusiastic and confident of his ability to steer DECL along the right path and that you all saw no reason to doubt this, particularly as it was so convenient for you to have someone whom you knew so well as managing director of DECL.

On the other hand, a cold appraisal of Mr. Masterman's qualifications would not have borne out any optimism on your part, unless at the time you felt that he would be called upon to do very little for DECL. In the first place, his background is heavy engineering, as you well know, and it is in this field that most of his best contacts lie. Secondly, he is a salesman by experience and by temperament, and by all accounts he has been an extremely good one, who has regularly sold each year for the past several years hundreds of thousands of pounds' worth of heavy equipment. He therefore had to transfer part of his attention from a profitable business in which he was selling very heavy equipment of high value to the day-to-day managerial responsibilities entailed in the running of an operation which was turning out parts one thousandth to one millionth the size of those to which he was accustomed, and which at best would have a turnover many times smaller than that of Masterman Engineering Ltd.—at any rate in the first three or four years of its life. Furthermore, Mr. Masterman, 55 at the time, was unlikely to be extremely flexible in breaking new ground.

This is perhaps a somewhat brutal commentary on a decision which must have had far more personal and subtle undertones than I could appreciate. But I am concerned to emphasise that the initial, and almost inevitable, liaison with Mr. Masterman was for this purpose very unfortunate. It led not only to the appointment of Jack Turpin but also to the appointment of Mr. Masterman himself as managing director. These appointments, in their turn, have done much to cause the misunderstandings which have generated so much frustration and lack of confidence on either side of the Atlantic. For over the last few months, you people at NEPCO have clearly felt an ever-decreasing confidence in Mr. Masterman and have consequently taken more and more of the DECL management decisions into your own hands. Meanwhile, Mr. Masterman himself has come to see more clearly than he did originally that he is not exactly the ideal man to run DECL on the spot, despite his considerable selling abilities. Furthermore, to this injury to his confidence is added the insult of having the decisions that he still regards himself as well qualified to make either ignored or taken out of his hands completely.

Before dealing in detail with various incidents in DECL's history over the past year, I am concerned to emphasise one other thing. I spent some time at Okehampton trying to make Mr. Masterman see how you at NEPCO probably visualised the DECL operation. I did my best to point out, in the course of a longish conversation which we had one morning, that NEPCO management was very busy indeed coping with a lucrative market, which was very much larger than a European market could ever hope to be and that as a result you were very often not able to give to DECL all the time and thought which a small subsidiary in a foreign country needs if it is going to survive. In turn, I feel obliged to point out to you some things about Mr. Masterman's present position since I think from some of the remarks that were made to me in Newark, you may be over-emphasising one or two aspects and not giving enough weight to others.

When I was in Newark, remarks were made to the effect that Mr. Masterman was throttling the growth of DECL by maintaining a tight control over everything that went on and by refusing to sanction the appointment of anyone designed to take some of this control out of his hands. I think this is a little unfair. First—and this is rather important—Mr. Masterman is undoubtedly, to use Shakespeare's comment on Brutus, "an honourable man." By this I mean that in his capacity as managing director of DECL he would not think of doing anything which was not in the best interests of the company; the same, I imagine, could be said of Colonel Sykes and Mr. Paton-Jones, and no matter what the relationship of the latter two to Mr. Masterman, I am quite satisfied that each of them would have no hesitation in speaking out against a particular course of action, even if Mr. Masterman had adopted it. Thus I feel that a conspiracy, as it were, between the three of them to keep the company in their pockets is a ludicrous concept. This leaves open the question as to whether their judgement is at fault and in this respect there is definitely a danger that you have underestimated and will continue to underestimate their shrewdness and experience as far as the English scene is concerned. It is true that they all know little about the world of electronics but their ignorance in this area should not necessarily be taken as an excuse for brushing aside their opinions in other areas.

Secondly—and this again is very important—Mr. Masterman definitely has better things to do than spending time at DECL from a strictly remunerative point of view. When I was in Plymouth seeing Williamson, I also called on the managing director of a firm for which Mr. Masterman does a good deal—by no means all—of his sales work. It was told that Mr. Masterman was spending too much time with DECL and that his sales work, and probably his health also, were suffering considerably. I understand also that because Mr. Masterman was not able to devote sufficient attention to his selling activities, Masterman Engineering lost a major client in the early part of this year.

Now all this raises the question—Why does Mr. Masterman persevere with DECL? I confess I find this the most difficult question of all to answer. Undoubtedly the main driving force is a strong sense of loyalty to you personally. Ironically enough (in the light of your feelings about Mr. Masterman and DECL), I think he feels that if he were to resign, it would make things very difficult for you. There may also be some future financial rewards in remaining with DECL and this you would know far better than I. However, I can find no trace of any payment to Mr. Masterman for his services. Incidentally, I would judge that he spends anything from two to six hours a day on DECL business, which is a great deal for a man who is supposed to be running his own business. And when he is treated, as he was in the matter of the dismissals, as a man whose opinion was of virtually no consequence whatsoever, small wonder that he feels the kind of anger and resentment that must have been obvious to Al Nelson on the telephone the other day.

At this point, I must again stress that the above comments are not made from any partial feeling on behalf of Mr. Masterman—(I, too, caught the rough edge of his tongue the other day). I have tried my utmost to be impartial throughout this report and produce some facts as evidence for every opinion in it. The only reason for my making the above comments is that I think they are things that you ought to know as they appear to a disinterested observer.

It remains now to go briefly through one or two incidents and matters which have caused some disagreement between NEPCO and DECL management. These are as follows: the dismissal of Harvey; the disagreement about Jones; the recent dismissals of six people; and the control over expenses.

1. **The dismissal of Harvey.** I must admit that I am still not entirely certain why Harvey was dismissed. The cause seems to have been a series of incidents rather than one particular one, with the main problem being that Harvey was far too often making decisions on the spot that he simply had not got enough knowledge to make. It is significant that all those to whom I talked who were in a position to know anything about Harvey at DECL tended to approve of Mr Masterman's action. Williamson, for instance, though critical of Mr. Masterman in some respects, seemed to think that he was right in getting rid of Harvey. One must remember that whoever runs the office at Okehampton is in control of the operation for a good part of the day and it is therefore essential that the person concerned should be reliable. After Harvey had quoted, for the third time within a short period, a ridiculous figure for the making of some part or other, it was understandable that Mr. Masterman should have felt a lack of confidence in him. It is true that Harvey was probably not guilty of anything that a competent general manager could not have cured in a short time, but this comment ignores the fact that there was no such knowledgeable general manager *permanently* on the spot. I tend to think that from the standpoint of reliability, you are far better off with Norris, who knows his own limitations full well, and who has complete honesty and much common sense.

The story behind Mr. Masterman's telephone call to Al Nelson the other day is as follows. I had many misgivings about going to see Harvey primarily because I knew it would be almost impossible for me to see him without Mr. Masterman knowing sooner or later that I had done so. It is difficult to exaggerate the speed and thoroughness with which news travels in a valley like the Okehampton one. I knew that if Mr. Masterman found out this way, he would be greatly offended and this would sabotage all good relations if you were to require me to make another trip to Okehampton. Nevertheless, I decided to see Harvey and then inform Mr. Masterman that I had done so, being as casual as possible about the whole business. I told him when I went to dinner with him on the Thursday evening and said that I had gone to see Harvey, not for the purpose of raking over the details of the dismissal, but to acquire more background information about the start-up of DECL of a kind which Harvey would be the best man to provide since he had been constantly on the spot for the first four months of DECL's life.

As I should have anticipated, Mr. Masterman was very angry, despite my full explanation. After a few minutes of strong talk, he decided to call Newark and I encouraged him to do so, feeling that it might be better if his anger were allowed to take its course. So, as you know, he called Al and used the Harvey matter as a peg on which to hang a lot of strong feelings. I should add that by the end of the evening he was again in a good mood and even expressed his admiration for the way in which Al had stood the blast.

After all that, I gained very little information from Harvey, and I doubt very much if I could add anything to what you have already learnt from that quarter. We didn't talk much about DECL but we talked enough for it to be clear that Harvey certainly does not bear Mr. Masterman any great ill will—and this is perhaps a sign that he recognises that there was some justice in his dismissal.

2. **The disagreement about Jones.** The whole Jones business showed clearly many of the weaknesses in the present DECL setup. It showed, above all, that there was no one on this side of the Atlantic in whose opinion the NEPCO management could have permanent confidence. One could say that the basic issue of disagreement between Sam Morey and the three English directors concerned the importance which should have been given to Jones's technical ability. Because the three English directors were quite unable to judge his technical qualifications for the position they naturally judged him on his general behaviour and tried to see what his character was like. In these respects, Jones was found sadly wanting, not only because of his conduct in the directors' meeting itself (conduct of which Williamson disapproved strongly as well as the three directors), but also because on a recent occasion he had drunk altogether too much in Mr. Masterman's presence and had actually been ill over the lunch table in a public place when sitting opposite him. When one considers the fairly narrow criteria by which the English directors judged Jones, it is not in the slightest surprising that they should have turned him down. Sam Morey, on the other hand, being satisfied completely as to Jones's technical ability and knowing that DECL very badly needed someone in everyday charge who knew something about electronics, was naturally disposed to take an optimistic view of Jones's character and to feel that all he needed was a strong guiding hand.

The Jones situation was aggravated by the lack of other possible candidates for the general manager's position. You on your side were far too busy to do anything but hope that the right man would somehow turn up on the English side, and because you were forced to pin so much hope on Jones being suitable, you were naturally very disappointed when he turned out not to be as far as the English directors were concerned. The English directors, on the other hand, regarded the finding of a general manager as being primarily an American responsibility, if I read correctly between the lines of a letter written by Mr. Masterman to Al Nelson on April 19th of this year.

The result was that no one set about finding a general manager in the kind of way that would, I think, have been obvious to you all had you not had so many other demands on your time and thought. Surely once you had decided that a general manager was needed at DECL and you had determined how much you were prepared to pay him, the next step should have been to find out how these things are done in England (and as far as I know, Mr. Masterman is right in thinking that advertising is the best way since I don't think we have any technical employment agencies). Then you could have collected five to ten candidates and would surely have been able to agree on both the character and the competence of one of them, particularly if you personally had coincided your visit with the selection process. I realise that you were reluctant to commit yourselves to the expense of advertising if it could be avoided, but the alternative has been five months of failure to find a general manager, during which time you have not had the flow of experienced information from any aspect of the DECL operation on which alone important decisions could have and should have been based.

I have tried with the above remarks to put the Jones business in its proper perspective, and in particular to show that it has received unnecessary emphasis in your minds because too many hopes were needlessly pinned on Jones. Let me now pass on to make one or two other comments on the matter. I sympathise a good deal with your feelings of bewilderment, because you were definitely led to expect at the beginning that Jones would be very satisfactory to all concerned (see Mr. Masterman's letter to Al Nelson of April 19, 1961: ". . . whilst I have every confidence in Jones. . ."). Jones rather tactlessly took his employment for granted long before he should have done and this is largely what upset the English directors, who strongly objected to someone saying that he would do this and that before he had any authority to give orders. Sam Morey made matters somewhat worse, probably because he felt that you in America would back his opinion against that of the English directors and would appoint Jones regardless. At any rate, I feel that Mr. Masterman is probably correct in thinking that Sam Morey promised Jones the job, even after the directors' meeting on May 12, and, as you can imagine, the English directors were very offended indeed. I wish I could have met Jones if only to satisfy my own curiosity; however, I didn't think it was worth making the attempt to do so. My tentative opinion is that an unreliable general manager, no matter how good he may be technically, is the last thing that DECL should have at the present time, and that most of the evidence points to Jones being unreliable.

3. **The recent dismissals.** Perhaps the less said about these, the better. As you probably well realise by now, your failure to pay enough attention to the opinion of the English directors or to acquaint them thoroughly in writing with the reasons for the dismissals was regarded almost as an insult, and I am a little surprised that all three did not resign there and then after it had been so clearly shown that you had very little respect for their judgement. I arrived at Okehampton to find Mr. Masterman almost beside himself with indignation and I had to agree that you could have been more tactful in carrying out your decision. Yet here again, I sympathise strongly with the American point of view. I realise that you were very concerned over the amount of money being spent at DECL and that you also felt strongly that the English management did not appreciate this. I realise also that you probably felt you had given way to Mr. Masterman—at great cost to yourselves—when you decided not to appoint Jones; and that, as a result, you were in a mood to be thoroughly firm about carrying out your intentions. I think you probably foresaw that if Mr. Masterman and the

other two English directors were consulted about the dismissals, then a long exchange of views would have resulted which would have taken time and money and perhaps got you nowhere. Therefore, in a gesture of semi-desperate frustration, you asserted your authority bluntly, and the fact that you had to do so surely shows that the situation at DECL cannot continue much longer as it is.

I have not, of course, read Al Nelson's reply to the Minutes of the directors' meeting which dealt with the dismissals, so I don't know how much attention was paid to Mr. Masterman's lugubrious comments about the labour situation in the valley. There is a danger that you may not now fully appreciate the kind of community feeling that can exist in a small English valley such as the one of which Okehampton is a part. It is something that should definitely be taken into account, if only because it is advisable to behave in Rome as the Romans do. The problem lies not so much in attracting labour to Okehampton (there seem to be a number of machinists within reach who could be attracted to Okehampton by good wages), as in the tarnish which the company's image will have acquired locally as a result of the dismissals. The locals naturally feel that the company is in danger of being closed down; this, in turn, upsets the present work force and will perhaps prevent you from acquiring good men when you need them. It may also affect the willingness of the National Park Planning Council to allow you to build further if you want to. In short, your action forfeited a lot of good will in the valley. I only hope this doesn't matter in the long run.

4. **The control over expenses.** Under this heading I would like to group one or two small things. It is always sad in a situation where serious misunderstandings have occurred to see how the smallest things thereafter combine to increase the righteous indignation felt on either side. I wonder if you at NEPCO realise the resentment which is generated at DECL by very small matters: e.g., the refusal to allow a cleaning woman at 2/6 an hour, coupled with a willingness to pay £1,500 for a piece of land that may never be needed; Sam Morey's querying of his Savoy bill and Al Nelson's comment that the bill was of surprising proportions; the complaints at the proposed directors' fees (complaints which were justified, I think); the querying of expense statements, which is interpreted almost as an accusation of dishonesty; the fact that Sam Morey on his sales visit promised gauges that were never sent; etc., etc. All these things have caused irritation and my mention of them is not intended as criticism of NEPCO but merely as examples of how far each side's appreciation of the other's point of view is lacking.

D. *Summary.* You have got yourselves into a difficult situation with DECL and to get out of it I think you must be prepared to supply a lot more money and time before the company is operating on a profitable basis. The root of the trouble lies in the preoccupation of the NEPCO management with the American market to a degree which has not allowed DECL to get the planning and foresight which the parent company should have exercised in starting a subsidiary in a foreign country—and England is sufficiently different from the U.S., despite the common language, to be called "foreign." The whole point of starting a subsidiary operation in a foreign country is that it enables the parent to transplant some of its skill and manufacturing experience to an environment in which these qualities will be sufficiently unique to earn profits. Therefore two major problems present themselves: the first is that of transferring the parent's skill and experience to the subsidiary, and the second is that of adapting them to meet the demands of a different environment. Many parent companies solve the first by making a sacrifice that you have not been prepared to make and sending a member of their top management to start up operations in person; and they solve the second temporarily by keeping him there for a year or two. By that time it is hoped that the subsidiary will be beginning to earn profits and that someone will have been trained sufficiently well in the ways of the parent company to be able to manage the subsidiary from that point on with the full confidence of the parent company.

By contrast, you at NEPCO have tried to mold DECL around two people whose qualifications for the task in hand were tenuous when judged from a coldly practical point of view. And you have tried to communicate NEPCO's skill and experience to the necessary degree by having Jack Turpin in Newark for a few weeks, by a few conversations with Mr. Masterman, by sending Bill Ryles over at the outset for six weeks, by a couple of fire-fighting visits from yourself and Sam Morey, and by a stream of correspondence—all this being effected over a long period of time. Thus in DECL's life to date there has at no stage been anyone who possessed simultaneously: (a) complete authority to direct DECL; (b) complete knowledge of the skill and experience which NEPCO hoped to bring to the English market to obtain a share of it; and (c) a day-to-day knowledge of the English environment as it related to DECL.

The first of these has been divided and this has not been very satisfactory. The second is possessed by NEPCO management who, however, do not possess the third and are therefore unable to foresee problems and take steps to meet them constructively, or to find the root of troubles that arise. No one in England has the third, with the possible exception of Jack Turpin, who hasn't got any authority to speak of. Mr. Masterman does not have the time to acquire the third properly.

This analysis is, of course, somewhat oversimplified, but I trust that it gets the point across that you are at present not giving yourselves a fair chance to succeed with DECL. It remains to consider briefly some possible courses of action now open to you. I feel myself unable to make any positive recommendations since I do not possess (b) and (c) above to the necessary degree; however, you have clearly a number of alternatives before you at this point and some of these are worth comment.

1. Obviously you can continue as at present in the hope that the lack of sales is due more to a slump in the English economy than to any fault of DECL's. But I don't think you can afford to drift indefinitely in this way and, as I said above, if sales do improve I have my doubts that the production side of DECL will be able to cope smoothly without a good

deal more help from NEPCO. Finally, the present situation is thoroughly unsatisfactory as far as Mr. Masterman is concerned, both from your point of view and his. Even if nothing else changes, Mr. Masterman's workload and responsibility at DECL must be cut down. Therefore:

2. You can stick to your original course of action and get a general manager as soon as possible, while leaving everything else as it is. This would certainly cut down Mr. Masterman's workload and, provided you pick a man of good experience, it should take care of any production problems that arise. However, you will still not have a man who possesses (*a*), (*b*) and (*c*) above. Even if you make the man you select as general manager a director to give him authority over Jack Turpin and the same status as Mr. Masterman, you will have to know him very well or else have great confidence in him to give him (*a*). Frankly, I doubt if an English appointee will know enough about NEPCO to avoid his spending two or three months in the United States. You may well think that a general manager need not be given as much power as I have suggested, but I am inclined to think that the more knowledge and authority you can concentrate in the hands of one person only, the better chance you will have of managing DECL efficiently and well, at any rate initially.

3. A third alternative is to send either Al Nelson or Sam Morey or some other member of NEPCO management over for an extended period of time. This will almost certainly not be easy to do, even if someone were ready to go. It is probably the best course of action, but, even so, it would not guarantee DECL's future profitability and anyhow I doubt if you care about DECL's success to the point where you would jeopardize the management of the American concern in this way.

4. You can also, of course, cut your losses (taking a pessimistic point of view) and close down, or

5. You might be able to come to some arrangement with an English or an American competitor who would be glad to spare the time and help to run DECL. Needless to say, I am instinctively against these last two courses of action.

I think you must now decide how much you care about the success of DECL and how much financial risk you are prepared to run on its behalf. You must also take some action in the near future with regard to Mr. Masterman since we have at present the ridiculous situation that he is spending a large amount o' time with DECL which he can ill afford, doing work which is far from being fully appreciated, in America anyway. I think he would be happy to see some qualified person take his place as managing director. If the change were tactfully done, and if he were retained as just a director, he would certainly be earning his keep in a way more satisfactory to all concerned. Incidentally, his influence and knowledge of the local situation in the valley should not be underestimated. He has done very well with the National Park Planning Council and he is a powerful ally to have when fighting the English Customs authorities.

I hope you will not resent those passages in this report where I have been somewhat critical of NEPCO management of DECL. I have deliberately not pulled any punches, since I think I was the only person in a position to deliver some of them at all. I sympathise very much with your problems—running a successful company like NEPCO with a small management is very much a full-time job, and I realise that by now DECL has assumed the status of a rather irritating nuisance which no one seems to have the time to deal with properly. Nevertheless, if you are to avoid further severe financial drain and get a hope of earning a return on your investment, matters cannot continue to drift.

.   .   .   .

Having finished his report, Ross despatched it to Newark with some trepidation.

4. Recognition Equipment Incorporated

THE PRINCIPAL BUSINESS of Recognition Equipment Incorporated was the design and manufacture of optical character recognition (OCR) equipment capable of use as the basic method of data input to large-scale electronic data-processing systems. During fiscal 1968, the Dallas-based company delivered systems with a purchase value of $27.3 million. This represented 39% of the estimated total of $70 million delivered by all manufacturers of OCR equipment. Reported revenue in 1968 was substantially lower than the purchase value of delivered equipment because of the high proportion of lease contracts.

In the seven years since the company's creation, Recognition Equipment had never made a profit. Total consolidated deficit at the end of 1968 amounted to $11,299,767. Consolidated losses for fiscal 1968 totaled $2,689,662. (Financial statements are presented in Exhibits 1 and 2, with notes in Exhibit 3.) However, as of October 31, 1968, Recognition Equipment's common stock price was quoted at $77, with 4,922,012 shares outstanding. (See Exhibit 4 for price range of common stock, 1964–1969, and Appendix B for comparative market values.)

Despite the sequence of seven unprofitable years, top management felt that a major objective had been accomplished in reversing on schedule the trend of increased losses. Profits were being forecast for 1969, but the management as well as the investment community knew that these profits would have to be both substantial and continuing if the stock price were to maintain its level of performance. Under this pressure for sustained profit performance, Herman L. Philipson, Jr., president of Recognition Equipment, and his top-management group were attempting to formulate a set of economic objectives and operating policies which would guide the company for both fiscal 1969 and the next five-year period.

Mr. Philipson pointed out that forward planning for Recognition Equipment had to take account of the company's subsidiary and affiliate companies which became publicly owned in 1967 through sub-

Exhibit 1

RECOGNITION EQUIPMENT INCORPORATED
INCOME STATEMENT

A. RECOGNITION EQUIPMENT INCORPORATED AND SUBSIDIARIES CONSOLIDATED STATEMENT OF
INCOME AND RETAINED EARNINGS (DEFICIT) FOR YEARS ENDING OCTOBER 31, 1966–68

	1968	1967	1966
Income from sales, lease rentals and other operating revenues (Note 9, Exhibit 3)	$13,680,948	$4,015,972	$ 665,478
Costs and expenses:			
Cost of sales and operating expenses (Note 2, Exhibit 3)	9,549,282	3,169,771	1,284,373
Depreciation of rental equipment (Note 5, Exhibit 3)	2,525,507	1,038,823	474,183
	$12,074,789	$4,208,594	$1,758,556
Selling, general and administrative	4,766,177	2,936,203	1,561,873
	$16,840,966	$7,144,797	$3,320,429
Operating loss	(3,160,018)	(3,128,825)	(2,654,951)
Other income and expense:			
Royalty income	323,100	42,000	....
Interest and other income	524,082	70,966	159,156
Interest expense	(590,392)	(669,759)	(397,565)
Amortization of debt issue expense	(15,390)	(44,884)	(43,997)
Minority interest	228,956	....	....
Net loss for the year (Note 3, Exhibit 3)	(2,689,662)	(3,730,502)	(2,937,357)
Deficit at beginning of the year	(8,610,105)	(4,879,603)	(1,942,246)
Deficit at end of the year	($11,299,767)	($8,610,105)	($4,879,603)

B. RECOGNITION EQUIPMENT INCORPORATED AND WHOLLY OWNED SUBSIDIARIES*
UNCONSOLIDATED STATEMENT OF INCOME (LOSS) FOR YEARS ENDING OCTOBER 31, 1966–68

	1968	1967	1966
Income from sales, lease rentals, and systems support	$13,535,731	$4,011,183	$ 665,478
Costs and expenses:			
Cost of sales, systems support, and continuation engineering	9,029,838	3,170,396	1,284,373
Depreciation of rental equipment	2,525,507	1,038,823	474,183
	$11,555,345	$4,209,219	$1,758,556
Selling, general and administrative	4,152,437	2,824,979	1,488,136
	$15,707,782	$7,034,198	$3,246,692
Operating loss	(2,172,051)	(3,023,015)	(2,581,214)
Other income (expense), net	29,816	(596,828)	(282,406)
Net loss for the year	($ 2,142,235)	($3,619,843)	($2,863,620)

* Excluding Corporation S and Docutel.

scription offerings to the parent company's shareholders. Docutel Corporation, 57% owned by Recognition Equipment, was developing an airline terminal baggage-handling system and had recently introduced an automated currency dispenser that was operated by the customer inserting a specially designed bank card. The Docuteller Currency Dispenser was the first in a family of automated equipment leading to the unmanned teller station for the banking industry. Corporation S,

Exhibit 2

RECOGNITION EQUIPMENT INCORPORATED

*Recognition Equipment Incorporated and Subsidiaries Consolidated Balance Sheet,
as of October 31, 1966–68*

Assets	1968	1967	1966
Current assets:			
Cash..................................	$ 3,092,663	$ 521,060	$ 1,659,468
Certificates of deposit.....................	14,475,000	—	6,450,150
Marketable securities, at cost which			
approximates market..................	550,000	—	—
Receivables:			
Trade notes...........................	171,970	664,180	—
Trade accounts.........................	2,917,988	1,028,990	118,694
Other................................	601,191	104,187	42,896
Inventories, at lower of cost (first-in, first-out) or market:			
Raw materials and parts.................	5,297,182	2,237,219	1,104,900
Work in process........................	2,067,086	1,068,147	164,095
Finished goods.........................	248,415	—	—
Other current assets.......................	105,579	171,614	36,017
Total current assets..................	$29,527,074	$ 5,795,397	$ 9,576,220
Properties, at cost, partially pledged (Note 6, Exhibit 3):			
Building, including construction in process of $735,822 in 1968....................	1,762,216	924,334	—
Machinery and equipment................	1,914,197	1,019,073	719,962
Systems for lease to customers (Note 4, Exhibit 3)..........................	18,437,692	9,747,668	5,009,534
	$22,114,105	$11,691,075	$ 5,729,496
Accumulated depreciation (Note 5, Exhibit 3)...........................	(3,417,149)	(1,183,522)	(588,555)
	$18,696,956	$10,507,553	$ 5,140,941
Land...................................	2,353,548	746,193	—
Total properties.....................	$21,050,504	$11,253,746	$ 5,140,941
Deferred costs and other assets:			
Research and development costs, less amortization (Notes 2 and 3, Exhibit 3)...	3,838,700	2,748,318	2,618,013
Long-term debt issue expense, less amortization based on the term of the debt...............................	34,004	495,091	771,897
Other assets...........................	508,218	197,460	27,703
Total deferred costs and other assets.....	$ 4,380,922	$ 3,440,869	$ 3,417,613
Total assets.....................	$54,958,500	$20,490,012	$18,134,774

Liabilities and Stockholders' Equity

	1968	1967	1966
Current liabilities:			
Notes payable..........................	$ 30,553	$ 149,902	—
Trade accounts payable..................	1,927,077	1,813,481	$ 781,023
Accrued interest........................	124,239	140,130	181,431
Other current liabilities..................	991,495	304,971	208,962
Total current liabilities...............	$ 3,073,364	$ 2,408,484	$ 1,171,416
Long-term debt (Note 6, Exhibit 3):			
Convertible subordinated debentures........	538,000	9,435,000	13,561,100
Bank loans.............................	8,000,000	3,000,000	—
Mortgage notes.........................	1,178,149	1,208,702	—
Total long-term debt.................	$ 9,716,149	$13,643,702	$13,561,100

Exhibit 2—Continued

	1968	1967	1966
Minority interest.........................	$3,743,069	—	—
Stockholders' equity:			
Common stock...........................	1,230,503	$ 928,327	$ 737,856
Capital in excess of par value...............	48,495,182	12,119,604	7,544,005
Deficit (accompanying statement)			
(Note 3, Exhibit 3)...................(	11,299,767)	(8,610,105)	(4,879,603)
Total stockholders' equity.............	$38,425,918	$ 4,437,826	$ 3,402,258
Total liabilities and stockholders'			
equity.........................	$54,958,500	$20,490,012	$18,134,774

49% owned by Recognition Equipment, concentrated on establishing service bureaus—called Optimation Centers—that provided a package of services to small and medium-sized companies including batch processing on OCR systems purchased from Recognition Equipment. Most centers were jointly owned with banks.

Mr. Philipson also noted that a long-range plan for Recognition Equipment had to take into account the company's particular characteristics. Not only did he feel that his organization (see Exhibit 5) had shown very little resistance to change in the past, but also that the company had an extraordinary ability to sustain a high degree of risk and uncertainty:

You must remember that this company was started as a small engineering group with very limited financial resources—about $175,000. We set out to build a product which when built most people didn't believe could work. Even if it did work, most people thought that there would be no market because of the cost of the equipment and that even if there were a market, the potential competitors were giants.

That was our first set of risks. A second set involved such questions as the following: Could we turn ourselves into a manufacturing company? Could we develop a professional marketing organization? Could we finance leased equipment and our growth at a time when we had no earnings and the banks had no money to lend?

Our current risk is quite simple. Can profit growth be produced at a rate which will satisfy shareholders and justify the existence of our company as an independent concern?

THE OCR INDUSTRY

Optical character recognition (OCR) equipment was designed to read printed characters directly from documents and to convert human language into a coded language understood by computers. All OCR units contained certain basic elements, such as a paper transport sys-

Exhibit 3

RECOGNITION EQUIPMENT INCORPORATED

Selected Notes to Consolidated Financial Statements, October 31, 1968

Note 2: Research and development costs are amortized on the unit of production method based upon estimated future sale or lease of systems, the total period of amortization not to exceed five years. Amortization to date amounts to $3,073,416, of which $1,300,642 is applicable to the current fiscal year. Amortization applicable to units sold is charged to income at the time of sale. Amortization applicable to units leased is included in the capitalized cost of such units and depreciated, by the double-declining balance method, over the estimated useful life, ranging from four to eight years.

Note 3: For federal income tax purposes, the company has elected to write off research and development costs in the year incurred. There is an accumulated net operating loss carryover for federal income tax purposes of approximately $13,600,000 at October 31, 1968. Because of the difference in timing of deductions for research and development costs for federal income tax purposes and similar deductions for financial accounting purposes, the net operating loss carryover for tax purposes exceeds the comparable amount for financial accounting purposes by approximately $4,000,000.

The federal income tax benefit of this difference in timing will be credited to a deferred federal income taxes account as the benefits are realized. The deferred federal income taxes will be transferred to federal income taxes currently payable as the research and development costs are amortized for financial accounting purposes.

Of the accumulated net operating loss carryover of approximately $13,600,000 at October 31, 1968, $1,300,000 will be available through fiscal 1969, $1,800,000 through 1970, $3,300,000 through 1971, $4,100,000 through 1972, and $3,100,-000 through 1973. There is an investment credit carryover of approximately $800,000 at October 31, 1968.

Note 4: Systems for lease to customers comprise the following:

Systems on lease to customers	$10,898,786
Systems available for lease	6,797,030
Systems in process, to be leased	741,876
	$18,437,692

Systems available for lease include: systems that have been completed, but not yet accepted by customers; systems that have been returned as part of a planned exchange program and are being refurbished to be available for delivery to customers; and systems being used temporarily in internal product test and development programs. In the opinion of management, all of these systems will be placed on lease during fiscal 1969.

Note 5: Provision for depreciation of the various system components is computed by the double-declining balance method over the estimated useful life, ranging from four to eight years. The company does not depreciate components during the periods that they are not on lease.

Exhibit 3—Continued

Provision for depreciation of other property classes is computed by the straight-line method. Machinery and equipment are depreciated over the estimated useful life, ranging from 2 to 15 years. Buildings are depreciated over an estimated useful life of 33⅓ years.

Note 6: The subordinated debentures due 1981 bear interest at 5¾%, are convertible into common stock of the company at $18.375 principal amount per share, and are redeemable after August 15, 1969 in whole or in part at 105% of principal amount plus accrued interest. The principal of and interest on the debentures is subordinated in right of payment to the prior payment in full of all senior indebtedness as defined in the indenture.

The company has an agreement with certain banks which agreed to lend the company a maximum of $18,000,000 prior to May 31, 1971, limited to a maximum at any one time equivalent to the borrowing base as defined in the agreement, with interest at the rate of 7% per annum on the outstanding principal balance. The company must pay a commitment fee of ½% per annum of the unborrowed amount of the commitment until June 1, 1971. On that date the principal amount of any outstanding notes under the agreement will be converted into instalment notes, bearing interest at the same rate, payable in not more than 36 monthly instalments of principal and interest; the first such instalment to be payable July 1, 1971. All notes under this agreement are secured by conditional assignments of the rental proceeds of system leases, and liens on the leased systems. Provisions contained in the loan agreement include, among other things, (1) requirements as to the maintenance of net worth and working capital, (2) limitations on borrowing, (3) prohibition against the payment of dividends other than in capital stock or, with minor exceptions, the purchase, redemption, retirement or other acquisition in respect to any of its stock and (4) a limitation of $75,000 of expenditures to redeem its convertible debentures.

The mortgage notes are secured by the pledge of the land and building. One note with a balance of $968,149 (net of current portion, $30,553) bears interest at 6¼% and is payable in monthly instalments of $7,676 (principal and interest), with the balance due January 1, 1973. A second note with a balance of $210,000 bears interest at 6¾%. Interest is payable semiannually on August 1 and February 1, and the principal is payable in semiannual instalments of $5,250 beginning February 1, 1972.

Note 9: Income is reported herein on a basis different from that in financial statements filed with the Securities and Exchange Commission. In the latter reports income from sales is segregated from lease rentals and other operating revenues. Sales in the 1968 fiscal year comprise approximately 59% of total income, as compared with 53% in the 1967 fiscal year. There were no sales in fiscal year 1966.

Exhibit 4

RECOGNITION EQUIPMENT INCORPORATED

Operating Revenues, Earnings per Share and Price Range
of Common Stock, 1964–69

	Total Operating Revenues ($000)	Earnings Per Share	Price Range of Common Stock
1964.........	$ 0.36	—	—
1965.........	0.54	d 0.46	11½–4¼
1966.........	0.67	d 0.97	17⅞–8¼
1967.........	4.02	d 1.06	47½–12
1968.........	13.68	d 0.55	102–36¾
1969.........	—	—	74–54

Source: Company annual reports and *Standard and Poor's Stock Reports*.

tem; a recognition system or reader; and a memory, code converter, and control unit.

OCR products were broadly classified by the type of reader device employed. As of 1969, there were three principal types of reader devices in use:

1. *Document readers* that could scan one or two lines in a specified location on a document.
2. *Page readers* that could scan large amounts of information arbitrarily located on a document.
3. *Journal tape readers* that could read paper tape rolls produced by cash registers and adding machines.

A further breakdown of OCR products was made according to the number of different fonts (or assortments of type sizes and styles) which a machine could read. Thus, single-font readers were only capable of reading a single stylized type, whereas multifont readers could read many different type styles.

From both a technical and a purely mechanical point of view OCR equipment was exceedingly complex. There were at least five different scanning techniques and four character recognition techniques in use. Despite this diversity in technology, it was felt by industry experts that the probability of surprising breakthroughs in OCR technology in the near future was very low. However, it was also thought that some important refinements would benefit innovators. For example, while scanning and recognition speeds were considered to be at appropriate levels, the opportunity existed to increase the flexibility and accuracy of character recognition and to develop more rapid document-handling systems.

Exhibit 5

RECOGNITION EQUIPMENT INCORPORATED
Partial Organization Chart, January 31, 1969

PRESIDENT (H. L. PHILIPSON)*

ASSISTANT TO PRESIDENT (BRUCE BOSS)

SR. VICE PRESIDENT MARKETING (P. A. MONAHAN)
- BUSINESS COMMUNICATION
- NORTH AMERICAN MARKET
- MARKETING STAFF SERVICES
- R.E.I. INT'L.
- JAPAN OPERATIONS

SR. VICE PRESIDENT ENGINEERING (I. SHEINBERG)

VICE PRESIDENT PRODUCT PROGRAMS (G. TINSLEY)
- PROG. MGRS.
- PRODUCT PLANNERS
- Q. A.

VICE PRESIDENT DEVELOPMENT ENGINEERING (L. NUNLEY)
- FIELD ENGINEERING
- SYSTEMS DEVELOPMENT
- SYSTEMS ENGINEERING
- SOFTWARE ENGINEERING
- MECHANICAL ENGINEERING
- ELECTRICAL ENGINEERING
- DOCUMENTATION

SR. VICE PRESIDENT FIN., PRODUCT PROGRAMS & PRODUCT OPERATIONS (M. J. VOLDING)
- VICE PRESIDENT PRODUCTION OPERATIONS (P. SOHOLM)
- FINANCE AND ACCOUNTING
- INVESTOR RELATIONS

* Mr. Philipson was graduated from Texas Agricultural and Mechanical University with a degree in Mechanical Engineering in 1947. Upon graduation, he attended the Harvard University Graduate School of Business Administration. Prior to founding Recognition Equipment in 1961, Mr. Philipson was president and general manager of Philipson's Inc. (1949–56), a Dallas clothing store, and co-founder, president, general manager and chairman of the board of National Data Processing Corporation (1957–60). National Data Processing developed and marketed a number of systems and devices for the encoding, handling, reading, sorting and processing of optically or magnetically encoded data.

After National Data Processing was acquired by UNIVAC, Mr. Philipson became president and director of Recognition Equipment. He was joined by several key executives and engineers from National Data Processing. In 1968 Mr. Philipson was also president and director of Techno Growth Capital Corporation and a director of Dawson Communication, Inc.

Most OCR products were designed to replace the punched card method of preparing data for electronic processing. This method of data input involved two manual steps: keypunching data onto cards and verifying the punched cards by keystroking the data a second time. Both the labor requirements and the error rate could be high under this method. Thus, newly developed OCR equipment aimed in part at eliminating these steps and reducing labor costs and input errors.

While there was some difference of opinion among industry analysts as to the economics of OCR versus traditional methods of data input, there was considerable evidence that OCR equipment offered time- and

TABLE 1

COMPARATIVE ANNUAL COST OF INPUT METHODS

KEYPUNCH		KEY TAPE		OPTICAL CHARACTER RECOGNITION	
Operators and Machines	Annual Cost	Operators and Machines*	Annual Cost	Operator and Machine	Annual Cost†
7	$ 46,200	5	$ 39,000	1	$ 70,000
10	66,000	7	54,600	1	76,800
13	85,800	9	70,200	1	82,740
20	132,000	14	109,200	1	96,600
30	198,000	21	163,800	1	116,400
50	330,000	35	273,000	1‡	156,000

Note: Assumptions—Keypunch equipment $ 600 per annum
                Key tape equipment   1,800 per annum
                Operator for above   6,000 per annum
                OCR equipment   48,000 per annum§
                OCR operator   9,000 per annum
    * Includes verification.
    † Assumes 30% of keypunch cost as not displaceable or substitute expense for control clerks and off-line editing expense.
    ‡ Over 50 machines, it is likely that a second OCR device or a more expensive, higher-performance OCR system would be considered.
    § Not based on Recognition Equipment systems.
    Source: Auerbach, Pollak, and Richardson, Inc., *The Allure of OCR* (December, 1968).

money-saving capabilities where large amounts of data were processed. One analyst's comparison of the annual rental costs for various input devices is presented in Table 1.

Together with the potential cost advantages of OCR equipment, the inability of conventional input devices to provide data at a rate equal to the processing speed of modern computers helped to create a market for high-speed data input devices employing OCR technology. For example, third-generation computers processed data 1,000 times faster in 1969 than computers did in 1953. Yet preparation of data for computer processing in 1969 took about the same time as it did in 1953.

This imbalance in data-processing systems created a market for OCR equipment which was related to the number of high-speed computers in operation. According to the National Bureau of Standards, over 70,000 computers of all types were in operation as of 1968. At the same time, only about 600 optical character readers were in operation, indicating that OCR equipment handled less than 1 per cent of the total keypunch volume.

Not every computer installation, however, could be considered a potential customer for OCR equipment. One study suggested that only computer installations with at least 13 keypunch machines could justify economically the purchase of OCR equipment. On this basis, it was thought that a potential market for 7,500 OCR machines existed at the end of 1968.[1]

The market for OCR equipment could be segmented by price ranges which related directly to the mix of technical characteristics in OCR systems. Important technical characteristics that affected price were paper handling capability, page versus document reading capability, multifont versus single-font capability, character recognition speed, and accuracy. Generally speaking, low-cost equipment required tight control over the format of data input, while the more expensive equipment required little control over data input because of superior OCR capability and could operate at far more rapid speeds than lower-cost equipment.

Figure 1 is the case writer's representation of key market segments. The triangle format suggests that fewer units of equipment were sold and fewer companies competed in the higher-priced segments. Companies included in the various segments are representative, not all inclusive. The price ranges refer to the price of the optical character recognition units alone. These prices would be substantially higher if total OCR systems, including such equipment as Ink-Jet Printers and Bar Code Reader/Sorters, were used as the standard of comparison.

In 1968 the OCR industry consisted primarily of two major computer manufacturers, IBM and CDC, and six independent OCR equipment manufacturers: Cognitronics, Farrington, Information International, Optical Scanning Corporation, Scan-Data, and Recognition Equipment. While industry experts reported that RCA, GE, NCR, Burroughs, and Honeywell all had OCR development programs, none represented a major force in the high-priced segments of the OCR market in 1968. However, in early 1969 GE signed an OCR contract

---

[1] Auerbach, Pollak, and Richardson, Inc., *The Allure of OCR* (December 1968).

with Farrington for the manufacture of OCR equipment, and there were some indications that RCA and NCR were interested in establishing the same kind of arrangements with independent OCR manufacturers.[2]

At least one industry analyst felt that the future for the independent manufacturers depended in part upon their ability to develop solutions to a wide range of data input problems. Since no generalized solutions were practical, the data input market was seen as one of multiple market niches. Given the already broad product lines of the major computer manufacturers, it was felt that these companies were not in as favorable a position as the independent manufacturers to develop a

Figure 1

PRINCIPAL SEGMENTS OF THE OCR MARKET

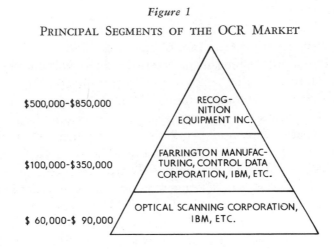

product line to cover all these niches. In addition, it was felt that the independents were in a good position to move from the manufacture of OCR equipment to total data input systems that could include, in a credit card system for example, the credit cards, point-of-sale imprinters, the OCR machine, and the software to tie it all together.[3]

In the past, the technical capability of OCR equipment was considered to be the most critical factor affecting competition; however, several other factors were said to be increasing in importance. Given the high price of OCR systems, effective marketing support was becom-

---

[2] Quantum Associates, *Technology Report: Optical Character Recognition* (September 8, 1969).

[3] *Ibid.*

ing an increasingly important factor affecting competition. Effective marketing depended upon a very special kind of sales force—one which needed to be highly skilled in systems engineering and in understanding the psychology of the data-processing marketplace. Even where cost analysis could demonstrate very clearly the advantages of OCR over keypunching, persuading potential customers to change from a time-tested method of data input to a relatively untried one—particularly in the face of substantial changes in data preparation procedures which were usually required—was a time-consuming, expensive, and rather sophisticated matter. In addition, the heavy financial investment in OCR equipment—often after a recent conversion to third-generation computers—meant that marketing efforts had to be directed against instinctively shy management groups. Thus, one of the requirements for an effective marketing effort was a sales force that could operate in this special environment.

Both the size of the investment and the complicated nature of OCR technology required a field engineering force that could help the purchaser to integrate new OCR equipment into existing data-processing systems as efficiently as possible. In addition, maintenance people had to be available in the customer's installation six or seven days per week.

Some industry experts felt that in the future price would become a more important competitive factor, especially at the middle and low ends of the line. This meant that efficient manufacturing would become in the future an important competitive asset in an essentially R&D oriented industry.

RECOGNITION EQUIPMENT'S PRODUCT LINE

When Herman Philipson and his small group of engineers drew up their initial product specifications shortly after the creation of the company, they deliberately rejected a limited performance system and committed themselves to developing a system with the greatest possible flexibility in terms of character recognition, paper-handling capability, and the ability to feed its input to the greatest variety of computer systems with minimum adjustment. Their decision was based on the assumption that the expanding market for OCR equipment was most likely to require a multipurpose system which could be adapted to a wide variety of situations, and that a small company could compete profitably only with a high average sale.

The core of Recognition Equipment's product line was the Electronic Retina Computing Reader (ERCR). This reader was multifont, operated with few restrictions on forms design, and possessed the ability to rearrange data to suit the needs of the main frame computer. Normally, either a Document Carrier or a Page Carrier or both was sold along with the reader. The Page Carrier provided simultaneous page feeding and stacking and aligned pages automatically. The Document Carrier accepted intermixed paper weights and sizes, handled documents with staples, clips, tears, and stickers, accommodated folds and dog-ears, and exposed paper transport for visibility and ready access. Recognition Equipment's paper-handling capability was considered to be the best in the industry.

In addition to the reader and the paper-handling equipment, a programmed controller (not manufactured by the company) provided real-time control of character recognition and paper handling plus on-line data processing. For example, the programmed controller computed while a document was being read, stored and formated data, prepared magnetic tape compatible in code and density with the main frame computer, performed balancing and verifying functions, controlled the sorting and collating of documents, and permitted the paper-handling and output units to operate simultaneously.

In 1968 two additional products were introduced: the Ink-Jet Printer and the Bar Code Reader/Sorter. These products extended the use of the reader into applications requiring economical, high-speed sorting of large volumes of documents.

Recognition Equipment's OCR system, including the Ink-Jet Printer and Bar Code Reader/Sorter, had a sales price of approximately $1.2 million.

SALES AND LEASES

As of April 30, 1969, Recognition Equipment had delivered or received firm orders for 56 optical reading systems (28 of which were equipped with Ink-Jet Printers) and 45 Bar Code Reader/Sorter systems. Historically, the sale-lease mix had been roughly 20–80. The recent shift in the mix to 50–50 was largely the result of increased shipments to overseas customers who generally purchased equipment outright.

All industrial leases were for over three years, with 50% of the leases being for five years. It was explained that this pattern would change only if some competitor announced its intention to market a revolutionary new machine in 18 months, for example, thereby making it difficult for Recognition Equipment to generate lease contracts for much more than 18 months into the future. It was also explained that leases were protected by the heavy investment in software that a customer had to make when installing OCR equipment. Thus, as a practical matter, it was very expensive to change OCR systems.

Each lease provided for a fixed basic rental, the amount of which depended upon the configuration of the equipment; thus, the amounts varied widely. The aggregate amount of monthly rentals of leased equipment was approximately $850,000. The rentals under all leases included personnel training to be provided by Recognition Equipment and Maintenance services. Rentals were subject to upward adjustment depending upon the number of hours per month a system was used.

Each lease gave the lessee an option to purchase the leased system for an amount related to rentals previously paid. The option prices of the systems under the various leases varied in amount and ranged from approximately $450,000 to $750,000. A percentage of the basic monthly rental paid by the lessee was allowable as a credit against the option price in the cases where the lessees elected to purchase. Each lease could be canceled by the lessee if the equipment failed to perform properly.

MARKETING

The initial marketing concept at Recognition Equipment was based upon two important requirements. First, it was felt that a successful track record with customers needed to be established very quickly if the company were going to survive. Secondly, this needed to be done with an extremely small sales and field engineering force.

As a result Recognition Equipment started marketing its product line by selecting two industries—the airlines and the oil companies—and by limiting itself to a single initial application within each industry. In the case of the airlines it was the processing of used tickets, and in the oil industry it was the processing of credit card receipts. In order to establish a credible track record, Recognition Equipment sought out such companies as United Airlines and Texaco as its first industrial customers. Sales were also sought out and made to national and local government bodies.

By 1968 this aspect of Recognition Equipment's market approach had paid off. Every so-called first-line oil company in the United States, except for Shell, had contracted for equipment manufactured by Recognition Equipment. In addition, many national airlines followed the trail blazed by the United Airlines contract.

As the opportunities for new sales outside these two industries developed, Recognition Equipment concentrated primarily on domestic sales to five key metropolitan areas: New York, Washington, Chicago, Houston, and Los Angeles. This was an effort to conserve the marketing resources and to reach for economies of scale wherever possible. Since field engineers needed to be on the spot to help install the equipment and to service the equipment in case of machine failure, grouping the relatively small engineering force at a few metropolitan centers was selected as the best route to take. In addition, a fairly concentrated group of customers eased logistics problems of providing spare parts and shipping new peripheral equipment as it was developed and sold.

Starting in 1966 Recognition Equipment sought to establish a position in the European market. As in the United States, Mr. Philipson saw an opportunity to establish Recognition Equipment's reputation very quickly if one or two prestigious organizations were to contract for one of their systems. Mr. Philipson saw that because of the degree of nationalization and industry centralization in Europe, there was a tendency toward the use of large, centralized data-processing installations which enhanced the potential for large-scale reading systems such as the Electronic Retina Computing Reader. The first such reader was sold in 1966 to the Swedish Postal Bank in Stockholm. This sale opened up the so-called Giro market.

Giros, such as the Swedish Postal Bank, existed in virtually every major Western European country and in many other parts of the world. These postal banking systems provided checking account, money transfer, and other banking services, and their branches were post offices throughout the country. Commercial banks in several countries also had formed Giros. Although the functions were slightly different, the method of using Recognition Equipment's systems was similar to that in the credit card industry. Thus, Recognition Equipment had some valuable experience upon which to build.

The volume of information to be processed by Giros in some of the larger European countries was greater than the combined volume of the five largest credit card organizations in the United States. In this growing market Recognition Equipment managed to follow up its Swedish sales with sales to France, Norway, Denmark, the British General Post Office, the German Bundespost, the Dutch Bank Giro, and several large clearing banks in Great Britain. As in the United States, subsequent sales were handled from offices in major metropolitan areas in Sweden, France, Germany, England, and Italy.

Mr. Paul Monahan, senior vice president for marketing, explained that Recognition Equipment's marketing goal for the future was to broaden the marketing coverage. The first step in broadening the geographic base was to expand out from the original five metropolitan offices to include Boston, Philadelphia, Kansas City, Toronto, Detroit, Cleveland, Dallas, and San Francisco. The original metropolitan offices became regional offices, taking in selected new offices under their wing.

It was clear to the top managers of Recognition Equipment that success in broadening the geographic base depended, in part, upon available marketing resources. As of 1969 the domestic selling organization was structured around so-called "marketing units." Each marketing unit was composed of one marketing expert, or marketeer, who acted as team leader, and two systems analysts. All three team members received a commission in addition to a base salary, so there was a vested interest in the marketing unit as a team. The team leader was responsible for allocating his time and that of his systems analysts among prospects and existing customers.

In addition to systems analysts included in the marketing unit, Recognition Equipment developed an approach to after-sale servicing which required a company-trained field engineer to be permanently on the customer's premises. He was expected to maintain and repair the OCR system, help the customer with forms design and other software problems, and even do some rudimentary programs upon request. No other company in the industry expected such a broad spectrum of capabilities from its field engineers. As a result, an important question for management was whether men of the requisite experience and talents could be found or developed in time to meet the growing requirements of this function. It was recognized that this could be a serious problem, since the absence of such people would be a drag of serious proportions on the company's growth efforts.

As of the beginning of 1969, 22 marketeers and 63 systems analysts existed in the U.S. marketing organization. Forty-five to fifty marketeers were expected to be at work by the end of 1969. One hundred systems analysts were also expected to be in service by the end of 1969.

It was explained by Mr. Monahan that about 8 man-months were required to train an already experienced EDP man to the point of getting results in selling OCR equipment. Of the $6 million marketing budget in 1969, 31% went for training.

A similar marketing structure existed for Recognition Equipment in Europe. At the beginning of 1969, 23 marketeers were in service, and an increase to 35 was expected by the end of the year. The ratio of systems analysts to marketeers was the same in Europe as in the United States, so an effort was also being made to enlarge the engineering staff. In 1969 a new office was opened in Japan which was also expected to require experienced marketing units in the near future.

MANUFACTURING

Recognition Equipment's manufacturing facilities in Dallas had sufficient capacity to handle about $60 million worth of shipments, although Mr. Per Soholm, vice president for product operations, thought that new manufacturing space would be required by mid-1970 as shipments reached the $80 million annual level. The Dallas plant, besides providing space for executive offices and engineering facilities, also included the fabrication departments, assembly areas, and inspection and testing areas necessary for the manufacture of sophisticated OCR systems. During 1968 land was purchased outside of Dallas for a new production facility.

Recognition Equipment's manufacturing process was basically an assembly operation. The fabrication departments machined parts and produced printed circuit boards, but fabricating costs represented only 5%–7% of total direct manufacturing costs. Seventy-five per cent of Recognition Equipment's direct manufacturing costs represented purchased parts and purchased subassemblies, which were principally semiconductor devices and electronic components, line printers, small computers, and various power supplies. The remaining 25% of the direct manufacturing costs was incurred by the company's own subassembly budgeted at $20 million for 1968.

Considering the low degree of self-manufacture, Mr. Soholm felt that there was considerable opportunity for vertical integration at Recognition Equipment. One such opportunity was purchasing or constructing a sheet-metal plant. Recognition Equipment used large amounts of sheet metal for cabinets, and Mr. Soholm thought that the manufacturers' high profit margins on sales could be saved. An investment in a 50-man plant was estimated to cost about $1 million.

Another possibility was the self-manufacture of power supplies that help transform electric current to a level suitable for transistors. This was not believed to be a very profitable item for suppliers, but in-house production could assure product uniformity which was difficult to maintain with three separate suppliers. In this case the investment in manufacturing facilities would not be high, since it would essentially require only assembly space. The heaviest investment in time and money would be product design.

A third possibility was the assembly of their own computer rather than purchasing complete units from the outside. Mr. Soholm estimated that a minimum of $100,000 would be required to set up for this kind of assembly work. A similar option existed for other electronic components, although in this case suppliers for components such as integrated circuits were giants and would be tough to match on a cost basis. An initial investment in a plant manufacturing electronic components was estimated to cost at least $2 to $3 million.

Despite the costs and the additional management problems associated with enlarging the manufacturing organization, Mr. Soholm argued for the serious consideration of at least some of his vertical integration proposals. He argued, first of all, that the profits of vendors could be eliminated on many items. In this context, he estimated savings for 1970 as shown in Table 2, assuming that his first three proposals for self-manufacture were accepted.

TABLE 2

ESTIMATED 1970 SAVINGS OF VENDORS' PROFITS
THROUGH PROPOSED SELF-MANUFACTURE

Sheet metal	$ 250,000
Power supplies	75,000
Computers	1,000,000*

* Based upon 95 computers at a saving of approximately $11,000 per computer.

Secondly, Mr. Soholm argued that with a larger working force general overhead could be spread over a larger number of workers so that the hourly labor rate would go down—at least to the point where new overhead expenses would be incurred. Third, Mr. Soholm felt that a greater degree of vertical integration would allow Recognition Equipment to exercise a greater degree of control over quality. Fourth, a large volume of self-manufacturing would mean better utilization of existing equipment, some of which was operating without "a base load." Finally, Mr. Soholm thought that the nature of competition would be changing in the future and that the competition in the 1970's may well be based upon price. This would require considerable attention to costs which, he felt, should be stressed now rather than later, when it would be too late.

Whatever the economies that could be made through vertical integration, it was not expected that they could change the essentially job-shop nature of the manufacturing process. An OCR system including a Document Carrier, Ink-Jet Printer, and Bar Code Reader/Sorter took as much as four and one-half months to manufacture and another two months to test by the quality control group. The most time-consuming aspect of this process was the installation and testing of complex wiring systems.

ENGINEERING AND NEW PRODUCT DEVELOPMENT

The three principal engineering activities at Recognition Equipment —development engineering, field engineering, and documentation— were the responsibility of Mr. Israel Sheinberg, a senior vice president. The largest group was development engineering, headed by Mr. Leonard Nunley, vice president. Mr. Nunley was responsible for both the development of new products and the solution of current engineering problems related to manufacturing and product performance. He was also responsible for several engineering support groups—software, mechanical, and electrical engineering—which provided specialists to product development teams.

The critical role of engineering at Recognition Equipment was signaled by Mr. Philipson's comments to company shareholders in early 1969:

In our field, technological leadership is a key element of success. This is true because profit results from leadership, not merely from competence. In addition, the leadership must be something of real value to our customers. Unless we maintain our leadership position, profits will become marginal. Since technological leadership is transitory, our position either improves or worsens continuously.

Recognition Equipment's engineering and research objectives were to preserve this technological leadership. As explained by Mr. Sheinberg:

We want to exploit new applications of data handling and data conversion techniques where there is poor automation at present and where there is the opportunity to compete on many service dimensions. This last point is important because if the value of our products to our customers is too high to price in very precise terms, then the road is open for a high rate of profitability for Recognition Equipment.

Sustaining technical leadership in OCR required both dollars and organization. Recognition Equipment's total engineering and research budget in 1969 was $5.5 million. Approximately half of this represented support money for existing products, while the remaining half went to new product development. Support money was expensed as incurred; product development costs were capitalized and depreciated over the life of the products, which averaged 6.5 years.

The company's research budget was expected to grow in proportion to the increase in shipments. For the near term at least, it was explained that Recognition Equipment would be attempting to develop a broader line of data input equipment. In an attempt to penetrate the market for smaller OCR systems, the development engineering group was working on a system that would sell for about $500,000. This new system, called Input 2, was designed to include a small Document Carrier and a Hand Print Reader Module. It was intended that this new system would be sold to public utilities, the various parts of the Bell System, brokers, and commercial banks.

The newest component to this system was the Hand Print Reader Module. Initial investments in the development of this module were expected to run around $1 million over a two-year period. This new reader utilized new OCR principles, including feature recognition rather than the current system of pattern matching.

Recognition Equipment's first experience with a hand print reader prototype had not been completely successful. An alphabetic and numeric reader had been announced in the summer of 1967, and the first prototype was to go into service at the Library of Congress. When the equipment was built, however, it was capable of reading only numerics and some symbols at an acceptable level of reading reliability. Since the machine's installation in December, 1968, Recognition Equipment's engineers were trying to develop an acceptable alphabetic performance capability.

In addition to this smaller OCR system with hand print capability other new product options existed, all of which could drain off substantial chunks of future cash flows. These options included special sorting and recognition equipment for the credit card industry, remote OCR systems to be adapted to time-sharing systems, and the like. All required substantial investments; thus, it was felt that investing in technological leadership had a very real impact on the level of both near-term and long-term profits.

Mr. Nunley explained that dollars alone could not insure technological leadership. Equally as important was an organization that balanced market-oriented product development with risk taking. According to Mr. Nunley, market-oriented product development was based upon identifying demonstrated needs in the marketplace. At Recognition Equipment these "demonstrated needs" were spotted through a very informal process. While three slots existed for product planners in a separate product programs department (see Exhibit 5), only one was filled. Actual product planning was therefore the result of feedback from the recently established marketing research group, the creative thinking of the development engineering group, and the principal company executives.

Mr. Nunley explained that risk taking referred to occasional leap-frogging of certain technologies which stood the chance of rising and falling very rapidly—such as was the case with hybrid circuits.

No basic research was undertaken at Recognition Equipment. In the words of Mr. Nunley, "Basic research is often like faith without works." Mr. Nunley explained that it was crucial for a company like Recognition Equipment, with limited financial resources, to base the product development program upon a realistic market concept.

The timing of new product introduction was also a critical concern of the engineering department. Often difficult trade-offs had to be made between development time, on the one hand, and product performance and manufacturing cost, on the other, which affected the company's market and financial position. For example, the development of the Ink-Jet Printer initially had to be slowed down because of limited financial resources, yet because of commitments of delivery certain risks in design and testing had to be taken at the end of the development cycle. While the manufacturing and performance problems were successfully worked out in the case of the Ink-Jet Printer, top management was aware that serious mistakes could be multiplied as sales volume built up. Mr. Philipson felt that no adequate approach had been developed to deal with this problem, although as a result of the Ink-Jet Printer experience the company adopted a system of product program management.

PRODUCT PROGRAMS

The function of product programs at Recognition Equipment was to provide a vehicle for relating the marketing, manufacturing, and research functions. These programs were drawn up by the Product Programs Department which had the task of planning new products, testing new and existing products, maintaining product quality, establishing company shipping schedules, and monitoring schedule performance and cost objectives. As such, a product program was basically a procedure for bringing new products from the laboratory to the marketplace. Figure 2 represents the steps in this procedure.

During the product planning stage market opportunities that were spotted by either the marketing or engineering departments were discussed by the Operations Committee whose job was to decide upon product objectives and design specifications. Once these objectives and specifications were established, a program manager normally entered the picture and was assigned to guide the project through manufacturing to final installation. His main function was to coordinate the network of engineering and testing activities. Program managers received assistance in product testing, quality assurance, and contract fulfillment from specialists located in the Product Programs Department.

Figure 2

SCHEMATIC REPRESENTATION OF A PRODUCT PROGRAM

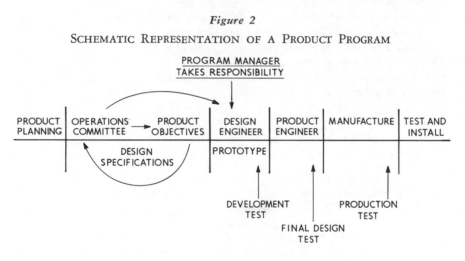

As of 1968 the Product Program Department was under the jurisdiction of Mr. Merle Volding, the senior vice president for finance, product programs, and product operations. In early 1969 top management was considering splitting up the department so that the product planning, product testing, and quality assurance functions would stay under Mr. Volding while the contract fulfillment and program management functions would be placed under a senior vice president of operations, responsible for all engineering, manufacturing, and marketing activities. Mr. Philipson was concerned whether or not this new arrangement would provide a more effective vehicle for resolving some of the painful trade-offs that affected new product development and introduction.

FINANCE

Mr. Tom Forman, treasurer of Recognition Equipment, offered these comments in reviewing the company's current financial position:

> If you look into our financial history and present position, I think you will see that Recognition Equipment has no serious financial problems. Without showing any current profits we have successfully managed five private and two public financings. We now have an $18 million line of credit with our banks, of which only $10 million has been taken down.

Mr. Volding added some historical perspective:[4]

> An important factor which enabled us to finance our company successfully under adverse conditions was the confidence of the financial community in our financial planning. We were able to keep our bankers' confidence by operating according to plan. After we made explicit certain key checkpoints in our plan, the financial community measured our progress in terms of achieving these goals. And two of our three checkpoints have already been met satisfactorily. The first was the bottoming out of monthly losses in late 1967, and the second was reducing our annual losses in 1968 below those of the preceding two years. Our third checkpoint is profits for 1969.

This third check point was a current topic of discussion for both the financial community and Recognition Equipment's top managers alike. Mr. Forman addressed himself to the issue in the following manner:

> Of course, everyone knows that when profits are finally made, they'll have to be big because then traditional market criteria such as P/E ratios may be used to value our stock. However, it's a ticklish job predicting profits due to our fluctuating lease-sale ratio. If the trend toward high ratio of sales continues, then we should be seeing a greater level of profits. If we find ourselves with a heavy lease ratio and accelerated depreciation on our leased equipment, then we will be deferring profits for the future, providing our leases are renewed.

Despite the challenge of Recognition Equipment's third checkpoint, both Mr. Volding and Mr. Forman claimed that the company was not faced with substantial financial risk. It was explained that the only potential financial problem would be an inability of the marketing group to generate long-term leases of three years or more which the company could borrow against. Such an inability, coupled with a high proportion of leases, could conceivably cause a squeeze on funds.

The finance group at Recognition Equipment acknowledged that even with the currently adequate levels of financing, primary attention in the future had to be given to balancing future cash flows with the

---

[4] See Appendix A for a detailed financial history of Recognition Equipment.

cash demands of growth. In addition, while the short-term financial goal was "to make a profit which will satisfy our shareholders," longer-term financial goals had to be established. This, however, posed a difficult problem for the finance group, since the company did not have a "profitable track record" that could serve as a forecasting base and no other companies were thought to be similar enough for the purposes of comparison. Thus, it was thought that return on sales and return on investment criteria had only limited usefulness in constructing a financial plan for the future at this time.

Despite the difficulty in establishing concrete financial goals, certain important decisions had already been taken regarding the company's operating subsidiaries. During 1968 Recognition Equipment reduced its equity position in Corporation S and Docutel by undertaking rights offerings to existing Recognition Equipment shareholders. (See Appendix A.) The purposes of reducing the parent's equity position were several in number. First, Mr. Philipson felt that new routes for future financing of the subsidiaries would open up if they were separate from Recognition Equipment. Equally important from an operating point of view was that this financial move allowed Mr. Philipson to segregate formally minor operations from major ones and to impose discipline upon these new ventures by giving them total exposure to the public. In this way, Mr. Philipson felt these small operations could attract top managers with stock options in fledgling enterprises and reward their managers in proportion to their own performance. Thirdly, the rights offerings gave shareholders the choice of whether or not to invest in other products and services while the manufacture and sale of OCR equipment was still unprofitable. Finally, those shareholders who did not want to reinvest could sell their rights and thereby, in effect, take a dividend payment although their company was unprofitable. Although a precedent had been established with Corporation S and Docutel, Mr. Philipson thought that both the advantages and disadvantages of this policy should be reviewed in the process of formalizing a financial strategy for the firm.

In 1969 about 15% of Recognition Equipment's outstanding stock was held by officers of the company and members of the board of directors. Table 3 lists the company's five largest stockholders as of October 31, 1968.

Ten houses made a market for Recognition Equipment's securities, including Merrill Lynch; Faulkner, Dawkins, and Sullivan; Blyth and Company; Troster Singer and Company; R. W. Pressprich and Com-

TABLE 3

RECOGNITION EQUIPMENT'S FIVE LARGEST STOCKHOLDERS, OCTOBER 31, 1968

Stockholder	Number of Shares	% Outstanding Stock
U.S. Trust Company of New York...........	463,000	9.4
Chemical Bank of New York................	381,000	7.7
Fireman's Fund Insurance Company.........	360,000	7.3
Techno Growth Capital Corporation*.......	320,000	6.7
Faulkner, Dawkins, and Sullivan†..........	213,000	4.3

* Mr. Philipson was a director of Techno Growth Capital Corporation.
† Mr. Richard Dawkins was a director of Recognition Equipment Incorporated.

pany; Singer and Mackie, Inc.; G. A. Saxton; Rotan Mosle, Wertheim and Company; and First Southwest Company.

MANAGEMENT OF SUBSIDIARIES

Despite the separation of Docutel and Corporation S from the parent company in a financial sense, operating relationships with Recognition Equipment remained very close. Most corporate staff work such as accounting was provided by Recognition Equipment.

In the case of Corporation S, the forward planning activities of the two companies were also closely tied together. For example, the Optimation Centers planned by Corporation S were to use Recognition Equipment's machines; thus, the growth of Corporation S would affect Recognition Equipment's order backlog. But even more important, the marketing activities of the two companies were seen as being closely interrelated. Optimation service marketing personnel were selling a concept quite like that sold by Recognition Equipment salesmen. Optimation was a computer input automation service that permitted a number of organizations in the same industry or geographical area to share use of the Electronic Retina Computing Reader. Subscribers paid a fixed unit price for each document processed—much like using an office copier. Except for the time-sharing aspect, the data input service was identical to that offered by Recognition Equipment salesmen. In addition, both companies were seeking the same kind of customers—airlines, banks, insurance companies, and government agencies. Size of customer was the principal dividing line in the sales territory. Yet, the two approaches were complementary and needed to be coordinated to avoid double coverage and competitive selling.

As of the end of fiscal 1968, neither Corporation S nor Docutel had shown profits. Docutel was experiencing encouraging success in placing its automated currency dispenser in major metropolitan banks. Corporation S had only one Optimation Center, although 12 more were planned to be in operation by November 1, 1969.

The break-even point of Corporation S was directly related to its rate of expansion. It was estimated that each center would require an initial investment of $1.5 million and would take between 8 and 12 months to break even. One way in which Corporation S was hoping to reduce the required investment was to enter into joint ventures with commercial banks or one-bank holding companies. Corporation S planned to participate with only one bank in a given area.

INITIAL STEPS IN LONG-RANGE PLANNING

As a first step in defining the most desirable role for Recognition Equipment in the world of the 1970's, Mr. Philipson asked Mr. Bruce Boss, assistant to the president, to take some time to think about possible strategies for the future. Mr. Philipson's only guideline to Mr. Boss was his goal that Recognition Equipment be a "major factor in the electronic data-processing industry by 1975." Mr. Boss interpreted this goal as meaning 3%–5% of total EDP sales, or as much as $750–$900 million in company sales. While internal growth alone would probably not be adequate to achieve this goal, Mr. Boss nevertheless concentrated his attention on the present business of Recognition Equipment. After initiating an informal study, Mr. Boss described three basic possibilities for the company.

The first possibility can be termed the "state-of-the-art" strategy and consists of concentration on the maintenance of increased technological leadership in large-scale OCR systems and OCR techniques. The resultant product line would be narrow but highly advanced, and the company would expect to assume in excess of 60% of the total market for its products. If technological advances were sufficient, the resultant market would be sufficient to produce acceptable financial results.

A second strategy can be called the specific market strategy. Under such a strategy an effort would be made to pinpoint specific areas in the general data processing market which can be expected to experience high rates of growth. Product innovations would be planned to fulfill the system requirements of the specific market sector so identified. One advantage would be maximizing the probability of success through concentration on high growth areas. In addition, the risk of running with a single product, as in the state-of-the-art strategy, would be decreased. However, there is always the risk of market miscalculation which could sap resources necessary for the continued development of our main line of products.

A third basic strategy can be termed an expanded market approach. This approach would provide for the programmed introduction of a broad line of peripheral devices and would have as an ultimate goal the ability to offer a full line of products covering all means of input, storage, and output. The desirable features of this approach are attractive. By 1973 it would be possible to offer complete systems for virtually any data-processing application. In addition the total market potential at this time would be about $14 billion annually. Against these desirable features are some negative factors. The capital requirements would be enormous. In addition, such a posture would mean head-to-head competition with present main frame manufacturers who may also anticipate the trend toward peripheral expansion and the less important stature of the central processor in the total systems of the 1970's.

The first alternative, in particular, suggested several different sub-strategies to Recognition Equipment's top managers. The first was to continue the past policy of concentrating on selling the largest companies in selective industries as had been done with the airlines and the oil companies. A second approach was to stick with the industries where Recognition Equipment was known and respected and to go after the smaller or second-line companies. A third approach was to search out sales from firms with large data-processing installations in a wide variety of industries. This would represent a marked departure from the proven approach of the mid-1960's. A fourth approach was to search out sales in diverse firms and industries with both large- and medium-sized data-pocessing installations.

The specific substrategies available under the remaining broad alternatives were less clear cut to the top management of Recognition Equipment. This lack of clarity resulted, in part, from the limited usefulness of highly tentative market and technological forecasts. Mr. Boss did attempt, however, to spotlight several potential markets for future exploration. As described by Mr. Boss, they were:

1. *OCR Input Automation.* This is essentially the business we are in now. It includes collateral devices such as the bar code equipment. Potential expansion of the basic OCR line could include such additions as an improved page reader, a reliable and economic hand print reader, a low-cost single-font system, and remote reading terminals.

2. *Financial Automation.* This may be described as the market for systems for automatic handling of all routine transactions of the financial community. It could include the entire range of functions from automated remote bank teller developments as currently being addressed by Docutel, through third-generation demand deposit accounting systems and on to securities exchange automation.

3. *Graphic Arts Automation.* This market is for systems and machines for extending automation in the printing and allied art fields, ranging from

improvements in automatic typesetting and computer controlled composition to automatic plate preparation and press operation.

4. *Retail Automation.* By this term is meant the machines and systems for making possible the "Automat" of the seventies. In addition to simply vending merchandise for cash, all types of goods can be vended in *credit* transactions (on- or off-line) and catalog orders accepted automatically for later automated delivery from warehouse.

5. *Retail Credit Automation.* Although there is considerable overlap with the preceding area, this potential market is conceptually distinguishable in that the emphasis is on accounts receivable automation beginning with point-of-sale capture of data and, with the possible exception of sales from bulk (such as gasoline), would not involve goods dispensing. However, the concept does extend somewhat into what was termed Financial Automation above. Examples of the Retail Credit segment include a credit card invoice billing automation system using bar code sorting equipment, credit card "pre-authorization" systems as being implemented with Bank-Americard, point-of-sale credit transactions data capture (on- and off-line), etc.

6. *Ticket Automation*—This would fundamentally consist of a specialized segment of automated retailing and include systems for automatically communicating (and displaying) space availability, accepting currency or credit instrument, vending ticket, updating computer account and space availability data, etc. Applications include transportation and spectator events, and perhaps others.

After considering these potential markets in the context of other EDP market opportunities, Mr. Boss ranked them all in order of gross revenue potential to the company in 1975. Table 4 gives Mr. Boss's rankings.

It was clear to Mr. Boss that successful exploitation of the various potential markets would depend upon the availability of certain important resources. Table 5 summarizes Mr. Boss's judgment of the

TABLE 4

RANKING OF 1975 REVENUE POTENTIAL FOR SELECTED MARKETS

Market	Rank
OCR input automation, federal government	4
OCR input automation, health care	10
Financial automation	2
Graphic arts automation	7
Retail automation	3
Retail credit automation	1
Ticket automation	11
Data communications systems	6
General purpose computer systems	9
Technical education services	5
Facsimile machines systems	8

TABLE 5

AVAILABILITY OF OPERATING CAPABILITIES REQUIRED BY SELECTED MARKETS

MARKETS	OPERATING CAPABILITIES*		
	Financial (a) initial cash (b) continuing cash	Marketing (a) personnel (b) office/facilities (c) orientation	Manufacturing (a) personnel (b) facilities (c) techniques
OCR input automation	(a)2 (b)2	(a)2 (b)3 (c)3	(a)1 (b)2 (c)2
Financial automation	(a)2 (b)1	(a)1 (b)1 (c)1	(a)1 (b)1 (c)2
Graphic arts automation	(a)3 (b)1	(a)3 (b)3 (c)2	(a)2 (b)2 (c)3
Retail automation	(a)3 (b)3	(a)3 (b)3 (c)2	(a)2 (b)2 (c)3
Retail credit automation	(a)2 (b)2	(a)2 (b)2 (c)1	(a)2 (b)2 (c)1
Ticket automation	(a)3 (b)1	(a)1 (b)1 (c)2	(a)2 (b)2 (c)3

* Key:	Symbol	Explanation
	1	Available internally through planned growth.
	2	Available externally, small effort.
	3	Available externally, considerable effort.
	4	Available with extreme effort, or unavailable.

availability of those operating capabilities that would be needed to enter each of the six potential markets that he was considering.

In Mr. Boss's opinion, technical capabilities were at least as important as the various operating capabilities that may be required to develop and exploit new markets in the 1970's. He acknowledged that Recognition Equipment had established a leadership position with respect to optical character reading, numeric hand print reading and document handling. In addition, he noted that some progress had been made with alphanumeric hand print reading and credit card reading, but that substantially more development work was needed before new products based on these technologies could be delivered.

Mr. Boss also noted that some technical capabilities which may be needed to exploit new markets were noticeably lacking. In particular, he felt that in-house expertise in the areas of data communications, video communications, voice recognition, data printers, and input keyboard devices were virtually nonexistent. He felt, however, that such expertise could be made available from the outside, except in the case of voice recognition. For all practical purposes, Mr. Boss thought that voice recognition would remain commercially unfeasible for some time to come.

It was clear to Mr. Boss after his initial effort at assessing alternatives for the future that his estimates by themselves could not serve as an adequate base for a strategy recommendation to Mr. Philipson. He felt that one of his most difficult tasks was evaluating the several possibilities in the context of recent developments and future opportunities in the OCR industry.

CURRENT INDUSTRY PROSPECTS

In 1968, IBM announced the development of a new fast-reading OCR machine with a hand print page reader. This new machine, called the IBM 1288, was scheduled for delivery in early 1971. Because this new machine aimed at page reading as opposed to document reading and included hand print reading capability, some industry analysts thought Recognition Equipment would have stronger competition than ever before in the market for second-generation OCR equipment. These very same experts also pointed out that such competition was coming at a time when Recognition Equipment—by virtue of its very success in selling expensive OCR systems—was running out of potential customers for large multifont systems. Other industry analysts noted that IBM's competitive threat would be tempered by the fact that IBM was (1) more concerned with the mainframe than peripheral equipment and (2) currently generating great profits from key punch machines and therefore reticent to push the OCR equipment too hard.

Future market potential for OCR equipment was closely related to the increased use of computers. By 1975 it was estimated that there would be between 150,000 and 170,000 computers in operation. By 1980 it was thought that the computer population could be breaking through the quarter million mark as new applications for computer technology were found in communications as well as in management information services. As the population of high-speed computers increased, it was also expected that the proliferation of input/output devices would not only continue but eventually outstrip the computer mainframe business. By as soon as 1975, it was expected by one expert that 70% to 80% of all electronic data-processing equipment would be ancillary to the mainframe.

Sales of OCR equipment were expected to participate in this trend affecting all peripheral equipment. For example, total OCR shipments were approximately $70 million in 1968, and one forecaster estimated that about $600 million worth of equipment would be sold during the 1969–72 time frame.[5] While forecasts were not broken down by price segment, there was some agreement that sales of low- and medium-priced equipment would show the sharpest gains.

There was also some agreement that the opening up of new industries to OCR technology was another development that affected Recognition Equipment's choice of a future competitive posture. To some industry experts, banks—like the oil companies and airlines—offered the next vast market for OCR products. For example, the potential existed for developing equipment that could read and sort checks so that bank customers could get a statement of their expenditures and the location of their purchases instead of a simple debit and credit account. The potential demand for this kind of service by the credit industry was judged as being very large. In addition, the recent bank sponsorship of credit cards signaled another potential market for OCR equipment. Between 1967 and 1969 some 30 different plans involving 2,400 banks were announced. It was generally recognized that the sorting of letters (in postal systems) represented the largest future potential market for OCR equipment. Another manufacturer had concentrated on this market and had installed limited-capability readers in several U.S. Post Offices. Recognition Equipment was completing work on two development contracts for the Post Office. One of these was to develop an effective machine to feed envelopes of various sizes and thicknesses. The second was to explore advanced OCR techniques required to read addresses on letters.

General industry perspectives were as important as sectoral developments. In February 1969 *Business Automation* summarized its review of the OCR industry with their own general forecast and a statement of the challenge facing companies such as Recognition Equipment:

Our guess is that there will continue to be a growing market for the whole range of equipment. Specialized, stylized systems seem assured of a good share of the market, as more and more standardization occurs in the forms used by various industries, making possible the use of effective turnaround documents. The key to growing markets in the specialized OCR area is low-cost machines, and they will be coming. On the other hand, the demand for more flexibility will increase the need for multifont systems. As to individual markets for OCR, it is almost impossible to find an area of paper flow related to EDP that would not

---

[5] Auerbach, Pollak, and Richardson, Inc., *op. cit.*

benefit from scanning capabilities. Even banking, though presently heavily committed to magnetic ink character recognition (MICR), must surely, eventually, move to the greater flexibility of OCR.

While the future of OCR seems unlimited, the same is not necessarily so for those whose total income is derived from the manufacture and sale of OCR equipment. In addition to the computer companies like IBM, Honeywell, Control Data, NCR, RCA, Burroughs, General Electric and others which market OCR equipment, there is a growing list of firms which are, more or less, exclusively in the OCR field. The list includes: Farrington Mfg. Corp; Recognition Equipment Inc.; Optical Scanning Corp.; Scan-Data; and Cognitronics, to name the major firms. The problem with the independents is profits. Take Farrington, for example, the oldest surviving company in the field, dating back to 1959 when it acquired David Shepard's Intelligent Machine Research Corp., which Shepard founded in 1951. Profit at Farrington is still a "tomorrow" thing, as it is with many of the independents.

Just as it happened in the computer industry during its formative years, many of today's OCR firms will probably see no tomorrows, from a profit standpoint. . . .

Appendix A: Recognition Equipment Incorporated

CHRONOLOGY OF EQUITY FINANCING

1. PRIVATE FINANCING, NOVEMBER, 1961–MARCH, 1965: $4.46 MILLION

   A. Common stock, A and B: A sold at $2, B sold at prices ranging from $8 to $40:

Class	Number of Shares	Price per Share	Proceeds
A	52,500	$ 2.0	$ 105,000
B	90,000	8.0	720,000
B	12,500	40.0	500,000
B	22,500	8.1	182,250
			$1,507,250

   B. Proceeds from sale of one- and two-year warrants exercisable at $8 . . . . $ 3,000
   C. Convertible subordinated notes ($2.95 million):

Date Sold	Conversion Price	Maturity Date	Amount
12/62	$12.50	12/31/77	$ 500,000
9/63	20.00	9/30/73	750,000
4/64	40.00	4/30/74	500,000
9/64	75.00	9/30/66	1,200,000
			$2,950,000
Total			$4,460,250

2. PREPARATION FOR PUBLIC FINANCING, JUNE, 1965
   A. Two-for-one stock split: A and B common stock ($2 par) exchange for twice as many shares of single-class common stock ($1 par).
   B. All convertible notes except $1.2 million maturing 9/30/66 converted.
3. PUBLIC OFFERING, JULY, 1965: $7.2 MILLION NET PROCEEDS

A. Securities offered: 60,000 units consisting of $100 principal amount 5¾% convertible subordinated debentures, due 1975, convertible at $25; two shares of common stock; and one warrant, exercisable at $25 and expiring July 15, 1969.

B. Offering price: $150 per unit.

C. Form of offering: 52,000 units sold to public through underwriters; 8,000 units exchanged for $1.2 million convertible notes maturing 9/30/66.

D. Other: Part of proceeds used to retire bank financing.

4. PUBLIC OFFERING, AUGUST, 1966: $9.1 MILLION NET PROCEEDS

A. Securities offered: $9.6 million principal amount of convertible subordinated debentures, due 1981, convertible at $73.50.

B. Form of offering: Sold to public through underwriters.

5. DOCUTEL RIGHTS OFFERING, JANUARY, 1968: $4.1 MILLION NET PROCEEDS

A. Securities offered: 425,000 shares of Docutel common stock.

B. Offering price: $10 per share.

C. Form of offering: Underwritten rights offering to Recognition Equipment stockholders at rate of two Docutel shares for each five Recognition shares.

D. Other: Prior to offering, Recognition Equipment owned 600,000 shares of Docutel common (96.7% of outstanding) and warrants to purchase 264,357 additional shares at prices ranging from $17.50 to $20.00. Subsequent to offering, Recognition's ownership was 57.4%. Offering resulted in conversion of $5.8 million principal amount of 1981 debentures and exercise of 49,858 warrants ($1.2 million).

6. STOCK SPLIT, FEBRUARY, 1968

A. Recognition common stock split four for one.

7. RIGHTS OFFERING, JUNE, 1968: $21 MILLION NET PROCEEDS TO RECOGNITION, $5.7 MILLION TO CORPORATION S.

A. Securities offered: 376,714 units consisting of one share of Recognition Equipment common stock and one share of Corporation S common stock.

B. Offering price: $70 per unit.

C. Form of offering: Underwritten rights offering to Recognition Equipment stockholders at rate of one unit for each 12 Recognition shares.

D. Other: Recognition owns 873,428 shares of Corporation S Class B stock, which accounted for 66.7% of all outstanding capital shares subsequent to this offering, and for which it paid $2.17 per share. Class B is convertible into common on a share-for-share basis prior to July 15, 1971, upon payment of $7.80 per share or at any time without payment if Corporation S consolidated retained earnings will be not less than $0.25 per share after conversion. Offering was over 99.9% subscribed. Offering resulted in conversion of $3 million principal amount of 1981 debentures and exercise of 20,553 warrants ($513,825).

8. CORPORATION RIGHTS OFFERING, JANUARY, 1969: $1.8 MILLION NET PROCEEDS

A. Security offered: 224,889 shares of Corporation S common stock.

B. Form of offering: Rights offering by Recognition to Recognition Equipment stockholders at rate of one Corporation S share for each 22 Recognition shares.

C. Other: Shares sold acquired by Recognition through conversion of Class B stock. Net proceeds of $7.80 per share paid to Corporation S by Recognition. Subsequent to offering, Recognition owned approximately 49% of all outstanding capital shares. Financial statements no longer consolidated. Offering oversubscribed.

9. RECOGNITION EQUIPMENT PRIVATE FINANCING, AUGUST, 1969: $4.5 MILLION

A. $4.5 million principal amount of 7½%, 10-year notes, subordinated to bank debt, to be sold to a large pension fund. Notes convertible into Recognition common at $72.

B. Convertible notes exchangeable for straight notes and 54,000 warrants exercisable at $60.

C. Notes redeemable after four years. Premium begins at 107.5% and declines 1.25% per year to 100% at maturity. Equal payments required in years five through ten.

Appendix B: Recognition Equipment Incorporated

EQUITY VALUATION DATA: COMPANIES IN VARIOUS CORPORATE SECTORS, 1968

Company	Market Value of Equity ($000,000)	Sales ($000,000)	Assets ($000,000)	After-Tax Earnings ($000,000)	Em-ployees (000)	Fortune* Index Ranking
Industrials						
General Motors......	22,614	22,755.0	14,010.0	1,732.0	757.0	1
U.S. Steel............	2,321	4,537.0	6,391.0	254.0	201.0	10
Boise Cascade........	1,115	1,026.0	1,028.0	45.4	29.9	100
Briggs & Stratton....	119	143.7	77.6	11.5	1.6	500
Recognition Equipment..............	354	13.7	55.0	(2.7)	1.2	
Electronic Data Systems............	467	7.7	9.6	1.6	0.4	
University Computing............	899	58.3	230.1	8.5	2.6	
King Resources......	483	48.8	105.7	12.0	n.a.	
Utilities						
American Telephone and Telegraph.....	29,111	14,100.0	40,150.0	2,052.0	679.0	1
Columbia Gas Systems..........	920	707.0	1,734.0	77.0	11.6	10
Southern N.E. Tel....	426	236.0	655.0	28.5	12.9	50
Banks						
Bank of America.....	2,536	n.a.	23,961.0	146.0	32.3	1
Security Pacific......	775	n.a.	6,288.0	50.5	13.0	10
Northwestern National............	n.a.	n.a.	1,196.0	7.9	1.3	50
Transportation						
Penn Central........	1,526	2,021.0	6,524.0	90.3	109.0	1
Eastern Airlines......	331	745.0	976.0	(11.9)	31.9	10
Spector Industries....	18	97.7	52.0	(0.2)	4.9	50

* Industrials and transportation ranked by revenues; utilities and banks ranked by assets.
Source: Prepared by William Fruhan from *Fortune*, May 15, 1969, and *Forbes*, May 15, 1969.
n.a. = not available.

PART III

Corporate Response to Social Change

THE FIRST two parts of this book deemphasize the problems of integrating public interests into corporate planning. The cases presented in Part III are designed to bring such issues into sharper focus.

The primary emphasis of the first three cases is upon administrative problems in responding to external social and political programs. The Clevite Corporation case, for example, raises the problem of financial contributions by corporations to noncorporate social programs. Equally relevant for corporate leadership today, the Auto-Start Manufacturing Company case focuses on those business policy problems associated with voluntary guidelines established by the government.

The case material entitled Corporate Performance and Private Criticism is drawn from two recent shareholder actions at General Motors which will undoubtedly have a profound effect on the development of corporate policy formulation. The Corporate Performance case raises important questions of shareholder democracy and the relationship between corporate policy and the goals of various shareholder groups. The task for the student in this case is to propose an appropriate response for General Motors to the Project on Corporate Responsibility and to analyse the implications of such shareholder actions for corporate policy makers.

The problems presented in Part III reflect an interesting paradox. While drawn from contemporary history, they reflect problems which have concerned corporate policy makers, political economists, and social reformers for decades. Little chance exists that these long-standing issues can be completely resolved after two case discussions. There is a far greater probability, however, that the issues will be clearly defined and argued, thereby providing a base for further study.

The concluding cases of this book should highlight the fact that decision-making at the general manager level is a continuous process. More dramatically perhaps than earlier cases, this material forces continual review of decision-making premises. However, the examination of decision premises and assumptions cannot be limited to the area where corporate policy and public expectations intersect. It is an essential element in all aspects of policy formulation.

In addition, this final part of *Policy Formulation and Administration* should also help students sample the most difficult aspect of administration—the coordination of many, often conflicting, social energies in a single organism so that they can operate as a unity. This is the central management task of the corporate leader and constitutes the basic skill which this casebook seeks to develop.

Section 6
The Business Leader and
Public Responsibility

1. Clevite Corporation

"AT THIS TIME Clevite does not have any plans for direct corporate involvement in the field of job training for the hard-core unemployed of Cleveland," began John Harris, vice president of Clevite Corporation in June, 1968. He continued:

We have discussed such involvement from time to time but feel that now the timing is not right for it, because of various conditions. Certainly there are the economic factors and the proposed mergers which make us reluctant at this time. Also, Clevite has a highly technical orientation. We are the largest employer in the Glenville[1] section of Cleveland, and our staff represents a mixture of races. We would like to employ a large number of Glenville unskilled people, but obviously we can't use our research building in Glenville to start training the hard-core unemployed for simple tasks. Finally, there is just the availability, or more appropriately, the plain lack of personnel to handle a major project. Our people, especially in management, simply have too many other tasks within Clevite that just have to be done before they can be assigned extra work on an inner-city project. We would need a major training staff to start any significant training program in the inner city; this is something we just don't have.

Although few of Clevite's executives were directly involved in the solution of Cleveland's inner-city problems in mid-1968, the corporation did contribute to the welfare of Greater Cleveland through corporate gifts to special projects and major charities, through the individual work of employees of the corporation, and indirectly through "Cleveland NOW!" and the Revolving Fund designed to alleviate ghetto housing problems. Throughout most of its corporate history Clevite had made monetary gifts to the Cleveland community, feeling that this was "part of the responsibility of a good corporate citizen."

COMPANY BACKGROUND

The Cleveland Graphite Bronze Company was founded in Cleveland in 1919 to produce a new type bushing made of bronze with graphite-

---

[1] Glenville is one of Cleveland's major inner-city ghetto areas. In the past 15 years it had changed from a predominantly white neighborhood to one inhabited almost entirely by blacks. In 1967 the unemployment rate was approximately 15%.

712

filled indentations. This product became the first self-lubricating bushing to gain widespread use in industry. With the acquisition in 1952 of Brush Development Company, an electronics firm specializing in electronic equipment and artificial crystals used in various acoustical products, the corporation's name was changed to Clevite to reflect the broadening product line. Clevite's products during the 1950's and 1960's could be classified into two major categories: mass-produced precision metal parts used by automotive companies, and electronic components and complete instruments. Through active work in research and development, Clevite entered into extensive production of a variety of piezoelectric devices.[2] In a move to strengthen its position in the field of electrical energy generation, conversion, and storage, Clevite acquired Burgess Battery Company and Sonotone Corporation in 1967. As Clevite grew internally and through various acquisitions, the company expanded geographically from its original locations in Greater Cleveland so that in 1967 it had major plants throughout Ohio and in California, Illinois, New York, and Wisconsin, as well as in several foreign countries. The main corporate offices, however, remained in Cleveland. In 1966 just over one half of Clevite's work force was employed in Greater Cleveland facilities. After the acquisition of Burgess and Sonotone in 1967, this figure dropped to approximately 40%.

In the decade prior to 1968 Clevite's revenues and earnings had grown consistently except for one year (see Exhibits 1–3). Many of Clevite's products faced strong competition, and thus Clevite's management was particularly cost-conscious. For example, William Laffer, the company's president, recently visited Detroit to negotiate with a customer in the automobile industry who wanted Clevite to drop the price of a particular bearing from 8.1¢ to 7.5¢. Annual sale of bearings to this manufacturer totaled around $4.3 million. A Clevite executive stated that three years ago it was thought that the price for this bearing would never be driven below 10¢, a price substantially below what the bearing sold for when it was first developed. In this particular situation Clevite held to the 8.1¢ price and as a result lost the contract, worth several hundred thousand dollars.

The problems of increasing competition and narrowing margins had

---

[2] Piezoelectric devices generate electric current when they are squeezed or twisted; they also work in reverse, changing shape when a current is applied to them. They are used as links between mechanical and electrical functions in such products as phonograph pickups, transducers in sonar equipment, and vibration producers in ultrasonic equipment.

Exhibit 1

CLEVITE CORPORATION

Consolidated Results of Operations, 1966–67

	1967	1966
Revenues		
Net sales	$162,743,294	$169,727,937
Other revenues	3,836,148	4,007,981
Total revenues	$166,579,442	$173,735,918
Costs and expenses		
Costs of goods sold	$115,924,046	$117,740,145
Selling, general and administrative expenses	32,309,771	32,138,348
Other expenses	2,249,481	2,380,976
Total costs and expenses	$150,483,298	$152,259,469
Earnings before income taxes	16,096,144	21,476,449
Provision for federal and foreign income taxes	7,806,000	10,497,876
Earnings	$ 8,290,144	$ 10,978,573
Retained earnings, January 1	65,465,750	54,337,088
Retained earnings of company acquired in "pooling of interests"	—	4,180,551
	$ 73,755,894	$ 69,496,212
Deduct dividends paid in cash:		
$2.50 preference stock, per share, $.86—1967	233,556	—
Common stock, per share, $2.10—1967; $2.10—1966	3,941,709	3,970,643
Dividends paid by merged company prior to acquisition	47,853	59,819
Retained earnings, December 31	$ 69,532,776	$ 65,465,750
Earnings per share of common stock (after dividend requirements on preference stock)	$4.05	$5.49
Pro forma earnings per share, reflecting conversion of preference shares into common	$3.85	$5.11

Source: Company annual report.

fallen to a relatively new "professional management," as one of the older officers described his colleagues. The resignation of James Myers in 1963 as chairman of the board marked the changeover of management to younger men who had not been with Clevite when it was founded. Although Mr. Laffer had been president since 1955, he was not part of the management team which operated Cleveland Graphite Bronze in the early years.

In early 1968 U.S. Smelting acquired 12% of Clevite's common stock and made a tender offer in an effort to acquire control. The company refused Smelting a position on the board in early February. By late June the question of control had not been resolved. Indeed, the control of the company was placed in further doubt by a merger offer

Exhibit 2

CLEVITE CORPORATION

Consolidated Financial Position, December 31, 1966–67

	1967	1966
Current assets		
Cash..	$ 8,899,411	$ 5,166,436
Marketable securities, at cost, which approximates market.........................	1,609,174	6,973,006
Receivable from customers and others.............	24,659,160	24,174,592
Inventories..................................	37,631,148	39,641,478
Total current assets........................	$ 72,798,893	$ 75,955,512
Current liabilities		
Notes payable................................	$ 2,420,752	$ 1,680,185
Payable to suppliers and others..................	15,418,323	15,740,304
Federal and foreign taxes on income..............	2,538,412	5,372,142
Total current liabilities.....................	$ 20,377,487	$ 22,792,631
Net working capital.............................	$ 52,421,406	$ 53,162,881
Property, plant and equipment...................	43,551,902	38,399,691
Prepaid costs and other assets...................	4,714,551	4,820,534
Cash for redemption of minority shares in consolidated subsidiary......................	622,136	—
Intangible assets acquired in purchases of businesses, less amortization...................	11,381,955	8,134,483
	$112,691,950	$104,517,589
Deduct:		
Long-term debt, less current portion............	24,387,326	11,493,957
Deferred federal income taxes...................	507,529	466,543
Liability to minority shareholders in merged company.................................	2,107,728	—
Minority interest in subsidiary companies........	5,263	9,453,245
Net assets....................................	$ 85,684,104	$ 83,103,844
Shareholders' investment		
Preferred stock—$5.25 cumulative................	—	$ 1,638,200
Preference stock—$2.50 cumulative convertible.....	$ 13,625,100	$ 13,550,400
Common stock—$1 par value		
Issued.......................................	$ 2,013,187	$ 2,010,039
Capital in excess of par value...................	6,531,227	6,440,931
Retained earnings.............................	69,532,776	65,465,750
	$ 78,077,190	$ 73,916,720
Deduct:		
Common treasury shares 134,100—1967, 133,700—1966, at cost.....................	$ 6,018,186	$ 6,001,476
	$ 72,059,004	$ 67,915,244
Total investment.......................	$ 85,684,104	$ 83,103,844

Source: Company annual report.

Exhibit 3

CLEVITE CORPORATION

Ten-year Statement of Operations, 1958–67
(Dollars in Thousands)

	1967	1966	1965	1964	1963	1962	1961	1960	1959	1958
Operations:										
Revenues	$166,579	$127,017	$118,223	$113,980	$105,341	$101,175	$91,874	$95,525	$86,183	$64,721
Income before income taxes	16,096	19,603	19,255	15,527	14,177	12,782	10,021	13,606	13,894	5,899
Earnings	8,290	10,230	9,704	8,003	6,927	6,562	5,143	6,826	6,494	3,109
Cash dividends:										
Preferred	234	—	36	95	115	136	157	176	197	211
Common	3,942	3,971	3,190	2,828	2,665	2,653	2,360	2,254	2,137	2,078
Stock dividend		2%	2%	2%	2%					
Retained earnings	4,114	6,259	6,478	5,080	4,147	3,773	2,626	4,396	4,160	820
Property, plant, and equipment additions	10,416	5,812	7,167	7,149	5,774	6,320	6,438	9,532	5,452	2,186
Depreciation	5,118	3,715	3,526	4,598	4,255	4,333	3,938	3,293	2,867	2,794
Financial position at year end:										
Current assets	72,799	56,239	54,321	54,658	48,230	44,260	41,112	42,136	43,070	35,839
Current liabilities	20,378	15,465	15,432	16,887	14,493	12,509	11,069	10,111	10,472	5,055
Net working capital	52,421	40,774	38,889	37,801	33,737	31,751	30,043	32,025	32,598	30,784
Property, plant and equipment, gross	91,636	69,410	64,095	69,372	67,891	63,443	58,570	53,896	45,274	41,109
Property, plant and equipment, net	43,552	31,174	29,141	31,778	32,268	31,305	30,269	28,224	22,201	20,147
Long-term debt	24,387	4,122	4,708	6,008	6,631	7,197	7,944	8,770	9,616	10,178
Par or stated value of preferred shares	13,625	—	—	1,937	2,403	2,852	3,338	3,768	4,283	4,563
Book value of common shares	72,059	72,140	66,539	65,027	59,843	55,504	51,551	50,085	43,835	38,032
Percentages:										
Income before income taxes to:										
Revenues	9.7%	15.4%	16.3%	13.6%	13.5%	12.6%	10.9%	14.2%	16.1%	9.1%
Shareholders' Investment (average)	19.2	28.2	29.2	24.0	23.5	22.4	18.3	26.3	30.1	13.9
Earnings to:										
Revenues	5.0	8.1	8.2	7.0	6.6	6.5	5.6	7.1	7.5	4.8
Shareholders' Investment (average)	9.9	14.7	14.7	12.4	11.5	11.5	9.3	13.2	14.1	7.3
Per common share outstanding:										
Earnings after preferred dividends	4.05	5.45	5.11	4.05	3.57	3.38	2.63	3.53	3.36	1.60
Assuming conversion	3.85									
Cash dividend	2.10	2.10	1.65	1.45	1.40	1.40	1.25	1.20	1.15	1.15
Stock dividend		2%	2%	2%	2%					
Book value (year-end)	38.35	38.45	35.19	33.27	31.33	29.21	27.24	26.60	23.42	21.05
Other year-end data:										
Number of employees	9,006	6,358	6,003	7,305	7,313	7,145	7,167	7,296	7,268	5,746
Number of common shareholders	10,514	9,605	9,199	8,704	7,716	7,410	7,406	8,558	8,610	8,335
Preferred shares	272,502	—	—	19,372	24,031	28,522	33,382	37,676	42,827	45,634
Common shares (000)	1,879	1,876	1,891	1,954	1,910	1,900	1,893	1,883	1,872	1,807
Common shares (000) to be issued as stock dividend	—	—	—	39	38	—	—	—	—	—

Note: The above tabulation summarizes the company's financial statements as contained in its annual reports for each of the years 1958 through 1967 and includes operations of businesses acquired under the pooling of interests concept from the beginning of the year in which the acquisition occurs.

from TRW in June, 1968. Consequently, a major portion of Clevite top management's time in the summer of 1968 was consumed by merger problems.

CORPORATE CONTRIBUTIONS POLICY

In an effort to form a more consistent policy and mechanism for corporate giving, Clevite management established a nonprofit, philanthropic foundation in 1951. Shortly after Clevite's action came the 1953 New Jersey State Supreme Court decision on a test case in which a stockholder of the A. P. Smith Manufacturing Company brought suit against the company for contributing to philanthropic causes. Although the court held the giving of contributions to be a legitimate corporate function, this test case reinforced Clevite's decision to work through a charitable foundation. (See Appendix.)

The formation of the Clevite Foundation also facilitated Clevite's ability to give to the community the same or an increasing amount each year. In order to maintain a more stable giving pattern, the corporate officers decided to keep the assets of the new foundation at an amount equal to three times the current contributions budget. Thus, in lean profit years the foundation's assets could be allowed to fall below this level, and then they would be built up again by the company in more profitable years. In this way it was also possible for the corporation to obtain certain tax advantages in good years by making larger gifts to the foundation than were given by the foundation to the community.

As was suggested by Ohio law, the Clevite Foundation's trustees were made synonymous with Clevite Corporation's board of directors. On the insistence of one Clevite director who opposed corporate contributions in principle, it was established that the trustees should vote on all gifts in excess of $2,000. This approval procedure differed from the approval necessary for normal business expenses. For example, while the purchase of one million dollars' worth of new equipment would be approved by a rather elaborate mechanism within the corporation, it would not be brought before the board of directors.

Beginning in 1956 the major responsibility for administering Clevite's contributions program rested with Mr. Charles Dilley. Since that time he was also responsible for the various employee benefit programs, and in 1968 the expenditures under these programs totaled nearly $5 million annually. Mr. Dilley devoted roughly 90% of his time to the employee benefit programs, and the remaining 10% was spent on matters related to corporate contributions. His secretary assisted him in doing the preliminary work of screening requests for contributions.

After Mr. Dilley had screened the many requests for funds, he prepared a succinct report of the proposals he believed should be supported by the foundation. These proposals were then reviewed by the company's Contributions Committee made up of the president, three vice presidents and Mr. Dilley. Once approved by this committee, the large proposals went to the trustees of the foundation. Mr. John Harris, one of the members of the Contributions Committee and a previous director, briefed the trustees as to the nature of the proposed gifts and the reasons why they had been selected. The trustees had long-standing confidence in the recommendations originated by Mr. Dilley and approved by the Contributions Committee. The trustees of the foundation had never rejected a proposal made to them by the committee.

CRITERIA FOR CONTRIBUTIONS

Clevite looked with greatest favor on those requests from institutions or projects which were concerned primarily with health, welfare, or education, on the ground that these were "good for the community." The United Appeal fitted this criterion well, and the Clevite Foundation typically allocated 30% of its total contributions to this cause. In addition, over 60% of its gifts was given to education and building funds.

Since the majority of Clevite's traditional operations were carried on within Ohio, and primarily within the Greater Cleveland area, the foundation trustees were usually not responsive to national campaigns for funds and attempted instead to play an important regional role. Indeed, Clevite's contributions as a percentage of profit before tax exceeded the national average of corporations by about 50%. (See Exhibits 4 and 5.)

Clevite directors believed that individual citizens should be responsible for the general areas of culture and religion, and thus Clevite did not normally become involved in these areas. Exceptions were occasionally made to this criterion; an example was the Cleveland Orchestra's new Blossom Center built in 1968. Two factors led Clevite to make a contribution to Blossom Center. One was the fact that Clevite's product line included acoustical devices. The other was that almost all other major Cleveland companies had agreed to contribute to this special project. Clevite trustees generally felt that they should carry their proportionate share in projects which were generally supported by the business community, even when they themselves had no particular enthusiasm for the cause. This policy came from their belief

Exhibit 4

CLEVITE CORPORATION

Annual Contributions Compared with Profit and Budgets, 1953–68

Year	4-Year Average Profit	Basis for Budget	Contributions Budget	Total Contributions	Per Cent of Average Profit	To Higher Education	Per Cent of Average Profit
1953.....	$ 7,931,226			$189,810	2.39%		
1954.....	7,357,419			156,183	2.12		
1955.....	7,936,712			243,558	3.06		
1956.....	7,818,652			178,605	2.28	$ 89,705	1.1 %
1957.....	7,676,000	4.4% after tax	$170,324	171,889	2.23	97,500	1.3
1958.....	7,746,000	4.4% after tax	175,164	131,535	1.69	73,416	.9
1959.....	8,719,000	4.0% after tax	175,600	166,175	1.90	87,775	1.0
1960.....	10,202,000	2.0% before tax	204,040	180,075	1.76	106,812	1.0
1961.....	10,855,000	1.8% before tax	195,400	182,300	1.67	108,323	1.0
1962.....	12,576,000	1.8% before tax	226,300	206,767	1.64	114,699	.9
1963.....	12,646,000	1.65% before tax	208,600	198,769	1.57	102,546	.8
1964.....	13,127,000	1.65% before tax	216,600	212,322	1.62	81,200	.62
1965.....	15,435,000	1.65% before tax	254,677	233,267	1.51	125,267	.81
1966.....	17,140,000	1.5% before tax	257,100	253,942	1.47	109,520	.64
1967.....	17,619,500	1.5% before tax	264,300	279,393	1.59	119,675	.68
1968.....	19,388,000	1.5% before tax	290,000	329,324	1.70	121,800	.62

Source: Company records.

that the average company can usually do very little to fund a worth-while project or organization all by itself, and thus most corporate contributions were "cooperative" contributions.

The foundation preferred to make annual gifts. For projects requir-

Exhibit 5

CLEVITE CORPORATION

*U.S. Corporate Contributions and Pretax
Profits, 1959–66*

(Dollars in Millions)

Year	Net Income before Taxes	Amount	Per Cent of Net Income before Taxes
1959..............	$47,034	$482	1.01%
1960..............	43,515	482	1.11
1961..............	47,034	512	1.09
1962..............	30,842	595	1.17
1963..............	55,599	657	1.18
1964..............	63,059	729	1.16
1965..............	74,200	785	1.06
1966..............	87,601	805	0.92

Source: U.S. Internal Revenue Service, U.S. Department of Commerce.

Exhibit 6

CLEVITE CORPORATION

The "Cleveland NOW!" Program

$177,000,000

Mayor Carl B. Stokes has called upon the entire Greater Cleveland community to dedicate itself to a $1.5 billion redevelopment and revitalization program for Cleveland over the next 10 years. The first phase is to start now and last through 1969 and cost $177,000,000. Of this amount $143 million is proposed federal funds, $22.75 million is proposed local and state funds, and $11.25 must come from private sources. The major emphasis of this first $177 million phase is aimed at the issues of jobs and homes for the disadvantaged, particularly Negro citizens of Greater Cleveland.

Let's Blast Off with Cleveland NOW

Mayor Stokes wants to wage total war against the city's troubles. He needs the help of the community and he needs it now.

That's the idea behind Cleveland Now, a bold, brave and extensive plan of action to rehabilitate this city.

The first thing that must be done is to raise $11,750,000 in seed money. Out of it should grow $177,500,000 that will pay for adequate programs and services long needed:

Improved housing inspection, job retraining and placement, youth training, rehabilitation of the worst vacant and vandalized homes, a Community Housing Corp. to spur construction and reconstruction, child day care centers, health and welfare facilities, aid to small businessmen.

And more than $60,000,000 would help accelerate six stymied urban renewal projects and help stimulate the downtown economy.

In his massive attack on the city's economic and social ills, the mayor has a major ally: the business community. As a full partner in urban restoration, businessmen will seek $10,500,000 in the next several weeks.

Other citizens concerned about their troubled city can do their share, too, by contributing to the $1,250,000 kitty from individuals.

This seed money will need the best soil conditions possible in order to grow to full and necessary size. It will need to be reinforced by an increased city income tax. Yes, the problems are that numerous and serious.

In the past The Press has vigorously supported efforts to help Cleveland. These efforts have been piecemeal works. This time things are different: This is a total struggle to be attempted swiftly and decisively.

Mayor Stokes' keen sense of urgency must become infectious if Cleveland Now is to succeed.

Clevelanders have shown time and again that when the chips are down, they can be counted on to rally.

This time all the chips are down.

Let's start with Cleveland Now.

Editorial
The Cleveland Press
May 2, 1968

Concentrated Code Enforcement on Near West Side, Tremont, Goodrich and Fairfax. Home Ownership program in Lee-Seville area for $10 million. Public Housing programs for Dike Park, Willson and Miles Heights at $36 million. Modernize 1500 homes for $18 million.	
Erieview I project for $10 million. University-Euclid for $12 million. Garden Valley, St. Vincent, East Woodland, Gladstone projects for $7 million. Demonstration projects for $3 million.	
Public and Private Job Retraining and placement program aimed at giving 16,000 unemployed persons jobs during the next 18 months Council for Economic Opportunities Program aims for 2000 jobs National Alliances of Businessmen aims for 4000 jobs Urban League on-the-job training program aims for 1800 jobs U.S. Labor Department Manpower development program aims for 1000 jobs Neighborhood Youth Council summer work aims for 1500 jobs U.S. Office of Education training aims for 500 jobs Cleveland Board of Education training aims for 200 jobs	

HOW THE MONEY

Amount	Purpose
$ 90.75	Neighborhood Housing Rehabilitation
61.	Accelerate Urban Renewal
18.25	Create 16,000 Jobs
2.	Expand Small Business Opportunities
1.75	Planning City's Future
1.25	Health, Welfare, Day Care Centers
.75	Recreation Programs for Youth
.75	Construction of Camp Cleveland
$177.00	TOTALS

City-wide youth program of work training, cultural enrichment, citizenship and recreation plus the substantial rebuilding and improvement of Camp Cleveland.

Cleveland: **NOW!**

George S. Dively

The major industry of Cleveland is being asked to come up with $10 million to help implement the *Cleveland: NOW!* program. The solicitation, undertaken as an official program of the Greater Cleveland Growth Association, is being headed by George S. Dively, Chairman of Harris-Intertype Corp., and John Sherwin, Chairman of Pickands Mather Co.

In addition, the private citizens of Cleveland are being asked for $1.25 million. This solicitation is being headed by George M. Steinbrenner III, president of American Shipbuilding Co., who is also founder and chairman of Group 66, a group of the City's young businessmen organized in 1966 to help improve the City.

John Sherwin

COMES AND GOES

000,000 omitted

Federal Share	State and Local Share	Private Share
$ 83	$1.75	$6.00
40	20.	1.00
17.5	1.	.25
1.5	0	.5
1.	0	.75
Operating Funds	—	1.25
0	0	.75
Operating Funds	0	.75
$143.	$22.75	$11.25

This includes $4.75 million over the next four years for financing a Community Housing Corp. to spur construction and rehabilitation by non-profit groups.

This includes $6 million to plan for CSU, Erieview II and University-Euclid II urban renewal projects.

Yet to be detailed program to aid small businessmen throughout the city to expand and create more jobs.

Used to finance 10 multi-service health and welfare centers plus 10 child day-care centers throughout the city.

Called "Policy Planning Systems Process for Policy Determination and Coordination" it is a brand new system employing computers and highly skilled professionals to coordinate and establish priorities for the city's needs.

Support Stokes' Plan

Mayor Carl B. Stokes' imaginative and bold plan for Cleveland is both a challenge and an opportunity.

The program conceived by the mayor and civic leaders is one of total commitment by the community.

There is a challenge in the 10-year program to marshal the financial and business power of the city in a $1.5 billion reconstruction and development project.

There is opportunity for cooperation never before proposed on such a magnificent scale involving the special talents of all facets of Cleveland's life.

The challenge should be answered.

The opportunity should be grasped.

The goal is a proud, progressive Cleveland where everyone can have the chance to live decently, to educate children and to have good housing and good job opportunities.

The Plain Dealer is enthusiastic about Mayor Stokes' plan, worked out with willing and generous leaders of Cleveland business, financial, welfare, foundation and housing agencies, for several reasons:

● It enlists the entire community in financing a common goal. Individuals as well as corporations can contribute to the great proposal which will combine federal, state, city and private funds and programs for the long-range task.

● It brings together the city's most knowledgeable people to implement the multi-purpose plan which aims at definite targets in full employment, resources for youth, health and welfare, neighborhood rehabilitation, economic revitalization and future civic needs.

● It arranges for an orderly attack on the city's major ills rather than a hit-skip schedule, starting in the central city with priority going to an immediate 18-month phase costing $177 million for things that urgently need doing.

It's an exciting plan. Cleveland should roll up its sleeves right now and get to work on it.

Editorial
The Cleveland Plain Dealer
May 2, 1968

ing support over several years, the foundation sent letters of intent rather than definite commitments in the form of pledges. Merger proposals had not changed this practice.

Mr. Dilley concluded:

> In summary, we are a wholesale giver. The things we give to are generally noncontroversial. A corporation, particularly in a large city, cannot become involved in creative giving, such as Project Afro, one of the high risk parts of Cleveland NOW! [See Exhibit 6.][3] This creative giving must be done by genuine philanthropic foundations which presumably "have money in search of a cause" and the expertise with which to distribute it. Corporations don't have this type of money; they only try to fulfill their social obligation. We try to be systematic, but make no claim to being scientific or sophisticated in our giving. Further, you don't have to follow up something like the United Appeal. Follow-up and control of gifts implies a sophistication in giving that just is not present in most corporations. This is why our method takes so little time. This is also the reason why an independent appeal has to be really good before we will consider it seriously; we much prefer to give to organizations that have proved themselves or been approved by some central screening authority like the Regional Hospital Planning Board or the Capital Accounts Committee of the Welfare Federation.

CLEVITE'S GIVING RELATIVE TO OTHER CLEVELAND COMPANIES

As the magnitude of corporate giving grew, Clevite management thought it would be desirable to compare their contributions practices with those of other companies in Cleveland. Thus, in 1957, the control group was established, consisting of some 20 large Cleveland-based companies which took their contributions seriously and published financial information. Clevite received the cooperation of the various participating companies because of the information they obtained from its biennial contributions studies. The total contributions of each company were compared to the average of their most recent four-year profits, and this ratio was then compared with similar ratios of the other corporations in the control group. This comparative data helped corporate gift officers justify their recommendation for contribution to their respective boards.

The control group was composed mainly of industrial companies.[4] While this facilitated comparison of data, the underrepresentation of the banking community and the utilities was probably due in part to

---

[3] Within the Cleveland NOW! program, Project Afro represented a $30,000 grant to blacks in the ghetto area to establish Afro craft shops to be used by children and teenagers during the summer of 1968.

[4] Membership in the group changed slightly over the years principally because of mergers and replacements.

the philosophy of the president, now deceased, of one of Cleveland's leading banks. He believed that corporations should not give away their assets to the public-at-large through charities. Other Cleveland banks and utilities apparently agreed to some extent with this point of view, since Cleveland banks and utilities over time had contributed a smaller percentage of their profits to charitable organizations than had industrial concerns.

When the Clevite control group was first formed in 1957, Clevite ranked third among the 20 companies in terms of percentage of profits given to charity. In 1957 Clevite gave 2.2% of its profit before tax (P.B.T.); this figure had declined steadily to 1.5% in 1967. (See Exhibits 7 and 8.) Clevite's position in the group in 1967 was tenth. Mr. Dilley attributed this decline to two factors in recent years:

Major national corporations give 50% less than we do [see Exhibit 5 above], and there have been pressures on our budget since 1966. In face of this situation, we have let our gifts, in percentage of P.B.T., decline recently so that our gifts can be justified to our 10,000 stockholders. In fact, now our position can be justified to anyone. I'm sure that if other corporations were giving 3% we'd be giving substantially more. These matters are relative, not absolute.

Following the practice of most U.S. corporations, Clevite did not specify the amount of its contributions in the financial statements published in its annual reports. The annual reports of 1963, 1966, and 1967, however, contained the following references to the company's philanthropic activities:

1963 annual report:

Through the Clevite Foundation, the corporation has given support to education, health, and welfare projects in various Clevite communities for many years.

Direct contributions in 1963 totaled $193,969. Some $81,189 of this was for colleges and schools, and the remainder for a variety of health and welfare projects. During the year, Clevite began a program to match contributions made by employees to their colleges.

1966 annual report:

During 1966, the Clevite Foundation, established in 1951, committed a total of approximately $254,000 for education, health, and welfare projects in cities where Clevite has installations. This breaks down as follows:

| Higher Education | $121,000 |
| Health and Welfare | $133,000 |

1967 annual report:

During 1967, the Foundation committed a total of $279,393 in funds, $119,675 for education and $159,718 for health and welfare.

Exhibit 7

CLEVITE CORPORATION
Sample of Data Furnished to Control Group Members, Clevite Report, 1966

Results of 6th Contributions Study   Prepared for: CLEVITE CORPORATION
1. *Totals from the Control Group for the Years 1965 and 1966*
    For the 20 companies in the control group (including Clevite), the information received for
    1965 and 1966 totaled as follows:

	1965 Only	*1966 Only*
a) Total employment..................	254,530	281,880
b) Cleveland employment..............	57,760	62,256
c) Total profit (before tax)............	$593,669,450	$711,872,948
d) Cleveland profit*..................	$152,712,303	$176,475,353

2. *Your Average Profit (1963–66) Compared with the Control Group*
    a) *Average* total profit of the control group.............. $554,659,932
        Your average total profit.......................... $ 17,141,000
        Your relation to the control group................. 3.1%
    b) Average *Cleveland* profit of the control group........ $144,813,951
        Your average Cleveland profit...................... $ 9,868,000
        Your relation to the control group................. 6.8%

3. *Contributions of the Control Group Related to Their Average Profit*
    a) *Total* contributions as percentage of total profit (before tax)

	1965	*1966*
Highest.............	3.81%	5.62%
MEDIAN...........	1.50	1.27
Lowest..............	.67	.63

    b) *Cleveland* contributions as percentage of Cleveland profit (before tax)

	1965	*1966*
Highest.............	7.79%	4.87%
MEDIAN.............	3.09	2.24
Lowest..............	1.35	1.28

4. *Your Contributions Related to Your Average Profit*

	1965	*Rank*	*1966*	*Rank*
a) Your total contributions as % of your total profit...............	1.5%	9	1.5%	5
b) Your Cleveland contributions as % of your Cleveland profit..........	2.2	13	2.1	13

* The "Cleveland profit" for each year is computed artificially by allocating to Cleveland that part of the published total profit of the companies involved that their Cleveland employment was to their total employment.

The past year was especially significant for our increased involvement in projects aimed to thwart the spreading decay of our inner-city areas.

Early in 1967, Clevite became one of six companies to form the Cleveland Revolving Fund. This organization has as its purpose to provide seed money to support homeowners in changing residential communities in Cleveland in their efforts to preserve their living conditions. Later in the year, we donated funds to the nonprofit Glenville Development Corporation to open and operate a recreation center in a neighborhood adjacent to our Cleveland Research Center facilities.

Exhibit 8

CLEVITE CORPORATION

Control Group Data, 1959–66

I. Clevite's Contributions Relative to Control Group Members
   A. For Total Contribution as Percentage of Average *Total* Profit

	1959	1960	1961	1962	1963	1964	1965	1966
Per Cent	1.9	1.8	1.7	1.6	1.6	1.6	1.5	1.5
Rank	5	8	9	10	8	9	9	5

   B. For Cleveland Contribution as Percentage of Average *Cleveland* Profit

	1959	1960	1961	1962	1963	1964	1965	1966
Per Cent	2.8	2.6	2.6	2.9	2.6	2.8	2.2	2.1
Rank	6	8	12	12	13	12	13	13

II. Data on Control Group Members' Contributions
   A. *Total* Contributions as Percentage of Average Total Profit (before tax)

	1959	1960	1961	1962	1963	1964	1965	1966
Highest	2.7%	3.6%	4.0%	4.1%	5.4%	3.5%	3.8%	5.6%
MEDIAN	1.1	1.2	1.6	1.6	1.4	1.6	1.5	1.3
Lowest	.6	.6	.6	.6	.6	.7	.7	.6

   B. *Cleveland* Contributions as Percentage of Average Cleveland Profit

	1959	1960	1961	1962	1963	1964	1965	1966
Highest	5.4%	6.1%	7.1%	5.0%	12.3%	6.7%	7.8%	4.9%
MEDIAN	2.0	2.4	2.7	3.3	2.9	2.8	3.1	2.2
Lowest	.8	.8	.9	1.0	.9	.9	1.4	1.3

Mr. Dilley remarked that since he had taken office in 1957, no outside stockholder to his knowledge had questioned the corporation's contribution practices.

DEVELOPMENT OF CLEVITE'S 1968 CONTRIBUTION BUDGET

At the beginning of each year the Clevite board determined what percentage of profit before tax would be allocated to contributions. Mr. Dilley then secured an estimate of profits for the year. In order to avoid distributing more funds than the actual year's profits might warrant, Mr. Dilley constructed a "Preliminary Reduced Budget" by reducing the estimated profits for the current year by a factor of 20%. This figure was then added to the total profits of the past three years and an average computed. (See Exhibit 9.) For 1968 this average profit figure was $18,597,000. In 1968 the board had decided to use 1.5% as a target for the level of contributions. Mr. Dilley's preliminary budget figure for that year was $278,900. As the year progressed Mr. Dilley was able to get more accurate data on what the profit for the year would be, and he adjusted his budget figure accordingly.

Exhibit 9

CLEVITE CORPORATION
Preliminary Reduced Budgets
(Dollars in Thousands)

A. PROFIT BEFORE TAX, 1962–68

Year	*Profit*
1962	$12,782
1963	14,177
1964	15,527
1965	19,255
1966	19,600
1967	16,096
1968 estimated full budget (12/67)	24,293
1968 preliminary reduced budget	19,434
1968 estimated full budget (11/68)	22,400

B. COMPUTATION OF CONTRIBUTIONS BUDGET

4 Years Ending	4-Year Profit before Tax	4-Year Average Profit before Tax	Contributions As Percentage of Profit before Tax	Contributions Budget
1957........	$30,705	$ 7,676	@2.2%	$153.5
1958........	30,985	7,746		154.9
1959........	34,874	8,719	@2.0	174.4
1960........	40,808	10,202		204.0
1961........	43,420	10,855	@1.8	195.4
1962........	51,304	12,576		226.3
1963........	50,586	12,646	@1.65	208.6
1964........	52,507	13,127		216.6
1965........	61,741	15,435		254.6
1966........	68,559	17,140	@1.5	257.1
1967........	70,478	17,620		264.3
1968 preliminary reduced budget....	74,388	18,597		278.9
1968........	77,351	19,338		290.0

Source: Company records.

A large fraction of any year's contributions budget went either to organizations that Clevite had supported regularly over the years or to organizations which had been given letters of intent indicating Clevite's intention of supporting particular projects over a fixed period of time. Exhibit 10 shows a worksheet prepared by Mr. Dilley in early 1968 which enabled him to control his individual recommendations to the Contributions Committee so that the total contributions figure stayed within the budget.

Exhibit 10

CLEVITE CORPORATION
Preliminary 1968 Contribution Budget

Items Approved by Trustees of Clevite Foundation at First 1968 Meeting
I. Contributions Already Made in 1968
  A. United Appeal..............................$10,000
  B. Schools..................................... 7,750
  C. Other...................................... 11,075

                                                              $ 28,825

Items with Tentative Approval
II. Contributions Already Committed by Letters of Intent
  A. Education (capital amount)....................$51,000
  B. Building funds 29,200

                                                              $ 80,200

III. Items Recommended to be Repeated in the Same Amount as Last Year
  A. Community funds............................$ 2,820
  B. Education (operating support)................. 31,800
  C. Health and welfare........................ 1,000
  D. Civic and governmental...................... 3,500
  E. Economic and other education.................. 2,500
  F. General causes (e.g., Planned Parenthood,
     NAACP, Cleveland Safety Council).............. 7,380

                                                              $ 49,000

IV. Minor Changes Recommended from Last Year

                                         1967   1968
  A. United Appeal of Cleveland
     (7% increase).....................$66,000 $70,620
  B. Education........................ 2,000   2,600
  C. Other (general causes).............. 23,510   25,000

                                                              $ 98,220
              Total $256,245

New Recommendations to be Considered by Board
V. Proposed New Capital Account Items
   3-year tentative commitment—$130,400 (1968)................$ 43,800
VI. Proposed New Operating Contributions......................$ 12,700
       Total...$312,745

Source: Company records.

When evaluating a new request for a contribution, Mr. Dilley asked the prospective recipient for detailed information about the proposed project and about the manner in which money for the project was to be raised. If he was satisfied that the proposal and method of fund raising were both logical and equitable, Mr. Dilley developed his recommendation to the Contributions Committee as to how much Clevite should donate. He did this by estimating the total gift he expected the control group members to make, based on prior giving patterns. For example, acting individually, the 20 companies in the group consistently gave approximately 22% of the total that the United Appeal received from all corporations. Naturally, for other requests which were less general in their appeal than the U.A., the companies in the control group carried a larger percentage of the total expected from all corporations (usually between 30 to 35%). Since Mr. Dilley computed Clevite's share of the control group based on financial ability, both on the basis of four-year average total profit and four-year average Cleveland profit, it was a simple matter to apply this percentage to the estimated amount that was needed from the control group in order to establish Clevite's "responsibility." This figure was used as the point of departure. Naturally it would be modified by special considerations, such as Clevite's greater interest in certain fields than others. See Exhibit 11 for a fuller statement as to how Clevite determined the amount it should give to an organization or project.

Exhibit 11

CLEVITE CORPORATION
Intracompany Memorandum
A NEW APPROACH TO THE CONTROL OF CORPORATE CONTRIBUTIONS

Few are the companies, particularly in large cities, that can undertake philanthropic projects single-handed. *Most corporate giving is cooperative giving*—a group of companies *cooperatively* help to build a hospital, expand a camp, fill a community chest, etc.

Most Cleveland companies, if at all interested in a project, want to carry their full share of the load, but none wants to be reckless in giving away stockholders' money.

The question is, "How much to give?"

Using a Control Group

Believing that "adequacy of giving" is relative, we decided to compare our giving with that of leading manufacturing companies which (1) had headquarters and operations in Cleveland, (2) published financial reports, and (3) took their contributions programs seriously. We chose:

Addressograph-Multigraph Corporation	National Acme Company
Eaton Manufacturing Company	Osborn Manufacturing Company
Ferro Corporation	Parker-Hannifin Corporation
Glidden Company	Reliance Electric & Engineering Company
Harris-Intertype Corporation	Republic Steel Corporation
Harshaw Chemical Company	Standard Oil of Ohio
Lamson & Sessions Company	Thompson Ramo Wooldridge, Inc.
Lubrizol Corporation	Townmotor Corporation
McKee, Arthur G., & Company	Warner & Swasey Company
Midland-Ross Corporation	Weatherhead Company
	White Motor Company

Average Profit as a Standard

Having chosen the companies for our control group, we then had to pick

Exhibit 11—Continued

the factor against which to measure adequacy of giving. Although realizing that employment, sales, and assets have all been suggested as standards for giving, we came to the conclusion that *adequacy of giving depended upon "ability to give"* and that, in a business enterprise, "ability to give" depended upon profit.

Since it is advantageous both to the company and to the recipient organization for the level of contributions to remain as even as possible, we relate contributions to *average* profit (four years) rather than the profit of any single year.

Allocating Profit to Cleveland

Since most of our appeals came from Cleveland, and since it does not make sense to ask national companies (even those with headquarters in Cleveland) to contribute to local appeals on the basis of their national profits, we felt the need for some simple device for allocating profits to a local community.

This we did for each of the companies in our control group by *allocating to Cleveland that portion of their total profits that their Cleveland employment was of their total employment.* The resulting figure we called the AVERAGE CLEVELAND PROFIT, and it is that figure which we use in measuring our share of any Cleveland project in which we are interested.

How Much Is Needed from Our Control Group?

While it is useful in retrospect to be able to compare our giving with that of a group of other responsible companies, this device is of limited value in determining a company's share in a current campaign unless it is known what percentage of that campaign is required from the companies in our control group. To get this information we wrote to charitable organizations and asked them what proportion of their contributions they had received from the companies in our control group.

Although the pattern of giving is different for different types of campaigns, it is quite consistent for campaigns of the same type. The broader and more complete the solicitation, the smaller the percentage that is required from our control group. For instance, in the United Appeal our control group recently produced only about 21% of the money that came from business and industry, but in recent building fund campaigns of four Cleveland colleges, the amount produced from our control group, as a percentage of the total received from business and industry, was as follows:

College	Per Cent of Business and Industry Money Given by Our Control Group
Case Institute of Technology	43%
Fenn College	44
John Carroll University	44
Western Reserve University	50

How Much to Give to Individual Campaigns—in Advance

By this time we not only had the information necessary to check our past gifts in relation to the standard which we had adopted, but also to estimate

Exhibit 11—Continued

ahead of time approximately how much was our share of a prospective campaign. This was done by:

1. Ascertaining the total goal.
2. Asking and evaluating the amount expected from industry.
3. Estimating on the basis of past experience the percentage of industry's support which would have to come from our control group.
4. Applying to this figure the percentage (of the support of our control group) that we had adopted as a standard for our own company.

FOR EXAMPLE, in a recent campaign the goal for corporations was $8 million. Since Clevite was one of the first companies approached, we estimated that $3,200,000 would be needed from the control group and that $192,000 would be needed from Clevite for the campaign to succeed. We conveyed this in our Letter of Intent, but indicated that *the final size of Clevite's gift would depend upon the giving of our control group.* To date, control group companies, other than Clevite, have pledged a total of $2,205,000, which suggests $132,000 from Clevite—some $60,000 less than the amount originally estimated. Here Clevite was able to use the Average Cleveland Profit approach to become a real bellwether in this campaign and still protect itself against the possibility that other companies might not be as generously inclined.

2/1/66
originally issued 8/6/63

There were many appeals which Mr. Dilley rejected: some did not fit Clevite's criteria, others appeared to be inadequately funded to be successful, and some were judged to be of a lower priority and were excluded in order to allow Clevite to stay within its contributions budget. A list of organizations which were denied support in 1965 appears in Exhibit 12.

TRENDS IN COMMUNITY CONTRIBUTIONS

Recognizing the difficulties and the costs of many independent agencies attempting to raise funds simultaneously, Cleveland established a United Appeal in 1919. Cleveland corporations, lacking the staff to evaluate many individual requests and feeling strongly that requests should be centralized for greater efficiency in fund raising, had applied financial pressure on organizations not joining the United Appeal. Clevite in recent years made it quite clear that they firmly believe that most of their contributions to health and welfare organizations should be made through the United Appeal. For example, Clevite and several other corporations even withheld gifts from the American Red Cross until it joined the United Appeal in 1958.

Exhibit 12

CLEVITE CORPORATION
Appeals Rejected during 1965

American Cancer Society
American Ceramics Society
American Civil Liberties Union
American Economic Foundation—Hall of Free Enterprise
American Freedom Center
American Home Economics Association Foundation
American Heritage Foundation
Assumption College, Worcester, Mass.
Atlantic Council of the United States
Board for Fundamental Education
Boys Athletic League, Inc., New York
Boys Club of New York—scholarship
Cleveland Club—membership
Cleveland Open Golf Tournament—advertising
Committee for Constitutional Government, Inc.
Committee on Electoral College Reform
Colgate University
Consumer Credit Counseling Service, Cleveland
Conference of American Small Business Organizations (gave $50 in 1964)
Epilepsy Association of America
Employment Enterprises Development, University of Michigan
Fine Arts Association, Willoughby
Fleet Reserve Association, Cleveland
Freedoms Foundation at Valley Forge
Freedom-to-Work Committee
Gallaudet College Centennial Fund
Greater Cleveland A.A.U. Junior Olympics
Greater Cleveland Bright Brigade
Goodwill Industries of Southern California
Heifer Project, Inc.
High Hopes School, Inc., for the Retarded Child, Euclid, Ohio
Ingleside Hospital
International Program of U.S. National Student Association
Institute for American Strategy
John Fitzgerald Kennedy Library
Karamu Foundation
League of Ohio Sportsmen
MacArthur Memorial
Mansfield School of Technology
Medico, A Service of CARE
Mercy Hospital, Hamilton, Ohio
Maur Hill School (private prep school)
National Achievement Scholarship Program for Negro Students
National Associated Businessmen, Inc.

Exhibit 12—Continued

National Association for Practical Nursing Education and Service, Inc.
National Commission for Cooperative Education
National Committee for Support of the Public Schools
National Council of Juvenile Court Judges
National Federation of Settlements and Neighborhood Centers
National Fire Protection Association
National Foundation, March of Dimes
National Fund for Graduate Nursing Education
National Kidney Foundation
National Jewish Hospital
National Library Week
National Merit Scholarship Corporation
National Music Camp, Interlochen Arts Academy
National Planning Association
National Scholarship Service and Fund for Negro Students
New York Public Library
Northern Ohio Opera Association
Ohio Information Committee
Ohio Science Education Association
Ohio University
Olivet Institution Baptist Church, Cleveland
Oxfam of Canada
Paralyzed Veterans of America
Phillis Wheatley Association, Inc.
People-to-People Sports Committee, Inc.
Recording for the Blind
Richmond Heights Hospital
St. John's Hospital
St. Alexis Hospital
St. John Ambulance (Ontario Council)
Salem College, W. Va.
Society for a More Beautiful Capital
Student Yearbook, American College of Switzerland
Thomas A. Dooley Foundation, Inc.
Tools for Freedom
Unitarian Universalist Service Committee
United Crusade of Los Angeles
United Epilepsy Association
United Nations 20th Anniversary Commemorative Book
United States National Student Association
University of Mississippi
University of the Pacific
Utica College
Westover Methodist Church, West Virginia
Winston Churchill Memorial and Library in the United States
World Center for Exploration Fund

While the United Appeal served the needs of some 155 organizations, it was by charter limited to subsidizing the *operating needs* of *established* organizations in the fields of *health and welfare*. Even in these fields the United Appeal insisted that organizations prove their value to the community over a period of several years before becoming participating agencies. Consequently, the U.A. performed no function in building-fund campaigns (even for member agencies) or for "ad hoc" projects such as those being proposed to solve the pressing problems of the inner city. As a result, Cleveland corporations received many requests to contribute to large, independent campaigns of local educational, and cultural organizations, as well as to building funds and new projects for the inner city. The number and size of these special requests presented problems for Cleveland businesses.

"For many Cleveland businesses the last straw came in 1967 when we read in the newspapers about two new campaigns with goals totaling $25 million," Mr. Dilley explained, adding:

Few corporate contributions officers knew anything about these drives until they read about them in the papers. We feel that if corporations are going to be asked for substantial amounts of money we should be able to discuss the objectives and need for campaigns before they are launched. The Welfare Federation already has such a screening authority for those of its agencies which wish to raise money. We need a more systematic approach to giving on a large scale.

This incident led to the formation of the Corporate Contributions Council of Cleveland in late 1967. It included the larger firms in Clevite's control group, plus representatives of the banks, stores, utilities and large "absentee-owned" plants (like Ford, G.E., and G.M.). In addition to discussing proposed campaigns before they were launched, the council tried generally to cut the overlap of projects requesting funds.

For example, in April, 1968, Mayor Carl Stokes announced the Cleveland NOW! project which was designed to use both public and private funds to solve some of the city's major inner-city problems. The Cleveland business community was asked to contribute $10 million over a two-year period. (See Exhibit 6 above.) One facet of the NOW! project was a proposal to build 12 neighborhood centers for recreation, child day care, and other activities. The Welfare Federation already had done extensive planning for the construction of four such centers through the Neighborhood Centers Association. The Corporate Contributions Council discussed the proposed plans with officials of the N.C.A. and NOW! and finally arranged to incorporate the NOW!

plans, somewhat diminished, into the Welfare Federation's existing plans.

Mr. Dilley summarized the attitude of the council:

Corporations are not geared to take the initiative in giving; through the council we hope instead to apply business methods to the problems of giving. We are trying to bring groups together, to set priorities, and to raise money for *groups* of agencies. Dr. James Norton, director of the Cleveland Associated Foundations, has made a beginning by setting priorities among the scores of appeals to help disadvantaged youth during the "long hot summer" of 1968. Nonetheless, corporations are being faced now with excessive demands for funds. The United Appeal has been losing ground since 1966 in the face of vastly increased requests for special causes which are made to appear more urgent. The council may just have to dry up some of the campaigns which attempt to work on their own for purposes we feel are not as urgent or as important as the ones funded through the United Appeal or reviewed by the council.

CLEVITE CONSIDERATIONS ON INNER-CITY INVOLVEMENT

Following the July, 1966, riots in the Hough area, Cleveland businesses reflected new concern about the problems of the inner city by changes in their corporate contributions policies and attitudes toward direct corporate involvement in the inner city. During 1966 the president of the Warner & Swasey Company, Dr. James Hodge, proposed a revolving fund with the purpose of guaranteeing loans to needy homeowners wishing to make major repairs on their homes to prevent further blight in Cleveland's Mt. Pleasant area. Clevite joined this fund along with five other major Cleveland companies, each of which pledged to contribute $25,000 to the effort. Mr. John Harris was appointed by Mr. Laffer to represent Clevite on the Revolving Fund's board of directors. This board worked through a community-based housing organization to allocate funds to homeowners.

In 1967 Clevite was approached by the Junior Chamber of Commerce to contribute to the "Tot Lot" program, a project to build playgrounds in the slum areas for younger children. Clevite decided to be a major participant in Tot Lot largely because one of the proposed playgrounds was scheduled to be near its research center. Although its Tot Lot was a great success, the city-wide program fell far short of its objectives because this program was judged by corporations to be of lower priority than some of the competing proposals for the inner city. In this instance Clevite gave $10,000 on a five-to-one matching grant basis, with the matching funds ($2,000) to be donated by the residents and small merchants of Glenville, an inner-city community. Clevite officers often preferred to match funds rather than to fund a project completely because they believed the most successful projects were ones in which the people who were benefited took some responsibility for their formation.

Mr. Dilley compared Clevite's action with that of other Cleveland companies working on inner-city problems:

Last year Clevite gave $25,000 to the Cleveland Revolving Fund and $10,000 to Tot Lot. But this is far from talking about setting up a Negro business or actually carrying out a new housing project. There is very little initiative in business for recognizing needs and giving appropriately. As far as I know Warner & Swasey is the only Cleveland company that has been really creative in tackling inner-city problems: they have been the innovators, others have been the responders.

There is no one at Clevite who has been given a responsibility like that of Jim Tinsley at Warner & Swasey; he devotes practically full time to work on inner-city projects and to keeping the company officers informed on the changes occurring in the inner city. At Clevite we feel we don't have the time or the money to be creative in giving. Our business must still be business.

IMPACT OF INNER-CITY PROBLEMS ON CLEVITE'S CONTRIBUTION POLICY

In June, 1968, Mr. Dilley reviewed some of his thoughts on Clevite's contributions policy in light of recent changes in the nature of requests he received. Prior to 1967 he felt the amount Clevite budgeted for contributions had usually been adequate to meet valid and worthwhile requests. In the past two years, however, requests for funds mainly to deal with the urgent problems of the inner city had increased by nearly $45,000 annually above the "usual" level of requests. As examples he cited such programs as the Revolving Fund, Tot Lots, and Community Family Planning, all of which focused on the inner city. There were many indications in 1968 that the number of such requests would increase. For instance, the Cleveland NOW! program asked all companies in Cleveland to contribute an amount equal to two thirds of their annual United Appeal contribution for each of the next two years. For Clevite this represented a request for $40,000 each year. If this amount were to come from Clevite's regular contributions budget, many of the gifts to existing programs supported by Clevite would have to be cut back. Mr. Dilley felt the programs currently supported were as important to the community as those designed for inner-city problems, although the latter were made to appear more urgent at this particular time. He felt strongly that once Clevite had undertaken the support of an organization it should continue to make contributions as long as that organization was in need of and deserved help.

Even though Mr. Dilley believed that Clevite's sales volume would be unaffected by changes in the company's contributions budget (he even speculated that the company could totally discontinue corporate giving and suffer no loss in sales because almost none of its sales came from the communities where its contributions were made), he knew that he and others in Clevite management shared the view that the company had very real responsibilities to the communities in which it operated. Corporate contributions had become an accepted cost of doing business and were an integral part of how Clevite attempted to meet its social responsibilities. In view of the fact he was now receiving an "excessive demand for gifts" from what he considered to be legitimate and urgent causes, Mr. Dilley wondered what new policy recommendations, if any, he should make to the Contributions Committee.

Appendix: Clevite Corporation

LEGAL BASIS FOR CORPORATE GIVING[1]

The granting of philanthropic contributions has been made one of the legal functions of corporations through the laws of most states and through the Internal Revenue Code in 1935. These statutes do not presently cover all states nor all types of businesses. A clear legislative trend was begun in 1952 by the New Jersey court ruling in the A. P. Smith case, in which New Jersey laws were upheld declaring that corporations may expend funds for those purposes they deem to be expedient and "as in their judgment will contribute to the protection of the corporate interest." This ruling went on to state that corporate boards may contribute for purposes which "will conduce to the betterment of social and economic conditions, thereby permitting such corporations . . . to discharge their obligations to society, while, at the same time, reaping the benefits which essentially accrue to them through public recognition of their existence within the economic and social, as well as within the legal, structure of society."

Following the A. P. Smith case, the American Bar Association recommended to the individual states to pass legislation similar to that which had been upheld in New Jersey. About three quarters of the states

---

[1] From Richard Eels, *Corporate Giving in a Free Society* (New York: Harper & Bros., 1956).

have since passed such legislation. One of the basic results of these statutes has been to limit the liability of corporate officers in stockholder suits in matters concerning the expenditure of corporate profits. However, most of these statutes in no way relax the requirement that a corporate officer exercise "good business judgment" when making such disbursements. For this reason, many corporations have established separate philanthropic foundations, free of any stockholder control, in an effort to further limit the liability of the officers and to allow them greater latitude in their contributions policies. Under the present I.R.S. Code, corporate gifts to nonprofit organizations up to 5% of profits before tax may be deducted for tax purposes in most types of corporations.

2. Albert Manufacturing Company

THE ALBERT MANUFACTURING COMPANY was founded in 1938 to produce various machined and fabricated components for industrial users. Shortly after the start of World War II the company began to make mechanical and hydraulic assemblies for aircraft. This part of the business grew and in April, 1947, was set up as a separate division. To house operations the company leased a newly constructed plant in Wichita, Kansas, with 1.2 million square feet of floor space. By the end of 1954 sales of the Wichita Division were running at about $120 million annually. The division had approximately 1,200 employees.

Early in January, 1955, Mr. Henderson, works manager of the Wichita Division and a vice-president of the Albert Company, called Mr. Paul Bellows to his office. Bellows was purchasing agent for the division. Henderson told Bellows he had just received a telephone call from the manager of the local office of the Federal Bureau of Investigation. The manager informed him that an investigation then in progress by the FBI had brought to light information involving certain of the division's buyers. Henderson said he had arranged for the investigators to visit the division the following morning. He asked Bellows to receive them and to keep him informed as to developments.

The next day Mr. Arnold Rand and Mr. Peter Thomas, FBI agents, called on Bellows. Mr. Ralph Nance, assistant purchasing agent, was also at the meeting. After a brief exchange of pleasantries the following discussion took place:

BELLOWS: As you can well imagine Nance and I are very curious about this matter. We have not mentioned it to anyone but we have speculated between ourselves as to the nature of the thing. What's the story?

RAND: Well, I guess I ought to go back to last fall. We were conducting an investigation on placement of government contracts at the P. B. Blake Company on the north side of town. After several weeks and rather by accident, Pete Thomas was interviewing a witness who was a buyer in Blake's purchasing department. The fellow confessed to having accepted a $4,500 bribe from a local tool supplier. Later we verified that he had received the money from the company he named. The supplier involved has gone on record that the money was a personal loan from their salesman and was to have been repaid. However, the buyer involved did not support this contention. The buyer turned state witness and gave us several other instances of similar occurrences, but they were not as serious—at least there wasn't as much money involved.

NANCE: Where is the tie-in with the Albert company?

RAND: This buyer has made a sworn statement that he knows three of your buyers have also been accepting expensive gifts and perhaps being bought off as he was. . . .

THOMAS: Bellows, this thing is nebulous as hell. We don't have much to go on, but there are enough basic implications that we think these three buyers of yours may well be tarred with the same brush.

RAND: I'd like to tell you about a fishing trip that our informant was on. He stated—and we have verified this—that he was one of 12 guests at an upstate fishing lodge over a three-day week end. The whole bunch were flown up to this lodge, spent the week end in substantial style and returned. All expenses were paid by the supplier. Now get this—your three buyers were there along with the chief tool designer and two manufacturing engineers from Albert. It was at this occasion that our informant states he learned of the arrangements, shall we say, between the supplier and your buyers.

BELLOWS: What can we do to get this thing off the ground? What can we do to help clear this thing up?

RAND: We would like to examine your records to see who placed orders with the specific company mentioned in the charge and two other companies also implicated. Then we think that sworn statements will be taken. After that if there are any concrete leads we will conduct an investigation outside the company to ascertain if the individuals have increased bank balances, are living beyond their means, and stuff like that. . . .

THOMAS: There is one thing that bothers us. We don't have jurisdiction.

BELLOWS: What do you mean jurisdiction?

THOMAS: At the P. B. Blake Company we could investigate because they held prime contracts from the government. You don't, and therefore we can't come in and do the same kind of thing.

BELLOWS: Could you if we asked you to?

THOMAS: That would take care of the matter completely.

BELLOWS: Well, that settles that. We are asking you now and will give you whatever you need in the way of an official request. Now then, when and how will you start the ball rolling?

RAND: In about three days if you can be ready for us. If possible, we would like to use a private office because of the secrecy necessary until we know where we are. We will also need personnel records, purchase order files, and a lot of other things.

BELLOWS: We will be ready for you. Let me say now I am more concerned than you are and want this cleaned up one way or the other as quickly as possible but with a minimum of disruption of the purchasing department. However, even if we have got to shake this department up hard, I will give you every support. Nance, get things organized to take care of this. Don't tell anyone what is going on until we decide the time is right . . . explain the presence of strangers by, well let them be headquarters auditors or something. Gentlemen, Ralph Nance will be your contact and will personally make all the necessary arrangements. Again, I want to assure you that you have our cooperation. Tell me, who are the vendors in question?

RAND: The Supreme Engineering Company is the firm specifically mentioned in the allegation. The other two are Superior Tool and Die, Inc., and Allied Tool Company.

NANCE: Thanks, you can be assured that things will be set up for you.

Mr. Bellows was especially concerned about this investigation because he had given special emphasis to a strict code of ethical conduct with suppliers since he had assumed his current assignment. The departmental policy was that no employee was to accept any gift or courtesy that he was not in a position to reciprocate. In a variety of ways Bellows had tried to get this standard of conduct understood and accepted by all those in the department. The topic was frequently discussed at weekly meetings with purchasing supervisors. All male employees of the department had attended a company school where one of the subjects discussed was the company policy on bribery. The issue had been discussed at the monthly dinner meetings held for male employees of the purchasing department. Bellows had authorized his buyers to make a fairly liberal use of expense accounts so that they could reciprocate in buying lunches, and so on, for suppliers' representatives and not feel under any obligation to them. He knew that some of the production and engineering employees had accepted Christmas gifts and entertainment from suppliers, but he had believed that his buyers had been completely honest in dealings with suppliers.

The Wichita Division was highly specialized in that it made only a limited line of small gear trains, landing gear assemblies, hydraulic pumps and actuators, and certain fabricated assemblies. The vast bulk of the more or less common components needed were obtained from subcontractors. In 1954 the purchasing department had paid slightly over $55 million to subcontractors, or about half of the total sales of the division.

Buyers for the division were divided into groups, each headed by a senior buyer. These groups were organized along product lines, each being responsible for purchasing items that fell within a broad classification. A service group typed purchase orders, maintained the files, expedited orders that were overdue, and performed other functions of a clerical or routine nature. The entire purchasing department employed 128 people.

The flow of work into the department was in the form of requisitions that specified the items required and the date they should be available. A requisition was first processed by a member of the service group, who entered it in a master log and then routed it to the proper buying group. The assistant buyer for the group upon receipt of a requisition determined what previous suppliers had furnished the item. Any specifications that applied were pulled out together with the blueprint of the part. Then invitations to quote were sent out to approved sources or, if there was only one source, the supplier's representatives were contacted for negotiation. After a supplier had been selected, the assistant buyer filled in on the requisition the supplier's name and the price per unit. Certain other details also were added, such as the storeroom that was to receive the goods, discount terms, shipping point, and so forth. The requisition then was passed on to the appropriate buyer.

In most of the groups the effective control in selection of suppliers was in the hands of the buyers. However, in all groups every requisition had to be signed by a senior buyer. At this stage it went back to the service group. The necessary number of copies were typed, hecto masters for receiving and accounting were prepared, the facsimile signature of the purchasing agent was applied, and copies were mailed to the vendor. The requisition had been transformed from a request to purchase into a contract with a supplier.

About a week after the FBI agents started their investigation, Nance and Thomas discussed progress made during the preliminary stage.

Thomas stated that he thought matters were progressing extremely slowly but that things should speed up in the near future. He and Rand had screened all the purchase orders placed by the division with the three suppliers in question during the past six months. All the orders had been for some type of tooling, primarily for tool repair work. All had been placed by the three buyers named in the original complaint.

Thomas gave Nance the following summary of the findings of the purchase order review:

1. All 1,976 purchase orders were initialed by the senior buyer for tools, Mr. Clinton Boles. The buyers that actually handled the orders and the distribution of orders among the suppliers in question were:

	Superior	Supreme	Allied	Total
Adolph Stimmer (assistant buyer)........622	257	48	927
John Lippen (buyer)................... 73	159	0	232
John Ruppert (assistant buyer)..........280	531	6	817

2. While only 54 purchase orders were placed with Allied, the total dollar value of these orders was $86,409. The dollar value for Superior Tool and Die was $234,765 and for Supreme Engineering it was $303,040.
3. Among the orders were three, all placed with Supreme, which radically increased in price during the period of manufacture. The original quoted prices for these orders were $257.75, $1,166, and $2,500. The final prices on the orders, as authorized by change notices to the purchase orders, were $1,186.50, $3,775, and $4,996.[1]

Nance had intimate knowledge of tool buying and of the tool buying group. He at one time had been responsible for buying tools at the home plant of the Albert Company, and Stimmer then had been an assistant buyer reporting to him. Any tool supplier usually could build a new tool. Quotations of delivery and price could be readily obtained by furnishing the supplier with blueprints and specifications. Repair of tools was an entirely different matter. It was necessary for someone from the tool firm to inspect the tool requiring repair before submitting a quotation. Time was important because the tool generally was needed for production of a scheduled part. Therefore repair jobs were often placed on an advise price basis; that is, the supplier would take the tool and after completing his inspection at his plant would submit a price. The buyer then would judge whether or not this price was fair. If he

---

[1] During the manufacture of tools, design changes often become necessary or desirable. Such changes sometimes cause revisions in the delivered prices. Change notices also may tempt the supplier, particularly one who deliberately quoted under his costs to get an order, to demand an exorbitant price increase. This practice is frowned on by reputable tool vendors but is sometimes resorted to by marginal producers.

decided it was too high, he either negotiated a new price or moved the tool to another supplier.

The tool buying group, unlike the other buying groups, dealt in general with small firms. A relatively low capital investment was required to start a tool shop and there were many local tool makers that were highly specialized and extremely small, sometimes employing no more than four or five men. Adequate credit and other information was difficult to obtain for these small firms.

About two weeks after they began their investigation, Thomas and Rand told Nance they were going to interview, under oath, Stimmer, Lippen, Ruppert, and Boles. They further stated that they wanted to discuss the progress made to date with Bellows and Nance as soon as they had had time to weigh the statements of the men. Nance suggested they meet the following afternoon. Rand and Thomas agreed.

The next afternoon Rand, Thomas, Nance, and Bellows gathered in Bellows' office. Rand opened the meeting.

RAND: Guess you will be surprised to learn that we are ending the investigation.

BELLOWS: You're all through already?

RAND: That's right. We have been unable to uncover any concrete evidence. We must have proof and, while there is no lack of suspicious circumstances, we just can't pin down anything definite.

BELLOWS: You can't come out here, tear into everything, arouse considerable doubt in our minds, and then pull out. We want these men either nailed to the cross or exonerated—-is this too much to ask?

NANCE: I thought you were making satisfactory progress.

THOMAS: Paul, you must realize we work for a boss too. He gave us almost five weeks to firm the investigation up. We just can't do it. There is a lot of smoke but no fire that we can find. So we want to give you everything we have and, if you come across some new evidence later on, we promise to give you all the help we can. That's all there is to it. We're sorry it turned out this way but. . . .

NANCE: Tell us what the score is now before we discuss this aspect further.

RAND: OK. First, Lippen is clean. He was recently transferred out of the tool group and actually was in the group only three weeks during the period of time the alleged offense took place. Both Stimmer and Ruppert absolutely deny the charge. They admit close knowledge of the suppliers but were rather evasive on the question of entertainment. Stimmer stated he was at the fishing party I mentioned to you earlier.

Ruppert says he doesn't associate with salesmen outside of the office.

THOMAS: I handled the outside investigation. We went over every phase of Stimmer's and Ruppert's personal affairs—bank accounts, recent large purchases, standard of living, and so forth. Both are clean insofar as concrete evidence is concerned, but there is considerable doubt in my mind as to whether these guys are on the level. Stimmer lives well but not too far over the level he could support on his income. Ruppert took a very expensive vacation last year—two weeks in Florida at a fancy hotel. I believe a supplier paid a large part of the bills while he was there, but again I have no proof.

RAND: I think you should also know that we have checked the suppliers very carefully too. I have tried to determine the expense account entries on the salesmen's reports turned into the companies. You realize that a company is in a box with the Internal Revenue if we catch it falsifying expenses. Again nothing conclusive, but, Paul, you should know that these companies all have substantial entries listing entertaining your people. I believe your name was even listed a few times.

BELLOWS: If you could check all of the 2,200 suppliers we do business with, I bet you will find my name quite often. Needless to say, I don't even know many of the salesmen, but a purchasing agent's name on the sales report for a lunch impresses the sales manager—and who is going to check to find the salesman is doing a little padding?

RAND: That is undoubtedly true, but there were still many of Albert's personnel on the statements. I was surprised that people outside of the purchasing department were mentioned freely. However, there was nothing to implicate Stimmer or Ruppert.

THOMAS: Well, what else can we say? We have a lot of suspicion that Stimmer and Ruppert are, at best, pretty close to these suppliers. Boles, of course, could be involved in this thing too. We didn't get around to checking his personal affairs as closely as the others, but I don't think he is completely out from under, from what little we have been able to determine.

BELLOWS: What do you say, Ralph?

NANCE: Well, I don't believe we can do much more. We have the information and can be on the lookout for future indications. It is regrettable that we can't run this thing into the ground, but there isn't anything we can do about it.

BELLOWS: Then I want to thank you gentlemen for your help so far and, if we do uncover anything, we will contact you.

Exhibit 1

The Albert Manufacturing Company—Wichita Division

Organization Chart—Purchasing Department

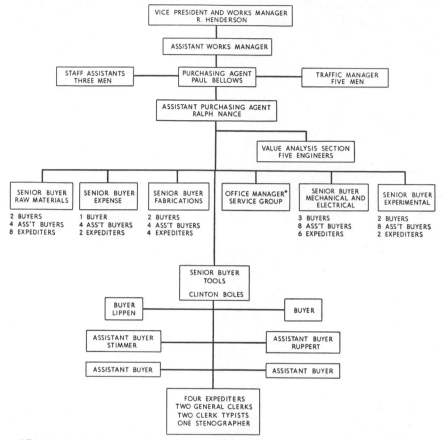

* Equal in classification to senior buyer. There were 18 women clerks, typists, and stenographers in the service group out of a total of 43 for the entire purchasing department.

Thomas: Feel free to do that—even if we can't get out right away we can tell you what move you should make.

After Thomas and Rand had gone, Bellows and Nance talked over the situation. Nance expressed the following views.

Nance: Paul, I'm not sure what I should do, but I'll tell you one thing: I don't want these guys in the tool group any longer. I've got to have a senior buyer that I can trust completely and buyers that are above reproach.

This whole mess is like shadow boxing. Just last November I rated Boles as ready for advancement and Stimmer and Ruppert certainly have always been considered as competent.

However, as I see it I have got to take action to make sure the situation is under control and guarantee this kind of thing doesn't happen again. Do you agree?

3. Auto-Start Manufacturing Company

THE AUTO-START MANUFACTURING COMPANY, a maker of equipment for automobiles, was concerned during the latter part of 1965 and the early months of 1966 with problems arising from proposed and actual changes in federal excise tax laws.

On May 17, 1965, President Johnson presented to Congress a detailed proposal calling for cuts in federal excise taxes representing about $4 billion in annual revenues. This was part of the administration's efforts to stimulate growth of the economy. The President urged businessmen to "translate lower excise taxes promptly into lower retail prices for consumers."

Congress acted promptly on the proposal, presenting an excise tax bill for the President's signature on June 17, 1965, that increased the reductions even beyond those asked for by Mr. Johnson, to $4.6 billion. The bill was signed into law on June 22.

A large number of items were affected at both the manufacturer's and the retailer's level. Relief for some items, automobiles for example, was staggered over a period of years and was not to be total. The excise tax on manufacturers' sales of automobile parts, on the other hand, was totally repealed as of January 1, 1966 (with the exception of items exclusively applicable to trucks and buses).

SUMMARY: FEDERAL EXCISE TAX HISTORY

The excise form of taxation had been used in the United States for many years. This form of tax so far as it affects the ultimate consumer is based on his consumption or use of goods and services instead of on his receipt of income or other revenues. The consumer does not pay the tax directly to the government; rather, manufacturers and the various business services act as tax collectors for the government.

The first excise tax in the United States was levied in 1791 on distilled liquors, which led to the so-called Whiskey Rebellion in 1794. Over the period 1792–1802 excise taxes produced 7.1 percent of total federal tax collections. They did not represent a substantial portion of total revenue until after the Civil War. From 1863 until 1919 they were a very important part of the total, reaching a high point of 55.2 percent for the period 1899 to 1902. After 1940, their importance declined, although not the sums collected from this source. For the period 1955–63 federal excise collections amounted to $102 billion and represented 13 percent of total tax collections. In 1965 the net collections were $14 billion.[1]

An excise tax was placed on automobile parts and accessories in 1919. The rate was 5 percent of manufacturers' sales. In 1932 the rate was reduced to 2 percent; later it was returned to 5 percent; from 1952 until its repeal as of January 1, 1966, the rate stood at 8 percent.[2] Total receipts from this tax were estimated at $255 million in 1965.[3]

COMPANY HISTORY

Auto-Start began operations in the early part of the twentieth century as a small manufacturer of various parts for the new and rapidly growing automobile industry. In recent years the company's annual volume had been approximately $100 million. The company had manufacturing and warehousing facilities in 10 states and more than 4,000 employees.

Product Lines.   A–S had three major product lines:

Item	Company's Brand Name	% of Sales
Spark plugs	Thunderbolt	50
Batteries	Fail-Safe	40
Ignition system parts	Geronimo	10
		100%

The company's products also were differentiated on another basis. Approximately 85 percent of sales were of items termed counterpart, that is, parts that were either original equipment on automobiles or, in the replacement market, items identical to original equipment. The remaining 15% of sales were of items called noncounterpart. These parts were manufactured as alternates for original equipment. They were primarily a "second line" of extra performance parts and were sold in the replacement market.

---

[1] Tax Foundation, Inc., *Federal Non-Income Taxes, an Examination of Selected Revenue Sources* (New York, 1965), chap. III.

[2] *Ibid.*

[3] Tax Foundation, Inc., *Facts and Figures on Government Finance* (13th ed.; Englewood Cliffs, N.J.: Prentice-Hall, 1965), p. 102.

Distribution.   A–S marketed its products under its own brand names
as original equipment for new cars and to over 500 domestic distributors as replacements. (A–S, like many producers of parts, sold to only
one automobile maker. In the replacement market, however, it sold
parts for virtually all automobiles on the roads.) It also sold to chain
operators under private-label brand names. The breakdown of sales (in
millions of dollars) by product lines to the various types of customers
was as follows:

Item	Automobile Manufacturers	National Chains	Distributors	Total
Spark plugs	19	8	23	50%
Batteries	6	14	20	40
Ignition system parts	—	3	7	10
	25	25	50	100%

A–S was one of the leading producers of automotive parts. It estimated that its share of the original equipment automobile market was
about 25 percent for spark plugs and 8 percent for batteries and, in the
replacement market, 30 percent for spark plugs and 25 percent for
batteries. The company had 10 competitors.

Annual sales of the automotive parts industry in the domestic replacement market were reported to be $3 billion at the manufacturer's
sales price based on federal excise tax receipts.[4] There were about 800
manufacturers of automotive parts producing one or more of the following product categories: ignition parts, mufflers and pipes, spark
plugs, batteries, filters and cartridges, motor and chassis parts, paint and
body supplies, brake linings and shoes, fan belts and cooling system
hose, shock absorbers, piston rings, fuel pumps, lamp bulbs, carburetors,
etc. There were approximately 25,000 automotive equipment wholesalers and jobbers and almost 300,000 dealer or retail outlets, including
service stations, automobile dealers, and automotive equipment and
parts stores. The 300,000 figure does not include department or general
merchandise stores.[5]

Exhibit 1 represents graphically the distribution network for A–S
and is generally representative for the entire industry. (As the exhibit
shows, A–S sales to distributors were made through A–S Sales, Inc. The
reason this extra step was interposed in the distribution process is

---

[4] *Jobber Topics,* November, 1965.
[5] *Ibid.*

Exhibit 1

AUTO-START MANUFACTURING COMPANY

Distribution Plan for Automobile Parts

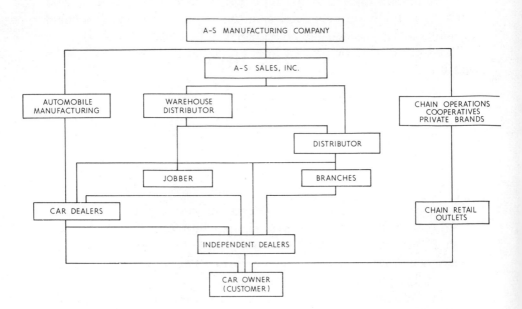

Definitions:

Nonstocking Dealer. Service station, garage, or other retail outlet that does not carry an inventory of parts but orders as needed from a jobber or distributor.

Stocking Dealer. Same as above, but carries a small inventory of the most popular parts.

Car Dealer. Automobile agency with service facilities; carries inventory of popular parts.

Jobber. Buys from another wholesaler and carries a small inventory.

Distributor. Medium-size wholesaler; carries fairly extensive inventory and buys from manufacturer or warehouse distributor.

Warehouse Distributor. Large wholesaler, carries extensive inventory and sells only to other wholesalers.

Chain. Buys direct from manufacturer, usually under private brand, and performs the warehousing and wholesaling function for company's owned or franchised retail outlets.

Automobile Manufacturer. Buys direct from parts manufacturer.

Primary Customer

Final consumer

Final consumer

Final consumer

Independent dealer

Independent dealer

Jobbers

Chain retail outlet

Car dealer

explained later.) Of A–S sales of parts to the automobile manufacturer, approximately 75 percent were used as original equipment on new cars; the remaining 25 percent were resold by the car manufacturer to franchised dealers for the replacement market. The more than 500 distributors used by A–S sold to approximately 10,000 jobbers, who, in turn, serviced about 180,000 dealers.

A–S AND INDUSTRY POSITION ON EXCISE TAX LEGISLATION

Original Position and Participation.   With President Johnson's announcement on May 15, 1965, that he would ask Congress for a reduction in the 10 percent federal excise tax on automobiles, A–S and other companies in the automotive industry through a joint committee formed by various trade associations—the Industry-Wide Automotive Excise Tax Committee—undertook to guard the interests of both car and parts manufacturers. The lobbyist for the committee sought the highest possible excise tax reduction. At that time, according to A–S president, Mr. Leadtoh, no one on the committee had thought out very carefully the full implications of the program. Nothing had been said about pricing philosophy in the event of a reduction in tax. However, it soon became clear that distributors and jobbers were opposed to any price reductions, for that would reduce their dollar gross margins. Moreover, in the parts business, the market was quite inelastic. Car owners had to replace parts when they wore out. They seldom purchased ahead of that time, no matter what the price. Thus increased sales were not likely to result from a price reduction.

The auto parts dealers and distributors were also much in favor of including in the law a floor tax refund provision. (Similar provisions had been proposed for other goods also.) Stocks on hand at the time an excise tax cut became effective would decrease in value if the tax saving was passed on to consumers. Therefore, it was claimed, provision was needed for refunding by the government of the amount of tax already paid on distributor and dealer inventories.

There was some concern by the manufacturers that the burden of administering a floor tax refund would be very costly to them. For a while some manufacturers opposed the refund, but the bill as finally passed included the refunding provision.

Management's Pricing Dilemma.   Under the new legislation the 8 percent tax on the manufacturer's selling price for auto parts was to be eliminated as of January 1, 1966. New price lists were usually issued at the first of each year in the industry. A–S prices had been increased in four of the last five years, the increase averaging 2.2 percent a year on spark plugs and 2.8 percent a year on batteries.

On counterpart items, which accounted for by far the larger part of A–S sales, the automobile manufacturers played a very important role in pricing. Mr. A. W. Distas, A–S marketing vice president, said, "On counterpart items, costs have little relevance to our pricing except in our negotiations with the car manufacturer over the original equipment price. But of course we sell relatively few original equipment items compared to the number of items in our aftermarket line. In our pricing of noncounterpart items, competitors' products, costs, and prices are important." On counterpart items, it was traditional for A–S and other parts manufacturers to follow car manufacturer prices. On noncounterpart items, there was no definite pattern, with A–S at times exerting price leadership and at other times following price changes of competitors.

Through bids and negotiations, A–S and the car manufacturer set the prices at which the manufacturer bought from A–S. The car manufacturer then set two prices, one at which it supplied its car dealers and the other a suggested retail price to the car owner.

When the car manufacturer announced new prices, A–S had in the past then calculated new prices for its distribution system. The basic A–S price was the distributor price, which averaged approximately 20 percent below the car manufacturer's price to dealers. Warehouse distributors usually bought at the distributor price less 20 percent, which represented a combination of functional and quantity discounts. Jobbers bought at about the distributor price plus 5 percent. Independent dealers who carried no inventory, buying parts as needed, usually bought at about one third off the consumer list price. Independent dealers who carried at least some parts in stock bought at 5 percent less than the price to the dealers with no inventory. For an example of typical price relationships throughout the distribution network before repeal of the excise tax, see Exhibit 2.

Computation of the amount of excise tax to be paid (as shown in Exhibit 2) had been as follows. An automobile part with a list price of $10 to the consumer was sold to the automobile manufacturer for $2.35 plus 8 percent federal excise tax, or $2.35 plus 19¢ for a total of $2.54. The 19¢ tax was equivalent to 7.4 percent of the total price paid by the automobile manufacturer. The price for the same part to large chain buyers was $3 plus 8 percent tax, or $3 plus 24¢ for a total of $3.24. The 24¢ was also equivalent to 7.4 percent of the total price paid by the

Exhibit 2

AUTO-START MANUFACTURING COMPANY

Typical Price Relationships and Gross Margins as of December 1965

Distribution Level	Approximate Price Relationships	Tax Paid by A–S as % of Sale Price			Gross Margin on Sales to Primary Customers
		At 23¢	At 24¢	At 19¢	
Consumer (list price)..................$10.00		2.3%	2.4%	1.9%	
Independent dealer (no stock)........... 6.75		3.4			$3.25
Independent dealer (stock).............. 6.45		3.6	3.7		3.55
Car dealer............................ 5.65		4.1		3.5	4.35
Jobber............................... 4.60		5.0			2.15
Distributor........................... 4.35		5.3			2.40
Warehouse distributor.................. 3.48		6.6			1.12
Large chain........................... 3.24			7.4		
A–S Sales, Inc........................ 3.10		7.4			
Car manufacturer...................... 2.54				7.4	3.11
A–S Cost............................ 2.00					
A–S Sales:					
Car manufacturer...................					.35
Large chain.......................					1.00
Warehouse distributor..............					1.24
Distributor.......................					2.11

chain buyers. In order to minimize the amount of tax paid on sales to warehouse distributors and regular distributors, A–S had established a separate, captive sales organization. A–S sold to this sales organization at a transfer price of $2.87 plus 8 percent tax (23¢) or $3.10. The sales organization was responsible for selling to warehouse distributors at $3.48 and to distributors at $4.35.

If the sales organization had not been incorporated into the distribution system, A–S would have been required to pay a tax of 7.4 percent of $3.48 (26¢) on sales to warehouse distributors and a tax of 7.4 percent of $4.35 (32¢) on sales to distributors. Thus, not only would the dollar amount of tax on the same part have been larger, but the dollar margin A–S received would have been less. The effect of the sales organization was to reduce the proportion that excise taxes represented of A–S total gross revenues from 7.4 percent to 5.5 percent. This was true because the 23¢ tax paid on the transfer price to the sales organization represented less than 7.4 percent of the revenues received from distributors by A–S. Also, a small portion of A–S sales were not subject to the excise tax. Use of the captive sales organization was acceptable to the Internal Revenue Service.

At the end of 1965, A–S reported revenues and sales for 1965 and projections for 1966. The percentage relationships were as shown below. Federal excise taxes A–S collected from its customers were not included as a part of gross sales.

	1965	1966 Projected
Gross revenues	100.0%	94.5%
Federal excise tax	(5.5)	—
Gross sales	94.5%	94.5%
Cost of goods sold	(77.5)	(77.5)
Gross margin	17.0%	17.0%

A–S distributors and dealers continued to oppose price reductions after repeal of the excise tax. Any price reduction that maintained the existing level of percentage mark-ups would reduce their dollar profit per item sold. These middlemen argued that it was not fair to them that they should earn fewer dollars for performing the same service and selling the same quantity just because federal excise taxes were removed.

The car manufacturer did not issue new price lists for its dealers until after January 1, 1966. A–S consequently delayed billing until it could establish its policy and prices.

A–S executives had a considerable difference of opinion as to how the excise tax cut should be reflected in new prices. Mr. Leadtoh believed quite strongly that his company should not reap any windfall gain because of the tax cut. He said:

I believe we should implement the tax cut in the manner requested by President Johnson. The consumer should receive the full benefit of the tax cut. I interpret this to mean (at least in theory) the final customer price should be reduced by the percentage of tax we have been paying, or about 5.5 percent.

But it is not that simple. We don't know what the car factories are going to do. It would do us no good to be below them—and we can't go above them. I suppose our competitors are in the same dilemma.

In addition, we must bear in mind the interests of our distributors and jobbers. They are already pressuring us not to reduce prices because they need the same dollar margins to cover their costs. If they are making a fair profit now, to reduce prices may induce other problems in the near future such as pressure for extra discounts, freight allowances, and the like. As you can imagine this could create a lot of havoc in the market as between both our customers and our competitors. If possible we would like to avoid this—it really helps no one and could potentially hurt our industry.

I'm just not sure what is right for everyone concerned or even if there is any action that we can take that will not end up hurting someone.

Another point of view was expressed by Mr. A. W. Distas, marketing vice president. Mr. Distas was in favor of retaining the prices in effect before the excise tax repeal. Mr. Distas said:

Prices are going up, material and labor costs are going up. Why reduce our prices? And most important of all, our customers don't want prices reduced. In my job, I certainly don't want to make them mad at us. The tax we pay is only around 2 percent of the final consumer price. Since we normally raise prices about that much each year, let's just leave things as they are.

A third point of view was expressed by Mr. M. E. Mantion, financial vice president:

I really don't see what the problem is. I think we should go along with President Johnson and pass the tax savings on to the consumer. On our sales at the distributor price, our tax amounts to 23 cents on each $10 item at the consumer level. Therefore, on a $10 item we would reduce the list price 23 cents. This is equal to 2.3 percent throughout the distribution network. This passes the tax savings on to the consumer and allows every one in the distribution network the same treatment.

Still a fourth viewpoint was expressed by Mr. Silas Eliot. Mr. Eliot, who reported to Mantion, was closely involved with the excise requirement, tax legislation, and pricing. Eliot explained his position:

Any additional profit resulting from the excise tax cut after passing on some saving to the consumer should accrue to us. Also you must remember our competitors are earning more money than we do as a percent of sales and return on investment.

I feel very strongly that we do not want to disturb the traditional percentage margins allowed in our price lists to the middlemen. Our customers understand this system. A percentage system allows great flexibility and is understandable. And it is fair and right that these people should have a given percentage margin to operate in. The margin in the past has been fair so any price reduction we make will be fair if we keep the same percentage for margins. Our customers now may want an equal reduction in dollars at each distribution level, which would change their mark-up percentages. But you can be sure that at the next price increase they will want equal percentage increases, not equal dollars.

We can't afford to upset our existing pricing system. That is why I think we ought to reduce prices for the excise cut and add on our normal annual price increase. That would mean reducing prices 5.5 percent and then increasing them 2.5 percent. In effect, this would be a 3.0 percent price decrease all along the line. To make our price increase publicly acceptable, we have to net it out rather than raise prices later.

Also, I don't think we ought to reduce our prices on noncounterpart items, even though they are covered by the excise repeal. We currently have a margin of about 14 percent on noncounterpart items and about 18 percent on counterpart items. If we do not reduce prices on noncounterpart items we will then have

Exhibit 3

AUTO-START MANUFACTURING COMPANY

Pricing Schedules Proposed Following Excise Tax Repeal,
January 1, 1966

Distribution Level	A–S Price Dec. 31, 1965	Car Manufacturing 1966 Prices	Base on Car Manufacturing 1966 Prices	Reduce Prices 5.5%	Reduce Prices 3.0%	Reduce Prices 23¢ (19¢ to manufacturing 24¢ to chains)	Reduce Prices 2.3%	Reduce Prices 2.3% Then Increase Prices 2.5%
Consumer (list price)	$10.00	$9.66	$9.66	$9.45	$9.70	$9.77	$9.77	$10.01
Independent dealer	6.75		6.52	6.38	6.55	6.52	6.59	6.68
Independent dealer	6.45		6.23	6.10	6.26	6.22	6.30	6.38
Car dealer	5.65	5.36	5.36	5.34	5.48	5.42	5.52	5.56
Jobber	4.60		4.44	4.35	4.46	4.37	4.49	4.48
Distributor	4.35		4.20	4.11	4.22	4.12	4.25	4.22
Warehouse distributor	3.48		3.36	3.29	3.38	3.25	3.40	3.33
Large chain	3.24		2.90	3.06	3.14	3.00	3.17	3.08*
Car manufacturer	2.54	2.35	2.35	2.40	2.46	2.35	2.48	2.41†
A–S cost	2.00	2.00	2.00	2.00	2.00	2.00	2.00	2.00

* Reduce price 24¢, increase price 2.5%.
† Reduce price 19¢, increase price 2.5%.

a margin of about 19.5 percent. If the company follows my recommendation on counterpart items we would have a margin of about 20.5 percent for those products. That would make the profitability of both types of products about the same, or at least much closer than it now is.

On Saturday, January 15, 1966, A–S received the newly published prices from the car manufacturers, which were as shown in Column 2, Exhibit 3. Mr. Leadtoh called a meeting for January 17 to discuss what pricing action A–S should take. It was essential for the company to act quickly. The president hoped to emerge from the meeting with a consensus as to appropriate action and a realistic appraisal of the effects of such action. Various pricing schedules that had been suggested are shown in Exhibit 3.

4. Corporate Performance and Private Criticism—Campaign GM Rounds I and II

EARLY IN FEBRUARY, 1970, the world's biggest automaker found itself under attack from a small, just-hatched, nonprofit corporation founded in Washington, D.C., by a group of mostly young lawyers. Called the Project for Corporate Responsibility, this fledgling venture announced that its first move would be a "Campaign to Make General Motors Responsible." Round I of this Campaign was fought in 1970; Round II in 1971. As of the end of the second battle, it was still too early to say whether the challengers would be in the ring again for Round III.

In seeking to change GM's corporate life style and values, the campaigners undertook to work from within, albeit from a very small base of operation. Thus, their initial act was to purchase 12 shares of GM stock—out of some 287.5 million shares outstanding. Small as it was, this investment would allow the Project to place proposals on the GM proxy statement—provided management either raised no objection or its objection was overruled by the SEC.

Besides this contingent right to bring its propositions to a stockholder vote via the proxy machinery, the Campaign arsenal started with only one heavy gun: This was a promise of support from Ralph Nader, the nation's best-known advocate of consumers' causes. For Nader, GM was an old adversary. In 1965 he had published a book, *Unsafe at Any Speed,* dedicated to the thesis that built-in deficiencies of automotive design were to blame for a high percentage of highway accidents. Singled out for particular criticism was a GM car, the strong-selling, rear-engine Corvair. Despite a colorful, muckraking style, this book might well have proved a "sleeper" had not someone at GM, reportedly without top management's knowledge, placed a "tail" on Nader, thus providing him with the basis for a celebrated $26 million lawsuit for invasion of privacy. The resulting publicity sent *Unsafe at Any Speed* onto the best-seller list, launched Nader on an influential

758

career, helped to bring about the passage in 1966 of the first federal automotive safety legislation, and helped also to send GM's Corvair, after a few declining years, into oblivion in 1969.

Nader's promise to introduce Campaign GM to the press[1] assured it of a wide publicity. Some of what might be called the campaign's underlying social philosophy was spelled out in his briefing as follows:

Corporations, [Nader] said, produce, process, and market most of the nation's goods and services and constitute a power grid that shapes the actions of men in both private and public sectors. Yet, he added, far less is known about the actual operations of the giant corporations than any other institution in America, including the national security agencies. . . . [But] corporate imprints are reflecting themselves in growing violence to our air, water, and soil environments, in imbalanced consumer and producer technologies that harm their users and dehumanize their operators, in the colossal waste and depreciation of consumer goods and services and in the Moloch-like devouring of a society's resources to the detriment of sane and human allocation of these resources to meet the needs of all the people by superior distribution and innovation.

According to Nader, the choice for citizens is one of either suffering increasing corporate predation or bringing about an "accountability of corporate power to the people" by gaining access to company information, asserting an effective voice in company policies, and insisting on remedies for unjust treatment.[2]

Insofar as size was a measure of corporate capacity for doing either harm or good, GM was an obvious target:

GM's officers are in truth the princelings of a private superstate. Operating worldwide, GM last year had 794,000 employees and gross revenues of $24,300,-000,000, a sum greater than the revenues of any government except that of the United States and that of the Soviet Union. In essence, what Campaign GM seeks to do is to call into question the "legitimacy" of management's near monopoly on corporate power.[3]

ROUND I PROPOSALS

On its February 7 launching date, the campaign sponsored only three demands for inclusion in GM's proxy statement. As summarized by *Business Week,* these were as follows:

---

[1] Nader did not himself join the campaign because of his pending suit against the company. In August, 1970, this suit, then reduced to $17 million, was settled out of court for $425,000, the largest award of its type ever made. Adding sting to the humiliation he had inflicted, Nader promptly announced that his net proceeds would be used to monitor GM's future behavior from a social responsibility point of view. See *The New York Times,* August 17, 1970.

[2] Luther J. Carter, "Campaign GM: Corporation Critics Seek Support of Universities," *Science,* April 24, 1970, p. 452.

[3] *Ibid.,* p. 453.

Amend the certificate of incorporation to put GM on record as limiting its business purposes to those consistent with the public's health and safety.

Expand the board from 24 to 27 members to make room for three representatives of the public interest. [The Campaign's] choices are former White House consumer affairs adviser Betty Furness, prominent biologist Rene Dubos, and the Reverend Channing Phillips, president of the Housing Development Corp. in Washington, D.C.

Require management to set up a shareholders' committee to watchdog the public impact of GM decisions and determine its proper role in society.[4]

Before GM could decide how to respond, these three demands were expanded into nine, the additions pertaining to car crash resistance, vehicle emissions, warranty provisions, pollution from manufacturing plants, GM support for public transportation, and opportunities for black employment (Exhibit 1).

GM's reaction, some three weeks later, was to opt for excluding the entire list, a decision which it backed by a 70-page letter and 320 pages of appendices. Accompanied by this dossier, the dispute then went to the SEC for settlement under the agency's guidelines. At that time these guidelines stated that a management could exclude a shareholder's proposal if (1) it was "not a proper subject for action by security holders" under the laws of the company's state of incorporation; if (2) it asked management to act on matters relating to the day-to-day conduct of the business; or if (3) it clearly was "submitted primarily for the purpose of promoting general economic, political, racial, religious, social, or similar causes."[5] Applying this last test, the SEC ruled out all of the campaign proposals except Resolutions II and III, and on Resolution III the wording of the full text had to be amended to allow GM (1) "to restrict the funds allocated to the Stockholders' Committee to reasonable amounts as determined by the Board of Directors"; and (2) "to restrict information to be made available to the Committee to areas which the Board of Directors does not deem privileged for business or competitive reasons."

Had the campaigners been unable to devise any proposal capable of passing the SEC screen, they could still have mounted at least a hit-and-run raid on GM by going to the annual meeting and making their suggestions from the floor, rather than by getting them on the proxy

---

[4] "Nader's Pitch to GM Stockholders," *Business Week,* February 14, 1970, p. 30.

[5] For a critical discussion of controversial features in these guidelines, see "Proxy Rule 14a–8: Omission of Shareholder Proposals," *Harvard Law Review,* Vol. 84 (1971), pp. 700–28, and Donald E. Schwartz, "The Public-Interest Proxy Contest: Reflections on Campaign GM," *Michigan Law Review,* Vol. 69 (1971), pp. 430–54.

Exhibit 1

CAMPAIGN GM: ROUNDS I AND II

Campaign GM's Original Round I Proposals

I. RESOLVED: That the Board of Directors amend . . . the Certificate of incorporation by adding the following language: . . . none of the [corporate] purposes . . . shall be implemented in a manner which is detrimental to the public health, safety or welfare, or in a manner which violates any law of the U.S. or of any state in which the Corporation does business.

II. RESOLVED: That . . . the By-Laws of the Corporation be amended to read as follows: The business of the Corporation shall be managed by a board of 27 [instead of 24].

III. RESOLVED:

1. There be established the General Motors Shareholders Committee for Corporate Responsibility.

2. The Committee for Corporate Responsibility shall consist of no less than 15 and no more than 25 persons to be appointed by a representative of the Board of Directors, a representative of the Campaign to Make General Motors Responsible, and a representative of United Auto Workers, acting by majority vote. The members of the Committee shall be chosen to represent the following: General Motors management, the United Auto Workers, environmental and conservation groups, consumers, the academic community, civil rights organizations, labor, the scientific community, religious and social service organizations, and small shareholders.

3. The Committee for Corporate Responsibility shall prepare a report and make recommendations to the shareholders with respect to the role of the corporation in modern society and how to achieve a proper balance between the rights and interests of shareholders, employees, consumers and the general public. The Committee shall specifically examine, among other things,

A. The Corporation's past and present efforts to produce an automobile which:

    1. is non-polluting

    2. reduces the potentiality for accidents

    3. reduces personal injury resulting from accidents

    4. reduces property damage resulting from accidents

    5. reduces the costs of repair and maintenance whether from accidents or extended use.

B. The extent to which the Corporation's policies toward suppliers, employees, consumers and dealers are contributing to the goals of providing safe and reliable products.

C. The extent to which the Corporation's past and present efforts have contributed to a sound national transportation policy and an effective low cost mass transportation system.

D. The manner in which the Corporation has used its vast economic power to contribute to the social welfare of the nation.

Source: The Project for Corporate Responsibility.

Exhibit 1—Continued

E. The manner by which the participation of diverse sectors of society in corporate decision-making can be increased including nomination and election of directors and selection of members of the Board of Directors.

4. The Committee's report shall be distributed to the shareholders and to the public no later than March 31, 1971. The Committee shall be authorized to employ staff members in the performance of its duties. The Board of Directors shall appropriate to the Committee all sums necessary to accomplish its tasks, including compensation to its members and staff. The Committee shall have the power to obtain any information from the Corporation and its employees as deemed relevant by the Committee.

IV. RESOLVED: That General Motors announce and act upon a commitment to a greatly increased role for public mass transportation—by rail, by bus, and by methods yet to be developed.

V. RESOLVED: That, by January 1, 1974, all General Motors vehicles are designed so as to be capable of being crash-tested—front, rear, and side— against a solid barrier at sixty miles per hour, without causing any harm to passengers wearing shoulder restraints.

VI. RESOLVED: First, that General Motors support and commit whatever funds and manpower are necessary to comply with the vehicle emission standards recently recommended by the National Air Pollution Control Administration for the 1973 model year; and to comply with these standards before 1973 if in the course of developing the emission controls this is shown to be technologically feasible. Second, that General Motors commit itself to an extensive research program (with an annual budget as large as its present advertising budget of about a quarter billion dollars) on the long-range effects on health and the environment of all those contaminants released into the air by automobiles which are not now regulated by the government. These would include, but not be limited to, asbestos and particulate matter from tires. The results of this research would be periodically published.

VII. RESOLVED: That first, the warranty for all General Motors cars and trucks produced after January 1, 1971, be written to incorporate the following:

1. General Motors warrants that the vehicle is fit for normal and anticipated uses for a period of five years or 50,000 miles, whichever occurs first.

2. General Motors will bear the cost of remedying any defects in manufacture or workmanship whenever or wherever they appear, for the life of the vehicle. Neither time nor mileage limitation nor exclusions of successive purchasers nor other limitations shall apply with respect to such defects.

3. General Motors accepts responsibility for loss of use of vehicle, loss of time, and all other incidental and consequential personal injuries shown to have resulted from such defects.

Second, General Motors raise its reimbursement rates to dealers on warranty work, making them competitive with other repair work.

Exhibit 1—Continued

VIII. RESOLVED: That General Motors undertake to monitor daily the in-plant air contaminants and other environmental hazards to which employees are exposed in each plant owned or operated by General Motors; that the Corporation report weekly the results of its monitoring to a safety committee of employees in each plant; that if such monitoring discloses a danger to the health or safety of workers in any plant, or in any part of a plant, the Corporation shall take immediate steps to eliminate such hazard; and that no employee shall be required to work in the affected area so long as the hazard exists.

IX. RESOLVED: That General Motors take immediate and effective action to allot a fair proportion of its franchised new car dealerships to minority owners; furthermore, that General Motors act to increase significantly the proportion of minority employees in managerial and other skilled positions.

statement. Indeed, a floor confrontation was all that had occurred in the pioneering drive made in 1967 to mobilize stockholder support of corporate social reform. Masterminded by Saul Alinsky, this drive had been directed at Eastman Kodak, where a civil rights organization bought a few shares of stock and then appeared at the annual meeting to accuse the company brass of not employing enough black workers. Although the dissidents had mustered only a few thousand shares—mostly church-controlled—out of Kodak's 161 million, in the end the company had stepped up its minority hiring.

Reflecting this success, the Kodak precedent was being followed in 1970 at several companies besides GM. Affected among others were Honeywell, American Telephone, General Electric, Boeing, Commonwealth Edison, United Aircraft, and Gulf Oil.[6]

ROUND I TACTICS AND COUNTERTACTICS

Besides outlining the rationale for Campaign GM in his introductory speech to the press, Nader also indicated where the campaign would seek for allies:

"It will go to institutions that own GM stock," Mr. Nader [said], "and, if they decline to respond, to the constituents of those institutions who will be contacted."

"The campaign will reach to the universities and their students and faculty, to the banks and their depositors and fiduciaries, to churches and their con-

---

[6] Robert W. Dietsch, "Whose Business Is Business?" *The New Republic*, April 25, 1970.

gregations, to insurance companies and their policyholders, to union and company pension funds and their membership and to other investors," he said.[7]

Of the possible alliances mentioned in this list, the universities soon became the campaigners' principal objective for reasons one observer identified as follows:

The corporate responsibility issue arises at a time when university students, who remain in a continuing state of ferment, seem especially susceptible to arguments for corporate reform. Fairly or not, large corporations are identified by many students with the Pentagon and the Vietnam War; Dow Chemical and its napalm contract (which Dow no longer has) have provided students with a symbolic target. And, this year, environmental problems are a major concern on campus and Campaign GM offers students an outlet for their desire to strike a blow against pollution.

. . . .

In Campaign GM, students seem to have found an ingenious alternative to staging sit-ins and picketing corporate recruiters as a means of prodding the giants of industry to move faster in reconciling profit objectives with the requirements of a humane society and a clean, healthful environment.[8]

Although attempting to use students and sympathetic faculty members to sway the trustees, boards, and regents who controlled the universities' stock, the campaigners readily admitted that this tactic, no matter how successful, could not suffice to assure victory in the vote at GM's annual meeting. The largest university holding, that of MIT, was only 291,000 GM shares, and the combined investment of all educational institutions was under 10% or so of GM stock. Under these circumstances, reporters were eager to know what the campaigners expected to accomplish. Replying to this query, one of the Project's principal sponsors, Mr. Geoffrey Cowan, reportedly predicted that the attempt to force socially conscious behavior on corporations might prove, "like the first lunch counter sit-ins," the start of "a whole new movement."[9]

Along with the campaigners and neutral observers, GM knew that its attackers could not win at the polls.[10] Nevertheless, having lost the skirmish about the proxy statement, the company had to decide whether to continue its active resistance, and, if so, what kind of posture —defensive or offensive—to adopt, as well as how much effort to de-

---

[7] *The New York Times,* February 8, 1970.

[8] Carter, *op. cit.,* pp. 452 ff.

[9] *The New York Times,* February 22, 1970.

[10] According to one authority on proxy battles, "Even a 10% or 15% vote against management would be unheard of for a shareholder's proposal." *Business Week, op. cit.*

vote to rounding up supporters, and where and how to proselytize.

How the company would answer these questions quickly emerged from a letter and a booklet, *GM's Record of Progress,* which the company had sent, along with its proxy, to all shareholders. The letter said in part,

> General Motors believes the purpose of this proposed committee is to harass the corporation and its management and to promote the particular social and economic views of the sponsors.
>
> If General Motors is to fulfill its responsibilities in the future, it must continue to prosper and grow. Indeed, the corporation can only discharge its obligations to society if it continues to be a profitable investment for its stockholders.

GM's booklet accused the campaign of misrepresenting the company's record. Far from being "against" greater automotive safety, low-cost mass transit, effective automotive emission controls, and social welfare, the company claimed to be "working diligently in all these areas—and more" and to have established an "excellent record of responsible progress."[11] The rest of the booklet's 21 single-column pages were devoted to spelling out in some detail just what the record to date had accomplished.

Besides documenting its past progress in the social sphere, GM took several new steps in the brief span of weeks between the start of the campaign on February 7 and the annual meeting on May 22:

1. In February, 1970, GM joined with Ford in expressing a willingness to produce engines capable of using lead-free gasoline, thus lowering certain types of pollution. The company said this change should be effected on 1971 cars.
2. In March, 1970, GM agreed to sponsor a new Minority Enterprise Small Business Investment Company (MESBIC) to provide low-cost loans to minority businesses.
3. In March–April, 1970, GM announced the coming introduction of a low-priced exhaust cleaner for pre-1966 cars, the unit to be available at least in California within a few months.
4. In March, 1970, GM set the fall of 1971 as the date for the availability of relatively low-emission turbine-powered trucks and buses.
5. In March, 1970, GM offered 10 oil companies the use of 27 modified GM cars in order to speed the introduction of nonleaded gasoline.

---

[11] General Motors Corporation, *GM's Record of Progress* (1970), p. 20.

In addition to reporting these new steps as they occurred, GM took special pains to place the whole story of its record of progress before the public press. As one newspaperman informed his readers, "An all-day program has been scheduled for April 16 to provide reporters, many of whom will be covering the annual shareholders' meeting, with General Motors' efforts . . . past, present and future . . . to curb industrial air and water pollution," etc. Commented one observer, "Some, or even all of this seems somehow to suggest overkill. There is little evidence in corporate history to indicate that socioeconomic issues tend to get much attention in actual proxy voting."[12]

In contrast to its efforts to reach stockholders and the general public, GM did relatively little—or relatively little that was reported—to carry its story to the campuses. Whatever quiet contacts GM may have sought with university trustees, it sought little contact with the faculties and students who were its detractors' principal allies. One notable exception occurred at MIT, where in mid-April the company agreed to send two spokesmen to "debate" a representative of Campaign GM. Selected for this mission were the company's treasurer and its director of emission control. Sticking closely to the line which the company had plotted in *GM's Record of Progress,* the former first charged the campaign with distortion, then listed all the areas in which GM claimed to have made social advances. Thereafter he turned the podium over to GM's second speaker for a much longer and more detailed presentation on the technical topic of emissions control. There followed what the *Boston Globe* described as "some tough and frequently hostile questions" bearing on the makeup of GM's board (Exhibit 2), the percentage of investment in social projects, the pace at which safety and antipollution advances were adopted in the absence of outside legislative pressure, the number of GM's nonwhite dealers, and how much lobbying the company had done to get government funds for public transportation. After the question-and-answer period, GM's representatives departed, leaving the field to the campaign spokesman, Mr. Joseph Onek, a young lawyer. His remarks, reported at length in *The Harvard Crimson* (Exhibit 3), encapsulated the criticisms which the campaigners hoped that MIT and other institutions would consider when voting their GM stock. He ended with a plea for university involvement:

In closing, I would like to say only this. In the last decade we have been made painfully aware of the shortcomings in our society—our racism, our excessive reliance on military force, our rape of the environment. Naturally, there-

---

[12] *The Christian Science Monitor,* April 15, 1970.

fore, some of the leading institutions in our society are being challenged and attacked.

Some of the attacks take the most primitive forms—bombing and killing. We are following a different route. We are using reasoned argument and legal process, the very methods which our major institutions say they respect. And many Americans will be watching to see how these institutions respond.[13]

Exhibit 2

Campaign GM: Rounds I and II
GM's BOARD 1969, 1970

BECHTEL, STEVEN D., JR.; b. 1925; Purdue 1946; Stanford Business School 1948; Pres. and Dir. Bechtel Corp.; Chrm. Bechtel International Corp. and Canadian Bechtel Ltd.
Director:
  Industrial Indemnity Co.
  Crocker Citizens National Bank
  Tenneco, Inc.
  Southern Pacific Co.
  Hanna Mining Co.
  Crocker National Corp.
Vice Chrm. and Trustee of National Industrial Conference Board

BEESLEY, EUGENE N.; b. 1909; Wabash Coll. 1929; Indiana Univ. (Law) 1943; Chrm. Bd. and Exec. Comm., Pres. and Dir. Eli Lilly & Co., Chrm. Lilly International Corp.; V.P. and Dir. Lilly Endowment, Inc.
Director:
  Eli Lilly subsidiaries (7)
  American Fletcher National Bank & Trust Co.
  United Fund of Greater Indianapolis, Inc.
  Procter & Gamble Co.
  Pharmaceutical Manufacturers Association
  Radio Free Europe Fund
  Indiana Univ. Foundation
  American Foundation for Pharmaceutical Education
Chrm. Exec. Comm., V.P. and Bd. Trustees Wabash Coll.
Bd. Mem. National Industrial Conference Board

BRACE, LLOYD D.; b. 1903; Dartmouth Coll. 1925; Dir. First National Bank of Boston
Director:
  Gillette Co.
  American Telephone and Telegraph Co.
  Stone & Webster, Inc.
  USM Corp. (and mem. Exec. Comm.)
  John Hancock Mutual Life Insurance Co. (and mem. Fin. Comm.)
  Mitre Corp. (and mem. Exec. Comm. and Trustee)
  General Motors Corp. (and mem. Fin. Comm.)

---

[13] "Is It a Kandy-Kolored Streamline Baby or a Safe, Non-Polluting Motor Vehicle?" *The Harvard Crimson,* April 24, 1970.

Exhibit 2—Continued

BRADLEY, ALBERT; b. 1891; Dartmouth Coll. 1915
Director:
  General Motors Corp.

BRANCH, HARLEE, JR.; b. 1906; Davidson Coll. 1927; Emory Univ. (Law) 1931; Chrm. and Dir. Southern Co.
Director:
  General Reinsurance Corp.
  U.S. Steel Corp.
  Southern Services, Inc. (and Chrm. Exec. Comm.)

COLE, EDWARD N., b. 1909; General Motors Institute 1933; Pres. and Chief Oper. Officer General Motors Corp.
Director:
  American Ordnance Association
V.P. Detroit United Foundation
V.P. Detroit Boy Scout Council
Mem. Business Executives' Advisory Council, Michigan State Univ. School of Business

CONNER, JOHN T.; b. 1914; Syracuse Univ. 1936; Harvard Univ. (Law) 1939; Chrm., Chief Exec. Officer, and Dir. Allied Chemical Corp.
Director:
  General Foods Corp.
  General Motors Corp. (and mem. Fin. Comm.)
  Chase Manhattan Bank
  Chase Manhattan Corp.
Former Pres. Merck & Co.
Former U.S. Secretary of Commerce

DONNER, FREDERIC G.; Chrm. Alfred P. Sloan Foundation
Director:
  Communications Satellite Corp.

GERSTENBERG, R. C.; b. 1909; Univ. of Michigan 1931; Exec. V.P. and Dir. General Motors Corp.
Director:
  General Motors Acceptance Corp.
  Motors Ins. Corp.

GORDON, JOHN F.; b. 1900; U.S. Navy Academy 1922; Univ. of Michigan 1923
Director:
  Consumers Power Co.
  National Bank of Detroit (and mem. Fin. Comm.)
  General Motors Corp. (and Chrm. Bonus and Salary Comm.)

KILLIAN, JAMES R., JR.; b. 1904; Massachusetts Institute of Technology 1926; Chrm. Massachusetts Institute of Technology
Director:
  Polaroid Corp.
  American Telephone and Telegraph Co.
  Cabot Corp.

Exhibit 2—Continued

KYES, R. M.*; b. 1906; Harvard Univ. 1928; Exec. V.P. Car and Truck Body and Assembly, Automotive Components Group, General Motors Corp.

LUNDIN, OSCAR A.†; b. 1910; Univ. of Michigan, 1932; Exec. V.P. (Finance) and Dir., General Motors Corp.

MCAFEE, J. WESLEY; b. 1902; Univ. of Missouri 1926; Chrm. Union Elec. Co. Director:
Anheuser Busch, Inc.
St. Louis Union Trust Co.
General American Insurance Co.
General Motors Corp.
First National Bank, St. Louis
St. Louis National Baseball Club
First Union, Inc.
Trustee St. Joseph Lead Co.
Trustee Barnes Hospital

MCLAUGHLIN, WILLIAM EARLE; b. 1915; Queen's Univ. 1936; Chrm. and Pres. Royal Bank of Canada
Director:
Capital Investment Corp. Ltd.
Shawinigan Industries Ltd.
J. & P. Coats (Canada) Ltd.
Elican Development Co. Ltd.
Metropolitan Life Insurance Co
Commandant Properties Ltd.
General Motors Corp.
Power Corp. of Canada Ltd.
Royal Bank of Canada Trust Corp.
Adela Investment Co., S.A.
Canadian Pacific Railway Co.
Genstar
Standard Brands, Inc.
Ralston-Purina Co.
Algoma Steel Corp. Ltd.
Niagara Insurance Co. (Bermuda) Ltd.
Ralston-Purina of Canada Ltd.
Chrm. Guildhall Insurance Co. of Canada
Chrm. Canadian Advisory Board, Sun Alliance & London Insurance Group
Trustee, Queen's Univ.
Governor, Montreal General Hospital
Governor, Royal Victoria Hospital

MAYER, JOHN A.; b. 1909; Univ. of Pennsylvania; Chrm. Mellon National Bank & Trust Co.

* Retired during 1970.
† Started during 1970.

Exhibit 2—Continued

Director:
  H. J. Heinz Co.
  Armco Steel Corp.
  Bank of London and South America Ltd.
  General Motors Corp. (and V.P., mem. Exec. Comm.)
  Western Pennsylvania Hospital
  Regional Industrial Development Corp.
  Aluminum Co. of America
Pres. Pittsburgh Clearing House Association
Mem. Federal Advisory Council, Fourth Federal Reserve District
Chrm. Pennsylvania Economy League
Trustee Univ. of Pennsylvania
Trustee Carnegie-Mellon Univ.
Mem. Association of Reserve City Bankers

MELLON, RICHARD KING*; b. 1899; Pres. and Dir. R. Mellon & Sons
Director:
  Aluminum Co. of America
  Gulf Oil Corp.
  Mellon National Bank & Trust Co. (and Hon. Chrm.)
  General Motors Corp.
Trustee, Carnegie Institute
Trustee Emeritus, Carnegie-Mellon University

MORGENS, HOWARD J.; b. 1910; Washington Univ. 1931; Harvard School of
  Bus. Admin. 1933; Pres. and Dir. Procter & Gamble Co.
Director:
  General Motors Corp. (and mem. Fin. Comm.)
  Owens-Corning Fiberglass Corp.
  Morgan Guaranty Trust Co. of New York
  Standard Oil Co. (N.J.)
  J. P. Morgan & Co., Inc.

MOTT, CHARLES; b. 1875; Stevens Institute of Technology; Chrm. and Treas.
  Charles Stewart Mott Foundation; V.P. and Dir. Northern Illinois Water
  Corp.; Treas. and Dir. Long Island Water Corp.; V.P. and Dir. Illinois Water
  Service Co.; Chrm. United States Sugar Corp.
Director:
  General Motors Corp.
  St. Louis County Water Co.
  Missouri Water Company

PERKINS, THOMAS E.; b. 1905; Univ. of Virginia 1928; Counsel, Perkins,
  Daniels and McCormack; Chrm. Duke Endowment; Chrm. Duke Power Co.
Director:
  American Cyanamid Co. (and mem. Exec. Comm.)

  * Retired during 1970.

Exhibit 2—Continued

Morgan Guaranty Trust Co. of New York (and mem. Exec. Comm.)
Penn. Central Co.
J. P. Morgan & Co.
Discount Corp. of New York
General Motors Corp.
Trustee and mem. Exec. Comm. Duke Univ.
Chrm. Fin. Comm. and Trustee Phillips Academy

ROCHE, JAMES M.; b. 1906; Chrm. and Chief Exec. Officer General Motors
Corp.

RUSSELL, GEORGE; Univ. of Minnesota 1927; Vice Chrm. and Chrm. Fin.
Comm. General Motors Corp.
Director:
General Motors Acceptance Corp.
Motors Insurance Corp.
Savoy Fifth Ave. Corp.

SIVAGE, GERALD A.; b. 1909; Carroll Coll. 1931; Pres. and Dir. Marshall Field
& Co.
Director:
First National Bank of Chicago
Metropolitan Life Insurance Co.

SULLIVAN, LEON H.†; b. 1922; West Virginia State 1943; Columbia 1947;
pastor, Zion Baptist Church, Philadelphia, Pa.; founder of Opportunities
Industrialization Centers Program (a 90-branch, nonprofit training organiza-
tion); co-founder of Zion Investment Associates (in real estate, construc-
tion, retailing, and manufacturing).
Director:
Zion Investment Associates, Inc.
Girard Trust Bank of Philadelphia
Philadelphia Saving Fund Society

WARNER, HAROLD G.; b. 1908; General Motors Institute 1932; Exec. V.P. and
Dir. General Motors Corp.
Director:
Oakwood Hospital
Detroit Symphony Orchestra Association
Oakland Univ.
Alma Coll.
Chrm. Bd. Regents General Motors Institute
Trustee Interlochen (National Music Camp)

WILLIAMS, ALBERT*; b. 1911; Beckley Coll. 1930; Chrm. Exec. Comm. and
Dir. International Business Machines Corp.
Director:
Mobil Oil Corp.

† Started during 1970.
* Retired during 1970.

Exhibit 2—Continued

First National City Bank
General Foods Corp.
General Motors Corp.

Source: GM annual reports and proxy statements; *Poor's Register of Corporations, Directors and Executives* (New York: Standard & Poor's Corporation, 1970–71) and *The New York Times*, January 5, 1971.

Exhibit 3

CAMPAIGN GM: ROUNDS I AND II
Remarks on Behalf of Campaign GM, Round I, by Mr. Joseph Onek, MIT, April 13, 1970

MR. ONEK: We are campaigning to Make GM Responsible. Obviously then, we believe that GM is now behaving irresponsibly. And the record bears us out.

Pollution Control

Let us look first at the question of air pollution. It has been estimated that GM vehicles and plants are responsible for 35 per cent of the nation's air pollution by tonnage. Yet for years, GM refused even to acknowledge that the automobile and air pollution were related.

This issue was already raised by GM. You saw the slides and the charts.* Everything was California models first and the rest of the nation afterwards. Why is that?

Well, it is true that the problem in California was somewhat worse, but certainly there were severe problems throughout the nation, particularly in New York. Why weren't controls applied to New York models until years later? The answer is quite simple. GM wasn't responding to legislation requiring it to act.

In addition, none of those devices they put on involved a new scientific breakthrough. They were old processes, old devices that could have been put on years before. It was a question of a little more money and GM wasn't ready to spend it until they were finally forced to.

And it is significant that even today, when GM recognizes the problem and purports to be concerned about it, that General Motors is spending only $15 million a year on anti-pollution research while it is spending $250 million a year on advertising.

Misleading Accounts

Instead of action, GM provides misleading accounts of what it has accomplished. In its Annual Report, and in the recent full-page ads it took out in the *Times*, GM states that its 1970 cars, as equipped for California use, reduced hydrocarbon emissions by 80 per cent. But this figure is based on tests made on finely tuned cars which were just off the assembly line.

* The reference here is to the previous remarks by one of GM's representatives, who discussed the company's progress in the area of emissions control.

Exhibit 3—Continued

What General Motors did not say is that the Department of Health, Education, and Welfare tests demonstrate that once the 1970 cars have been on the road a while, as many as four-fifths of them fail to meet the standards which GM claims to have met.† This is an example of GM's commitment to honesty and to pollution control. We have asked the Securities and Exchange Commission to require GM to recall this misleading statement about pollution control efforts. And if SEC does not take action, we intend to appeal to the courts.

Safety

GM's record in automobile safety is equally poor. Fifty-five thousand Americans die in automobile accidents each year, more than have died in the entire Vietnam war. GM has done little to prevent this bloodletting. It delayed for years before installing seat belts and collapsible steering wheels. Nor does it appear interested in constructing a truly crash-proof car.

In 1963, a GM safety engineer wrote that it was impossible to protect against injury in collision at 30 miles per hour. Now, just seven years later, the National Highway Safety Bureau has already tested successfully a prototype vehicle that can withstand impacts at 47 miles per hour, without injury to passengers wearing a normal shoulder belt. I think it is a disgrace and a tragedy that this prototype had to be developed by the Federal Government rather than by the automobile industry.

Another aspect of the auto safety picture is the high cost of property damage of even very minor accidents. . . .

Racial Disaster

General Motors' record in the field of racial justice is a disaster. There are 13,000 Gm dealers in this country. Seven, only seven, are black. And even in blue-collar employment, GM has consistently lagged behind Ford and Chrysler.

For the sake of fairness, I should add that ever since those riots in Detroit, GM has been doing much better in the racial area. But I always thought that we were trying to build a society where progress can be made without the need for riots and killing.

Mass Transit

The mass transit issue involves both air pollution and racial justice. The lack of mass transit in this country has clogged our cities with polluting automobiles, has driven white men's roads through black men's homes, and has deprived blacks of access to the new jobs in the suburbs. And GM is a charter member of the powerful highway lobby which has fought for years to prevent federal funding of mass transit programs.

Let's get back to what GM said earlier about going on record for mass transit. They have always been on record for mass transit as long as the money isn't funded.

The big controversy in the mass transit area for the last ten years has been what is going to be done with the federal highway trust fund. Millions of

† Auto makers have argued that declining efficiency indicates inadequate maintenance.

Exhibit 3—Continued

dollars have been set aside for national defense highways. . . . Can't we take some of those highway funds which are already there and use them to build monorails, bus lines, or some other forms of transportation?

And the answer of General Motors and the automobile manufacturers' association has been no—thou shalt not touch money from the highway trust fund. Therefore there have been no new funds appropriated for mass transit because most of the people who want more mass transit thought that money should come out of the highway trust fund.

Warranties

If I had more time, I would talk about automobile warranties, an area where the performance of GM and other manufacturers has been strongly condemned by the Federal Trade Commission. I have a feeling, however, that many of you have sufficient first-hand experience with that problem.

In short, then, GM is a corporation which has acted irresponsibly in many areas of vital concern. We at Campaign GM contend that shareholders can and should do something about the record of the company they own. We have proposed two resolutions which we believe would have a significant impact.

First, we have proposed the addition of three new members to the GM Board of Directors.

Special Interests?

GM strongly opposes our candidates for the Board. It says that they represent "special interests." It is significant that GM now has on its Board directors of oil companies, banks, and insurance companies. Apparently oil companies and banks are not "special interests." Only consumers and blacks are.

We recognize that the election of three public interest board members, although significant, is not the be-all and end-all. So we have proposed the establishment of a Committee on Corporate Responsibility to examine not only GM's performance in the problem areas I have already described, but also the structural changes which may be needed to make GM responsible.

GM opposes this proposal, even though the Commission's recommendations would be advisory only. The reason is obvious. GM does not want independent and respected experts examining what it has done and what it could be doing for society. It does not wish to have its closed and archaic decision-making process exposed and challenged.

Resolution Change

I recognize that an MIT General Assembly Task Force‡ recommended that MIT abstain on this proposal because it felt that even though the need for a Committee on Corporate Responsibility was manifest, the method of selecting Committee members was inadequate.§

---

‡ One of the bodies at MIT that studied Campaign GM's proposals and advised the Executive Committee of the MIT Corporation how to vote.
§ See Exhibit 1, Resolution III.

Exhibit 3—Continued

We at Campaign GM had a great deal of trouble determining what the selection process should be. We did not want to leave the matter entirely in GM's hands and we could not think of groups other than the UAW and Campaign GM with sufficient knowledge and interest to participate in the selection process.

I would like to make two announcements, however. First, Campaign GM is ready to provide MIT and other shareholders with a list of types of persons we would nominate for the Committee on Corporate Responsibility.

Second, we at Campaign GM will gladly relinquish our role in the selection process, if a better process is suggested. The Committee on Corporate Responsibility is too important to be jettisoned simply because of the difficulties in selecting its members.

We believe that every responsible shareholder should support our proposals.

Source: *Harvard Crimson*, April 24, 1970.

DENOUEMENT OF ROUND I AT THE ANNUAL MEETING

Not until the voting at the annual meeting would it be clear exactly how many votes Campaign GM Round I would have won. Some strange bedfellows had, however, declared their commitment to the cause. These included a number of colleges: Tufts (9,300 shares), Brown (4,700), and Amherst (37,000 for at least one proposal). Still other colleges would at least abstain—an action that was counted as a moral victory. This contingent comprised Yale (86,000), Williams (21,000), Stanford (24,000), Swarthmore (2,200), and Rockefeller University (63,000). The absence of MIT and Harvard from these lists was a special disappointment to Campaign GM, but the governing committee of MIT had at least indicated that it would formally ask the company to concern itself with socially desirable goals.[14] Similarly, a number of other large colleges and foundations, though supporting management, had "also cautioned that they might not do so the next time around." Most notable of these was the Rockefeller Foundation, which had castigated GM for its " 'defensive and negative attitude' toward its critics."[15] Besides these sources, more announced support would come from such scattered quarters as U.S. Senator Hart (315 shares); The New York City Pension Fund; the new chief of the

---

[14] This Committee included four academic administrators (three *ex officio*), the physician-in-chief of a research hospital, three company presidents, a corporate board chairman, a former executive vice president, and a retired corporate director. See *MIT Institute Report,* Special Supplement, May 22, 1970.

[15] "Businessmen in the News: James M. Roche," *Fortune,* June, 1970, p. 31.

United Auto Workers (UAW), who had come to the annual meeting to speak on behalf of the shareholders' committee—disclosure proposal; and, most quixotically, the son of GM's senior board member—Mr. Stewart R. Mott (2,000 shares). Another well-known figure in the campaign corner was Mr. Robert Townsend of *Up the Organization* fame. At a pep rally just before the meeting, he echoed a favorite campaign theme by telling his hearers how soon GM could build a clean car if only the company would divert to this purpose $200 million of the $240 million annually spent on advertising.

At 2:00 P.M., when GM's Chairman James M. Roche gavelled the annual meeting to order, it had already attracted an overflow crowd of some 3,000 people. Present along with the Campaigners and Middle America were what *The New Yorker* called the familiar *"enfants terribles* of the annual meeting circuit." These included Mr. Louis Gilbert, champion of cumulative voting, and—wearing a paper money hat and a gilded gadfly pin—Mrs. Wilma Soss, champion of limits on executive pay. "Warming up" in another corner was Mrs. Evelyn Y. Davis "in white tights and a black bathing suit, with a sash reading 'Miss Air Pollution' across her chest." Less familiar were a peace movement chairman and a Nobel laureate who had come to "sneak in" a nomination to the GM board for the younger Mott, supported by speeches against the war in Vietnam.

Planned and unplanned scenes with all these actors took several hours, and then attention turned to the first campaign proposal. A "footloose correspondent" sent by *The New Yorker* described what happened next:

> It was 5:06 P.M. before the proposal on the Shareholders' Committee came up formally. Whether by calculation or not, the chairman had managed things so adroitly that much of the audience was by then impatient to go home. Betty Furness got the floor, and had barely opened her mouth when she yielded graciously to a challenge from Mrs. Soss. Then Mrs. Davis—without anybody's yielding to her—broke in. Soon another lady shareholder was recognized and was allowed to deliver a rambling tirade against Ralph Nader, and even to suggest, if I understood her correctly, that if Nader's youthful followers would stop drinking and taking drugs there would be fewer splendid General Motors cars involved in accidents. Not long after she finally braked herself, a male stockholder told Mr. Roche that by repeatedly calling upon certain predictable filibusterers in the room he was in effect conducting a filibuster himself. . . . Shortly thereafter, discussion was closed and a vote on the Shareholders' Committee was taken.[16]

---

[16] E. J. Kahn, Jr., "Our Footloose Correspondents—We Look Forward to Seeing You Next Year," *The New Yorker,* June 20, 1970, pp. 40–51.

When the vote was finally counted on both campaign proposals, management had won handily, as shown in Table 1.

TABLE 1

Proposal	Number of Shareholders for	Number of Shares for	Percentage of Shares for
Shareholders' Committee......	61,794	6,361,299	2.73%
Three additional directors......	53,495	5,691,130	2.44%

Undaunted by this count, a spokesman for the campaign first complimented GM's top officer on "the courtesy and stamina he had displayed" in chairing the day's tumultous proceedings, then added, "Mr. Roche, we look forward to seeing you next year."[17]

GM UNDER THE GUN

In picking GM for the two-time target of an effort to make U.S. corporations more "responsible," the campaigners had selected the world's largest auto maker and one of the world's largest companies. Despite its blue-chip status, however, GM was beset by a wide range of conventional business problems. Not just social critics, but dealers, customers, investors, labor, government agencies, and competition all posed difficulties calling for managerial attention. The following list of company problems is drawn from press notices for only 15 months through 1971's first quarter:

1. In January, 1970, reflecting a growing unrest over car sales felt to be subsidized, car dealers threatened to take the four major auto companies to court over discounts made to large fleet buyers. Responding in May, the "Big Three" auto makers halted these allowances—and by year's end found themselves defendants in antitrust suits filed by eight states and several cities, charging a conspiracy to eliminate competition in sales of government fleets.
2. In February, 1970, in the wake of past complaints from customers, dealers, and the FTC over defects and warranties, the company told a Nixon aide that inspectors had been put into all plants. A few days later, Chairman Roche was reported as blaming auto workers for the industry's quality woes.
3. In April, 1970, owing allegedly to slumping sales and rising costs, the Big Three reported their worst first quarter since the 1958 recession. In GM's case the drop was 33.4% in earnings, and it followed an 11-year low in profit margins for 1969. Investors responded with a "pasting" for automotive stocks.

---

[17] *Ibid.*

4. In June, 1970, canvassing ways to cut costs, GM and Ford were reputedly mulling the purchase of Japanese steel, currently making well-publicized inroads against hard-pressed domestic suppliers.

5. In July, 1970, hoping to control the net costs of the new contract soon to be worked out between the auto makers and labor, GM's Chairman Roche charged that the UAW had "shirked its obligations," and he reiterated an April demand for greater productivity and efficiency.

6. In August, predicting the "rout" of foreign-made autos by Detroit's upcoming minicars, GM's Chevrolet Division made ready to introduce its own contender, the "Vega," at a price still undisclosed. When the announcement came, the price was so high ($2,091) that analysts questioned the dent on import sales, and leading import makers announced themselves "unafraid." Two days later, Ford set the price on its "Pinto" minicar to undercut the Vega by $172.

7. Early in September, Nader charged GM with having "lied" about company data that showed Corvair to be unsafe. Repudiating this charge the next day, the firm called this attack "false and vitriolic" and offered the U.S. Secretary of Transportation any information desired. Evidence from both sides was later turned over to the National Highway Safety Bureau, which indicated in November that Corvairs tipped over and that carbon monoxide emission was a problem, but which reportedly did not support Nader to the extent he had hoped.

8. In mid-September, contract negotiations having broken down, the UAW selected GM as the sole target of a strike which turned out to last at least 10 weeks in GM's U.S. plants and 14 weeks in Canada. Strike results for the company included a half-year loss of $210 million, a 64% decline in yearly earnings, omission of bonuses for top executives,[18] omission of the customary extra year-end dividend, and bids by Ford and Chrysler to lure customers away.

9. Late in November, GM's strike was settled by a contract giving labor gains estimated at 30% over the next three years. Besides setting an at least mildly inflationary wage-and-benefit pattern, the strike had reportedly cost Michigan's economy $4 million a week in revenue losses, and it had cost the federal government a $1.4 billion drop from GM's 1969 income tax. National social costs were also high, as suggested by the charts in Figure 1.

10. Late in November, following the labor settlement, GM added an average of $24 to its 1971 model prices, bringing the increase from 1970 to a total of 6.9%.

11. In November, maintaining a position it had adopted the previous year, GM refused to agree that the wheels on some 200,000 of its trucks were defective, and, in the first such action of its kind, the company was ordered to institute a recall on a nonvoluntary basis. This action followed a Nader intervention and a 10-month study of possible safety defects

---

[18] In 1968 bonuses and salaries for 63 top officers and directors had been respectively $4.9 million and $9.9 million. In 1969 parallel figures for 67 recipients were $5.6 million and $9.4 million.

Figure 1

COST OF GM STRIKE

A. How the GM Strike Can Affect the Economy

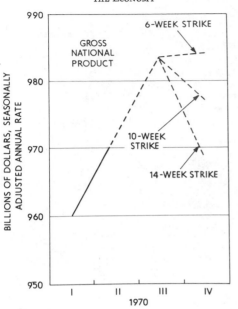

B. Estimated Daily Cost of the GM Strike

$14 million	in wages to 403,000-plus workers in United States and Canada
$90 million	in lost sales of 26,000 cars and trucks in United States and Canada
$40 million	in payments to suppliers
$20 million	in taxes related to sales, but not including state, local, and federal income taxes

Source: *Business Week*, November 7, 1970, p. 19.

Note: Data from Wharton econometric model, University of Pennsylvania.
Source: *Business Week*, October 3, 1970, p. 18.

in GM trucks and buses by the National Highway Safety Bureau, during the course of which the company had voluntarily recalled almost 47,000 vehicles, including 19,000 school buses. GM promptly filed in the courts to have the government's order set aside.

12. In December, Nader reported that the break-up of Ford and GM had been recommended by agents of the Justice Department.

13. In February, 1971, the annual report for the previous year revealed that GM's profit from foreign operations had fallen 26%, despite a rise of 8% in overseas sales. Strikes in Britain were a major cause, with some of the problem being contributed by Peruvian government decrees which forced termination of assembly in that nation. Even so, GM's non-domestic operations contributed $377 million to the U.S. balance of payments, bringing the post–World War II total to $12.3 billion.

14. Making up a sales backlog from the strike, GM's sales pattern through 1971's first quarter was very strong—but still difficult to interpret. Overall, analysts wondered if domestic minicars had "flopped." According to *The Value Line* for April 16, "The introduction of U.S.-built sub-

Exhibit 4

CAMPAIGN GM: ROUNDS I AND II
GM Financial Data
(Dollars in Millions)

A. SELECTED GM FINANCIAL TRENDS, 1965–70

	1965	1966	1967	1968	1969	1970	Estimated 1971*
Assets	$11,479	$12,213	$13,273	$14,010	$14,820	$14,174	—
Sales	20,734	20,209	20,026	22,755	24,295	18,752	$27,800
Operating margin (%)	21.6%	18.7%	18.0%	18.1%	16.7%	7.9%	15.0%
Working capital	$ 3,685	$ 3,606	$ 4,006	$ 4,230	$ 4,352	$ 3,011	$ 3,480
Net plant	4,617	5,130	5,330	5,438	5,645	6,396	6,500
Net worth	8,030	8,514	9,048	9,548	10,021	9,680	10,250
Net income	2,126	1,793	1,627	1,732	1,711	609	1,870
Earnings/net worth (%)	26.5%	21.1%	18.0%	18.1%	17.1%	6.3%	18.0%
Earnings/sales (%)	10.2	8.9	8.1	7.6	7.0	3.2	—
Average annual PE ratio (%)	13.8	13.3	14.3	13.5	12.9	3.8	—

B. GROWTH RATES PER SHARE, ANNUALLY COMPOUNDED

	Ten Years	Five Years	Three Years	1969
Sales	7.9%	7.4%	6.4%	6.8%
Net income	6.9	−0.3	−1.5	−1.2

* Estimated by *The Value Line.*
Source: *The Value Line,* April 16, 1971, p. 131, and General Motors annual reports.

compacts . . . failed to stem the tide of imports which continue to post new records."[19] Worse still, relatively low-margin minicars were eating into large-car sales; thus "the home-grown small cars . . . appear to have realized Detroit's worst nightmare."

Over the longer run, downturns in earnings (Exhibit 4) and certain unfavorable trends in sales caused some observers to wonder if "mighty GM" could be faltering:

There are many who say GM's engine has been missing badly in recent years. Once, the race between Chevrolet and Ford was strictly no contest, with Chevy regularly winding up the year leading by more than 300,000 cars. Last year the lead was under 200,000 and for the first six months of this year, Chevy leads by about 80,000. GM has been noticeably tardy in recognizing some emerging market segments. Ford's Mustang had the sporty car market to itself for 2½ years before GM countered with the Camaro. Cynics wonder if GM has missed the market on occasion because the world a GM executive sees

---

[19] According to a GM speaker at the Harvard Business School, GM regarded the "competitive threat of the foreign car manufacturers as the principal most important determinant of the American industry's future prosperity." *Harbus News,* April 15, 1971.

from his pinnacle can be distorted. Says a man who once was close to the pinnacle: "The top executives tend to be too isolated from what goes in the market place."[20]

ROUND II CAMPAIGN PROPOSALS AND CONCURRENT PRESSURES

True to the promise given at the annual meeting in May, Round II of Campaign GM was initiated the next November. This time, only three demands were made (Exhibit 5), all of which reached the proxy statement:[21] As summarized by *The Wall Street Journal,* these demands were as follows:

A "proposal on shareholder democracy" that would require GM to list on its proxy statement for next year's annual meeting all candidates nominated by nonmanagement stockholders. In the past, GM has listed only the management slate on its proxy.

A "proposal on constituent democracy" that would require GM to allow three groups—GM employees, purchasers of new GM vehicles, and GM auto dealers—to each nominate a director candidate. The three candidates thus selected would be voted on by all shareholders.

A "proposal on disclosure" that would require GM to publish in its annual report specific facts and figures regarding its progress on auto-pollution control, auto safety and minority hiring.[22]

Besides having to contend with Nader's friends in Campaign GM, the company concurrently had to contend with other challenges sponsored or abetted by Nader. Thus GM, along with other corporations, could be affected by at least three of Nader's prime reformist schemes: one a plan for breaking up monopolies and oligopolies, another a Code for Professional Integrity, and the third a Federal Incorporation Act. Of these, the first would operate by setting ceilings on market share.

---

[20] "Mighty GM Faces Its Critics," *Business Week,* July 11, 1970, p. 72.

[21] Since the previous year, the path to inclusion had become easier following a successful court challenge to an SEC ruling based on its social issues guideline. This challenge had come from shareholders in Dow, who had asked the D.C. Court of Appeals to overrule an agency decision supporting Dow management's resistance to an antinapalm resolution. After the court had remanded this issue to the SEC for a more formal finding so that "the bases for its decision" could "appear clearly on the record," many resolutions on behalf of social issues found their way onto 1971 proxy statements. Meanwhile the SEC had asked for a ruling from the Supreme Court on the adequacy of its procedures, claiming that these had to be informal to enable it to cope expeditiously with the growing volume of its work.

[22] *The Wall Street Journal,* November 20, 1970. Besides the three Campaign resolutions, GM's proxy statement bore five others. Four came from such familiar critics as Mr. Gilbert, Mrs. Soss, and Mrs. Davis and bore on such relatively mundane matters as the locus of GM's annual meeting. The other, from a missionary unit of the Episcopal Church, sought to end GM's manufacturing in South Africa.

Exhibit 5

CAMPAIGN GM: ROUNDS I AND II
*Summary of Campaign GM's 1971 Proxy Proposals with
Campaign and Company Comments*

Proposal 1: On Shareholder Democracy

Proxies are solicited in support of an amendment to the by-laws that will provide a process for shareholder nomination and election of Directors.

The stockholder has submitted the following statement in support of such resolution:

Reasons: "This proposal would, for the first time, give shareholders a real choice in the selection of Directors. Under the present system the only candidate shareholders have any opportunity to consider are management's nominees. This proposal would permit shareholder nominees for Director to be listed on General Motors' proxy, so that all the shareholders would have a chance to consider nominees for Director in addition to those proposed by management. The proxy would in effect become a ballot giving shareholders a choice among opposing nominees."

The Board of Directors favors a vote AGAINST this resolution for the following reasons:

The adoption of this Proposal would place the stockholders of General Motors at a serious disadvantage. In the opinion of the Board of Directors, it would not be in the best interest of those stockholders who look forward to the continued success of General Motors.

A corporation's board of directors should be a group of qualified individuals dedicated to the business success of the company and the interests of its stockholders and the public as they relate to the corporation. Directors should not have any commitment or interest in conflict with those of the corporation and its stockholders. To provide such a board, General Motors, like other companies, presents in its proxy statement a slate of nominees for directors that it recommends for election by the stockholders at their annual meeting.

If a group of stockholders wishes to propose an alternative slate, or even a partial slate, corporate procedures are already available which permit these stockholders to solicit proxies. . . .

. .   .   .

This represents an attempt to secure the benefit of the Corporation's proxy solicitation facilities by groups of stockholders who have not demonstrated that they have broad stockholder support. These facilities would be theirs to use without cost. But the cost would be borne by GM stockholders.

The proposal would permit director candidates to be placed on the Corporation's proxy by only $\frac{1}{100}$th of 1% (0.01%) of the 1,300,000 General Motors stockholders, or by the owners of $\frac{1}{2}$ of one-thousandth of 1% (0.0005%) of General Motors 286,000,000 shares of stock.

. . . Continuity of a successful Board of Directors is of utmost importance. The proposal would substitute an intentionally cumbersome procedure designed to permit small groups with little stake in the company's success to force the entire body of stockholders to vote on candidates that these groups might choose

Exhibit 5—Continued

on the basis of their own interests. This is more than a proposal to experiment as it is a proposal to discard procedures that have contributed to the economic success of General Motors and to the economic well-being of its stockholders.

Proposal 2: On Constituent Democracy

Proxies are solicited in support of an amendment to the Corporation's by-laws that would allow for constituent participation in the selection of Directors. . . .

The proposal on Constituent Democracy would provide that regardless of the size of the Board of Directors, three of the Directors would be nominated by constituent groups of employees (including nonunion employees), consumers, and dealers. One Director would be nominated by each constituency. It is contemplated that this number would be a small minority on the Board of Directors.

The stockholder has submitted the following statement in support of such resolution:

Reasons: "This amendment recognizes the need to broaden the decision-making base of the Corporation by adding to the Board persons chosen by groups who have a vital interest in the Corporation's affairs. Employees, dealers and consumers are unable at present to influence significantly the policies of the Corporation. The Corporation will better serve the interests of the larger community if these groups can participate intimately in decision-making. At the same time, the shareholders' ultimate ownership right to choose Directors is maintained since they can veto absolutely any candidate."

The Board of Directors favors a vote AGAINST this resolution for the following reasons:

This proposal goes a step beyond the Stockholder Proposal Number[1]. It would provide for the nomination of three directors by groups that are not stockholders. These nominees would be chosen in a kind of "popularity contest" among loosely defined groups. In size these groups could range from some 20,000 in the case of GM dealers in 115 countries to 800,000 in the case of GM employees throughout the world and up to 30,000,000 in the case of users of GM cars, trucks, and buses in all parts of the world. There would be no real means of verifying the eligibility of those voting.

The proposal would require General Motors to poll the members of each of these three groups to determine their nominees. . . . This proposal is hopelessly impractical. No reliable poll of these groups could be conducted without setting up voting procedures as elaborate as the election processes of some of our States. Under the Project's proposal, the expense of conducting such polls would be borne by all the stockholders. It would be considerable; the cost and effort incident to the polling of 800,000 employees and of as many as 30,000,000 "GM consumers" on a world-wide basis would be prohibitive.*

The proposal ignores the fact that each member of the Board of Directors is charged by law with representing *all* of its stockholders. It seems inevitable that directors elected under this proposal would soon find themselves in a conflict of interest. They would be divided between their allegiance to the group which

Exhibit 5—Continued

nominated them—the dealers, employees or consumers—and the entire body of stockholders to whom each director has a legal responsibility.

The basic purpose and underlying philosophy of the proposal are wrong. The Board of Directors of a corporation in the United States is neither a political institution nor a legislative body. It consists of representatives elected by the stockholders to run the business on their behalf with due regard to the legitimate rights and interests of the stockholders, employees, dealers, customers, and the public at large.

Each of the three groups which would select nominees under this proposal has existing channels of communication and representation which have operated well for many years. . . .

Proposal 3: For Disclosure on Minority-Hiring, Air-Pollution, and Auto-Safety Policies

Proxies are solicited in support of a proposal to require the Corporation to disclose in its annual report data in three areas of immense concern to shareholders and the public: air-pollution control, auto safety, and minority hiring and franchising.

The purpose of this proposal is to provide information that is currently not available to shareholders in order that they may accurately evaluate the performance of management in meeting public responsibilities in these areas.

The stockholder has submitted the following statement in support of such resolution:

Reasons: "Shareholders have both the right and the responsibility to be concerned about the policies of the Corporation which affect the community. Shareholders require information about the Corporation's activities and its policies in order to assess their adequacy. The proposal would require management to furnish to the shareholders in the annual report the minimum information needed in three key areas of concern to the Corporation and its shareholders: minority hiring, pollution, and safety. Unless this information is furnished, the shareholders would be prevented from carrying out their proper role as owners."

The Board of Directors favors a vote AGAINST this resolution for the following reasons:

General Motors in its annual reports, its quarterly reports, its special mailings to stockholders, and its numerous formal statements to the press has an enviable record of open disclosure to its stockholders and the public generally. Detailed information is also filed with city, state, and Federal agencies. These filings are available to those having a legitimate interest in them. The final decisions as to matters to be included in stockholder reports, the degree of detail and the timing of the information should be determined by those charged with the successful operation of the company. The degree of success they have achieved over the years is evidenced by the many awards General Motors has won for the excellence of its reporting.

.   .   .   .

While the proposal would permit omission of information if a competitive

Exhibit 5—Continued

disadvantage would result, the Board of Directors would be required to demonstrate "clear and compelling reasons" for any such omission. The question of
what facts or circumstances might constitute "clear and compelling reasons" is
clearly one on which there can be—and undoubtedly would be—disagreement.
This could lead to protracted argument and even to expensive litigation.

．　　　．　　　．　　　．　　　．　　　．　　　．　　　．　　　．　　　．

* According to one expert in the field of stockholder solicitation, it might cost GM as much as $100 million a
year to carry out the consumer portion of this proposal alone. *Wall Street Journal*, May 12, 1971.
Source: Summary statements of the Campaign resolutions from the Project on Corporate Responsibility, *Campaign GM: Round II Proxy Statement* (Washington, D.C., November 19, 1970), pp. 5, 8, 11; supporting and opposing
statements from General Motors Corporation, *Proxy Statement*, April 5, 1971.

The second would encourage and protect engineers and other professionals in business in reporting what they believed to be "illegal,
hazardous or unconscionable" behavior by their employers. The third
would, among other things, broaden the requirements for corporate
disclosures and would even "pierce the corporate veil" to make officers
personally responsible for acts which currently resulted only in indict-
ments of the corporation. As a precedent for this idea, Nader pointed
out that brokers could be suspended by the SEC for violating the securities law. He continued: "Suppose you suspend the president of General
Motors for six months. He would be crawling up the wall, wondering
who's going to usurp his power. It's a tremendous built-in deterrent.
. . . Another idea would be suspending advertising."[23]

GM, along with the whole auto industry, would be affected by
Washington's increasingly rigorous climate of legislation and regulation, a climate which Nader had helped as much as anyone to create
(Exhibit 6). Spurred on in part by critics who suspected all regulators
of a flaccid backbone and all industry of needless foot-dragging, units
such as the National Highway Traffic Safety Administration (NHTSA)
and the Environmental Protection Agency (EPA) were making demands in 1970 and 1971 that, according to the auto industry, were
"unattainable" within the time-frame specified. One dispute erupted
over a government demand that car occupants be protected by airbags
as a form of "passive restraint" (i.e., one requiring no positive human
action) as early as 1973. Another storm broke over emission control
requirements, when standards for 1975 as proposed by the Department
of Health, Education, and Welfare were suddenly replaced within
about two weeks by much stiffer standards from the EPA, which GM

---

[23] *The New York Times,* January 24, 1971.

Exhibit 6

CAMPAIGN GM: ROUNDS I AND II
Meet Ralph Nader

Within three years of authoring *Unsafe at Any Speed,* Nader had been credited with providing most of the impetus for major federal legislation on auto safety and meat inspection codes. His crusades and his life style continued to capture attention in the press. The following excerpts are from write-ups in *Newsweek* and *Business Week.*

EVERYMAN'S LOBBYIST AND HIS CONSUMER CRUSADE

Diseased fish, higher auto prices, dental X-rays, tires—you name it. Ralph Nader was upset about it last week. As Everyman's self-appointed lobbyist in Washington, the lanky, sallow-faced lawyer raced through six eighteen-hour days, propelled by a fine sense of what his admirers call "controlled outrage" and his detractors describe as "fanaticism."

.　　.　　.　　.　　.　　.　　.　　.　　.　　.　　.　　.

The possibles for Nader have grown infinitely since he achieved his sudden fame in auto safety. Critics complain that he is too "emotional," too "vindictive." But his charges and denunciations now command headlines at home and abroad, and a simple letter of inquiry from Nader to a Federal agency or industrial firm gets immediate attention.

.　　.　　.　　.　　.　　.　　.　　.　　.　　.　　.　　.

To finance his crusade, Nader currently has only his own resources—and by the standards of most of Washington's lobbyists, they would support perhaps one medium-size cocktail party at the Shoreham. . . . He couldn't care less for material things; his wardrobe numbers four suits, he eats in cut-rate cafeterias and he owns no car.

An ascetic? Obviously. But Ralph Nader's principal quality . . . is a well-honed sense of society's shortcomings and a practical view of how [to deal with them]. He summed up his own view of his special mission in a recent interview with *Newsweek* correspondents in Washington:

"I'm not really a reformer; so many reformers leave a lot to be desired. A dreamer? No, I've got to be practical. But the real question is [not] why I'm doing what I'm doing but why so many people don't care. What we do about corporate air and water pollution, corporate soil and food contamination, corporate-bred trauma on the highways, corporate inflationary pricing, corporate misallocation of resources and corporate dominance over state, local and Federal agencies—to suggest a few issues—will decide the quality of our lives." Then, in the very next breath, Nader denied he is either anti-business or convinced that businessmen themselves are evil.

"It's a disservice to view this as a threat to the private-enterprise economy or to big business," he insisted. "It's just the opposite. It is an attempt to preserve the free-enterprise economy by making the market work better; an attempt to preserve the democratic control of technology by giving government a role in

Exhibit 6—Continued

the decision-making process as to how much or how little 'safety' products must contain."

.   .   .   .

Last week, he was gathering evidence and charting strategy on a long list of new issues: drug safety, the sonic boom, mine safety—even the venerable and seemingly unpregnable oil-depletion allowance.

CRUSADER WIDENS RANGE OF HIS IRE

.   .   .   .

More than his relative penury, Nader seems to feel that material possessions and self-indulgence constitute hostages to fortune, and he includes both wife and children in that forbidden category. He watches his facts, watches his step, and remains invulnerable.

One curious by-product of Nader's style of life and career is the awe in which he is held by law students, especially those from the prestigious Eastern colleges. *The Harvard Law Record* said in an editorial that though Harvard has had some great lawyers, the school "should recognize that Ralph Nader may be the most outstanding man ever to receive a degree from this institution."

Last summer, Nader was able to recruit a group of Harvard and Yale law students and recent graduates dubbed "Nader's Raiders," to work in Washington at their own expense and produce the . . . report [on the deficiencies of the FTC].

Sources: "Everyman's Lobbyist," *Newsweek*, January 22, 1967, pp. 65–72; "Crusader Widens Range of His Ire," *Business Week*, January 25, 1969, pp. 128–30.

felt it could not meet, as shown in Table 2. Still another source of friction was the bumper code. Here the auto makers won an adjustment. Whereas NHTSA had at first suggested that both front and rear bumpers be able to protect cars from damage in 5-mile-an-hour crashes by the 1973 model year, the rear-bumper requirement was later reduced to 2.5 miles an hour.[24]

TABLE 2

AUTOMOTIVE EXHAUST EMISSION REQUIREMENTS FOR 1975 AS A PER CENT
REDUCTION FROM UNCONTROLLED LEVELS

CONSTITUENT	TODAY	HEW PROPOSAL (February 10, 1970)	EPA PROPOSAL (February 26, 1970)
Hydrocarbons	80%	95%	97%
Carbon monoxide	69	86	96
Oxides of nitrogen	33*	83	90†

* California only.
† For 1976.
Source: General Motors, *Progress in Areas of Public Concern* (February, 1971), p. 8.

[24] *The Wall Street Journal*, April 15, 1971.

Given the high pitch of public interest in safety and ecology during the start of the 1970's, the evolution of government standards and industry's reaction to them attracted considerable coverage in the press.

ROUND II CAMPAIGN TACTICS

Whereas Round I of Campaign GM had won considerable press attention for its proselytizing on the campuses, Round II earned more coverage for seeking the support of financial institutions. *The New York Times* reported on evolving versions of this tactic, one account going as follows:

The Project on Corporate Responsibility asked the nation's 12 largest mutual funds today to adopt a whole new standard for their investment decisions, under which the funds would consider corporate policies in two areas of social policy before investing. . . .

. . . These were environmental policies and minority hiring. . . .

The project itself did not attempt to dictate standards of good corporate behavior in these areas. Instead, it asked the funds and the [Investment Company Institute] to adopt standards of their own.

.   .   .   .

The project . . . suggested that the institute and industry leaders consult with church groups, minorities, environmental and other organizations in formulating the code.

The project's letters represent the first time that the mutual fund industry, on a broad basis, has been asked to formulate investment policies that would take social policies of companies into account. Individual funds have previously been approached on specific issues, such as the campaigns to bring issues before the General Motors shareholders' meetings.[25]

According to an earlier story, the campaign had written to the 350 largest mutual funds, asking them to vote their GM shares on the basis of a shareholder poll—or, if a poll would be too expensive, on the basis of a 5% sampling. At the same time, the campaign had also written to the major brokerage firms holding customers' stock in "street names." These brokers were warned that, in the campaign's opinion, they could not legally vote their stock without instructions from the beneficial owners. Commented *The New York Times*, "This argument appears to be disputed."[26]

GM'S ROUND II COUNTEROFFENSIVE

Forewarned well ahead of time, GM's management had ample chance to reconsider, if it wished, the tactics it had followed during

---

[25] *The New York Times*, April 21, 1971.

[26] *The New York Times*, April 14, 1971.

Round I. A well-known apostle of conservatism, Milton Friedman, had recently penned a widely read statement attacking the position of corporation critics. Published under the title, "The Social Responsibility of Business Is to Increase Its Profits,"[27] this statement could have furnished GM some ammunition. Some observers, moreover, were eager to see the company assume a more aggressive posture. For example, *The Wall Street Journal* gave space on its editorial page to a long article by Jeffrey St. John titled, "Memo to GM: Why Not Fight Back?"[28]

In the event, GM undertook a countercampaign composed of (1) statements outlining the company's attitude toward the profit/social obligations issue, (2) enumeration of past achievements in the area of social responsibility, and (3) stepped-up action in the social sphere.

Among the spokesmen who undertook to enunciate what might be called GM's philosophic position was Chairman Roche (Exhibit 7). He made two major statements on this topic, one in a booklet distributed to a wide audience including all GM stockholders, the other to an urban executive club. In the first of these statements, Roche wrote in part as follows:

> Every executive must recognize that social progress throughout the nation in the long run is beneficial to his business. The modern businessman and his company are expected to engage in activities that are beyond the traditional concerns of a business. People and institutions still invest in a business with the expectation of earning a return. . . . Therefore profit must always be a primary concern. But now it is more widely recognized that profits and social progress must go hand in hand.
>
> The corporate executive, therefore, must balance the responsibilities of the corporations to various publics. At General Motors, for example, we have responsibilities to our customers, to our employees, to our dealers, to our suppliers, as well as to our stockholders. We are anxious to live up to the expectations of each. . . .
>
> .   .   .   .
>
> This corporation and every other must serve the society in which it operates. GM responds to society's expectations. When society in the competitive marketplace demands a different automobile, we try to make it. When society, through the various groups to which we are responsible, asks us to involve ourselves more in national problems, we attempt to do so.
>
> However, we do not believe that corporations are the best equipped to answer every social problem. Corporations should take leadership only where

---

[27] *The New York Times Magazine,* September 13, 1970, p. 122 ff. (Reprinted with permission as a case by the Harvard Business School under the number 3–371–106/AM/P320.)

[28] May 21, 1971. Mr. St. John was identified as a columnist and radio–TV commentator and as the moderator of the business segment of the "Today" show.

Exhibit 7

CAMPAIGN GM: ROUND II
James M. Roche—Portrait

In June, 1965, when James M. Roche was appointed to GM's presidency, short write-ups appeared in several magazines, including *U.S. News & World Report* and *Newsweek*, from which the following excerpts are taken.

UP FROM THE RANKS—GM'S NEW PRESIDENT

A man who has never personally sold a car and who didn't attend college is the new president of General Motors.

.   .   .   .

Mr. Roche was born in Elgin, Ill. After graduating from high school, he augmented his education with correspondence courses, then went to work for Cadillac at the age of 21. He rose steadily through the ranks. . . .

.   .   .   .

Mr. Roche had been a favored candidate for the GM presidency because of his wide experience in GM's international operations, which last year accounted for 13 per cent of the company's earnings. Colleagues describe him as "thorough and capable—a man with tremendous loyalty, brains and ability."

GM'S NEW DRIVER

The average man, when he gets a promotion, takes his wife out to dinner, and that's just what James M. Roche did one night last week. The whole evening was fairly average: a trip to the New York World's Fair, with two rounds of drinks, tours of a few pavilions and a climactic ride through the Pepsi-Cola exhibit. In fact, as a celebration, it hardly measured up to the promotion, but it's difficult to imagine what could. At 58, Roche had just been named president of General Motors Corp., the world's largest manufacturing concern, a job that paid his predecessor $740,000 last year.

In a ritual press conference after the New York board meeting that made his new job official, Roche engagingly confessed to "sort of being overwhelmed by the responsibilities." Within the huge corporation, where he has been a front runner for the job for well over a year, the consensus is that he needn't be awed at all; and in the company plane heading back to Detroit next day, Roche was clearly unflustered. "We're all so accustomed to working as a group," he said, "in a sense, this is just carrying on."

In another sense, Roche is a triumphant example of GM's widely admired management-in-depth technique; it is a school for bosses in which literally any one of a dozen men could step into the top job at any time. (Ultimately, Roche may do just that when chairman Frederic C. Donner, 62, retires in three years.) Roche joined GM's Cadillac division in 1927 as a statistician, and piled up experience in sales, business management, personnel, labor relations, public relations and as general manager of the Cadillac division. In 1962, he was named executive vice president in charge of a huge and diverse chunk of the company: household appliances, engines, miscellaneous products and the Overseas & Canadian Group. Last week, asked if there were any phase of the vast business

Exhibit 7—Continued

that he's not acquainted with, Roche could honestly say: "No, I don't think so."

No Fish: A lean, affable 6-footer, Roche is on first-name terms with a surprisingly large number of lower-echelon executives. As is normal with GM's top brass, his 8:30-to-6:30 working day has eaten heavily into such former hobbies as fishing, gardening and golfing. A devout Roman Catholic, he attends Mass daily before driving his own Cadillac on the 45-minute crawl from his Bloomfield Hills home to the GM Building in Detroit, and he intends to make almost no changes in the routine. "I may dip into the driver pool more often, when I have a lot of reading to do on the way home," he says, "but I enjoy driving."

Roche's background in sales and overseas operations is sharply different from retiring president John F. Gordon's engineering emphasis, but no sweeping new policies are imminent. "I think we have a very good system, and I want to preserve it," he says. "I don't visualize any major changes." Nevertheless, it's a safe bet that GM's recent overseas stress will be intensified. In the past five years, GM has budgeted $1.5 billion to beef up its foreign operations, which now account for 13 per cent of its business. The result, Roche says, has been "some improvement, but it has not been as great as we would like to see. We still have a long way to go."

Sources: "Up from the Ranks," *U.S. News & World Report,* June 14, 1965, p. 14; "GM's New Driver," *Newsweek,* June 14, 1965, p. 38.

they are best qualified. Other institutions—colleges, churches, government—all have a role to play. General Motors is determined to do its full share in meeting its obligations to society—alone where we are best able, together with other elements of society where that is more effective.

We want to know what you think of all this. As long as you as a stockholder express your will, General Motors will continue to respond. . . . If you are impressed with some of the progress you are seeing today, then some satisfaction belongs to you. If, on the other hand, you think we should follow other directions and have constructive suggestions, we hope you will give us the benefit of your counsel and support.[29]

Mr. Roche's other major statement was given before the Executive Club of Chicago. As characterized by *The Wall Street Journal,* this speech was "one of the toughest attacks ever made on corporate critics by GM."[30] Commenting, Nader called it "unvarnished GM, a massive display of GM's malignancies."[31] A campaign spokesman simply said, "He's flipped his lid."[32]

---

[29] General Motors Corporation, *Progress in Areas of Social Concern* (February, 1971), p. 33.

[30] March 26, 1971.

[31] *Business Week,* April 10, 1971, p. 101.

[32] *The Wall Street Journal,* March 26, 1971.

After charging unnamed critics with threatening the entire free enterprise system, impugning America's reputation, and creating an unfairly negative picture of U.S. business, Mr. Roche went on in part as follows:

An Adversary Culture

Corporate responsibility is a catchword of the adversary culture that is so evident today. If something is wrong with American society, blame business. Business did not create discrimination in America, but business is expected to eliminate it. Business did not bring about the deterioration of our cities, but business is expected to rebuild them. Business did not create poverty and hunger in our land, but business is expected to eliminate them.

As citizens and Americans, we heartily endorse all these objectives. . . . But every thoughtful American must face the fact that new aspirations entail new costs.

.   .   .   .

The Contributions of Business

Business does its job when it provides useful jobs at high wages, when it provides useful products at fair prices, when it provides economic growth that produces taxes for government and earnings for stockholders. These are the long-standing responsibilities of business. Their fulfillment by American business over two centuries has made our America what it is. It is an achievement to be proud of—an achievement to talk about.

Earlier, I said we must be ready to accept change. And business today is expected to respond to the new aspirations of the society it serves. This broad public expectation must be recognized, and these new challenges must be accepted. The costs of many are not prohibitive. . . . However, in other areas, for example in the control of pollution, costs are usually substantial. To the extent that they cannot be absorbed, they will raise the price of the product and in turn the overall level of prices in our economy.

Aspirations and Their Cost

As a nation we must be mature enough to face up to the costs involved in meeting our new aspirations. It can mean a weakened competitive position in the world. It can mean higher prices for the consumer, and higher taxes for the citizens. This no dire forecast. This is already a fact.

.   .   .   .

It is not enough that management should be aware of what benefits—and what costs—are involved in fulfilling social objectives. The owners of American business . . . must make the ultimate decision.

In the end, management must be responsive to the wishes of the stockholders. Management is obliged to inform stockholders as to the problems and short-term costs as well as the potential long-range benefits of a greater and more direct involvement in social objectives. Then, management must abide by the owners' decision.[33]

The documents that in 1971 undertook to tell the story of GM's achievements in the social sphere included both the annual report and a much expanded version of the previous year's *GM's Record of Progress*. Titled *Progress in Areas of Public Concern,* the new booklet dealt with such topics as automotive safety, emission and pollution control, urban transportation, abandoned car disposal, minority opportunities, etc. (For excerpts, see Exhibit 8). Like the earlier *Record of Progress, Progress in Areas of Public Concern* not only went to all GM stockholders but also provided the theme for a conference just before the annual meeting. Invited this time, among others, was a group of prominent educators and representatives of foundations and investment institutions. By special invitation of Mrs. Roche, key campaigners were invited too.

In the area of action, GM's countercampaign got under way well before Round II started. Although Nader indicated that most of what was done was, in his opinion, simply "cosmetic," and a campaign spokesman saw GM's actions as aimed at "destroying our credibility,"[34] the press gave these moves extensive coverage, as indicated by the following list, mostly based on reports in *The Wall Street Journal:*

1. From June through November, 1970, GM negotiated purchase of the German-patented Wankel rotary-type engine, in the expectation that with further development the Wankel could prove the eventual answer to auto pollution. Investment was put at $50 million.
2. In June, 1970, GM planned to start a model project in a small Michigan city to retrieve junked and abandoned cars; usable materials were to go to foundries, in an effort to demonstrate the economic feasibility of the sponsored system.
3. In June, 1970, GM took on a $1 million government contract to design safety cars.
4. In July, 1970, GM reported that a two-months' test-marketing project revealed car owners were reluctant to pay $20 for kits to curb used-car pollution.

---

[33] James M. Roche, *Address before the Executive Club of Chicago,* 1971, pp. 9–12. Regarding the cost point raised by Mr. Roche, one study reported, "Auto men now say that pollution and safety hardware already ordered will slap as much as $500 onto the price tag of a new car by 1975, and other proposals under discussion could raise the total to $1,000." This estimate has been disputed by Mr. Douglas Toms, head of NHSTA. "He has told the industry, 'I am confident that you can build a safe car for the same price that you can build a dangerous one.' " See "The Crash Program That Is Changing Detroit," *Business Week,* February 27, 1971, pp. 78–84.

[34] "A Black Director Pushes Reforms at GM," *Business Week,* April 10, 1971, p. 101.

Exhibit 8

CAMPAIGN GM: ROUNDS I AND II
Excerpts from General Motors Corporation,
Progress in Areas of Public Concern*

Automotive Emission Control

Behind much of the problem are two basic misconceptions: first, that most of the air pollution problem is caused by the automobile; and, second, that the automotive industry, and particularly General Motors, is doing nothing. . . . Both of these are grossly in error.

First, let's look at the air pollution problem in the United States and the role of the automobile. Figure 2 shows estimates by the Federal government as to atmospheric tonnages of various pollutants—hydrocarbons, carbon monoxide, oxides of nitrogen, oxides of sulfur and particulate matter.

Unfortunately, using only the weight of pollutants is somewhat misleading. It doesn't illustrate the real picture of the air pollution problem—particularly as it relates to human health and plant life. Figure 3 shows that when both the total tonnage and health concern issues are considered, transportation is responsible for less than 10% of the total U.S. air pollution problem for the 1968 calendar year.

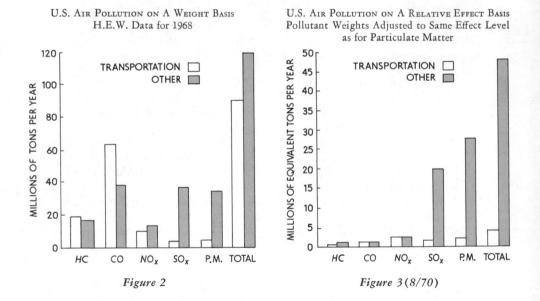

U.S. AIR POLLUTION ON A WEIGHT BASIS
H.E.W. Data for 1968

U.S. AIR POLLUTION ON A RELATIVE EFFECT BASIS
Pollutant Weights Adjusted to Same Effect Level
as for Particulate Matter

Figure 2   *Figure 3 (8/70)*

Let's look now at the second popular misconception: that we have done nothing to correct this contribution to the nation's air pollution. Just what has been done to minimize automotive emissions? Figure 9 illustrates what has happened to the total automotive hydrocarbon contribution to the atmosphere. Until about

---

* Deletions not indicated. The original booklet contained 49 pages, 8″ × 11″ in size.

Exhibit 8—Continued

1966, this contribution rose steadily. This would have continued if no control equipment had been added. As shown by the two lower curves, however, this trend was arrested because of the control systems on new cars. Figure 10 shows the same information for the carbon monoxide situation. These curves are graphic demonstrations of why GM believes we will take the automobile out of the air pollution problem for this decade.

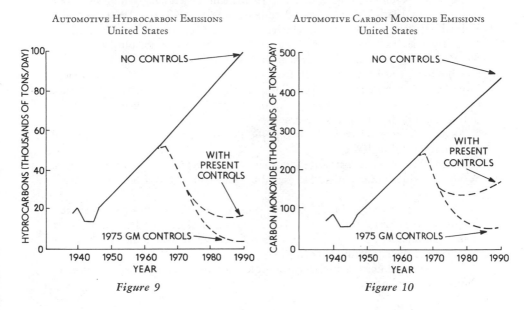

AUTOMOTIVE HYDROCARBON EMISSIONS
United States

AUTOMOTIVE CARBON MONOXIDE EMISSIONS
United States

Figure 9

Figure 10

Now you may ask, "How about beyond this decade; will those curves ever turn up again beyond 1980 or 1990?" General Motors is not blind to the long-range future. What we see are possibilities for dramatic changes in our overall transportation system, changes in which General Motors will play a big part.

We think the future system will be a balanced mix of mass transportation, private vehicles, and blends of the two. This system will reduce traffic density to such an extent that the automotive emission problem should never again rise to its present level. In this future transportation we see the opportunity for a variety of power plants.

We have extensively researched the alternative to the spark-ignition gasoline engine over the years—including gas turbine and Stirling engines, electric and electric hybrid power plants, and the steam engine. Some of these power plants have certain emission advantages, while others do not. All of them have tremendous development problems ahead.

In the future transportation system—beyond 1980—each of the feasible low emission power plants will compete with all the rest for the various transportation jobs which will need to be done. And don't be surprised if the spark-igni-

Exhibit 8—Continued

tion gasoline engine still has a major portion of the market. It will still be a very strong contender when we've finished cleaning it.

Industrial Pollution Control

Briefly, I would like to trace the trend of legislative concern, give you a report on General Motors' policies and progress, and suggest where we are headed.

In water pollution control the first permanent Federal legislation was not enacted until 1956. This law was amended in 1961, 1965, and 1970. The first Federal legislation concerned exclusively with air pollution was enacted in 1955. By today's standards it was only a token effort. It was not until the enactment of the 1967 Air Quality Act that the issues of industrial air pollution were met head-on. The point that I wish to make is this: In spite of the emotion, impatience, and criticism directed at industry and its pollution control programs, the fact remains that meaningful criteria and guidelines have been established only within the past four to six years.

General Motors recognized the significance of Corporation-wide industrial pollution control in 1946.

Since 1947, we have installed more than 100 water pollution control facilities at our operations in the United States and Canada. Our record, I feel, is outstanding in industry.

GM's industrial air pollution control program in the past has shown similar progress. It has been directed primarily at the removal of dust from our power plants and foundry operations, which has been considered the major problem by industry and the regulating agencies.

The last decade has seen about a tenfold increase in capital expenditures to control plant pollution.

Urban Transportation

In planning the transportation of the future, our objective should be a system which has the proper balance between private transportation and high quality, convenient and flexible public transportation. And that balance will differ from city to city.

Public transportation today, however, is facing extremely difficult challenges. It is obvious that financial aid and other forms of assistance from government agencies will be necessary. . . . The Federal Urban Mass Transportation Assistance Act of 1970 provides that $3.1 billion be made available over the next five years and a total of $10 billion over the next 12 years. General Motors supported this legislation.

General Motors—both as a responsible corporate citizen and for obvious business reasons—has a vital stake in promoting improved transportation systems for metropolitan areas. In fact efficient, balanced transportation systems are necessary to the long-range success of our major product—the automobile. It is important that we help to minimize the problems created by the automobile so that it can continue to operate as a useful and necessary part of the urban environment. And this is what we are attempting to do. Let me discuss some of our work in this field.

One of the most promising systems developed by General Motors is called

Exhibit 8—Continued

Metro-Mode. Buses would enter an exclusive lane on the freeway—and travel at 60- or 70-miles-per-hour to downtown destinations. The real questions, of course, are: Will such a system work? How many passengers can be transported? GM conducted a research project to get answers. Using platoons of 12 buses each, this study showed that a capacity of 27,000 passengers could be transported in each lane per hour.

Two other concepts were developed in special studies for the U.S. Department of Housing and Urban Development. One is the Network Cab, designed to provide improved mobility in the downtown areas. Another proposal is Dial-A-Bus. In this case the proposed service would be provided by small, 10- to 15-passenger buses summoned by telephone as with a taxicab, but on a share-the-ride basis to reduce the fare. Our studies indicate that [this system] would operate more effectively in cities of about 200,000 population with the proper population density. This could apply to perhaps 100 cities—such as Lansing, Michigan; Rochester, New York; and Cambridge, Massachusetts.

Our studies involve not only new concepts of propulsion but also new types of vehicles. Included are small, special-purpose, low-emission vehicles which could be used for two-passenger commuter service. In the bus field [we have] introduced an experimental rapid transit type coach that could be readily adapted to the Metro-Mode concept.

Research at GM's Electro-Motive Division includes developing advanced concepts for trains. One involves a modern high performance locomotive. Another is a so-called "corridor train," a short-range, relatively high-speed passenger train for use between major urban centers.

Minority Opportunities

For many years, our policy, like those of other large companies, [was] one of nondiscrimination. However, in recent years we made a significant shift. We chose no longer just to be against discrimination. We chose instead to work actively to assure equal opportunity.

New programs have produced encouraging results. In 1965, about 67,000 of our 593,000 employees were from minority groups. This was 11.2%. Today, General Motors is the largest private employer of minority Americans. At the end of 1970, GM employed more than 92,000 minority Americans in the United States. This was 15.3% of GM's total employment.

To help recruit, we follow a number of approaches. We write every year to [educational] institutions seeking referrals of minority graduates. General Motors was one of the first major corporations to recruit actively on the campuses of predominantly Negro colleges.

In 1967, Pontiac Motor Division launched a program to provide jobs for the hard-core unemployed. The experiences [thus] gained proved useful when, in April 1968, General Motors began participation in the JOBS program of the National Alliance of Businessmen—a nationwide effort to hire the hard-core unemployed.

Since these programs were started, General Motors, up to the end of 1969, had hired 45,132 so-called hard-core unemployed. Nearly 21,000 of these—46.5%—were still on the job, a percentage only slightly less than that of other

Exhibit 8—Continued

employees hired during the same period. During 1970, however, declining auto sales made it necessary for General Motors, like other companies, to lay off many employees. About 3,5000—one-sixth—of the 21,000 former hard-core unemployed had to be laid off in 1970. The remaining 17,500 continued to work. However, all with seniority have recall rights.

Some will point out that, while the overall percentage of our minority employment is relatively high, a disproportionate number are in hourly rather than salaried jobs. There is no denying this.

But we must recognize that every job at General Motors is a good job. The typical hourly employee, the man who assembles our cars, earns more than $12,000 a year with normal overtime.

Hiring, however, is only half the task. Giving disadvantaged workers equal opportunity to advance is the other part. To attain this objective, we engage in other programs to qualify our employees for advancement. Partly as a result, the number of minority workers among journeymen, apprentices, and employees-in-training for skilled trades has risen to nearly 2,300—a 50% increase—in three years.

General Motors works for greater economic equality in other ways than employment. We have several activities by which we assist minority enterprise.

General Motors has 65 automotive dealers who are minority Americans, including 12 blacks. In addition, 160 other minority businessmen sell and service General Motors products throughout the United States. A year ago we had only seven automobile dealers who were black, and a year before only two.

We regard the growth from two to 12 as a measure of our progress. But we also consider the fact that there are still so few—in spite of our efforts—as a measure of the difficulty we face. Even a small dealership is a good-sized business in most communities. It is a high-risk, intensely competitive business, and clearly not for the inexperienced manager.

To overcome these obstacles, General Motors is making intensive efforts to locate potential new dealers. We are also encouraging our dealers to place promising individuals in their businesses so they can acquire the experience and background that may qualify them for dealerships. Where a qualified applicant may lack sufficient capital, General Motors stands ready to join in the enterprise through capital investment.

We encourage minority enterprise in other ways as well. Last year, we formed a Minority Enterprise Small Business Investment Company—MESBIC. MESBICs provide low-interest funds together with managerial help and technical assistance to small minority-owned businesses. Ours was the seventh MESBIC to be formed. GM has committed an investment of $1 million to this venture.

Since 1969 General Motors has been depositing in minority-owned banks. This year we will maintain $5 million in 32 banks as part of a governmental program that is seeking total deposits of $65 million from private industry, and $35 million from government.

General Motors is also providing interest-free loans to two non-profit corporations acquiring land for low-cost housing projects. The first loan is for up to $1.1 million. The second is for up to $1 million.

Exhibit 8—Continued

Automotive Safety

At General Motors, we are committed to the advancement of safety through sound engineering. We have demonstrated this commitment by introducing safety features whenever they have reached production stage, often in advance of our competitors.

The GM Safety Research and Development Laboratory [dedicated in 1968] probably is the most extensive facility of its kind in the industry. Here we have the great variety of equipment necessary to conduct tests that ultimately provide data leading to safety improvements.

The result of utilizing safety test devices is that we have GM cars that are second to none in overall safety. Our energy-absorbing steering column, for example, has much greater performance than required by Federal safety standards, and its success in real-life accidents has been well documented. Present instrument panels, seat backs and other interior components also are much superior than minimum standard requirements, and are performing very well in real life.

The improvements we have made in the vehicle thus far have not interfered with normal usage of the vehicle. However, it is becoming an increasingly difficult challenge to continue adding major vehicle improvements without affecting vehicle utility.

The great majority of safety work we do here at the Laboratory is directed primarily at occupant protection. The rest of the Proving Ground, with its 85 miles of varied road systems, tests and evaluates the performance, durability and reliability of our vehicles so that they can enable the driver to avoid accidents, if at all possible.

[During the discussion period] an individual asked about the Corporation's budget expenditures in these areas. Mr. Richard C. Gerstenberg, Vice Chairman, said that U.S. expenditures of $124 million are forecast for 1971 for automotive emissions research, engineering and related activities. He said GM will spend another $64 million for controlling air and water pollution from plants, an expenditure almost four times as large as three years ago. He pointed out that these figures do not include the cost of automotive emission control hardware being installed on GM models. As for safety, Mr. Gerstenberg said the estimated expenditures for 1971 are over $400 million.

Closing Remarks

This whole meeting was concerned with the need we at General Motors recognize to do better—to build even safer cars, to clean up the environment, to promote minority oportunity, to work for better mass transportation, to do all that is expected of us.

We are determined to do all these things—not only to benefit our customers, not only to benefit our stockholders—but to benefit the whole of society.

Source: GM, *Progress in Areas of Public Concern*, a booklet based on a conference held in February, 1970, at the GM Proving Ground, Milford, Michigan, "for a group of prominent educators and representatives of foundations and investment institutions."

5. In August, 1970, GM created a Public Policy Committee of five non-officer members of its board, charged with making sure that the company was meeting rising expectations in matters of broad national concern.
6. In September, 1970, GM announced plans to install catalytic converters on some 1973 models and hoped that this device to control emissions could be included on all 1975 cars. (These hopes were later reported as having been overoptimistic.)
7. In November, 1970, GM was reported to have devised a 90% effective way to cut fumes from coal-fired power plants.
8. In December, 1970, GM reported that nearly $160 million out of $1.1 billion planned capital expenditures for 1971 would go for air-pollution control, for a 7% increase over 1970.
9. In January, 1971, GM appointed its first black to its board. He was activist Leon H. Sullivan, Philadelphia pastor, sponsor of self-help programs and advocate of black business. Indicating that his main concern was improving the position of blacks in America, Sullivan set three-year targets for GM: (1) 50 new black dealers; (2) 1,000 black executives moving up the ladder, and (3) inner-city training centers for mechanics, capable of handling 5,000 trainees a year. "My role is an expression of my ministry," he said. "When I'm not effective I'll resign."[35]
10. In January, 1971, GM undertook to make deposits of $5 million in banks owned by minorities.
11. In February, GM went outside the fold to find an environment chief and appointed Professor Ernest S. Starkman of the University of California at Berkeley to a clean-air post.
12. In February, 1971, unfolding a new national program to mollify critics of quality, GM announced that dealers would be paid to inspect and fix new cars on their lots.
13. In February, 1971, GM established an advisory panel of six "top" scientists to study the environmental effects of products.
14. In February, 1971, GM's annual report announced the following expenditures.

	1970	1971 Budget
	(in millions)	
For control of automotive emissions and development of alternative power sources	$119	$124
For air and water pollution from GM plants	35	64

DILEMMA FOR MONEY MANAGERS AND COLLEGES

Regardless of how many votes it would garner in the test at GM's annual meeting, the campaign and the issues it raised were reportedly

[35] *Business Week,* op. cit., p. 103. (Whereas the campaigners reportedly characterized other GM actions as "window dressing," Nader himself acknowledged his approval of the Sullivan appointment.)

taken seriously by both important financial institutions and important universities. Making up their minds how to vote—and even how to reach a decision—posed a real dilemma.

According to a survey of "money managers" conducted by *The Wall Street Journal,* the management companies in charge of the Putnam and Wellington Funds both created special committees to review the year's crop of social-action proxies. Putnam's included the management company's chairman, among others, and the well-known scientist Vannevar Bush. Similarly, the executive vice president of the First National City Bank reported, "Every proposal, no matter how humble, is given attention at the highest level." An official at the Chase Manhattan Bank expressed an often stated view that it was becoming easy to vote against management on social issues while basing that decision on investment implications. "A company that continues to pollute the air may not be around very long," he said.[36]

Taking an approach approved by the campaigners, the Dreyfus Corporation undertook to poll the holders of one of its smaller funds on how it should vote the GM shares held in this fund's portfolio.[37] Of wider impact, the SEC ruled in response to a dispute that a fund management company had to include on its proxy statement a shareholder proposal that, if ratified, would require the management company to consider the social policies of corporations before investing in their stock.[38] Indeed, one small management company even announced formation of a "Social Dimensions Fund" to invest in companies that would "contribute to society beyond satisfaction of basic material needs and the traditional goal of maximizing profit to the exclusion of all other ends."[39]

At the universities, many hard questions were posed initially by Campaign GM; these turned out to have far-reaching implications on which serious study was needed. For example, did it really matter how the college stock was voted, given the fact that the largest university holding (MIT's) was only 291,000 shares and that all educational institutions together held only 10% or so of GM's stock. If the college vote did matter, could the trustees properly ignore their student and faculty constituencies and vote only their own conscience, whatever this might be? If so, did GM deserve to be reprimanded, or had it been

---

[36] *The Wall Street Journal,* April 28, 1971.

[37] *Ibid.*

[38] *The New York Times,* May 11, 1971.

[39] "A Fund That Bets on Social Progress," *Business Week,* May 1, 1971, p. 29.

unfairly singled out, and was the economic system threatened by attacks on so prestigious a company? Even if the goals of the campaign merited respect, did an overriding obligation exist to vote the university's shares in whatever way would bring the maximum financial support for its primary goals of teaching and research? If, on the other hand, social values should be protected, could Campaign GM be treated as an isolated case, or was a long-term policy needed to cover all investment decisions? If the college did recognize a basic, long-term obligation to shape financial choice in the light of social considerations, what limits and what scope should this obligation have, what guidelines should be followed, what extra costs incurred, and what administrative structure should be created to implement this policy?

After all, as a Harvard University Committee observed (apropos of the idea of screening corporations for responsibility prior to making an investment), "Sophisticated criteria are likely to require elaborate machinery for gathering and processing information. Relatively simple low-cost machinery could cause the University to make decisions that are both intellectually and ethically shabby"[40]

ROUND II OUTCOME

Looking to the outcome of Round II about three weeks before the decision, *Business Week* reminded its readers that something important was riding on the vote count, even though that something was not the question of which side was sure to be declared the winner:

> The key question is whether Campaign GM—or any other dissident proposals—can win 3% of the shareholders' vote. If not, SEC rules allow management to keep the proposals off the proxy statement for three years. And that could stall the inchoate drive for reform through proxy power.[41]

Going into the meeting on May 22, campaign sponsors predicted they would get at least this meaningful 3% vote. Known supporters in the campaign corner included some colleges (Antioch, Bryn Mawr, and Vassar); the College Equities Retirement Fund, an organization with $1.5 billion in assets and 750,000 GM shares;[42] and the First Pennsyl-

---

[40] Harvard University Committee on Governance, *Harvard and Money,* cited in the *Report of the Committee on University Relations with Corporate Enterprise* (H.B.S. Professor R. W. Austin, chairman), *Harvard University Gazette,* March 5, 1971, p. 4.

[41] "The Moral Power of Shareholders," *Business Week,* May 1, 1971, p. 78.

[42] Characteristically, funds did not make their decisions public, but the Dreyfus Corporation did disclose that the poll of shareholders in its Leverage Fund resulted in a verdict favorable to GM. See *The Wall Street Journal,* May 21, 1971.

vania Banking & Trust Co., the largest bank in Philadelphia. Some time earlier First Pennsylvania had reportedly "stunned GM and the banking community" by declaring its intention to vote for at least one of the campaign's three proposals—that pertaining to disclosure through the Annual Report of what GM was doing to minimize pollution, to maximize minority employment, and to increase the safety of its cars. Although the Carnegie Fund would support GM, the Rockefeller Fund planned to abstain on at least two of the campaign resolutions.[43]

Given this encouragement, campaign workers were "clearly surprised" as well as disappointed by the vote when it came. Management had won a "smashing victory." The campaign's three proposals, faring worse than in the year before, got only 1.11% to 2.36% of the shares voted. Conceding their dismay, members of the campaign board now also reportedly "questioned the efficacy of their effort to force social change on the corporation through its shareholders." Said the campaign chairman, "We are going to have to reassess the kind of strategies we pursue in the future."[44]

---

[43] *Business Week, op. cit.; The Boston Globe,* May 18, 1971; *The Wall Street Journal,* May 19, 1971.

[44] *The Wall Street Journal,* May 22, 1971.